I0187934

Better than Cure

The life and times
of the ebullient and resilient

William Redfern
1775(?)-1833

Surgeon & Doctor

(VIRTUS ET VERITAS PREVALEBUNT)

Volume I

Wellbeing in the
Wooden World

Published: April 2019 by
The Book Reality Experience

ISBN: 978-0-6484471-8-4
Hardback Edition

For frontispiece latin motto, "Power and Truth Prevail", see J. M. Antill & Rose Antill-de Warren. The Emancipist, (Printed inside front cover of an Autographed Edition).

Cover design Luke Buxton | www.lukebuxton.com

Better than Cure

Volume I
Wellbeing in the
Wooden World

Arthur Raymond Jones

REDFERN

Suburb of Sydney, New South Wales,
&
William Redfern Orations

(RANZCP)

Commemorating

Redfern's contribution to
Public Health & Preventive Medicine.

Volume 1 of 2

See separate Volume:
Volume II: Wellbeing in the Colony
ISBN: 978-0-6484471-9-1

Table of Contents

ACKNOWLEDGEMENTS

This book is presented in two parts (as separate volumes):

Jones AR (2019) Better than cure: The life and times of the ebullient and resilient William Redfern 1775-1833 Surgeon & Doctor.
Volume I: Wellbeing in the Wooden World
&
Volume II: Wellbeing in the Colony

At the outset let me say that this study would not have developed and grown the way it has without the love, concern and active interest of first, Muriel, my wife of just days short of 72 years, and of our children, Howard, Lynette, Ian, Susanne and Peter and in turn their partners, children, and close friends. I am particularly indebted to Howard for first introducing me to Macintosh computers and guiding me ever since.

I have made every effort to acknowledge the sources of the written material of this book. In doing so I thank the authors, their publishers and guardians, for the efforts made to record and protect their work, ideas and visions.

Reading the book will reveal my indebtedness to a wide-ranging community of people outside my family, mentioned above, from young to old. I thank them each and everyone. The study began with the school community at Minto, NSW. Campbelltown and Airds Historical Society provided an early audience. The papers of Dr Norman Dunlop and Sir Edward Ford, and the accounts of the Great Mutinies of 1797, I read at the Mitchell and State Libraries, Sydney. Further reading at the Archives Authority of New South Wales provided much needed detail.

Paul Brunton (in 2007) read the mutiny chapters, and Shirley Fitzgerald (in 2008) read the whole manuscript as it was then. Dr John Turner of Newcastle University advised me to publish while on a history study tour of Norfolk Island in 1994. William Redfern being a surgeon required me to broaden the study base to include health and medicine. Librarian Brenda Heagney saw to that at the History of Medicine Library, the Royal Australasian College of Physicians, Sydney. I acknowledged her invaluable help in my study of William Redfern in the refereed *Journal of Medical Biography* (1999) and am happy to do so again. Brenda read some of the earlier chapters of this book and Alison Holster had read most of the book in some form or another. Their support and constructive criticism have proved invaluable. Dr Bryan Gandevia, from our first meeting, became a supportive and most challenging mentor. He also read earlier versions of this work. Their encouragement led me to join both the New South Wales and the Australian Societies of the History of Medicine and the association of Health and Medicine Museums. In those years I became aware of the contribution to History of Medicine by a widening range of people, medical and nonmedical, academics and others. Many of them I met at Society meetings and the History of Medicine Library (RACP).

I regularly attended meetings, acted on committees where appropriate, and was given full support when I proposed and organised a seminar around the life of William Redfern at the Campbelltown Campus of Western Sydney University. I thank all concerned for their support. Over the years, Campbelltown, NSW has achieved city status and an excellent library service. I acknowledge the contribution of each to this study, and to the opportunity to serve as an Alderman, and member of the library committee for six years, half the time as chairman.

Following family agreement Campbelltown City Council, NSW, accepted our offer to donate to their library some six hundred books collected in the course of this study of William Redfern. Grant White, Manager of Library Services, Campbelltown City Council, has advised that the '*Arthur and Muriel Jones Collection* is now in place in the custom made Tasmanian Oak book case' (Email: 18 November 2014).

I am most grateful to Lynette Abbott and Sarah Lumley for editorial assistance.

Arthur Raymond Jones
Campbelltown, New South Wales
April 2019

PREFACE

Some guiding thoughts.

"The prevention of diseases is an object as much deserving our attention as their cure. The means of prevention are also more within our power than those of cure".

"More may be done towards the preservation of the health and lives of seamen than is commonly imagined; and it is a matter not only of humanity and duty, but of interest and policy".[1]

With such thoughts in mind, Gilbert Blane, in 1780, while physician to Admiral Rodney's Fleet in the West Indies, set out to determine "the causes of sickness in fleets, and the means of prevention".

The half title of this book, *Better than cure,* is relevant across the broad concerns of its content, not only for health and medicine. The failure by management to meet the social needs of the seamen led to the great fleet mutinies of 1797.

Nicholas Rodger's *The Command of the Ocean, A Naval History of Britain 1649-1815,* confirms that simple truth.[2]

This book bears witness to the opening sentence of David Crystal's second introduction, 'real' in contrast to the 'standard' *Stories of English.*[3]

"It is not what the orthodox histories include which is the problem; it is what they omit, or marginalize".

At the same time I have been cognisant of Alan Frost's reminder to "*bear in mind Sir Keith Hancock's 'rule of contextual congruity', by which it is wrong - in every sense of the word - to measure the thoughts and actions of people in the past by a measuring rod of knowledge and experience which did not come into existence until after those people were dead*".[4]

L.P. Hartley's perception,[5] *"The past is a foreign country: they do things differently there",* gave David Lowenthal a book title[6] and George Parsons a text to "be engraved above the study doors of the historians of early Australia".[7]

Lowenthal's emphasis on historic preservation of physical artefacts has revealed the past as "an ever more foreign realm, yet one increasingly suffused by the present".[8]

More recently, Alan Atkinson accepted that the past still lives, not only as "a foreign country but a region thick with competing voices". From these

"We have to decide whom to listen to, and to shut out everything else in order to give ourselves room to understand".[9]

Atkinson, in acknowledging his selection of voices to be somewhat perverse, takes advantage of the moment to assert "the belief that whole-hearted perversity is the best gift of the Europeans to Australia".[10]

I have noted the admiration of C. J. Cummins, for the early colonial doctors.

"They lived in rough and turbulent days and their responses to their environment were colourful and direct, with an abruptness and disregard of consequence, which in these days of conformity can be admired in the perspective of history. They were generally men of character and determination who became influential and prominent in the social and political movements of their times. Because of this they were involved often in controversy, sometimes in scandal, and frequently in conflict with authority as well as with each other. They had the opportunity because of status and education to proffer leadership and occupy important positions in the social and political structure of the Colony". [11]

Some final references are not out of place with emotive words such as *ebullient* and *resilient* in the title. *Emotions and the Economy* is among six general concerns of economic sociology, today.

"It is arguable that the project of modern social science from its European nineteenth-century origins to its contemporary variations defines emotion out of social action in general and economic action in particular".[12]

No better example of this process may be found, than the displacement by economists of Adam Smith's *The Theory of Moral Sentiments* of 1759 by his *Wealth of Nations* of 1776.

"How selfish soever man may be supposed, there are evidently some principles in his nature, which interest him in the fortune of others, and render their happiness necessary to him, though he derives nothing from it, except the pleasure of seeing it. Of this kind is pity or compassion, the emotion which we feel for the misery of others when we either see it, or are made to conceive it in a very lively manner".[13]

V.A.C. Gatrell's *The Hanging Tree*, was "not only a history of emotions" but "in a measured sense", the author hoped, "an emotional book". Nevertheless, it was awarded the Whitfield prize by the Royal Historical Society.[14]

INTRODUCTION[15]

Who was William Redfern? I needed to know, having arrived at Minto in 1961, to take charge of the Public School, and finding his early home sitting just over the ridge.[16]

S. Elliott Napier, an experienced journalist, had answered my question as best he could in articles published in The Sydney Morning Herald, in 1926.[17] However, I did not find them until my book was nearing completion in 2010.

What I did find were two short but useful biographies of William Redfern at the Mitchell Library, Sydney, New South Wales, where I acquired a reader's ticket. Norman Dunlop published the first in 1928,[18] and Edward Ford, the second, in 1953.[19] Subsequently, I bought a copy of the Royal Australian Historical Society's *Journal and Proceedings*, containing Dunlop's paper. Ford gave me one of the last remaining copies of his own paper, following a phone call to his office.

My next acquisition was Frank Clune's book,[20] while Roger Pescott sent me a copy of his university study, as I had been in contact with him at the time.[21]

Jacqueline Grant and her husband Peter were our guests on their visit to Campbelltown. Subsequently we attended Jacqueline's book launch and added a copy of her book to this nucleus of a study cell.[22]

Last in line was my own contribution published in the *Journal of Medical Biography,* London, in two parts.[23]

George Rudé, in answering his wider question "Who were the convicts?" described an evolution of responses. Dunlop was closer to the idea of the 1920s when "Australian historians, like the Hammonds in England, began early in the century to picture the convicts as more sinned against than sinning".[24]

Rudé placed William Redfern among the 3,600 political and social protestors, so defined in the introduction to his published account.[25]

Dr Norman J. Dunlop opened his paper, which he read to the Royal Australian Historical Society on 27 March 1928, with these words - "William Redfern was a convict. It would be, perhaps, nearer the truth if we called him a martyr. He may have been indiscreet on one occasion in his youth; but he was never a criminal, and always a gentleman". Time will tell.

Sir Edward Ford, MD, presented the Annual Post-Graduate oration based on the life of William Redfern, in the Great Hall of Sydney University on 29 April 1953. He thought well enough of Redfern to celebrate his life, and his contribution to preventive medicine and public health, in the bicentennial year of the publication of James Lind's *A Treatise of the Scurvy.* Ford paid tribute to "the records of the day, stored richly in the Mitchell Library, and...the biographical work of the late Dr Norman Dunlop".[26]

This was not the last of Ford's evaluations of William Redfern. In the following year he delivered "The Charles Mackay Lecture" which made special mention of "the work and influence of [surgeons] John White, William Redfern and William Bland".[27]

Ford also contributed a short biography of Redfern to *The Australian Encyclopaedia* in 1958. A later entry, "William Redfern", in the *Australian Dictionary of Biography, Volume 2: 1788-1850,* in 1967, over Ford's name, was compiled from his 1953 paper. Ford was overseas at the time.[28]

Redfern and Ford, though separated in time, had shared the professional practice of public health and preventive medicine. Their experience of war contributed to a closer bond of understanding between the two. Each had crossed swords with military officialdom in a theatre of war, Redfern, on board a man-of-war, and Ford, in New Guinea.

Frank Fenner, eminent scientist, detailed in his autobiography Lieutenant Colonel Ford's successful request to meet with General Blamey, and the positive outcome.[29] This confirms the story told by a colleague in the Sydney University *Gazette* on Ford's retirement.

"When two or more older army medical officers are gathered together the talk will turn to [Ford's] legendary interview with General Blamey, in December, 1942, the outcome of which was not only the enforcement of rigorous anti-malarial measures - this undoubtedly saved an untold number of lives - but also the acceptance of the doctrine that preventive medicine was the concern not of the medical services alone but of the army as a whole".[30]

Ford had another disease apart from malaria in mind. On his advice all supplies of sulphaguanidine available in Australia were sent to New Guinea to fight dysentery, "a bold and fully justified" action .[31]

Ford concluded his study of William Redfern with these words. "The proud and rugged figure of William Redfern stands out in added importance as the years pass. He was rich in the attributes that men admire. He was stalwart in adversity, a helper of the weak, a spokesman for the oppressed, a great citizen, and a good doctor".

In turn, Bryan Gandevia saw the character of Ford, himself, mirrored in this fine character portrait, and proclaimed his belief in a talk, given on 25 July 1998 to the N.S.W. Society of the History of Medicine, which I attended.[32]

Fenner followed his reference, above, with an insert, *Sir Edward (Ted) Ford,* which noted and confirmed Bryan Gandevia's belief that "Ted Ford had several personal qualities rarely seen in one man: an ever-present gentleness, a great depth of kindness and understanding, a wonderful generosity and a sincere humility, and a keen sense of humour and wit, none of which precluded determination and firmness when the occasion demanded (as was evident in his conversation with General Blamey)".[33]

Clune brought Redfern to the attention of a wider reading public. He inspired Scottish friends to find and photograph Redfern's tombstone in the New Calton Burial Ground, Edinburgh.[34] A nearby site has a memorial to the Scottish Martyrs. Clune celebrated their lives, too, in another of his lively accounts.

Less than six years later, Pescott was at work on his own study. He considered, at the time, that he had "gathered more information concerning Redfern than other writers...because it seems not enough has previously been sought".[35]

Of the four authors, only Clune, with the help of a research assistant in London, tapped the record of Redfern's court martial, but did not find the Redfern letter.[36] Clune argued for the Redfern case to be re-opened.

Each of the above authors produced a variation on Dunlop's basic themes, enriching the core evidence with associated documentation, and strengthening the account with a wider and deeper reading of events. My own two papers, above, shared similar themes and intention, as does this study.

One would hope that as the fields of commentary widened to include other sources and authors, 'a fruitful dialectic' developed 'between data and interpretation, with limitations of vision being successively superseded, and better-directed observation opening horizons onto new problems'.[37]

Dunlop held degrees in arts and medicine and practised in Newcastle, New South Wales. Failing health leading to his retirement from Newcastle Hospital, he moved to Sydney to be close to the Mitchell Library and to the Royal Australian Historical Society. Dunlop made good use of the Mitchell and played an active part in the affairs of the Society. In return his papers were published and he was rewarded with its highest honour, a fellowship.[38]

Ford had been appointed to the Chair of Preventive Medicine at Sydney University after a distinguished army career in World War II in which he became Australian Army Director of Hygiene, Pathology and Entomology. Before the war he worked in the field of Public Health and Tropical Medicine and surveyed native health in Papua.[39]

"A keen collector, he...achieved an internationally known collection of rare books and manuscripts. An authority on the history of medicine, Ford made a number of notable contributions to Australian medical history" including his *Bibliography of Australian Medicine 1790-1900*, "a superlative work", in the estimation of Dr Bryan Gandevia, MD.[40]

On 19 February 1987, Bryan Gandevia as Chairman of the History of Medicine Library Committee, acknowledged the Committee's "profound debt of gratitude to Sir Edward Ford and his family but also the responsibility which it acquires to preserve and develop the legacy inherited from an inspiring leader".[41] His curatorship and benefaction of the *History of Medicine Library* of the Royal Australasian College of Physicians exemplify other significant contributions. Chapters in this book, relevant to the study of the history of medicine, owe much to the work of Ford, Gandevia, and to others, of course. Some are mentioned along the way. Dedicated librarians and their libraries are there, too.[42]

Frank Clune, with the assistance of his "ghost writer" P. R. Stephensen, told the *Hillsborough* story, prompted by convict William Noah's diary.[43] They gave an account of the lives of some of the passengers before and after they went aboard that "Death Ship".[44] Sarah Wills was a child passenger on *Hillsborough.*[45] Her subsequent marriage to William Redfern gained him entry to Clune's book.

Clune devoted some four chapters to William Redfern, and further chapters to the Wills family. A veteran of Gallipoli, Clune had wandered the world. He "prided himself on coming from the school of hard knocks but he also suffered from a sense of educational and cultural inferiority, especially among his writer friends, so he took on the Oxford-educated P.R.Stephensen, a former Queensland Rhodes scholar, to make up the deficiency".[46]

Stephensen served first as Clune's "editor" and then as his "ghost writer". "When their partnership was well under way, Clune provided the principal research material and anecdotes from his travels, and Stephensen put together and polished the narrative".[47]

Roger Pescott worked on his Redfern study, *Emancipist and Autocrat*, while a postgraduate student at the Australian National University. From 1971 to 1980 he was posted overseas in the Diplomatic Service. In 1985 he was the Liberal Party Member for Mitcham in the Victorian Parliament, and became known, nationwide, as a politician who put principle before practice and resigned.

Jacqueline Grant made her contribution to a biography of William Redfern by widening our understanding of the Redferns - Sarah and William - through the lives of their convicts, and the Ireland of those days that gave birth to them.[48]

John Grant had been selected by Redfern to work on his farm. Jane O'Brien was assigned to Sarah. The two Irish convicts fell in love. Sarah and William Redfern are portrayed as caring and compassionate, extending helping hands to the young Irish couple whose life together was tragically short.[49]

This book detailed John Grant's contribution to Redfern's farming activities and to their expansion over time. It was Grant who pushed the frontier of Redfern's land holdings into and over the Blue Mountains area - "Ultra Montane" - to use Redfern's own description, claiming acres for himself, along the way.[50]

The origins for my own contribution are to be found in an experience of teaching in the primary field of education that began in one-teacher country schools. It developed strong links with local communities and their beginnings.

Cessnock Municipal Council supported my proposal for an historical society affiliated with the RAHS. It held its first meeting on 27 September 1954. For my local initiatives in the field of school and public libraries I was nominated successfully for Affiliate Membership of the Library Association of Australia (NSW) by Elizabeth Hill, head of the School Library Service, and Ron McGreal, Secretary to the Library Board.[51]

Effective education proceeds from the known to the unknown. The rain that fell on the school playground at Bingara, when I was teaching there, gave birth to a teaching unit on the inland river system of New South Wales. In turn, Minto School's historic neighbours, the Redferns, would inspire the teaching of local studies. The interest and motivation of children both demanded and deserved a knowledge-based response to their presence. And, since nothing stimulates the interest of children more than a good story, what was the story of William and Sarah Redfern?

From what has already been said, my search started with the published accounts of Dunlop and Ford but continued by retracing their steps through the Mitchell Library with the help of librarians and card index. On only one of innumerable library cards did I find a minor historical slip.

Members of the school's Parents and Citizens Association were among the first audience for my discoveries. It was essential that they should hear the story, as *Campbellfield,*[52] Redfern's name for his property, had been changed to *Buena Vista.*

Had associations with William and Sarah Redfern been lost with the name? Perhaps there might even be resistance to the idea of presenting a former convict in a positive light? I need not have worried. At my suggestion, and in full knowledge of the source, the parents adopted as a school motto, "Truth and Courage", freely translated from the Latin *Virtus et veritas prevalebunt* on a coat of arms said to be William Redfern's.[53] An agricultural motif suggestive of Redfern's farming interests was central to the design of a school badge that won a competition among district high school students.

By August 1963 I was rash enough to write to the Department of Education, suggesting a name change for the school from *Minto,* to *Campbellfield,* where the school was now sited. The district[54], that gave its name to school and village, stretched from the Nepean River to Liverpool. It was large enough to be subdivided into Upper and Lower Minto, but from the school's point of view lacked that close association with the Campbellfield homestead site on which it stood.[55]

For a National Trust open day at the Redfern homestead I typed a two-page chronology of William Redfern for visitors,[56] and as a reference for the local school community. In 1967 I was able to feature the William Redfern story in an exhibition, part of the centenary celebrations of Saggart Field Provisional School.[57]

This had been the first local school built by parents of the children on land given to the Catholic Church for school purposes, on the western ridge of Bow Bowing Creek.

Eventually a school was built nearby and given the district name, Minto. When the school at East Minto burned down a decision was taken to have children from both schools, east and west, attend a new one, Minto Public School on the corner of Pembroke and Redfern roads, its present site.

The search, and a widening resource base.

By then, I had sighted much of the primary Redfern material, documents, letters, etc., for which cards were available in the Catalogue of Printed Books, the manuscript catalogue, the Bigge index, and the *Sydney Gazette.* My library visits were on alternate Saturdays in the afternoon. In the mornings I attended the Council meeting of the N.S.W. Teachers' Federation as the representative of teachers from Campbelltown, Camden, and Picton. I caught a train pulled by a steam locomotive.

One of my early aims was to find descendants of the Redferns.[58] The Society of Australian Genealogists had no knowledge of any, but gave me the address of a Councillor of the R.A.H.S., James Antill. He, in turn, referred me to the author, M.H. Ellis, of whom more will be heard, later.

On 19 August 1964, I wrote to the Deputy Principal Librarian, M. Hancock, Mitchell Library, Sydney, in appreciation, and seeking further help in my enquiries. I was particularly interested in Redfern's portrait, his first wife, the route taken by the *Estramina,* carrying Redfern from Norfolk Island, and whether the Library had any books that had belonged to Redfern. [There was one, but it was not known as such until years later.]

On the same day, letters went to M.H. Ellis, early chronicler of the Macquarie era, and to a Fred Redfearn, of whom little more was known than a name and address on a catalogue card at the library. Ellis provided insights into the character of Redfern, which I was seeking. The letter to Fred Redfearn opened a friendly correspondence that further stimulated our mutual interest in William Redfern.

Some references have been excluded in order to keep this opening account of the Redfern study focused. *The Emancipist,* "written round the life of Surgeon William Redfern...and incidentally of Governor Lachlan Macquarie" seemed inviting.[59] Published in 1936, and with only Dunlop's account of the Nore mutiny as its source, it is not surprising to find *Act 1,* a work of pure fiction. On the other hand, a short introductory account of Redfern contains an item rarely mentioned then or later: "Redfern was returned to Sydney in 1803". While that was correct, what followed was not. He did not stay, being returned to Norfolk Island.

The Mitchell Library, Sydney: Historical and Descriptive Notes, was published in the same year. "Issued by the Trustees of the Public Library of New South Wales in the Centenary Year of the Founder", the book revealed the wealth of material possessed by the *Mitchell* and pointed the way to a future use of the treasure, be it in the writing of works of fact, or fiction. I bought a copy.

Ellis would make good use of this library, publishing a biography of *Lachlan Macquarie,* in 1947, positioning Redfern on a larger canvas in a positive light. Ellis continued his study of the colonial period, with a biography of *Francis Greenway,* in 1949, and of *John Macarthur* in 1955. Each work has contributed to this study.

Ellis made further references to Redfern in the first edition of the *Journal and Proceedings* of the Campbelltown and Airds Historical Society. In his address to the Society, Ellis mentioned Macquarie's party having called at *Campbellfield* for "a very handsome cold Colation" on their way to the foundation ceremony for Campbelltown, on Thursday, 1 December 1820, in which William and Sarah Redfern participated.[60] "Dr Redfern's old home, near Minto" was the first in the list of buildings recommended for preservation under the heading, "The Society's Formation, Aims and Activities".[61]

1954 saw Morton Herman's *The Early Australian Architects...,* while *Macquarie's Journals of his Tours...*appeared in 1956, and *The Australian Encyclopaedia* in ten volumes followed in 1958.

The first two volumes of the *Australian Dictionary of Biography* covering the period 1788-1850 were published in 1967, providing both inspiration and a handy source of information.

Treading the same soil as Sarah and William Redfern at *Campbellfield,* Minto, gave this study its Australian roots, but wider studies were crucial.

On retirement from teaching I enrolled at Wollongong University to read urban geography and sociology, with an eye to conservation values, in both the built and natural environment. These studies linked to my experience in local government, and provided understanding and incentive for my third age activity as community member of a Macarthur planning and implementation authority; first in its planning role and again at a point where attracting industry to the burgeoning community had become the primary object.

At Wollongong University my ongoing study of the life of William Redfern would benefit from the economic, political and historical emphases of the subjects taken, on the one hand, and on the other, from the constant demands of reading, and of juggling ideas, information and sources in discussion and writing, disciplined by word counts and time frames.

History of medicine.

A chance reading of a notice board, at Campbelltown Public Library, while I was waiting to give a talk about William Redfern, led my wife and me from 20 to 28 February 1994 on "a history tour" of Norfolk Island, under the guidance of Dr John Turner, of Newcastle University.[62] One day on the Island, over lunch and by invitation I talked about some of Redfern's local experiences. Fay Heikkila asked whether I had ever been to the Library where Ford had contributed so much. My answer being in the negative I was told how I might make good my omission.[63]

On my return to Sydney I kept an appointment with the librarian, Brenda Heagney, at the History of Medicine Library, Royal Australasian College of Physicians, Macquarie Street, Sydney.[64] There on the table, in front of me, was a midwifery text that Redfern had brought with him to Australia on the convict transport, *Minorca.*

This was typical of the thoughtful attention I received at the College. Beside the Redfern text was "An Annotated Bibliography of the History of Medicine and Health in Australia", a most useful guide for my reading. This was a major revision and updating of an earlier *Annotated Bibliography* published in 1956 by Bryan Gandevia, who gave credit to Alison Holster for her stimulus in getting the revision under way and her enthusiasm that brought completion.[65]

As a professional librarian of the History of Medicine Library from 1969 to 1986, Alison Holster was held to be "mainly responsible for the development of the Library into a nationally respected service",[66]a reputation ably maintained and extended by her successor Brenda Heagney, who had wide experience in the field of history of medicine librarianship.[67] Each was actively involved with Health and Medicine Societies.

Likewise, Megan Hicks, of *Health and Medical Museums,* was active in promoting the association of people enthused by the materials of practice in health and medicine, their study, provenance and collection. This has taken her to the Sydney Powerhouse Museum, first as curator of health and medicine, and presently as commissioning producer of permanent galleries.

The History of Medicine Library of the Royal Australasian [now Australian and New Zealand] College of Physicians had developed a keen interest in our present concern, preventive medicine. Some notable scholars closely associated with the library, included Dr Leslie Cowlishaw[68], Sir Edward Ford, and Dr Bryan Gandevia.[69] The latter propagated the idea that the "history of medicine permeates all aspects of history".[70]

The truth of this concept would grow on me as I embarked upon an extended and profitable voyage in the company of Royal Navy surgeons and seamen of the eighteenth and nineteenth centuries. A collection of rare books of the period would light the way.

That was not all. Membership of History of Medicine, and Health and Medicine Museum societies brought contact with others actively engaged in the study and writing of medical history. At meetings of these societies I met, heard, and came to understand the people involved.

As well as regular meetings of the New South Wales Society I attended two biennial conferences of the Australian Society, one on Norfolk Island, on my second visit, and the other in Sydney. These challenged me to further comprehend important changes within the study of medical history itself, and the importance of contributions to health and medicine literature made by persons other than practising professional workers in those fields.[71]

My understanding of both points of view was fed by these experiences and by the opportunity to read at the Library. They were exciting years of education, of challenge and reward, both for myself, and for my ongoing study.

I am particularly grateful to Bryan Gandevia and Brenda Heagney for seeking my advice on a priority need for William Redfern studies, adding a copy of the minutes of Redfern's court martial to the collection, and allowing me first use. The paper I wrote at the time remained unpublished but now contributes to the relevant chapter of this book.

Talking and writing about William Redfern.

I often wondered why no one had published a book-length study of William Redfern. He had certainly captured the interest of each of the five authors, whose work has been discussed, and others, too. People who have formed the audience for story, lecture and display, or shared a conversation about William Redfern have shown more than a passing interest.

The idea of a book fed upon the notion that William needed to be seen for himself, centre stage, where past conclusions might be contested and new interpretations given space to develop to full flowering.

Consider the fleet mutinies. It was not enough to read *about* the minutes of Redfern's court martial. A copy of the minutes needed to be in front of one.

It was essential but insufficient to read about the Nore fleet mutiny simply because Redfern was involved. Understanding the Spithead fleet mutiny, which preceded that at the Nore, was essential reading, too.

And so it went on. One pebble - a book, paper, or idea - made ever-widening ripples on the pond. Widen the pond. Make it a sea. Fill it with ships. Make war. Change pebbles into cannon balls. Out of the storm of the sea rescue your story.

Progress on the book was also a little stormy, unlike the day I went aboard another wooden ship the *Endeavour* replica, with Frank, formerly of the RN and RAN, neighbour and friend. Both within and without Sydney Harbour the sea remained as still as a millpond for the few hours of its journey.

Inspiration came from many sources. A biennial conference of the Australian Society of the History of Medicine planned for Norfolk Island was important. The theme, "Mutiny and Medicine", fitted nicely with my own studies, so I settled upon contributing a poster and prepared an abstract to go with it.[72]

Although restrictive, a poster challenges selectivity and demands quality in visual presentation.[73] A poster does have the advantage of stretching the presentation time over the whole conference. Since then, this Redfern poster has lent itself to talks and exhibitions associated with open days at Campbellfield.

Dr Bryan Gandevia threw out the next challenge to my Redfern studies. What might be included about William Redfern in six hundred words? This was the length of the entry that he had been invited to write for the *New English Dictionary of National Biography*. The final statement was his, alone, of course.[74]

My study of William Redfern had everything to gain at that point from the critical acumen of a man twice endowed by a doctorate in medicine, and a lifetime of studies and writing of the history of health and medicine. I was mindful too, of the fact that Dr Gandevia had taken a special interest in my Redfern study since our first meeting at the History of Medicine Library.

There was another exchange, too. Relevant Gandevia files housed in the basement of the History of Medicine Library were opened to my search. In return I was able to satisfy his requests for specific items of information. My literature review in an early state of preparation came under the critical gaze of a man selected to place the stamp of his experience and skills upon a special edition of the *Medical Journal of Australia*.

This led to the London *Journal of Medical Biography*. Drs Bryan Gandevia and Ian Chapple encouraged me to submit an article. I was familiar with this quarterly journal, having read the full series at the History of Medicine Library. In due course I submitted two papers. Chronology structured the first, and themes the second. Each proved acceptable to the referees and was published in 1999.

Towards a table of contents.

The purpose of the literature review to this point has been threefold. An early intention was to introduce and link authors, biographical details, and primary and secondary records. An emphasis on histories of health and medicine followed. These authenticated Redfern's experience in those fields. A third intention was to lay the foundation of central themes that helped structure this work.

These ideas will continue to work throughout the book. Their true measure will be found in the text as place and circumstance change over time. The process of getting knowledge appropriate to the task has evolved with information technology but has taken time.

At first, large volumes of the Bigge Transcripts, on request, trundled into the Mitchell Library Reading Room on metal book trolleys. These have been supplanted by stripfilm on open access shelving and film readers. Macquarie's *Journals of his tours* is now online with much else.

Visits in person to librarians and libraries provided opportunities to search bookshops along the way. Interlibrary loans came into play. Electronic search engines have had their impact on this study. One needs of course the spider's ability to reach its prey and return without becoming ensnared at some point of intersection of ideas in a world wide web.

Writing has been done in pencil and pen, typewriter and word processor. As it stands, this book is a work of reference, providing an entry to the life and times of William Redfern, through a miscellany of primary and secondary records. It has attempted to be definitive, dividing fact from fiction wherever possible.

Redfern, as place, is a suburb close to the heart of Sydney, Australia. It is associated now with Aboriginal people and inner city renewal. It is a reminder that William Redfern had early connections in the colonial era with both Aboriginal people and places. He farmed formerly Aboriginal lands.

The one-time simple country home of Sarah and William Redfern, *Campbellfield*, at Minto, faces Sarah Redfern Public School, which provides education, for infants, primary and high school students, as well as special education.

The old saw that prevention is better than cure stands well enough for the whole book. Gilbert Blane was aware that this emphasis, in health and medicine, was peculiarly appropriate to ships. But even there, an emphasis on prevention paid due regard to what Erwin Heinz Ackerknecht described among revolutionary French physicians as "due in part to a loss of confidence in the available therapeutic methods".[75]

In the more diverse and rapidly changing environment of land warfare, where death from disease exceeded wounds, the pace of public health improvement was slower. Even so, it had its outstanding activists, among them being Donald Monro, Pringle, Fitzpatrick and McGrigor.[76]

Presently the annual William Redfern Oration honours the man and the theme, in both its medical and wider social imperative. Each, in turn, exemplified in the work of Edward Ford, professor in that discipline, and by members of the College of Physicians working in Public Health, who conceived the idea of a commemorative Oration.

The words in the title of my opening chapter 'Ground bait for further fishing' came from Harold B. Carter. *The Sheep and Wool Correspondence of Sir Joseph Banks 1781-1820*, 1979.[77]

A sea change follows. This time it is not only "the fishermen of England [who] go down to the sea in ships" (from a song for male voice choirs) but Royal Navy seamen.

1797 was the year William Redfern joined the Royal Navy, and of two great victories. In February, at St Vincent, Admiral Sir John Jervis (later, Earl St. Vincent) attacked a numerically superior Spanish Fleet and Horatio Nelson helped secure victory. In October, an earlier mutinous North Sea Fleet, under Admiral Duncan, defeated the Dutch at Camperdown.

Yet, between those two battles, several fleet mutinies, centring upon Spithead, and the Nore, occurred around the shores of England. Professor Conrad Gill made an exhaustive study of the mutinies and came to a conclusion that service in the navy at that time involved hardships, which were in no way essential to a seafaring life.[78]

Paul Brunton contrasted these fleet mutinies with the single ship affair on Bligh's *Bounty*.[79]

"The ship was not engaged in great affairs. Her crew was not the first or even the second rank of British seamen. It included a blind fiddler, a drunken surgeon, a couple of inexperienced boys taken on as a favour to their relatives, a troublesome and troublemaking carpenter, an ageing master and a ship's corporal completely unsuited to the role of policeman".

"There was no passionate aim on behalf of the mutineers to improve the conditions of sea life, as was the case with the large scale mutinies which would immobilize an entire British fleet in a few years' time".

Forgetting has bedevilled these larger mutinies, and remembering has been the lot of the *Bounty*, which "became one of the most famous; recounted again and again in the nineteenth century and re-enacted five times on film in the twentieth". Perversely, this mutiny, "the most celebrated of all maritime mutinies, was of no importance". [80]

Greg Dening wondered whether the idea, "That the whole fleet should mutiny not once but twice in home waters in the shadow of a revolution in France, was a shock that the British seem best to have survived by forgetting". [81]

While there were common grievances throughout the Royal Navy it is not correct that the Royal Navy, as one "whole fleet", [82] mutinied as claimed by Greg Dening, above,[83] and his critic, Keith Windschuttle on a subsequent occasion.[84]

Windschuttle did provide a partial reason as to why the 1797 mutinies have been forgotten: "Most of the handful of books and articles published on the 1797 mutinies are now out of print and familiarity with most of them was, anyway, largely confined to professional historians".

The English Channel Fleet mutiny, off Southampton, at Spithead and places nearby, confront the reader in the second chapter of my study. To their credit, the seamen petitioned for change, time and again. By ignoring these petitions, as well as the advice of certain admirals and captains of ships, the chances of preventing the mutinies were lost.

A later Board of Admiralty, forgetting the political lessons of the 1797 fleet mutinies again failed to prevent a similar debacle at Invergordon in 1934.

"The naval mutiny of 1797 is the most astonishing recorded in our, or perhaps any history; astonishing by its management rather than for its results, for other mutinies have been successful. Though a thoroughgoing and alarming mutiny, which shook the country from end to end since it occurred in the middle of a war, in one part at least it was ordered with rigid discipline, a respect for officers, and unswerving loyalty to the King. If throughout its course it was sensationally dramatic, marked by swift changes, halts and rebounds, and in many ways mysterious, in its chief manifestation it never overstepped the bounds it had set itself in the beginning. Moreover it was so rationally grounded that it not only achieved its immediate end, the betterment of the sailor's lot, but also began a new and lasting epoch in naval administration. Thus besides being a part of Naval History, it also forms a chapter in Social History, a queer, poignant, naked-nerved chapter, which even at this the present day [1935] contains lessons that have never been properly learnt".[85]

The authors of these observations, Manwaring and Dobrée gave full credit to "the invaluable piece of research by Professor Conrad Gill, *The*

Naval Mutinies of 1797, published in 1913". Their own work differed in having access to material not available to Gill, and in that he "seems to have had less sympathy with the sailors than we have".

Even so, Gill considered that at Spithead, "The cause of the mutineers was such as might commend itself to a sober and normally well-disposed seaman". And, again, "The seamen had good cause to ask for a reform in naval administration...There was some justification for their refusal to weigh anchor when they found their petitions had been ignored".

For the early chapters of this book, I have accessed each of these studies, and a later work by Dugan, whose singular title, "The Great Mutiny", collapses the several mutinies into "an isolated major event in industrial history".

In 2006, when Nicholas Rodger's *The Command of the Ocean, A Naval History of Britain 1649-1815* became available to me these earlier works were critically reviewed.[86]

Rodger dismissed the idea that "designing landmen [Quota men] had been introduced into the Navy to corrupt the simple sailors".[87] Rodger also reported "a variation on this theme a contrast [which he said] has been proposed between the 'unpolitical' (benign, morally justified) Spithead mutinies, and the 'political' or 'revolutionary' (malign and dangerous) mutinies on the East Coast".[88]

In following chapters these matters will be discussed in some detail.

For Redfern, it mattered little whether he had joined the Channel, or North Sea Fleet, as far as mutiny was concerned, as each fleet mutinied in 1797. On the contrary, the outcomes displayed the 'two faces of paternalism', forgiveness at Spithead and punishment at the Nore.

Grievances, a driving force in the mutinous fleets, were common to the whole British Navy. These are considered in the third chapter in their naval, historical, political, and social settings, against a background of peace and war.

The health and medical implications of the grievances are examined in the fourth chapter that serves as well to introduce the surgeon and his mate to their wooden world. This called upon my reading at the Library of Medical History, RACP, Sydney.

"Statesmen, I believe, seldom or never read the medical history of fleets and armies. They are afraid that such gloomy narratives would alarm conscience, and bring on fits of hypochondriacism. Yet by these means, they might be made wiser ministers, if not better men". Thomas Trotter, M.D., physician to the Channel Fleet, held this opinion in 1807. [89]

In chapter five, ships from the North Sea Fleet, including H.M.S. the *Standard*, with Redfern aboard, mutinied and sailed south to join the Nore mutiny at the mouth of the River Thames. Redfern's court martial takes up the following chapter, the sixth.

Gigantic disturbances form the subject matter of the seventh. This material is well within the natural bounds of concern of this book, at this point. Social change had national and global dimensions. A contemporary increase in the gaol population and convict transportation set the scene for later chapters.

One unresolved grievance of the mutinous seamen, shore leave, and the presence of women aboard ships of war, at sea, leads into a search for understanding. This, in turn, raises questions of the status of women on ships and in the world at large, in the late 18th and early 19th centuries. Contemporary and later women's voices will be heard in this eighth chapter which leads into a discussion of childbirth since William Redfern practised as a male midwife.

The strong focus on preventing disease on wooden ships, at sea, moves from Royal Navy seamen to convicts en route to Botany Bay, in chapter nine.

Chapter 10 has William Redfern's personal experience of transportation in the convict ship, *Minorca*, to Port Jackson, and from there, to Norfolk Island in the *Harrington.* This chapter concludes Volume I.[90]

Volume II has Redfern returned to the mainland where he was appointed acting Colonial Surgeon and placed in charge of the Convict General Hospital at Sydney Cove. Volume II, chapters 1 and 2 have that story.

Redfern's farming activities are described in chapter thirteen. As a social process Redfern is involved in feeding the "gaol", which was, of course the whole convict settlement. This was a significant expression of Redfern's twin desires of being "restored to society" and of "bettering himself".

Redfern's *Report on Convict Transports* provides a contemporary handbook on preventive medicine at sea. While it had particular reference to the convicts, other people on board - master (captain), crew, marines, soldiers, and those who came free - stood to gain from a healthy ship, and to suffer the consequences, on the contrary. Over time, Redfern's report would benefit immigrant ships. This is chapter 4 in Volume I.

With matters going well for Redfern, certain policies of the British Government, with some help from colonial critics, came into play, with devastating effects.

Commissioner John Thomas Bigge paid a visit to New South Wales. He was reminded before leaving London that "transportation to New South Wales is intended as a severe punishment, applied to various crimes; and as such must be rendered an object of real terror to all classes of the community".

Volume II builds upon exchanges between Bigge, Macquarie, and Redfern in Sydney and in London from 1818 to 1824.

During this time the Redfern family travelled to London in the emancipist cause. Sarah had a second son. Trowbridge in Wiltshire claimed attention and Redfern enrolled in the Medical School at Edinburgh University.

References in the literature to Redfern's religious, philanthropic, and educational beliefs, practise and experiences give rise to two thematic chapters.

In *Acting Chaplain* (Volume II) providence and prudence come into play with benevolence, caring and believing. In *Mind Furniture* emphasis is on education.

The final chapter (Volume II) sees William, unwell in London, unsettled on his return to the colony. He vacillated between country farm and city practice, and again between farm and bank. His directorship of the Bank of New South Wales proved to be a mixed blessing. Amending his *will* he left for Edinburgh with his elder son.

A chance discovery on the one hand, put in doubt the accepted and depressing account of his Edinburgh years, and on the other directed my research to a more edifying conclusion in favour of William Redfern.

Chapter 1

GROUND BAIT FOR FURTHER FISHING[1]

William Redfern: Birth and Death?

What did the first group of biographers, discussed in the *Introduction,* discover about the life of William Redfern? Dunlop led the discussion, with an account of Redfern telling Bigge that he was about nineteen years of age at the time of the Mutiny at the Nore in 1797.[2] This gave a birth year around 1778.

Dunlop's single page "post scriptum"[3] reported the discovery of a certificate of burial for William Redfern that pointed to the New Calton Burying Ground, Edinburgh, Scotland. Dunlop credited Dr Scot Skirving with this discovery.[4] This showed William Redfern to have died in Edinburgh in July 1833, at the age of fifty-eight, providing a year of birth as either 1774 or 1775.

Dunlop told how the *Sydney Gazette* scotched an earlier rumour of Redfern's death at sea.[5]

1774-5(?) should have been accepted now, but Ford held with 1778.[6] Although he mentioned Dunlop's postscript in his paper, he held to fifty-five as against fifty-eight for Redfern's age at death.[7] 1778 will be found in his entry in the *Australian Encyclopaedia.*[8]

Fred Redfearn, a Victorian surveyor, came on the scene, obtaining from London in 1955 a copy of the "Muster Log of HMS *Standard",* the ship on which Redfern had served.[9] This gave Redfern's age as twenty-two years on joining the Navy in January 1797. This supports the possible birth year derived from the certificate of burial mentioned earlier. A decision between 1774 and 1775 rests upon the month of birth, as noted by Pescott.

Dougal Hay, a Scottish friend of Frank Clune had also contributed, finding Redfern's gravestone.[10] Clune, subsequently, published a photograph taken by Dr Alexander Dunbar. The stone shows that William Redfern had died on 17 July 1833.[11] James Rillie, Assistant Recorder of City Burial Grounds, replied to a request from Fred Redfearn for information about the grave.[12] It had "an upright tombstone in good condition, which measures approx. 5 feet high by 3 feet wide. On it is carved in clear lettering the following,

"William Redfern Esq.,
Died 17 July, 1833".

Rillie continued: "The grave [in the New Calton Burial ground] is well kept, in good order and what beautiful surroundings, as is the whole burial ground, which overlooks the Abbey of Holyrood where ancient Scottish Kings are buried, also the Palace of Holyroodhouse, H.M. the Queen's official residence in Edinburgh".[13]

Clune's "certificate", called by him "a Death Certificate",[14] in hindsight was the certificate of burial of 23 July 1833 mentioned by Dunlop.[15] For some reason, Clune did not give priority to Fred Redfearn for his Muster Log discovery,[16] but when the oversight was brought to his attention he sent Fred a copy of his book, gratis.

Clune's general conclusion stands. Redfern's "age, 58 years [at death], agrees with the statement [he] made...in 1797, when joining the Navy, that he was twenty-two".[17]

Pescott thought the Muster could have been "lax or carelessly recorded", and that it was in Redfern's interest to impress Bigge with his youth at the time of the Mutiny.[18] Evidence in the first case, and understanding in the second, contradict these suggestions.

Clune noted a reference to Redfern's death in the *Australian* newspaper of 27 December 1833. "[T]he melancholy intelligence has been received of the death of William Redfern Esq., M.D., which happened at Edinburgh in July last. Mrs Redfern who left this port on the 10 March 1833...to join the Doctor did not reach London till two days after his interment (sic).[19]

Dr Betty Iggo, genealogist, of Edinburgh, working on my behalf, confirmed the particular references of Dunlop and of Clune. Her account follows. "A record of the death of William Redfern may be found in the Old Parish Register 692/2, Vol 34, South Leith, New Calton Burying Ground. "The Record of Mortality" kept in the Calton Burying Ground for July 1833 has a record of the burial of William Redfern, aged 58, formerly Surgeon of 18 Lothian Street, in the New Ground in the grave purchased for his executors by Mr David Walker.[20] No disease, or cause of death, is shown".[21]

A primary reference to Redfern's birth, perhaps in a family letter - not presently known to the writer - is needed to clarify such temporal uncertainties as day, month, and year of his birth.[22] Not to mention the names of his parents, and place of birth.

A Place to be Born?

Since the HMS *Standard Muster Log* correctly recorded Redfern's age on joining the Navy, is there any reason to doubt the Log's reference to Canada, as his place of birth? Canada does lack corroboration, but Clune accepted a Canadian birthplace on the strength of the *Muster Log* record.[23]

Pescott did not, adding two more arguments against Canada to his idea of muster log unreliability. Redfern had a brother and two sisters settled in England.[24] However, there is a gap of some thirty-five years between Redfern's birth year, 1774 or 1775, and 1810, for the "brother in England", ample time for the family to leave Canada and settle in, or return to England, or Ireland, after William's birth.

In my own limited search on this point, a Canadian correspondent advised, "1775 is a very early date for an English birth in Canada. There was no settlement in Ontario at that time and although founded in 1749 Halifax in Nova Scotia would not have been described as Canada. Montreal is therefore the most likely place of birth. As it became British territory only in 1760 the English Population in 1775 was still very small and was largely confined to army personnel, merchants and fur traders. Quebec City is likely the only other possibility".[25]

There is a story here, interesting, but not definitive. Let us suppose that Canada linked the Port Jackson triumvirate, Governor Lachlan Macquarie, his aide-de-camp, Major Henry Colden Antill, and Colonial Surgeon William Redfern. What a talking point that would have made on the Macquarie tours they shared and where they got on so well together.

Macquarie volunteered for the army in 1776, and was posted to Nova Scotia, arriving there when Redfern would have been a year or two old. Might Macquarie have known Redfern's parents?

Antill was born of British stock in New York on 1 May 1779. His father fought for Britain in the war of American Independence and as a result lost his property and moved to Canada. Henry grew up there and joined the British Army in 1796.

Antill's presence at Port Jackson followed from his Indian service friendship with Captain Lachlan Macquarie, with whose 73rd Regiment he travelled to Port Jackson. Redfern arrived there as a result of being found guilty of mutiny at the Nore, one of the whole fleet mutinies of 1797.

The three friends were together on the Governor's crossing of the Blue Mountains in 1815 and although others were included in the party including Mrs Macquarie, Antill could not "help mentioning with satisfaction, the unanimity and good understanding which subsisted between every individual, composing our small society. Not a word of ill humour passed the whole time: on the contrary, everyone appeared to use his endeavour to make the time pass as pleasantly as possible".[26]

After Commissioner Bigge's arrival, time did not pass so pleasantly for them[27]. This present context seems appropriate to introduce two aspects of the commissioner's impact, his inquiry method and his reports, which have a critical role in this study.

Bigge recalled this interview and the circumstances associated with it in his *Report* of 1822. The question at issue was: "How should persons, once convicted, be regarded when they had served their time or had been emancipated?"

"Major Antill, accompanied by Mr Redfern," Bigge observed, "called upon most of them [the officers of the 48th regiment], and with the exception of Lieutenant-colonel Erskine, Major Morisset, and Major Druitt, was denied admittance, under circumstances that must have been very painful to Mr Redfern, and ought to have speedily convinced Major Antill of the bad effects of his injudicious friendship". [28]

Macquarie, Antill, and Redfern remained close friends, in spite of the commissioner.[29]

Returning to the quest for Redfern's birthplace, it should be noted that neither Dunlop in the postscript to his 1928 paper, nor Ford writing in 1953, knew of the *Muster Log* record, so neither mentioned Canada. Dunlop, on the strength of possibly two of Redfern's medical texts, looked to Scotland. Ford thought more of a brother in Trowbridge.

Pescott took this brother to be *Robert*, the only brother mentioned in Redfern's *Will*.[30] As it turned out, it was Thomas, also a surgeon, who lived in Trowbridge with his wife and son. Already told in my published paper this story will reappear below with the reason for Thomas being left out of the will.

Clune followed Fred Redfearn's story of "red ferns" - bracken in autumn, in this case - and a place of that name. However, after diligent search, Clune gave up. No one seemed to follow the red haired Viking, Eric the Red! M. H. Ellis, biographer of Macquarie, Macarthur and Greenway, assured me that

William Redfern did have red hair and all the qualities that went with it. Was Ellis confusing Redfern with D'Arcy's son, William Charles Wentworth? [31]

Ireland appeared as a pointer to Redfern's place of origin but was not followed up by the early writers. Elizabeth Macquarie, the Governor's wife, understood Redfern to have had a brother in Ireland. Joseph Holt described both Darcy Wentworth and William Redfern, as "from the north of Ireland".[32] Clune published material from Joseph Holt's original memoirs four years after his *Hillsborough* book. Peter O'Shaughnessy published the full text in 1988.[33]

Patrick O'Farrell omitted Redfern from *The Irish in Australia.*[34] Anne-Maree Whitaker, in her biography of Joseph Foveaux, described William Redfern as a native of Belfast.[35] Redfern was mentioned again as Irish, in Whitaker's book about United Irishmen, but not as one of them.[36]

It was Redfern himself, however, who confirmed a later Irish link. In 1988, Professor John Pearn published his account of finding William Redfern's signature in the Matriculation Roll of the University of Edinburgh for the year 1822, the first for that year; an original observation in the William Redfern story.[37] Subsequently Dr Iggo, genealogist, found that Redfern had given Londonderry as his address in the years 1830-31, when he again enrolled at Edinburgh University.[38]

A Bedside Manner?

The mind boggles at the idea, or even imagining, let alone writing about a doctor's "bedside manner" in the largely convict colony in which Redfern lived and worked. Nevertheless, most of his outpatients would have been visited in their homes.

Robert Howe,[39] who followed his father, George, as editor, wrote of Redfern's "bedside manner"[40] in the *Sydney Gazette* of 6 September 1826. "His methods, or his manner...may not be so winning or seductive as might be wished". There was, too, an "absence of overflowing politeness". [41]

Dunlop described Redfern as "not possessing the soothing voice and gentleness of Dr. Bland - he was even brusque with his patients".[42] To Ford, Redfern was "brusque and direct".[43]

Pescott used most of editor Robert Howe's material.[44] The "absence of overflowing politeness" was there, and Redfern's "medical reputation was not enhanced by any social grace, and his bedside manner was described as being less 'winning and seductive as might be wished'". Pescott's early mentor, John Ritchie, went further. Redfern was "brusque, even violent",[45] but not, of course with his patients, one would hope.

What is to be made of all of this? Was Howe's observation accurate, or was he putting Redfern down? If so, why? Below, and in the penultimate chapter, further light will be thrown on this matter. In that context, take note for comparison, that "the soothing voice and gentleness of Dr. Bland", considerate and clever surgeon though he was, came from a person who had killed an opponent in a duel.

Stephen Jacyna's more recent commentary is relevant. "The personal qualities deemed to constitute an eligible medical practitioner varied widely between national and local contexts, and with the kind of patient they were designed to attract. Manners and deportment remained important: a London consultant, for instance, was expected to visit patients in a 'chariot' as a sign of his status. Some practitioners, such as the surgeon John Abernethy (1764-1831), flourished by adopting a contrarian approach and *affecting* [my italics] a bluff, even rude, manner when dealing with the most socially distinguished patients".[46]

Returning to Howe, why was he believed? Was it for the observation in itself, or because it fitted another stereotype of Redfern, the "bluff, hearty, British sailor", Dunlop's description? Possibly. Redfern's "early career in the Navy" was the reason that his "bedside manner was not perfect".[47]

But, think for a moment. Could a few months of navy service turn a young medical student into a "bluff, hearty, British sailor"? I doubt it. While he thought well of Royal Navy surgeons, Redfern was not impressed by the Navy in general, and tried to leave it. Anyway, life in the Royal Navy at that time, as the Royal Navy physicians, Dr Thomas Trotter and Sir Gilbert Blane will confirm in later chapters, tended not to produce that kind of person. Nevertheless the seamen were revered by each of them for other qualities.

Yet, Dunlop, Ford and Pescott accepted this overnight metamorphosis of an urban educated medical student. It seemed they succumbed to the temptation to suck up scarce information as nectar to the brush tongue of the honeyeater. Give Dunlop his due, he started by publishing the *Gazette* article in full, but finished with a qualification - Redfern "had the skill and that quality of character that carries conviction and inspires confidence - compensations that more than balance honeyed phrases or flattering remarks".[48] That Dunlop's alternative character assessment was correct would be supported in a very private letter, to be considered in a later chapter, from one of Redfern's teenage patients, Elizabeth Macarthur, junior, to her friend.

Redfern, in another private letter that has become public, "Redfern to Bigge", spoke of the qualities of commissioners. While he was not dismissive of "amenity and a finished polish of manners", Redfern expressed a preference for "wisdom & integrity" in a commissioner. The two might be combined, however. One gains the impression that Bigge might have been wiser in watching his manners when interviewing Redfern.[49] Though, why should he worry when his secretary, Scott, was his brother-in-law and shared a similar conservative outlook?

The relationship between William Redfern and Robert Howe was different from that between Redfern and Robert's father, George. For one, the fact that George Howe had married Redfern's mother-in-law brought family into the picture. Clune revealed instances of subsequent family discord.

There was friction between Robert Howe, on the one hand, and the Wills' sisters, who supported their young brother, Horatio Spencer Howe Wills. Robert had thrashed Horatio, his apprentice, who, in turn, came to Redfern's assistance when the latter, having taken a horsewhip to Robert was overwhelmed and 'given as good as he gave'.

Redfern was duly charged, found guilty, and fined. Horatio discretely disappeared.

If, in reading the first one hundred and seventy five pages of Clune's book you wonder why there are so many references to members of the Wills' family, you will find on the page that follows a surprising link with Horatio's disappearance. Extensive research for the book to that point had resulted from Clune's search for the missing Horatio Wills.[50] He will return, as this study comes to an end.

Redfern as a Young Man?

1797 produced the first written references to William Redfern that have been uncovered. At that time he would have been twenty-two years old but what he looked like is anybody's guess. His only known portrait, privately owned, is a miniature painted the year before he died.[51]

Dunlop, Ford and Clune had to be satisfied with a black and white photographic copy. For Grant, Norrie,[52] and myself a colour photograph was available.

At first glance the colour photograph appears to refer to a different portrait, but a closer view reveals congruency of lines. The facial bone structure stands out in b & w, but is smoothed in the colour print.

I have not seen the original but have seen instances of difference in effect between art works as exhibited, and as illustrated in a catalogue; and, as in this case, between b & w, and colour. Again, with no other likenesses of William Redfern for comparison it remains to consider the artist's other works. Some exist, but I am not aware of any study that throws light on the problem of how good a likeness he might have achieved.

Beaglehole, in search of the character of Captain James Cook, had several portraits at his disposal.[53] Did that make it easier? One observer of these portraits, Sir James Watt, saw not so much *character*, as such, but evidence of Cook's state of health.[54]

Certainly William Redfern was not well at the time, earlier considering retreat to a Mediterranean climate. He died in 1833, but there is no evidence of the cause of death.

In contrast to the dearth of precise biographical details of Redfern, as a young man, is the wealth of contemporary references to that same period 1775-1797. For Eric Hobsbawm, on the one hand, and Albert Boime, on the other, it was "an age of revolution" encapsulated in the titles of their studies.[55]

The American Colonies, restive at Redfern's birth, would become independent in the early 1780s. The French would follow in 1789. All the while an industrial revolution, based firstly on the power of running water then upon wood and coal combined with iron technology, was pouring forth a stream of molten minerals that had grown to a raging torrent by the end of the century in Great Britain.

Asa Briggs reflected contemporary understandings from a research literature of primary materials, when he wrote that people "were divided about the merits of 'improvement', but they were at one in admitting that it existed". Briggs' chapter, "Economy and Society in the 1780s", underpinned his study, relevant through periods of war, repression, reform and social cleavage, the social-time scale of this book.[56] This historian will become a familiar voice, but he will not be alone.

Edward Thompson will also make an appearance. He it was who sought "to rescue the poor stockinger, the Luddite cropper, the 'obsolete' hand-loom weaver, the 'utopian' artisan, and even the deluded follower of Joanna Southcott, from the enormous condescension of posterity". Thompson found the compelling reason for paying attention to these people, was the "exceptionally high valuation [placed] upon egalitarian and democratic values".[57]

These same values were at home among the seamen of the mutinous fleets. But were they found at large in British society at that time? Not in practice. As a result, parliamentary reform was central to the demands of those seeking political change, so called "radicals",[58] who had to wait until 1830 for their First Reform Bill.

Surgeon and Sailor of the Enlightenment, Miriam Estensen's subtitle to her biography, *The Life of George Bass*, when joined with the text, confirms Bass as not unsympathetic to such changing political opinion. His wide reading and books in his possession encourage this idea, while his interest in the Scottish Martyrs and readiness to provide medical care for them at Port Jackson confirm it.[59]

Redfern's siding with the seamen against authority, so soon after joining the Royal Navy, suggests that William Redfern had been affected by the revolutionary temper of the times, and like Bass, had not neglected his medical studies.[60] Redfern told Commissioner Bigge that he had gained a medical education in England and had passed an examination of the College of Surgeons.

Ford accepted Redfern's own statement that his medical education was obtained in London[61] and said that it "almost certainly consisted of some years of apprenticeship to a surgeon, during which he lived with his master and assisted him in his daily tasks. The training of Redfern's apprentices, James Shears and Henry Cowper, was probably based on his own experience".[62]

The Great Fleet Mutinies of 1797?

Dunlop's concern for the seamen matched a need for an improvement in their treatment but showed little understanding of what happened when the seamen took matters into their own hands. In 1928 he described how "the men of the Navy normally loyal and docile, ran amok", and "succumbed readily to the insane virus of insurrection".[63]

Professor Conrad Gill's studied conclusion published in 1913 by Manchester University Press revealed a different story.

Professor Nicholas A. M. Rodger[64] recently concluded, "The outstanding feature of this mutiny - appreciated by the seamen themselves, by their officers and the Admiralty, by the Parliament and the nation as a whole - was its respectability".[65] Amazingly, this mutiny of the whole Channel Fleet in a time of war also had "the support of public opinion".[66]

If that has been difficult for some people to accept today, it was all the more difficult for Pitt and the Lords of Admiralty to accept in 1797. The unanimity, resolution and reasonableness of the seamen led Pitt to call upon Admiral Howe to settle the first great fleet mutiny at Spithead.

Pitt did not accept Howe's offer to conciliate at the Nore, where the second great fleet mutiny was under way, even though concessions made at Spithead had "prevented far worse troubles".[67]

Ford, writing in 1953, had both the work of Conrad Gill, *The Naval Mutinies of 1797*, and, *An account of the Mutinies at Spithead and the Nore in 1797,* by G. E. Manwaring and Bonamy Dobrée,[68] available to him. The latter, first published in 1935, was in 1937, the eighth of the original Pelican Books. Ford, by using these sources, including Surgeon Snipe's letter at the Nore in 1797, moved away from the outdated Tobias Smollett, as chief witness for conditions in the Royal Navy in that year. [69]

Clune, by publishing extracts from the *Minutes* of Redfern's court martial, stole a march on James Dugan, whose book was accessed by Pescott.[70] Dugan, alone, of the mutiny authors, wrote of William Redfern in a short chapter, appropriately named "The Mutineer Surgeon".

Clune dealt with the fleet mutinies in his thirteenth chapter.[71] "Under the heading 'Proceedings of a Court Martial', the story is told in five notebooks of about seventy pages each, 'copied from Mr Gurney's shorthand notes'".[72] Clune's "friend in London, Jeffrey Gibian", who did "diligent research at the Public Record Office", supplied the copies of the court martial minutes.

Gibian found no reference to William Redfern, by name, in "the log books of Captain Parr and John Rorie, the *Standard*'s Master". However, Redfern would have been the "surgeon's mate" in Gibian's quote from the Master's log for 14 June 1797: "Came on board 80 privates of the Warwick Militia with their officers, sent on shore to prison for mutiny 37 marines, 1 surgeon's mate, and 23 seamen.

William Redfern and a Medical Upbringing?

Let us accept the Muster Log and give Redfern a Canadian birth. Who might his parents have been? His mother's name would be most acceptable, but his father's profession is more likely to be indicated. Assuming British origin, there is a possibility that his father was in the British army, or navy, in Canada at the time, or perhaps in the Hudson Bay Company.

Next, it may be supposed, that Redfern's father was a surgeon, as three of his sons had a medical background.[73] Irvine Loudon pointed out, that "[m]any surgeon-apothecaries in the late eighteenth century", were "the sons of medical practitioners. One advantage for a father who practised medicine, and wanted to train his son, was that he paid no premium".[74]

Neither did he have to register his son as an apprentice. To increase the probability in this case, the names of the brothers should not have been recorded on an apprentice register. I did not find their names in a comprehensive computer printout of names of apprentices, masters, and relevant parents.[75] This need not of itself produce a conclusive result.

Dunlop tentatively suggested that Redfern might have "received the whole or part of his professional training in Edinburgh, Scotland". The germ of this idea came from two medical texts that were once owned by Redfern. Admittedly their authors were Scottish but each had taught in England, so that the idea of Redfern's association with Scotland lost its point.

Commissioner Bigge, in his questioning of Surgeon Redfern asked two questions that related to his medical background. "Are you a member of any Medical Society in England Scotland or Ireland?" The written record has Redfern saying "I passed an examination in London before the examiners of the Company of Surgeons but I am not a member of any Medical Society".

"In London", was the answer recorded for Bigge's second question, "Where did you perform your Medical Studies?"[76]

If Redfern had not written a number of letters to Bigge he would not have earned the reputation of critic of the commissioner, nor would posterity have ever known what happened at that inquisition. That is why the word *minute* has been carefully avoided. Redfern's criticisms were concerned with an earlier *draft* that Bigge had sent to him. The published version, above, is the amended version and shows Bigge to have accepted Redfern's criticism, which now follows: [77]

"I must beg leave to remind you Sir; of the great astonishment which you affected at my having said I had passed the usual examination before the Court of Examiners of the Company of Surgeons in London, observing 'Mr Redfern you must mistake, I think they are called "The Royal College of Surgeons". I then explained that 'at the time I had undergone examination (Jany.1797) the[y] were then the Company of Surgeons'".

"I do now contend", Redfern continued, "that my explanation ought to have been noted down as part of My answer to your query, & that omitting it would convey to all those unacquainted with the History of the rise & progress of the Royal College of Surgeons, that I had asserted a deliberate falsehood & that I had undergone no examination whatever And I will further contend, Sir, that from your manner of conducting the examination, from your appeal to your Secretary, Mr Scott, to know whether he knew anything of the matter, that you intended to depreciate my Moral & Medical character by such omission".

Jane Beck, connected by descent from a sister of Redfern, obtained confirmation for Redfern's stand in the reply to her letter to the Royal College of Surgeons, London, in 1992: "A William Redfern attended the Court of Examiners of the Company of Surgeons (our predecessors) on 19th Day of January 1797. No address is recorded. He passed as 3rd Mate on any Rate of Ship".[78] A separate request for information in 2001 brought a similar reply.[79]

Redfern, in his letter, quoted an official Navy document to show that the term, *Surgeons Mate* was in use until 28 January 1805. It was only then that *Assistant Surgeon* came into use in the Royal Navy.[80]

What possible reason could Bigge have had, not only to question Redfern, on a matter so much within his experience, and to bring his secretary into the dispute to back him up, in an argument the commissioner could not possibly win?

Was Bigge deliberately trying to belittle Redfern? Of course, each knew that *Assistant Surgeon* was in use by the time of the interview. That was not the point at issue. (Governor Macquarie had also got it wrong.)

John Ritchie incorporated Redfern's criticism of Bigge's "manner" in a conclusion he had reached about this precise interview in his study of Commissioner Bigge. "Whatever the manner in which Bigge examined Redfern, he set down nothing incriminatory against him. If the interview was not impersonal, the evidence recorded was".[81]

The next year, Ritchie published a variation of this conclusion to fit a wider context. It comes at the end of this sentence: "While it is true that the commissioner's questions occasionally wounded the feelings of his informants, and that such questions, together with the informants' answers, were sometimes omitted by Mr Secretary Thomas Hobbes Scott in his minutes of interviews, it is clear that if the *manner* of Bigge's interviews was not impersonal, in general the evidence recorded was".[82]

As a taste of what lies ahead, let Redfern be heard in a letter to Commissioner Bigge. "You were also pleased to rate my Professional Abilities in examination, very low, & that my expectations in the way of My Profession were raised more than they ought to have been". Prompted by this "impersonal" conclusion, like others that follow, Bigge set out to "ascertain from Redfern what other opportunities [he] had enjoyed of learning & studying [his] Profession beyond those very limited ones that were to be found in the Colony".

As Redfern considered these remarks from Commissioner Bigge to be "in the Judgement of any thinking Man...as unfair, [and] illiberal an attack on My Medical character as the Most predetermined Malice could invent", he dismissed a related question from the Commissioner with less dignity than it might have deserved.

Bigge asked whether Redfern had a Diploma, by which he meant, "belonged to a Medical or Surgical Society". To this, Redfern replied that most "Medical Men" entered the Navy as he had and that service in the Army or Navy of itself could bring entitlement to most of the priviledges of College or Company".

Furthermore, "How Many Medical Men are there in the Colony", Redfern asked the commissioner in return, "who have any other claims than to 'Chalk & Grinding' - and some of them not even that - merely the Fee for St Andrews Degree of M.D.?"

"In those days it was not quite so fashionable to be dubbed an M.D. from St Andrew, where I might for the customary fee have procured one for My Horse".[83] Attendance at lectures or examination, in such cases, was not required from the medical imposter.[84]

Later, in London, worse was to come when Redfern read the commissioner's first published report. "Mr Redfern's professional skill was acknowledged, and that, aided by great assiduity and good natural talents, he had overcome the want of early study and experience, yet, that the irritability of his temper constituted a well founded objection to his appointment to the magistracy. My objections, however, were not confined to this defect alone".[85]

One significant task of my objections to Bigge's conclusions, is to determine whether the source of that "irritability" was in Redfern's nature, or in Bigge's revisiting of the Nore mutiny, or from "Mr Redfern's disappointment for the loss of the situation of principal surgeon, and to which, I believe, there are many, would have gladly seen him succeed", as Bigge noted, a couple of pages on, in this same report.

Bigge is to be congratulated for this last acknowledgment. However, he made no mention of the denied promotion, formerly promised to Redfern by two Secretaries of State for War and Colonies, Viscount Castlereagh and Earl Bathurst, and strongly supported by Governor Macquarie.

Again, as a commissioned officer, by the hand of His Royal Highness the Prince Regent, Redfern had a right of succession to the principal surgeonship. Bigge made no mention of this right, although he did see the ornate *Commission,* as Redfern had sent it to the commissioner and asked for it to be returned. It was, and is now at the Mitchell Library, Sydney.

In contrast to the Commissioner's attitude to Redfern was that of one military Commandant, Foveaux, on Norfolk Island and of Governor King, R.N. on the mainland. The latter granted what the former recommended, conditional and then full emancipation.

Foveaux had such good reasons, personal and public, to approve of Redfern's application to his medical tasks on Norfolk Island that he appointed him in due course acting colonial surgeon in charge of the convict hospital on the mainland. Governor Macquarie confirmed Foveaux's appointment mentioning Redfern's positive "abilities and character" when communicating with Lord Castlereagh.

"I Consider Mr Redfern, as a professional Man, a Very Great Acquisition to this Colony - his Talents, as a Surgeon, being far Superior to those of any other Person of that Description in this Country, and perhaps equal to those of the most Skilful Medical Men in any other Country. With such Talents, and such Claims, Mr Redfern, unquestionably looks forward to filling the highest Situation in the Medical Department of New South Wales, in the regular Rotation of Seniority - being able to produce Satisfactory Proofs of his Eligibility, both with respect to professional Abilities and Character".[86]

The present discussion will conclude with references to a changed appreciation, in recent years, of the preparation of surgeons and apothecaries, from the middle to the end of the eighteenth century, when Redfern gained his medical background.[87]

Firstly, consider the attitude of writers before the reassessment took place. According to Loudon, "The rank-and-file practitioners of the eighteenth century have, on the whole, had a poor press. The famous are acknowledged, but only as giants amongst that race of pygmies, described as the 'quasi-irregular' apothecaries and surgeon-apothecaries of the back streets and villages, implying that the formation of a corpus of trained and regular doctors for the great majority of the people only occurred with the arrival of the general practitioner in the nineteenth century".[88]

"This kind of assumption," he said, "is part of a general tendency, noted by Porter, to treat medical developments in the eighteenth century not in their own right but as mere forerunners of what was to come later".[89] As W.F. Bynum put it, more recently, Porter "rescued [eighteenth-century medical history] from the clutches of historians blind to its medical richness".[90]

It should be mentioned at this point, if necessary, that the above references are to the late Roy Porter, who 'pioneered the now fashionable concern with patients (instead of doctors)'. Porter was elected "a fellow of the British Academy in 1994" and "made an honorary fellow by both the Royal College of Physicians and the Royal College of Psychiatrists".[91]

He has among his histories of medicine, *The Greatest Benefit to Mankind*, as author, *The Cambridge Illustrated History of Medicine*, as editor and major contributor, and jointly with W.F. Bynum, editor of a *Companion Encyclopaedia of the History of Medicine*, in two volumes.

A social history of London, and of England, came from his pen. His "first ever lectures [typed in 1974] given to the Cambridge history faculty were on the English Enlightenment". A full-bodied prize-winning *Enlightenment: Britain and the Creation of the Modern World* appeared in 2000. With Jeremy Black he edited *The Penguin Dictionary of Eighteenth-Century History*.

Porter also edited with Mikulas Teich, *Sexual Knowledge, Sexual Science*. Beginning in 1981, "The purpose of these and other envisaged collections is to bring together comparative, national and interdisciplinary approaches to the history of great movements in the development of human thought and action".

Returning to our reassessment of late eighteenth century medical training, a second critical stance needs to be taken, this time to Bigge's questioning of Redfern. It needs to be evaluated, afresh, in the light of what was then known about medical education when Commissioner Bigge was in London.

"By the 1770s", according to Christopher Lawrence, "London was competing vigorously with Edinburgh as a centre of medical education".[92]

Hear what John Pickstone had to say: "Oxford and Cambridge universities were stagnant but Edinburgh medical school boosted that city's finances by attracting students from England and North America. In Scottish universities and in the private schools of London, teaching was good business. Indeed, in a sense, education was the most dynamic aspect of the medical economy - knowledge changed much faster than therapies".[93]

Sir James McGrigor, "Father of Army Medicine", would not have agreed more. He went to India with a larger stock of books than most surgeons. After the war, on his advice, a great number of medical officers "betook themselves to Edinburgh, Glasgow, Dublin, Paris and the German schools.[94]

It would be fair to suggest that Bigge's thinking about Redfern's medical education was out of touch with the reality of the medical market place. However an Oxbridge mindset would have strengthened another conservative element. "Clear hierarchical relations were...held to obtain between...branches of medicine", which placed physicians, products of Oxbridge universities, at the top.[95]

On the other hand, if by any chance Bigge, and others since, had in mind *The Adventures of Roderick Random* at Surgeon's-hall,[96] he might be forgiven, but not excused for so meagrely addressing Redfern's London medical experience.[97]

It is hoped that Bigge's low estimate of medical education outside the universities of Oxford and Cambridge, will give way in the light of contemporary evidence of the 18th century scene, emphasised in the late 20th century reassessment. The new studies replaced a persistent judgmental view of the past.

As an aside, one might note Commissioner Bigge's correct use of "Mr" for surgeon, as title for William Redfern. Governor Macquarie wrote: "Mr Redfern's singular abilities are well known here". It was not the title but the description that impressed Pescott, who considered this to be Macquarie's most expressive description of Redfern's medical abilities.[98]

Over time, however, Macquarie changed the title to match the widening service provided. *Mr* became *Doctor* Redfern. Confirmation is in Macquarie's *Tours* and cover notes for Redfern's report, as other skills than surgery directed his daily medical rounds. This had a parallel with contemporary trends in Great Britain. The idea of doctor as "general practitioner" included varied skills - surgeon, bonesetter, apothecary, physician, obstetrician, male midwife, etc.

(For the above reasons, neither title, *Mr* or *Dr*, had the lifelong continuity of meaning appropriate for use in the title of this book.[99])

Was William Redfern an Educated Man?

There is strong evidence for Redfern having received a sound general education, and a supposition that it may have been a liberal one.

To Governor Macquarie, Redfern possessed “universal knowledge”. To William Wentworth, son of his old friend, D’Arcy, he had the education of a gentleman.[100] In Sydney, he had a library. In later years he was accepted as a matriculant at Edinburgh University.

Ford, speaking of Redfern’s letters, “written in a small, legible hand [with one exception, on board ship, at Rio (ARJ)], showed that he had a greater mastery of English than the majority of medical graduates today. He wrote with clearness, sometimes vividly, and with occasional classical allusions. In some of his letters, especially those to his enemy, Commissioner Bigge, which were written in circumstances of rankling injustice, he combines bitter invective with powerful advocacy”.

These letters may be found in later chapters, as does Redfern’s report on the convict transports, which Ford held up as a pattern for such writings.[101]

A good education for Redfern, then, can reasonably be accepted. Where it was obtained and what it included still remain to be determined. Did he attend a grammar school? Which one? An answer to that question would be most useful, bringing with it vital information about his early years, his parents, his home life and influences. It could have enlightened Redfern’s role at the Nore.

Perhaps Redfern had attended a liberal non-conformist school or academy of the kind encountered in Braithwaite’s study of publisher Joseph Johnson, or as experienced by John Macarthur’s sons.

Juanita Burnby in discussing ‘An Examined and Free Apothecary’, told of education before apprenticeship in “the excellent Non conformist academies such as that at Warrington where John Aikin received his schooling”.[102]

Remember, too, that there were surgeons in the “radical” London Corresponding Society. Possible influences abounded, but proof remains stubborn, hidden, or non-existent, or as Pescott considered, ‘not sought’.

Loudon, again, has something useful to say: “Practitioners from a medical family and others who were the sons of the clergy, attorneys, naval and army officers, ‘gentlemen’ and minor landed proprietors accounted for two-thirds of the total”.[103]

Where were these sons educated? The “typical surgeon-apothecary of the second half of the eighteenth century was a grammar school, not a public school boy, leaving school somewhere between the age of thirteen and sixteen to take up an apprenticeship varying from three to seven years”.[104]

Samuel Taylor Coleridge and Charles Lamb described one such school, Christ's Hospital Grammar School, where they were enrolled.[105] Coleridge started there in September 1782 at the age of nine (when Redfern would have been about seven). Coleridge and Lamb showed the advantage of having a local contact when it came to food. According to Cecil, "The boys had little to eat, and what there was unappetising. Sometimes a meal consisted of no more than a chunk of stale bread washed down by a mug of stale beer". Green vegetables were not on the menu at the school, which has interest for the scurvy conscious.

With the passing of years and examinations, pupils were streamed into a hierarchy of subordinate schools within Christ's Hospital Grammar. The mathematical and drawing schools retained pupils till sixteen or seventeen and provided midshipmen and schoolmasters for the navy. William Wales, of Cook's second Pacific journey, taught there.[106] Coleridge, marked out for University, followed a different curriculum.

On Saturdays an elder brother came to town "to walk the London Hospital". There Coleridge met him to "hold the plasters or to attend the dressings". This was "bliss" to the young Coleridge who "became wild to be apprenticed to a surgeon". To this end he read incessantly - English, Latin and Greek books of medicine. "Blanchard's 'Latin Medical Dictionary' [he] had nearly by heart".

Latin was still a link between grammar school and university medical examinations.[107] While the vernacular was the language of lectures and increasingly of texts, Robert Dalziel Lobban showed that it wasn't until 1833 that "English was substituted for Latin as the language for the examinations" in Edinburgh.[108] Before that, if one's Latin had become a little rusty, "grinding" would help.[109]

Let us suppose - again - that Redfern did attend a grammar school, stayed till he was fifteen or sixteen, then left to study as a surgeon-apothecary for five or six years. This would provide him with a typical education, both academically and medically, to enter the Navy as surgeon's mate at age twenty-two, as the *Muster Log* recorded.

If no record can be found of a grammar or independent school enrolment - still insufficient proof of it not existing - how might one deduce that it probably occurred in Redfern's case? To find pointers, it is needful to reconsider in greater detail, references to Redfern as an educated man.

First let us return to William Charles Wentworth's claim of Redfern having the education and manners of a gentleman.[110] How would he know? From an early age, Wentworth would have come close to Redfern as a frequent, welcome, and friendly visitor to his father's house.

Redfern's offer to fund a term at Cambridge University for William, son of his old friend D'Arcy, had been accepted.[111] Later, Redfern and Wentworth were in a position to compare and contrast the Oxbridge and Edinburgh scenes and the need for a university in London.

After Madeira, the two Williams would spend more time together, on their way back to Australia with Wentworth's friend, Robert Wardell, accompanied by Robert's mother, Sarah Redfern with her newborn baby, Joseph Foveaux Redfern, and elder son, William Lachlan Macquarie Redfern, and other persons to be mentioned in due course.

As Wentworth and Wardell were lawyers, who would found a newspaper in the Colony, one can imagine the wide range of topics they would cover; the Bigge *Reports*, Redfern and Eagar's presentation in London on behalf of the emancipists, possible changes to the legal system, law and order, trial by jury, limitations on the Governor's powers, freedom of the Press, farming and agriculture, the convict system, medicine and health, and so on. Not forgetting Wentworth's long poem on Australasia, and his book, recently revised.[112]

William Charles Wentworth, I suggest, had sufficient reason for describing William Redfern as "well educated".

What now of the Governor? Lieutenant-Colonel Joseph Foveaux had introduced Mr Redfern, in person, to Governor Lachlan Macquarie. That gesture, in itself, was commendation enough, but had gained additional strength from Foveaux's placement of Redfern in the colonial medical service at Port Jackson, after having previously given Redfern a similar task on Norfolk Island.

There was a further and unexpected parallel to be realized between Redfern's medicine and his two masters. Foveaux's health had benefited from Redfern's medical advice, which had included a sea trip for his asthma. No doubt this information was also passed on to Macquarie. Little did Redfern know, at the moment of meeting Macquarie, that he too, and his wife, would come to rely heavily on his medical knowledge and skills.

This path by which William Redfern moved close to power has been lost in sweeping generalisations.[113] One follows: "In his first five months in New South Wales Macquarie chose for his administrators and confidential advisers those men over whom their conviction and his benevolence had given him unlimited power...They were placed entirely at his mercy. As he had raised them in society, so he could reduce them. While he regarded his actions as humane, they were also convenient. Macquarie's desire for subordination strengthened the autocracy of his government and made sycophants of his counsellors".[114]

Ritchie, while writing his biography of Commissioner Bigge, found a source for such ideas in the *Sydney Gazette* of 18 March 1826, reprinted from the *South African Commercial Advertiser* of 23 November 1825.[115] In his later biography of Lachlan Macquarie, Ritchie repeated this account almost word for word, except then, Macquarie had "made his counsellors satellites to his planet".[116]

Admittedly, in this instance, Ritchie first presented Macquarie's emancipist policy in a positive light, before alerting the reader to "less altruistic motives behind his intent". Macquarie's "favourites were not the struggling ex-convict farmers; more often than not, the opulent emancipists attracted his notice and higher promotions". [117]

However, it was Foveaux and King who made Redfern a free man and again it was Foveaux who had appointed Redfern to the hospital both on Norfolk Island and at Port Jackson. Redfern's unique relationship, first with Foveaux, and then with the Macquaries, arose primarily from his ability to meet their medical needs, both personal and colonial. That a friendly feeling, or some form of attachment or dependence, may arise as a result, is not an unlikely outcome. To the unwary that critical fact could be lost in generalised remarks about "sycophants", "satellites" and more particularly "opulent emancipists". This brief sequence pleads eloquently for a Redfern study of some length, such as the one now undertaken.[118]

Ford noted that Macquarie had described Redfern as "a man of very eminent talents and an excellent scholar and possessing universal knowledge".[119]

Although Redfern carried books with him to the colony, 'the world was his classroom'. On Norfolk Island he learned colonial ways from farming to finance, and made his own contribution. Nevertheless, Redfern's portrait, painted in miniature in 1832, shows one arm resting upon a book, and books were with him when he died in Edinburgh in the following year.

Personal book collections, 'libraries', were not unknown at Port Jackson and books were often listed for sale in the *Sydney Gazette*. In 1823, George Reiby told how "we obtain [books] here almost with as great facility as in England, by giving a discretional order".[120] His mother, on a trip to England, bought a copy of the *Encyclopaedia Britannica*. However, Redfern was the first to admit, as he did to Bigge, that distance from London, the centre of knowledge, had its effects on his [speed of] access to information.

The disappearance of Redfern's library is a matter of some regret, which will be expressed at appropriate moments. It is not a unique problem. E. P. Thompson faced a vastly more complex problem with William Blake. His library has never been identified, either.[121]

Thompson extended the idea to known collections that Blake might have accessed and also added "ulterior questions", such as, "Who was Blake? Where do we place him in the intellectual and social life of London between

1780 and 1820 in his mind?[122] "I have no unexpected disclosures to offer. I must commence with conjectures, and conclude with some firmer evidence, out of which further conjectures will arise".[123]

On the contrary think what a useful resource the known contents of the personal library of many a luminary has proven to be.

Bigge mentioned Redfern's library twice. It would have been housed at that time in the southern wing of the Sydney Hospital in Macquarie Street, Sydney. Typically, Bigge did not mention the books. He was more concerned for the keys or hospital records that Redfern might have kept there.

Dunlop named two only of all the books that Redfern might have had, and that might have survived.[124] Their Scottish associations suggested to Dunlop the possibility of Redfern having received his medical education in Scotland. Noted above.

The first was an edited version of *William Smellie's Treatise on the Theory and Practice of Midwifery* with a set of Anatomical Tables, published in Edinburgh, in November 1783.[125] In due course Ford obtained it for the R.A.C.P. History of Medicine Library. It will be discussed in some detail in a later chapter.

Smellie (pronounced Smiley) published his midwifery texts in England, originally. According to Irvine Loudon, "By mid-century, the centre for the publication of treatises on midwifery had moved from Paris to London". William Smellie headed a list that followed. "For originality and clarity they were seldom equalled by anything published in obstetrics in England during the nineteenth century".[126]

Dunlop had a "John Bell" as the author of the second book, *The Anatomy of the Human Body.* K.F. Russell gave 1797 as the date of publication of the first of four volumes with this title. The other volumes were completed by 1804. The brothers John and Charles Bell[127] were the authors, their texts enriched by a wide range of material from comparative anatomy, as I found by reference to another copy of that edition at the History of Medicine Library.[128]

Elizabeth Windschuttle has a delightful account of Charles Bell and his wife as regular visitors to the Macleays' country house in Surry, of Bell introducing Fanny Macleay to Gilbert White's *Natural History of Selbourne* and of giving her and her sister lessons in drawing.[129]

According to Russell, "for most of the eighteenth century the important unit in London anatomical teaching was the private school, run by a surgeon-anatomist".[130] The Bell brothers were teaching in London at the time. Such opportunities were open to Redfern for extra curricular studies. He certainly was aware of them.

A Missing Book?

Ford described a third book that could not be found at the History of Medicine Library, RACP.[131] It had Frederick Thomson, a Royal Navy surgeon, as the author, and *An essay on scurvy* as its title. The book was published in London in 1790. According to an inscription, on the half title page, the author presented this copy to Capt. Wm Bligh in 1791. In due course, Bligh gave the book to William Redfern. The inscription on the title page, read "From His Excellency Gov. Bligh to Mr Will Redfern, 13 Feby 1809". Wm Bligh's signature followed, above that of a "W. Bell".[132]

Bligh agreed to leave Port Jackson in February 1809, but reneged, eventually sailing for the Derwent on 17 March, in the *Porpoise*.[133]

While the idea of Bligh giving Redfern a book, raises a number of questions, it does illustrate, again, the need for a definitive biography of Redfern to draw a clearer line between fact and fiction. Assuming at this point that this book did exist, what is the evidence for Redfern doing Bligh a service, which attracted such a gift?

There is a story that Redfern was present at Government House when Bligh was arrested on 26 January 1808. He was there to provide medical aid to Bligh's daughter, Mary, whose husband, Lieutenant John Putland had died only three weeks previously.

Dunlop used this story to show Redfern's "loyalty to the King". [He need not have. The fleet mutineers had expressed their loyalty.] Though Dunlop added a footnote, he provided no reference.

Cowlishaw, an earlier medical historian, had also concluded that Redfern "seems to have been friendly with Bligh" because his name was not included with the surgeons, Wentworth and Mileham, "attached to the letter to Major Johnston asking for the removal of Bligh". For Cowlishaw this idea was strengthened by the story of Redfern's "attendance on the Governor's daughter when the soldiers came to arrest her father".[134]

Ford did not retell this story. Clune did. His quote was from an unnamed "short, well-written biography of Redfern", clearly Dunlop's, but his conclusion was his own. Redfern was on Norfolk Island at the time. The story was false.

Pescott repeated the story but provided an interesting source, mentioned above, in passing, in the context of Bigge's attack on the triumvirate.[135] In more detail that unfortunate business will be debated in a later chapter. What did Macquarie have to do with this Redfern/Bligh story? In what follows, the governor was arguing strongly and emotively for his friend, Redfern.

"I have hitherto omitted to lead Your Attention to the Consideration of the Feelings of the Man, thus singled out, as it would Seem, for Persecution! a Man, who for the last Seventeen Years has been actively employed for the

Benefit of his Fellow Creatures; who has during that time been One of the Most Loyal and Useful Subjects to the Government in this Country; a Man, who while the persons, who have been principally instrumental in Exciting the Bias felt by you and Others against him and All those in his Unfortunate State, were treating His Majesty's Representative with every Indignity and Violence, Short of that of taking his Life, *Exerted himself in preserving an Existence most dear to him, that of His own Daughter, the Governor's only Companion in that Hour of Horror and Misery".* (My italics).[136]

This, then, was the original source for an account of Redfern assisting Bligh's daughter.

Reflect upon the Governor's state at that time. He had been rocked by reports of his being attacked by Mr Grey Bennett and others in the British House of Commons. Physically weak, he was stressed by the vehemence and unfairness of Bigge's attack, and his drive to counter it.

Macquarie erred in confusing Redfern with the Rev. Mr. Henry Fulton. He, too, was well educated and a political convict. Fulton had been implicated in the Irish Rebellion of 1798, found guilty of seditious practices and sentenced to transportation for life.

Fulton, who had been on Norfolk Island with Redfern, was in Sydney when Bligh was arrested. It was Fulton not Redfern who "was in attendance at Government House for the greater part of the day of Bligh's arrest".[137] Redfern was still on Norfolk Island.

On 27 December 1819 [Macquarie] wrote in his *Journal* of four weeks of illness, during which time he was "extremely weak, reduced in flesh and very much debilitated. - Doctors Wentworth and Redfern...were assiduous and kind in their attentions. -But had it not been for the extraordinary exertions, unwearied solicitude, and most affectionate attentions and exertions of my good beloved Mrs, M. I think I should have fallen a sacrifice to my disease. To her therefore-under God- I may chiefly ascribe my recovery".[138]

At the start, Redfern was most apprehensive of Macquarie's condition and begged Wentworth not to lose a moment in coming to see him.[139]

Perhaps Macquarie did have a memory of Redfern helping the Blighs, but it could not have been the occasion attributed to Macquarie, and accepted to this point in time, as far as I am aware. When was it, then?

While Redfern was on Norfolk Island, Bligh's son-in-law, Captain Putland, visited on two occasions during 1807, on HMS *Porpoise* (2). Putland arrived first in June, leaving on 13 July, and returning in October. He left in the same month for the Derwent.[140]

Putland was a sick man, suffering from the effects of tuberculosis, known then in medicine, as *phthisis pulmonalis.* In October he must have been in a bad way, as he died on 4 January of the next year. Was Redfern able to be of assistance to Putland while the latter was on Norfolk Island? It seems likely.

After 21 June 1808, Redfern was at Port Jackson. Either Bligh, under arrest, or his recently widowed daughter, Mary Putland may have claimed Redfern's attention. Bligh's evidence at the court martial of Lieutenant-colonel George Johnston puts this in doubt: "From the 26th of January 1808 until the 20th of February 1809...every person in the colony was ordered, upon pain of punishment, not to supply me or my family with any food or article whatever".[141]

Surely medical assistance was not proscribed. Foveaux arrived from London on 28 July 1808, a month after Redfern, and appointed him acting colonial surgeon in September 1808. Here, again, Redfern could have earned Bligh's reward.

One final suggestion could place Redfern on board the *Porpoise* to receive the book from Bligh himself on 13 February. Doing what? Perhaps, checking and making good the medical supplies on an outgoing ship (as he would do for the ships *Kangaroo* and *Emu* in 1815). With Bligh promising to sail in February this is a plausible story, even if he did stay till March 17.

It is interesting to contemplate what thoughts were uppermost in Redfern's mind when they met. Did Redfern see the Bligh of the *Bounty*, or of the *Director* (at the Nore), or of the governor not too well disposed to the medical fraternity at the time, nor to himself as boat builder on Norfolk Island?

Eventually, Bligh had sanctioned the boat's voyage to Sydney,[142]even though Redfern was out of order in building a sea-going ship, beyond allowable size limits set by earlier Governors for such a vessel. Redfern could face the deposed Governor with a clear conscience on that score, at least.[143]

Whatever; it was pleasing to receive a gift, and an important work on scurvy, at that.

Commissioner Bigge was not inclined to let the matter rest and put some pointed questions to William Redfern, who had this to say:

"You were aware, Sir, that I had expressed my opinion on the arrest of Govr. Bligh in strong terms of reprobation and condemnation of that measure. You questioned me on it, by way of conversation".

Bigge's disbelief was clear from his 'sarcastic sneer', which Redfern noted and added to the above statement. Was he thinking of Redfern as a mutineer by habit? Or perhaps associating Redfern with his friend D'Arcy Wentworth, who suffered with other surgeons under Governor Bligh, Herbert Vere Evatt's *Rum Rebellion,* notwithstanding.[144]

If the latter, you may find some pertinent comments in a letter Redfern wrote to D'Arcy Wentworth from Norfolk Island. It may be found in chapter ten, below.

Remember? This story of a Bligh gift book had its origin in Ford's catalogue card. I accepted his scholarship and assumed the book existed. But where, that was the first question, and others followed.

Alison Holster, formerly librarian of the History of Medicine Library, had worked with Edward Ford. It was natural to discuss the card with her at the start of my quest. So, years later, seeing the book on display in an exhibition of works forming part of David Scott Mitchell's original bequest, in the library that bears his name, Alison lost no time in ringing me with the news.

Paul Brunton, senior Curator, Mitchell Library, Sydney, explained how the book came to light. For the Mitchell Centenary, a book-by-book search for the donor's signature, had revealed this book's history.

Brenda Heagney, who followed Alison at the History of Medicine Library, and also knew of the quest, kindly gave me her copy of the catalogue, arthritis having prevented my visit to the exhibition.

As you will have noticed from the beginning, there are two parts to this story. It started with a missing book, a gift to Wm Redfern from Bligh. It continued with a search for an explanation for Bligh's action.

The book was found and the gift confirmed but did Macquarie ever say what he was supposed to have said about Redfern attending Bligh's daughter? Here is what Macquarie did say to Bigge:

"I have hitherto omitted to lead Your Attention to the Consideration of the Feelings of the Man, thus singled out, as it would Seem, for Persecution! a Man, who for the last Seventeen Years has been actively employed for the Benefit of his Fellow Creatures; who has during that time been One of the Most Loyal and Useful Subjects to the Government in this Country; a Man, who while the persons, who have been principally instrumental in Exciting the Bias felt by you and Others against him and All those in his Unfortunate State, were treating His Majesty's Representative with every Indignity and Violence, Short of that of taking his Life, Exerted himself in preserving an Existence most dear to him, that of His own Daughter, the Governor's only Companion in that Hour of Horror and Misery".[145]

Macquarie contrasted Wm Redfern's deeds as a 'most loyal and useful subject' with the misdeeds of those 'exciting bias' who treated Bligh, when governor, 'with every indignity and violence'. It should have been sufficient. Macquarie had done well. Unfortunately, his emphasis has been lost by a succession of writers who misread these words - *Exerted himself in preserving an Existence most dear to him, that of His own Daughter.* This could only mean that it was Governor Bligh who exerted himself. To insert, or even to imply, someone else makes no sense, or does it?

Go back to the end of the fifth and onto the following lines in the above extract. What follows logically, *A Man, who...*? It can only be *A Man, who Exerted himself in preserving an Existence most dear to him*, that is, to Governor Bligh's daughter.

The 'story of the missing book' may remain as told.

The Character of William Redfern?

"What shall we call the eighteenth century? How often, and how vainly, has it been summarized in a phrase! - stuffed into a single garment, as it were, from which it bursts at every seam, its uncontrollable, magnificent, startling life forcing itself upon the eye of the beholder in lavish and indecent contradiction".[146]

How shall we describe the character of a person?

To Paul Carter, holding the belief that "the soul of the object was, or could be, contained in a word" was "to indulge in a form of linguistic animism".[147] At the same time he argued that "the cultural place where spatial history begins" is "not in a particular year, nor in a particular place, but *in the act of naming*. For by the act of place-naming, space is transformed symbolically into a place, that is, a space with a history".

In Australia, of course, places already had a "spatial history" acquired by Aboriginal naming, but Redfern renamed his land holdings at Minto, *Campbellfield*, after the maiden name of Governor Macquarie's second wife, and to honour her.

Is it too much to suggest that the act of name-calling may have an analogous effect? What of the naming of a character trait?

One such space in Redfern's character was transformed in 1997, as if to commemorate the events of the mutiny two hundred years before. John Ritchie, in describing the reaction of Macquarie, Redfern, Eagar and William Wentworth to Bigge's first report, described them behaving "as men maligned", but "Redfern's rage was unseemly, as befitted a bully".[148]

Ritchie also linked Redfern to "eaves-dropping and intrigue" along with Campbell, Antill and Fitzgerald.[149] Later, Liston would single out Redfern, making 'eaves dropping', *his* real offence. Ritchie and Liston each gave the same source, an anonymous, incomplete, and undated letter to Macquarie.

"His [Redfern's] presence in homes when their occupants were most vulnerable exposed him to many secrets which he carried back to the governor".[150] No mention was made of Redfern's detailed knowledge of the needy being put to positive use in the working of the benevolent societies with which he was closely associated.

Brevity can be dangerous. It may also be "the soul of wit", or the essence of a motto. It is far too constricting in prose. In the media, too often the need is for the headline "grab", the jam bottle label. Yet, even here a fuller disclosure is now compulsory. Tell me in a word? Indeed!

Caricature, too, remains an abbreviation, and may publish a partial truth, or be a lie. Caricature may also be positive, suggestive, and powerfully reinforce a notion of character, and even illustrate, with panache, a serious biography. But caricature is essentially ironic.

I ask myself, what is the character of a man - in a word - who could be found guilty of mutiny, given a life sentence, held in a hulk, sent off to a convict colony, allowed to assist the surgeon on the way, trusted to keep a record of the sick, trusted to be free again, and again to be written off as a danger to society, trusted with people's health and lives, be guilty of assault, be a bully, as well as a friend of low and high, convict and governor?

William Redfern? Every lesson taught, every conversation carried on, every talk given about this man, by this writer, has had the character of the man in mind. Yet the search for a title, like drowning, "wonderfully concentrated the mind". All resistance to concentration was swept aside. *Ebullient* and *resilient* emerged as words highlighting character phases of this man. But the reservation remains, they are but partial indicators. They do not encompass all, but when linked with external as well as internal states they *suggest* a broad picture and traces of finer detail.

This use of *ebullient* and *resilient* resonating from outside as well as inside the person, not only has a person boiling over, but the external world exploding. Events may be stubborn, but so may the person, refusing to bow down to despair, or if forced to bend, having the resilience to spring back again.

As an unknown youth, the William Redfern of this book steps out of two Royal Navy records of 1797, one, the *Muster log of HMS the* Standard, and the other, the minutes of his court martial. While the *log* tells little of character, the *minutes* provide a sense of constrained ebullience, of a tightly coiled spring. His outburst against the court martial reveals its naked force, and impotence, against an overwhelming reaction from the court.

Generally, Redfern was restrained during his court martial but exercised his right to ask questions and to cross-examine witnesses, being both sharp and persistent at times.

While Redfern's mutiny was a rather muted affair, "acting as surgeon" at the request of the mutineers, its implications were serious. His trial's outcome changed dramatically from the certainty of imminent death by hanging to an undefined and prolonged punishment by imprisonment and transportation.

But he survived, to be put down again by the Tory Government, in London, and its Commissioner, Bigge, in Sydney. Certainly, some few reactions to his tormentors were less restrained and more physical after those events.

The record showed that fortune could sometimes smile on him and provide a helping hand. Jacqueline Grant called it *Providence.* It was providential that the emancipist Redfern had selected the Irish convict John Grant. Each gained much from it. *Providence,* the title of her biography of John Grant, commemorated both the idea, and the name of the ship, which carried the convict to Australia. For Jacqueline Grant, the hand of God was there, too.[151]

Perhaps it was fortunate for Foveaux's health that Redfern was on Norfolk Island, but was it "providential" that the Surgeon had been drowned in the surf? Certainly Foveaux was able to appoint Redfern, at once, in his place. Did Redfern have other qualities that appealed to Foveaux?

Ann Maree Whitaker's life of Foveaux suggests that as a probability. A secondary cause for Redfern being on Norfolk Island at that time may be discerned in his own initiative in asking for his transportation to be brought forward. Through his work, serving surgeon and convicts on the transport that brought him to Port Jackson, Redfern undoubtedly caught the eye of Acting Governor King who sent him on to Norfolk Island where his medical skills would be appreciated and given free rein.

It is well to remember that Redfern was on the island at the time of the first white settlement. For good and ill, that first settlement more closely resembled the contemporary colony at Port Jackson and served Redfern as a schoolroom where he learned the first principles of survival in a convict colony. The sapling must bend before the storm.

As Cummings observed, educated surgeons, like Redfern, took advantage of opportunities for leadership, and occupied "important positions in the social and political structure of the Colony". The life of Surgeon William Bland,[152] to whom reference has already been made, provides another good example.

Bland's story is essential reading in its own right. At the same time, contemplation of the lives of Redfern and Bland, highlights similarities and differences and helps in the appreciation of individual strengths and weaknesses, but bear in mind that Redfern left the colonial scene for Edinburgh in 1828. Bland would continue to contribute to the life of the colony, and to the wider world, till his death in 1868.

Surgeon William Bland refused to be examined by the Board of Competency,[153] of which surgeon Wiliam Redfern was a member. This put an official appointment as colonial surgeon out of Bland's reach, but did not prevent him from opening the first private practice in the colony.

A contemporary appreciation has Bland, "a brave and accomplished man, an incorruptible asserter of civil rights, an elegant scholar, a man of science whose surgical skills and inventions had excited admiration in Europe".[154]

"Sensitive, quarrelsome and flamboyant, Bland rode in brightly-coloured carriages yet showed selfless affection for those physically or mentally crippled. In 1858 grateful citizens gave him a candelabra in recognition of his services; three years later they declared him bankrupt".[155]

One outline character sketch of William Redfern might be drawn from the early writings of Dunlop, Ford, Clune/Stephensen, and Pescott. It could read something like this.[156]

"Redfern was rich in the attributes that men admire. He was affable, friendly, reliable, and loyal. At the same time he was frank, independent, uncompromising, forceful, and strong-willed. He was brave and stalwart in adversity".

"Well educated, even scholarly at times, his talents found expression as a surgeon, male-midwife and physician. He was highly regarded as a doctor and as an assiduous worker".

"William Redfern was acknowledged to be a great citizen, benevolent and generous. Impatient of injustice, he was moved by suffering, helped the weak and became a spokesman for the oppressed. At the Nore, Redfern was ready to support his convictions with his life".

"Commissioner Bigge, on the other hand, saw William Redfern's involvement in the Nore mutiny as evidence of his 'criminal guilt' in a 'most foul and unnatural conspiracy'".

"To Bigge, Redfern's temper was volatile, even violent at times to both inferiors and superiors". "Redfern's physical attack on his apprentice, and on Robert Howe fits this opinion".

"Redfern remained unashamed of his history. Nevertheless, there was evidence to suggest that his health was failing, over time. He found it difficult to settle down, and, in the end, his mind broke under the strain".

Each of these opinions has been followed to its source. Acceptances, rejections, revisions and fine tunings have been applied according to the nature and relevance of primary and other references. Wherever possible new evidence or fresh insights have been brought to bear upon earlier conclusions. Some have already been revealed in this opening chapter. Others will follow as the study progresses, to be recorded within the twenty-one chapters of the two books comprising this work.

William Redfern, on HMS *Standard*, appeared as an intelligent non-commissioned medical officer, no slouch when it came to work, courageous in adversity, and willing and able to express himself fluently and with confidence as bespoke an educated gentleman. He was young, in the youthful company of seamen of a man-of-war of some 500 persons, ebullient, impetuous, perhaps brash at times.

As a surgeon's mate, Redfern took his work seriously. The result was that one seaman witness, who had been his patient, told the court that Redfern could not have done his work better as a surgeon than he had as a surgeon's mate, an opinion shared by the mutineer leadership, who were determined to have him as their surgeon, whether he came willingly or not.

How did William Redfern see himself, over time? All of his letters, sparse as they were in total, are valuable in this regard. His correspondence with Commissioner Bigge revealed him as a bold critic.

If, as assumed, Redfern had a coat of arms,[157] it may be said that he owned its content, the motto, *Virtus et veritas prevalebunt*, in particular. Accepting this ownership would help provide an answer to the question, raised above.

This was Redfern's motto, his reason for being. It was his desire that virtue and truth prevail. The wish was father to the deed. Long held, it anticipated the coat of arms and was at work on board *Standard*. That was why he became involved in a mutiny, that particular kind of mutiny that was about the virtue of command and the true nature of the condition of the seamen.

For *virtus*, the dictionary [S.O.E.D.] gives *virtue, manliness, valour,* and *courage*, while for *veritas* it has *truth*. So often these qualities are restricted to physical events, to war in particular. They are equally valid in civil society.

"Commanders of His Majesty's Ships [were] strictly required to shew in themselves, a good Example of Honour and Virtue to their Officers and Men". This will be found in the fourth chapter.

Virtue, as a word, was in common use at the time, finding a place in *The Penguin Dictionary of Eighteenth-Century History*. There, Sylvana Tomaselli situates *virtue* in the intellectual climate of the times.[158]

Did Redfern see virtue in male terms, in manliness, from its Latin root, *vir*, for man? Was this the quintessential male civic virtue of classical studies and of popular belief? At the same time, womanly virtue was seen in terms of sexual morality.

Mary Wollstonecraft would not have it that way, describing "manly virtues" as "the attainment of those talents and virtues, the exercise of which ennobles the human character". "Let woman share the rights," said Wollstonecraft, "and she will emulate the virtues of man".[159]

Dorinda Outram, too, stressed the differences, and the restrictions placed on women as a result. "Nowhere was this process of exclusion and differentiation more marked than in the case of the most important word of the [French] Revolutionary political vocabulary: 'virtue'. There was an immense gulf between public male virtue personified by Brutus and private female virtue as shown by Lucretius".[160]

Did William Redfern, even handed, apply morality to civic and sexual roles, or did the double standard apply? Was Sarah, in particular, able to pursue her civic interests in the knowledge of William's faithfulness to his marriage vows? These are questions at the heart of Redfern's relationships with women. Where little is known, discussion is muted.

Being a Surgeon, a Mixed Blessing?

William Redfern's medical training and practice gave him entry into the Royal Navy in 1797. In that same year his practice as a surgeon's mate first brought him to the attention of the fleet mutineers on the *Standard,* and then to the captain of that ship, as a mutineer surgeon. In turn, this same professional experience, root cause of his being found guilty of mutiny, would lead to his being thrown upon the mercy of King George III. That proving successful, Redfern exchanged hanging for transportation. Being a surgeon provided a ladder of escape from his lost place in society, and a new life in a strange colonial world.

Chapter 2

SPITHEAD AND THE CHANNEL FLEET IN 1797

Calm before the Storm.

"On 30th March [1797] the Fleet once more rode placidly at anchor at Spithead".[1] *This was continued: "The graceful lines of the ships swung gently on the tide, the occasional sunlight cheerfully reflecting the paint - black from the water to the lower gun-deck, then bright with various yellows, sweeping up to the vivid red or blue of the poops above the quarter-deck guns - a gallant, heartening sight to those on land. Every now and then gleams of gold, or scarlet, or pale blue flashed from the forecastles, while the Admirals' flags or Captain's pennants fluttered from their appropriate topgallant mastheads. Boats, with their crews gaily tricked out in any uniform that struck their captain's fancy,*[2] *rowed busily as active ants over the wind-dappled water between ship and ship, while the bum-boats*[3] *swarmed rapaciously out from the shore. All was peacefully everyday, innocent of omens; and Admiral Lord Bridport*[4] *went on leave until the 10th of April".*

All was not as it appeared, however, as seamen of the Channel Fleet had been chewing over their grievances for months.[5] Grievances, did you say? What grievances? Surely everybody loved a sailor.[6] Certainly, while he was helping Britannia to rule the waves there was much talk about "love", but little was being done to translate words into action.

Take the matter of pay for a start. Sailors were not happy about it. Why should they be? Their present wages had been settled, not under Charles I or

II, as stated in their petitions, but under the Commonwealth, when "From 1st Jan. 1652-3 the wages of A.B'.s [sailors rated as Able Bodied] were raised from 19s, to 24s, a month. Ordinary Seamen continued at 19s".[7]

The sailors' wage freeze had lasted 144 years. Cold comfort, when it is known that the Lords of Admiralty intended it to continue. No increase in pay for seamen had been included in the *Estimates* for 1797.

"'The fleet,' Pitt told the Commons in 1796, was 'more respectable and more formidable than ever before'. For ordinary seamen life in the navy was certainly formidable. Unfortunately nothing was done to make it respectable. Indeed so far from sailors' conditions having improved, they had deteriorated".[8]

What dramatic action did the seamen of the Channel Fleet take? They sent petitions.[9] This was a legitimate form of protest or request at the time both within and without the Royal Navy. Not only legitimate, part of a process by which institutions change.[10]

Although the following petition was sent to their former Admiral, Earl Richard Howe, known affectionately to them as *Black Dick,* it was not signed. It was not considered wise to attach names to written forms of protest.[11] Nor was it sent through their ship's commander. Caution was instructed by earlier mutinies[12] in the Royal Navy and by the conditions of repression then existing, reflecting governance in England, supposedly spurred by events in France.

"To the Right Honourable Richard, Earl Howe, Admiral of the Fleet and General of Marines,[13]

The humble petitioners on board His Majesty's Ship *Queen Charlotte*[14] on behalf of themselves and their Brethren on Board of the Fleet at Spithead. Most humbly sheweth that your petitioners most humbly intreat [sic] that your Lordship would be pleased to take the hardships of which they complain into consideration and lay them before the Lords Commissioners of the Admiralty, not doubting in the least from your Lordship's interference in their behalf they will obtain a speedy redress.

It is now upwards of two years since your petitioners observed with pleasure the augmentation which had been made to pay of the Army and Militia, and the provision that took place with respect to their wives and families, of such soldiers as were serving on board,[15] naturally expecting that they should in their turn experience the same munificence, but alas no notice has been taken of them, nor the smallest provision made for their wives and families except what they themselves sent out of their pay to prevent them being burdensome to the parish.[16]

That your petitioners humbly presume that their loyalty to their Sovereign is as conspicuous and their courage as unquestionable as any other description of men in His Majesty's service as their enemies can testify, and as your Lordship can witness who so often led them to victory and glory and by whose manly exertions the British Flag rides triumphant in every quarter of the Globe.

And your petitioners humbly conceive that at the time when their wages were settled in the reign of Charles the Second was intended as a comfortable support both for themselves and families, but at present by the considerable rise in the necessaries of life, which is now almost double; and an advance of 30 per cent. on slops,[17] your Lordship will plainly see that the intentions of the legislature is counteracted by the before mentioned causes and therefore most humbly pray for relief.

Your petitioners relying on your goodness and benevolence humbly implores that my Lords Commissioners of the Admiralty will comply with the prayers of this petition, and grant such addition will be made in their pay as in their Lordships' wisdom they shall think meet.

And your petitioners will in duty bound ever pray,"

28th Feb. 1797.[18]

A second petition followed. There are minor variations, of importance in the main as indicating that the people on different ships had a limited right to make changes around a central theme. Once again, only ship name and date appear. It was addressed to the Right Honourable the Lords Commissioners of the Admiralty on *28th Feb. 1797.*[19]

On the surface these petitions appear innocuous and unthreatening. The seamen were behaving as members of the lower orders were expected to behave to those above them, showing due deference to their Lordships' "wisdom and goodness".[20] They would need a great deal of that, for, according to W.J. Neal, "on the 25th April 1797 (the date is significant) the Navy Office estimated the debt of H.M'.s Navy, as it stood on 31 December 1796, to be as follows:[21]

"Due to pay the men unpaid on books of ships paid off £435,395 15 2

To ships in sea pay on aforesaid 31st Dec. £973,324 12 9".[22]

On 3 March the Grand Fleet called at Plymouth showing no sign of disorder.[23] While 7 March was suggested as the original date to dispatch petitions to Lord Howe, these had to be sent at sea off Brest,[24] as Lord Bridport cruised there for most of the month.[25] In "March 1797, Sir Roger Curtis was sent with a small squadron to Plymouth to cruise in the western part of the Channel.[26]

All of which demonstrated the men's willingness to co-operate in containing the French within their harbour at Brest, as part of the Blockade,[27] and in patrolling the English Channel. During this time the men kept strictly under wraps their own private campaign for bettering their wages and conditions, including the sending of petitions from ships at sea.

Eleven copies of the petition for increased pay, of which two examples were given above, were sent to Lord Howe. They found him at Bath suffering badly from his gout. Nevertheless, Howe read them carefully, concluding them to be the work of one and the same person disguising his handwriting.[28] Howe put them on one side. Later, having second thoughts, he wrote to Lord Seymour, another Admiralty Lord, asking him to check at Portsmouth for "any discontent in the Fleet". Seymour replied that all was well, there.[29] As the Channel Fleet was at sea, how did he know? In London, on 22 March, and still uneasy about the petitions, Howe handed them to Seymour who showed them to George, Earl Spencer, the First Lord of the Admiralty.[30]

Spencer's reaction was one of shock and horror.[31] "Here was this deplorable question of increased pay, which meant, naturally, swollen estimates, cropping up again!"[32] At the next Board meeting Spencer dealt with the matter. Everybody thought it was clearly "impossible to do anything officially on the subject without running the risk of unpleasant consequences by a public agitation of so delicate a topic," and so "it was judged advisable by the Board to take no notice of the circumstance".[33]

In reviewing the ill-conceived responses to the petitions sent to Lord Howe, Manwaring and Dobrée decided that "Spencer was more to blame[34] than Howe; he was young, he was imaginative: and Howe, after all, though he has been upbraided for not insisting on a searching investigation, had done all that could be expected of a war-worn veteran. He had cogitated (a little), he had made enquiries, and had handed the documents over to the proper authority. If he had acted with more vigour...but then history is made up of ifs, and in a few days the game passed to other hands".[35]

Petitions - the Third Wave.

The seamen decided on further action, not having heard any news of their petitions, not only of the eleven of 1797 but those of the previous year. Bridport found that those, too, had been sent to the Admiralty, and were ignored.[36] So there was nothing precipitous about petitioning the Admiralty again, and, as well, "Charles James Fox,[37] fat, debauched, a gambler, but a fiery defender of libertarian ideas, and leader of the opposition".[38]

Meanwhile action was taken by the majority to bring the waverers into the fold because the men would take over and send "the officers and women out of every ship on 15 April, the day the petitions were to be sent to London".[39]

Captain Patton of the Transport Office, getting wind of this on 12 April[40] informed the Port-Admiral, Sir Peter Parker,[41] and "then hastily [was] rowed out through the darkness to the *Royal George* to give the tidings to Lord Bridport". Next morning Bridport contacted Spencer asking to be told about the petitions for an increase in pay, in particular what had been done about an increase. He anxiously needed "instructions", Bridport continued, as "some disagreeable combinations were forming among the ships at Spithead".[42]

Bridport was not impressed by Spencer's reply,[43] and on the 15th wrote to Evan Nepean, Secretary to the Admiralty, sending copies of the latest petitions, one from his own ship. He considered "the latter to be the sense of the Fleet". Bridport advised Nepean that their Lordships will not direct the squadron to proceed to sea before some answer is given to these petitions. In this letter he sent a copy of a petition from the *Queen Charlotte*, "whose people have taken the lead in this business",[44] repeating an aside in the above letter.[45]

The Admiralty, in their wisdom - or lack of it - ignored Admiral Bridport's on-the-spot and contrary advice and ordered him to prepare for immediate sailing on Easter Sunday, "a bright, sunny day, with a south-west wind scudding a few black clouds along like ominous watchers for a possible tragedy".[46] Bridport restricted the order to Gardner's squadron. Ships' crews read the message of the flags on Gardner's ship, the *Royal Sovereign*. They also read the language of body movement of officers and men. It clearly told them that the men were resisting the order.

Queen Charlotte's crew manned the fore-shrouds and gave three cheers. The mutiny had begun.[47] Delegates from the *Queen Charlotte* rowed from ship to ship telling the people to send two delegates to their ship that evening.[48] Boats from the other ships joined *Charlotte's boat* in a procession. Admiral Colpoys on the *London* offered resistance to the mutineers coming aboard but was warned to desist by a message from Lord Bridport. The commanding Admiral also "ordered each captain to muster his men and ask them to state their grievances".[49]

The delegates of the fleet responded to Admiral Bridport's order with a written list.[50] Five additional grievances were now added to the original wage claim of the petitions.[51] Briefly, the list (summarised) included:

That wages are too low. That provisions be increased and with better quality.

That flour not be served instead of meat while in harbour and sufficient vegetables be provided. That the sick on board be better attended to. That some liberty be permitted when in harbour. That any man wounded in action be paid till he is cured and discharged.

Delegates signed on behalf of each individual ship's seamen who had elected them. Only Delegate John Fleming did not sign, as he had not then been elected.[52]

Dr Thomas Trotter, physician to the Channel Fleet, believed that "the original cause of this mutiny was a seaman's grievance, and not to be charged to the levelling doctrines of the times". The bounties paid to landsmen disgusted the seamen and "its rankling effects" helped excite the mutiny.[53]

More recently N.A.M. Rodger expressed a similar point of view. "Though they did not say so, it is clear that a major grievance was the operation of the bounty system, especially the extra bounties paid under the Quota Acts, which had the effect of giving latecomers, mainly landmen, far more than the seamen who were really valuable. This outraged their sense of fair play".[54]

Who Were the Seamen?

Since the petitioners and delegates were seamen it is necessary to start with this question. Who were the seamen?

Writing today, in the context of mutiny in the navy, one would begin with N.A.M. Rodger whose "Social History" strand included the subheading, "Men and Manning" for the years 1763-1792, 1793-1802, and 1803-1815. His twenty-ninth chapter, already mentioned above, is concerned with the 1797 mutinies. It opens with these words: "No serious study of the manning of the Navy during the Revolutionary and Napoleonic Wars...has ever been written, and much about the subject remains conjectural".[55]

Nevertheless, my own readings, above and below, did provide useful understandings, which had prior Rodger publications, set out above, among their sources. Earlier still, Professor Michael Lewis of the Royal Naval College at Greenwich worked out a summary "composition of a typical ship's company, circa 1812".[56] Percentages, however, varied from ship to ship, and during the course of the War, 1793-1815.

Lewis held that about one quarter of the seamen came willingly. Volunteer numbers consisted of men, two thirds, and boys, one third. Impressed men mainly British, accounted for half of the crew. Foreigners made up an additional fifteen per cent. Volunteers among them, about two per cent, have already been included. Quota-men, starting in 1795, grew in number to twelve percent by 1812. This author considered that only about a quarter of the total intake, from all groups were really new to the job.

To Lewis, the volunteers were "the cream", pressed men were "good sound stuff" (45% seamen or water-men) with those among them not seamen (5%) "unlikely to be weaklings", while the foreigners would be "handy about a ship". This combined group accounted for 88% of seamen; "all of them had their strengths, some in personal qualities, some in seamanship, some in both...they were by no means 'riff-raff' ".[57]

Poverty, unemployment, debt, misfortune, governance and its failure to attract sufficient Navy recruits,[58] drove the Quota Act. Quota-men did much harm, giving "the whole Navy a much worse name than it deserved". Their presence aboard, given their reputations and behaviour, was resented, as was their £70 bounty, which compared with the volunteer bounty of £5. Quota-men called down upon themselves more and more brutal punishment, and became the raw material of a caricature of the British seamen of the time, as composed of "gaolbirds, ne'er-do-wells and puny starvelings".[59]

Wars create problems. The manning of the fleet was but one of them. Apparent solutions themselves created further problems. Impressment as a policy was problematical to say the least. While the Admiralty's manning policies as carrot attracted one seaman, the impressment stick brought two more.[60]

Press gangs worked the harbour taverns and environs.[61] Royal Navy ships stopped, and their officers boarded, homeward bound merchant ships in coastal waters. There, the best crewmen from these ships could be exchanged for unwanted men from the Royal Navy ship, which stopped it. This was wartime.

This practice, shown by Rodger to have been well established mid-century,[62] was continued until the end of the war in 1815. Gill considered the removal of seamen on their home run "particularly and needlessly objectionable".[63]

The younger Nelson would not have agreed. Soon after taking command of the 28-gun frigate *Albemarle* on 23 August 1781, he chased four Indiamen, merchant ships headed for London docks. The fact that these ships were British did not deter Nelson from firing a broadside and forcing them to stop.[64] It is not surprising that Nelson and many of his crew "came down with scurvy" in the months ahead, having spent too long on sea food.[65]

Marcus Rediker pointed to "the single most powerful determinant of the seaman's life in the early modern era". It was "[w]hether England and its colonies were at war". "The simultaneous mobilization of the Royal Navy and of enormous privateering forces generated furious competition for the skills and strength of Jack Tar. Wages in the merchant service increased sharply during wartime, not only as compensation for the possibility of attack, seizure, and incarceration by the enemy but also as compensation for the possibility of attack, seizure, and incarceration by Jack's own government through impressment".[66]

Brian Lavery's figures speak competition, indeed. 118,000 merchant seamen in 1792, "on the eve of the French Revolutionary War", run neck and neck with 120,000 Royal Navy men voted by parliament five years later. "In general," according to Lavery, "the navy expected its seamen to have been trained in the merchant marine, and it persisted in the fiction that they were serving temporarily in the navy before returning to the merchant service".[67]

Adam Smith could be found to support Lavery's contention with respect to merchant navy training. Giving a monopoly to British Ships over the Dutch at once diminished 'the naval power of Holland' and increased that of Britain. The Navigation Act of 1651 had the security of Great Britain depending on the 'number of its sailors and shipping'.[68]

Given that impressed men, mainly British merchant seamen accounted for half of the crew, why has so little thought been given to their probable influence on the mind set of Royal Navy trained seamen? Marcus Rediker may have an answer.[69] In American history, "The eighteenth-century deep-sea sailor is still by and large an unknown man", and in "eighteenth-century England, where seamen played a major role...they have been largely invisible". So, as late as 1987, Rediker was able to describe those merchant seaman as either "unknown", or "invisible".

Rediker asked, "what did these working people do for themselves and how did they do it?" "[S]pecial attention [was given] to the efforts made by seafaring workers to free themselves from harsh conditions and exploitation. Seamen devised various tactics of resistance and forms of self-organisation".[70]

"The seaman's dilemma went beyond the menacing, seemingly boundless forces of nature he confronted," contrary to the romantic image. "The tar was caught between the devil and the deep blue sea: On one side stood his captain, who was backed by the merchant and royal official, and who held near-dictatorial powers that served a capitalist system rapidly covering the globe; on the other side stood the relentlessly dangerous natural world. Many important ideas and practices emerged in the social zone between the man-made and natural dangers that governed the seaman's life".[71]

On land, with the sea behind them, or in port, merchant seamen were less constrained, not amiss to expressing labor militancy in the "strike", a word that originated with the idea of striking or lowering sail, to prevent the ship from moving.[72]

Mid-century rioting by sailors, aimed at rescuing bodies of the hanged at Tyburn from the surgeons, led Peter Linebaugh to include sailors among "five kinds of solidarities" to whom the felons had previously appealed.[73] Linebaugh held sailors to have in common "a large and historic experience of 'the deep-sea proletariat', the labour force of mercantilism" of a size exceeded only by agriculture and textiles.[74]

Rediker, in the concluding paragraphs of his study of merchant seamen, opposed the perspective of "capital", captain and merchant, to that of "labour", the seamen. Thousands of merchant seamen "spent much of their lives - and in many cases, all of their lives - battling 'authority and privilege". "Obedience was indeed a rule of the sea, but it was continuously contested, as were the limits of authority".[75]

Lavery referred to a report of merchant seamen as "the ringleaders of all disturbances for raising wages", and separately of a seaman being "indifferent" to "the treatment and the fare", which a new recruit from the Royal Navy considered to be an improvement on what he had received there.[76]

Once aboard a Royal Navy ship, did the impressed merchant seaman respond to a fresh challenge? Not being well received at first, he probably kept his peace. Over time, it could be expected that some would have exhibited those qualities already outlined, and again stressed by Rediker, in the last pages of his book.

"Jesse Lemisch has shown how the seaman's struggle against authority paralleled and contributed to a broader political struggle against absolutism and kingly authority in the American Revolution. But matters did not end there. When the sea captain, in the later guise of the factory master, sought to make 'authority and obedience' the 'rule of the land', he confronted Jack Tar's heirs, the weavers, the Wobblies, the industrial workers, who continued the fight for democracy and freedom".[77]

There does not seem to be any need to go too far from the ships, whether Royal Navy or merchant marine. By mid century, according to Rodger, the former was "the largest industrial unit of its day in the western world, and by far the most expensive and demanding of all the administrative responsibilities of the State".[78] "In a sense", said Dugan, in his 'Author's Interjection', "the great mutiny was an isolated major event in industrial history", taking "the Georgian Admiralty as a major concentrator of wage labour".[79]

There was ample evidence in the Royal Navy in 1797 of the need to "contest" "the limits of authority".[80] By 1797 the merchant seaman's traditional opposition to "the spirit of tyranny and oppression", then active within the fleets, must certainly have made its contribution. The reality of increasing conflict was there, inherent in the merchant navy as argued by Rediker, and in the Royal Navy as evidenced by individual complaints, statement of common grievances, and finally, by Admiral Howe's disciplinary action after the Spithead mutiny against a "spirit of tyranny and oppression" active among a number of officers and other ranks.[81]

Yet, the only concerted action the Royal Navy seamen of the Channel Fleet had taken was in the matter of wages, and that by means of petitions.

Here, a reading of E.P. Thompson's *Customs in Common* will not go amiss. "All the studies in [his] book are connected by different paths with the theme of custom as it was expressed within the culture of working people in the eighteenth century and into the nineteenth". Thompson's thesis was "that customary consciousness and customary usages were especially robust in the eighteenth century: indeed, some 'customs' were of recent invention,[82] and were in truth claims to new 'rights' ".[83]

One characteristic of such culture was an oral tradition "with its heavy freight of 'custom'", maintained by the denial of education to the 'poor'. As well, 'language' [highly significant in the case of seamen] comes into play 'as not only the carrier but as the constitutive influence upon consciousness' ". "Many of the classic struggles at the entry to the industrial revolution turned as much on customs as upon wages or conditions of work".[84]

Thompson's "plebeian culture", similar to that derived from Rediker and Linebaugh, was not "self-defining or independent of external influences". It was "a more concrete and usable concept...located within a particular equilibrium of social relations, a working environment of exploitation and resistance to exploitation, of relations of power which are masked by the rituals of paternalism and deference".[85] An illustration of this last phrase may be seen in the petitions of the seamen.

Following a resume of "the characteristic features of the eighteenth century plebeian culture", Thompson describes its reproduction of "practices and norms...down the generations" as 'vigorous'. "This, then, is a conservative culture in its forms, which appeal to and seek to reinforce traditional usages. The forms are also non-rational; they do not appeal to 'reason' through the pamphlet, sermon or platform; they impose the sanctions of force, ridicule, shame, intimidation".

However, Thompson immediately qualified the adjective "conservative" by saying that "the content or meanings of this culture cannot so easily be described as conservative. For in social reality labour is becoming, decade by decade, more 'free' of traditional manorial, parochial, corporate and paternal controls, and more distanced from direct client dependence upon the gentry".

"Hence one characteristic paradox of the century: we have a rebellious traditional culture". Thompson later added, "but rebellious in defence of custom. The customs defended are the people's own".[86]

At that time, on land or at sea, simply talking about wages in a group was rebellious. Taking action was even more dangerous, resulting in "the sailor's creation of a cultural form, the instrument of protest known as the Round Robin...a means of organizing resistance".

A "round robin" was a form of petition on a large sheet of paper with two concentric circles. In the inner circle "they will write what they have a mind to have done". Their names are written in the space between the circumferences, starting with the cardinal points and gradually extending around, so that nobody can say who is the ringleader.

Rediker described the round robin as "a cultural innovation from below, an effort at collective self-defence in the face of nearly unlimited and arbitrary authority". This form "eloquently expressed the collectivistic ethos of the seaman's oppositional culture, demonstrating how the equal distribution of risks was often essential to survival".[87]

The petitions of the seamen, of course, had an extra protection, anonymity. But what protection was there from the likes of "Admiral Sir Thomas Trowbridge, a brave sailor who had commanded the *Culloden* and had a distinguished career under Nelson?"[88] According to Gilmour, Trowbridge "thought trouble was always caused by 'lawyers', by which, he meant 'fellows that can read and write'. Asked to define mutiny, he replied: 'Whenever I see a fellow look as if he was thinking, I say that's mutiny'".[89]

While the present emphasis is upon the writing and sending of petitions, mutiny is never far away. "Combinations", so-called by Bridport, must have formed in 1796. Did he have proof that it began on *Queen Charlotte*? He gave that impression, but it has been suggested that he was really 'taking a shot' at Howe. Did it start in 1795, a year of "outrageous prices" for bread,[90] bearing in mind the reference to wives and families in the petitions, and not wanting them to be "burdensome to the parish"?

Out of seamen's talk, everyday, unstructured, came complaints, of the person and of the ship. Some complaints would soon wash off. Others would bind like barnacles. With crews of 500-1000 - not all "seamen" of course - on each battleship, and with countless wordy exchanges, there would seem to be little chance of one complaint rising to the surface. Nevertheless, on the strength of it, one did. It was that matter of a pay increase.

That the sending of petitions continued, but unproductive, reflects their undoubted support as a fleet based, and service wide issue. "As the men had told Fox, '[we] are not actuated by any spirit of sedition or disaffection whatsoever: on the contrary it is indigence and extreme penury alone that is the cause of our complaint'".[91]

Some senior officers shared this opinion. Captain Pakenham had advised Spencer, the First Lord of the Admiralty, on 11 December 1796, that "there was a strong feeling among some of the officers that the people whose pay really ought to be increased were the men", and that "the seamen also would apply for a rise unless something was done for them". Manwaring and Dobrée drew from Pakenham's text a sense of the justifiable strength, even anger, of the men's feeling.[92]

Pressure was building and would impact upon whatever clandestine group was overseeing the sending of petitions.

It is not known when or how a particular grievance captured the attention of the seamen on a ship, or how it spread around the fleet. The wage problem could well have started a ball rolling.[93] But no doubt there were times when any one of five, or more, other grievances could come to attention, spurred by some pressing example.

The seamen of the Channel Fleet being a mixed bunch, it hardly seems likely that the sending of petitions was the only strategy being talked about, or that seamen who put aside a different approach, say for direct action, would not feel inclined to take it up again when petitions were ignored by Howe and the other Lords of Admiralty. Tempers might rise, but experience was an effective moderator of extreme positions.

It would seem therefore that communication among "active" seamen both within ships and the fleet would need to increase over time. Cheap postage, allowed to seamen, was already helping.[94] It is unbelievable that the Royal Navy might assist, but it did, as an unintended consequence of a local option for an open blockade of the French Port of Brest. Bridport followed Howe in adopting this policy, which kept the fleet in port, in extremes of weather, and so provided more opportunities for seamen from different ships to interact.[95]

Netted by the seamen in fishing for a richer haul of ways and means, the Admiralty's failures nourished and strengthened the seamen's resolve. Now they would be wiser, opening their wage grievance to parliament and indirectly to the press. This was the third and last wave of such petitions, with petitioning now having given way to mutiny of the Channel Fleet at Spithead with a committee of elected delegates from the ships in charge.

A Seaman, Settling in, on a Royal Navy Ship.

How could such disparate groups of individuals become united as seamen in the Royal Navy of 1797?[96]

On being brought aboard ship, the seaman faced a dilemma, to stay, or to run: to "do a runner", in the language of the sea. Rodger critically examined this phenomenon in the Royal Navy, to mid-century.[97] He graphed *desertion against length of service*, and sampled *rates of desertion* and *rates of turn-over*. His first finding agreed with naval physician Thomas Trotter's view, at the end of the century that most desertions occurred in the early months aboard ship.[98] Rodger also found that the "rates, stations and commanding officers of the ships...were three of the most important factors affecting desertion". Not only pressed men ran, but also volunteers, and men on ships with a high rate of turnover. Denial of shore leave, both as cause and effect, was an official recognition of the tendency to run.

Rodger held "the most frequent motive of all which tempted men to run from one ship to another was the desire to be reunited with their former shipmates. The cohesion of a settled ship's company was by far the strongest force which bound the Navy together, and officers and men were at one in intensely disliking any idea of breaking one up".[99]

Lewis reported 12,302 cases of desertion for the period May 1803 to June 1805, closer to the time of our mutinies.[100]

Having decided to stay, seamen still had to face the reality of life on a wooden ship, at sea, and the fear of drowning. Few seamen could swim at that time in either navy.[101] Rediker included a description of a storm at sea, early in his book, to highlight this fear. "The winds blew 'most dreadfully' and the sea crackled like a 'continuous flame' ", he wrote. "What a terrible cry the people gave, expecting to go every minute".

Rodger also noted this fear among Royal Navy seamen and its contribution to the discipline of the ship.[102] Even so, there were times when pumps and swimming were futile. 13 000 seamen perished by the sea.[103]

Having decided to stay, how did the new hands help to keep the ship seaworthy? "Clearly, the first task of the first lieutenant was to ensure that enough competent men were on duty at any given moment to keep the ship safe. To achieve this, it was normal to divide the crew into two watches".[104]

Christopher Lloyd[105] described the make-up of the ship's crew.

Not all ships had 100 guns, but all the following were men-of-war, ships of the line of battle. Their names may be found in Gill (6n2)[106], Manwaring and Dobrée (257-8), and James Dugan (482-4). The latter's table indicated which ships, both large and small, were involved in each of the several 1797 mutinies.[107] For the First Spithead Mutiny he included 18 battle ships - the *Defence* (74 guns), *Defiance* (74), *Duke* (98), *Glory* (98), *Impetueux* (74), *La Juste* (80), *London* (98), *Marlborough* (74), *Mars* (74), *Minotaur* (74), *Monarch* (74), *La Pompee* (80), *Queen Charlotte* (100), *Ramillies* (74), *Robust* (74), *Royal George* (100), *Royal Sovereign* (100), and *Terrible* (74). Manwaring and Dobrée listed no delegates for the ships *La Juste* (80) and *Monarch* (74).

The rating of a ship defined its size not its quality.[108] Most importantly the rating defined the numbers of officers allocated to the ship and their rates of pay. "[F]irst and second rates were three deckers; those of the third and fourth were two-deckers, while virtually all those of the fifth and sixth rates were frigates, with a single complete deck of guns".[109] As the frigates were sent by the delegates to do convoy duty they are not among the sixteen ships discussed above, and below.

Three ships, each armed with 100 guns were first-rate men of war and had a crew of 850-950. The three 98 gun ships were classed second rate with complements of 740-750. Of the rest, two carried 80 guns and ten carried 74 guns each. These were all third raters with complements around 700. From this information a simple calculation can be made to arrive at an approximate number of people embroiled.[110] For this first mutiny there were on 1st rate ships [900x3] 2700, on 2nd rates [745x3] 2235 and on 3rd rates [700x12] 8400, giving a grand total of 13,335 rounding to 13,000 men.

Paul Brunton was taken by the size difference between the Spithead fleet mutiny [largely forgotten] and the more famous mutiny on HM Armed Transport *Bounty* with its crew of 45 all up.[111] The contrast occasioned Brunton to declare that the mutiny on the *Bounty* was "of no importance", lacking the "passionate aim...of the mutineers to improve the conditions of sea life".

Again, those supporting any mutinous action at Spithead would have had to "run the gauntlet", as it were, of from 700 to 1000 men who were not of quarter deck status among the crew of a particular ship. After that they would need to convince the Fleet, a daunting task.

The Delegates of 1797.

From ship *Muster Books* in the Public Record Office, service details of the thirty-two who signed this new petition, were set out in a table by Manwaring and Dobrée.[112] Sixteen ships of the line had two delegates each to represent them. The *London* had three, hence the total of 33. They were young men, reflecting the general youthfulness of the fleet. To support this, I have averaged the ages within each category and included the result in parentheses. Overall, it was 29 years of age.

Brian Lavery classified sixteen of the delegates as petty officers.[113] Thirteen delegates were rated able seamen, A.B., (average age, 28).[114] This was the highest rating reached by the majority of seamen. Below them were ordinary seamen and landsmen. All other delegates were rated above A.B., and were paid according to the rate of ship, from one to six, on which they were serving.

From the gunner's crew were two quartergunners (34), one gunner's mate (23), and one yeoman of powder room (39). No delegates came from carpenter, armourer and ropemaker crews. Six quarter masters (29) and one quarter master's mate (25) were from crews responsible for steering the ships. There were four yeomen of sheets (29).

Five[115] delegates were midshipmen (32), who came usually from middle or upper class families and who depended on patronage for their first appointment as boys of 11 or 12 years of age as captain's servant. Experience at sea, education and examinations aboard ship, and a 'nod' from the captain, were preconditions for promotion as lieutenant by the Crown through the Admiralty.

Manwaring and Dobrée spoke well of the delegates as "trustworthy seamen", "hardy men, no longer youthful, many of them in responsible positions, and all of them apparently competent". Having drawn attention to their skilled positions, they declared the delegates to be "no rabble of discontented scum, knowing nothing of the sea, but men whom their companions had learned to trust, the flower of all that was not quarter-deck".[116]

1797-1997.

In 2004, Rodger agreed with these assessments of the Spithead delegates, adding, "none of them was a Quota man, and only four out of thirty three were Irish", thereby rejecting two groups of subversives - others followed - alleged by "modern historians' to have been responsible for the mutiny.[117] "Here we are", Rodger argued, "in the presence of the conspiracy theory in its purest form, in which the entire absence of evidence only serves to prove the fiendish cunning of the conspirators".[118]

Rodger's long-time studies culminated in *A Naval History of Britain.* His considered opinion of the delegates was strengthened by generous access to "The 1797 Mutinies - Papers [unpublished] of the Spithead and Nore Bicentenary Conferences, 1997", which he acknowledged.[119]

Before encountering this late work of N.A.M. Rodger my own earlier searches had noted the tendency of "modern historians" to do as he suggested.

Gill was convinced that the mutinies occurred in 1797 and not "in any one of the previous 250 years" because they were "closely connected with the revolutionary movement and the wave of humanitarian feeling which overspread the country at the end of the eighteenth century".[120]

John Keane noted that " 'vast numbers of Paine's pamphlet [*Rights of Man*] were distributed both to regiments and ships' on the second anniversary of the fall of the Bastille".[121] With a third, fourth, fifth and sixth edition appearing rapidly with 50,000 copies sold.[122]

Using Paine's figures of " 'between four and five hundred thousand' copies within ten years of publication", Keane estimated that one reader in ten purchased a copy of *Rights of Man.* "More astonishing was the fact that *Rights of Man* was read aloud and talked about to the illiterate on an unheard-of-scale".

Gill found a basic commonality of opinion among the men that was rooted in "the ideals of liberty, equality and fraternity and the conception of the rights of man", he believed these ideas had permeated the navy, *helped* by the quota-men.[123]

Of Gill's wave of humanitarian feeling, Asa Briggs had this to say. "The eighteenth century was rightly proud of its 'improvement' in manners and its ripening sense of social duty. For the care of the sick, the aged, prisoners, foundlings and poor children, new institutions were created during the course of the century, particularly after 1750. 'We live in an age when humanity is in fashion', wrote the London magistrate Sir John Hawkins in 1787, and its influence could be traced in many places inside and outside London both in individual lives and in the growth of voluntary social organizations: on scores of tombstones and memorial plaques in parish churches we read of men like William Whyte, a surgeon of Castor, who died in 1788 and was 'equally distinguished for professional Abilities, the strictest integrity and an active Discharge of the Duties of Humanity' ".[124]

Lewis had a problem. Having generalised the seaman as "a simple soul, obstinately conservative, ill-educated, and, as we have much cause to lament, unvocal", looked among the educated quota-men for the more "subtle and sophisticated" qualities of the delegates.

Lewis credited some of the educated quota-men with performing "a useful service" by bringing to the seamen "some realization of how grossly they were exploited,[125] and inducing them to assert their rights". He noted their talents of organisation and the quality of the Spithead fleet leaders.[126]

An Irish influence appeared with Dugan, who thought that "[a]bout a third of the names appear to be Irish",[127] although Manwaring and Dobrée had found "only a small sprinkling of Irishmen" among the delegates at Spithead.

Gilmour discussed the Fleet Mutinies of 1797 under the heading, "Ireland and the mutinies".[128] He went on to argue for the influence of Irish and quota men on "a significant number of sailors affected, or disaffected, by French Revolutionary and United Irish ideas".[129] "In Ireland, as in Britain, the French Revolution fertilised radical ideas and produced reform societies. The Society of the United Irishmen, founded in Belfast and Dublin to unite Protestants and Catholics, sought to make 'all Irishmen citizens - all citizens Irishmen'. The instrument was to be parliamentary reform; like the English radicals, the United Irishmen had virtually no social programme".[130]

Gilmore continued: "To meet their quotas, local authorities had to offer bounties to volunteers, which attracted men in debtors' prisons, 'disqualified attornies and cashiered excisemen, clerks dismissed from employment and other individuals in similar cases'. Such men were more literate, of a higher social standing, less inured to brutality, and likely to be more politically conscious and more radical than previous naval recruits'".

According to Gilmour, "suspected Irish Defenders" were sent illegally to the British Navy by the Commander in Chief, Ireland, as well as by many magistrates, resulting in Irishmen making up "more than 10 per cent of the fleet". "[O]n some ships more than half the seamen were Irish".[131]

"Most of them had been dispatched to the navy to reduce the danger of an explosion in Ireland. Their likely effect on the British fleet was ignored".

Similar arguments that have been used to "explain" the delegates, Irish and Quota men, have been applied to the search for a leader. "There was no official leader of the mutiny," Gill wrote in 1913, but four "delegates from the flagships of Howe and Bridport, seem to have had a predominant influence". Valentine Joyce was one of the four delegates missing from the meeting with Admirals Gardner, Colpoys and Pole on *Queen Charlotte*. Gill reports the effect of the return of the four on Gardner's work of reconciliation. The sticking point was that "the King's pardon should be actually in their hands".[132]

Manwaring and Dobrée considered that "If one of them was leader, which cannot be proved, it was probably Valentine Joyce of the *Royal George*, twenty-six years old, nearly the youngest man there but a sound, experienced, authoritative sailor, or he would not have been Quarter Master's Mate".[133]

Dugan noted that the delegates did not elect a chairman, that Joyce continued to sign documents as a delegate of *Royal George*, but appeared to act as spokesman.[134]

Lewis, and Gilmour, agreed on Joyce as a likely candidate but accepted that his leadership role was not proven. Gilmour's description of Joyce included a reference to him as "a United Irishman who had been imprisoned for sedition". [135]

Of the leadership, Gilmour concluded, they "retained unanimity among their followers, used minimum violence, kept their demands moderate and maintained strict discipline. Even flogging survived. Continually stressing that if enemy ships appeared they would immediately go to sea to fight them, they conciliated traders and commercial men by continuing the defence of merchant ships. In short, nothing was changed except that the fleet was ultimately under the control of the men's 'delegates' or 'General Assembly', not its officers".[136]

Seamen delegated. Delegates, so empowered, acted on behalf of, and for, the seamen. The power of the Spithead mutiny came through its unity of purpose expressed in the decisions of its committee or "general assembly" of delegates speaking for the seamen.

The Making of a Delegate.

Understanding the making of a delegate is still a concern. This task needs to be conceptualised for the period 1796-7 in the Channel Fleet, as described above. Pitt was Prime Minister under George III, and at times, the Prince Regent. On 1 February 1793 France declared war and by 1797 the war was not going too well for Britain. Spencer was 1st Lord of the Admiralty and Admiral Bridport was in command of the Channel Fleet.[137]

Pressure on decision-making was increasing for the unknown seamen who were directing the clandestine operation. Strategy would have had to change as well. Over time, the more active seamen had to grow the range, intensity, and speed of decision making to meet the change from crafting words to striking sail. Uniquely, at that time, they appeared to have retained a communal committee structure as opposed to a hierarchical one.[138]

E. P. Thompson wrote of it as a time when "the plebeian movement placed an exceptionally high valuation upon egalitarian and democratic values", including the right to vote, held and propagated at considerable risk.[139] Self-activating and self-organising processes among the common people were the concern of tradesmen, shopkeepers, and mechanics, who debated for five nights their right to obtain parliamentary reform. They decided that they had that right and proceeded to exercise it as members of the London Corresponding Society, turning away from "any notion of exclusiveness, of politics as the preserve of any hereditary elite or property group".[140]

Thompson, more recently described the 1790s as "times of great excitement in London with the accelerating events in France, with the passionate debates provoked by Thomas Paine's *The Rights of Man* (part one, 1791; part two, 1792) and with the formation and rapid growth of the popular reform societies, culminating in the failed attempt of the government to convict the leaders of the London Corresponding Society for high treason in 1794".[141]

Thompson declared that "every advanced member" of this Society of "master craftsmen, shopkeepers, engravers, hosiers, [and] printers" "could have bought a tiny cheap edition of a work", other than Paine's, "to carry around in his pocket". This was Constantin's radical text, translated from the French, and available in England by 1792.[142]

Volney delighted in the response of the people. On being "freed...from parasites and tyrants" they proceeded to select "delegates" "to frame...a system of government and laws" with the understanding "that to-morrow [these delegates] will descend from [their] stations, and rank again with us; that [they] will have acquired no distinguishing right, but the right to our gratitude and esteem".

Volney's delegates duly reported "that in the order of nature all men are equal", "are created free, and from the idea of equality immediately flows that other idea of equity and justice".[143] The delegates of the seamen saw their role as Volney's delegates had done, acquiring no right but that to gratitude and esteem.[144]

Perhaps some of the Fleet readers had passed through *The Ruins...*[to] *the Law of Nature* and discovered why fraternal love is a virtue. If they had they would be familiar with Volney's account of the Scythian king and the bundle of arrows, which while bundled together could not be broken but individually broke like reeds, suggesting metaphors for the mutinies at Spithead and the Nore.[145]

Here, however, the concern is with the making of delegates of the Fleet before they freed themselves from "tyrants". This was the situation in which "trade unions", by and large, found themselves in the eighteenth century. Workers were underpaid, deliberately and continually, whether in money or in kind.

If one is looking for a process of development of such people at that time then one was available, as Weber argued. Positive gains have been made when men have come together freely and have had to prove themselves among their equals in work of mutual benefit. This applied to the situation in the fleet. Add "autonomous decision making, good sense, and responsible conduct" - in the view of the seamen - and there is a possible contributory process.

John Keane argued that Tom Paine was the better for his early contact with Quakers, and from being a Methodist preacher. But as R.H. Tawney argued, while "Puritanism helped to mould the social order...it was also itself increasingly moulded by it". Methodists, within a different context - factory management - became more efficient "in their peculiar mission to act as the apologists of child labour".[146]

Beginning in the years of our immediate concern from 1790, and 1830, Thompson noted "an appalling declension in the social conscience of Dissent. And above all, there are the proverbial Nonconformist mill-owners running on to, with their Methodist overlookers, and their invidious reputation as week-day child-drivers, working their mills till five minutes before midnight on the Saturday and enforcing the attendance of their children at Sunday school on the Sabbath".[147]

Such ideas came out of a study of seventeenth century protestant sects in Europe usually associated with Max Weber who saw similar processes in play in nineteenth century "clubs" in the United States. In the following quote, the authoritarian State to which Weber referred was his own native Germany.

"According to all experience there is no stronger means of breeding traits than through the necessity of holding one's own in the circle of one's associates". [148] If the Delegates were as good as they were said to have been, then some such process may have contributed. It had. In their working lives as seamen they had developed leadership skills, proven by their promotions.

"Organizing a mutiny was a supreme test of character and leadership. Only those who were really admired by their shipmates would be followed. ...

Almost without exception, mutinies were led by petty officers or long-serving leading hands, the natural aristocracy of the lower deck".[149] Rodger continued. "It was precisely these men, experienced, responsible, fully alive to the necessity of organization and teamwork at sea, who were the officers' essential allies in establishing discipline".

Greg Dening also sought answers in the ships to essential questions about the eighteenth century Navy.[150] "The structural tensions of a fighting ship were created by the division of authority between those who were given it by sovereign power and those who earned it by experience", or as Norbert Elias had it, *Gentlemen* and *Tarpaulins.*[151]

Dening was seeking to understand "how Bligh's language could have been 'bad' in a time of institutional transformation". He moved away from expletives to "patterns of discourse", "regulated through the forms of corporate assembly in which they are produced". "Discourse space is never completely independent of social space and the formation of new kinds of speech can be traced through the emergence of new public sites of discourse and the transformation of old ones".[152]

"Add a ship to this list of places of discourse. Add the space created by the collective sense of being 'navy'. Add tonality, silence, looks and glances, winks and nudges, and a sense of corporate reaction to our understanding of the ways in which language and discourse are expressed. The Wooden World of sailors was classified in a complex system of signs whose mastery gave seamen their identity and set them apart".[153]

"That the realisations and politics of this world should turn on such apparently trivial matters as ducking, yarning and dancing should not surprise us. Institutions in the end are talk, and, in the social dramas that talk makes, institutional men become the most adept critics. Of such criticism and theatricality politics are easily born".[154]

To Dening, power on ships was a matter of negotiation and failure in this process led captains to make their own mutinies.[155] The Admiralty, at a higher level, by failing to negotiate, helped make the Great Fleet Mutinies of 1797.

In the making of a delegate, power was also a matter of negotiation, but with the seamen. Their task was twofold. They had to master 'the patterns of discourse' among the seamen of the ship's wooden world, and of the fleet beyond. They would need to be sensitive to the manners and moral economy that regulated their special spaces of discourse within a man-of-war. It was a crowded place. Within the walls of the smaller battle ships at Spithead were upwards of 700 men and, in port, a varying number of women depending upon circumstances. These ships were built for the convenience of war. The people were appendages of war and of a machine called a man-of-war. They acted over time with the economy of machines in space, assisted by the communal mind-set of their particular ship.

Even in self-centred moments private thoughts merged with public space. Dreams of heaven and hell swirled and intermingled as in a Blake vision. Prizes of war, the cream on the cake, richest at the top, thinning on the way down to be gripped in hands knotted by hard labour, accident and disease. Not for nothing were seamen called "hands". Life itself so often depended upon their ability to grab and to hold. Not prize money, though, they soon drank what little trickled down to them.

A delegate would need to understand and to be able to tap into the abilities of those "hands" to make, see and interpret signs, in the unique language of sailors and the sea. In the collective experience of every day living on board ship, little was missed. Not only did rumour spread like wildfire but civil and violent contacts between officers and "hands" were noted and passed around. A body language of acceptance and rejection told it all. Action and inaction at such times spoke louder than words. Silence did not mean consent.

So they would have lent a hand and pulled their weight. Seamen disliked shirkers. Would delegates, too, need to be as fond of their long ribbon-tied hair[156] and chewing tobacco as the next one - as hard drinking and as coarse tongued, unless affected by Methodism's inroads on that navy tradition? Did they bawl sea shanties in the rhythm of work, and reel off songs of liberty with true feeling? Denied the pleasures of shore leave did they also stamp many a lively jig - and more - with wives, girl friends, or prostitutes, on the decks they shared with the guns, giving rise to the expression "son-of-a-gun"?

These men would know the old fear of the sea and could be trusted not to forget it. They would defer to officers, even in a state of mutiny, on matters of ship safety. They would become knowing men of their ship. Their ratings suggested it. Like the sailors in private merchant ships, however, these delegates to be, would side with the men and not with the captain and officers in an industrial action. These loyalties would strengthen as the men's unresolved grievances increased and were ignored.

What led to action? Accepting Gill's subjective and objective causes, and the change agents of Gilmour, and Lewis, it still is not clear how united action came about.[157] Surely the repeated failure of the authorities to respond to the petitions of the seamen did not encourage a suppressed response.

Another important factor was the mindset of the delegates-in-waiting, and those closest to them, for, alone, they could not have succeeded as they had. These new men believed that change was not only possible but achievable. It was an age of improvement.[158] But improvement waited upon men of the ships to take action. Negative responses had to be changed to positive action and had to come from the seamen. The reflexive action of men against the sea had to be locked in against the Admiralty itself. "There is no more effective way of bonding together the disparate sections of restless peoples, than to unite them against outsiders".[159]

Thinking of "outsiders" from another point of view, one might join those who asked, "Did delegates and committeemen receive direct help from outside the Royal Navy?" Was there evidence of the new kind of working class organisation revealed in the first meeting of the London Corresponding Society [L.C.S.] with its "working man as Secretary", its "low weekly subscription", mix of "economic and political themes", meetings serving "social and political" ends and having "procedural formalities"? "Above all", said Thompson, was "the determination to propagate opinions and to organise the converted, embodied in the leading rule: 'That the number of our Members be unlimited'".

John Binns of the L.C.S. was sent to Portsmouth "but was recalled when the London committee learned that he was being shadowed and was liable to arrest".[160] Visits to the dockyard by the L.C.S. members led Thompson to consider them as "one among the threads which link the Jacobins to the naval mutineers at Spithead and the Nore in 1797". The L.C.S. collapsed towards the end of 1796, although suggestions of underground activity have been made.

Aaron Graham, magistrate, was sent out to find links between subversive groups and the mutinies. He was not alone in his failure. This adds credibility to the belief that the Spithead Mutinies were essentially industrial disputes. But this does not take away their subversive nature for as mentioned above, even getting together to talk about wages and conditions, on land, was illegal at that time.

Further comment on the mutinies appears in Gilmour's concluding chapter where he asked whether "A revolutionary situation?" could have come about in eighteenth century England, particularly in its later years. Gilmour concluded that "the mutinies were not instigated by the United Irishmen or by the radical societies, but the United Irishmen had planned a naval revolt in the previous year and might well have taken advantage of Spithead and the Nore in 1797. When he learned what had happened Wolfe Tone lamented the loss of a marvellous opportunity. Even as it was, members of the United Irishmen were prominent in the mutinies. Similarly a number of the leaders had been members of the "Jacobin" societies, and Painite ideas are discernible in their petitions. Lord Gordon's former secretary, Dr Robert Watson, a prominent member of the London Corresponding Society, was active in Portsmouth at the time. Because Joyce and the other leaders, mindful of the need to maintain unanimity, stuck to the industrial grievances, which were all that concerned the great majority of the loyal seamen, the Spithead mutiny appeared much less political than its successor at Sheerness. Yet, though divisive political notions were kept beneath the surface, sedition was not absent from the Channel Fleet, some of which talked of sailing to Brest".[161]

However difficult industrial action had become on land it appears even more so on the ships of the Royal Navy. At all points and on all levels power was surely arraigned more strongly against the seamen.

Committing seamen to such an objective, on one ship, was difficult enough. How much more difficult would it have been to unite the Fleet. An understanding of seamen and more than ordinary powers of observation, perception, foresight and patience were needed. Careful, clever and cunning the leaders would need to be, to match the misdirected care, cleverness and cunning of the Lords of Admiralty. Success in the task had to come in the face of entrenched authority, institutionalised power, and the majesty of the crown itself. As if that concentrated power was not enough the country was also at war. It was united against a common enemy and even more strongly bonded by patriotic fervour and the too obvious need for self-defence.[162]

However, to Thompson "the mutinies posed in the most acute form possible the conflict between the republican sympathies and the national loyalties of the members of the London Corresponding Society". The latter position triumphed at Spithead. Eric Hobsbawm agreed with Thompson, claiming "the real weakness of British Jacobinism is indicated by the fact that the...fleet at Spithead...clamoured to be allowed to sail against the French once their economic demands had been met".[163]

Two delegates from each ship had won the confidence of the majority. Why two? Was it because of an ingrained practical sense of the ship, that two hands, meaning two sailors, in this case, are better than one? Two delegates appear to reflect the communal sense of the Fleet, abroad at that time. Perhaps, too, the people felt a second voice carried a clearer and stronger message to and from the ship and were more comfortable with that.

Secrecy[164] had been essential before but was no longer required when the seamen had taken over the Fleet. At that point, Delegates became known to the ship's officers as those to whom the seamen had delegated power to act on their behalf, and in their interests, under the red flag. To this end the seamen had sworn an oath.[165]

The delegates-to-be, by putting the communal good before self interest, whether egotistical or revolutionary, put their mark upon events. True to each other, neither cause nor man was put at risk. Their sincerity was their strongest defence against betrayal. Their secrecy remained inviolate - to the last moment - when their unity was unshakeable. It was further protected by the seamen's ownership of words and actions the fruit of democratic labour.

Democracy, an idea that hardly existed in the world at large, was active among the men. The Delegates encouraged it. Of a rough and ready kind, it persisted under the constraints of secrecy. There it was expressed in the language of the sea, and a mixture of banter, cussin' and swearin', of winks and nods, of clear agreement by head or hand. This down on the lower deck democracy released the energy required to separate the wheat of action from the chaff of grievance, the grain from the dross.[166]

During the stage of secrecy, democratic processes had driven decision-making and had bonded the seamen. The sense of the fleet, read by Bridport when at boiling point, had been weeks and months in the making. Activists, potential delegates, had fostered and confirmed it from the seamen's everyday body language and from their lips. Skilful and committed persons had drawn out and moulded this sense of the fleet from extreme emotions, loud resentments, strong grievances, deep hurts to body and mind, fear and hatred of the Royal Navy and its masters - and patriotism. There were, as well, subdued yet audible murmurings, a whole range of possible and impossible, probable and improbable, outcomes and solutions. Some of the men themselves were for doing nothing, others for "doing a runner".

There should not have been a mutiny. The petitions made a modest request dampening extreme emotions and winning over the more timid. Each time the petitions were ignored, stronger action was encouraged.

With Melville's words in mind that "the *might-have-been* is but boggy ground to build on",[167] it is interesting to reflect on what might have followed had the first decisions of the seamen been crowned with success. In a conservative mood, combining patriarchy with patronage, they had petitioned their popular commander to interpose on their behalf in a claim for wage justice. Success could have strengthened conservative opinion still more and mutiny most probably avoided. It was not to be.

The effective management of their cause reassured the seamen. The whole Fleet had been included and were now united in a mutiny. Draft petitions and amendments at first, and later the agreed petitions, with forwarding instructions, had been circulated and sent off undetected.[168] When fleet movements threatened the timetable, the petitions were sent at sea. Such detailed and successful actions carried out under a cloak of secrecy were all the more impressive.[169] Direct contact between ships bonded seamen taking part in this work.[170]

It did not end with the petitions. Leading up to the mutiny, grievances were aired and listed. At the same time a set of rules of conduct was worked out, eventually circulated as "A caution from the delegates to the Fleet".[171] This, while binding the mutineers, helped maintain discipline within individual ships, and in the long run, the readiness of the fleet to go into action.

They would be ready to sail when the Admiralty met their demands.

Let Conrad Gill have the final word before returning to the action in the fleet. After carefully considering their grievances, he wrote - "The seamen had good cause to ask for a reform in naval administration. And we must admit that there was some justification for their refusal to weigh anchor when they found their petitions had been ignored. It may be assumed then that the mutinies were not part of a movement inspired by sheer caprice or malice; but that there was justice, at least in the earlier demands of the mutineers that service in the navy involved hardships which were in no way essential to a seafaring life".

"The cause of the mutineers was such as might commend itself to a sober and normally well-disposed seaman", Gill concluded. But that was written in 1913, what were their masters thinking and doing about their cause in 1797?[172]

The Exercise of Power: Admiralty and Delegates.

"The Admiralty still thought that the disorder could be suppressed", replied Gill. "They directed Parker to see to it that all captains of ships at Portsmouth should sleep on board, and should repress any display of insubordination. The ringleaders were to be arrested, and no communication was to be allowed among the ships, or between the fleet and the shore".[173]

From 15-17 April, "Bridport, better informed, knew that resistance was hopeless, and from the first...advised conciliation".[174] On 16 April, at Spithead, delegates from each of the sixteen line-of-battle ships in the fleet determined three primary objectives - to achieve the unanimity of seamen, to maintain the discipline of the fleet, and to prevent rumours on shore.[175] On this day written petitions were signed by delegates from the whole Channel Fleet,[176] the fleet was ordered to put-to-sea, and the whole fleet struck sail.[177]

On 17 April 1797, oaths were sworn[178] and the rule of delegates began in earnest at Spithead.[179] The delegates directed *Romney* and *Venus* to do escort duty as they supported the convoy system to avoid "injury to trade".[180] A decision, well calculated, Gill wrote, to please the Admiralty and the nation as a whole, and it showed sound judgement on the part of the delegates.

The same day an Admiralty Deputation left London for Portsmouth.[181] It included Spencer, 1st Lord of the Admiralty. On 18 April, the deputation arrived at Portsmouth and Bridport acted as an intermediary between the Admiralty deputation[182] and the ships' delegates.[183] Next day the Board met at Portsmouth to discuss the details of the delegates' demand for wage increases.[184] On the 20th at Portsmouth the Board considered whether to resist or conciliate.[185] It accepted the financial terms of settlement[186] but ignored food, pensions at Greenwich, and leave.[187] The Navy Board resolutions were read out next day to the seamen,[188] but, later in the day, Admiral Gardner on *Queen Charlotte* was angry and impatient.[189] As a precaution the delegates met again and decided to mount guns.[190] Expressing their indignation at the Mutiny, officers struck the Admiral's flag on *Royal George*.[191] In response, a conciliatory letter was written to Bridport, by the delegates on 22 April,[192] demanding an Act of Parliament and a King's Pardon.[193]

In London, the Admiralty sent a Memorial to the Privy Council on the cost of the pay increase,[194] while at Windsor, Spencer met the King and obtained a Royal Pardon.[195] On April 23, copies of the pardon reached Admiral Parker at Portsmouth. These were passed on to the captains who read them to their crews.[196] The delegates' response was a request to see the original, and being satisfied, the mutiny ended.[197] In London a Privy Council Committee was appointed to consider the increased pay proposals.[198] The Fleet assembled at St Helens on 28 April but due to westerly winds it was impossible to put to sea.[199] However, in spite of these conciliatory moves, four ships at Plymouth showed signs of mutiny on 26 April.[200]

On 1 May, from London, the Admiralty ordered the commander of the fleet to enforce regulations,[201] a decision described as "a masterpiece of folly" against the need to "soothe the men while the 'Seamen's Bill' was being prepared".[202] On the other hand the Privy Council committee gave a favourable report on the estimates stage[203] and Bedford asked for information on the bill in the Lords.[204] Questions in the House provided newspaper reports, which had the effect of unsettling the crews.[205] On the 4 May, *Estimates* were prepared and Pitt gave notice to the House of Commons.[206]

A Fresh mutiny at St Helens.

Contrary winds and contrary comments, both parliamentary and press, conspired to bring on a fresh mutiny at St Helens. It was organized from the 5-6 May. The seamen believed they had been betrayed.[207] On 6 May seamen on the *Royal George* were upset and a *Pompee* letter raised doubts.[208]

On the 7th the Delegates moved to Spithead to bring the ships there back to St Helens as a "more compact and formidable", though mutinous Fleet.[209] The process of sending officers ashore began that day. At least 100 officers from eighteen different ships were landed.[210]

The condition of the Fleet on 7 May is set out by Gill, who referred to 13 ships.[211] He quoted from "letters to Bridport from the captains under his command" which, he said, "give a vivid impression of the helplessness of the officers in the face of an overwhelming majority of the mutineers".

On 8th, delegates concentrated the fleet at St. Helens, at a safe distance from the guns at Portsmouth.[212] "The condition of the Fleet on 9 May" followed in the text its "condition on 7th".[213] Gill noted that the "*Royal William* must have been the only ship of the line left at Portsmouth". He also reported, that "dispatches of Bridport and Parker showed that on 9 May officers had been sent ashore from nearly every ship".

Delegates were seriously opposed in only one instance, by Colpoys, on the *London*. Manwaring and Dobrée,[214] and Gill,[215] provide lively accounts of this situation. The delegates' experience on board the *Marlborough* where the Captain made no resistance is contrasted with Colpoys' reaction. He, it was, who had been ordered by Bridport on the first mutiny to allow the delegates to come aboard.

However, on this second occasion, shots were fired. Amid "general confusion, shouting, trampling, and explosion of firearms" three sailors were killed and several men were wounded, including a delegate, two or three marines, an officer and a midshipman.[216] When Colpoys cooled off and surrendered to the delegates he faced his crew bent on revenge.

In this extremity it was the two delegates Valentine Joyce and Mark Turner, who quietened tempers and prevented further bloodshed. And it was the ship's doctor who persuaded the men to listen to Colpoys, who explained that Peter Bover, the first lieutenant who had opened fire was obeying "very recent instructions from the Admiralty". A copy was demanded and being fetched, Colpoys, Griffen and Bover were locked up and "the bloody flag once more displaced at the masthead the Admiral's serener banner of St George".[217]

In London the wage increases were again discussed and an amount of £372 000 was voted by the House of Commons on the 8th to cover them.[218] The Government, by asking for a silent vote aroused the ire of the opposition who had much to say about "early mismanagement and subsequent bad handling", of "a degree of guilt or incapacity or both, that has led us to the brink of destruction".[219] "After more fulmination by Sheridan, who pointed out that the sailors were very properly suspicious of promises, and that a resolution was only a promise and would probably not satisfy the seamen, Pitt moved to bring in a 'seaman's' Bill to make the resolution law. It was brought in on the spot, rattled through all its stages, and sent up to the Lords, who had been asked to wait; and indeed, after passing the Bill, they postponed their adjournment until a message came to say that the Royal Assent had clinched the affair".[220]

Next day at Portsmouth, only the *London* received a copy of the parliamentary decisions, because of heavy seas.[221] As a result, the men promised to release Colpoys and Griffiths. With Bover, the three "were summoned on shore for a civil trial by the court sitting as coroner's jury upon the body of a wounded man who had died in Haslar Hospital".[222] The matter was closed with a verdict of justifiable homicide. Bover, having promised to return to the ship, did so against the advice of his friends and was received with cheers.[223] The same day the delegates restricted the fresh mutiny to ships of the line, returning frigates and smaller ships to Spithead.[224]

At this point of their account of the mutinies, Manwaring and Dobrée assessed the situation.[225] For both the Government and the seamen a sticking point had been reached. After the second mutiny, Delegate authority based on ship power was more firmly entrenched than ever. At the same time the Admiralty order of 1 May, and Colpoys reading of it, "suggested clearly to the seamen that as matters now stood the instigators would be hunted out and vindictively hanged".[226]

A Dazzling Gleam.

From the government viewpoint, unrest at the Nore made a solution to the Spithead affair all the more urgent. "A picturesque vision of the fitting end came in a dazzling gleam to either the King or Pitt", to invite the "venerable Lord Howe...armed with lavish powers to treat with the men, to occup[y] the centre of the canvas".[227] Burke opposed it.[228] "Among all the parts of this fatal measure the Mission of my Lord Howe has been by far the most mischievous". He wanted "a great naval commander" to be sent down "to awe the seditious into obedience". Bridport,[229] as well, was none too happy about Howe for not telling him at once about the petitions he had received. After all, he, Bridport, was in charge of the Channel Fleet with Howe, sick, and off duty.

Addington and Spencer sent Bridport "emollient letters" excusing themselves from the decision to send Howe. Pitt wrote to him on the 10th explaining that it was "a civil commission in order not to interfere with the military command of the Fleet". Manwaring and Dobrée said of Bridport that while he "may not have been a brilliant sailor...he was, as he showed all through the mutiny, a man of unruffled sense and great moral courage; that he was a man of unusual generosity as well is revealed in his reply. He swallowed the affront, put his pride in his pocket in the good cause, and wrote to Pitt the next day, 11 May 1797, promising his full support to Howe in endeavouring to restore regular order to the fleet at Spithead. He added...I have always considered peevish words and hasty orders detrimental, and it has been my study not to utter the one or issue the other. I wish that rule had guided the conduct (of) those in higher situations, as I think it wiser to soothe than irritate disturbed and agitated minds". Wise words, indeed.[230]

On the day Pitt's letter arrived, Bridport distributed thirty copies of the *Act* at St. Helens.[231]

A statement, "The Effect on the Estimates", explains what happened. "The estimates were first worked out for a full year then reduced by nine lunar months to 24 April. Since Bridport had promised that the increase would begin on 20 April, four more days were added at a cost of nearly £4 000. The additional wages bill for the whole year was fixed at £351 000. The estimates for victualling were based on the old rate of 19s. a month for every man. The one-eighth increase granted was added. With 120 000 men in the Navy at the time including marines the increase for victualling amounted to £185 250. The request of the mutineers for the full sixteen ounces was apparently resolved by the Admiralty adding two ounces in the estimates instead of it being subtracted from the rations". [232]

Howe travelled down to Portsmouth[233] about the same time as Aaron Graham.[234] Graham represented "people who could not understand how sailors could fail to be contented with their lives unless seditious - Jacobin or Irish revolutionary - elements had been at their horrid work". His mission failed to make a "possibly lurid discovery [that] would exonerate the high and mighty from a charge of maladministration".

Howe arrived at Portsmouth with his wife on May 11,[235] and went at once to visit the ships at St Helens. Bridport received Howe on his flagship the *Royal George*.[236] "Black Dick then talked to the men of [that ship]. He had first of all to re-establish himself in their confidence as the sailors' friend, and then to convince them that the Act was water- tight, that the Admiralty meant to deal squarely by them, and that the Royal Pardon was all-embracing. From the first he met with them as man to man; there was no getting upon the high horse for him, or refusing to recognise the authority of the Delegates, as there had been on the part of Spencer's Board when it had come down in April. His own intuition guided him there, though it may have been strengthened by the advice of Lady Howe, a woman of 'discretion and excellent understanding', according to Benjamin Franklin. But apart from all other difficulties, there was one that lay deep in the old hero's nature, and a grave one in the circumstances – sheer incapacity to state his meaning directly. He meant what he said honestly enough, but it was not always easy to discover what, precisely, he had tried to convey".[237]

After the *Royal George*, where he read a fresh Proclamation of a Royal Pardon,[238] Howe moved on to his old state cabin in the *Queen Charlotte*, and finally to the *Duke*, before giving up for the day. Next day he moved "from ship to ship, till he had been to every one, arguing, explaining, cajoling. His patience was infinite, his manner at once sympathetic and sorrowful".[239]

His sympathy was for their condition, his sorrow for their behaviour. They must ask him to interpose for the King's pardon. The seamen made their "mild gesture of humiliation" but refused to accept a "promise" of pardon. The sentence, "we do hereby promise our most gracious pardon" had to give way to "meaning further to extend our most gracious pardon".[240] And so it became.

For the next two days Howe was rowed once again to the ships in turn, climbing up and down ladders until he had to be lifted in and out of his boat.[241] On the 13 May he decided he would be visited and invited the Delegates to meet him on the *Royal William* at Spithead. Howe met the "Delegates as Spokesmen of the Fleet",[242] when the disposal of officers was discussed.[243] Howe decided that each concerned ship should forward a petition to him in the form of "a prayer to His Majesty to indulge them with the appointment of other officers". The officers were in the wrong. As Howe said, "However ineligible the concession, it was become indispensably necessary'". He repeated an offer of the Board for courts-martial but the men refused.

Manwaring and Dobrée considered that "Howe undoubtedly did the sensible, the humane, and the statesmanlike thing; all through he had shown that at last he realised the implications of the mutiny, and in dealing direct with the Delegates he gave the first example of the proper way to settle industrial disputes. Such an innovation, in the Navy, too, of all places, revealed surprising imaginative powers. And besides, the unflinching dismissal of fifty-nine officers and warrant officers, including one admiral and four captains, was the very thing to impress the men with the sense that the country had confidence in its sailors".[244]

Finally, it can be said that Howe "had been instructed to let the officers go, rather than fail in his mission:[245] About one half of the total number of officers sent ashore by the Mutineers were allowed to return to their Ships.[246] The deposed officers were placed on full pay until they could find another ship.[247]

The conference on the *Royal William* had completely cleared the air.[248] Pay, food, and redress of grievances had been won. All that was needed was a solemn ratification in the form of the King's pardon. Next day, Sunday, on the same ship, all would be concluded. But his day's work was not finished for Curtis arrived from the west with his squadron of eight ships of the line flying red flags, in a state of mutiny.[249] Howe went on board the *Prince* and convinced the squadron to return to duty. The men agreed but insisted that sixty-five officers and warrant officers should be removed. Some were.[250]

According to Gill[251], Howe wrote to Nepean on 14th May noting that he was "much tired...with his daily employment there...to quiet the most suspicious but most generous minds he thought he ever met with in the same class of men".

Festivities on the Sunday were deferred because the revised pardon had not arrived, but it would, and in anticipation "a superbly jubilee procession" was planned for the Monday. "At midday Lord Howe went ashore again, to be received by an immense multitude shouting itself hoarse with acclamation".[252] Whether true or not, Joyce is said to have met Howe to ask for a time to start the procession next day but Howe left it to Joyce who suggested seven o'clock when the tide would serve. Encouraged by Howe's tone, Joyce invited Lady Howe to join the procession. She accepted. Howe then invited Joyce into the Governor's house to drink a glass of wine with him. Joyce accepted "with a manly freedom, unaccompanied by the least particle of familiarity or rudeness".[253] Before the day was out the Admiralty telegraph gave the news that the Pardon was on its way.

Conciliation, Reconciliation, and Celebration.

Early in the morning of Monday, May 15, 1797,[254] the Delegates rowed to the Sally Port and marched up to Sir William Pitt's house with their bands playing "God Save the King" and "Rule Britannia" and joined by the band of the marines. Invited in to the house, they partook of refreshments and appeared on the balcony. At about eight, when all was ready, four men in plain clothes came up to Joyce and were invited by him to join in the festivities. They were the sailors from the Nore come to help.[255] The first boat in the procession flew the Union Jack and carried the band. Lord Howe followed in the Royal Barge. Next came Sir William Pitt and the Lieutenant-Governor with aides-de-camp. Lady Howe, Lady Pitt and other ladies followed, with the Marine band bringing up the rear. The Delegates' boats with crews smartly dressed formed in line ahead on either side. On they rowed to St Helens.

Howe, the 'peacemaker' and 'conciliator'[256] started with the *Royal George*, reading out the Royal Pardon on the quarter deck. It was shown to some literate sailors then passed around for all to see, with its Royal Seal attached. "The enthusiasm was immense; the crew gave vent to three ear-splitting cheers, tore down the now outmoded yard-ropes, and replaced the bloody flag with the Royal Standard". Howe visited nearly every ship where this scene was repeated and in the afternoon was taken to Curtis's squadron where things were still uncertain but he need not have worried the *Prince* soon displayed the Union and Standard under a royal salute. At the end of the day the Delegates hoisted Lord Howe on their shoulders and carried him to Sir

William Pitt's house with the Union Jack fluttering over his head. There Richard, Earl Howe, once more the old beloved *Black Dick*, threw off the hero to become the host, and entertained the Delegates at dinner in all the forms.[257] Then the Delegates rowed back to St Helens and reported for duty.

"An Act of Total Oblivion"[258]

Neither delegate nor seaman suffered for his involvement in the Spithead mutinies. The Royal Pardon led in that direction and "at the very end, on the 14th, the myopic Admiralty itself had gone so far as to make a sensible, even a generous gesture. In an order of two paragraphs, issued to all flag officers, captains and commanders, they promulgated an act of total oblivion for all or any deeds of disobedience, mutiny, breach and neglect of duty, and ordained that no seaman or marine should be 'disquieted by any reproof or reproach' in respect of any deeds".[259]

Chapter 3

GRIEVANCES OF THE SEAMEN - I

Conditions.

"It is also unanimously agreed by the fleet, that, from this day, no grievances shall be received, in order to convince the nation at large, that we know when to cease to ask, as well as to begin, and that we ask nothing but what is moderate, and may be granted without detriment to the nation, or any injury to the service". [1]

The petition from which these words came was considered by Christopher Lloyd to be "[t]he most important document representing the grievances of seamen at the end of the eighteenth century".[2] Requested by Admiral Bridport, it was addressed to the Right Honourable the Lords Commissioners of the Admiralty, and was handed to the Admiral on board the *Queen Charlotte*, by the delegates of the fleet, on 18 April 1797. It was the first signed petition as the delegates felt secure when protected by the united seamen of the Channel Fleet who had mutinied with them.

With the command of the Fleet turned upside down, the "General Assembly" of the delegates awaited a response from Admiralty and attended to the internal discipline of the mutiny. "Except for the cheers at eight o'clock and at sunset, the normal routine, dull and harassing, went rigidly on, under the usual officers, to whom the greatest respect was shown. No violence, not even rudeness, was hinted to any, though some were politely told that boats would be waiting for them at a certain time to take them and their belongings ashore. They went, but the others were not allowed out of their ships, except on official business".[3]

The delegates also circulated a caution to their fellow seamen "as a security and bulwark against the fair speeches of designing men, who will use all their eloquence to defeat our laudable intentions". All were reminded of the aims of the mutiny - that the petition be fully answered, that verbal answers were to be ignored, that pay and other concessions be backed by an Act of Parliament, and, following that, a King's pardon be issued to the whole Fleet.[4]

These sentiments were reiterated in a letter sent to the Board of Admiralty on 22 April reminding their lordships that unless the petition's grievances were met, "the fleet now lying at Spithead...will not lift an anchor; and this is the total and final answer".[5]

The delegates were secure in the knowledge that they had made a good start with their mutiny. The fleet had unanimously agreed on a cut-off point after which no new grievances would be received. Their intention could not have been expressed more precisely[6] than in the words which concluded their new petition and open this chapter. Peter Kemp would conclude in the twentieth century that the Spithead mutiny had been "conducted throughout with great decorum and a proper sense of responsible behaviour".[7]

The Tempestuous 1790s.

The formative years of Redfern's late teens and early twenties, while he was acquiring his medical education in London, will become the focus of immediate attention. Described as *the tempestuous 1790s* they provide a social and political background to the fleet mutinies based on events both on land and on sea. The Royal Navy, in 1797, the year William Redfern joined, had its management exposed to public view by the Spithead and Nore mutinies and was found wanting.

Asa Briggs is the source for the view that worsening economic conditions, largely resulting from the nature of Pitt's financing of the war with France, were impacting on lower wage earners. This has a bearing on the pay claim, the initial and continuing grievance at Spithead and among the first echoed from the Nore, with the support of the North Sea Fleet, in which Redfern served as a surgeon's mate.

Edward Thompson's material supports his picture of a nation divided between stirring workers and supporters, on the one hand, and on the other, politically repressive individuals and forces. Thompson held these forces to be independent of the reasons for war against the French Revolution.

Asa Briggs.

Economic and social conditions in England had been growing progressively worse in the 1790s for the lower wage earners. These formed the great mass of the people who carried the social pyramid[8] on their back.

Soldiers and their families with wage increases just two years before, were again feeling the pinch.

"England at the beginning of 1797 was weighed down by war-weariness. The spirits of men sagged, and everything that happened was either shot with stridency or muffled with a blanket of depression".[9]

Why was this? According to Briggs, the war with France had been a controversial war from the start.[10] Prime Minister Pitt, relying on British economic strength and sea power,[11] concentrated his efforts in the colonies. At the same time, 'gold' to the value of £16 million went on guaranteed loans and subsidies between 1791 and 1803[12] to maintain Britain's allies on the Continent. Among them were Prussia and Austria - and later Russia - all of whom needed financial aid to keep their armies in the field.[13] Unfortunately, while this finance did not buy victories, it aggravated social problems in England.

Napoleon proceeded to conquer Northern Italy, and Austria. The latter signed a peace treaty in 1797 confirming Napoleon's gains in Italy and French power in the Low Countries which formed France's "natural frontier" on the Rhine.[14]

Appointed "Commander-in-Chief of the Army of England", Napoleon eyed the English Channel and began organising Spanish, Dutch and French fleets to make a crossing. France occupied Holland, came to terms with the Prussians (1795) and formed an alliance with Spain (1796).

"[E]vents outside England, the French Revolution and its Napoleonic aftermath, dictated much [but not all[15]] of what happened inside England in the long period from 1789 to 1815. The way into the nineteenth century led across the battlefield[16] as well as through the cotton mill and the iron foundry".[17]

In 1797 Pitt suspended cash payments by the Bank of England and moved at once to increase taxation.[18] A serious financial crisis had resulted from Pitt's preferred use of loan money to finance the war effort. "The size of the loans raised increased from £11 million in 1794 to over £32 million in 1797...Unbalanced budgets, foreign remittances in loans and subsidies, abnormal imports of grain, the re-establishment of a metallic currency in Paris and finally, after paper credit experiments, a run on the English country banks, led to a drain of gold from Britain and a serious fall in reserves".[19]

From 1793 to 1801 prices rose as a result of the inflationary policies of the government.[20] "The price of food, of bread especially, was disturbingly high, and going higher - rises agreeable to profiteers, but bringing distress and even starvation to the masses". "Dear food meant...starvation for the poor...of the new towns [and] the village labourers themselves.[21] "Wages did not keep pace with prices".[22] People on fixed incomes, and particularly the poorest and weakest sections of the community suffered most. Briggs described these "sections of the community [as] politically paralysed and [with] fewer opportunities of ventilating their far more serious tax grievances".[23]

Edward Thompson.

Edward Thompson detailed the events of the early 1790s that bear upon this "paralysis", in his work, *The making of the English working class*, in its own way as much a classic as was Briggs' *The Age of Improvement.*

Society was divided, Thompson argued. [W]orking men in villages and towns over the whole country [were] claiming *general* rights for themselves.[24] '[S]omething unusual' was affecting "pitmen, keelmen, cloth-dressers, [and] cutlers; not only the weavers and labourers of Wapping and Spitalfields, whose colourful and rowdy demonstrations had often come out in support of Wilkes".

On the other side of the divide was a reaction to this general awakening, for as Thompson declared, "It was this - and not the French terror - which threw the propertied classes into panic".

Dissenters agitated between 1789 and 1790 against "disabilities" placed on them but failed to have them repealed.[25] In this period, on the reform side, Constitutional Societies were born. Their aristocratic opponents formed "Church and King" Clubs,[26] which, "From May 1792 [their] anti-Jacobin demonstrations were more highly organised...and more openly directed towards the intimidation of plebeian reformers".[27] Dr Joseph Priestly had lost his church, house and laboratory in 1791.[28]

Thompson returned to this theme to describe rampaging gangs beating up Jacobins and destroying property, while a "magistrate refused to stir from his home, a few score yards from the scene of the riot, and the parson stood on a hillock pointing out fugitives to the ruffians". Thompson was convinced that more was involved than "war fever". It was as if the authorities sensed some sea change in the opinion of the masses, as if some slight event might be enough to set all that "combustible matter" aflame.[29]

"Reformers must be watched and intimidated, the societies isolated and ringed round with suspicion, the prejudices of the ignorant whipped up and given licence. In particular, professional men with access to printing-press, bookshop, pulpit or rostrum, who associated with plebeian reformers, were the subject of intimidation".[30]

In May 1792, "a Royal Proclamation against seditious publications was issued, aimed in particular at [Thomas] Paine". "In December, Paine was outlawed (in his absence) and *Rights of Man* was condemned as seditious libel". Thompson was "inclined to accept the claim of two hundred thousand sales [of Paine] in England, Wales and Scotland (taking account of both parts, and of abridged editions issued by local clubs) in 1791 to 1793".[31] "In January 1793 [King] Louis [of France] was executed, and in February, war between England and France commenced". "Pitt's long-delayed decision to prosecute Paine signalled the opening of the era of repression".[32]

"Cries for peace became louder and more frequent than ever, and to the alarm of timorous Conservatives the radical Corresponding Society was swelling its ranks, and holding more open-air oratorical displays than ever; while, on the other hand, the suspension of Habeas Corpus brought sharply home to lovers of liberty that the forces of reaction were ready to pounce. It was a bleak, grey period, threatened with winds of adversity".[33]

While wives and children suffered penury on land, husbands and fathers were fleeced at sea. On the ships themselves, pursers had increased the cost of slops - replacement clothing - by thirty per cent. Sufficient has been said to appreciate Ian Gilmour's more recent claim that the fall in the value of the seamen's pay due to inflation was the only respect in which their conditions had worsened since the war started.[34]

Thompson's material shows that people were stirring on land, as well as in the Royal Navy, in the 1790s. Seamen were not alone in experiencing repression, and the denial of basic human rights. The wonder of it all is that against the background of events on land the seamen were successful at Spithead. How much longer might they have had to wait for wage justice and other benefits without their mutinies? A history of the Reform Bills suggests a general, and the continued denial of shore leave, specific answers.

Gilmour held the government to blame for what happened at Spithead by not having raised the wages of seamen previously. As a result of his study of *Governance and Violence in Eighteenth-Century England*, Gilmour concluded that "violence is usually a reaction against somebody or something, and to leave out those causes would make it incomprehensible. More particularly, violence often arises from the actions or inaction of government, and popular resistance cannot be divorced from this. It is for this reason that governance must be considered together with violence - especially as the violence itself may come from the government".[35]

The Added Grievances.

The added grievances were mentioned in chapter 2. Briefly they were all those grievances additional to the pay increase. They related to the quantity and quality of provisions, better care of the sick on board, shore leave, the needs of those wounded in action, and grievances, specific to particular ships.

With regards to the second grievance, there is some confusion in the footnotes of Gill.[36]

Addressing the Grievances.

The seamen had made their position clear. They wanted to go on living, but as men, with their manhood intact. Conrad Gill recalled how the seamen at Spithead, in their first petition, reminded the Admiralty of the respect due to them as petitioners. Later, at the Nore they were even more determined. "Long have we been endeavouring to find ourselves men. We now find ourselves so. We will be treated as such".[37]

The "real grievances" referred to above, were described by Gill as "hardships...in no way essential to a seafaring life".[38] Lord Howe thought so too, and removed fifty-odd Officers who had contributed to that unnecessary hardship.

The need to revisit this issue will be found in later chapters dealing with the Nore mutiny in which William Redfern was involved.

The fourth grievance, the refusal of leave to seamen when in port, was not resolved by either mutiny. It was mentioned in passing in the previous chapter in connection with seamen running from their ships. This is not considered to be an adequate discussion of such a critical matter. It will be further discussed in a later chapter when the presence of women aboard ships at sea will be investigated. Many more women were there at times, in the main, as an unintended consequence of the refusal of shore leave to seamen.

The Health of Seamen.

Those grievances concerned with provisions and the care of the sick and wounded go to the heart of the greatest threat to seamen, to their continuing health, threatened by disease, whether caused by nutritional deficiency, or contagion.

The health of seamen has had [and continues to have] a critical role in naval warfare. The Napoleonic Wars were no exception. A healthy seaman has an obvious advantage over a sick one, enemy or not.

Diseases of seamen, combined with individual accidents, were responsible for about eight out of every ten deaths at sea. Deaths from this same combination of causes were some four times heavier than those resulting from ship accident and enemy action. Ship-accidents were just about twice as deadly as the Enemy.[39]

William Redfern's story slots into this contemporary study of health at sea for he joined the Royal Navy as a surgeon's mate in the year of the Great Mutiny. Although brief, his experience of life on a battleship provided him with a practical entry to medicine in the Navy. Both specific and general understandings of Redfern's medical experiences will become available to us in the chapters that follow.

In time, his early medical education and Royal Navy and convict transport experience would come together to inform an acclaimed and influential report on preventing disease on Convict Transports. Later to influence Immigrant Ships. [40]

Victualling the Fleet.

Nicholas Rodger gave to the victualling process a national as well as a naval role in *The Command of the Ocean.* "In the period in which Britain rose to greatness, there were only three significant economic activities in the British Isles: agriculture, foreign trade and war", he argued.

"The achievements of British sea power were national ones, the product of government and society as much as of the Navy as an institution. Without the courage and professional abilities of officers and men at sea they would have been impossible, but the most crucial developments in the period covered by this volume were not naval but financial and administrative. It was the capacity of naval administration ashore, above all the Victualling Board, which transformed the operational capabilities of British fleets at sea".[41]

Here, "Victualling", the name given to the process of provisioning the fleets, will be narrowed to a concern with food and drink. The *Regulations* detail the nature and items of such provisioning in some twenty "Articles".[42] The daily allowance comes first in the form of a weekly table (Article I). The men are to be paid the difference in any shortfall, which the Officers must suffer equally with them (II).

Variations in the allowance, for good reason, require the equivalence of various items to be set down. For example, "a Pint of Wine, or Half a Pint of Brandy, Rum or Arrack, hold Proportion to a Gallon of Beer". Similarly, "Half a Pound of Currants, or Half a Pound of Beef Suet pickled, are equal to a Four Pound Piece of Beef, or Two Pound Piece of Pork with Pease" (III).

Detailed instructions are given for cutting up pickled meat into just weight (IV & V). "Pudding Bags, proportions of Butter and Cheese and Olive Oil for Foreign Voyages, and new Casks for water and beer" were the concerns of Articles (VII-XI).

There were a number of references to provisions. They might be purchased overseas if stocks were running low. Vessels bringing provisions are not to hang around. Proper officers are required to condemn old provisions as unfit for keeping. Checking supplies is to be frequent. There were rules for supplying other ships. Fresh beef or mutton was to be available for two days in the week - one in lieu of salt beef and one of salt pork. Provisions from enemy prizes were also covered.

The Purser.

Here the quantity and quality of provisions will be examined against the role of the ship's purser, a middleman between Navy authorities and crew. If the Purser wanted to protect his investment he would need to be word perfect in the *Regulations* and diligent in applying them, particularly when he was at risk of loss from his negligence.

If Samuel Pepys is to be believed, and he should be, considering his long connection with the Royal Navy, albeit of an earlier age, it is not surprising that sailors' rations were high on the list of grievances. Pepys held to the view that "Englishmen, and more especially seamen, love their bellies above everything else, and therefore it must always be remembered in the management of the victualling of the navy, that to make any abatement of them in the quantity or agreeableness of their victuals, is to discourage and provoke them in their tenderest point, and will sooner render them disgusted with the king's service than any other hardship that could be put upon them".

"Indeed," according to Christopher Lloyd,[43] whose original quote brought Pepys' reference to this present notice, "more mutinies have been caused by complaints about food than those caused by low pay or tyrannical behaviour. In the forefront of the demands of the mutineers of 1797 is a request for more vegetables and better quality of food". As we have discovered.

The quantity, quality and variety of food items available on Royal Navy ships came within the domain of the purser ("pusser"), a non commissioned officer. Greg Dening was obliged to give serious thought to this position when he wrote of Bligh and his *Bounty* mutiny, for Bligh was his own ship's purser,[44] as Captain James Cook had been, although Cook delegated much of the work.

"Pursers were objects of almost universal suspicion because they distributed provisions, accounted for every ounce of food and every farthing of expense. Pursers were the brokers of every transaction on a ship and had to find a profit in these transactions if they were to win back the surety they had laid down. They were responsible to the Naval Victualling Board. The Board, out of long experience, had learnt every trick there was to squeeze a farthing. It made all its own rules, none to its disadvantage. It took any amount of time between six months and fifty-seven years, as Rodger has written in *The Wooden World* (1986) to settle its own debts. Shipwreck, mutiny or accident was never a reason to compensate a purser for his losses. Any man who became a purser had to have some genius for knowing what would adversely affect him, and had to labour instantly to record whatever he counted and measured. A mean spirit and calculating shrewdness were his chief defences. The altruism expected of a captain glimmered lowly behind the parsimony anticipated from a purser".

Light is thrown on this Dening text from an occurrence at Spithead in 1787, ten years before the Great Mutiny. That was the year Bligh sailed off in *Bounty* for the Pacific Ocean and the First Fleet headed for Botany Bay. On 12 May 1787, Arthur Phillip gave the order to sail to his fleet. Observing some hesitation, Phillip sent his aide, Lieutenant P.G. King, to investigate. King described the incident in his *Journal.*

"A disagreement...took place between the Seamen of the Transports & Victuallers, with the Masters of them, in which I think the Seamen had a little reason on their side. They had been in employ upwards of seven Months, during which time they had received no pay except their River pay & one Months advance. The great length of the Voyage rendered it necessary that they should have more Money, to furnish themselves with such necessarys [sic] as were really indispensable. But it became the Masters interest to withold their pay from them, that they might be obliged to purchase those necessarys from them on ye course of the Voyage at a very exorbitant rate; However our sailing, obliged some of them to return to their Duty, others compromised with the Masters, & ye *Fishburn* lost 5 Men which never returned".[45]

Victor Crittenden thought this incident might almost constitute "the first Australian 'strike' ". He went on to suggest that the first strike breakers, Navy men at that, were the sailors from the *Hyena* who replaced the discontented seamen.[46]

To Lloyd, as well as Dening, the eighteenth-century purser was primarily a businessman.[47] And no wonder, that the purser's pound, was a target for the Fleet Mutineers of 1797. But there was another term to the equation. The purser had his own problems, as Lloyd explained. "In consequence of a petition in 1776 he was allowed to deduct one-eighth of the value of his stores or to issue them at 14oz. to the pound in order to recover loss 'of Bread by its turning to Dust;[48] of Cheese by its decaying Mold and being eaten by Mites; of Peas and Oatmeal by their being eaten by Cockroaches, Weevils and other Vermin'". Lloyd added a reference to the "principal demand of the mutineers in 1797...that their provisions should be raised to the weight of 16 oz., to the pound 'and of better quality'". So the petition was used on each side of the argument over food, sandwiching the Admiralty in between.

In passing, the sailor's diet, in spite of its condition, "made up in quantity what it lacked in quality". The weekly ration of biscuit, beer, beef, pork, pease, oatmeal, butter and cheese was "superior to that enjoyed on land by [people of] the class from which pressed seamen were drawn, for meat was seldom eaten by the poor".[49]

Lloyd widened the discussion of victualling and again is very much to the point.[50] "The victualling of the Navy was the responsibility of the Commissioners of the Victualling Board, whose contracts were paid by the

Treasury but whose policy was dictated by the Admiralty and the Navy Board". "What they required were foods which could be preserved and easily transported, and which were sufficient to maintain life under adverse and varying conditions". The guiding principles of purchasing policy were durability and economy.

Here technology lagged. For example, it was 1813 before canned beef was supplied to the fleet.[51] "Technology [was] both the problem, and its own solution".[52] New technology had produced the deep-sea ship, but sadly, not the means of ensuring a healthy voyage. People had to work and to die for that. Anson circumnavigated the world but lost most of his men from scurvy.[53]

Scurvy's Challenge to the Victuallers.

James Lind, who started his navy career in 1739 as a surgeon's mate, was appalled by the Anson record and driven to find answers, searching anecdotes, learned tomes, and Admiralty backed recipes. Lind found that "scurvy", as a generic term, had become a receptacle for ill-defined symptom and unexplained disease.[54] To him, no authority was sacred. The need for certainty was too pressing.[55]

Scurvy is no innocuous complaint. It was described by Kenneth J. Carpenter as "probably the nutritional deficiency disease that has caused most suffering in recorded history", with the exception of famine.[56] An estimated two million lives were lost at sea from scurvy alone between 1500 and 1800.[57]

Lind described the effects of this disease, beginning with the early mild stages, which Banks had experienced on the *Endeavour*.[58]

"[W]hen the several causes productive of the scurvy, act with combined and uninterrupted force, it then becomes a most dreadful distemper. It reduces the most stout and vigorous constitution to the weakness of a child; and the bloom and strength of youth, to the imbecility of age. The feeble knees tremble, and cannot support the weight of the body; nor the back, the weight of the trunk. By walking a few steps, the sick are out of breath, and often faint away; the countenance, the whole appearance, the groans, and complaints of the patients, denote the most piteous and abject state of weakness and of misery".[59] Gums degenerated, teeth fell out, old wounds opened and even rib bones came away from the sternum.[60]

In May 1747, Lind, now a ship's surgeon, tested six accepted Royal Navy "cures" on board H.M.S. the *Salisbury* in the English Channel. He selected twelve scurvy patients at a similar stage of development of the disease. All received a common base diet. Each pair of patients received one of the following six 'cures' as a supplement - cyder, elix. vitriol,[61] vinegar, sea water, oranges and lemons, garlic and mustard. Only those given oranges and lemons were cured. Among the other patients, those receiving cyder improved, but all the others got worse. This was the first ever, controlled clinical trial.[62] It found a certain cure for scurvy and should have disposed of a number of mythical ones.

Although Lind published his *A Treatise of the Scurvy* in 1753, Carpenter was unable to find any other "reference to the experiment itself in literature published between 1750 and 1900".[63] This was in spite of the fact that Lind described his *Salisbury* trials in English, against the Latin tradition of the time for such works.

A macabre dance with scurvy and death continued throughout the eighteenth century. It would be almost the end of that century before lemons, lemon juice and green vegetables became more readily available to Royal Navy seamen.

One may wonder why. The fully reasoned story includes the unexpected, and to some, the unbelievable. While Carpenter presented the history of scurvy in book length form in 1986, Christopher Lawrence's concise paper of 1991, "Scurvy, Lemon Juice and Naval Discipline" is worthy of attention.[64]

Lawrence described a marked change in the practice and theory of medicine in eighteenth century Britain, associated with "a new breed of self-assured medical men, many of whom were dissenters". He contrasted the small ship of exploration with the large man-of-war of the Royal Navy and "the close-knit paternalism" of Cook with "more modern forms of discipline", quoting Blane to the effect "that cleanliness and discipline [at sea] are the indispensable and fundamental means of health".

"The Cook-Pringle-Admiralty nexus was a very specific formation...never exactly reproduced again", while the Banksian Learned Empire "played scarcely any role in the massive expansion and disciplining of the Fleets which occurred in the late eighteenth century".

Gilbert Blane and Thomas Trotter did play a role, and a successful one at that. Pupils of William Cullen, representing the new breed of medical men, as will be seen in Lawrence's paper, and in this study, were active in the campaign against scurvy in the Royal Navy of the time.

Lind dedicated his book about scurvy to Lord Anson, who may have appointed him to the new Haslar hospital for seamen, as a result. There were those at the time who considered the curative power of a simple lemon beyond belief. By comparison, Lind's "own theory of the disease...is extremely difficult - even painful - to read, let alone summarize, and few have attempted it".[65]

While Lind's controlled experiment had also proved that "elixor of vitriol" did not cure scurvy it was still recommended by "the College of Physicians as an efficacious Medicine in Scorbutick [scurvy] Cases". As late as the 1790 edition of the Royal Navy *Regulations* it was supplied to the fleets for that purpose.

Lind himself was somewhat reticent to see himself as more than one who finds rather than implements new ideas.[66] Nevertheless, in attempting to make easier the supply of lemon juice to ships, Lind reduced bulk by boiling the juice. Unwittingly this destroyed the vitamin C. His rob[67] of lemon did not work, and Lind's well-intentioned efforts were counter productive.

Blane (1785) knew "for certain" that the "virtues" of the juice were impaired when "fire" was involved in the preparation of rob, such as Lind's. He recommended that the juice be expressed and bottled with a small quantity of spirits added to preserve it. Blane's observations in the West Indies revealed fresh vegetables and the juice of lemons, oranges and limes as the most reliable cures. Essence of malt was not as good.[68]

Again, Lind gave "no clear final message to those in authority" on the victualling of ships in the 1772 revision of his *Treatise*, but Nathaniel Hulme had done so in his work, *A Proposal...*, published in 1768. Hulme argued, "to supply every ship with enough citrus juice to provide 11/2 ounces per man per day, together with two ounces of sugar, was both practicable and economical".

Carpenter considered some extreme positions taken on Lind's contributions that ranged from extreme adulation to the overly critical. His final evaluation was that "we should honor Lind for what he was and for his truly pioneering controlled clinical trial". Beyond that, "not every one of Lind's recommendations is seen now, with our benefit of hindsight, as being antiscorbutic, but if his recommendations, *taken as a whole*, had been adopted, there can be no doubt of their favourable effect. Let us respect the man in the context of his period and by what he *did*, rather than by what, from our viewpoint, we think he *might* have done".

Captain James Cook, that great navigator, also became part of the problem. Considered to be a paragon of all the virtues associated with running a healthy ship, Cook is held to have contributed to a twenty year lag in the supply of citrus fruit to the Navy. This proposition, well researched, follows.

Sir James Watt showed how closely Cook had followed Lind's recommended *Health Measures* with one critical difference, a stated reliance on "MacBride's malt, rather than Lind's lemon juice as a general antiscorbutic". Cook's broad and largely successful approach to maintaining health on his ships, coupled with the lack of controlled experiments by his surgeons, made it difficult for him to elevate the contribution of one alleged antiscorbutic against another.[69] Nevertheless, Sir John Pringle, speaking on behalf of Cook, who was at sea, did offer support to MacBride's malt, and partly as a result, scurvy continued unchecked. The Channel Fleet in 1780, after a six weeks' cruise, returned with 2,400 cases of this easily cured disease.[70]

Joseph Banks, with Cook on the *Endeavour,* discovered in himself the early signs of scurvy, although he had made use of all the antiscorbutic 'treats' on board. Banks was grateful for the lemon and orange juice he had with him and which he had good reason to believe had proved the effective agent in his cure.[71]

Hulme had written to Banks on 1 August 1768. He mentioned the juice sent to Banks by order of Dr Fothergill, detailing what each case contained, methods of extracting the juice, suggesting he take some empty containers for collecting fresh juice along the way, and gave page references to his book, published that year. One may suppose that Banks already had a copy since the juice had been sent to him.[72]

Later, in September 1769, Mr Monkhouse [surgeon] prescribed some of Hulme's juice for Dr Solander, who was unwell. Obviously Banks was not selfishly guarding his store.[73]

It was to Hulme, introduced above by Carpenter, to whom Watt gave the credit for keeping Lind's work alive. Hulme influenced the surgeons and captains of discovery vessels fitting out in the Thames. By 1776 he was President of the Medical Society of London and a Fellow of the Royal Society".[74] Watt also attributed the success of Cook's health measures to the advice of Wallis and his surgeon, Hutchinson, although he also acknowledged that Hulme had advised both Wallis and Banks.[75]

Phillip, of the First Fleet, in 1787, was well aware of the means required to combat scurvy, having had earlier experience of it in the Portuguese Navy. Phillip also had the will to take necessary action in the victualling of his Fleet. Alan Frost offered conclusive evidence for this in his *Botany Bay Mirages.*[76]

He explained: "Modern knowledge tells us that scurvy, the scourge of sailors before the nineteenth century, arises from a deficiency of vitamin C; the human body needs a minimum of 10milligrams of ascorbic acid daily to prevent its onset, with the recommended intake being 30-45 milligrams. Without replenishment, the body's store of this vitamin is exhausted after about 68-90 days and the depletion rates increase when people labour in wet and cold conditions and consume salt and alcohol. We also know the vitamin contents of a very large number of fruits and vegetables".

The complex story of scurvy may be followed in the literature through every intricate twist and turn. Lind's *Treatise* was reissued in 1953, in its bicentennial year, edited and with notes by C. P. Stewart and Douglas Guthrie. Christopher Lloyd told the story in "The introduction of lemon juice as a cure for scurvy" in the *Bulletin of the History of Medicine* (1961). Sir James Watt was at his compelling best in *Starving Sailors* (1981). Kenneth J. Carpenter's

The history of scurvy and vitamin C (1986) is a classic text, an absorbing read. Today one would start with Carpenter.

As told in the first chapter of this book, above, Governor Bligh gave William Redfern a copy of Frederick Thomson's *Essay on scurvy.*[77]

Scurvy entered its decline in the Royal Navy on the very eve of the Great Mutinies, from 1795-6. Nathaniel Hulme, as explained by Carpenter and Watt, had kept Lind's work alive, but Gilbert Blane, physician, then elevated to the Sick and Hurt Board and Thomas Trotter, physician to the Channel Fleet, were strategically placed to bring that performance to a conclusion. [78]

"The Admiralty orders to this effect were issued between August 1795 and April 1796, and a general order was promulgated in 1799". Lloyd gave "Sick and Hurt Records, July 19, 1799" as his reference.[79]

However, it was not all plain sailing as Trotter pointed out. "The frost in the month of December 1794 set in extremely severe; and a cold north-easterly wind prevailed for three or four months". [The Thames froze over in 1795.] "Independent of the effects which an extreme degree of cold, long continued may possess in predisposing the body to Scurvy, it had at this time destroyed all vegetation in the neighbourhood of Portsmouth. Even the bum-boat women, who are in the practice of bringing vegetables to sell in the ships, could procure little of the kind or at a price that put them out of the reach of the sailor".[80]

In the remaining years of the Napoleonic Wars over a million gallons of lemon juice were consumed by the Royal Navy. Nelson, having earlier suffered from scurvy on his 28-gun escort frigate *Albemarle* after successive Atlantic crossings,[81] took no chances in his Mediterranean campaign. Providing cheap lemons for the Home Fleet cost the life of John Snipe, physician to the Mediterranean Fleet. Snipe died from an illness contracted at Messina while negotiating the supply of lemons. In Sir James Watt's opinion, Nelson displayed not only his "interest in individuals, but the priority he accorded health" when he commended Snipe's service to the Admiralty.[82] As ship's surgeon, Snipe appeared to his credit at the Nore, as will be seen below, but not as a mutineer surgeon like Redfern.

Vegetables.

Lind also stressed the value of vegetables in preventing and curing disease in his *Report on Scurvy* published in 1753. Yet, the Delegates in their petition of 18 April 1797 "grievously complain and lay under the want of" "a sufficient quantity of vegetables, of such kind as may be the most plentiful in the ports to which we go".[83]

Vegetables, had they been in regular supply, would have gone a long way towards preventing scurvy. Anson was aware of the capacity of greens, grass even, to cure his scorbutic crew, getting them ashore when he could.[84] Neither Anson nor Lind was aware of the underlying reason. In his *Treatise,* Lind had referred on numerous occasions to the antiscorbutic properties of vegetables and had organized a regular supply of green vegetables from Plymouth for Admiral Edward Hawke's blockade of Brest in 1759. The purchase of vegetables, sanctioned after that, "died out during the American War of Independence, when the number of seamen was at its height and their health at the lowest".[85] Lloyd noted the absence of vegetables in the official dietary scale and pointed to this as "the principal reason for the ravages of scurvy".

Thomas Trotter, a follower of Lind, called for vegetables and fresh meat in port. He was able to make his own special contribution when appointed physician to his Majesty's Channel Fleet, on April 3, 1794, under the command of Admiral Richard Earl Howe.[86] This placed him on board and in charge of the hospital ship *Charon.*

Trotter took pride in going in person to the markets to purchase fresh vegetables, salad, cabbage, onions, apples and other fruits. At the same time he prompted a positive reaction from the authorities so that after 1796 an order allowed an issue of 50lb. of greens to every 100 men. Trotter claimed that the extinction of scurvy may be reckoned from that event. There was some truth in what he claimed, for lemons at first were restricted to outgoing ships and fresh vegetables built up the sailors' reserve of vitamin C before he went to sea.

Trotter's contribution to this debate is of special significance as he was the senior health official in the Channel Fleet at the time of the mutiny. It seems strange to have the seamen there, making such a complaint when Trotter was doing the rounds of the markets buying fresh vegetables for them.

The allowance to ordinary ships had only been authorized in the previous year and supply problems had not been overcome by the time of the mutiny. There would be recurring seasonal shortages but onions and potatoes would help, in time.

The Navy, as expected, but within reason, as Trotter pointed out above, argued in response to the Spithead petitions that fresh vegetables were not always available, even in port, as noted above. Matthew Flinders, in the *Investigator* at Cape Town, wrote that "vegetables were not to be purchased, but we several times received small quantities, with oranges and lemons, from the naval hospital" there.[87] The later blockade of Brest in the Napoleonic War benefited from the strategy of growing vegetables on the Channel Islands.

Outside the Navy, the need for vegetables was not always recognised as Coleridge found while at Christ's Hospital as a student. There, as mentioned in the opening chapter, "appetites were damped, never satisfied, and [they] had no vegetables", a poor preparation for a life at sea.[88]

Lemons, Weapons of War!

If it appears that too much has been made here of the story of scurvy, bear in mind the following comments, the first two from Christopher Lloyd and the third from Gilbert Blane.

"One can almost argue that the American colonies were lost because of the incidence of scurvy".

"Of all the means which defeated Napoleon, lemon juice and the carronade gun were the two most important".[89]

"Blane was right when he said after the war that if the mortality [to which scurvy contributed] had been equal to that of the preceding war 'the whole stock of seamen would have been exhausted...for there would have died annually 6674 men which, in 20 years, would have amounted to 133,480, a number which very nearly equals the whole number of seamen and marines employed in the last year of the war".[90]

There is one contrary thought on the subject of scurvy included by James Watt in his report on "Nutritional disorders in 18th-century British circumnavigations", part of a symposium in *Starving Sailors.*

"In concentrating upon scurvy, however, we may have ignored the neurological effects of vitamin B deficiencies seen most tragically in the death of Captain James Cook but evident also in the decisions of other circumnavigators".[91]

Victualling of the Fleet, in Retrospect.

This discussion of the grievances of seamen linked to the quantity and quality of provisions began with the role of pursers in victualling the Fleet. That first section concluded with a brief reference to technology as promoter of change, with scurvy as an occasional, but serious, unintended consequence.

Scurvy took centre stage in the section that followed. While Lind drew attention to the facts that lemons cured and vegetables prevented scurvy, a maze of mixed signals confused decision makers and held back the regular issue to seamen of lemons and lemon juice for fifty years, with dire consequences for the Fleet. The fluctuating supply of vegetables to seamen proved to have a history with close parallels to that of citrus juice. In each case the incidence of scurvy was a measure of success or failure in the supply of preventive foods, fruit and green vegetables, and fresh meat when in port.

From this brief account, Guenter Risse might detect an enlightenment glimmer of "faith in the progress and perfectibility of society with the help of science and technology",[92] at a time when "military and naval medicine' were seen as part of a broad medical mission to meet the needs of 'national power".[93] "The underlying premise...was that disease could be controlled, removed, and perhaps prevented by the conscious and deliberate application of 'enlightened' views about health hitherto individually employed in the private sector of both middle and upper classes".[94]

Risse claimed that "for the first time in history" physicians were enabled to "make significant contact with sectors of the lower classes of society",[95] in this case the seamen of the Fleet.

The History of Medicine, a Study.

Along the way, this study has converged with the field of study of the history of medicine. Now that we have arrived at the last of the seamen's grievances, the care of the sick and wounded, this relationship appears to be more natural. But no more so than the presentation to this point since the *prevention* of disease had become central to the practice of enlightened medical practitioners in the Royal Navy.

While the study of the medical history of the Navy depends upon books and other records held in public and private collections, writing that history is another matter. John Burnham, looking over the whole field of the history of medicine, saw the challenge now is to come to terms with a body of knowledge enriched by "a process of cross-fertilisation" between the work of medical practitioners and academics writing medical history.[96]

An earlier attempt to bring historical and medical studies to bear on problems of health at sea has provided a useful source of material, *Volume III* of *Medicine and the Navy* (1961), for this chapter. There the academic historian, Christopher Lloyd, F.R.Hist.S., *Assistant Professor, Royal Naval College, Greenwich,* collaborated with the surgeon, Jack L.S. Coulter, F.R.C.S, *Surgeon Captain, Royal Naval Medical School.*

Burnham saw all of medical history at the end of the twentieth century, enlivened by "intellectual, technical, social, and cultural questions". Its quality was the proper focus and not the formal qualification of the writer.[97]

Concentration on outstanding medical persons runs against a trend of current studies in the history of medicine. However, Lind, Blane and Trotter[98] are germane to this text for their high degree of involvement in conceiving, propagating and implementing a critical mass of ideas for the improvement of the health of seamen in the second half of the eighteenth century.[99] At the same time they were neither infallible, nor alone, and were not without opposition.

Additionally, the publications of these three naval surgeon-physicians, provide a concise history of the main features of eighteenth century naval medical theory, practice and change. Publication dates and titles flag a sequence of events in that history. The content of their books shows clearly that these three were 'participant observers', practising, proposing, and more than once, effecting major changes in medical practice in the Fleet.

James Lind's *A Treatise of the Scurvy* had been published twice [1753 and '57] by 1757. In this year he also published the first edition of *An Essay on the Most Effectual Means of Preserving the Health of Seamen.*[100] By 1780, the *Scurvy* volume had seen a third edition [1772] while his *Essay* had gone through several editions as well [1762, 1774 and 1779]. *Two Papers on Fevers and Infection* appeared in 1763. *An Essay on Diseases Incidental to Europeans in Hot Climates* [1768] ran through six editions to 1808.[101]

Gilbert Blane's publications, as listed by Lloyd and Coulter, began with *A Short Account of the most Effectual Means of Preserving the Health of Seamen* (1780) followed by his *Observations on the Diseases Incident to Seamen.* First published in 1785 there were further editions in 1789, and 1799. In 1815 came his Statements of the Comparative health of the Navy, in *Med.-chir. Trans.*, 6, 490-573. *Elements of Medical Logick* followed in 1819 and *Select Dissertations* in 1822.[102]

Thomas Trotter's list of publications also starts with that of Lloyd and Coulter. His *Observations on the Scurvy* was dated 1786. *A Review of the Medical Department in the British Navy* [1790] was followed in 1792 with a second edition of his *Scurvy.* Remarks on the Establishment of the Naval Hospitals [1795], was followed by *Medicina Nautica,* 3 vols [1797-1803].[103] *An Essay Medical, Philosophical, and Chemical On Drunkenness and Its Effects on the Human Body* was published in 1804 and reprinted in 1988.

To the Trotter list, Roy Porter added the following - *A View of the Nervous Temperament...* [1807, reprinted 1976]. *Suspiria Oceani: A Monody on the Death of Richard Earl Howe,* K.G., Admiral of the Fleet, etc. [1800]. *A Practical Plan for Manning the Royal Navy...* [1819]. *Sea Weeds. Poems Written on Various Occasions...* [1829].

Lloyd and Coulter frequently cited the work of these three authors, while Lloyd published selections from their writings, giving as one reason the fact that their published books "are almost as rare and inaccessible as manuscript materials".[104]

His publishing project was conceived as having relevance to a number of studies - naval history, medical history, public health services (naval), epidemiology, and preventive and tropical medicine. These writings, as Lloyd pointed out, "provide admirable evidence on such subjects as the manning of the fleet, living conditions on board, the ventilation and construction of ships and the victualling of the Navy – with its consequences".

Lloyd concluded with three more compelling reasons for such a publication.

Disease was the major cause of deaths of seamen (Lind).

Navy historians' had neglected the study of health - 'the great thing in all military services' (Nelson).

The advice of Lind, '(which had to be repeated by his disciples Bland and Trotter on account of Admiralty obscurantism) certainly saved the lives of untold thousands of men'.

James Lind's *Essay* alone, in its 1779 form, contained all the essentials for preventing the shocking conditions on the guard ship at the Nore, in 1797.[105]

Finally, these authors and their works would have to be seen as contributing to the medical making of William Redfern, as critic and reporter of disease and its prevention on Convict Transports. Redfern's involvement, and the sheer numbers of convicted and free people brought to Australia by ship, make invaluable the presence of 18th century works on health at sea in the collection of the History of Medicine Library, Sydney.

But, what of Sydney's Mitchell Library? Paul Brunton, Senior Curator, had some exciting news to deliver in the *State Library of New South Wales Magazine*, July 2008:16-17; also available online. Lind, Blane and Trotter volumes assembled by Robert and Mary Anne Parks of Detroit had found their way to the Mitchell Library.

Specifically mentioned here are Lind, *A Treatise of the Scurvy* 1953; Blane, *Observations on the diseases of seamen* 1785; Trotter, *Medicina Nautica: An essay on the diseases of seamen* (3 volumes 1797-1802).

Factors that drove Lloyd to publish a volume of extracts from these three works apart from their resource value was rarity and inaccessibility (see above). Brunton reported not a single copy of Lind or Trotter was found in any public collection in Australia and Blane in only one institution in Victoria (Ibid. NSW State Library, 2007). [This, of course refers to first editions.]

The Sick and Hurt Board.

Lloyd and Coulter opened their first chapter[106] by introducing the Sick and Hurt, or Sick and Wounded, Board, whose Commissioners were appointed, by the Admiralty. The first Board was appointed in 1653 and from 1702 responsibility was extended to include prisoners of war. This dual role continued throughout the eighteenth century until 1796 when the care of prisoners was handed to the Transport Board, where it was so well administered that the Sick and Hurt Board followed in due course.

From 1795 to 1802 the Commissioners of the Sick and Hurt Board were Drs John Johnstone, Robert Blair, William Gibbons, John Weir and Sir

Gilbert Blane, 'the most distinguished naval physician of the day'. "Before this date there had been considerable criticism of the inefficiency of the Board".[107] Now, important innovations were introduced by the Board, as prime mover, from the issue of lemon juice to new regulations for surgeons, which...'Blane took personal care to see properly implemented'.[108]

In the context of the present discussion the concern is with the administration of medicine in the Navy up to the date of the Mutiny. But the decision to amalgamate the Board for Sick and Wounded seamen with the Transport Board as from January [6] 1806 reflected 'the deplorable state of the business' in that department which 'has long been known' as Barham [Sir Charles Middleton], the First Lord, advised the King in his letter of November 4, 1805.[109]

What was the business of the Sick and Hurt Board supposed to be? Lloyd and Coulter included among its work, responsibility for 'the salaries, expenses and standards of the whole medical department', 'the issue of necessaries for the sick and the supply of drugs'. The drugs (medicines) came from the Society of Apothecaries, 'viewed' by the senior physician at Greenwich Hospital.

The Board tried to maintain a reasonable standard of service among its surgeons and hospitals by visitations and inspections carried out by a Board member, its Agents, or the local commander-in-chief with special responsibility, rarely met, to visit local hospitals. With surgeons scarce in the middle of a war, 'it was difficult to dismiss even the most dishonest or inefficient'. One example given was of a ship's surgeon, in 1804, not preparing his chest for action and of having rusty instruments.[110]

Hospital inspections in 1785 had in mind siting that was open and elevated, 600 cubic feet of air space per patient, and 3 feet between beds. Cubicles were discouraged, and hair mattresses preferred over flock, in each case to reduce infection. All new patients were to be washed and their clothes fumigated to contain infection.

Trotter called Deal hospital 'a place in every way calculated to generate contagion and lengthen disease'. It seems to have enjoyed the worst reputation, not forgetting 'a five-ounce lead weight...found attached to the provision scales'.[111]

In a submission to the Admiralty in 1796 the Board summarised its responsibilities. Blane, Blair, Gibbons and Johnstone signed the document. Comments on five of these responsibilities were added by Lloyd and Coulter in their chapter. A complete review followed.

Lloyd and Coulter concluded that, by "such recommendations, and by the reforms in the status and pay of surgeons which the Board suggested soon afterwards and which were implemented in 1805, it was hoped to make the medical department of the navy autonomous, efficient and respectable, none of which it could justifiably have claimed to be before".

How far the Sick and Hurt Board's Ideas of 1796 had already infiltrated the practice of selection of "respectable and well qualified medical candidates" would be difficult to determine. In any case, 1797, the year of William Redfern's acceptance by the Royal Navy, seems to be too soon for automatic inclusion among this better selected group of surgeon's mates particularly as their examination remained within the hands of the Surgeons' Company.

For the concerns of this chapter, however, the Board's own assessment of the need for change in 1796 strengthens the claims of the seamen at that time for better care of the sick and wounded.

Gilbert Blane's 'Observations'.

Gilbert Blane demonstrated the enlightenment approach to the study of health at sea. In 1780, while personal physician to Admiral George Rodney in the West Indies, Blane was appointed Physician to that Fleet and Rodney issued an order to every surgeon in the Fleet to send in a monthly return. This allowed Blane 'to collect and compare a great number of facts'. As he said, in the preface to his book, "I endeavoured to analyse and collate these facts, by throwing the monthly returns...into the form of Tables, as the most certain and compendious way of finding their general result'.

He had three steps in mind for a book. A record of "the health, disease and mortality records of sea voyages and hospitals" would come first. Deductions would follow "from observations founded on these facts, and also from the former experience of others, the causes of sickness in fleets, and the means of prevention". Finally, he hoped to "deliver some practical observations on the cure of the most common diseases incident to fleets, particularly in hot climates".

In October 1781, soon after arriving back in England with Lord Rodney, who aimed to recover his health, Blane presented a memorial to the Board of Admiralty "proposing such means for the preservation of the health of the fleet as had occurred to [him] during [his] past service". This memorial appears in the Appendix to Part II of his book. In conclusion, Blane highlighted the alarming waste of British seamen.

On July 16, 1782, Blane, back in the West Indies sent a supplement to his Memorial advising that a general improvement had occurred in the health of the Fleet [about 40 ships of the line]. However, he was "persuaded [that losses] should have been still less had the improvements proposed been complied with in a manner more extensive and complete, and had the general rules of discipline and cleanliness been kept up with due and equal strictness throughout the fleet".

In 1780, prior to his Memorial, Blane had prepared "a small treatise for the fleet, containing general rules for the prevention of sickness". This was reprinted in later editions of a larger study as *Observations on the Diseases of Seamen.*[112] What follows I first noted in the 1789 edition of Blane's book.

Blane concluded his observations with these words. "My trouble would be compensated, should it prove the means of health and comfort to a single ship's company; nay, I should not repent my labour, could I enjoy the conscious certainty of its being the means of saving the life of one brave and good man". [Words similar to these, from William Redfern, will be encountered later in this book.]

In footnotes, Blane acknowledged chiefly Dr Lind and Capt Cook. He referred to Lind's "most accurate observations on the health of Seamen in hot countries". He gave as a reference to Captain James Cook, Sir James Pringle's "Discourse before the Royal Society on the occasion of adjudging a prize medal to Capt Cook for his paper upon this subject".[113]

Blane's *Observations* resulted from the convergence of certain of his social and intellectual dispositions. He was at ease with the propertied class of people on the quarter-deck, and in Admiral's and Captain's cabins. He was privy to their conversations and discussions and soaked up their commentary and asides on death and disease. He was also the Admiral's personal physician and had been given the task, somewhat irregularly, of keeping his eye on health matters affecting the Fleet, in the West Indies.

Blane's 'Observations' in Brief.

To Blane, "acute diseases [we]re as much artificial as any others, being the offspring of mismanagement and neglect". Having a feeling for truth and courage he addressed his observations to those who directed the navy in a civil and military capacity.

What Blane was saying of the Royal Navy seamen in the eighteenth century still rings true for the health care of people to day, in peace and in war.[114]

Much may be done to maintain the health of seamen. Humanity and duty prompt and interest and policy demand such action.

Able and healthy sailors are a truly inestimable order of men, the real resources of a state, and the true sinews of war.

Maintaining the health of seamen was preferable and cheaper, than restoring it, after the ravages of disease.

Preventing disease was stressed repeatedly as its cure was not the great strength of eighteenth century medicine.

Health on board ships depended more upon officers than surgeons.[115]

Blane, himself, added a footnote. "It is not meant by this to insinuate that every commander is absolutely accountable for the health of his ship's company, and censurable when they are sickly; for this may depend on his predecessor in command, or a stubborn infection may have prevailed from the original fitting out or manning of the ships which he may not have superintended".

Over time, "Fleets and expeditions with the best health records were distinguished by close and effective collaboration between the commander and his physicians and surgeons. Rodney developed a close relationship with Blane, Nelson with Gllespie and Snipe, Wallis with Hutchinson, Cook with Patten and Anderson, La Perouse with Rollin, and Malaspina with Gonzales and Salvaresa".[116]

William Redfern described the tragic consequences when dislocation, not collaboration prevailed on the convict transports. His recommendation that a surgeon-superintendent be appointed and empowered to stimulate collaboration reflects both an acute perception of the need and first hand knowledge of the situation. Contributions to his experience would have come from his Royal Navy service, short as it was, from his voyage on a healthy convict transport, his medical inspections of hundreds of other such ships on arrival, and from his study of the works of Blane and others of his kind. Only the last of these influences has had to be inferred from his report.

Seamen as Described by Blane, and Trotter.

For the immediate concern of our mutiny study it is useful to bring to mind what was said of Royal Navy seamen at that time. According to Trotter, the diseases affecting seamen "spring from causes peculiar to a sea life; laborious duty, change of climate, and inclement seasons, bring on premature age, and few of them live to be very old".[117] Blane agreed.

In *Medicina Nautica,* now rare and expensive to purchase, Trotter first discussed "the follies and vices of the sailor", following with his virtues, "of the finest cast". "Was I ever to be reduced to the utmost poverty", Trotter claimed, "I would shun the cold threshold of fashionable charity, to beg among seamen; where my afflictions would never be insulted by being asked through what follies or misfortunes I had been reduced to penury".

Constrained to follow with a reference to the officers, Trotter explained that "some of the gentler virtues which adorn the naval profession in watching the health and comfort of their people, will receive abundant testimony from the...pages" that follow in his book.[118]

In *A View of the Nervous Temperament,* Trotter contrasted the seamen's behaviour with "the general effeminacy of manners, that is rapidly consuming the manly spirit and physical strength of this age, and...may ultimately annihilate all that is great in the character of Britons".[119]

Chapter 4

GRIEVANCES OF THE SEAMEN - II

Health.

In their petition, the seamen asked *"That [their] lordships will be pleased seriously to look into the state of the sick on board his majesty's ships, that they may be better attended to, and that they may have the use of such necessaries as are allowed for them in time of sickness; and that these necessaries be not on any account embezzled".*

The last point was taken up by the Admiralty in its order of 1 May 1797, when surgeons were warned not to embezzle the drugs and medical comforts consigned to their care.[1] Gill, Manwaring and Dobrée, and Dugan reflected on the Navy surgeons over the time-span of their writing, 1913-1966. However, it was Lloyd's 1965 publication of selections of the work of Lind, Blane and Potter[2] that provided essential background to health and medicine in the Royal Navy at that time.

Dugan, alone, had a reference to William Redfern, commemorating him in a brief chapter, "The Mutineer Surgeon". There, Redfern was credited by the mutineers as having "behaved very well to the sick since he had been in the ship".[3] Redfern, to his credit, declared at his court martial that his age and the fact that he had not been long on board made him more acceptable to the people than the older surgeon.[4]

Of the Admiralty order, Dugan said, "Surgeons were inferentially accused of stealing. Everyone knew many were dishonest, but to have it officially from the Lords Commissioners of Admiralty was a novelty".[5]

"Some of the doctors, of course, did their work well, and were regarded by the men as their best friends", according to Manwaring and Dobrée, "but many of them were of the kind typified by Bell - sodden, rough and incompetent". The crew of *Minotaur* formally complained about a surgeon Bell, in response to Bridport's request for their grievances.[6]

Merchant seamen were not well disposed to sea doctors, who were mainly on slave and other large ships. Since they sided with steward and captain they fell foul of the seamen's antiauthoritarian disposition. Edward Barlow's journal contained a 'bitter' reference to "surgeons and doctors of physic" being "very careless of a poor man in his sickness".[7]

Gill discussed the surgeons under a chapter headed, "Discipline",[8] which is a little strange, considering it is concerned with "indiscipline" on the part of the officers. Its opening sentence reads, "A third grievance was the harsh conduct of some of the officers" and of course was not restricted to surgeons.

Gill admitted "this grievance fills a larger space than any other in the official documents relating to the Spithead mutiny". Tucked away in that chapter is the record of the officers' ill treatment of the men, "taken from the records of the Channel fleet".[9] Such treatment was described as "unnecessarily cruel" - as if "cruel" were acceptable - "unendurable", and as "examples of brutality that largely justified the mutineers in revolting".[10]

At least these complaints were heard and investigated at Spithead. "Heartrending documents, written by illiterate men who had not the education to state their case lucidly or even well...sporadically loaded the Admiralty post-bag", and had been ignored in recent years, and would be again at the Nore. Manwaring and Dobrée spread their sorry tale of ill-treatment by captains, and "flogging [as] their portion", dating back to 1793.[11]

One item that did not appear in the above accounts of the Mutinies of 1797 may be found in Brian Lavery's text. In a discussion of "Shipboard Life" in *Nelson's Navy,* he wrote: "Courts-martial show quite numerous cases of child molesting by officers. In the first few months of 1808 alone, there were three such cases. A boatswain was tried for 'taking improper familiarities with the persons of two boys'. He was dismissed and imprisoned. A lieutenant took 'indecent liberties' with a boy, taking him into his cabin and committing a sexual offence with him in his cot, on more than one occasion. A sergeant of marines was acquitted of indecency with a drummer".[12]

Two years before the mutinies, Admiral Lord Duncan, in charge of the North Sea Fleet, addressed the Admiralty on a whole series of matters ranging from a limitation in the number of lashes, regulated leave, the serving of tobacco, soap and lemon-juice, and even a more equal distribution of prize money.[13]

Admiral Philip Patton reported to Spencer in 1795 that a general mutiny was possible, and in December, 1796, Captain Packenham advised him that "there was a strong feeling among some of the officers that the people whose pay really ought to be increased were the men".[14]

This stands as proof that not only seamen, but Admirals, too, were ignored by the Admiralty Board, in spite of "The Rules of Discipline and good Government to be observed on Board His Majesty's Ships of War", at the time.[15]

"In the first Place, the Commanders of His Majesty's Ships are strictly required to shew in themselves a good Example of Honour and Virtue to their Officers and Men..." Truly "honour" and "virtue" were at home in such an eighteenth century document.[16] And just as truly preaching and practice could be at odds. Hence, mutinies in the fleet.

Returning to Gill and to the surgeons it is found that complaints are on record against one surgeon from *Minotaur* of "inattention, cruelty and drunkenness" and against another from *Marlborough* of continually disregarding the state of health of the men to the extent of allowing, and even reporting, a sick man to be flogged. Three other surgeons were sent ashore at Portsmouth, and Gill supposed that several were dismissed from other ships.[17]

Understandably, Gill was not at ease[18] while giving an account of the dishonourable behaviour of a number of officers and surgeons. His account still gave only a sampling. He wavered between charges that were "trivial and foolish", and the most serious, "a needless amount of cruelty" once again begging the question of how much cruelty was "needful".[19]

The Care of the Sick.

In 1782, according to Watt, approximately 1 in 3 seamen were discharged to hospital. The mortality rate was 45 per thousand, double that of a comparable group in the general population in England.[20] Lewis showed that disease and occupational accidents accounted for 81.5 % of all naval deaths between 1778 and 1806 compared to 18.5% from major disasters and enemy action.[21]

Nevertheless, improvements were under way. Scurvy provided a case in point.[22] Trotter noted that it was this subject, which "first drew [him] into notice as a medical author".[23]

Thomas Trotter, M.D., physician in charge of *Charon* a hospital ship in the Channel Fleet, responded to the complaints of the seamen by taking delegates to inspect his ship. They were amazed, he said, to see the provision for the sick. However, the sailors' collective memory of disease in Royal Navy ships at sea over several centuries, had been etched too deeply to be erased by the ever so recent official issue of antiscorbutic vegetables and lemon juice.[24]

A comparison of the actions of Blane and Trotter would tend to show that these issues were still patchy at the time of the mutinies. That no cases of scurvy could be found at Haslar hospital in 1797 reflected both an improvement in its prevention by means of fresh meat and vegetables in port, and its cure on board ship with lemon juice.

While the specific grievance of the seamen referred to "the state of the sick on board" - and this will be given due consideration - the separate provision for the sick on hospital ships and on land will also be examined. These hospitals contributed to the care of the sick and wounded from individual ships in the longer term.

Hospitals at Sea and on Land.

"Howe's tactics at the beginning of the war were those of the Open Blockade of Brest. This allowed for frequent returns to port for replenishment, but Trotter usually accompanied the fleet in the hospital ship *Charon* if the cruise was extensive, in order to supervise the victualling. Thus in June, 1795, he demanded 5000 cwt. daily of fresh vegetables, an increased supply of lemon juice (now first issued on a large scale) and other necessaries such as cocoa, sugar and portable soup".[25]

Thomas Trotter as physician-of-the-fleet had his cabin in the hospital ship, otherwise Admiral Howe, commander-in-chief of the Channel Fleet would have directed him to another ship. Admiral and physician, had a good working relationship. The service benefited by Howe's readiness to advance Trotter's ideas at the highest levels of naval administration.

Charon,[26] described as "ill-named" and "singularly ill-named" for the reason that in Greek and Roman mythology, Charon was the ferryman who conveyed the shades across the Styx, a river of Hades. It is only fair to say that *Charon* was the name of the ship on its earlier active service, and not one given by some ghoulish imagination as more appropriate to its use as a naval hospital.

Nevertheless, hospital ships in general, "[w]ith their ancient hulls, rotting timbers, low deck space (5 feet 10 and 1/2 inches), and grim atmosphere, [could] never have been very salubrious craft". This was the conclusion reached by Lloyd and Coulter in a brief discussion of eighteenth century hospital ships.[27]

In spite of this, and no doubt because of the experience of troops on land with malaria and yellow fever, Trotter and Johnstone recommended a hospital ship be sent to the West Indies in 1795.[28] Though the ship was not approved, their advice provides useful information on medicine and diet for the sick.

"Additional supplies [were suggested] of antiscorbutics - lemon juice, malt and cream of tarter, as a sop to the conservatives - and also of bark, calomel, opium, mercury, rhubarb, antimonial powder, camphor, magnesia and ipecacuanha. For daily diet they suggested gruel with wine or cocoa for breakfast; 1/2 oz. pickled cabbage, 1/2 lb. potatoes, and 3/4 pint of wine, in addition to the regular salt provisions for dinner; cocoa with sugar for supper".[29]

On the hospital ship *Nightingale* in 1775, diet was varied from full to low. "Patients on a low diet were given rice, whey, milk and panada (i.e. bread and butter pudding); those on half diet had for dinner 8oz. mutton, 1 pint broth, 8 oz. vegetables, 16 oz. bread and 3 pints of small beer. For breakfast they had 1 1/2 pints of milk pottage. Their full diet was twice this amount".[30]

At sea, weather permitting, the worst cases of the Channel Fleet sick would be transferred to Trotter's hospital ship. In port, such cases would be sent to whichever was nearer, *Charon,* or a neighbouring port hospital.

The history of the care of the sick and wounded in the eighteenth century Royal Navy began in 1714 with "the system of contracting for naval beds in...civilian hospitals" and of "boarding out the sick in private lodging-houses".[31] In the hospitals that followed, "at Greenwich,[32] Haslar and Plymouth, the Crown provided establishments for the care of the aged and infirm, and for the cure of the sick and wounded seamen, on a more munificent scale than was to be found in any other nation of the world".[33]

Of these hospitals, only Haslar will be discussed here, partly because it was adjacent to Spithead and also because Lind (and his son) and Trotter had associations with it. Dr James Lind was appointed as Physician to Haslar Hospital on May 24 1758 and advised his wish to retire in 1783. His resignation was received with regret and a pension of £200, equivalent to his salary, was approved. But almost at once "the money for James Lind's pension was found by promoting his son John into his father's shoes and at the same time dispensing with the services of a Second Physician", the position John had held.[34]

Trotter, who had been "a pupil of Lind's at Haslar, was fond of referring to his master as a 'man of observation' and was 'always ready to pay tribute to Lind as a physician' ". He was, however, critical of Haslar hospital from an administrative point of view. Lloyd and Coulter consistently supportive of Trotter were "not prepared to condemn James Lind out of hand" and provided evidence for and against. The debate is lengthy and detailed, spilling over into the situation at Plymouth in 1795 and extending to a special section on Trotter himself.[35] There, "Trotter's *Directions* for the conduct of affairs in the wards which had been under his charge at Haslar" were described by Lloyd and Coulter as "perhaps, a model of their kind".

Care of the Sick on Board Ship.

The care of the sick and the duties of the ship's surgeon were laid down in *Regulations and Instructions.*[36] What surgeons did in practice depended upon their individual will-to-do, negotiated as always with captain and officers, and not always to the advantage of the sick. Medical skills came next, modulated by the materials of practice, that were to hand, and individual knowledge and experience.

"Rules for the Cure of Sick or Hurt Seamen on Board their own Ships" were restricted to one page of the *Regulations.*[37] Their intention was to have set aside a convenient place for the sick, to appoint carers, to have conveniences made, and provide fish, fresh from the sea. Negotiation was inherent in the articles, I to IV, as sick-bays were not a fixture, "attending and serving the sick" varied with numbers, the cooper was needed to construct toilet buckets and the carpenter for cradles for fractured bones. The responsibility also rested with the captain to "employ some of the Company in Fishing". With good will between captain and surgeon an effective delegation could solve all. And, on the contrary?

The surgeon had his own set of rules ("articles") beginning with his responsibility "to provide himself with Instruments and a Chest of Medicines according to the Rules of the Navy".[38] Having obtained printed "Sick" and "Smart Tickets" (III) he was then to "examine the Necessaries sent on Board for the Use of the Sick Men, and if they are not good, in their Kind, to acquaint the Captain" (IV).

That "article" continued - "He is to keep the said Necessaries in his Custody, and not embezzle or misapply any Part thereof, but take Care that they are well husbanded, and duly served out for the Relief of the sick Men". So. They *had* been told.

The surgeon was to visit the Men at least twice a day, and oftener if needed, and arrange for their continuing care by the surgeon's mates and assistants (V), the loblolly "boys".

Difficult cases were to be brought to the attention of the fleet or squadron physician, if there was one (VI). A daily sick report was to be given to the Captain with special mention to be made of "infectious distempers". These would either be sent out of the ship or isolated (VII).

Sick men sent off to hospital, whether on ship or on land, were to be accompanied with a written case history that included their medical treatment (VIII).

"In an Engagement [the surgeon] is to keep himself in the Hold where a Platform is to be prepared for the Reception of the Wounded Men; and himself and his Mates and Assistants, are to be ready, and have every Thing at Hands for stopping their Blood, and dressing their Wounds (IX)".

The surgeon was also required to keep "a Day-Book of his Practice" (X).

The cockpit was the site of the surgeon's struggle with life and limb, when the ship engaged in battle. Brownlee described "a pile of tourniquets [being placed] beside each gun while, below, the cockpit was turned into a hospital and operating theatre. Trunks and cases belonging to the junior officers were carefully arranged with tarpaulins thrown over them to form resting and waiting couches for the wounded. The large dining table was cleared and scrubbed down and lanterns hung above. This was now the operating table where the only anaesthetic was a glass of rum and a piece of leather to bite upon".[39] Shock from the injury, also had a "dulling" effect, a kind of natural anaesthetic, of assistance if the operation followed quickly.[40]

Wounded in Action.

Robert Young's description of "the scene in the cockpit of H.M.S. *Ardent* at the battle of Camperdown in 1797" appears in Lloyd and Coulter. "He had no mates to assist him, because the recent naval mutinies had driven many out of the service". Speaking of himself as surgeon, he wrote:

"A man who is at once Physician, Surgeon and Apothecary, upon whom in these characters, the health and lives of so great a number of valuable subjects of the State are often solely depending, ought to have every means and every instrument and every accommodation to favour and aid the exercise of his industry and skill..."

Lack of accommodation for the sick and wounded on board, of which Young complains, was a constant feature of the overcrowded warship under sail. "The normal operating theatre was the cockpit, situated on the orlop deck below the water line and illuminated by lanterns; but...in an emergency, temporary platforms were erected in any of the lower parts of the ship which were available".

Operations were conducted in order of arrival of the wounded in the cockpit without regard to rank.

Samuel Leech, "in one of the few genuine autobiographies of that date", and that, too, of a boy seaman, described conditions on board after a hard action, as seen by a layman. This extract concludes with the following..."We saw two of our mess wounded. One was the Swede. We held him while the surgeon cut off his leg above the knee. The task was most painful to behold, the surgeon using his knife and saw on human flesh and bones as freely as the butcher at the shambles. Such scenes of suffering I saw in that wardroom I hope never to witness again. Could the civilised world behold them as they were, and as they often are, infinitely worse than on that occasion, it seems to me they would for ever put down the barbarous practices of war by universal consent".

Together with Robert Young (above), and others, such collective accounts begin to furnish minimal understanding of the practice of surgery in a ship, in action, or in an "engagement" as the *Regulations* described it.[41]

Much has been said to this point about sickness, but little about wounds.[42] While disease was a greater killer than enemy action, as Lewis and others have pointed out, 6,500 men died from wounds.[43] In the British Army the proportion of death from disease to wounds was 24:1 while for the Peninsular War (British under Wellington) it stood at 7.5:1.[44] Even so, the British Army suffered 12,000 deaths from battle casualties.[45]

Nelson's wounds were varied.[46] A shell splinter's effect was mainly bruising but a compound fracture of the right arm, caused by a musket ball, led to an amputation. (After that, surgeons were instructed to heat their knives before operating.) Nelson also suffered much pain while the ligature rotted away. He also developed septicaemia.

In the Corsica campaign, Nelson received a 'sharp cut' in the back and was knocked over by "a shower of earth from a heavy shot". Later, he "[w]as much bruised in the face and eyes by sand from the works struck by shot". His right eye was permanently damaged. At the Nile he was hit by a fragment of shot, which struck him on the forehead above his right eye cutting the flesh to the bone. Finally, at Trafalgar he was killed by a ball from a sharpshooter in the mizzen top of the *Redoutable*.[47]

In action, the impact of projectiles on wooden ships gave rise to showers of flying "splinters" and large "spears" of wood, resulting in a range of bodily effects from the superficial to the deeply serious and death.

So it was with fire, an ever-present fear. *Redoubtable* caught fire at the Battle of Trafalgar and *Orient*, the French flagship, blew up at the Battle of the Nile.[48]

Watt, in his paper, "The Burns of Sea Battles", traced the complicated nature of burn injuries and their treatment from the Armada to his time of writing, 1974.[49] Fireships and cannon had "added, the hazard of gunpowder, strewn over the deck and readily ignited in action, to the longstanding danger of sudden conflagration caused by tallow candles and fires used for cooking, for ventilating and fumigating the ship, or perhaps for preparing some complicated apothecary's prescription". [50]

From the Armada came wounds that varied from "superficial flash burns from the accidental ignition of powder horns carrying the gunpowder used for priming the guns, localised full-thickness burns from contact with red hot metal, burn wounds caused by the explosions of cast-iron, muzzle-loading guns and the combined effects of oxygen deprivation, smoke and the toxic products of combustion, together with the liberation of noxious gases and infections which had been locked up in the hold, upon men already debilitated by disease, scurvy and malnutrition".[51]

Some 200 years later Blane reported that "scorches from the accidental explosion of gunpowder" were still "the class of wounds most peculiar to a sea engagement" and were in his experience "very frequent and fatal". Blane's preferred treatment was with linseed oil, mixed with either limewater or cerusse. Watt, after contrasting the high mortality from superficial burns reported by Blane with the good results with these burns from reports of 16th and 17th century surgeons asked whether the true cause was the use of cerussa, lead dissolved in vinegar. He added, "If so, it is by no means the last time that history records the serious consequences of surgeons failing to anticipate the results of absorption of toxic local agents".[52]

In the interim, Watt had drawn attention to an early report of rehabilitation of burn victims in 1588, to the cleaning of wounds of "all the powder that sticketh to the flesh, for it hindereth the cure" of 1617, and to a reference in 1686 to "the great controversy, which has continued to the present day, between the calefacient school (those who applied heat) and the refrigerant school (those who applied cold). [53]

In a text enlivened with accounts of treatment under fire and enriched by contemporary references to a largely botanical pharmacopoeia for cures, Watt moved to prevention. He turned to Blane for accounts of the urgent need for, and the results of taking preventive measures against fires at sea.[54]

Blane reported "one-fourth part of the whole killed and wounded was from the explosion of gunpowder" "in the battles of 1780 (St. Vincent) and 1781". By contrast, on 9 and 12 April 1782 only three lives were lost from two accidental explosions of gunpowder.

Blane attributed the improvement to better training of gun crews, the practice of wetting the wads, replacing large ox horns with goose-quill tubes and small priming boxes, and gunlocks. All but the first of these he attributed to Sir Charles Douglas.

The fitting of glass ports in the ship's side, reducing the need for candles, a fire risk, was the other important innovation of the 18th century for which a surgeon William Thompson has been given credit.[55]

Watt held, that "18th and 19th century naval surgeons were very much influenced by Benjamin Gooch whose 'Chirurgical Works' were published in 1767 and established principles of burns treatment the modern equivalents of which are followed in many burn centres today".[56]

Watt concluded the section of his paper on "Burns in Nelson's Day" with a reference to "the second recorded controlled clinical trial in the Navy". On this occasion Ralph Cumming, surgeon of HMS *Pegasus*, described in the Medical and Physical Journal (1805) "how he cut away one blister which he used as a control and aspirated the others, finding that the open burn took longer to heal". He also described "the beneficial effect of cold water treatment on a scalded Sergeant of Marines".

Watt concluded:

"There are few accidents or maladies to which mankind are subject, which have met with a greater variety of treatment than burns; and, as it appears to me, these various methods have in general been received and adopted as things of course, and handed down without any fixed principle or determined idea annexed to them...applications made use of which entirely vary from each other in nature and effect".[57]

The Sick-berth.

From the records of Redfern's court martial it is known that the surgeon on *Standard* had his own cabin with a dispensary just large enough to keep medicines, a table and chair. To Lloyd & Coulter this was usual. Not surprisingly, Blane defined the sick-berth as a space "between two guns, or any space between decks" partitioned by canvas. Trotter's first sick-berth was near the galley and its unwelcome smoke.[58]

"Lind's advice (as usual) was sensible enough, but it was not (also as usual) widely adopted. He demanded a well-ventilated wing berth, isolated from the rest of the ship, under the forecastle and not near the gunroom or the hold, "which is the most damp and unwholesome part of the ship".[59] Lind also provided evidence of at least one "neat, spacious and well-ventilated Sick Berth...[on] a remarkably healthy ship" to show what could be done.[60]

Once again the request of the seamen was *moderate, and could be granted without detriment to the nation, or any injury to the service,* as was demonstrated by Admiral Markham, captain of the *Centaur* in 1800. Markham was chiefly responsible for improving accommodation for the sick.[61]

Markham's sick-berth was "[p]laced between the two forward guns...had access to the heads [toilets] and included a necessary house of its own. It was covered with a skylight, panelled with canvas to exclude smoke from the galley, and furnished with cots, kids,[62] wash-tubs, settees, a stove and its own cooking utensils. Funds for the mess were provided, not by Authority, but by the ship's purser, who credited the unused victuals of the sick to a sick fund. Wine and other delicacies often found its way down there from the Captain's or wardroom tables. This arrangement was copied in other ships in the Channel fleet...and the attention of St Vincent, the Commander-in-Chief, was drawn to it by Trotter as Physician of the Fleet".[63]

St Vincent had pigsties removed from the forward part of the ship, and ordered that "no sick are to be kept below the upper deck of any line-of-battle ship, and that a sick-berth is prepared in each under the forecastle, on the starboard side, with the round house enclosed for the use of the sick". St Vincent, when First Lord [of the Admiralty] issued an order in 1801 for this to apply to all ships.[64]

Surgeons, Mates, and Loblolly 'Boys' and Women.

As mentioned above, a naval surgeon was required to act as physician, surgeon and apothecary as Redfern had been, on HMS *Standard* at the Nore in 1797.[65] Recognised as more a craftsman than a professional, the surgeon ranked with the master in pay but not status, of higher status than the purser and perhaps level with the chaplain. Surgeons were styled "warrant officers of wardroom rank", along with the master and the purser, in order to distinguish them from boatswains, gunners and carpenters. He could not be considered "an officer and a gentleman" until after the reforms of 1805. Only then did surgeons have an official uniform.

Lloyd and Coulter gave the evolution of surgeons to quarterdeck rank as the main theme of their third volume.[66] Their history of change brings to mind a dispute between Redfern, and Commissioner Bigge who drew Scott, his secretary, into the argument.[67] Redfern's stand, on the five points below, finds confirmation in Lloyd and Coulter and at the same time flags some important changes in the organization of surgeons.[68]

The barbers and surgeons were separated in 25 June 1745 by an Act [which also removed the ban on private dissection].

Entry to private practice was open to any army or navy surgeon after three years service without further examination or apprenticeship fee following an *Act* of 1749.

Examination for entry to the Navy was by the Surgeons' Company [called Company of Surgeons by Redfern] irrespective of prior medical education and attainment.

The Royal College of Surgeons came into existence in 1800 replacing the Surgeons' Company for which Redfern sat his examination in 1797.

The designation "surgeon's mate" was changed to "assistant surgeon" by an Order in Council dated 23 January 1805.[69]

It would seem that there were certain evergreen topics of relevance to surgeons throughout the eighteenth century - their education, examinations, service attractions, conditions of work, pay and allowances, instruments and drugs, work journals, retirement rights and right to private practice. These matters were quite relevant to the Colonial Medical Service in Sydney in Redfern's time.

Thomas Trotter was actively engaged in bringing the needs of surgeons to the fore. In 1790 he published his *Review of the Medical Department in the British Navy, with a method of Reform proposed.* In September 1797, he was among a group of surgeons who petitioned the Admiralty.[70]

Trotter preferred a board of naval surgeons to the College of Surgeons for examinations, and physicians of the fleet, rather than the Society of Apothecaries, to decide on the suitability of naval drugs, which should be issued free. The *Monthly Review* in June of that year, in support, claimed the medical department of the navy "was bad in its first institution, and it had gradually been growing worse". John Bell of Edinburgh, "the most respected anatomist of the day" supported "a thorough reform" (1800).[71]

Blane, in 1799, in the third edition of his *Observations* was suggesting the need for surgeons to be "still more respected and encouraged" by "flattering attentions and a certain degree of estimation in the eyes of other officers". The "strict and distant behaviour" of commissioned officers to surgeons needed to give way and pay to be increased to attract the best people. Trotter claimed that only 125 out of 500 were eligible for half pay on retirement. The 1797 surgeons' petition included parity of pay with the Army.[72]

After the war, Blane could say, that "a better type of man was now attracted to the service by the prospect of improved pay, status and conditions", backed by "a more efficient medical department".[73]

Trotter's contribution to such improvements was acknowledged when "a number of his colleagues presented him with a gold snuff-box".[74]

Medical Education Ashore.

Commendable as these efforts were, they still relied on the training available on shore for the men recruited by the Navy. At a point where William Redfern's medical background could provide enlightenment, the only certainty about his medical education was that it was obtained in London.

Roy Porter asked what the role of medicine was in England and what it achieved. In an uncharacteristically slim volume he provided a concise answer. "[M]edicine was, in fact, far more than a placebo, or just a bedside manner. It could not vanquish the fatal diseases, but it could reduce pain, palliate discomfort, patch people up, and help them to cope with chronic disorders and disabilities - leg ulcers, abscesses, rheumatism, gout, dyspepsia and so forth. True, what the doctor ordered often differed little from what common sense dictated. The gout-ridden readily discovered for themselves that they hit the bottle at their peril. But the good clinician knew by training and experience how to manage such conditions as dropsy - severe and painful, though rarely fatal - that might be completely beyond the know-how of the layman. Similarly, he was an invaluable surgeon who could set a fracture, or deliver a malpresented baby that had thwarted Nature and baffled the midwife's art".[75]

With this as starting point, what was the status of medicine in the Navy in the eighteenth century? "Naval medical practice under the influence of percipient naval writers such as James Lind, William Northcote, Charles Fletcher and Sir Gilbert Blane was often more advanced than that of contemporary orthodoxy represented by the College of Physicians and the Royal Society". This was Sir James Watt's conclusion. [76]

Support for Royal Navy medical practice may be found in the following comparative figures. When the number of seamen reached over 100 000 for the first time in 1782, there was a sick list of 23 000. In the year of Trafalgar (1805) there were 120 000 men in pay and only 8 000 sick.[77]

"Blane was justified in the pride he took in the comparable figures for the rates of sickness and mortality between 1778 and 1815. In 1778, 1 in 2.4 seamen was sick and 1 in 42.0 dead. In 1814, 1 in 10.7 was sick and 1 in 143.0 dead.[78]

While a physician might have the care of a Fleet, each ship had its surgeon and surgeon's mates, determined by its rating. Loblolly "boys" assisted.[79] Not uncommonly, as a later chapter about "women aboard" will canvass, one or more women, sometimes wives of seamen, traditionally assisted the surgeon.

Illness: Fever, a Common Symptom.

The sea shanty tells what was to be done with a drunken sailor and the reason for special attention. But what would lay the seaman low and land him in the sick bay? Commonly, it would be a fever.[80] "Scurvy and typhus march together through the history of eighteenth-century warfare. Both being associated with the extremes of human misery, the one weakened the body so that the other could easily take hold. From the days of Vernon's expedition to Cartagena to those of Napoleon's retreat to Moscow, these diseases flourished in the wretched, crowded conditions prevailing in ships and camps. The history of war is usually written in terms of victorious generals and admirals, and as Zinsser says, 'the epidemics get the blame for defeat, the generals the credit for victory: it ought to be the other way around'".[81]

Fevers, their nature, perceived causes and treatments have long medical histories.[82]

Dr John Huxham "distinguished 'intermittent fever' ('ague' or malaria), slow nervous fevers (possibly enteric) and the putrid malignant or pestilential fever (typhus), in which the usual fever symptoms are intensified and accompanied by a rash of livid spots or *petechiae*. He also included accounts of smallpox, 'peripneumony', to which seamen are peculiarly prone and which seems to include tubercular fever, and 'pleuro-peripneumony', or pleurisy".[83]

Dr Richard Mead directed "his attention to the problem of contagion" and rejected "the traditional explanation of acts of God".[84] Mead talked of contagion, "propagated by three causes, the air, diseased persons, and goods transported from infected places", including stagnant water, rotting vegetable matter, or "putrid exhalations from the earth, for which he used the comprehensive word *miasmata*".[85]

Blane's "prevention is better than cure" approach, typified miasmatists, who shared this concept of the origin of disease with his fellow naval surgeons and physicians. The idea of miasma, in one or other of its many variant forms, had a long history and has persisted. Brian Bracegirdle pointed to the difficulties "of our predecessors, threatened quite frequently with death from epidemic disease, but having no knowledge of how it was transmitted, and faced also with death after sustaining a possibly quite simple injury when it was followed by fever and infection". Many problems had to be overcome before the germ theory of disease was able to take root, but even then, "needed the genius of...Kock (1843-1910) to establish it".[86]

Fevers and their cures were a recurrent theme of text and receipt [recipe]. "Neither Blane nor Trotter were fever experts of the calibre of Lind or Robertson[87], but at least half their works are devoted to the subject because of its importance".[88] The first pair accepted that medical skill was unavailing against yellow fever, of which West Indian campaigns provided such dreadful evidence, right up to the eve of the Spithead and Nore mutinies.

Following a "cold fit", treatment might begin with restoratives while a "hot fit" would suggest bleeding and purging. This assumed that all fevers were the same. In fact the literature found as much confusion with "fevers" as Lind had found with "scurvies".[89] Blood-letting was the only agreed procedure during the first half of the 18th century.

In view of the miasmatic influence, both on the Navy's and Redfern's practice of medicine, more will be said about it here. Caroline Hannaway,[90] discussing "the air as the cause of disease", made the observation that "miasmas, which resisted detection by scientific instruments, invariably led back to their perceived source in a particular locale. What usually revealed their presence was a smell.[91] For this reason, such fetid sites as graveyards, tanneries, refuse dumps, cesspools, and so on, became the foci of attention of health reformers towards the end of the eighteenth and the beginning of the nineteenth centuries. There developed strong movements to clean these sites up".

Dorothy Porter[92] drew attention to "the Hippocratic treatise on *Airs, Waters, Places* (c. fifth century BC)" which "divided diseases into 'endemic' and 'epidemic' and attempted to identify the environmental determinants of local endemicity and to provide practical advice for colonization, suggesting that climate, soil and water were crucial". The treatise advised that "[n]ew settlements should avoid marshy lowlands, and houses should be built on elevated areas to be warmed by the sun and catch salubrious winds".

Such ideas persisted, encouraged and modified by early colonial experiences and travellers' observations. Bryan Gandevia saw them at work in the much-travelled Governor Phillip's search for a settlement site, and in the rejection of the low lying Botany Bay for Sydney Cove.[93] The selection of windy Macquarie Street as a site for the new General Hospital at Sydney exemplified such ideas and probably showed the hand of Redfern. Certainly, Redfern's elevated cottage, *Campbellfield*, at Minto, was "warmed by the sun" and did "catch salubrious winds".[94]

Dorothy Porter saw the twin themes, of personal and public hygiene, influencing actions to regulate environmental conditions, and individual behaviour for the benefit of the community. It is her view that "it was French revolutionaries who added health to the rights of human beings" an idea that resonates in the context of the early chapters of this book. 1791 saw the right to work and subsistence to the unemployed, while health was added to the state's obligations to citizens in 1793.[95]

She noted: "The citizen's charter of health, however, was double-sided. The ideologue Constantin Volney (1757-1820) raised the issue of the citizen's responsibility to maintain his or her own health for the benefit of the state. In the new social order, the individual was a political and economic unit of a collective whole. Thus, it was a citizen's duty to keep healthy through temperance, both in the consumption of pleasure and the exercise of passions, and through cleanliness".[96]

Earlier, when discussing "a renaissance of health", Dorothy Porter referred to the Quaker cloth-merchant John Bellers (1654-1725) recommending "municipal street-cleaning, refuse collection, regulation of dairies, abattoirs, and noxious trades", and "constant water supply to towns". "The philanthropist John Howard (c.1726-90) studied gaols, bridewells, lazarettos, and hospitals in Britain and on the continent in the 1770s and 1780s. He concluded that their filthy conditions and closed contaminated atmospheres were lethal, responsible for such endemic conditions as "gaol fever" (typhus). James Lind and John Pringle campaigned for ship and camp cleanliness to eliminate typhus. Pringle and Hales recommended ventilation for ships and gaols.[97]

"Cleanliness being of great Consequence to the Health of the Men, all Commanders of His Majesty's Ships and Vessels are strictly required to cause the following [five] Rules to be punctually complied with". Both men and the air were to be kept clean. Centinels (sic) were to protect the hold from its use as a toilet or garbage bin. No fruit or strong liquors were to be sold on board ship and the presence of women was to be discouraged.[98]

Specific Diseases or Ailments.

Those discussed below were seen by Lloyd and Coulter as "some of the diseases or ailments to which seamen were particularly prone".[99]

Smallpox.[100]

Smallpox probably attacked more people in eighteenth-century England than any other serious disease and was most virulent between 1770 and 1800 with one estimate of 45,000 deaths a year. In the Navy it was of lesser account than typhus or scurvy. Nevertheless when Jenner[101] published his work on cowpox in 1798, the Navy was quick to respond.

Interestingly, 1797, the year the mutineers called for action on matters affecting the health of seamen, stands between a year marking the beginning of the end of scurvy as a major threat to the Royal Navy seaman and a fresh start on mastering smallpox.[102]

Inoculation.

Inoculation by living organisms was used on occasion by the Navy but it was 1795 before Trotter used it against smallpox. British troops had earlier been inoculated in Boston in 1776.

This process was described in a letter written by Lady Mary Wortley Montagu, wife of the Ambassador to Turkey, and sent from Adrianople to her childhood friend Sarah Chiswell on 1 April 1718.[103]

"A propos of distempers I am going to tell you a thing that I am sure will make you wish you were here. The smallpox, so fatal and so general amongst us, is here entirely harmless by the invention of engrafting, which is the term they give it. There is a set of old women who make it their business to perform the operation". They make parties of fifteen or sixteen for this purpose in autumn. The old woman rips open the offered vein with a long needle and puts in 'as much of 'the best sort of smallpox' as can lie upon the head of the needle'. After that, the wound is bound up and the procedure repeated on four or five other veins. On the eighth day the children or young patients begin to be effected by the fever and 'they keep their beds two days, very seldom three'.[104]

Lady Mary decided to try it on her son and was considering writing to a doctor to have inoculation introduced in England.[105]

Jennerian Vaccination.

With the support of Blane, on the Board, the authorities moved with unusual promptitude to extend opportunities for voluntary vaccination, a worthy accompaniment to the issue of lemon juice. Trotter had a role in each case. He was one of the earliest supporters of Jenner and hoped to vaccinate the whole of the seamen at Spithead but it was not until September 1800 that a general order for voluntary vaccination was issued.

Fisher accepted this latter position. Richard Dunning, the Plymouth surgeon who coined the word 'vaccination', was an associate of Trotter who organised the first public testimonial Jenner was to receive, a gold medal from the surgeons of the fleet sent to him on 20 February 1801.[106]

An illustration of the medal appears as a frontispiece to Trotter's *Medicina nautica,* vol. 3. 1803.[107]

In 1803, Trotter wrote a dedication to Dr Jenner, for his *book An Essay...on Drunkenness.*

Lefanu remarked on Jenner's own "strenuous campaign to propagate his gospel throughout the world" in the process becoming "an active pamphleteer and letter writer, ready for every opportunity to expound and defend his discovery".[108]

For example: "I have a pamphlet just ready for the press intended as a supplement to my former publication on the subject of cow-pox...A candid and judicious public will not fail to discriminate between the man who sedulously employs the greatest part of his time in making experiments for the complete investigation of a confessedly complex subject, and him who appears peremptorily to decide on the truth or falsehood of a theory..." Edward Jenner, *26th Feb, 1799. To* Dr Beddoes.[109]

William Redfern was wrongly held to have introduced cowpox vaccination into the colony of New South Wales.[110] In chapter eleven a detailed account will make clear Redfern's involvement in vaccination - quite an active one, both on Norfolk Island and on the mainland.[111]

Hernia.

Hernia was considered by Lloyd and Coulter to be the commonest among many occupational hazards facing seamen in the days of sail.[112] Among the predisposing factors was the work the seamen did, "hauling on a rope, working the windlass, or lifting heavy weights", straining the body.

The extent of the problem may be read from the size of the Board records with first supply of trusses dated 1744. 1 in 7 of those serving in the years

1808-15 must have been in some degree ruptured according to calculations from the annual issues of trusses. Some help came from the increasing use of blocks for running rigging and fixed iron storage-tanks for water in place of casks.[113]

The conclusion reached by Lloyd and Coulter was that the "alarming incidence of hernia" was due to a combination of these factors acting "upon an abdominal musculature which in any case would be weakened by deficiency diseases". "So that we are able to confirm the statistics with some truth", they continued, "by stating that the seamen of the eighteenth century had his physique so undermined that hernia as an occupational hazard was only to be expected among the numerous disabilities by which these unhappy men were bound to be affected".

According to Roy Porter, Trotter suffered a hernia in 1795, and this perhaps precipitated the early end to his naval career in 1802.[114] At forty years of age, Trotter settled in Newcastle and took an active interest "in the intellectual and cultural life of the town, being prominent in the Literary and Philosophical Society and contributing to the local newspapers and journals".[115] There Trotter met the great English engraver on wood, Thomas Bewick, whose first volume of *British Birds* was published in the year of the mutinies.[116]

Kidney Stones.

Ghislaine Lawrence discussed renal stone, in the context of traditional surgery, as "prevalent throughout western Europe until the nineteenth century, particularly in country areas and in children. Calculi formed in the urinary tract became impacted and obstructed flow".[117] Lithotomy developed as a surgical treatment for the removal of stone.[118]

Sir James Watt alerted the reader to renal stone, in the Royal Navy, by his reference to Governor Arthur Phillip as suffering its effects. "Stones in the urinary tract were an occupational disease in the Navy," according to Watt, "caused by restricted fluid intake, excessive sweating and the use of Madeira wines to which lime was added to preserve them".[119]

Joseph Black (1728-1799) wrote a famous chemical/medical thesis associated with the use of lime water to dissolve urinary calculi (see below: chapter 7).

Drunkenness.

Lloyd and Coulter pointed to the contradiction structured into the Navy's provision of "a liberal issue of grog" and "barbarous forms of punishment" for drunkenness.

Intoxication on board ship was responsible for "innumerable accidents". "Turnbull called it 'a frequent evil among seamen', and its treatment 'one of the most frequent duties of a Navy Surgeon' ".[120] Conditions of service and tradition provided a "right to get drunk. The trouble was that the seaman did so too frequently and on shocking liquor", taking advantage of every opportunity, not excluding spirits smuggled aboard beneath the skirts of numerous fair skinned women in British ports, and by their darker sisters in the West Indies, in coconuts.[121]

Naval surgeons "deplored intoxication as the root of most of the troubles they had to deal with on board".[122] "Robertson considered that grog contributed to scurvy by destroying the digestion. Blane held that in the West Indies the consumption of new rum...[led to] "malignant fever". Blane also argued that "lead from the stills" used to produce this rum led to "many cases of 'flux' (whether dysentery or gastro-enteritis)".[123]

"In medical language," Trotter wrote, "I consider drunkenness, strictly speaking, to be a disease: produced by a remote cause, and giving birth to actions and movements in the living body, that disorder the functions of health". [124]

Towards the end of his book, Trotter held, that *The habit of drunkenness is a disease of the mind* [his italics]. "This disease, I mean the habit of drunkenness, is like some other mental derangements; there is an ascendancy to be gained over the person committed to our care, which, when accomplished, brings him entirely under our controul [*sic*.]. Particular opportunities are therefore to be taken, to hold up a mirror as it were, that he may see the deformity of his conduct..."[125]

Porter linked Trotter's book to his original MD thesis, *De Ebrietate*... defended at Edinburgh University, and published in 1788. While each has a common structure two concerns are "crystallized" in the later work. "The *Essay* is noteworthy for the scope of Trotter's concern with the problems of habit and habit-forming substances in general, within the context of (a) the analysis of a drug-consuming culture, and (b) the notion that drunkenness is a disease of the mind".[126]

Porter discussed Trotter's work in the context of the eighteenth century "spread of ardent spirits ['potent, dangerous, and often extremely cheap'] which raised the problem of drunkenness onto a new plane". To this he linked another of Trotter's works which "engages with the [Enlightenment] debate over the gains and losses of man's emergence from 'rudeness to refinement' ", and to which reference was made in the previous chapter.[127]

Drunkenness in "the ignorant and illiterate man is to be shunned in proportion to its excess: it is human nature in its vilest garb, and madness in its worst form".[128] However, rather than sitting on his hands, Trotter had "200 gin shops shut up" in the Port of Plymouth.[129] This action is in keeping with his treatment of the disease, through total abstinence from alcohol.

According to Watt, "alcohol made the largest contribution to the energy requirements of the eighteenth-century sailor", but at the same time "multiple nutritional deficiencies [were] aggravated by a very high alcohol intake".[130]

Insanity.

Insanity was shown by Blane to have a higher incidence in the Navy, 1 in 1000, than in the wider population, 1 in 7000. His figures for the years 1809-13 are only for Hoxton and show a total of 425 patients received. Of these 56 were discharged cured, 14 discharged to friends and 228 to Bethlem. 76 died during that time. From an accumulation of patients from these and the preceding years there were 643 insane patients remaining at Hoxton in 1813.[131] The increases suggested to Lloyd and Coulter the strain of a long war.

Again, Trotter has something original to say. "[A] species of nervous disease did make its appearance during the late war. It occurred among both officers and men; but was, by no means, a general malady. The hard duty of a stupid blockade, had a chief share in its production".[132]

Trotter said of the blockade, "it was abhorred by Howe and Nelson, as inconsistent with the genius of our seamanship". "A duty so severe, without variety to give spring to adventure, benumbs the faculties, exhausts the bodily powers, and in habits predisposed, brings on nervous irritability that shortens the span of life".[133]

Blane suggested head injuries resulting from intoxication were a contributing factor. Here the occupational hazard is given as height between decks, never more than 5 feet 10 inches. To this, Lloyd and Coulter add the consequence of shock or blast, particularly for gun crews. At one London asylum the majority of inmates were seamen who had fought at the battle of the Glorious First of June in 1794.[134] One seaman on HMS *Standard* became violent from the combined effect of alcohol and earlier head injuries sustained when a musket fell on him from a height.[135]

"George III's first attack of derangement [in 1788], played out in a blaze of publicity...brought with it a fundamental change of attitudes. No longer could insanity be equated with ignorance or sin or superstition...Insanity ceased to be a matter of shame or blame, Furthermore...it could be cured".[136]

An increase in patient numbers and madhouses followed, which gave rise to a fear that insanity was on the increase. There had been increases starting in 1790 and again in 1810 as demonstrated in the first histograms in medical literature. Conclusions drawn were that moments of great public interest sparked each rise - the King's madness, and Parliamentary inquiry and report on insanity.[137]

"Like other movements for social reform, that to improve the lot of the insane can also be traced to the last decades of the eighteenth century. The sympathy aroused by the royal malady opened people's minds and eyes to the whole field of mental derangement and stirred the national conscience about the fate of the poor and the mad...It may properly be called the 'asylum era'".[138] So wrote Ida Macalpine and Richard Hunter of George III and his porphyria-induced state, not altogether helped by his treatment as the following extract suggests.[139]

"George III appears to have had a particularly virulent form of the disease. To an extent this may be attributed to the way he was treated, which at least must have aggravated and prolonged the attacks. He was also kept on 'a low diet' and for long periods was given no meat. He was further reduced by blood-letting, leeches to the temples and cupping, and for months was regularly given vomits and purges. Of all his treatments 'blistering' probably had the worst effect, since it set up a running infection which persisted for weeks. It is also a question how far his ebullitions of passion, his turbulence and obstreperous behaviour were in response to his harsh management and the forcible administration of drugs - often only after a bitter struggle - to bring down his 'fever' and high spirits, slow his pulse, calm his nerves and make him sleep - all of which may have aggravated the underlying conditions and certainly exasperated the patient".[140]

In the first half of the century insane seamen were sent to public asylums such as Bedlam (Bethlem) and given a subsistence allowance. Later they were sent to Hoxton or to York where they were assured of 'the same mild treatment'. There were also special wards at Plymouth and Haslar. At Greenwich, the insane, chiefly senile, were usually sent to Hoxton or Bedlam.[141]

Hysteria.

Among sick seamen at the Nore, Thomas Trotter noted 'many cases of hysteria, accompanied by convulsions and passionate outbreaks of weeping characteristic of shock'. Picked up by Lloyd and Coulter (1961:164) from Trotter's *Medicina Nautica vol II,* p.28 it was included in Jones (1999; 7:36).

Mark S Micale's *Hysterical Men* (2008) again brought Trotter's observations to attention. This time he accessed the original work, showing page, title, volume, to have been correctly attributed, and found further references in *Medicina Nautica.* Trotter's generalisations in *View of the Nervous Temperament* (1976) do not hit the mark. [Trotter's *On Drunkenness* (1988) received a comment, unconnected with hysteria.]

At the point of entry to his text, 'British Hysteria Theory, 1790-1870' (p.76), Micale wrote: "The transfer of the seat of all hysterical manifestations from the uterus to the brain by Jorden, Willis, and Sydenham had constituted a major turning point in the history of hysteria, Similarly the culture of nerves and sensibility in eighteenth-century Britain encompassed extensively, if not quite equivalently, men and women. That it is reasonable to expect that nineteenth-century physicians would build on these impressive precedents and practices. But this was far from the case".

Venereal Disease.

In a list of diseases in order of importance in the Channel station in 1806 "venereal" appeared last.[142] Typhus heads the list, followed by "intermittent fevers or agues, rheumatism (with lumbago and sciatica), consumption ('a hopeless complaint'), dysentery (probably gastro-enteritis), smallpox, scurvy and venereal. Cures of a sort had been found for the last three, but very little was known about the rest".[143]

Venereal Disease, or "the pox" as it was called, was extremely prevalent in the eighteenth century, particularly in the ports. With shore leave at a premium, or not allowed, "boatloads of prostitutes came out to the ships as they rode at anchor".[144]

Affected sailors "were mulcted two weeks pay, or 15s. per cure, as a fine to be paid to the surgeon".[145] Trotter considered "venereal fines...to be iniquitous, because the men delayed reporting the disease until it was too late for a mercury cure".[146] £5 was also allowed to surgeons "for every 100 cases of venereal disease".[147]

Credit goes to Trotter for having these practices abolished on advice given in 1795. "Thus terminated a practice illiberal from its institution, inhuman in its practice and impolitic from its continuance. It forms an epoch in naval improvements, for hundreds of seamen have annually fallen victim to its effects".[148]

Milton Lewis in *Thorns on the Rose* claimed venereal disease is known to have been "very prevalent in both the Navy and Army" accounting for 1,308 of 5,861 cases in regimental hospitals in 1808. This figure of 25 per cent of all cases of illness remained constant over a long period". Of interest in a later context were references to the likelihood of "representatives of the Army in the infant colony" as "probably much afflicted with venereal disease".[149]

The Necessities of Life for Seamen.

Brian Lavery used this heading in his book, *Nelson's Navy.* In this context he discussed seamen's clothing, slops, washing, food and drink, hammocks and beds, heating, ventilation and lighting, and other every day concerns.[150] Some of these items come within the field of Miasmata, discussed in relation to fevers. This was believed to be associated with the generation and spread of diseases, to which ships were known to be prone.

Clothing.

There was no official uniform for seamen before 1857 in spite of the advocacy of Lind, Blane and Trotter. Some captains moved towards a uniform in individual ships. For practical reasons seamen had a liking for short jackets with buttoning cuffs and loose trousers that could be rolled up. Check shirts were common. Naturally their hat of choice was small brimmed, or was a woollen or fur cap. Slops tended towards some uniformity due to mass buying. Dungaree, a coarse calico, served for a good seaman wanting to make his own clothes.[151]

The wife of Admiral Howe arranged for woollen garments next to the skin of the Channel Fleet seamen. St Vincent also ordered them. Trotter advised care in their use. The aim was to ensure that the men had a change of clothing after a wet watch. Keeping dry was essential in conserving body energy.

Keeping clothing clean was needed to reduce body fomites[152] and disease. Great concern was shown for the state of cleanliness of both body and clothing but an issue of soap was not general.

It was common knowledge that guard ships were a source of infection from newly impressed seamen. A guardship at the Nore in 1779 that received the "imprest Landsmen" of London, was reported by Lind as being "hitherto...the most fatal and general cause of sickness in the royal navy". (There was still a problem at the Nore in 1797, to be discussed in the next chapter.)

Ten years after Lind, Sir Gilbert Blane, still recorded poorer health on ships manned from guardships but reported improvements at Portsmouth in 1781, "planned and executed by Sir Charles Middleton, Comptroller of the Navy", who required recruits to be medically examined, "stripped, washed, and provided with new apparel".[153]

Hammacoes and Bedding.

Regulations used the Caribbean word (S.O.E.D.) for hammocks, two of which were desirable for health reasons. Each was a piece of hempen cloth, six feet long, and three feet wide gathered together at both ends, and slung horizontally below the deck. It was a receptacle for the bed, which was a mattress preferably of flock or wool, but rags or old clothes[154] were substituted. In addition a seaman had a blanket, a coverlet and a bolster or pillow.[155]

In a 74-class ship some 500 men had to sling their hammocks in an area of 6000 sq. feet. Canvas screens were sometimes provided as protection from draughts and rain. Hammocks were rolled and stowed in the daytime in netting along the sides of the ship. In bad weather the hammocks were usually kept below decks.

Heating, Ventilating and Lighting.

Lighting was by candles placed in lanterns for safety, with 'lights out' strictly enforced by the evening watch. The heat generated by 5-600 seamen on the lower deck was sufficient to keep the place warm to "overpowering". Portable stoves were more for helping to dry the ship.

"Ventilators, operated by bellows, had been fitted aboard ships since the 1750s, and Admiralty Instructions demanded that they be worked continually".[156] In hot weather, men were allowed to sleep in other parts of the ships that were cooler, but not on deck.

Samuel Sutton extracted foul air by means of pipes and a furnace while Rev. Stephen Hales developed a system of fans operated by windmills.[157]

Roy Porter noted that Trotter's solution to the problem of explosive and other gases in deep coalmines, "an effective ventilation system", "surely reflects his years of experience in keeping ships' holds salubrious".[158]

Sanitary Arrangements.

For the crew, the main toilet accommodation was in the heads of the ship where seats were provided. Some ships had primitive urinals at the side. Chamber pots were in common use, or for the sick, wooden buckets. These were simply emptied over the side. Needless to say in such crowded ships insanitary short cuts were taken, requiring sentries by the gratings over the hold as noted in the Regulations, above.

Driving Away Dull Care.

Recreation, in the sense of re-storing the life force by escaping from boredom, and releasing "animal spirits" and tension, was recognised widely by perceptive officers. In addition, Matthew Flinders and others had linked "The Necessities of Life" and "amusements" with the earlier concern with scurvy. For example, on Sunday 9 August 1801, after leaving Madeira, Flinders ordered "lime [lemon] juice and sugar to be mixed with the grog" and "to be given daily to every person on board'.[159] While, on 7 September he wrote, "It was a part of my plan for preserving the health of the people, to promote active amusements among them, so long as it did not interfere with the duties of the ship".[160]

Flinder's entry for Friday, 16 October was made in the knowledge that all were in as good health as when they left Spithead, and gave credit to "the beneficial plan, first practised and made known by the great Captain Cook". Here is that plan.[161] "It was in the standing orders of the ship, that on every fine day the deck below and the cockpit should be cleared, washed, aired with stoves and sprinkled with vinegar. On wet and dull days they were cleaned and aired, without washing. Care was taken to prevent the people from sleeping upon deck, or by lying down in their wet clothes; and once in every fortnight or three weeks, as circumstances permitted, their beds, and the contents of their chests and bags, were opened out and exposed to the sun and air. On the Sunday and Thursday mornings, the ship's company was mustered, and every man appeared clean shaved and dressed; and when the evenings were fine, the drum and fife announced the forecastle to be the scene of dancing; nor did I discourage other playful amusements which might occasionally be more to the taste of the sailors, and were not unseasonable".

Brian Lavery also moved on from "necessities" to the "rewards and pleasures" of shipboard life. He included among them, shore leave, recreation, music, religion, drunkenness, sex, personal belongings, tobacco, and "crossing the line".[162]

Rewards and pleasures of shipboard life?

Sex.

Heterosexual seamen: Among the main grievances of the seamen, the refusal of shore leave will be discussed in a later chapter. The inhibition of the role of sex in heterosexual familial pair bonding must be accounted one of the chief arguments against warfare as appropriate to human beings. Moderation was possible when some wives did manage to meet their husbands on board ship in harbour.

Promiscuous heterosexual seamen on the other hand might run to "any port in a storm", fall into the arms of one of many prostitutes who came on board.[163]

Homosexual seamen: "Sexual 'drive' must not...be confused with its mode of expression," argued Shuster and Shuster, "and while the former may be largely genetic and developmental, the latter is greatly determined by environmental circumstance and opportunity".

"This explains the level of homosexual activity in jails, and single-sexed boarding schools, but this homosexual *activity* should not be confused with homosexuality as a state of *sexual preference*".[164]

Rodger in discussing homosexuality during the seven years' war referred to "a score or so of known instances, over a period of nearly nine years during which at least a hundred thousand individuals must have served in the Navy".

He gave as reasons for this "very insignificant total" a largely heterosexual population of seamen, their general abhorrence of sodomy, the difficulty of concealment on board ship with so little privacy, and the death penalty.[165] Obviously, what was not observed was not recorded!

Drunkenness, and Tobacco.

The first of these has already been discussed. "Until 1798, seamen were allowed to buy tobacco from the purser, the price being deducted from their wages. After that, it was issued free, at the rate of 2lb per month for seamen who wanted it. Some men had clay pipes, though smoking was not allowed below decks because of the danger of fire, and was generally permitted only on the forecastle. Others chewed it. Tobacco was issued to the ships at the main victualling ports".[166]

Recreation, music.

Seamen often turned to their former trades of painter or makers of shoes or hats to pass the time. Some sewed and mended, learned to read, write or cypher, or taught others. Others gambled. "One is a good singer, another can spin tough forecastle yarns, while a third will crack a joke with sufficient point to call out roars of laughter. But for these interludes, life in a man-of-war with severe officers, would be absolutely intolerable; mutiny or desertion would mark the voyages of each ship".

Bearing in mind Bligh's "blind fiddler",[167] and Flinder's "drum and fife",[168] one can readily accept Lavery's conclusion that "[m]usic played a large part in the seamen's lives". A favourite recreation was "playing the violin, flute or fife, while others dance or sing thereto". Remarkably, one person (Bowker, 1978:169, self-published), who wrote of Bligh, thought that asking the men to take part in all male dancing "must have seemed to them to be the height of absurdity"!

Marcus considered the "seamen of old revelled in the melancholy ballads of which the tune was as doleful as the words. Sung in a minor, dirge-like key, these airs centred on such subjects as drownings, mutiny, pestilence, and piracy on the high seas. The more dismal, the more horrific, the more generally ghastly they were, the better the seamen were pleased".

A midshipman[169] of 1811 would have agreed. "It is ridiculous to hear the sailors lie and sing in their hammocks of an evening. They chant the most dismal ditties in the world, and the words be ever so merry, yet the tune is one and the same, namely "Admiral Hosier's ghost. They never seemed to dance with any spirit unless they had an old black to fiddle to them". They sing and dance not because they are happy but "because they feel miserable, just to drive away care".

Conrad Gill included three songs composed during the Nore Mutiny. As one was 'Song no. 13' Gill concluded that the seamen must have made a large collection.[170]

Another side of singing in the wooden world was about the rhythm of work and sea shanties. Stan Hugill began with the capstan.[171] "The first piece of ship's furniture with which a crowd of new hands would come to grips on joining a fresh ship was the capstan", in the centre of the fo'c'slehead. The mate calls for a "nightingale" to set the shanty rolling and from the cavernous throat of some true son of Neptune comes the hurricane reply: "Oh, say wuz ye niver darn Ri-i-o Grande?" The sailormen answered with "Way-a-ay darn Ri-O!" As the men sang and heaved together, the anchor rose from the deep.

Religion.

In practice, Lavery held that "Religion played very little part in the life of the seaman" in spite of the *Regulations*. Evangelical captains supported it, while clergymen on board could find themselves "awkwardly situated...in a ship of war; every object around him is at variance with the sensibilities of a rational and enlightened mind". These were the words of Edward Mangin, Chaplain of the *Gloucester*, 74. "Visiting the sick was worse than useless" being seen as a fatal signal. Profane swearing might just as well pass unnoticed, for rebukes had no effect. Sunday services and burying the dead were regular enough to provide employment. Converting a crew to Christianity would prove to be difficult.[172]

Personal belongings.

Given the restricted life of seamen and the crowded nature of the ships-of-war there was less need for possessions nor room for personal storage. Clothes were kept in a bag slung against the side of the ship. Sea chests had to be shared by several men and were stored in the hold or on the orlop desk when at sea. More chests were allowed on frigates and were stored on deck.[173]

Crossing the line.

This was a well-established custom, to shave and duck those who had not yet crossed the equator.[174] On the *Investigator*, Flinders allowed the ceremonies of crossing the line to proceed, "the seamen were furnished with the means, and the permission, to conclude the day with merriment".

Dening reflects upon ducking, yarning and dancing.

Greg Dening would have one pause at this point. "Ducking, yarning and dancing need a moment's reflection," he wrote.[175] "The ways human beings exercise power over one another in an institution such as a ship, whether exaggerating it or fending it off, are subtle and complex. Hegemony is made of trivia. If a description of these trivia deflates an expectancy that high drama is caused only by momentous action, so be it".[176]

Dening compared "ducking" with "skylarking", "exuberant physical play [in the dogwatch], to transfer the conflicts of messes and watches and the tensions created by the skilled work that stratified them to giddy games".[177] "The spontaneity of skylarking was fragile and needed to be managed by those who knew what the games really were about. Skylarking did not need careful management by the very power whose authority was being metaphorically tested".[178]

"Bligh's estranging carefulness had also been shown in that other reverse ceremony of a ship, the "Crossing of the Line".[179] He had forbidden ducking over the ship's side as cruel and dangerous.[180] Yet, to the seamen, enduring successive duckings before paying a fine, "was a matter of personal achievement and boasting". "Bligh spoke badly to them in not allowing them to find their own levels of authority independent of his".[181]

Dening opened a more detailed account of "Crossing the Line" in the eighteenth century, as "no affair of starched whites and excited squeals" that it would become later. Indeed it was "play of a serious and disturbing sort",[182] "play on the edge of not being play".[183] "Certainly its brutality and inhumanity were a satire on the brutality and inhumanity of sailors' lives.[184] But the bravado with which the brutality was endured could be a social quality of the crew as well as a sign of the individual's strength".[185]

Of "yarning", Dening is reflecting upon a ritual of sociability that may be experienced "high up in the yards and in secluded niches in the sails" in the normal course of the day. But it would occur, as well, in times set aside for relaxation. "In verbalising their way of life, let us say, they were peculiarly susceptible to language that got it wrong". Mr Bligh's language was getting it wrong on "duckings", and was "bad" in that critical sense.

As mentioned above, "dancing" was certainly implied by Flinders' "drum and fife", and Bligh's "fiddler". Here, each has a particular reference to an idea, which Carpenter traced back to Sir Richard Hawkins' *Observations* of 1693, finding it among his recommendations for keeping scurvy at bay.[186]

Carpenter returned to this idea later.[187] He held "that these observers were reversing cause and effect". He gave credit to the early observation, now confirmed, that fatigue and lassitude were the first effects of scurvy. Being unwilling or unable to dance might also confirm this, rather than being lazy, or difficult.

So, when surgeon Thomas Huggan reported that Jo Valentine, able seaman, had died of scurvy, Bligh flew into a rage. He had the crew "vigorously pumping the bilges, drinking half a pint of elixir vitriol and eating barley and essence of malt. Above all, he would have them 'chearful', so they must dance. When two of the crew refused to dance, he cut their grog and promised something worse".

"Bligh's language was getting very bad". His antiscorbutic remedies were not much better.

Perhaps it was well that a variety of fresh fruit, vegetables, and meat would soon fall upon them like manna from heaven. Nor was proven antiscorbutic food the only measure of their garden of delights. The men would soon have an "opportunity to taste the sweets of liberty on shore", which in 1797 would become part of the wish list of the men of the Channel and North Sea Fleets.

Chapter 5

THE NORTH SEA FLEET & THE NORE MUTINIES, 1797

1797 was the year William Redfern passed medical examinations to obtain a warrant from the Board of Sick and Wounded for entry into the Royal Navy as a surgeon's mate. He joined Admiral Duncan's North Sea Fleet as surgeon's first mate of HMS *Standard*, a battleship or ship of the line with a total of sixty-four guns mounted on two decks.[1]

William Redfern would have been one among some 500 people on *Standard* with general life experiences and expectations little different from those in the ships at Spithead. The two fleets, North Sea and Channel, had similar roles in the British war strategy. Each had the task of containing an enemy fleet within its homeport, and of destroying any ships that ventured out. Duncan's responsibility was the Dutch fleet on which he kept watch off Texel.[2]

With so much in common it is not surprising that there were murmurings among the crews of Duncan's ships as there had been at Spithead and the Nore.[3]

The Nore.

The Nore continues to be famous for its light, saving ships from its sand bank, and infamous for those who knew for its guard ship anchored there, which harboured disease to spread through the fleets of Royal Navy ships.

According to Francis Ross Holland, a lightship at the Nore "goes back only to 1731, when a British entrepreneur received a patent which permitted him to place a lightship at the Nore Sandbank in the estuary of the Thames River and collect duties from ship owners. The first lightship was a single-masted sloop, and its light consisted of two ship's lanterns suspended twelve feet apart on a crossarm attached to the mast. The lightship proved an immediate success and was most popular with navigators".[4]

While there is evidence of a Roman version, the Nore lightship is the original modern example according to Holland.

"The Great Nore anchorage was about a half mile wide and four miles long, marked out from the prevailing mud shoals by a depth contour averaging six fathoms. It lay in the mainstream, north west of the town of Sheerness, which jutted into the junction of the Thames and the Medway. Off the town was a pocket anchorage called the Little Nore".[5]

"The seat of the big new mutiny, the Nore, was the most populous naval and merchant shipping anchorage in Britain...Tens of thousands of wooden vessels a year passed the Nore up the sea-river to London or to the shipyards and docks along the way, or into the meandering Medway, at the head of which lay the major naval dockyard of Chatham. At this period, in the infancy of canals and conception of railways, Britain's domestic bulk cargo was carried mainly in coasting sail. In the coal trade alone there were about two thousand colliers rounding her dangerous shores".[6]

Pause and give thought for a moment to those "colliers", which feature in an account of the London River by G.J. Marcus.[7] The coal trade served to emphasise the volume of sea traffic and the challenge to shipping presented by the intersection of wind, weather, wave and tide on shallow coastal and outer Thames waters where many of the dangers of the sea were concentrated and where most of the losses occurred in wars.

A measured response to this challenge came from a detailed knowledge of these well-charted waters,[8] the use of shallow draught colliers, and the consummate seamanship of their crews. So effective a combination resulted in the colliers' owners generally preferring to carry the risk of losses themselves and thereby to save insurance.[9]

Contemporary accounts described the colliers in their race to market and return. Gales and contrary winds might bring fleets of colliers, numbering 2-300, working to windward, out of port. Marcus described such a fleet snowballing and sailing together, with each vessel striving to outsail the other, passing and crossing each other in so little time and room. This is said to have caused a French observer to exclaim, "there, France was conquered". [10]

James Cook's "astonishing skill in seamanship and navigation" was a product of this same proving ground and led him to select a collier, the *Earl of Whitby*, better known by its new name, *Endeavour*, for his first Pacific journey of exploration. This first choice, having proved so successful, Cook selected two more Whitby colliers, *Resolution* and *Adventure* for his second journey, and *Resolution* again and *Discovery* for his third and last.

The Nore Command.

The Nore was geographically and commercially different from Spithead, and in the nature of its Royal Navy command and usage. "The Officer in Command of HM Ships and Vessels in the River Medway and at the Buoy of the Nore...was a troubled old vice-admiral named Charles Buckner...the admiral of everything and nothing", according to James Dugan. "Nothing", that is, in the way of fleets and squadrons, which were the concern of Sir Peter Parker at Spithead.[11]

Everyone petitioned Buckner to redress grievances. There were captains begging the Admiralty to take over payment of their private servants, and crews complaining of cruel treatment by their officers. "Among these petitions there were several from crews begging the sea lords *not* to take away their captain or first officer, or else to transfer the company with them to the new ship".[12] This reflects good leadership on the one hand, and on the other, what Rodger called the "cohesion of a settled ship's company...by far the strongest force which bound the Navy together".[13]

Of all the problems Buckner faced, one of the worst was on his own flagship, *Sandwich,* of 90 guns. A former splendid vessel built in 1759, she had become "an old corpse of a ship" and "now stank with decay".[14] Gilbert Blane knew it in its earlier days as Admiral Rodney's flagship in the West Indies.

Surgeon Snipe and 'A Situation...Replete with Anxiety'.

HMS *Sandwich,* whose reduced "harbour flag-and depot-ship complement of 400", had been increased by some "1,100 to 1,200 supernumeries, recruits of various kinds, and men paid off from other ships, waiting for transfer", with many in a shocking state of health. Surgeon John Snipe left little unsaid in a medical report of 22 March 1797 to his captain, Mosse, who forwarded the report to Admiral Buckner for action.[15]

He commenced his letter, dated 22 March 1797[16], by stating that "The infection which has existed for some time in His Majesty's Ship *Sandwich* under your command having of late become more virulent, and resisted the methods that have been taken to check it, which is solely owing to the ship being so crowded, I beg leave to acquaint you that it is absolutely necessary to reduce the numbers of men already on board".

In conclusion he stated "I never was in a situation more replete with anxiety, than the present as Surgeon of the *Sandwich.* I only have to add that the whole of the evil herein stated originated from the ship being crowded with supernumeraries, and those men permitted to remain such a length of time on board to the very great detriment (both physically and morally) of His Majesty's Service".

Nothing so confronting had faced the Spithead mutineers. Action was imperative. On the 5 June 1797, "the Delegates collected some fifty or sixty of their sick...put them on board the *Nancy* tender, and sent them to be received at the hospital ship. Buckner, after consulting with Mosse and other captains, was inhuman enough to order the master of the *Nancy* to return the sick men to their respective ships".[17]

Perhaps it was "as well they never reached the hospital ship *Spanker*, because her surgeon cut his throat and his mate had taken refuge on shore; her sick were removed to Deal".[18] Dugan reported the Admiralty as advising Buckner to take the seamen to task for the death of Mr Saffray [surgeon], since delegates had threatened the surgeons after seamen patients had charged them with maltreatment.[19]

If the care of the sick was questionable at the start of the mutiny, Gill considered that it grew worse after the mutiny,[20] and figures do confirm a worsening of health in the Navy in 1797.[21] Gill, and later, Lloyd and Coulter agreed on the effect delegate pressure had on the surgeons at Sheerness on 15 May.

Nevertheless, one must not overlook or lessen the responsibility of Royal Navy mismanagement for the overcrowding on HMS *Sandwich*. This had led to an increasing number of sick seamen in the first place. Never before had Surgeon Snipe been in a situation "more replete with anxiety". You can believe him. This surgeon's ultimate sacrifice in the interests of the health of seamen was brought to notice above. (See chapter 3).

What makes the authorities the more culpable was that it had all happened before. Indeed, the Lords Commissioners of the Admiralty had authorised the publication of the second edition of James Lind's *Essay...of preserving the Health of Seamen* (1762), which contained the solution. No, not buried in the text. The second sentence of the synopsis points to it, and the details occupy the opening pages of the first chapter.[22]

"A guardship is usually stationed at the Nore, to receive those [imprest Landmen] who are taken up in London. But experience has shewn how fatal she has often proved to the health and lives of many seamen; and that this ship has become a seminary of contagion to the whole fleet. One diseased person from the street, or clothes from a prison, have often conveyed infection on board, which it has been extremely difficult afterwards to remove. For the confined and corrupted air in a large crowded ship, greatly favours the spreading of this contagion, and the exertion of its utmost malignity...

"This has hitherto been the most fatal and general cause of sickness in the royal navy, especially on the fitting out of ships. In the commencement of the late war, the seeds of infection were carried from the guardships into our squadrons, to all quarters of the world..." That threat was there in *Sandwich*, again, in 1797.

Lind's solution was detailed and included a particular innovation, a receiving ship for the imprest men, where bodies may be washed and clothes burnt or fumigated. The sick should go "immediately" to hospital. No. James Lind would not have been surprised - disappointed, more likely - by the content of surgeon Snipe's letter.

According to the First Lord of the Admiralty "the persons concerned [at the Nore]...do not appear to have any specifick [sic] object of complaint". As for Buckner's decision on 5 June to send the sick seamen back to their ship, Conrad Gill gave the landing of invalids from the Mediterranean Fleet at Sheerness hospital on 24 May as a possible reason.

However, neither admiral nor admiralty can so easily escape responsibility for the unhealthy state of HMS *Sandwich* and its continuing and increasing demand for medical care in hospital, on shore or in hospital ship.

Seamen at the Nore not only had good reason to be concerned for their health, but fearful for their future, having in mind Admiral Buckner's response and the denial by the first Lord of Admiralty of any special need.

Growing a Mutiny at the Nore.

In his account, Dugan described how the "King's navy resorted to the Nore more than to any proper base, including Portsmouth, the grand fleet base".[23] Bligh had taken his ship *Director*[24] to the Nore for a refit. A "rickety ship", it "had spent January and February at anchor in the Humber River and Yarmouth Roads, as part of Duncan's North Sea Fleet".[25] Andrew Hollister, one of the four Nore delegates to Spithead,[26] came from this ship, a 64, like *Standard.*

"At the Nore, frigates made rendezvous with merchant convoys for the Baltic and the Atlantic Ocean,[27] ships came in to be provisioned, paid or repaired, or to be sheltered from the stormy Channel, and ships came down from the big Thames' yards on builder's trials. Ships wandered or blown in from squadrons lay by for orders or were sent out to reinforce the blockaders – Adam Duncan at the Texel, or Bridport at Brest or Old Jarvey [Jarvis] at Cadiz. There was as well a clutter of prison hulks, guard ships, receiving ships, sheer hulks, captured bottoms, storeships, and all the lesser watercraft required to serve the big ones. The Nore was a catch-all".[28]

At Spithead, the Delegates, secure in the mass of support in the battleships, were able to send the smaller frigates about their convoy business.

Here at the Nore, the Delegates' strength - for what it was - came from a host of such lesser ships and nondescript navy vessels, until reinforced by battle ships from the North Sea Fleet.[29] Using Dugan's ship list, below, approximately 9,000 men were embroiled [both for and against, officer and seaman] at the Nore, as against 13,000 at Spithead.

Dugan described the difference between these two theatres of mutiny in terms of leadership. "At Spithead," he said, "leaders looked for people: at the Nore, people looked for leaders".[30] Even Richard Parker had to be pressured to accept a leadership role.

It is too simplistic to see failure of the Nore mutiny resulting solely from this one decision over leadership but it might have ended the mutiny sooner than expected as Dugan suggested. The germ of this idea is in the sequence of events related in his fourteenth chapter, *The Red Flag*.[31]

"On Tuesday 30 May, the morning after their lordships went back to London, President Parker and the moderate delegate William Davis, of Sandwich, went to Sheerness to induce the authorities not to cut off victuals from the fleet". Though they soon found out how unpopular they were among the townspeople, and even ran the risk of being arrested, they failed to meet with the authorities.

Those worthies were too busily engaged "smuggling the King's pardon and the Acts of Parliament through fog and drizzle to the ships" causing friction between delegates and pardoners on nine of them. A brawl broke out on *Director*. Parker watched and listened to the seamen and in turn was critically noticed by the delegates. According to Dugan, Parker "must have felt that there was hope for a peaceful adjustment at the Great Nore".

If it ever existed that thought came to a dramatic end when the delegates decreed that the President of the Fleet was to be elected each morning, preventing him "from concluding any agreement the delegates did not desire". Dugan described this as "one of the most unusual constitutional safeguards of a legislature against an executive in parliamentary history".

This was in extreme opposition to the outsider view of the King's men who called Richard, 'Admiral' Parker, thereby holding him to be in command of the mutiny and focussing blame for the uprising and any implied threats upon his head. The haste with which Parker was condemned and hanged confirms the efficacy of such a process.

Rodger, more recently has argued against other and equally false understandings.[32] As he reported, the great mutinies "demanded explanations, and contemporaries rushed to offer them", "only outside subversion could account for them". Modern historians incorporated quota-men into the outsiders theme. Rodger's is the latest, and most telling rejection of this "conspiracy theory".

Earlier, Dugan, by using the singular title *The Great Mutiny* collapsed space and time - Spithead in April and the Nore in May - into one event, and gave priority to a common cause, the condition of seamen in the Royal Navy, over differing effects.

Rodger was in concert with the idea, expressed by Dugan, of placing *cause* above *effect.* Find the major causes. Remove them. Block their return. That way, change is more effective, as was the active practice of preventive medicine in the Royal Navy, at that time, as featured in this book.

Rodger attacked, too, a variation on the theme of difference, which held the Spithead mutinies to be "'unpolitical' (benign, morally justified)", while "the mutinies on the East Coast [the Nore], became 'political' or 'revolutionary' (malign and dangerous)".[33]

Earl Howe, at the time, "analysed the new rising...[and] imputed the neglect of the seamen's complaints to 'the incompetency of the persons who have the immediate superintendence in the department'. He declared that 'preventive measures rather than correctives are to be preferred for preserving discipline in fleets and armies'".[34]

Howe's offer to conciliate would be rejected, as the Government and Admiralty had a *'corrective'* in mind. They intended to crush the Nore mutineers.

Today, William Redfern's reputation gains from such insights. It remains to be seen in this and the following chapter how the Nore mutiny ended and what were the real and persistent effects on William Redfern.

While the Nore, as Dugan described it was a "catch-all" for Navy vessels across the fleets, it was also a point of exchange for information and ideas. Seamen talk, at least to one another. From the banks of the lower Thames came a fruitful harvest of new recruits, people who had rubbed shoulders with other workers, including men from the naval dockyards, increased the flow of "radical" opinion and "excitement" into the Royal Navy.

While that same Admiralty and Government that had turned a blind eye to the Nore as a source of disease, were acutely aware of this 'excitement' and proactive against it. A sense that prevailed, after the mutinies were over. Marcus described how the pressgang "went into action with unparalleled speed, secrecy and efficiency" at the Thames, taking "close on a thousand seamen...in a single night", in 1803. That was after the brief Peace of Amiens between Britain and France, which had commenced the year before.[35]

During that peace, *Standard* ceased to be a man-of-war. (See the first endnote in this chapter.) This calls into question its seaworthiness just a few years before. If deficient, it would not have been alone.

Authorities were aware of Nore ship-based grievances long before the Spithead eruption.[36] When did the Nore seamen consider taking action?

According to Dugan, "Spithead seamen wrote and sent envoys to the Nore to solicit support and to carry their regulations as guides. The men in the Thames estuary recognised that if their messmates at Spithead succeeded, they, too, would benefit. The trouble was that there was no forecastle organisation at the Nore. They could not translate feeling into action, sensibility into sense, until they had united the lower deck in a miscellany of vessels".[37]

"After Sir Alan Gardner's tantrum and Sir John Colpoys's blood letting [at Spithead], the Nore seamen suspected perfidy.[38] They could no longer remain passive. It was time to demonstrate real unity with Spithead. Individual ship's companies produced their own spokesmen. On 6 May, midway in the second Spithead remonstrance, they circulated a resolution for a delegates' meeting on *Sandwich,* to adopt a fraternal oath,[39] which would be given to all sailors at the Nore and which imitated the Spithead oath".[40]

The oath read, "I, A.B., do voluntary make oath and swear that I will be true in the cause we are embarked in and I will to the laying down of my life be true to the Delegates at present assembl'd, whilst they continue to support the present cause, and I will communicate to them at all times all such things as may be for the good of our undertakings and all conspiracies that may tend to the subversion of our present plan. I will also endeavour to detect and suppress as full as in my power everything that may lead to a separation of the unity so necessary [to] completing our present system".[41]

Mutiny at the Nore was heralded, by cheering on HMS *Sandwich,* on 12 May.[42] That was the day four delegates from the Nore arrived at Spithead to offer their support. As was noted in the first chapter, the visitors were surprised to find the Spithead mutiny at its end. On being invited, these Nore delegates had joined the victory celebrations, and the parade of the Royal Pardon by Earl Howe.[43]

George III Receives News of the Mutinies.

Soon after this event, King George III received a note from Spencer.[44]

"Earl Spencer has the honour of laying before your Majesty a letter received from Lord Howe this morning, together with a message just come up by the telegraph, in consequence of which he flatters himself he may congratulate your Majesty on the termination of the disorders on board the Fleet under the command of Lord Bridport, and it is hoped that the other divisions of your Majesty's Fleet which have been affected by the contagion of their bad example, will now follow them in returning to their duty.

"Earl Spencer likewise lays before your Majesty the letter received from Vice-Admiral Buckner subject of disturbances at the Nore and Sheerness which he hopes will very speedily be terminated, as the persons concerned in them do not appear to have any specifick [sic] object of complaint".

The King replied:

"I receive with pleasure Earl Spencer's report of the well-grounded hopes that the Channel Fleet, by the cool conduct of Earl Howe, is returning to reason. As soon as it is known what officers have been obliged to quit particular ships I desire I may have a list of them and of those sent to relieve them. I trust the disturbance at the Nore, as it seem[s] ungrounded, will, when it is known that the Channel Fleet has sailed, will cease".

The Nore Grievances.

Far from being "ungrounded" the Nore Mutineers had their own "ultimatum" of eight articles.[45] The formal signed copy at the Nore was dated 20th May 1797, about a month after the expanded Spithead list of 18 April 1797.

"Article 1 - That every indulgence granted to the fleet at Portsmouth be granted to his Majesty's subjects serving in the fleet at the Nore, and on places adjacent.

Article 2 - That every man, upon a ship's coming into harbour shall have liberty (a certain number at a time, so as not to injure the ship's duty) to go and see their friends and families; a convenient time to be allowed to each man.

Article 3 - That all ships before they go to sea, shall be paid all arrears of wages down to six months, according to the old rules.

Article 4 - That no officer that has been turned out of any of his Majesty's ships shall be employed in the same ship again, without the consent of the ship's company.

Article 5 - That when any of his Majesty's ships shall be paid that may have been some time in commission, if there are any pressed men on board that may not be in the regular course of payment, they shall receive two months advance to furnish them with necessaries.

Article 6 - That an indemnification be made any men who run, and may now be in his Majesty's naval service, and that they shall not be liable to be taken up as deserters.

Article 7 - That a more equal distribution be made of prize-money to the crews of his Majesty's ships and vessels of war.

Article 8 - That the articles of war, as now enforced, require various alteration, several of which to be expunged therefrom, and if more moderate ones were held forth to seamen in general, it would be the means of taking off that terror and prejudice against his Majesty's service, on that account too frequently imbibed by seamen, from entering voluntarily into the service".

"The committee of delegates of the whole fleet, assembled in council on board his Majesty's ship *Sandwich*, have unanimously agreed that they will not deliver up their charge until the appearance of some of the lords commissioners of the Admiralty to ratify the same.

Given on board his Majesty's ship *Sandwich*, by the delegates of the fleet, May 20th, 1797.

Richard Parker, President".[46] Parker, a quota man, came from a debtor's prison in Scotland.

The eight articles were also signed by delegates from the 40 gun *Sandwich*, the 74 gun *Montagu*, eight 64s - *Director, Inflexible, Belliqueux, Standard, Lion, Nassau, Repulse, and Monmouth.* Smaller vessels ranged from the 50 gun *Isis*, to the 28s, *Proserpine* and *Brilliant*, the 20s, *Grampus*, and *Champion*, the 16 gun *Swan*, *Inspector*, and *Pylades*, and finally *Comet* of 14 guns and *Tisiphone* of 12.[47]

It is not surprising that the Nore's first article asks for those indulgences granted at Spithead to be extended to them. As shore leave had not been granted it was included as the second article.

Further detailed references to pay, not taken up by the Spithead mutineers, included the payment of arrears before a ship sailed and an advance to pressed men under stated conditions.

The ban on officers returning to ships from which they had been removed followed on from the successful removal of such officers at Spithead.

A concern for men, who ran from their ships, had in mind inhumane causes that overcame the fear of punishment. The distribution of prize money and the effects of the articles of war, were matters that had long rankled in the minds of the people of the Navy ships.

Manwaring and Dobrée Review the Nore 'Articles'.

Manwaring and Dobrée commented on each of these articles, in turn.[48] Four addenda followed from a combined meeting of delegates from the North Sea and Nore Ships held on *Sandwich*.[49] "It was decided that courts-martial for accused seamen should be made up of seamen instead of officers" and that the composition of the court should vary to take into account other ranks and marines. Wages of ten pence a day were sought for marines.[50] Immediate payment of bounties was demanded. The proposed changes in payment of prize-money included claiming three-fifths of the prize-money for seamen and petty officers, with the balance going to the quarterdeck, that is, the officers.

The Marines.

Two references to marines in the Nore *Articles* deserve a further comment. Lavery, early in his discussion of the *Marines* noted their association with the suppression of mutiny.[51] Perhaps that was why their pay increase, referred to in the petitions in the first chapter, preceded that won by the seamen.

Traditionally the marines were kept separate from the seamen and "under St Vincent during 1797 - the year of the great mutinies - these rules [for separation] were greatly reinforced". St Vincent called his marine captains to his flagship "to give them some sense about keeping a watchful eye, not only upon their own men, but upon the seamen".[52]

The Marine officer sent ashore from *Standard* in the North Sea at the request of the men, was simply doing his job, suppressing a mutiny. If so, he probably took some satisfaction from the fact that punishment was meted out to marines when the mutiny ended. It is clear from the *Minutes*[53] of Redfern's court martial and from Lavery's account that there were times when marines supported the seamen in a mutiny. Some paid dearly for it.

"St Vincent's policy of favouring and encouraging the Marines to sustain authority against mutiny was extremely dangerous. It worked, in the short run, for the Marines like other landmen had always been the butt of seamen's disdain, and their resentments could be turned to account. What he was doing, however, was dividing the ships' companies, setting the officers against their natural supporters, and undermining the petty officers' authority with their men".[54]

Rodger's conclusion reads, "The Marines deserved their improved status and the title 'Royal' which St Vincent obtained for them in 1802, but it would have been better for the Navy if they had won it in action against the enemy".

Admiral Buckner's Reply to the Nore 'Articles'.

Charles Buckner, Vice-Admiral of the White, and Commander of his Majesty's ships and vessels in the river Medway and at the buoy of the Nore, conveyed to the Nore delegates the orders communicated to him by the Lords Commissioners of the Admiralty on 27 May 1797.[55]

His Majesty's most gracious pardon was offered to the Nore mutineers, with an "order to all the officers to bury in oblivion all that has passed", "notwithstanding all that [they had] done". Apart from this offer, "At the Nore there was no warmth, no humanity, to alleviate the hardness of official stone, the chill of an abstract system". So, claimed, Dobrée and Manwaring.[56]

That probably went some way to explain Dugan's comment about the Nore mutiny being the bigger and more violent".[57] Undoubtedly, some of the blame rests with governance. Overcrowding and fever on HMS *Sandwich*, and cutting off supplies to the ships, come readily to mind.

However, the more violent scheme, was being planned by the authorities, not by the mutineers. What was intended was revealed on 22 May in a letter from Evan Nepean, Secretary of the Board of Admiralty, to Admiral Duncan, who was being asked to consider an attack by the North Sea Fleet on the Nore mutineers. Duncan replied the next day. He saw problems in such an idea and suggested an alternative. Caste "the *Sandwich* adrift in the night and let her go on the sands, that the scoundrels may drown; for until some example is made this will not stop". Drown they most certainly would have done as few seamen could swim. Sick seamen would have been doubly handicapped.

Nepean saw his original suggestion as an alternative to "submitting to conditions which would be highly disgraceful". Little had changed at the Admiralty. They sent the same deputation to the Nore as they had at Spithead and again its members refused to talk directly to the delegates.

This time they had in mind blowing the mutineers out of the water, and out of contention to avoid what Nepean feared, further public revelations of mismanagement at the Nore, and in the North Sea Fleet. That was not how Nepean described it. If the Admiralty was planning to make war on the Nore mutineers it is not too much to imagine the authorities smarting over what they must have conceived as their defeat at Spithead.

What hope did these seamen have of a successful conclusion to their mutiny when the Admiralty planned on taking two pounds of flesh, one for Spithead and the other for the Nore?

After the letter to Admiral Duncan the Admiralty sent Bligh to Yarmouth on this same "very delicate business". Duncan had left, so they did not meet on this occasion as they would have done previously. Bligh had been with the North Sea Fleet. What he found now was the mutinous North Sea ships anchored in the Roads. Bligh sent a report to the Admiralty describing their plan as "doubtful and hazardous".[58]

Another vigorous measure was neither. Orders were issued to stop provisioning all ships at the Great Nore. This would help to bring the mutiny to an end in the longer term. Its immediate effect, however, was to inflame the seamen and to push the moderates towards the militant faction.[59] This strengthened a mutiny lacking the unanimity and cohesiveness of Spithead, in part because of the hoped for flow on from the earlier success.

Geography favoured the authorities. Linebaugh had described the Thames as the jugular vein of Empire.[60] Mutinous ships at the Nore, at the sea gate to the Thames, posed a threat to commercial interests. A local response was an increase in the membership of "volunteer corps not so much to fight for survival against the French, as to defend their shops, homes, businesses or land against the more seditious and riotous of their own countrymen".[61]

"The evidence suggests," Linda Colley argued, "that in the early years of the war the British Government was - rightly or wrongly - as afraid of its own people as it was of the enemy". "Labouring men might be the bedrock of the regular forces and fill the ranks of the militia, but they were neither welcome nor much trusted in the less structured world of the volunteers. Not an armed people, but a propertied and respectable home guard to restrain domestic disorder was what the authorities were most anxious to create at this stage of the conflict". [62]

The reinforcing of Sheerness by General Fox with two regiments of militia on 21 May flagged a growing opposition to the mutineers by the Authorities.[63]

In turn, mutineer response was evident on 24 May when their ships were brought from the Little Nore and concentrated at the Great Nore anchorage.[64]

On the same day and on 26-7 May mutineer ships entered the Long Reach of the Thames to recruit additional ships for the mutiny.[65] They struck opposition at Gravesend and Tilbury.[66] Two mutineers found themselves under arrest on their fourth recruiting expedition up the Thames.[67]

Cabinet decided, after some procrastination, on 27 May, to send a deputation, which included Spencer, Arden, Young and Marsden,[68] but was not bent on negotiation. Mutineers faced the alternative of pardon or punishment.[69] Surrender was a precondition for talks. By refusing the delegates entry to the Board,[70] the same Admiralty deputation was repeating the stand it had taken at Spithead. It dug in its heels. At the Nore, there was no Admiral Bridport, on the spot, advising on a "sense of the fleet".

The North Sea Fleet Brings Redfern to the Nore.

The same day, 27 May, ships of Admiral Duncan's North Sea Fleet were in a state of mutiny off Yarmouth. Ships refused to return to their blockade station, centred on Texel, where the Dutch Fleet was bottled up.[71]

HMS the *Montague* became the first of Duncan's Fleet to start for the Nore.[72] Later that day other ships from his Fleet were seen approaching the Thames with red flags flying,[73] bringing much needed reinforcements to the mutinous seamen at the Nore.

Back at Sheerness, crews heard their Captains read an Admiralty proclamation.[74] The Admiralty Deputation returned to London.[75] On 30 May, *Clyde*, *San Fiorenzo*, and several gunboats surrendered.[76] Parker learned how unpopular he was and near to being arrested,[77] when he and Davis went ashore at Sheerness.

31 May brought HMS the *Standard*, with William Redfern aboard, to the Nore from Yarmouth with other ships from Duncan's Fleet.[78]

That same day also brought from the King "A Proclamation for the Suppression of the mutinous and treasonable Proceedings of the Crew of certain of our Ships at the Nore".[79]

Reference was made to the Admiralty orders of 27 May to crews at the Nore "to return to their due obedience". It said that some crews desirous of doing that have been prevented by violence, some ships have been fired upon, etc. After "repeated admonitions and offers of our gracious pardon" such "rebellious and treasonable attempts against our crown and dignity" make it "necessary for us to call on all our loving subjects to be aiding and assisting in repressing the same".

The call went out to all such subjects in "their several stations" "to use their utmost endeavours, according to law, to suppress all such mutinous and treasonable proceedings, and to use all lawful means to bring the persons concerned therein, their aiders and abettors, to justice".

Moreover the King's loving subjects were strictly enjoined and commanded "not to give any aid, comfort, assistance, or encouragement whatsoever, to any person or persons concerned in any such mutinous and treasonable proceedings, as they will answer the same at their peril".

Finally people were likewise to do all they could "to prevent all other persons from giving any such aid, assistance, comfort, or encouragement".[80]

Supplies Stopped. The Noose Tightened.

At Sheerness, the stoppage of supplies brought a protest from the delegates,[81] with a "final determination" from Parker, Widgery and Wallace.[82] Under a flag of truce, delegates went ashore to demand stores.[83]

Pressure continued to build against the Nore mutineers. On 1 June 1797, in London, both houses of Parliament received the King's message on subduing the revolt.[84]

Next day the central committee of delegates responded by ordering a blockade of the Thames.[85]

The ship, *Firm,* a floating battery, surrendered on 2 or 3 June.[86] On 3 June a Bill passed against the seduction of sailors and soldiers.[87] That day, Parker, as President, wrote to Buckner on behalf of the Delegates of the whole Fleet about "the highly improper conduct of the administration".

"The foolish proclamations which have been received are only fitted to exasperate the minds of a sett of Honest Men, who would never be more happy than in really serving their country", Parker added.[88]

The refused entry of sick seamen to a hospital ship, already discussed, occurred on 5 June.[89] On this same day seamen "seized the opportunity of the King's birthday to express their loyalty". Many of the ships were dressed with colours, the *Sandwich* flew the Royal Standard at the fore, and the Fleet fired the resounding salute, which did such alarming damage to the old brick merlons of Sheerness fort.

There might not have been the same eagerness to honour the Sovereign had the men known that he had written to Spencer a few days before that 'the preventing of their getting fresh water will soon oblige them to submit'.[90]

Two more ships, *Serapis* and *Discovery* surrendered that day,[91] and Parker called off the blockade.[92]

On 6 June, Bills passed to stop contacts with the shore, to restrict communication to Buckner, to declare ships in mutiny and rebellion, and to separate the leaders from the led.[93] A proclamation was read at the Sheerness dockyard.[94]

Outgoing buoys and lights in the Thames were removed on 7 June to prevent the escape of the mutinous fleet.[95] The task of installing such essential navigational aids in the first place, and in providing a pilotage service, was the Corporation of Trinity House, which levied shipping dues to fund their work.

Ships Continue to Surrender.

Tightening the ropes was having its effect. *Leopard* and *Repulse* surrendered on 10 June.[96] Surrendering ships did not go unnoticed. On 11 June the Nore delegates still prevailed but factions on various ships came to blows.[97] The Admiralty kept up the pressure, sending Vice-Admiral Peyton to the Nore to demand unconditional surrender. *Ardent* was next to surrender.[98] A boatload of seamen, probably from the Nore, escaped, and were chased by a cutter.[99]

On 12 June blue flags flew amongst the red and half masted, but next morning only blue flags were flying. The Nore Mutiny had virtually ended.[100] *Agamemnon, Nassau, Standard, Vestal,* and *Champion* surrendered the following day.[101]

HMS the *Standard* was persuaded to surrender by her first lieutenant.[102] Wallace, the chief delegate from *Standard* would shoot himself next day.[103] He was one of the three, associated with "the final determination of the fleet".[104]

Former surgeon's mate William Redfern was discharged from *Standard* at Gravesend on 14 June 1797 for his involvement in the Nore Mutiny.[105]

On that day, the ships *Iris, Sandwich, Monmouth, Isis, Brilliant, Proserpine, Pylades, Swan, Comet, Ranger, Tysiphone* and *Grampus surrendered.*[106] On 15 June 1797, *Inflexible, Director, Montague(?),*

Belliqueux(?), Lion and Inspector also surrendered[107] while *Inflexible* mutineers in *Good Intent* sailed to Calais.[108]

Buckner announced that the last vessel submitted on 15 June, at the Nore.[109] Williams reported next day from Sheerness that the Nore was not in a perfectly tranquil state. Crews were kept to their ships, the site of recent disputation with the Royal Navy and among themselves.[110]

Pardons, Arrests, Courts Martial, and Punishments.

"At Gravesend, when the Nore mutiny had broken up," according to James Dugan, "560 men were pointed out and imprisoned as delegates or activists, and 412 of them were held for trial. At least 59 were sentenced to death and at least 36 hanged. Not more than 200 actually received legal process".[111] Gill numbered some 400 mutineers, with their leaders, removed from their ships at Chatham on 16 May. They were taken to the *Eolus* hulk and to Chatham and other gaols. Ships were provisioned, as some were destitute of supplies.[112]

After the first court martial, which lasted from 22 to 26 June, Parker was hanged on 30 June 1797 from a ship's yard arm on HMS *Sandwich.*[113]

Some mutineers were luckier than others. King George boarded the royal yacht to visit Admiral Duncan, after Camperdown, only to be thrown out of bed while still in the Thames. When they did meet, Duncan presented a petition from 180 repentant Nore mutineers, offering to take them into his fleet. They were pardoned.[114]

Courts Martial.

What was a court martial? Ten Articles and Orders relating to courts martial were set out in an official Royal Navy document printed in London and viewed in an edition of 1790 in the collection of the History of Medicine Library, Sydney.[115] In order for him to be even better prepared, Counsel had been arranged, separately, for William Redfern, supposedly by his family and friends. Having Counsel had also separated the seamen from men of rank at Bligh's *Bounty* court martial.[116]

Death, and Other Punishments.

All the grim detail, the pomp and ceremony of killing, could be read in *The Times* of 10 August 1797, over the signature of "P[eter]. Parker". On this occasion convicted Nore Mutineers from the *Standard's* sister ship, H.M.S. the *Montague*, were to hang.

There was more to this particular hanging than met the eye. The place was Spithead. As the previous chapter reported, the mutineers there had been granted a Royal Pardon. In addition, all reference to the Mutiny was expunged from their records. Promotion was open to those involved. Afterwards they had resumed active duty with the Channel Fleet and sailed to restrain the French navy.

But all had neither been forgotten nor forgiven. Just months after those events at Spithead, some repressed feelings would out. Mutineers from another mutiny, at the Nore, would hang there.

Sir Peter Parker who signed the order, above, had come to our attention as Port-Admiral at Plymouth during the Spithead mutiny. He was one of the first to know of the planned uprising and received copies of the Royal Pardon for distribution to the Fleet. He was there when Lord Howe took the Royal Pardon around the Fleet and was aware that those same mutineers were now on active service with their old Channel Fleet. Nevertheless, the Admiralty, in its wisdom - or, out of revenge - or, fear of recurrence - wished to "impress on the minds of all persons in the fleet, a due sense of the crimes for which the said prisoners are to suffer".

Later, at the Nore, Thomas Trotter, Channel Fleet physician, noted some effects of this Draconian measure implemented by the Admiralty, 'an unusual despondency and dejection of spirits among the patients. The outrageous fury of late precedings had subsided, the horror induced by some awful examples of punishment was now operating'. There were 'many cases of hysteria, accompanied by convulsions and passionate out breaks of weeping characteristic of shock'.[117]

Crimes indeed! *Mutiny*, pardoned after Spithead, was punished after Nore. Why? Whose voices were being heard, and were there other voices still to be heard?

'The Wooden World' of N.A.M. Rodger.

Nicholas Rodger wrote of "a common opinion derived in considerable measure from Masefield's *Sea Life in Nelson's Time*, that naval discipline was harsh and oppressive, officers frequently cruel and tyrannical, ratings drawn from the dregs of society, ill-treated and starved". Rodger set out "to test th[is] traditional view of the internal life of the Navy by studying the evidence in detail for a limited period". He chose the Seven Years' War (1756-63) with extensions back to 1749 and forward to 1775.[118]

Rodger had described the eighteenth century British Navy as "the largest industrial unit of its day in the western world, and by far the most expensive and demanding of all the administrative responsibilities of the State".[119] He concluded that the Navy in the middle years of the century "in its fundamentals, in the ways in which people dealt with one another and thought of one another...closely resembled British society ashore. In the last analysis, the wooden world was built of the same materials as the wider world.[120]

"A ship's company, large or small," according to Rodger, "was a microcosm of society with a manifold division of ranks and ratings, of social class and status, of skills and professions, and of age.[121] The life of the ship can only be understood in relation to these overlapping patterns. In their dealings with one another, in tension and accommodation, in fear and affection, in persuasion and command, men acted within the constraints imposed by the complex internal structure of shipboard society".[122]

Highly relevant in our context is his six-part chapter headed, "Discipline".[123] *Obedience and Command* (part A) which opens with a challenge to the traditional view of Navy discipline. Rodger draws to our notice an opinion, that "The Icelandic language is said to have one hundred and fifty words for the cod's head..." On the other hand, "The eighteenth-century Navy, by contrast, lacked even a single word for discipline". "[W]hen men lack a word for something it is safe to assume that they do not often think and talk about it".[124] When they did think of discipline it was more in the sense of "training". "Where modern officers expect to command, mid-eighteenth-century officers hoped to persuade. The fact that this did not alarm them was partly because it was a feature of Service life to which they were completely accustomed, and no different from the weakness of civil authority, ashore or afloat". [125]

Rodger, by contrasting the sailor's life at sea with that in port, suggested an alternative to a command structure. This was based on "the collective understanding of seamen" and "of intelligent co-operation in survival". In the absence of this survival imperative "[i]n port, and even more on shore, seamen were notoriously riotous and insubordinate". "Once the anchor tripped and the last liberty men sobered up, they became a different breed of man, alert, intelligent, and obedient. This was not because the officers suddenly recollected their duty, it was because the prospect of drowning concentrates a man's mind wonderfully".[126] This author described as "fantasy" the "total society" view of the Navy at that time "as a strictly ordered, hierarchical society, brutally repress[ed]".[127]

Violence and Humanity (part B) introduces the eighteenth century [in Britain, at least] as "the age of benevolence, an age in which Christian virtues were almost universally approved, and not infrequently practised.[128] The man who helped the needy, protected the weak, and used power with justice and mercy was respected, if not always imitated. In this, as in most other matters, the officers and men of the Navy accepted the values and attitudes of the community from which they came. Almost all of them were Christians..."[129]

Asa Briggs[130] told how in the 1780s, "each man had his station and each station its peculiar responsibilities...not always met - for every charitable action there were many callous and brutal ones - but the concept of social order itself often blossomed out in works of corporate as well as private philanthropy".

"The eighteenth century" Briggs continued, "was rightly proud of its 'improvement' in manners and its ripening sense of social duty. For the care of the sick, the aged, prisoners, foundlings and poor children, new institutions were created during the course of the century particularly after 1750. 'We live in an age when humanity is in fashion' wrote the London magistrate Sir John Hawkins in 1787...William Whyte, a surgeon of Castor, who died in 1788, was 'equally distinguished for professional Abilities, the strictest integrity and an active Discharge of the Duties of Humanity".

Rodger agreed that "brutal officers" did exist but being "inefficient", were "distrusted by the Service for reasons both moral and practical".[131] But flogging was widespread as was the tendency "to settle affairs with a blow".[132] Despite improving manners suggested by Briggs, "[T]he eighteenth century was an age in which personal violence was more common than it is now". The Navy was no exception.

On the other hand, and more in keeping with the idea of benevolence having practical and positive outcomes, intelligent efforts were being made "to improve the conditions of the people aboard ship". With numbers of five hundred and more, individuals lost their identity in the shipboard mass. Grouping these people in divisions, each the responsibility of a Lieutenant was "like all great ideas, simple, elegant and obvious".[133] Though the health of seamen improved as a result, this was only a beginning.

Lord Howe[134] became an early exponent of this divisional system, first conceived by an individual, Vice-Admiral Thomas Smith, and not by the Admiralty Office.[135] Captain Charles Middleton and Captain Richard Kempenfelt were enthusiastic supporters of this system.[136] Middleton, in the *Ardent*, divided his crew into four divisions. One result was 'adequate periods of rest between their spells of duty. Middleton was one of the few who allowed limited shore leave to seamen. He may be taken as an exemplar of Christian leadership that brought positive benefits to seamen. More will be heard of him in later chapters.

Crime and Punishment (part C) accepted that any organized community, such as the Navy, "is bound to encounter the need to repress crime",[137] but "everyone was anxious to avoid courts martial if at all possible". "If the alternative were a court martial, it seemed to many officers far better to dispose of the matter with relative leniency, informality and speed by ignoring the regulations".[138]

A court martial was described as "an unwieldy and unpredictable instrument, assembled by authority only if it seemed unavoidable, and viewed with considerable trepidation as a weapon which was quite likely to misfire".

At sea, a "panel of captains, all of them legally untrained [were] assisted by a judge advocate who was usually the admiral's secretary and might have some passing knowledge of the law".[139] The decisions of courts martial were on the "whole, extremely inconsistent, and taken individually, often quixotic". Not even an Admiral, such as Byng, was safe, as he found to his cost.

The conclusion reached was that discipline in the Navy appeared on examination "to have been largely an organic response to the nature of life at sea, overlaid with a ramshackle legal structure, and not an attempt to sustain an artificial authority by force".[140] If true to 1775, it will be asked below whether it was still true of the Navy of 1797?

Continuing his analysis of discipline, Rodger takes the reader through *Complaint and Consultation* (part D). He considered that '[t]he absence of any official mechanism for complaint meant in practice that any method was accepted as legitimate'.[141] A sailor might speak to the captain or even a port admiral. Petitioning was "common enough to provide a living for 'the petition writer at the Admiralty gate'". Letters were also used.[142]

On a different scale, the complaint of a ship's company "was a powerful weapon against real oppression".[143] "[T]wo or three junior flag officers or senior captains"[144] visited ships and followed-up allegations against officers. Action also followed justified complaints about surgeons[145] and unseaworthiness.[146] Miscarriage of justice balanced malicious or frivolous complaints, over time.

The system of complaints and consultation worked because the smaller size of the Navy in the middle years of the eighteenth century allowed for a larger degree of informality, even of intimacy between officers and ratings.[147] It was 'almost unconscious of class'. Again, was that conclusion applicable to 1797?

In *Mutiny* (part E), Rodger described two senses in which the word was used in this period, "neither of which corresponds to the usual modern usage".[148] Violent insubordination as in striking an officer was one sense, while collective actions of whole ship's companies was the other.

This latter approaches the modern usage. Rodger, however, rejected emphatically the "Cecil B. de Mille school of history...of the violent seizure of a ship from her officers, on the high seas", as virtually unknown in the Navy.[149] The *Hermione* and *Bounty* mutinies were exceptional.[150]

When Bligh lost his ship, *Bounty*, to the mutineers, the Admiralty took a dim view of it and sent Captain Edward Edwards in HMS *Pandora*, a sixth-rate frigate of 24 guns, to find and arrest the mutineers.[151] Some of those found and arrested were imprisoned in "Pandora's box" or in irons and were lost when *Pandora* struck a reef.[152] Mutineers who survived were returned to England to face courts-martial.

According to Lavery, *Hermione* was the most notorious of the rare type of mutiny in the Royal Navy. Captain Pigot, whose behaviour was largely responsible for two topmen falling to their death, ordered their bodies to be thrown into the sea. "That night, the crew began by rolling shot about the decks (a well-known sign of impending mutiny), and then rose, killing the captain and eight other officers".[153] Many of the mutineers were eventually captured and hanged.

"The kind of mutiny which did happen, and happened quite frequently, conformed to certain unwritten rules...".[154]

The removal of intolerable officers was a proper and traditional object of mutiny. Another common cause of mutiny was related to delays in pay resulting from "the cumbersome naval accounting system". On land, riots had developed among seamen over late payment.

Pepys, of course, knew all about that. In October 1665 he was threatened with physical violence by a hostile crowd of "poor seamen that [were] starving...for lack of money".[155] In November "Sir William Batten had his cloak torn from his back and his servant assaulted by demonstrating sailors". "The very same day Pepys was 'much troubled to have one hundred seamen...cursing us and breaking the glass windows. [They] swear they will pull the house down... There was a charitable fund, The Chatham Chest for Stricken Sailors, in which Pepys took considerable interest, but it was totally inadequate to meet their needs".

Such behaviour was atypical. The "precise objects" of "pre-industrial crowds" rarely involved "indiscriminate attacks on either properties or persons".[156]

The sufferings of the seamen and their dependents, denied their promised pay and given "tickets" or IOUs, were so acute that in July 1666, a mob of women demonstrators - over 300 of them - surged into the yard of the Navy Office, and stayed there. In Pepys's words, "clamouring and swearing, and cursing us". Many were demonstrating on behalf of their husbands, who had been taken prisoner and were lying penniless and starving in foreign prisons. The Navy Board ordered the relief of the prisoners was to be done "without any trouble to be given to any of their relations demonstrating here".[157]

This is in conformity with Rodger's view that punishment of mutineers was secondary to the removal of causes for a mutiny.[158] While in three accounts of mutinies the idea of punishing mutineers was not raised, in two other instances leaders were court-martialled. "These two mutinies were exceptions which prove the rules by which other mutineers conducted themselves...When other methods failed, mutiny provided a formal system of public protest to bring grievances to the notice of authority. It was a sort of safety-valve, harmless, indeed useful, so long as it was not abused. It was part of a system of social relations which provided an effective working compromise between the demands of necessity and humanity, a means of reconciling the Navy's need of obedience and efficiency with the individual's grievances. It was a means of safeguarding the essential stability of shipboard society, not of destroying it".[159]

To which category belonged the Fleet Mutinies of 1797? Did the passage of years explain changing responses by authorities and the public to mutinies in the Royal Navy? Or were there other reasons?

These and other questions raised above will now be addressed.

Rodger's detailed study was essentially "mid-century" so he was constrained to write a brief conclusion to his book to confront the challenge of the large scale, fleet-wide Mutinies of 1797.

"Except in being collective movements in which ships co-operated," he wrote, "these mutinies followed more or less the 'unwritten rules' which had long governed such affairs [in the Navy]. Like popular riots throughout the century, they were essentially conservative,[160] aimed to restore the just system, which had formerly obtained, to rescue the Navy from the deformations recently introduced into it. To men, both on the lower deck and the quarterdeck, who had seen the excesses of the French Revolution, the mutinies of 1797 seemed very dangerous. Certainly they displayed evidence of class and political sentiments which would have been unthinkable a generation earlier, but it is not clear with hindsight that they were really as novel or as revolutionary as they then seemed. In forty years material conditions in the Navy had worsened. Inflation had ground away the value of the naval wage, and the coppering of ships had removed the chance of frequent leave. The Service had expanded not only absolutely but relative to the population as a whole, to recruit many more men (and officers) unacquainted with the traditional accommodations of seafaring". "When all these things have been considered, however, we should still beware of exaggerating the changes of forty years". [161]

Rodger's study of the Royal Navy continued. In 1994[162] he published a chapter based on an earlier research paper of 1992.[163]

Rodger opened his 1994 chapter with his usual and careful consideration of his research findings. "The period which Patrick O'Brian has made his own, the Great Wars against France, is at once the least known and the best known part of all British naval history". This invited the elucidation, which followed, and, that "we still know far too little about the daily life of the officers and men of Jack Aubrey's day".[164]

However, one thing was clear. The "social life of the Navy changed greatly during that time. These changes may be divided into the material and the psychological". "The manpower situation had undoubtedly worsened over fifty years" with "the ratio of skilled to unskilled...virtually reversed". "A worsening manpower situation was bound to affect life on the lower deck in many ways, mostly adversely", making more work for the skilled seamen, increasing turnovers from ship to ship, and affecting shore leave, at a premium due "to coppering of the ships". Increased turnovers unsettled seamen and "acted powerfully to destroy men's loyalty to their ship and their officers".[165]

"Perhaps the gravest material decline in seamen's conditions between 1750 and 1800 was caused by inflation". This, Rodger accepted as another material disadvantage, "which had grown up, or, at least grown much worse since the 1750s", but "were not the only or even the most serious social problems of the Service". The French Revolution was largely responsible for a breaking down by the 1790s of the "solidarity, almost intimacy between officers and men" from an earlier period when the "almost feeble authority of the Admiralty counted for much less than the officers' powers to reward, and their need of reliable followers".[166]

A growing class-consciousness and tension between officers and men was evidenced in "an increasing intolerance of complaint, and a notably harsher attitude to mutinies". For example, the 1797 Spithead mutiny, held by Rodger to have been "conducted with great moderation and good sense for entirely traditional objectives", was described by one captain as "perfectly French" and as establishing "a system of terror". "By 1797 the Admiralty no longer felt that officers' promises to their men needed to be kept if it were inconvenient to do so".[167]

"With growing class-consciousness", to which Rodger added, "mutual suspicion between quarterdeck and lower deck went a steady rise in the severity of punishments both formal and informal, and a growing tendency to indiscriminate brutality. Although we have little systematic research, it is certain that court martial sentences increased as the century went on, and probably that the same was true of flogging at captains' discretion". The growth of state power and centralisation weakened personal bonds. "Where officers' powers to reward had weakened, their powers to punish had to grow to compensate". "Commanded by officers to whom he was an entire stranger, cut off from them by a gulf of mutual incomprehension and suspicion, subject to harsh discipline (and in some ships to capricious brutality), forbidden leave for years at a time, his lot was undoubtedly worse than his predecessor's in the Navy of Anson's time".[168]

As described in an earlier chapter these published steps in Rodger's research and thinking on the mutinies of the 1790s culminated in his major history of the Royal Navy in 2004.

What of Lord Howe in 1797? Did he consider the mutineers to have played according to the rules? He evidenced some disappointment with the delegates but did not shun them. He talked directly. The Navy Board, as reported above, had refused to negotiate face to face with the delegates at Spithead, and again at the Nore.

For this and other reasons both delegates and seamen in general responded positively to Howe. According to Brian Lavery,[169] Howe's credit had been enhanced for the men by his resolution of the *Janus* affair in 1783. He had also been the popular commander-in-chief of their Channel Fleet.

None of these items, by itself, provides an answer to the question that opened this paragraph. Was it simply that Howe was of "the old school" and was playing by the old rules of preference for eliminating grievances, rather than punishing the victims?

Had new men come to positions of power in an increasingly larger navy? Certainly there was murmuring among the officer-classes against the so-called soft options of Howe's conciliation, supported at Spithead and rejected at the Nore by government. Just as there had been admirals like Duncan who had spoken up for the seamen years before the mutinies broke out.

No doubt some of the opposition to Howe was generational, youth versus age. Some was linked to Howe's more open approach to the blockade of Brest. Critics argued, that this strategy resulted in the Channel Fleet spending more time in port, and in making mutinies. Others were critical of Howe's victory at the "Glorious First of June" where the French "had sacrificed the warships to keep Howe away from a convoy of 116 vessels" bringing essential food supplies from America.[170]

Ian Gilmour reached his opinion on Howe's involvement, in his study of *Governance and Violence in Eighteenth-Century England*.[171] Burke and many others feared that Howe's concessions had put an end to all naval discipline, said Gilmour, who argued to the contrary that they prevented far worse troubles; had governmental obduracy driven the mass of loyal seamen to embrace the ideas of their Irish or "Jacobin" leaders, the consequences would have been explosive. Yet, neither concession nor punishment prevented further unrest in the navy, as Lavery noted.

Thomas Trotter obviously had Howe, in mind, when he discussed a "nobleman of my acquaintance". Of him, he said, "A life so valuable ought to have been spun to its last thread!"

What if Howe had been asked to spin "to its last thread" a cloak of conciliation at the Nore, as he had been asked at Spithead? Would Trotter have found such 'unusual despondency and dejection of spirits among the patients', or have observed so 'many cases of hysteria, accompanied by convulsions and passionate outbreaks of weeping characteristic of shock'?

Would this horror (already brought to attention above) induced by some awful examples of punishment have been operating at the Nore?[172]

Dugan's research revealed that of the fifty-nine seamen and marines sentenced to death, thirty-six were hanged.[173]

These were the outcomes of governance by violence, the rejection by government of Howe's conciliation, and search for the causes of unrest at Spithead, being continued at the Nore.

Terror, as expressed government policy, would later be applied to the transport of convicts to the colony of New South Wales.[174]

'Between the Devil and the Deep Blue Sea', with Marcus Rediker.

Earlier accounts of the mutinies did not have the benefit of Rodger's work on the Georgian Navy, or an equally useful study of merchant seamen, by Marcus Rediker, *Between the Devil and the Deep Blue Sea.* Rediker sought "to recover the experiences of the common seaman in the first half of the eighteenth century".[175] He argued that merchant seamen, critical players in the century of trade, were largely invisible in its history.

Merchant Navy influence in the Royal Navy has also been overlooked, even though Michael Lewis, while Professor of History, Royal Naval College, Greenwich, considered "they were actually the same people". Just as the "similarities between British warships and British merchant ships have always been greater than their differences", Lewis wrote, "the same is even more true of the 'rating' and the 'deck-hand', the seamen who manned the respective services".[176]

In 1960, Lewis held that some "three-quarters of the men comprising any ordinary Ship's company were, by upbringing and training, seamen: and seafaring in this country was a markedly hereditary calling",[177] especially in the sea shires.

Rediker's contribution as well as Rodger's is needed to assess the likely influence of one service upon the other. In the earlier text, Lewis argued that impressment, used to make up Navy numbers, was unsound economically, because merchant seamen were better paid.[178] To their loss of income, Lewis added the following.[179]

"Compulsion meant lack of liberty when on board, since unwilling men, if allowed on shore, were tempted to desert; and lack of liberty, as well as poor conditions on board, led to further unwillingness to serve, and, therefore, to the continued need for compulsion".

The title of Rediker's book, with its play on the word "devil" for ship and its captain, placed the seamen between man and nature.[180] "Maritime culture was forged from [these] two related confrontations, each of which was central to seafaring work. The first was the confrontation between man and nature...[The second]...the class confrontation...over the issues of power, authority, work, and discipline'.[181] "Maritime culture...was fractured".

Rediker's first confrontation was similar to Rodger's, keeping the ship afloat, a survival imperative. A clear language of "technical necessity" directed the labour process in "one of the early modern world's most sophisticated pieces of technology" - the deep-sea ship.[182]

For this same period, according to Rodger, the Royal Navy experience was different. "Naval discipline was by modern standards feeble and anarchic, but it rested on a fundamental stability which no longer exists. Disorder was tolerable then, as it would not be now, because order did not seem to be essentially threatened". [183]

Significantly for this discussion, Rodger continued, "The officers and men of the Navy in the 1750s and 1760s [the period of his study] were the last generation to be unconscious of the class structure in which they moved. Their problems of discipline were all problems of detail, which carried no implication for the basic stability of the system".[184]

When the implication of Rodger's statement is noted - that post 1760s generations of officers and men were *conscious* of the class structure in which they moved - Rediker's position is approached. He argued "that it is impossible to separate the work experiences and the cultural life of the merchant service and the Royal Navy in the seventeenth and eighteenth centuries", even if "in modified form".[185]

Were the wooden worlds of naval and merchant seamen so distinctive and so different? Naval ships because of their guns were jammed full of people to operate them. Merchant vessels had fewer guns and, as a result, fewer seamen to manhandle them. Nevertheless there were other differences that had a profound effect on attitudes to direct action and particularly to the idea of a mutiny. Mutiny in the Royal Navy has already been considered. What was the Merchant Navy experience?

Rediker, in contrast to Rodger, held that "Maritime culture...was undergoing a long and uneven transition in which something similar to craft organization was being eclipsed by that of class".[186] This was related to "cultural dissociation based on class" that was occurring in the wider society ashore.[187] One result was "that merchant capitalists and captains did not bank upon the seamen's voluntary acceptance of capitalist relations of production in shipping". Maintaining discipline and obedience became "increasingly vicious".

For the Royal Navy, if not in the first half of the eighteenth century, certainly thereafter, a change occurred, culminating in the last years of that century. Manwaring and Dobrée referred to a "constant if thin stream of piteous letters which trickled in to the Admiralty" about the cruel practices of officers, that went unanswered.[188]

One persistent attitudinal difference between the two navies has been noticed in the provision of health care that extended into the middle years of the next century. As Christopher Lloyd pointed out, the introduction of lime juice into the merchant navy mid -[19th]century required "Shipping Acts, and a long and laborious process because of the avarice of shipowners".[189]

What then of mutiny? According to Rediker, "Captains often applied the term to the most minimal disobedience. Mutiny as used here is an organized, self-conscious revolt against constituted authority, aimed at curtailing the captain's powers or seizing control of the ship". "It is remarkable that historians have devoted so little attention to mutinies in the merchant shipping industry".[190]

Sixty mutinies are listed in *Appendix E*[191] and are said to "represent an unknown (perhaps only a minor) portion of the mutinies that actually took place" in the first half of the eighteenth century. Involving merchant vessels and privateers they fit the stereotype that has come to mask the Royal Navy experience.[192] Of the sixty, nine belong to years of war in the period between 1702 and 1748, forty-nine to times of peace between 1700 and 1750, while twenty-one mutinies took place in the period 1715-1737.[193]

Half of these mutinies used or threatened violence. One in five involved the death of one or more officers. In one half of the rebellions, mutineers succeeded in taking control of the ship. Piracy was the end of about one third of the rebellions. Mutinies followed from multiple rather than single issues.[194] Among the causes were oppression, mistreatment, and complaints about the condition of the ship. There were too few hands, too many officers, and too much work. Provisions were inadequate, health care was poor, and "ready money" was hard to find. "Mad" captains and breaches of the wage contract rounded out the list. The minimal support of 20-30 per cent of the crew could bring about a mutiny if the others remained neutral. The captain's side almost always consisted of the steward and the surgeon, both generally regarded as "tell-Tales to Capns".[195]

Although grievance-based, with shared naval themes, mutiny as expressed in merchant ships clearly differed from the Navy experience. This supports Rodger's contention that such mutinies were virtually unknown in the Navy. The comparison also helps strip away the stereotypically violent and antisocial label - *mutiny* - that adhered to the Great Fleet Mutinies of 1797, and to those who participated in them, well on into the 1800s, and within my experience, to the time of writing, with but a few exceptions.

William Redfern and the Thames Court Martial.

With fresh voices ringing in our ears it is now time to return to the court martial and to the Admiralty's sense of place. The hanging of Nore mutineers on Royal Navy ships for maximum impact on seamen is not out of place with the idea of conducting the courts martial on the decks of Royal Navy ships open to routine comings and goings. In Redfern's case it was the deck of the *Neptune*, which was being made ready to sail within the week. The ship, in turn, stood there in the great public concourse of the River Thames with its bulging waterway traffic. Contemporary prints and printed words confirm a forest of masts of wooden sailing ships parallel to the river's banks on each side. Between them, vessels of all shapes and sizes passed with time and tide, harnessing wind and human energy.

By the 1790s, overcrowding, delays and alarming theft levels threatened the Port of London[196] pointing to the perceived need for a marine police force and the building of walled docks that were to follow. Patrick Colquhoun's contemporary *Treatise on the Commerce and Police of the River Thames,* which includes a table of shipping for 1797, supports this vision.[197]

A contemporary drawing showed ship masts still forming a dense fringe along the Thames' banks even after the West India Docks had been opened in 1802. It required many more great docks in that decade to make any lasting impression as trade was increasing. Roy Porter[198] described the congested Thames, further up river, where ships from across the world offloaded "their cargoes into thousands of hoys and barges". That year Thames business approached £18 million, "more than all the other ports combined". Porter said that "Everything came to London" and selected more than forty items from Colquhoun's lists to prove his point.

Linebaugh's "jugular vein" aptly described the Thames with its life-blood of commerce surging through.[199] A mutineer fleet at the Nore, at London's throat, was too close for comfort. An acute commercial reaction followed and government nurtured their interest against the mutineers.

As a result the Nore mutineers were denied the support of public opinion that their fellow mutineers had enjoyed at Spithead, when they made their decision to release frigates for convoy duty.

There were some who saw as fitting punishment, the hanging of Nore mutineers along the Thames.

What Happened on HMS 'Standard' at Yarmouth?

An answer may be found in the Minutes of Redfern's court Martial. To set the scene, Prosecutor Captain Parr of HMS the *Standard* called his first witness, Fourth Lieutenant Delafons, to describe what happened at Yarmouth

Roads aboard *Standard*, while part of the North Sea Fleet under the command of Admiral Duncan.[200]

According to Delafons, *Standard* lay to all that night and in the morning went into Yarmouth Roads. *Montague* was coming out with a Red Flag flying and gave *Standard* three cheers, which were returned. The Red Flag and the *Standard*'s answering cheers went aloft together.

"On the Evening of the 28th the Command was taken from them but they allowed the officers to work the Ship as they said for the safety of her, they had no further command. This was from 28th May till about the 14th of June". This concluded the account Delafons gave in response to Parr's first questions.[201]

How were the Six Prisoners Involved at the Nore?

The Prosecutor, Captain Parr, having established the fact of the Mutiny,[202] questioned Lieutenant Delafons about some of those involved who were of course the prisoners.[203] Delafons described the first prisoner as having been "particularly active as officer of a watch - after our shifting to the Essex shore - repeatedly...firing musquets [sic] at passing vessels to bring them to". This mutineer had also pointed "one of the Quarter deck guns forward in the direction of the *Leopard* [on its way to surrender]". Delafons had been kept busy dashing between decks to stop the firing. He had found this prisoner "in a violent rage", telling Capt. Parr, "nobody had the right to interfere" in his watch.

When "Lieut. Walker solicited the assistance" of the second Prisoner, "for the Standard to follow the *Leopard*", this mutineer replied that he "wanted none of his parlaver (sic)". The third Prisoner, was seen by Delafons, "filling the Marine Cartouche Boxes with Cartridges". The fourth "relieved the Sentinel over the Marine Arm Chest on the Starboard side of the Poop. Both sentinels had pistols. It was not usual before the Mutiny for any sentinels to have pistols". Delafons also remembered having "frequently seen [another prisoner] in boats as a Sitter firing...at vessels passing...to bring them to and make them anchor".

To the ship's company, Capt Parr had read a letter, which he intended to send to the Admiralty. Delafons confirmed the captain's action, and told how some seamen made their intention clear, not "to give the Ship up until they had got their pardon". One prisoner added, "Yes and that pardon must be dated up to this day at noon on stamped paper and signed with the seal of the Admiralty to take on the business of last night and what we have done this day".

Delafons specified these events, as "the firing at the *Leopard* and the *Repulse* and stopping the Merchantmen".

One of the Prisoners had been particularly active after the ships came to the Nore, "In looking out for Signals - having them answered and in giving repeated orders to the Ships Company. Delafons had seen ships shorten sail on being fired on". Once, this prisoner had to be pushed from a gun and taken in a bear hug.

Fifth Lieutenant Benjamin Walker of the *Standard* was sworn. He "supported Delafons in most points adding rather than subtracting" from his account. Three cheers were given on the order at 8 o'clock each morning as the Red Flag was hoisted. He had seen Merchantmen being fired on and coming to anchor as a result but couldn't say how many. Holdsworth was the Principal when the Ship was moved to the Essex Side. All hands were on deck at that time.

John Williams, Carpenter of the *Standard* was sworn. He was the first to use the word 'Delegate' when referring to Holdsworth.

The Court-martial from the 'Minutes'.

This chapter concludes with some references to the members of the Court Martial. Presiding was Sir Thomas Pasley, Kt Baronet, Vice Admiral of the White and Commander in Chief of His Majesty's Ships and vessels in the River Thames.[204] Other members were Commodore Sir Erasmus Gower Kt,[205] and Captains John Markham,[206] Edward Riou,[207] Sir Francis Saforey Bart, and Richard King. Each will receive the honour of introduction by brief but relevant comment.

Sir Thomas Pasley had earlier been sent to persuade the North Sea mutineers to return to duty. Manwaring and Dobrée[208] suggested that his visit might have had the opposite effect, confirming the sailors in their belief that nothing was to be gained by staying at Yarmouth. The mutineers proceeded to the Nore, instead. Pasley had no more luck than Bligh.[209]

Pasley appears again in the narrative of the Nore when Nepean wrote to him on 11 June 1797 advising that 'no proposition short of unconditional surrender can be listened to by their Lordships'.[210] This letter ordered Pasley to South End in Essex to join with His Majesty's military forces to capture sailors trying to escape. One runaway was taken.

It was Pasley who had presided over the first court martial in the Nore series. That was the one that condemned Richard Parker to be hanged.[211] Parker had the misfortune to be elected to lead the mutiny already under way at the Nore, in the Sea Reach of the River Thames. After being sentenced, he expressed the wish that his life would be the only sacrifice.[212] This was not to be. Moreover, the King and Pasley shared the view that Parker's 'body should be hung in chains on the most conspicuous land in sight of the ships at the Nore'. This did not happen.[213]

"Nepean, in a letter, which does not read very pleasantly, egged him [Pasley] indecently on to convict the accused" Parker. After the trial, Pasley wrote to Nepean in these words, "My Dear Sir, The conviction of the villain Parker must have been so very dear to you at the Admiralty that the place and time of his execution might have been previously settled".[214]

Sir Erasmus Gower, in that part of the Thames known as Long Reach, had been ordered to prepare his 84-gun *Neptune* to attack the mutineer ships. His task was to organise a naval force, composed of 'middle class' volunteers backed by 'smug City merchants who could not conceive that horrible conditions could have produced the mutiny'. The East India Company put its ships and men wholly at the disposal of the Government'.[215]

Admiral Sir Richard King, was commanding officer at Plymouth at the time of the Spithead affair.[216]

Nepean, mentioned above, was secretary to the Board of Admiralty and in that capacity involved with courts martial. "Nepean himself never played a prominent part in the dealings with the mutineers; nor is there any indication of the influence which he may have had on the policy of the Admiralty. But he did a vast amount of work in connection with the Mutinies. From the number of " 'out-letters' which he wrote, and the number of 'in-letters' docketed by him", Gill judged that he must have been one of the busiest men in the country.[217]

Rodger described the secretary as the "link between the politicians of the Board and the clerks of the Admiralty office" reading and answering all the incoming correspondence "in their Lordships' name or his own. Only about one letter in five was actually referred to the Board, and the Secretary judged what should and should not be laid before it. He controlled the administration of the Office, and he acted as political manager for the First Lord, looking after the Admiralty's extensive patronage, and managing naval affairs for the ministry in the House of Commons, in which he invariably sat. It was a position of crucial importance, and it was almost unique in eighteenth-century politics".[218]

"This combination of the professional authority of long experience in the affairs of the Navy with considerable political consequence gave the secretaries of Admiralty a weight out of all proportion to the apparent importance of their office".[219]

Nepean was appointed secretary of the Admiralty in 1795, possibly through the influence of Sir John Jervis.[220] All owed their advance to powerful patrons, but the opinion of Jervis (St Vincent) was that "Nepean had made 'his way...by superior talents for business, unremitting diligence, and integrity'." Created a baronet in 1804 he was a lord of the Admiralty in 1804-06. Earlier, as under secretary of state in the Home Department, Nepean was concerned with arrangements for the First Fleet to New South Wales and the administration of the colony in its early years.

Chapter 6

WILLIAM REDFERN'S COURT MARTIAL

As mentioned in the preceding chapter, HMS *Neptune*, floating on the Thames at Greenhithe, up river from Tilbury Dock and Gravesend, provided a Royal Navy stage setting for the court martial of William Redfern.[1] Actors were the court members, senior naval officers, HMS the *Standard*'s Captain as prosecutor, and a number of the officers, all in court dress, and other ranks as witnesses, and of course the *Standard's* six prisoners - sailors, marines and one surgeon's mate.

Pause for a moment and hear Marc Baer speaking of *Theatre and Disorder in Late Georgian London.* "[T]he behaviour of English people in their disorders reflected the importance of both theatre and theatricality in British life".[2]

Greg Dening, from a study of *Passion, Power and Theatre on the Bounty*, had this to say. "What was remarkable at Nore was the form of their politics. The sailors showed that they knew that in the presentation of power the forecastle must be as dramaturgical as the quarterdeck. Alas, in the end, they were too innocent and too trusting in the 'gentlemen' of their institutions of discipline. They mistook the navy's notion of 'gentlemen' for that of the gentlemen who would honour responsibilities for their welfare. They believed their old metaphors of their captains as 'fathers'. Such innocence cost thirty-six of them their lives".[3]

This Court Martial - No Singular Affair.

Presiding was Sir Thomas Pasley Kt Baronet, Vice Admiral of the White and Commander in Chief of His Majesty's Ships and vessels in the River Thames. Other members were Commodore Sir Erasmus Gower Kt, and Captains John Markham, Edward Riou, Sir Francis Saforey Bart, and Richard King.[4]

The court proceeded to try John Burrows and Joseph Hudson (seamen), William Redfern (surgeon's mate), Thomas Lunniss alias Linnos (serjeant of marines), Bryan Finn alias Fenn and Joseph Glaves (privates, marines) being persons in and belonging to His Majesty's Fleet [the North Sea Squadron in particular].[5]

The Charges.

The charges levelled against the six *Standard* prisoners, collectively and individually were -

> "for making and endeavouring to make a Mutinous Assembly and Assemblies on board His Majesty's Ship the *Standard* and on board divers others of His Majesty's Ships and vessels... on 26th Day of May last and for several days afterwards and for concealing traiterous and mutinous words spoken to the prejudice of His Majesty's Government and for being present at a Mutiny without their using their utmost Endeavours to suppress the same and for behaving themselves with Contempt to their Superior Officers in the Execution of their Duty and for disobeying the lawful Commands of their Superior Officers and for any of the said offences committed on or after the 26th Day of May last". [6]

The King's Proclamation of 31 May 1797 (Appendix 8 in Dugan, 1966) is clearly visible in the above.[7]

The Minutes.

There are two preliminary sheets attached to the copy of the Minutes. The first is a cover note to Evan Nepean; the second is the title page, which lists the six *Standard* prisoners, William Redfern among them.

Page 1 of the minutes includes the hearing dates, the names of those present, and the Admiralty order for assembling a court Martial. This runs on to page 2 concluding with the names of the prisoners before the court and the charges against them. Leave-of-absence for Captains concludes this page and opens the third page which records a warrant for the appointment of the Judge Advocate, the taking of the appropriate oaths required by Act of Parliament relating to offences committed on or after the 26th day of May last [1797]. At that point, the witnesses were ordered to leave the court. The Judgement of the court took up the last three pages of the Minutes and documented the final day of the Proceedings, Friday August 25th, 1797. Before the verdicts were announced all counts were read relating to offences committed after the 26th Day of May last.

The *Minutes* provide a concise document, easy to follow. Parr prosecuted each of the six prisoners within the daily time frames but independently of each other. Their defence documents followed as attachments. After their presentation Parr concluded the prosecution case.[8]

Which prisoner was the focus of attention at any point is made clear by questions from the Prosecutor, the Court, and the prisoner.[9] The minuted sequence runs through Tuesday 22nd and Wednesday 23 August 1797.[10]

References to William Redfern have been extracted and a running record follows this paragraph. Critical examination of the prosecution case and of the defence will follow in due course.

Prosecutor Captain Parr Called Witnesses.

Hamilton FitzGerald.

Hamilton FitzGerald, midshipman[11], was sworn.[12] Captain Parr asked "Did anything pass between you and the prisoner Redfern during the mutiny?" To this Fitzgerald replied, "While we were at the Nore Mr Redfern told me he could get a case of Pistols and I advised him against it at this time". Fitzgerald, in answer to Redfern, said that he did not know of him ever using any arms. Later, the court (p.22) asked what had induced him to answer the prosecutor's question the way he had. He said that the finding of the pistols in 'Mr Redfern's clothes bag' had brought it to mind.

The court further questioned the witness, asking why Redfern wanted the arms and the place and the context of this conversation. Fitzgerald said they had often talked about the Mutiny, which "was always generally condemned by Mr Redfern and every other officer". The court was assured that Redfern's condemnation remained steady both before and after his talk about pistols. Fitzgerald, answering Redfern, said this conversation took place after the Officers were disarmed. The Prosecutor asked, for the second time, whether anything had passed between Mr Redfern and himself, or between the Prisoner and any other person, to lead him to speak to Mr Buller [Lieutenant]. Fitzgerald answered each question in the negative.[13]

(During the mutiny, Fitzgerald and Redfern were messmates. The Prosecutor, Capt. Parr, drew to the attention of the court (p 22) that on one occasion Redfern had accepted his invitation to dine with him [Capt. Parr]. Fitzgerald remembered that Redfern had dined with the Captain.)[14]

Nathaniel Dyer, Midshipman.

Nathaniel Dyer, Midshipman, was sworn (M 26).[15] The prosecutor asked if Redfern was confined with the petty Officers (p 27). Dyer believed not and remembered neither tarpaulins thrown over the grating nor Redfern asking "if they meant to smother us". Redfern's questions pointed to his own confinement. He asked Dyer if he remembered him "going up with a sentry" at Dyer's request, again implying that his movement was restricted. Dyer remembered his request but associated it with Redfern's freedom of movement. The court was told that although the Committee commanded the ship at that time, Dyer made no use of Redfern's name to go on deck. While the Officers were confined from about 3 o'clock one afternoon till about 9 or 10 the next morning, Redfern was free to go up and down and attended the sick without the surgeon.

Thomas Branston, the Pilot, was sworn. To the Prosecutor's question, he said he had been before the Committee of the *Standard* and had seen Sergeant Linnes and Redfern there, sitting at a table with Holdsworth. Redfern sought details from Branston who remembered he was sitting on the larboard side but was not doing anything. It was about 1 or 2 o'clock in the afternoon of 8th or 9th June. He was taken there by Wallace (p 31), but he didn't know why Redfern was there or whether he was still there when he left. He couldn't swear that Redfern was there when he produced the *Chart*.

The court wanted to know whether Redfern was there is his capacity as surgeon; had he any medicine, surgical instruments or plaisters with him and was Holdsworth in good health. Branston's answers denied Redfern any such medical reason for his presence.

Branston hadn't seen Redfern at the Committee before. He did not speak to Holdsworth and didn't appear to be like a Member of the Committee as he sat mute.

Redfern asked whether Branston had attended in fear and if he thought it would have been safe to refuse an order to attend or to leave. Branston wasn't too sure of his answers. Redfern also questioned Branston closely about his eyesight and why, being as close as six feet, he couldn't tell whether Redfern was there all the time or not. Branston explained that he "was not taking notice of the prisoner".

Lieutenant Delafons Returns.

Lieutenant Delafons[16] was called in again and asked by the Prosecutor if he had ever watched Redfern writing (p 38). On saying that he had, Delafons was shown a letter and asked: "Do you believe the letter produced to be his hand writing?" He replied, "I can't say it is. I have seen some of his writing and it is something like this". The Prosecutor came back, "Do you believe that it is or that it is not his handwriting?" "I can't say whether it is or is not". The question came for the third time. "Having seen Mr Redfern write do you believe that letter to be his hand writing?" Instead of an answer, the court was cleared (p 40). On resuming, Delafons was advised by the court that he wasn't swearing that it was the hand writing of the prisoner - "the question was whether from having seen the prisoner write he had formed a sufficient knowledge of his handwriting to be able to swear that he believed the paper produced to be his writing". On the question being put, the Prosecutor got the answer he sought, "Yes". [A copy of the letter was written into the *Minutes* (*Minutes* 39-40).][17]

The Redfern 'Letter' / 'Paper'.

Redfern questioned Delafons till the court adjourned to the next day [pp 39-45]. He asked how Delafons came to know about his handwriting and signature and whether he had knowledge of the alleged letter before its production in court. Delafons was close to Redfern while he was writing a prescription of about six to eight lines. He had also seen him copying something at the same time but had not paid such close attention. Delafons did not know the subject matter of this other writing.

Delafons denied, at first, any prior knowledge of the "letter" but then admitted that he had seen it. It was placed on a table with other items. He did not read it, simply looked at the name. He didn't say why he was shown the letter. He couldn't say that it was the same letter that was produced in court. Redfern asked if it was presented as "his letter". Delafons said that it was not particularly shown to him but to Mr Buller. He admitted to being asked questions concerning his knowledge of Redfern's handwriting. His reply at the time was that he had seen the prisoner write and thought he should know his handwriting or words to that effect. Delafons did not say that he believed this to be Redfern's handwriting, but he thought the writing like it and particularly the name.

Delafons had seen Redfern sign his name, *Wm Redfern*, after copying a prescription written in Latin. Redfern asked whether Delafons remembered sending such a prescription back to be translated. Delafons was positive that he was present when Redfern wrote the Latin copy. The court asked whether Delafons had seen Redfern's signature on the surgeon's mate's sick lists. Delafons said he had not (pp 43-4).

[The court met pursuant to Adjournment and was opened and the Prisoners brought in.][18]

Prosecutor Captain Parr Called Further Witnesses.

Mr Robert Kirkwood late surgeon of Standard.

Mr Robert Kirkwood late surgeon of the *Standard* was sworn (p 45). The Prosecutor asked if he had done the duty of Surgeon of the *Standard* during the Mutiny. Kirkwood said that "[a]bout a week after we arrived at the Nore I was told by the prisoner Mr Redfern the Surgeons Mate that the Ships Company had ordered him to do the duty of Surgeon and from that time I did not act as Surgeon although I still remained on board". Kirkwood said while Redfern had done the duty of Surgeon, "there was very little to do as most of the Sick were on Shore".

Captain Parr then asked Surgeon Kirkwood if he had seen Redfern in the act of writing (p.45) and was he acquainted with his handwriting. To the first question he answered "no" and to the second, "yes". At this point Redfern began a series of questions to Surgeon Kirkwood (p 46). What did he mean by Redfern "acting as Surgeon"? Doing the whole duty of Surgeon was Kirkwood's reply. Redfern asked if he did this to "displease" Kirkwood. To which Kirkwood replied that he didn't know "what was intended by it". Redfern suggested that he was following orders from the Ships Company and that Kirkwood had believed what Redfern told him. Kirkwood accepted that there were still some sick on board and a surgeon was needed. He also agreed that after he ceased to be Surgeon, Redfern had asked for his help, and he had given Redfern orders (p 47).

The Prosecutor asked if Kirkwood had "any reason afterwards to disbelieve that the Prisoner Mr Redfern had received his orders from the Ships Company". Kirkwood thought not (p 48), saying that Redfern had told him twice, first one night and again the following morning. Redfern also told him that the Ships Company would speak to Mr Kirkwood, but they never did.

The court then asked Kirkwood whether Redfern had shown "any reluctance in displacing" him. He replied that Redfern had "said he was sorry that they had done so, that it was not his wish, he did not want to be the Surgeon of the Ship".

Mr Patrick Conway, Purser of the Standard.

Mr Patrick Conway, Purser of the *Standard*, was sworn (p 48).[19] The Prosecutor asked: "Do you remember examining some papers in the Captain's Clerks office on board the *Standard*?" Conway answered: "Yes I do on the day the prisoners were sent on shore which I believe was the 14th of June". Conway said that the Letter was amongst them but he didn't know how the papers came to be there. He was ordered by Lieut Buller "to examine Mr Redfern's papers" which the Clerk produced.

Redfern found from his questions that there were several papers in the Clerk's Office and a separate bundle called "his papers". Conway examined all of Redfern's papers, some of which were printed but mostly written. He believed them to be Redfern's papers by seeing private letters addressed to him and by what Lieut Buller and the Clerk had said. Redfern asked whether "the letters addressed to [him would] satisfy you that the whole bundle was my papers?" To this Conway answered, "No not if I had not been told that they were the prisoners bundle of papers". The court asked: "Were there any papers in the bundle signed with the prisoners name besides the papers produced before the court?" Conway didn't recollect any (p 52).

Mr Archibald Ingram, and 'the Pistols'.

Mr Archibald Ingram, second master, was sworn (p 64).[20] The Prosecutor asked Ingram about pistols found when the prisoners were sent out of the *Standard* at Gravesend. Ingram said that two Ship's Pistols and pistol-ball Cartridges were found in Redfern's bag. Ingram said he saw them taken out of the bag by the Loblolly Boy. The bag was taken from the dispensary and opened in the Cockpit at the Corner of the medicine chest. The dispensary was assigned to Redfern. There he used to sit and keep medicines and other things. The Prosecutor was told that the bag was being searched at Redfern's request for shoes and boots. At the time the Prisoners were being sent out of the Ship (p 66).

Redfern asked Ingram if he had seen the bag taken out of the dispensary. Ingram only saw the man coming from the dispensary with the bag. Redfern also asked if the bag was locked or fastened. Ingram didn't know. He did know that the dispensary was large enough for one person to enter, sit down and close the door. He had been in it with another person but did not know how the Arms came to be in the bag.

The court had already asked if the dispensary was generally locked or open. It now appeared to follow up Redfern's leads. As the questions were numerous and sometimes repeated, both questions and answers have been separated and grouped as follows: "The dispensary", "what happened there", and "who owned the bag". [Questions F1-3 and Answers F1-3].

Thomas Cheeseman, Seaman.

Thomas Cheeseman, seaman on board the *Standard,* was sworn (p 72).[21] The Prosecutor asked if he had ever been before the Committee. He said that he had and had seen three of the prisoners there, including Redfern. Further questions revealed that he was uncertain when he first saw Redfern there but remembered it was in the forenoon. Cheeseman was sitting at the table but, the place being full of people, got up to make room for Redfern, and left.

Cheeseman answered Redfern's first questions by saying he had been present "different times" at the Committee, knew its members but had never heard of Redfern being one.[22] He said he was present when Branston discussed the [Thames] chart and thought Redfern was there. He couldn't swear to it but thought this was the second time he had seen Redfern at the Committee. He was uncertain about who else was there.

The court asked Cheeseman when he first saw Redfern in the Committee. He thought it was soon after we came to the Nore but once again could not remember whether it was before they moved to the mouth of the river. "What was passing at the Committee when Mr Redfern came in?" Cheeseman thought it was the matter of Redfern being sent for to know if he was willing to act as Surgeon as Holdsworth had proposed. The court asked what objection the people had to the Surgeon and was told he did not properly attend the sick and they would sooner have Mr Redfern. The court asked, "Do you mean positively to say that Mr Redfern did not use to frequent the Committee". Cheeseman answered, "I never saw him but as I have before mentioned".

The attention of the court now moved to the consideration of a letter, alleged to have been written by Redfern, and previously read into the court record. Cheeseman's answers to a long series of questions provided the following summary [pp 74-6].

He said, "A letter from Redfern was read on the forecastle I think in the evening of the same day I saw him in the Committee. It was read to the whole Ship's Company but I don't remember who read it. It could have been read in Committee but not to my knowledge". Redfern said, "He was agreeable as it were to aid and assist during the time of the mutiny in serving the Sick". Cheeseman said he could read but was not closer than three or four yards to the person reading the letter. He was never in Committee when a letter was received from Redfern. No, he didn't know of another letter. He gave the same answer when the question was rephrased. When asked had he ever seen the letter in the Committee afterwards he replied, "I might but I never read it" nor any part of it. No, he could not remember anything else in the letter. He then restated his earlier answer as to what Redfern had said. "Whatever was to happen in the Ship he was agreeable to serve in it as far as serving the Sick and Wounded". Cheeseman believed the letter was addressed to the Committee but couldn't tell who received it. On being asked who generally received them, Cheeseman said, "I can't tell unless it might be the Captain of the Ship". To the court's question, "Who do you mean?" Cheeseman replied, "Holdsworth".

The court asked a few final questions about attendance at Committee Meetings. Due to falling attendance it was decided to beat a drum as a reminder. "At any times when the Drum beat did you see Redfern there?" Cheeseman: "I can't say that I ever did". "Did then more people meet there than the Committee?" Cheeseman: "Yes, more people used to come there".

The Prosecution closed.

Additional to the above précis.

As only the Tuesday and Wednesday sittings of the court martial have been included it is fair to ask what happened on Thursday. On that day the court heard the prisoners' defence submissions and the witnesses, if any, whom they called.

While this will be considered a little later, it too will reflect the general form of the prosecution's plan of attack on Redfern and the nature of Redfern's response through his Counsel.

Defence in Law, is the opposing or denial of the truth or validity of the prosecutor's complaint. It is not constrained to go further. The defendant's written statement is a pleading of his case [S.O.E.D.].

To the extent to which the *Minutes* reflect these opinions, they cannot provide a rounded and even-handed account of Redfern's involvement in the *Mutiny* that the biographer might desire.

Nor can any interpretation of Redfern's involvement in the Nore Mutiny be made in the light of his experience before joining the Navy. That period of his life is virtually unknown.

Similarly, it would be unwise to read back, later understandings of Redfern into that period of his life. Might not such post-mutiny traits have developed as a result of the mutiny and its aftermath?

From introduction, this account turns now to analysis.

The Prosecution Case Against William Redfern.

While the charges remain unchanged, as set down by the Court, what comes to light from the above précis is a co-ordinated plan of attack by the prosecution. Five matters were of special interest to them.

In order of introduction these focussed on one of the following-

a. A Brace of Pistols,

b. Redfern's "freedom of movement",

c. his being "seen at the Committee",

d. his "acting as Surgeon", and

e. 'the letter in question'.

William Redfern was constrained to take issue with each of these matters through his cross-examination of witnesses, and with the help of his Counsel.[23]

Whether from studying the original text or the précis it becomes clear that the first four matters received less attention than the fifth.

A Brace of Pistols

Mr Hamilton Fitzgerald, midshipman of the Standard, told how Redfern had raised the matter of getting a case of pistols. This was after the officers had been disarmed. Fitzgerald assumed that the pistols would have come from mutineer sources and advised Redfern against the idea. (M17-23.)

A brace of pistols, was allegedly found in a bag supposed to belong to Redfern. The Prosecution case reduced to this. The mutineers carried pistols after the mutiny in the North Sea Fleet. Redfern had pistols. Therefore Redfern was a mutineer.

Redfern did not deny his interest in a brace of pistols. He wanted them for his own safety aboard ship, and ashore, if he managed to escape. Rather than a wholehearted support of the mutineers - necessary if he was to acquire pistols from them - he went in fear of them.

Redfern did not mention having acquired pistols. One witness said he had never known Redfern to fire a pistol.

Under arrest, and preparing to leave *Standard,* Redfern sent a loblolly boy for his boots and shoes.[24] This resulted in a brace of pistols being found, supposedly in Redfern's bag.

Redfern argued that there was no proof that they came from his bag and engaged in a lively cross-examination of witnesses over the pistols.

Mr Hamilton Fitzgerald, a midshipman of the *Standard,* told how Redfern had raised the matter of getting a case of pistols. This was after the officers had been disarmed. Fitzgerald assumed that the pistols would have come from mutineer sources and advised Redfern against the idea. Fitzgerald held firmly to the view that Redfern condemned the mutiny.[25]

Captain Parr obtained from his witness, Mr Archibald Ingram, second master, an apparently clear account of the discovery by the loblolly boy of a case of pistols and ammunition in Mr Redfern's bag. But, on Redfern's first question, Ingram couldn't "exactly" say whether the bag was taken out of the Dispensary.

The court followed Redfern's lead with a series of questions that appeared to erode the prosecution case. Ingram did not know whether the dispensary was generally locked, or open, or whether the door of the Surgeon's room was open at the time.

He was uncertain of the lighting as well, and admitted that although close to the scene it was the discovery of the pistols that really focussed his attention.

Finally, Ingram could provide no proof of the ownership of the bag but thought it went in the boat to Mr Redfern.[26]

Redfern's "Freedom of Movement".

Redfern's claim that he was put under constraint with the other petty officers was not supported by Mr Nathaniel Dyer, midshipman of HMS Standard (M23-38).

The Prosecution held that from the start of the mutiny Redfern had not been constrained like the officers. The mutineers had that freedom. Therefore Redfern was a mutineer.

Redfern claimed that he had been put under constraint with the officers. He had complained at the time about being smothered [more fear than reality]. His subsequent freedom of movement followed solely from his professional duties as acting Surgeon.

Mr Nathaniel Dyer, another midshipman of the *Standard*, contradicted Redfern's claim that he was put under constraint with the other petty officers.[27]

His Being "Seen at the Committee".

Redfern did act as surgeon but it was not in that capacity that he was present in the committee room of the mutineers according to Thomas Branston, the pilot. On the other hand the latter's evidence did not support the idea that Redfern was a committeeman (M23-38).

"Being seen at the Committee" was considered by the Prosecution, to be proof that Redfern was one of, or at least one with, the Mutineers.

Redfern argued that he was at the committee because he had been ordered to attend by the mutineers. He was afraid to disregard such an order. He was there to be informed that he was to do the duty of surgeon. One witness confirmed that Redfern sat "mute" and didn't behave like a committeeman.

This same witness said he could be certain of Redfern being at the committee once. He may have attended twice but he was not a committeeman.

On being questioned by Redfern, Cheeseman admitted that he himself had been at the committee several times but had not heard of Redfern being a member.

To the court's questions, Cheeseman said Redfern was at one committee meeting by command to hear a request for him to take over as surgeon, as Holdsworth had suggested, because Redfern was the preferred surgeon.

On the second occasion Thomas Branston, the Pilot, had been present but Cheeseman left and didn't know what took place.

On again being asked whether Redfern was "a frequenter of the committee", Cheeseman replied, "I never saw him there more than twice and am not quite certain as to the second time".[28]

His "Acting as Surgeon".

Redfern did act as surgeon but it was not in that capacity that he was present in the committee (M23-38).

The Prosecution called witnesses to confirm, that Redfern had acted as surgeon. This was the fourth targeted offence.

Redfern did not deny it, but said that he had not wanted to be surgeon. He accepted for the same reason that the surgeon had stepped aside when ordered by the mutineers. It was to calm the people and to reduce disturbances.

[Redfern was aware of a potentially explosive situation among the people. Internal and external evidence confirmed this position.]

While Redfern did act as surgeon, it was not in that capacity that he was present in the committee room of the mutineers, according to Branston.[29] A member of the court had specifically asked whether Redfern had plaisters or other evidence to show he was there to treat a patient.

From the *Minutes* it is known that Redfern alleged that he had been ordered by the ship's company to take over as surgeon about a week after coming to the Nore. Mr Robert Kirkwood, late surgeon of the *Standard*, had accepted Redfern's word that the mutineers wanted him to cease doing that work. Kirkwood was not told to cease work by the mutineers directly.

While most of the sick had gone ashore [at Yarmouth] there was still a need for a surgeon. Redfern had done the full duty as surgeon but was open to Mr Kirkwood's advice and had received an order from him during the time he was in charge.

The court understood from Mr Kirkwood that Redfern had shown reluctance in taking over his job.[30]

'The Letter in Question'.

In the case of each of the prosecution's first four matters of interest there was little disagreement during the proceedings about what was meant by the words - "a brace of pistols", "freedom of movement", "seen at the Committee", or "acting as Surgeon". The evidence for this opinion is in the minutes, and in the discussion above.

On the contrary, meaning is central to the disagreement between the prosecution and the defence in the case of the final matter of interest. What the prosecution called 'a letter' was 'a paper' to the defence. But as it turned out there was a further variation.

The prosecution case was that a letter was found on Redfern when he was arrested. It was their trump card. It is no wonder that Captain Parr, the Prosecutor, had it read into the *Minutes*.

To Parr, the first paragraph has the hallmark of a friendly letter from a fellow mutineer to the ship's committee of management. Words such as "concordance", "frankness", "warmest", and "gratitude" fit well with a letter from one adopted as "a brother in the Cause".

The next four lines help confirm the author as one with some insight into medical practice, though, in no way necessarily restricted to surgeons of ships. To the prosecution, however, it would have pointed to Redfern.

Who, more than Redfern, would want to keep his involvement a secret? This third paragraph makes the reason quite clear.

After due consideration, he allowed his name and opinion to be used by the committee.

To cap it all, he promised the mutineers that he would stay with the ship no matter what happened. With talk of sailing to France this was the most damning statement of them all.

Captain Parr felt confident that "the letter in question" would serve his case well, but he was not over confident. He continued to examine witnesses on the subject. The handwriting, its signature, its being read to the people, what it was heard to contain, each came under scrutiny.

The Prosecutor aimed to prove that the letter Redfern had sent to the Committee and the one found when he was arrested, were one and the same, and by Redfern's own hand.

Witnesses called to throw light on this matter.

Mr Patrick Conway, the purser of the *Standard*, examined a bundle of papers that had been pointed out to him as belonging to Redfern. While some were addressed to Redfern these did not of themselves prove that all the papers belonged to him. Some were printed but most were in long hand. The only one supposed to exhibit Redfern's signature was that produced in court.[31]

Cheeseman had seen and heard a letter read at the forecastle to the whole ship's company. He had not read it himself. He knew of only one letter, and that expressed Redfern's agreement to serve the sick and wounded during the time of the mutiny. He was not aware of anything else in the letter.[32]

Redfern's handwriting next came under scrutiny. Lieutenant Delafons could not say whether it was Redfern's handwriting on the paper he was shown. The Prosecutor repeated his question but Delafons gave the same answer.

After Captain Parr asked the question for the third time the court was closed before Delafons could answer. Upon resuming, the court ruled that Delafons need only "swear that he believed the paper produced to be his writing". Delafons then replied in the affirmative, giving Captain Parr the answer he sought.

Redfern Cross-examined a Witness.

Taking advantage of his right to cross-examine witnesses, Redfern questioned Delafons on the basis of his knowledge. Delafons had closely watched Redfern writing a prescription of six to eight lines in length, and less attentively to some other writing, on the same occasion.

Of the letter itself, Delafons at first denied any prior knowledge, then admitted having been shown it, or one like it. At the time he had been asked about his ability to recognise Redfern's writing.

He was unclear about his precise answer but said, without actually reading the letter, he thought the writing like Redfern's and particularly the name. Taking him to mean his signature, Redfern found Delafons's knowledge of it to be restricted to the writing of the one prescription. This opinion was strengthened when the court discovered that sick lists signed by Redfern had not been sighted by Delafons.[33]

Testing the Sensitivity of the Court.

Redfern remained silent when witnesses spoke of a letter, attributed to him, that only promised his help to the sick and wounded, during the mutiny. This was in accord with the Defence strategy to accept such a letter, but to attack references to the Prosecution's letter, which had much wider implications.

Redfern cross-examined vigorously in attempting to undermine evidence relating to his handwriting. It was Captain Parr's persistent questioning of Lieutenant Delafons on this subject that led to a sudden closure of the court, mentioned in passing, above.

As Redfern had it, an opportunity presented itself when "Captain Parr strangely eager to convict [him] if possible, pushe[d] a middle question about "belief" [w]hen a member of the court" interjected in a manner critical of the Prosecutor. Redfern's counsel prompted Redfern to make an objection, which had the dramatic effect of closing the court.

Ebullient behaviour, but counterproductive as it turned out, since the court resumed its sitting with a ruling inimical to Redfern. It was no longer necessary to *swear* that it was Redfern's writing. A witness needed only to *believe* it to be so.

Redfern explained "this interval [as] most unfortunate" for him. It "seems to have operated like a charm upon the intellect of the witness", who changed his mind about the signature, saying it was his belief that it had been written by me.

Redfern's Defence Submission.

This discussion will now turn from the general *Minutes* as presented in the *précis* for Tuesday and Wednesday of the court martial to the defence submissions of Thursday, 24th August, 1797. The court had called for these individual submissions. Redfern's twenty page *Defence Submission* may be contrasted with eleven pages in all, for the five other prisoners.

It is not known what Redfern contributed to his defence submission separately from his counsel.[34] The opening paragraph of his "Introduction"[35] is submissive, bowing to the Military Profession in the hope of an "impartial" and "indulgent hearing". He wished some allowance to be made for "uninstructed youth, imperfect reason and total inexperience in Naval Affairs".

"He freely consented to die", he said, "if he had deliberately excited Mutiny".

Redfern was persuaded that the court "will discriminate infirmity from bad intention" in the circumstances he illustrated (para.3). The "propriety of lenient discrimination" by the court, followed (para.4).

With the mutineers in control of the ship the situation altered. Officers knew "that dignity must stoop and authority bend" to "soothe and palliate the movers of sedition". They exercised discretion (para.5). This approach prevented the excess of violence (para.6).

Expressed in another way, Navy orders and articles are primarily concerned with the prevention of mutiny. After the mutiny, with the mutineers in charge of the ship, the situation had changed (para.7). Some mitigation was then appropriate.

Redfern, in the remaining paragraphs of his "Introduction", contemplated his possible guilt and punishment. "Indiscriminating severity" is not appropriate to his conduct, "in a season of dread and difficulty", even if it was not precisely according to the *Articles.*

If he had been forced to choose between "deceiving or suffering", Redfern must have been on the horns of a dilemma He also admitted to "unguarded and doubtful expressions", in the main unproved, which may have escaped him.

In the final paragraph appears the germ of the idea, taken up by the court, that Redfern's "profession...will suggest a general reason..." why he, "alone of all the Gentlemen on board should have any connection with the Mutineers".

"The prisoner William Redfern being called upon delivered in the following defence which was read by his counsel".

'Introduction' (in part - first statement).

"Sensible of the important and awful situation in which I am produced before this honourable court it is my wish to avoid every thing which might be deemed in the least degree accrimonious [sic] or offensive..".

Defence in Reply to the Prosecution's Matters of Interest.

Counsel, after reading the *Introduction,* in full, moved to consider Mr Fitzgerald.[36] He was described as more adverse to the prosecution since he maintained that Redfern condemned the mutiny. This freed the defence to concentrate on other specific targets. Counsel claimed the pistols were not intended to support the mutiny and Redfern's freedom of movement was due to his acting as surgeon.

Being 'seen at the Committee'.

The pilot, Thomas Branscombe, was able to confirm that Redfern was present at the committee on one day that he attended. Although quite close to him, Branscombe took little notice of Redfern but did remember that he sat in silence, i.e. was taking no part in the discussion. Counsel added the following:

"When this witness said I neither did or said any thing in the Committee Captain Parr ingeniously enough endeavoured to turn this against me by saying he would charge me for doing nothing to repress the Mutiny".[37]

This is Redfern reporting to his Counsel.[38] His meeting with Parr would have been before the trial started. The notion of 'repressing mutiny' was the key idea in the King's Proclamation of 31st May, where people were "to use their utmost endeavours, according to law, to suppress all such mutinous and treasonable proceedings".

The prosecution's evidence showed Redfern at the Committee and at a time when the matter of escaping from the Thames was under discussion with the pilot, Thomas Branscombe.[39] This I assume was Parr's allusion. It was a serious matter not brought out in the evidence against Redfern but in associated parts of the prosecution of the other five prisoners.

If the beacons had already been removed, Branscombe would have advised against any such attempt. Redfern would have nothing to add to such a decision. On the other hand, if escape was still possible, the idea of going over to the French could well have been on the agenda. Redfern's silence could have been regarded as a serious matter by the prosecutor. The words in the Redfern letter, "let the Ship go where she will", left it open to such interpretations as escaping from the Thames, and going over to the French.

The letter in question.

Six of the twenty pages of Redfern's defence statement were devoted to Lieutenant Delafons who had caused some concern. This has already been mentioned but will be discussed again.

Redfern, through his counsel, begged the court that his remarks might not prejudice the court against him but he was constrained by endeavouring to save his own life to make remarks painful to himself and apparently disrespectful to this witness.

Lieutenant Delafons first considered the handwriting on the "paper in question" to be like Redfern's but could not swear whether it was or not. Following the clearing of the court, he changed his mind.

Redfern then questioned the grounds for this decision by Delafons whose observation of him while writing was far too brief for him to be able to identify his writing style. This would be particularly so for Delafons with Redfern writing in Latin, a language foreign to him. Although Delafons alleged he had watched Redfern twice he only gave evidence that related to this one occasion.

Redfern made it clear that physicians simply initialled their prescriptions, so Delafons could not have seen Redfern use his full signature. Again, to sign a copy of someone else's prescription was 'unusual, unprofessional and even dishonest'.

Under these circumstances Redfern would not have signed "Wm Redfern", the signature supposed to have been on "the paper in question", according to Delafons, and neither would Delafons have seen him sign that way.

The letter in question and the closure of the Court.

The closure of the court was not in the prepared "script". It was unforeseen by the prosecution. Fresh and unexpected, its impact was compounded. While it enlivened the proceedings it called into question the official court record of events. Details are known only from this defence submission.

Captain Parr's persistent questioning invited an intervention from an unnamed member of the court, who exclaimed:

"Lieutenant Delafons I am sure does not appear to prevaricate you may ask him as many questions as you please Captain Parr but he cannot consistently answer otherwise than that which he has already said upon his oath that he is not able to tell whether the letter in question is Mr Redfern's writing or not".

Redfern's counsel seized upon this implied criticism from the court as the opportune moment to attack. To this end he sparked Redfern to rise and object, which he did. This was instantly repelled and the court ordered to be cleared.

Redfern expressed himself wholly ignorant of the reasons for clearing the court but had no doubt that the interval was most unfortunate for him as it seems to have operated like a charm upon the intellect of the witness,

"What before was dark is suddenly and surprisingly illuminated what hitherto waxed low and weak is wonderfully raised and supported my handwriting which before he could not ascertain he is at once a perfect judge of and without any reserve or hesitation he avers the paper in question to be so".

Delafons was advised by the court, after the hearing resumed, that he wasn't swearing that it was the handwriting of the prisoner - "the question was whether from having seen the prisoner write he had formed a sufficient knowledge of his handwriting to be able to swear that he believed the paper produced to be his writing". It was then that Delafons changed his mind to Redfern's regret and the parosecutor's satisfaction.

More may be read from the defence submission about Redfern's "objection". Consider the following: "Here with all submission and due deference [sic] to the court I must venture to say that I am much surprised and hurt to be thought troublesome or impertinent in my question as to the difference between a court Martial and the old Bailey".

So that is what stirred the court. But, there was more: "If more indulgence is shewn to a prisoner at the old Bailey than at the Court Martial, I would wish to have been tried there".

Redfern's objection, prompted as it was by his counsel, was a substantial one, calling into question important differences between a court Martial and the old Bailey in the indulgence shown to prisoners.

The clearing of the court and reprimand showed that the court was not impressed, certainly not as counsel might have hoped. Wiser counsel made amends for Redfern's outburst by having him express his belief that "[he was] however by no means dissatisfied with [his] present judges".

Redfern's counsel, however, in advising him to rise when he did, appears to have doubly erred. That advice had the unintended consequences of offending the court, and easing the Prosecution's task. Perhaps, though, counsel and Redfern had achieved what they had set out to do, to place an indelible stain upon the fabric of the court. Or was there another reason?

An Echo from Bligh's Bounty Court Martial.

One might well ask "Who was Redfern's counsel?" for Greg Dening has something interesting and relevant here to say about a similar occurrence at Bligh's *Bounty* court martial. Muspratt's defending lawyer exploited an opportunity "to show that in a matter of life and death there was a serious discrepancy between civil and military law".

Sir Thomas Pasley, now presiding, had been a Member of that *Bounty* court martial. Furthermore, "[w]hile the others were executed, Muspratt was freed with an admonition about his future conduct".

Pasley had also presided over the first court martial in the Nore series that had condemned Richard Parker to be hanged. In turn, Parker found his way (p.539) into Ala Alryyes' discussion of *Court Martial Narratives in the eighteenth century*; Described as 'a little noticed eighteenth-century genre...worth reading and analysing for the insights it offers into how geographic realities, literary styles and rhetorical practices inflected representations of the empire and its sorrows'.[40]

Alryyes was concerned with 'crafted literary texts, in which a narrator/editor claims to incorporate a court-martial's minutes'. Such court martial narratives 'reveal the ubiquity of war in a century whose major literary genre, the novel, under-represents the period's ever-present military strife. Like poetry, but unlike the novel, [such narratives] portray aristocratic passions and heroic virtues'.[41]

But, at a point where Redfern and Counsel were contrasting 'old Bailey' with 'Court Martial', 'civil' with 'military law', was Alryyes forthcoming? Yes. Under a heading, 'Military Law and History' (and, indirectly by quoting one of the court martial editors) appear 'two experts on military law [Tytler, and Stephen Payne Adye] who both open their treatises with an attempt to defend military law from attacks by famed British civil jurists. One of these authorities, Alexander Tytler,[42] is aware of the tenuous legal status of military 'law'. Claiming that 'the Military Law has never been systematically treated,' Tytler justifies his treatise further with the observation that 'in these latter years...Britain has become an armed nation. The Military Law has obtained a more extensive field of operation than at any former period of the national annals'.

Tytler opposed his view of military law as 'part of the law of the land' to Sir William Blackstone's hostile notions that 'Martial Law...built upon no settled principles... entirely arbitrary in its decisions, is...in truth and reality no law'. Tytler stressed the occasional necessity of the harsher measures of 'Martial Law', for example 'in times of actual rebellion, Martial Law and the mode of summary trial by courts-martial, is enacted for a limited time, either over a part or a whole of the kingdom'.

Just as the *Mutiny Act*, 'War's child, takes after the father', quoting Merman Melville, following Alryyes, so may it be argued do *Martial Law*, and *Court Martial*. Civil conciliation resolved the Spithead Fleet Mutiny peacefully. Yet Military Law, in courts martial, bloodied the aftermath of the Nore Fleet Mutiny, as if it had been a foreign engagement. How necessary was that?[43]

The paper in question.

This was the one and only time that legal precedent was mentioned in argument at the court martial. Counsel for Redfern cited the case of Algernon Sidney as a significant moderator on the court's decision making on "the letter in question". The relevance to the case may be found in Sidney's "Speech on the Scaffold", delivered to the sheriff, December 7th 1683, wherein these words appear - "[T]he whole matter is reduced to the papers said to be found in my closet by the king's officers, without any proof of their being written by me, than what is taken from suppositions upon the similitude of a <u>hand</u> that is easily counterfeited, and which hath been lately declared...to be no lawful evidence in criminal causes. But if I had been seen to write them, the matter would not be much altered. They plainly appear to relate unto a large treatise written long since in answer to Filmer's book".[44]

J.P.Kenyon considered it to be "strange that we do not know who originated and conducted this skilful campaign against the Whigs", of whom Sidney was one.[45]

Since that time, the defence argued, the decision had been "roundly condemned".[46] Adam Smith was among those who did, publishing a reference as late as 1790. "The heroes of ancient and modern history [including Algernon Sidney], who are remembered with the most peculiar favour and affection, are, many of them, those who, in the cause of truth, liberty, and justice, have perished upon the scaffold, and who behaved there with that ease and dignity which became them".[47]

Redfern's question to the court was "What kind of a mutiny can a man make by carrying a piece of paper concealed about his cloaths [sic]".

Redfern denied that a paper directed to nobody and shown to nobody by himself could provide evidence of mutiny. Nevertheless, it was "the paper found upon him".

Having made clear where "the paper" came from, Redfern pointed out to the prosecution that it still had to prove that he wrote it and having written it published it abroad to encourage the Mutineers. He said that they had proved neither. Mr Conway proved nothing against him. Saying a paper was his was not proving it to be so. Redfern concluded that Mr Kirkwood, the ship's surgeon, was not examined as to the paper found upon him, perhaps because

Redfern cut in with his own questions, and from what appeared to pass in court confidence was no longer placed in it.

Surgeon Kirkwood's evidence.

Redfern considered Mr Kirkwood's evidence was more favourable to himself than he ever expected. Kirkwood admitted that he had done the duty of surgeon during the Mutiny until Redfern told him that he had been ordered by the Ships company to take over. He was first told in the evening and again the next morning whereupon he ceased to do the Surgeon's duty leaving that department wholly to Redfern. There were some sick on board and it was proper that they be attended.

Mr Kirkwood allowed that Redfern declared himself to be sorry to have displaced him and that it was not his wish to do so. Mr Kirkwood stood down from his position as Surgeon and Redfern took over that position on an order from the Ship's company.

Redfern suggested, in effect, that his and the surgeon's actions were symmetrical. Kirkwood was ordered by the Mutineers to vacate his position as surgeon. Redfern was ordered by the same Mutineers to act as surgeon. Each responded in a way that was more likely to calm than arouse the mutineers.

'A brace of pistols', again.

Redfern then turned to Mr Ingram's evidence. When strained to the utmost it can prove no more that this, a Brace of the Ship's pistols unloaded, with some a[m]munition, were taken out of a certain Bag supposed but not proved to be his. When and how they came into this bag is not attempted to be shown nor has a word been said as to his actually having or using any arms at any time during the Mutiny. If the evidence were supported it would go to establish an embezzlement of the Ships Stores with which he had not been charged. Redfern said it certainly proved nothing on any substantial part of his charge. Noting that the fact of the pistols being in his possession had not been proved he didn't need to say or prove a syllable about them. (See the lengthy cross examination at M64-68).

Being 'seen at the Committee'.

Thomas Cheeseman's evidence is followed [as in my summary]. Cheeseman saw Redfern at the Committee once before the *Standard* went to the other side of the River. He gave up his seat and left so could not say whether Redfern sat down or not. On his crossexamination he made it clear that he went often to the Committee. He never knew or heard that Redfern was a Committeeman. He was hesitant about saying Redfern was there when the Chart was discussed. This witness was very strictly examined by the court, cautioned to speak the truth and reminded that he had been at this Bar before. He could not say whether the time he first saw Redfern there was before or after the *Standard* came to the Nore. (See Dugan, p.134, below).

That 'letter' again.

Cheeseman said Redfern was sent for to see if he would act as Surgeon, a suggestion made at the forecastle because the Ships company objected to Mr Kirkwood. Redfern said this confirmed the truth of what he had told Mr Kirkwood and that he deserved the credit which he says he gave to me. Cheeseman said he saw a letter read at the forecastle. The subject of it was that Redfern informed the Ships company that he would continue to attend the sick and would while affairs were unsettled.

Redfern argued that there was no satisfactory evidence that the letter read at the forecastle was very different from the contents of the paper produced in court. Nothing about being a Brother in the cause or in the least degree of an inflamatory [sic] nature or tendency but a simple assurance that I would comply with their order and attend the sick as they desired till matters became composed and restored to their former course. He could not tell the contents from hearing only. He had not heard Redfern read a letter to the Committee nor had any other letter of his been read there. As attendance fell off a drum beat was used to call Committee men. This procedure was adopted after the letter was written. After the drum beat summons Cheeseman had never seen Redfern at the Committee. This was proof that Redfern was not a committee man. As non members also assembled on the drum his absence was further proof of his disinclination to attend.

Redfern's prayer to conclude his submission.

Redfern would, "Trouble the court with few witnesses because so much is proved in my favour by the prosecution witnesses neither intended nor inclined, except by the love of truth or dread of perjury, to advance anything tending to my acquittal or exculpation".

Redfern thanked the court for this Indulgence. "He committed his life into their hands as to Gentlemen duly alive to the impressions of and the suggestions of Conscience to the value of an unimpeachable character and the importance of religion.

"May the author and upholder of everlasting truth justice and mercy who hath made us all ameanable[sic] to his unerring tribunal direct you in this awful moment that by his infinite rectitude and goodness you may be preserved from error and I from undeserved Death".

Redfern's Witnesses.

Doing the Surgeon's Work.

Arthur McLoughlan, Seaman of the *Standard,* sworn, and in answer to Redfern's questions recalled his acting as Surgeon and gave a fresh account of the meeting on the forecastle.

There stood William Wallace and William Holdsworth abaft the foremast. They said that they had heard grumbling against Mr Kirkwood. The people with one voice called for him to be turned on shore. Bill Holdsworth asked if they had any objection to Mr Redfern doing the duty as surgeon. They all said 'no' that he had behaved very well to the sick since he had been aboard. On Bill Holdsworth saying that he didn't know whether Redfern would do it the people said they would make him.[48]

Mr Hamilton Fitzgerald was asked by Redfern if he had ever been in the dispensary with him particularly when an order came from the Committee for Redfern to attend. Fitzgerald confirmed that Redfern, as a result, left the dispensary, returning within about ten minutes. Fitzgerald also agreed with Redfern that Mr Kirkwood was there at the time and the two talked together. Fitzgerald could not remember the conversation but agreed that Redfern had told him the Ships company wished him to do the duty as Surgeon.

James Carr, Seaman of the *Standard,* sworn, said that he had heard Holdsworth tell Redfern that he must act as Surgeon. This took place while Redfern was on his way down to the cockpit and Holdsworth to the lower gun deck to stop the people from firing. It was the day the *Repulse* went away.

The Prosecutor asked, "Did you understand that Mr Redfern did the duty as Surgeon before the *Repulse* went in?" Carr couldn't say. To his mind Redfern never could do it better as a Surgeon than he formerly had done as a Surgeons Mate. Therefore there was no practical difference to mark the change.

Lancelot Nicholson, Seaman of the *Standard,* sworn, agreed with Redfern that he was with him, Mr Kirkwood and a number of sick during the Mutiny while the Ship was at the Nore. Mr Kirkwood had said that he had orders to do no more duty as Surgeon. Mr Redfern told him not to think that he was trying to get preferment, he had not had a hand in it and was obliged to do it by the consent of the Ships company. "Consent", asked Redfern, "or 'by order' of the Ships company?" "To the best of my understanding it was consent," replied Nicholson.[49]

At this point Redfern asked if he had said anything to Nicholson about a Surgeon's warrant or a sum of money. Nicholson heard Redfern say that he had written for his discharge twice and had offered a sum of money to get clear of the service. In answering the court, Nicholson said the Ships company obliged Redfern to do it, that it was to Mr Kirkwood he was talking about his discharge, etc. Because he had been ill for about three months he knew nothing of the meeting on the forecastle or of the letter. Neither was he able to fix the time of the cockpit conversation by reference to specific ship movements.

Freedom of movement.

To a further question about Redfern's freedom of movement compared to the other petty Officers, Fitzgerald replied that "[h]e never appeared to me to be under confinement".

Redfern then asked whether Mr Kirkwood was confined during the Mutiny. Fitzgerald understood that all the Ward Room Officers were confined, including Mr Kirkwood for eight and forty hours at the most. He did not know whether Mr Kirkwood ever slept out of his cabin during the mutiny.

The Letter.

To the Prosecutor, McLoughlan replied that Holdsworth hadn't given an answer for a day or two and then a Letter was read on the forecastle. The letter was said to be from Mr Redfern saying that he would do as much as he could to serve the sick. That was all he could remember. Seeking further details the Prosecutor asked for any particular word at the conclusion, or the first words. McLoughlan couldn't remember.

The court followed up the Prosecutor's questions to Fitzgerald on Redfern's handwriting. Fitzgerald, Redfern's messmate during the Mutiny repeated his answers. He had "very frequently" seen Redfern writing. Carefully the court explained its next question. "You will observe that it is not necessary to swear that the paper produced is the hand writing of the Prisoner but the question is whether from having seen the prisoner write you have formed a sufficient knowledge of his hand writing to enable you to swear that you believe it to be so". Fitzgerald replied - "I believe it is".

Delafons' evidence of Redfern's writing was limited to a single observation. It didn't amount to much. The Defence made much of this to the point of saying that the "paper in question" was no longer of importance. On the contrary if the charge of "concealing traiterous and mutinous words spoken to the prejudice of His Majesty's Government" applied to Redfern it is not likely that the opportunity presented by Fitzgerald's presence in court would be missed. It wasn't. Prosecutor Parr must have been particularly pleased at the turn of events especially as Redfern had referred to Fitzgerald, originally called by the Prosecution, as more adverse to their case than his.

The Defence of the prisoner William Redfern closed.

The Judgement.

The Judgement of the court occupies the last three pages of the Minutes and documented the final day, Friday August 25th. Before the verdicts were announced all seven counts were read relating to offences committed after the 26th Day of May last [1797]. These appear early in this chapter.

"[H]aving examined the Evidence produced on the Part of the Prosecution and on the Part of the Prisoners respectively and having heard what the Prisoners had severally to offer in their Defence and having very maturely and deliberately considered the whole, The court is of the opinion that the charges have been proved against [four, including] William Redfern".

[The court] "therefore adjudged the four [including William Redfern] to suffer Death by being hanged by the Neck until they be dead".

The pattern of final arrangements for the hangings was then set down. Only at this point was it announced that first, one of the condemned, and then another, Redfern, was to be recommended for commutation.

"And with respect to the Prisoner William Redfern the court in Consideration that the Exercise of his profession in the Situation in which he was required to act by the Mutineers might be the means of leading him into his Connection with them does therefore recommend his Case likewise to His Majesty's Consideration for a Commutation of his Punishment".

Twenty years later - Commissioner J.T. Bigge.

In a letter to Commissioner Bigge on 5 February 1821,[50] Redfern referred to an interview conducted by the Commissioner on 26 June 1820, at 9 o'clock at night, in the depth of winter. He wrote, "It had been reported to you, at least so you said, that I had been Secretary to the Mutineers at the Nore, and even to Parker. I told you then, Sir, as I tell you now, that I never wrote a line for any Mutineer nor for any person connected with the Mutiny; nor did I ever see Parker".

For some time Redfern had tried unsuccessfully to obtain a copy of the minutes of that meeting. Having finally received a copy, he had written in reply on 8 February 1821.[51] Redfern was dissatisfied with the record of his interview and only accepted it as corrected up to the "9th query" [out of 40].

Redfern told Commissioner Bigge, that his "questions but more particularly [his] conversation...on the subject of the Secretaryship to the Mutineers & to Parker; on My Sentence and Pardon...was most artfully & cruelly calculated to harrow up, wound & insult my feelings".

Bigge's 'accusations' in the Light of Events at the Nore.

If actions speak louder than words, then Captain Parr's actions following the end of the mutiny on HMS *Standard* would suggest that it was highly unlikely that Redfern was close to Parker, the president of the Nore mutiny, as Bigge claimed.

Captain Parr had listed Redfern among the mutineers. Over time, as Redfern was considered for court martial, certain procedures were set in motion to determine the charges to be levelled against him.

The requirements, set down in *Regulations*, may be found in the previous chapter, in full. "The Judge-Advocate is to examine the Witnesses upon Oath, take down their Depositions in Writing, and shew the same to the Commander in Chief, who is to order him to send timely, before the Tryal, an attested Copy of the Charge or Accusation to the Party accused, in order to his being better prepared for his Defence [V]".

The judge-advocate also attended the sittings of the court, took minutes, and gave advice as required. Neither the charges against Redfern, nor the official transcript of the minutes of the court martial, made any reference to Redfern acting as "Secretary to the Mutineers at the Nore" or "to Parker". While their absence provides a conclusive rebuttal of Commissioner Bigge's remarks, the following strengthens that denial.

Had Redfern been involved as suggested, he would have had to be continually going to and fro, and have come under scrutiny by Captain Parr and his officers who remained on board *Standard* during the mutiny. Their officers were not sent ashore by the mutineers, as happened in some other ships.[52]

Captain and officers therefore had both opportunity and reason to observe the comings and goings of those on board. Remember too, that they were in close contact with the crew, as they still were responsible for the safe conduct of the ship, even with the mutineers in control.

Taking back full command was foremost in the mind of Captain Parr and his officers. The attitude of the crew, in general, was balanced on a 'knife's edge'. For Parr and his officers to succeed in taking back the ship only the most complete intelligence could bring success. An intimation of that knowledge may be gained from James Dugan's sketch of the final moments of the mutiny on board *Standard*.[53]

At the court martial, Cheeseman, a mutineer turncoat on the above account, claimed that he had seen Redfern at two mutineer meetings, but denied that Redfern was a committeeman. At one meeting Redfern had not acted like a committeeman as he had sat mute. The other time he was there by order of the committee about acting as surgeon.

If Redfern had been close to Parker, he would have been seen at more than two meetings. He would have been an active, not mute committeeman, and a delegate to combined meetings of ship representatives, as was Wallace, who in the event, saw death beckoning in the not too distant future, and after his arrest, shot himself.

As to the rest of Redfern's denial of Bigge's charges in 1821, that at the Nore, he "never wrote a line for any Mutineer nor for any person connected with the Mutiny", all that can be said at this distance has been said in the course of his court martial.[54]

Bigge's More Sweeping Allegations Against Redfern.

On 10 November, 1819, at Sydney, in New South Wales, Commissioner Bigge wrote to Governor Macquarie. The subject of that letter[55] was whether this same William Redfern, by then assistant colonial surgeon, was a fit and proper person to be appointed to the magistracy, in Sydney.

Bigge argued that Redfern had failed to be promoted principal colonial surgeon, in spite of an earlier promise, because of his convict past, ignoring completely his official appointment as Colonial Surgeon. The same reasoning applied, he said, in rejecting Macquarie's plan to appoint Redfern a magistrate, in spite of precedents for the appointment of emancipists to such positions.

Bigge went further. He said that Redfern's qualification was 'negatived' by "the peculiar Character of Mr. Redfearn's [sic] Crime", being implicated in 'the most foul and Unnatural Conspiracy that ever disgraced the Page of English History'.[56] And "that Mr. Redfearn's Crime is unparalleled even amongst those of his unfortunate Brethren". The reason for this assessment by Bigge, set down in his letter, was that Redfearn's crime coincided with "the only moment...in which it Could be truly said, that England was in danger".[57]

Danger, yes, but not *under direct attack* from an enemy fleet.

In degrees of guilt, Bigge measured a case of theft that brought seven years' transportation to one emancipist magistrate, as insignificant compared to the "Enormity of Mr Redfern's" crime. But whether the crime was great or small "the fact of Transportation" provided "a perpetual Ground of Reproach" whether or not sufficient atonement had been made for it. Bigge continued, "that Altho' his Crime may be forgiven by Englishmen, it Never Can be forgotten by them".[58]

Yet, just months before the Nore the actions of mutineers at Spithead were expressly forgiven and forgotten - their involvement expulged from the records - by the order of the King, himself.

A Considered Response.

"Sir Ian Gilmour, a barrister by profession...served as Secretary of Defence under Edward Heath...and Lord Privy Seal and Deputy Foreign Secretary in Mrs Thatcher's first cabinet", did not see things quite like Bigge. Gilmour said, in his *Preface,* "violence often arises from the actions or inaction of government, and popular resistance cannot be divorced from this".[59] By the end of his book he was pointing the finger of blame directly at the Pitt government for the fleet mutinies of 1797, which, "[b]y turning a blind eye to all the warning signals of impending trouble in the fleet, precipitated [the] mutinies".[60]

Admiral Bridport's response at the time, and on the spot, showed up Bigge's "most foul and Unnatural Conspiracy" for what it was, punitive, ignorant and unhelpful. It placed Bigge in the camp of those who would have turned their back on Admiral Howe and conciliation at Spithead, and did, at the Nore, settling for repression and punishment.

Gill[61] argued that "[t]he fact that it [i.e. the Spithead Mutiny] was begun without violence was due to Bridport, who saw no hope of regaining his authority by any other method than conciliation. He had allowed the men of the *Queen Charlotte* to board all the ships with impunity, and he had raised no objection when the delegates met in the admiral's cabin. Bridport explained his position clearly in the letters he wrote to the Admiralty on this day -

"With respect to the using vigorous and effectual measures for getting the better of the crews of the ships at Spithead, their Lordships will see that it is impossible to be done, or securing the ringleaders. I therefore see no method of checking the progress of this business but by complying in some measure with the prayer of the petitions".[62] "I trust vigorous measures will not be necessary, as the men on board the *Royal George, Queen Charlotte* and several other ships have no objection to go to sea, provided an answer is given to their petitions".[63]

"I have always considered peevish words and hasty orders detrimental," wrote Bridport, "and it has been my study not to utter the one or issue the other. I wish that rule had guided the conduct [of] those in higher situations as I think it wiser to soothe than irritate disturbed and agitated minds".[64]

Of course in 1797 there were others who held strong views about the mutiny. As Gilmour wrote, "Burke and many others feared that Howe's concessions had put an end to all naval discipline. In fact they prevented far worse troubles: had governmental obduracy driven the mass of loyal seamen to embrace the ideas of their Irish or 'Jacobin' leaders, the consequences would have been explosive".[65]

Among the "many others" was Nelson, who "had sympathy for the just grievances of the sailors: they were ill paid and, when discharged, 'shamefully treated'".[66] "He had no sympathy at all, however, with mutineers [at the Nore, and]...raised no objection to the severe punishments inflicted on the ringleaders". "[Nelson] would have been happy to command a ship against"..."the Nore scoundrels".[67] "At present", said Nelson, "we are all quiet in our Fleet, and if Government hang some of the Nore Delegates, we shall remain so".[68]

A Spithead execution would not be overlooked simply because earlier mutineers at that place had received a Royal Pardon. But then they had also "won the day".[69]

A more precise complaint has been made of the mutineer North Sea ships of deserting in the face of the enemy. There was no battle action. The ships were on their way to resume their Texel watch on the Dutch Fleet.

Duncan was well aware of the problem he was having with his squadron but chose to return to his station. As his ships fell away and made for the Thames Duncan sent messages to his now non-existent squadron. This ruse was effective. The Dutch accepted the signals as real, and proof that Duncan's ships were ready and waiting if and when the Dutch Fleet came out of harbour.[70]

Duncan was fearless and determined to sink his ship to block the Dutch if they attempted to come out. It had the makings of a great tragedy, for Duncan was one of those who had tried to alert the Admiralty, years before, of the need to improve the conditions of the seamen. Admiral, or not, he had been ignored.

Bigge's Persistence.

Bigge could not let the matter rest. He revised minutes but he continued to raise the matter of Redfern's involvement at the Nore. There it was again in his first published report on the colony of New South Wales for all to see. Worse still, Bigge was giving the impression that Redfern was helping to write the text.

"In the course of my inquiry," wrote Bigge, "I learnt from Mr. Redfern himself that he had been sentenced to death by a naval court martial, for being implicated in the mutiny at the Nore in the year 1797". Correct.

This sentence concludes with these words - "and that the nature of his offence consisted in having *verbally advised the leaders of the mutiny 'to be more united amongst themselves'*. Such a statement does not appear in the minutes of the court martial or of Bigge's interview with Redfern.

Often quoted, with Bigge's estimate of his age, also incorrect, at least he got *Standard,* the ship's name, correct.

It is inconceivable that Redfern would have made such an admission after so vehemently denying any written incrimination at the Nore. Unity generated the power at Spithead that brought victory and a Royal Pardon. Disunity at the Nore was handing power back to government and the mutineers to punishment.

There is no reference in the minutes to Redfern's advising seamen to be more united. This was tantamount to reminding them to be true to their oath of allegiance to their delegates - "I will also endeavour to detect and suppress as full as in my power everything that may lead to a separation of the unity so necessary [to] completing our present system". As one seaman described it, standing "true to the Cause until the King's Pardon was obtained".[71] One can understand what Captain Parr would have made of such an admission. The people on *Standard* were almost evenly divided between going on and giving in. Can you imagine more critical advice?

But hold hard, did Redfern say in which direction he wanted the united push or pull to go? Redfern's own self preservation makes it pretty clear, however.

The original oath was sworn on 17 April 1797, at Spithead.[72] Gill published a copy.[73] On 6 May 1797 ships were notified to send delegates to draw up an oath at the Nore.[74] Dugan claimed the Nore oath imitated that from Spithead, and published a copy identical with that in Gill, included in the previous chapter of this book.

Wasn't It More a 'Strike' Than a 'Mutiny'?

Strike has its origin in the wooden sailing ship in the phrase to strike sail, which means to take the sail in, to furl it. It could also mean not to raise the sail at all, leaving the ship powerless, as "In 'striking' the sails the river workers prevented the ships from sailing".[75] In Royal Navy usage, it applied to flags as well. "On the conclusion of the trial of the people [including William Redfern] of the *Standard,* Vice Admiral Pasley struck his flag on board the Centaur...as [he]...is under orders to join the Channel fleet".[76]

Some might prefer "strike" on the grounds of "mutiny's" infamous and unpalatable layers of meaning - and confusion with that other navy as argued in the previous chapter - but strike also carried every ignominy that could be put upon it, including the Georgian government stamp of illegality.

Dugan, in an "Author's Interjection", offered a brief commentary in *The Great Mutiny,* his singular title which included both Spithead and Nore. "In a sense the great mutiny was an isolated major event in industrial history. Considering the Georgian Admiralty as a major concentrator of wage labour - 120,000 men in several 'plants' - the cruising squadrons and fleet anchorages - Valentine Joyce and his confederates at Spithead led the first successful mass sit-down strike in history...". Dugan mentioned that it would be a hundred years before the London dock strikes, a comparable event, and one hundred and fifty years before the Invergordon mutiny in the Royal Navy in 1931, "virtually a repetition of Spithead in steel instead of wood".

Mutinies they were seen to be, and believed to be, and "were real in their consequences", so dire that Government decided to expunge all references to the Spithead mutiny from the records of individual seamen. As unity fell away at the Nore nothing could hold back the storm of mutiny's punishing consequences on those who had stepped over the line. William Redfern felt that blast, more perhaps than others, if the following has the significance attached to it by their authors.

Dugan had Captain Parr describing the six *Standard* mutineers sentenced in the earlier court martial as "amongst the best of the ship's company". Of the second *Standard* court martial, Dugan claimed, "one of them renewed public interest in the proceedings". "William Redfern, a surgeon's assistant, was the highest ranking person of all the accused in the mutiny trials. He was a warrant officer, a gentleman, and a member of the wardroom. He was one of the few defendants who was able to secure counsel".[77]

Manning Clark had earlier told how "Between 1787 and 1823 four hundred and fourteen men were transported from the army and navy for offences punishable by transportation in their regulations. At least ninety-nine per cent of these came from the rank and file though, as with so much in the history of the convict system, one exception survived as a person in the history books. For, amongst them was William Redfern, a surgeon in the navy, who as a young man of nineteen had joined in the mutiny of the Nore in 1797".[78]

What did the Court Martial tell us about William Redfern?

He apparently took his medical work seriously. One witness told the court that Redfern could not have done his work better as a surgeon than he had as a surgeon's mate. The mutineers must have held a similar opinion for they were determined to have Redfern as their surgeon. Redfern, himself, played down their preference, excusing the surgeon, Kirkwood.

Redfern's medical background was shown to have the range typical of the times. As physician he had taken sick parades, compiled daily sick lists, and then as apothecary made up medicines in a cupboard-sized dispensary adjacent to the surgeon's cabin.

After the replacement of Surgeon Kirkwood, Redfern had both sought advice from him, and on a separate matter had accepted advice. Kirkwood feared trouble on one occasion and alerted Redfern, who would have taken the necessary action to have everything ready to receive casualties.

Redfern's capacity for medical work and his broad medical background are to be found here, recorded for the first time, in the minutes of the court martial.

Redfern's courage in adversity is also revealed in his uninhibited cross examination of witnesses and his questioning of the whole proceedings, when deemed timely by his counsel.

There is evidence too - in this cross examining - of a nimbleness of mind and a fluency of expression, reflecting his education and the confidence it gave, even at a life-threatening court martial.

It is now possible to conceive of William Redfern as an intelligent young medical officer, broadly trained in the manner of his times, with a good attitude to his patients, mostly young like himself, no slouch when it came to work, courageous in adversity and willing and able to express himself fluently and with confidence as bespoke an educated gentleman.

Perhaps though, a little 'out of place' in the wooden world - perhaps the reason for his wanting to leave it - and somewhat immature, when compared with his ship mate the midshipmen - if he had wanted a set of pistols at that precise moment for whatever reason.

Redfern spoke well of the surgeon, had not wanted to take over his job, but did throw in his lot with the mutineers. Fear, or courage – or contiguity, as the Court held - moved him?

Unlucky Redfern, to have joined the wrong fleet! Or did he? How significant were his Irish connections? Holt, the Irish general, said Redfern was from the north of Ireland.[79] Among fourteen Naval mutineers who came out with Redfern, "most if not all were Irish" according to Anne-Maree Whitaker, who claimed seven as "members of a branch of the United Irishmen aboard HMS *Defiance*".[80]

One would like to know why Redfern joined the Royal Navy? Why did Captain Parr have his invitation to Redfern to dine with him, and Redfern's acceptance, written into the evidence of the court martial? Who arranged for Redfern to have a lawyer? What might this signify? Who might that lawyer (counsel) have been?

Redfern's defense submission has some intriguing contents. What was implied by the alternative, "deceiving or suffering"? Who would be deceived, and by whom? Who would be suffering and on what grounds? Was it Redfern, himself? He also admitted to "unguarded and doubtful expressions", in the main unproved, which may have escaped him.

It is remarkable that in the final paragraph of Redfern's defense submission appeared the germ of the idea, taken up by the court, that Redfern's "profession...will suggest a general reason..." why Redfern "alone of all the Gentlemen on board should have any connection with the Mutineers".

If that was so, it was strange indeed. Being a surgeon was the cause of his involvement in a mutiny for which he faced the death penalty and led to his imprisonment and transportation. At the same time being a surgeon, and forced by his work to have close contact with the mutineers, was used by the court to snatch him from the deadly grip of the noose, and bend him before the clemency of the King.

Imprisoned.

What of the immediate aftermath of conviction? Where would Redfern await his journey to Botany Bay? Was it to be in another ship, a former man-o'-war reduced to a shell of its former self, soon to be the fate of HMS *Standard,* like Redfern himself? What was it to be? There was little choice between a land gaol, bad enough as a hotbed of disease, and a prison hulk floating among the flotsam and jetsom of a tidal river or coastal port.

Alan Frost has much to say about hulks by which is meant of course, the shells of ships that had known 'better' days and had become prisons to convicts at labour,[81] instead of to men at war.

Frost was questioning *Botany Bay Mirages, Illusions of Australia's convict beginnings.* One of those illusions was of "Overcrowded Hulls, Foetid Sinks", to quote his relevant chapter head.

He began with punishment. Transportation to North American and West Indian colonies became permanent in 1717-18 'to introduce more flexibility into penal practice' (Ibid. 9) - hanging, branding, whipping, exposing in the pillory, fine and imprisonment.

"In providing for transportation for seven or fourteen years (and later, for life), Parliament not only broadened the range of punishment, but also gave justices means of taking account of previous good character and mitigating circumstance, and of distinguishing between degrees of violence or callousness".

The first of two other aims was to gain from the labour of the convicts and the next, to give them a chance to reform in a new environment.

The central government had only a minimal role in transportation, that being left to the merchant.

Between 1718 and 1775 some 50 000 British men and women were transported across the Atlantic.

Since the convicts were sold on arrival there was an incentive to see that they arrived.

Thus "Transportation to the American colonies was really a neat penal practice, from which central government gained in three ways: by 'exporting' a social problem; by doing so at little cost; and by obtaining a benefit for the nation from the convicts labour via the mercantilist system" (Frost, 12).

The North American colonists changed this neat practice by gaining independence through force of arms from Great Britain, and by simply refusing to accept any more convicts. Partly, as a result, convict numbers grew within the British Isles.

They were kept in land and hulk prisons while some new destination was found for them and transportation ships found a new route. Government settled upon New South Wales. Something of that story will be told in later chapters, but for now, where was our man?

"William Redfern convict", entered into the Google search engine with a reference to an alleged Public Records document, discovered him in a prison hulk, moored at Portsmouth.[82]

In columnar form beside his name on a list, his crime was described as mutiny, his place of conviction *Neptune*, the date of conviction 22 August 1797, his final destination N.S.W., and his prison term was for life. The only error was in his age, 32. It should have been 22. The final column shows that he was sent from the hulk on board the convict transport *Canada,* on June 6, 1801.

Canada, Nile 1 and *Minorca* kept company as they sailed for New South Wales and arrived together. Their story is for a later chapter.

A rough idea of Redfern's 'shipmates' may be formed by taking the names of twenty convicts immediately above and below William Redfern's name, forty-one in all, just short of this one page of the record book [nos 178 to 218].

Only two of these convicts definitely escaped transportation - or death by hanging. One was pardoned. The other died.

All had been convicted from courts up and down the country. General terms descriptive of their crimes range in frequency from 'felony' [25], 'grand larceny' [5], 'petty larceny' [4], and mutiny [1]. For the remainder, one is a blank entry and the other five are shown as 'cap. respite' having been 'granted a respite from death or execution'. Sounds ominous.

Of, this 'cap. respite' group, two were for life and three for seven years. One 'lifer' was transported, as was one serving a seven years term. One other died.

The eldest convict was fifty and the youngest, thirteen. The average age of 10 convicts in the 13-19 was 16 years of age, 23 for 18 convicts in the 20-29 range, and 32 for 9 in the 30-39 range. 41,42, 44, and 50 were the ages of the four remaining.[83]

The average age for 35 of these 41 convicts was 25. Youth then, was a common factor of both the Royal Navy and this selection of prison hulk convicts.

Canada took 11 of these 41 convicts and *Coramandel* took 16.

Some of the former British and captured foreign Navy Ships were reduced to hulks and used to imprison both convicted civilians and captured sailors. Having in mind from years before, a painting of a line of hulks hanging in an Australian Art Gallery, it took little time to find the details and the artist's name, Louis Garneray.

Soon after, I was reading Richard Rose's translation of Garneray's book *Mes Pontons* and studying in text and illustration the nature of *The Floating Prison* in which this French prisoner-of-war spent nine years of his life. Remarkably, during this time he was able to paint and sell his paintings.[84]

I wonder if William Redfern found an opportunity to practice medicine.

Chapter 7

'GIGANTIC DISTURBANCES' TO WAYS OF LIFE AND THOUGHT

The Great Irish Rebellion.

With Redfern imprisoned, awaiting the King's pleasure, there is time to gaze about the landscape of coercion. A quasi-natural history beckons like the dried-out figure of a long-dead highwayman, conspicuous at some cross roads, on its gibbet tree. This history is objectified in gaols and hanging 'trees', as part of the built environment.

It is not a pleasant view, because of its inhumane content. The year after the Great Fleet Mutinies, for example, saw the Great Irish Rebellion of 1798.[1] Thomas Pakenham described how "[i]n the space of a few weeks, 30,000 people - peasants armed with pikes and pitch forks, defenceless women and children - were cut down or shot or blown like chaff as they charged up to the mouth of the cannon".

"The result of the rebellion was no less disastrous: Britain imposed a Union on terms that proved unacceptable to the majority of the Irish people, and there was a legacy of violence and hatred that has persisted to the present day".[2]

How might the story have been different had an invasion of Ireland by the French succeeded?[3] On the night of 16 December 1796, due to the Channel Fleet's open blockade of Brest, a French fleet of "thirty-five ships with 12,000 troops" escaped with "slightly-built thirty-three year old Dublin barrister Wolfe Tone"[4] on board.

With General Hoche separated from his fleet and the weather turned against him, disaster struck the French invasion fleet. Success, on the other hand, might have kept the Channel Fleet so busily engaged with the French that the fleet mutinies of the ensuing year might never have been.

The Irish Rebellion increased the convict colony of New South Wales,[5] where "Irishmen made up a quarter of the population" by 1802.[6] Far fewer Nore and North Sea fleet mutineers would go to 'Botany Bay', as many were accepted back into the Navy,[7] which urgently needed them.

Convict surgeon William Redfern would find himself eventually attending to the health of the "artisans: weavers, carpenters, smiths, masons and so on", who made up the Irish numbers.[8] Redfern would also get to know some Irish political prisoners from the Rebellion. One of them, Joseph Holt, wrote of Redfern's links with Northern Ireland.

Packenham also mentioned the Irish convict James Meehan, who was to survey and measure Redfern's early land grants, and to become deputy surveyor-general of New South Wales.

Unlike the martyrs for Parliamentary Reform, the men of '98 have their own memorial in Sydney. There are no memorials to the fleet mutineers. As noted above, Redfern had a Sydney suburb named after him.

War!

Warfare fits well the title of this chapter. For obvious reasons, war at sea took precedence over land wars in preceding chapters of this book, but naval ships and land armies knew integrated roles.

They also shared common themes. 'Rats, lice, and disease' was one of them as was scurvy. However, as Richard Blanco noted, "[w]hile the navy, under the inspiration of James Lind, Gilbert Blane, and Thomas Trotter, had progressed in preventive medicine, the army lagged behind".[9]

But sick troops in army camps or navy transports, or left wounded on the field of battle for days, unattended, also aroused compassion *in a very lively manner* among certain army doctors, and others, as participant observers.

Sir Jeremy Fitzpatrick (mentioned by William Redfern), inspector of health for the Land Forces, "stunned by his visit to embarking ships filled with dying men" [the army was in retreat] wrote of their being "inhumanly treated". Formerly "as inspector general of prisons in Ireland, Fitzpatrick had often witnessed the degradation of convicts, but he was shocked at the state of hospitals at Arnheim, where 'such misery and wretchedness as I found can scarcely be described'".[10]

Another outstanding army medical practitioner described by Blanco also took notice and kept a record. He was Donald Monro (1727-1802)[11] who formed a trilogy of Army doctors with Sir John Pringle (1702-82), and Sir James McGrigor.

At the same time, and within the limits of his understanding, each surgeon attempted to ameliorate or prevent some at least of the major failings of military leadership, at home and abroad, in maintaining the health of soldiers.

McGrigor met typhus fever in Jersey camps and in the Army's retreat from the Lowlands, yellow fever in the West Indies, overcrowding in transports in India, and plague in Egypt. Following a further stint in Army camps and hospitals in England, Wellington selected him as his Surgeon General.

Reminiscent of an earlier comment (Chapter 3, above) on naval health being dependent upon a close working relationship in Royal Navy ships between commander and medical officer is that between Wellington and McGrigor. The latter was required, and desired, to report each morning, in person, to his Commander, and did so to good effect.[12]

Oliver MacDonagh revealed a similar relationship between key Irish Parliamentarians and Sir Jeremiah Fitzpatrick, where a legislative response was essential to improve conditions in gaols, prisons, and Charter Schools.[13]

McGrigor believed, "It is not only in the sense of humanity, but in that of a sound policy and real economy, that the state should provide able medical and surgical advice for the soldier when sick or wounded. I look upon it to be an implied part of the compact of citizens with the state..."[14]

He found, in practice, "the medical board, in demanding reports and returns from the medical officers of the army, as in all their correspondence, seemed to look solely to the fiscal concerns to the neglect of all that was professional. The most minute and scrupulous attention was...exacted in the number of ounces of soap, salt, oatmeal, etcetera given to each patient...while no notice was taken of any new or extraordinary feature of prevailing diseases, no proposition made for the trial of new remedies and for the return of reports thereon, nor any injunctions issued to notice post mortem appearances".

To McGrigor's critical gaze, regimental surgeons and assistant surgeons had become clerks. When opportunity allowed he activated their reports towards "professional duties in the interest of science".[15]

With such encouragement, regular reports from surgeons in the field began to interact with McGrigor's own experience, and reading from his personal field library.

McGrigor's *Medical Sketch of the Expedition to Egypt from India*, even though abridged in the published copy of his autobiography (2000: appendix 9:292-318) clearly reflects his experience in the field. An opinion supported by Blanco's biography (1974).

There is no doubt that the surgeon's role in the commonly accepted sense at that time, included much more than *surgery.* Reading McGrigor shows how ready he was to include short-term needs - that day's battle - in long-term strategies of preventive medicine. So, transport vehicles bringing in supplies took out the sick and wounded.

Earlier, Monro had described the wide range of health and medical conditions he encountered as a physician in 'British military hospitals in Germany from January 1761 to March 1763'.

For each condition described, Monro added the treatment given, medicines used, pharmacopeia, diet, convalescence, etc. The whole report concluded with *Observations on the Means of Preserving the Health of Soldiers* (1780).[16] Works of similar intent for Seamen by Lind (1757) and Blane (1780) come to mind.

Perhaps the best way to preserve the health of victims of war is to look upon war, itself, as a social disease, and to act accordingly by peaceful moves to prevent an outbreak. Some look to medical reports of war caused disease, including the venereal, to reduce the worst or more common effects of involvement.[17] [For emotional effects of modern wars see Micale, 2008:282ff.]

Warfare, in its intended and unintended consequences, is intricately linked with the economy of nations and with the lives of non-combatant men, women, and children.

The London Hanged.

Biographies of "The London Hanged" provided Peter Linebaugh with the raw material of his research.[18] He believed that "[u]nlike the historian of class relations in the nineteenth or twentieth centuries, whose subject-matter is studied through the glass of money, the eighteenth-century historian needs sources of information that are as particular as the things of the eighteenth century and as concrete as the labouring history of eighteenth century persons".[19]

To Linebaugh, "The eighteenth-century historian has greater reason than those of subsequent periods to search for evidence of the organisational and technical aspects of the labour process, since these decided both the value and use of what was produced and the ability of the living worker to take, in exchange for work, what was necessary to live, whether such taking was 'allowed', or 'customary' or otherwise".

"Only then", Linebaugh argued, "can we be in a position to understand the contentious exchange between living, labouring people and their rulers. Since the exchange was disputed, it was very often disputed in law, and therefore, for London, there are fewer sources of information better than the documentation left by the criminal courts. The archives of the criminal jurisdictions of London and the printed *Proceedings* of the Old Bailey give us a history of misappropriated things. From them we may derive *a history of taking*. Rarely do they provide information permitting us to understand how things were made or the exact combinations of materials, tools and expenditure of labouring creativity. For that information we need to begin with the biographies of the men and women who were hanged – from these we may obtain *a history of making*".

Linebaugh's discussion of "ships and chips" exposed the twin themes of "making and taking" in the context of what he describes as "technological repression and the origin of the wage". The construction of eighteenth century wooden warships provided a site for Linebaugh's investigation of "the [evolving] organisational and technical aspects" of a specific "labour process".[20]

What was at issue was "the form and value of payment. For most workers in the eighteenth century the payments were not made in money, or, when they were, such payments were only one of several forms".[21] "Chips",[22] the customary perquisites[23] of workers in the shipbuilding yards, and their exchange for a cash allowance play a significant role in this study. As Linebaugh explained, the word "chips", "refers not to the wood itself but to the right of the worker to appropriate a certain amount of it - a prescriptive right since 1634",[24] and which "became associated with some deeply held working-class ideas of freedom and slavery".[25]

But "ruling class corruption" was there as well, taking from the labourer's product, an unearned share.[26]

Linebaugh compared the eighteenth century Samuel Bentham with Frederick Winslow Taylor, a century later.[27] Each was confronted by "the forms of workers' power in a labour process", which required its destruction. To do so, "tools of adequate measurement" of work done were needed. Piece-rates followed that would "increase profitability and raise wages". "Both knew too that an increase of wages was fully consistent with an increase in the rate of exploitation. Finally, each was aware that before mechanization could be satisfactorily introduced a prior revolution in the labour process was required".[28]

To Linebaugh, there were many such changes over the eighty years from 1724. "These were the result of a serious protracted struggle, whose consequences in ship design, in nautical engineering, in mechanical operations, in productivity - perhaps even the victories of the Navy during the Napoleonic Wars - are well known". But he wondered about "improvements", bringing John Charnock of the *History of Marine Architecture* (1800) into play.[29]

Charnock revealed "avarice, luxury, and ambition" as "the moral qualities that promoted the technical changes". [Not the comfort of the seamen?] "The application of changes, he observed, had two important effects. First, they 'augmented the general inquietude of man'. Second, they promoted 'those horrid scenes of slaughter or desecration which, during so many ages, have disgraced the universe' ".[30]

But as Linebaugh acknowledged, philosophic moralism has its own limitations, and while Bentham and Charnock belonged to a "republic of letters" the chip men and women belonged to a "republic of wood".

"Their profession was no less intelligible than philosophy or engineering - at least to those admitted to it. It had its ways of doing things - its arts and mysteries, its circuits of exchange and barter, its solutions to the ecological and energy crises of working people, its social structures between men and women, adults and children, the healthy and the infirm, and as we have seen, its characteristic ships".

While wooden ships have played a significant role in the Redfern story to this point and will continue to do so, their building and the analysis of the work processes and human relations involved have drawn attention here to the complex nature of payment to workers. In the imposition of the wage, perquisites became criminalized and later in New South Wales, William Redfern would be caught up in a similar process involving the pay and perquisites of colonial surgeons.[31]

Patrick Colquhoun, "a Scotsman who had twice served as Lord Provost of Glasgow...had come south to seek new worlds to conquer. Colquhoun was in his mid-forties, bursting with ideas, ambition and energy". Donald A. Low saw him as "a practical man of the Scottish Enlightenment", telling how "he prospered as a trader in Virginia" and returned to establish "a successful business in Glasgow". His business interests took him to London, where he became "a leading magistrate", and "threw himself wholeheartedly into what he undoubtedly judged to be a necessary war against crime".[32]

Not surprisingly Linebaugh saw him in a different light. "Colquhoun was the London agent for the planters of St Vincent, Nevis, Dominica and the Virgin Island. He worked tirelessly for the West India Merchants' Committee in London. He worked closely with the Home Secretary and the House of Commons, testifying frequently to the Finance Committee on the subject of police and drafting its legislation on that subject. Edmund Burke, Edward Gibbon and Adam Smith were visitors to his home. He collaborated with Jeremy Bentham on police schemes and reformation of the dockyards".[33]

"If a single individual could be said to have been the planner and theorist of class struggle in the metropolis it would be he," Linebaugh said. Melville Lee called him the 'architect' of the police. The Webbs called him its 'inventor'. His influence goes far beyond the establishment of the Marine Police Office, because his books, although written for the practical purpose of establishing a police force, contain the combination of law, economics, flattery and class hatred that together have exercised a powerful influence upon subsequent conceptions of law and order".[34]

Colquhoun's writings have found their way into the Goldsmiths'-Kress library of economic literature.[35] Colquhoun was a great compiler of facts and figures. From his *Treatise on Indigence* (1806), Dorothy George (1931) was able to compare estimates of population change, wealth and poverty, over one hundred years from the end of the seventeenth, to the start of the eighteenth century.[36] Roy Porter drew upon Colquhoun's records of commercial traffic in his description of the Thames River flooded with shipping.

The Hanging Tree.

From *The London Hanged* to *The Hanging Tree*[37] is but a short step in my reference book collection but a much longer one in reading and understanding. Gatrell was not unmindful of ordinary working class men and women. He said it was "an emotional and imaginative engagement with their plights that pushed [him] forwards, and at last took [him] into a history of emotion itself".[38]

From his reading of stories overlooked in the archives "it became clear that for many thousands of those past people the law was neither an ideal nor something to which consent was spontaneously given, but an arena of unequal negotiation and despair; moreover, it was knitted into their lives and could shape destinies irretrievably".[39]

In that history there is much to provide data for our present concern, the extent (and the nature) of crime. "It has been a conventional wisdom that 'crime' inevitably increased in these demographically explosive decades [1770-1830], and that in the interests of security, prosperity, and work discipline, there was a growing demand for a broader and more effective punishment than that applied to the few felons who had been prosecuted and convicted hitherto".[40]

There is a present day relevance in Gatrell's understanding that, under "conditions of heightening anxiety about order, from Bentham and Colquhoun in the 1780s on...the appeal to rational and efficient punishment always sounded out more loudly than the appeal to 'humanity' did".[41]

Gatrell argued, "these pressures were by no means concerted. For a start, many contemporaries knew better than some historians do that 'crime' was less obviously increasing in the early nineteenth century than anxieties about it and the publicity given to it, along with the facilities for its higher prosecution: up went *prosecution* rates, therefore - not crime rates".[42]

Since Gatrell was concerned with the ultimate punishment, hanging, he gave some thought to "measuring the subject". "75,000 people are thought to have been executed in the century 1530-1630, and nothing like this was seen again. Execution rates declined in the second third of the seventeenth century [with] transportation to the American colonies...and political stability kept hanging rates stable across the next half-century".[43] He continued with the account of a dramatic fivefold increase in London hangings in the second half of the eighteenth century from the 281 of the first half. "The slaughter rate thereafter stayed high. As many were hanged in London in the 1820s as in the 1790s, and twice as many hanged in London in the thirty years 1801-30 as hanged in the fifty years 1701-50".[44]

The two periods, the 1790s and the 1820s, were significant in the life of William Redfern. He experienced each decade in London. In the first, he almost ended on the gallows. In the second, Commissioner Bigge robbed him of his good name.

Remembering Redfern's life-threatening experience, and with convicts in mind, the following estimates from Gatrell, are of particular interest. "[S]ome 35,000 people were condemned to death in England and Wales between 1770 and 1830. Most were reprieved by the king's prerogative of mercy and sent to prison hulks or transported to Australia. But about 7,000 were less lucky".[45]

Gatrell takes us past the range of this Redfern story but it is well to note his argument "that hanging came to be repudiated for reasons greater than the fact that some people began to feel bad about it. We also take it for granted that many came to feel bad about it because they could afford to do so - as new controls bit deeper and made them safe. Hostility to the scaffold on humane grounds was never so vehement as when the perceived need for it was waning. Wakefield wrote his letter from the hangman when change was in the air. Thackeray announced his shame and disgust at watching Courvoisier hang in 1840 when most capital statutes had been dismantled and debate on root-and-branch abolition was swelling. So let it be axiomatic throughout what follows [in his book] that humane opinion had influence chiefly in so far as it bore a plausible and justificatory relationship to processes which were working to change punishment anyway".[46]

The Age of Silk.

"If the seventeenth century were the 'Age of Wool' and the nineteenth century the 'Age of Cotton', then the eighteenth was the 'Age of Silk'. It was the fabric of power and class command".[47]

"The producer is rarely seen, but must be imagined: tens of thousands of men, women and children massed on the other side of London, winding, throwing, dyeing, weaving, drawing, cutting, designing, stitching in hundreds of attics and garrets down the alleys of Spitalfields and Bethnal Green, whose magistrates kept a close watch upon their alehouses".[48] In his summing up "of the struggles among the weavers in the 1760s",[49] Linebaugh described how "many were forced to migrate to escape the hardness of life: they went as indentured servants to America, they became sailors in the East India fleet, they returned to Ireland as tramps. And a certain number of them were hanged. Yet the struggle had not been a complete failure. Its greatest accomplishment was the pressure that induced Parliament in 1773 to pass the Spitalfields Act (13 George III, c.68) [which] introduced a system of binding collective bargaining between the workers and their employers". "Magistrates...were empowered to 'settle, regulate, and declare' the wages of the trade. In doing so, they would consider the price of provisions and the balance of power between masters and workers".

Bearing in mind industry's supposed antipathy to regulation it is not surprising that greener pastures were found in Paisley, but see below for additional reasons. Now a humble young weaver provides a starting point.

Scotland.

An early patron and friend of William Redfern was Lachlan Macquarie, Governor of the convict colony of New South Wales. Hear his biographer John Ritchie.

"Those who care to know the history of this particular man, of the elements mixed in him, of the role he played in governing events and as pawn of circumstance, of the good and ill he did to others and they to him, and of why he was as he was, must turn for his beginnings to North Britain in the eighteenth century".[50]

While the 'gigantic disturbances' of the Highlands[51] and Western Isles of Scotland [Ritchie's 'North Britain'] cry out for inclusion in this chapter, it was the Lowland South and East of the country, which had its magnetic attraction for William Redfern.

Here, Alexander Wilson's story[52] will open that account. Born in Paisley,[53] Scotland, on 6 July 1766, Wilson had an eye for the colour and form of birds, and an ear for their calls. No doubt he would have appreciated the melodious singing of a canary many years and miles away in the coal town of Cessnock, in New South Wales.[54] This was a caged bird, and while Wilson would come to know that feeling of being entrapped, his life was not cut off suddenly, as was that avian songster's by a grey butcherbird. This predator so confused the canary that it flew to the bars of its cage and was killed.

While this conjunction of songsters, of poet and bird, is both true and metaphoric, there are other implications. Birds attacking birds, poets falling prey to their fellow men and questions of right and wrong within and across species. The butcherbird's behaviour and subsequent events are etched into the memory of this writer whose father expressed the family's rage by setting snares of horsehair on the cage. One did its deadly task.

Time has brought new understandings that challenge earlier responses. Judith Wright's lines, "Whatever the bird is, is perfect in the bird", and "Whatever the bird does is right for the bird to do", stand for behaviour in the natural world.[55] People, on the other hand, 'being human because they think', must govern their behaviour with this faculty. Duties of care to one's fellows and to the biosphere are the ideal outcome but take time to mature and remain widely variable in interpretation from person to person and over space and time.[56]

That most human and humane of Scots poets, Robert Burns, felt "man's inhumanity to man", but was also "...truly sorry man's dominion / Has broken Nature's social union". Burns expressed his sympathy "*To a Mouse",* a '"Wee, sleekit, cow'rin', tim'rous beastie" on turning her up in her nest, with the plough, in November 1785. While not doubting that the mouse "may thieve" asks, "What then? Poor beastie, thou maun live!" Burns does not begrudge the mouse an occasional ear of corn among a stack of sheaves. Some there were at the time who did begrudge their fellows, near starving women and children, even timeless rights to glean.[57]

This present author's interest in birds, converging in the 1960s on printed works and bookshops, turned up a sheet from a book of bird drawings by Alexander Wilson and later, at a book sale, Robert Cantwell's biography of the artist, the original source for the present account.

Wilson was described by Cantwell as weaver, poet, observer and painter of birds and "one of the first, if not the first, to begin the creation of a democratic culture" in the United States. "No American poet before Whitman sang of nature with the confidence of Alexander Wilson".

Yet the forces that helped drive Wilson from his home have been encountered already. Patrick Colquhoun gained experience, there, in the "disciplining of the spinners and weavers of Paisley".[58]

Scotland, with the rest of Great Britain, was experiencing at that time a clash of cultures, of past with present, of confirmed ways and disturbing changes, an age of revolutions, industrial, political and other.[59] Industrial change accelerated in England and spread throughout Britain in the 1780s.[60]

Country villages, of which Paisley was one, had supplied labour and swiftly flowing streams to energise burgeoning factories. Wealth was generated and middling groups of people felt the stirring of new ideas about governance that they hoped would set them free from inherited practices, and increase their own power.

Spithead, Nore, and now Paisley, pointed to "the fine soil" where the seeds of democracy sprouted in the late eighteenth century. "At that time, of course, not only was there no democratic government, nobody even called themselves a democrat till the century was nearly over".[61]

Braxfield, the lord justice-clerk of Scotland,[62] came down heavily on such ideas. It will be clear in due course who felt the force of his judgments. To his way of thinking it was "the landed interest" alone, that "has a right to be represented" in government.[63] And, his was not a lone voice, but extreme. The hungry birds, rocky places and thorny ground of the parable[64] were more likely to be found among this same "landed interest" where the seeds of democracy failed to grow.

When Alexander Wilson's father "Saunders Wilson gave up smuggling for [the sake of his wife] he profited beyond what could have been expected. Paisley was the fastest-growing city in Scotland, and one of the first manufacturing centers (sic) of Britain. The town had a monopoly of the thread-making industry. Silk gauze had become fashionable, and the silk gauze trade brought into Paisley some £450,000 a year; twenty large silk firms, with payrolls reaching £500 a week, operated their own Paisley mills and their fashionable retail shops in London, Paris and Dublin".[65] Paisley and its pattern became synonymous.

Links with America were mixed. Local smuggling had its own contacts through illegal American sugar and tobacco importing. Some connections were family with ties that were intimate and close, of marriage and property. Some were of trade, linked with Scottish woollen goods, guns, and later clandestine sales of gunpowder during the revolution.

The democratic church practice of Paisley clergyman Dr John Witherspoon also found a response in the American colony,[66] resulting in an invitation for him to become president of Princeton College. He accepted, giving his support to the American cause on arrival. Witherspoon believed the colonial rebels expressed *the sense of the grievances*, a conclusion similar to that reached by Admiral Bridport confronted by the Fleet mutineers at Spithead. Each saw conciliation as an answer.

But, neither after the Nore Fleet Mutiny, nor in the case of England and her American colony, was conciliation the order of the day. Witherspoon, however, went on to become the only clergyman to sign the Declaration of Independence.[67]

Wilson benefited from an early grammar school education,[68] which ceased with his mother's death. Then he left for Beith to work as a "little boy blue" on a farm, keeping cows from the corn. Returning to Paisley at thirteen years of age in 1779 he became an apprentice weaver.

On Saturdays in summer, Alexander walked to Lochwinnoch, near Beith, where his father now lived, and where he learnt to operate a still and acquired a gun. His poaching in the moorlands at the base of Misty Law, fostered his interest in nature and of solitude, but long-tolerated illegality was becoming a lethal crime.[69] Fortunately for Alexander, the local landowner, Colonel M'Dowell, head of Dunlop and Houston in Glasgow was not concerned.

This firm owned the Ship Bank, the biggest in the country. M'Dowell's wealth had gained an infusion from slave-powered sugar plantations. Sugar was "the most important foodstuff imported from the tropics and the one whose sweetness has created more human bitterness than any other".[70]

As a weaver, Alexander worked with his brother-in-law and periodically peddled their products, walking from door to door, "selling printed muslin, silk, handkerchiefs, ribbons, flags and other products of his own and Duncan's looms".[71] At times he sat down and wrote poetry. This was not out of place in Paisley. Poetry writing there and more widely in Scotland "sprang from the literate tradition of the community, the conditions of the weavers' trade, and the tremendous impetus that Burns gave to native poetry of all kinds".[72]

Unrest, at the time, was associated with change, noted above, across a wide spectrum. Changes in technology often made former skills obsolete. Consumerism also had dramatic effects. "In 1786 fashions in dress changed overnight, and silk went out of fashion. The Paisley weavers converted to linen, that same year turning out 2,000,000 yards of linen...a change possible only because the weavers adapted themselves so quickly".[73] But, while Paisley weavers survived, those in the outer villages suffered from loss of work and underemployment.

At Lochwinnoch, McDowell and Company dammed the Calder and erected a water-powered cotton mill that was so successful that it led to the construction of "one of the biggest factories in the world, five stories in height, lighted with 192 windows, and employing 650 people".[74] Whirring factory wheels fascinated, ended old drudgeries and inspired a Wilson poem, but factory owner supervision and greed increased with working hours. Alexander regretted the loss of free time spent in the open air.

The fascination of new labour-saving technology gave way to the monotonous repetition of its use, made tedious by the narrowing of skill levels through the division of labour.[75] As Augustus Comte had it, "The inconveniences of the division of functions increase with its characteristic advantages".[76] Comte was here thinking less of a specific labour task. He was hopeful that society would not lose its sense of "the common intercommunication" between "temporal and spiritual power".

Wilson may have doubted it. He began to attend meetings of the weavers and was remembered as "the most expert writer of reports and resolutions...in a style of elegance most astonishing to his compatriots".[77] Resolutions adopted at these meetings were published as advertisements in local newspapers. As they included support for the French Revolution, for universal suffrage, or more frequent sittings of Parliament, authorities took exception to them.

More blatantly they were then printed as handbills and stuck to walls, for public display. Wilson's poems, too, became handbills. One, *The Shark*, was sent anonymously to the person targeted, a local mill owner. Unfortunately, a request was attached for payment of five pounds for the manuscript of the poem with a threat to publish.[78] Wilson was named by the mill owner in a petition for the discovery and punishment of the person or persons involved.

This matter, which began on 22 May 1792, continued until 4 January 1794. During this period Wilson was in and out of gaol, largely due to non-payment of fines, reflecting his poverty.

The point of the poem was that the mill owner had reduced the length of the standard measure by which weaving was measured. The owner was a "shark" devouring the honest product of his workers. The point of the charge against Wilson, extracting money by threat, was that the real issue never came to court. Based on certain admissions of Wilson, and implications drawn from them, but not necessarily correct, he was fined on that count. Wilson took the blame for blackmail and bears the calumny to this day. The mill owner's perfidy went unpunished.[79]

Clark Hunter drew attention to the records of an earlier Wilson court case, overlooked by Cantwell, concerning a poem "The Hollander, or Light Weight".[80] "At a parochial level 'The Hollander' reached its targets, but it also reached out further, for, in its way, this was one of the first poems to comment on the factors associated with the social transformation inherent in the Industrial Revolution which led to the formation of trade unions".[81]

Hunter continued. "To William Henry the poem was defamatory and inflammatory, particularly dangerous in the growing manufacturing town, but his immediate reaction was to ignore it. Wilson, however, quickly became something of a folk hero to the weavers. That - together with the continuing frightening news from France; pressure, no doubt, from other manufacturers; and the realization that almost everyone in Paisley and its environs had read or been read the poem - now prompted Henry to take action, and he sought the aid of the law".

Hunter concluded his discussion of this matter by saying that court action appears to have been allowed "to go to sleep", and with no evidence to the contrary we may put this down to the generosity of William Henry and the court.[82]

As a subsequent story will confirm, events may have turned out differently, and Wilson could well have joined the Scottish Martyrs, a convict in New South Wales, as was William Redfern. Instead, it was to America Wilson decided to go as a free man. He slipped away under cover of darkness taking ship finally on 15 May 1794. There, life was not easy for him but he renewed his love of the outdoors and eventually published a pioneer work, *American Ornithology*, renowned as much for its original observations as for its illustrations.[83] His life reflected the traumas of his country of birth and the birth pains of the new nation to which he had escaped. Wilson spent the rest of his life there, dying in America after a bout of dysentery, on 23 August 1813.[84] Wilson's memory is kept alive through his biographers, in his poetry, prose, and his *Ornithology,* and in the *Wilson Bulletin* and *Ornithological Society.*[85]

The Rape of Africa.

While Wilson was pushed by circumstances to seek refuge in America, the final decision was his. But it was brute force that propelled countless unwilling Africans in this same direction. Many would die on the way.[86]

Slavery was, "by virtue of its duration and scale, the greatest tragedy of human history"; words penned by Jean-Michel Deveau and recalled by Doudou Diene.[87]

"The reign of King Sugar and King Cotton had begun across the Atlantic, and it called for millions of slaves, with the dead continually replaced by the living. This set in motion a process of forced migration larger than any other in history. It laid the foundations of American development. It nourished the English and French economic growth that led to great technological and scientific progress. The human record knows no combination more grimly contradictory: the piling up of wealth on one side, but the misery of mass enslavement on the other".[88]

"Historians calculate", Basil Davidson argued, "that about 10-12,000,000 captives were landed alive in the Americas during the four centuries of the slave trade. We have estimated that another 2,000,000 or more died on the Middle Passage. As for those who died in Africa before enshipment, or as a result of slave raids and wars, the total was certainly large but it is impossible to estimate".[89]

Since only the "young, healthy and of sound physique" were taken, the "ground for economic development...[in Africa] was continually undermined". This situation was made even worse by the effect of the "guns-for-captives contract" creating new levels of violence and increasing slave numbers.[90]

"So the bloody partnership between 'kings, rich men and prime merchants' on either side continued, adding one new violence and degradation to another".[91]

Africa lost its potential for future development and Europe and America harvested "the burgeoning fruits of a three-sided enterprise in profit: first, from the export of cottons and other goods to West Africa; secondly from the sale of captives into American and Caribbean enslavement; and thirdly, from the sale in Europe of slave-grown produce".[92]

From Basil Davidson (1984) and Channel Four this discussion moves to Ali A. Mazrui (1986) and the BBC, and from films to books of the series. Mazrui confirmed the Davidson account, for the eighteenth century, and extended it to the time of writing, arguing that in the last 300 years Africa's contribution to the wealth of Europe and North America had been to its cost.[93]

Slave labour led Africa's contribution driven by "Europe's sweet tooth". "Expanding demand for sugar in Europe resulted in expanding demand for slave labour in South America and the West Indies from the seventeenth century onwards".[94]

"In the eighteenth century technological change in the West" and "new factories of Europe needed more labour-intensive crops such as cotton and indigo". Resulting prosperity created a demand for still more "labour-intensive crops [such] as rice, coffee and tobacco [from] South America, the Caribbean and the southern states of the United States".[95]

Mazrui asked why black Africans were taken for slaves and found the answer linked to "a racial identity imposed on them by Europe", and what seemed to be the absence of concrete remains [of civilization] and of written records.[96] "Slavery was at once the consequence of racism and the mother of newer forms of racial degradation".[97]

Mazrui pointed out that American Blacks have always been named after a physical feature, a racial characteristic - their skin colour - almost the exception among ethnic groups there. At the same time, common English names forcibly erased given cultural names, and identification by place of origin. Cultural loss followed negative indoctrination as 'niggers' or 'negroes', separation from their religious springs whether indigenous or Muslim - many had been converted - and by loss of language, of their archival memory.[98]

A new phase of the study of slavery has opened with the launch of UNESCO's International Slave Route Project. "Its purpose was to consider ways and means of enabling black peoples, formerly oppressed and reduced to slavery, to rise together, with the support of all the nations of the world, to the challenge of development".[99]

Paul E. Lovejoy, in his contribution to the UNESCO publication, *From Chains to Bonds*, set out to examine the condition of African slaves in the Americas. He wrote, "I have chosen to concentrate on a neglected theme in the consideration of the slave condition: the African identity of the slaves themselves as perceived in the historical context of the period in which individual slaves lived. As a focal point for reflection, I want to emphasise the central place of Africa in the slave experience. By bringing Africa to the fore, my intention is to highlight the importance of agency...Africans brought with them real issues and live interpretations of their predicament. How these were subsequently interpreted in the Americas lies at the base of the African contribution to the process of creolisation and of resistance to and accommodation with the slave experience".[100]

The Jacobins abolished slavery in the French colonies[101] more as a means of encouraging the black population of San Domingo to fight for the republic against the English. In effect they helped create in America the first independent revolutionary leader of stature in Toussaint-Louverture,[102] brought to life by C.L.R. James, in his book, *The Black Jacobins* (1938).[103]

Pitt and Dundas for years hung grimly on to their hope of taking that island. In November 1795 Dundas was offering freedom to mulattoes to gain their support. "But the drain of men and money was too great. By the end of 1796, after three years of war, the British had lost in the West Indies 80,000 soldiers including 40,000 actually dead, the latter number exceeding the total losses of Wellington's army from death, discharges, desertion and all causes from the beginning to the end of the Peninsular war".[104]

Early in 1797 the British Government decided to withdraw from San Domingo.

An Age of Revolutions.

The world into which William Redfern was born was shaken by revolutions, political in America and France, and industrial in Britain. Wars raged with but 'a decade of peace (1783-1793)', noted by Donald B. McIntyre as no 'ivory tower' for geologist James Hutton, whose life he was documenting.[105]

Shock waves of change from the late eighteenth century washed across the world. Olivier Bernier's global time band fluctuated around the year 1800.[106]

Felicity A. Nussbaum's edited work, *The Global Eighteenth Century,* involved historians (6), art historians (2), a geographer, an anthropologist and a dozen literary scholars. The aim was 'to forge a broader, sharper, and more collaborative understanding of the eighteenth century', that included the people of the peripheries of empires.[107]

British colonists in North America had rebelled, setting the scene for the first revolution, 1775-83, and the birth of America as an independent State. There the political activist Tom Paine produced his radical text, *Common*

Cause, believed to have achieved "the greatest sale that any performance has ever had since the use of letters".[108]

The American Revolution aroused early sympathy in Scotland until the war closed its factories and devoured its children. In 1789,[109] the French Revolution proved to be the catalyst of both reform and repression, which Wilson, Paisley - and Redfern, in the Royal Navy, - experienced at first hand.

Major revolutionary changes were associated with other 'disturbances', different in kind, modulated by a slower evolutionary process. Roy Porter published a short view of *The Enlightenment* (1990), and a longer work, *Enlightenment...*(2001). The latter's emphasis on process finds rock-solid support in his study of *The Making of Geology. Earth science in Britain 1660-1815.*[110]

There was no 'pitched battle against religion' as 'most eighteenth century scientists were men of piety' and helped develop the tools for the later science, but 'the Enlightenment was the era which saw the emergence of a secular intelligentsia large enough and powerful enough for the first time to challenge the clergy' (Porter, 1990:72).[111]

To Eric J. E. Hobsbawm, enlightenment's "object was to set all human beings free" - in theory.[112] In reality it was more complex, as Hobsbawm was only too well aware.

Dorinda Outram understood this period as providing a "social setting" for *The Enlightenment,* a set of ideas, some with a Scottish imprint.[113]

Outram, 'historian of eighteenth- and nineteenth-century French science', considered the enlightenment encompassed a time "capsule containing sets of debates, stresses and concerns which however differently formulated or responded to, do appear to be characteristic of the way in which ideas, opinions and social and political structures interacted and changed in the eighteenth century".[114]

Outram's conclusion, following in part her overview of both *enlightenment* and subsequent studies, was that "by the 1960s, it was increasingly difficult to see the Enlightenment as in any way a unitary phenomenon, dominated by a few, mainly French, 'great thinkers'. 'Enlightenment' was increasingly seen as different from state to state,[115] region to region, and thus it followed that the relationship between government and the crucible of concerns and debates that made up Enlightenment, would also be different'.[116]

Outram concluded that "the Enlightenment was much better at creating new relationships among élites...than it was in reaching out to lower social classes,"[117] or in embracing the rights of women[118] (see the following chapter, here.)

Alexander Wilson[119] on the one hand, and Mary Wollstonecraft[120] on the other, bear witness to these sites in enlightenment endeavours, or lack of them. Also, in chapter two above, Heilbroner and Malone (1986) called to witness the failure of Enlightenment philosophes, including Adam Smith, to imagine a future sovereign role for the lower orders.

In 1997 out of a year immersed in the Max Planck Institute for the History of Science would come Outram's study, *On being Perseus: New Knowledge, Dislocation, and Enlightenment Exploration.*

'[W]hat explorers reported about human societies they encountered, made the whole issue of human difference itself a central problem in the Enlightenment. Enlightenment knowledge posed such questions as: If there was one human nature, then why did human societies differ so profoundly? If there was one human history, one human rationality, then how could the social world be ordered with such absolute difference in its particular manifestations?'[121]

David Daiches, in *A Hotbed of Genius,* described as 'one of the paradoxes of eighteenth-century Scottish thought that humane, enlightened and progressive thinkers tended to be politically conservative', with the opposing Calvinists, the more radical.[122]

In this same text, Archie Turnbull described such failings as 'a substantial criticism of the political effect, or lack of it, of the Scottish Enlightenment at home', but as he went on to explain, played 'a more significant role' 'in the birth and development of the Unites States of America'.

To Turnbull, the 'process of transatlantic exchange was not just one way', 'many Americans went abroad to study'. Higher education, both general and medical, sought *principals* [see Dr John Witherspoon, above], and wealthy fathers, *tutors for their sons,* from among the Scottish educated.

The contribution of 'wealthy fathers' brings to mind Roger L. Emerson's commentary on Scottish gentry, or one in particular, Archibald Campbell, 3rd Duke of Argyll (1682-1761). He it was, 'who gave support, jobs, pensions, and social roles' and, 'whose prestige and even power allowed the enlightened to have an impact on the world in which they lived'.

Emerson (2009) advised 'Scholars of the Enlightenment...[to] spend more time on the patrons who made possible the careers of enlightenment figures'; Individuals such as 'Archibald Campbell (1682-1761), Earl of Ilay (1706-d.), and 3rd Duke of Argyll (1743-d.) - one and the same person.[123]

The study of patronage in the arts, music, sculpture, painting etc. needs no such special pleading.

For certain workers, hear William Cobbett on *The Evils of the Factories in 1824,* contrasting them with the earlier and favourable period of manufacturing, in association with agriculture, which was "a great blessing to the labouring people themselves" as well as to the landowner. At that stage families were kept together, now they are separated and "the masses [drawn or driven to manufacturing] are still more miserable than the wretches left behind them in the agricultural districts".[124]

Conducing to their misery, Cobbett reported, were the conditions of work. "In the cotton-spinning work these creatures are kept, fourteen hours in each day, locked up, summer and winter, in a heat of from EIGHTY TO EIGHTY-FOUR DEGREES. The rules which they are subjected to are such as no negroes were ever subjected to".[125]

Later, he wrote: "If we wanted any proof of the *abject slavery* of these poor creatures, what proof do we want more than the following list of fines? "Any Spinner found - with his window open (1s.), - washing himself (1s.); Any Spinner - leaving his oil-can out of its place (6d.), - putting his gas out too soon (1s.), –spinning with his gas-light too long in the morning (2s.). Any Spinner - *heard whistling* (1s.), - being five minutes after the last bell rings (2s.), - being sick and cannot find another Spinner to give satisfaction, to *pay for steam*, per day (6d.)".[126]

"What had once been the exciting vision of 'man the machine' (free of original sin) became the nightmare reality of factory life in the machine age" (Porter, 1990:75).

John Gascoine saw 'Banks...as a useful guide to the limits of the English Enlightenment'. On the one hand he noted his 'willingness to approach political and social problems in a secular spirit, to promote science-or, more broadly, useful knowledge-and to question tradition where it conflicted with observation and reason'. But, not so much as to weaken 'self-confidence in themselves as a [elite] class', privileged and destined 'to direct the affairs of the nation'.

Bank's support for Joseph Lancaster's methods and materials of schooling[127] [opposed by the established church] was mediated by his belief that schools improved 'the manners and subordination' of youth.

'Though the Enlightenment was a central impulse in Bank's life and work it was...subject to the limits imposed by his social position and his support to the traditional order in Church and State'.[128]

Political Radicals of Scotland and England.

Scotland was a place where "money and position were used to keep the Scots subservient and willing" and where forty five Westminster Members of Parliament were chosen by only 3844 Scots in a population of 2,000,000.[129] "Because Scotland's traditional ruling class, the aristocracy, now exercised minimal power, merchants, lawyers, academics and doctors increased in wealth and importance more rapidly than in England. But this rising class was still excluded from burgh government. The French Revolution was the catalyst that showed up latent antagonism".[130]

"'Tammy Paine the buik has penned, And lent the courts a lounder"', wrote Alexander Wilson.[131] Paine published the first part of his book *The Rights of Man,* in 1791. Some of the 1,000,000 sales of copies were made in Scotland, helped by a Gaelic translation. David Craig quoted Wilson's comment that Paine's book was "read by mony a hunder".[132]

Some years later, when seeking subscribers for his *Ornithology,* Alexander Wilson "made his way to Greenwich Village to interview Tom Paine". Paine received him in his dressing gown, at a table covered with newspapers and his writing materials. He asked to be remembered to [William] Bartram[133] and to [Charles Wilson] Peale[134] when Wilson got back to Philadelphia, looked over the *Ornithology* with a penetrating and intelligent eye, and signed up for a set of the books, though his death a short time later terminated the contract".[135]

John Keane, biographer of Paine, added to this account of the meeting,[136] describing Alexander Wilson as "the prominent ornithologist", and attributing to him the observation that Paine's "keen eyes symbolized his brilliance as a public figure". "The penetration and intelligence of his eye bespeak the man of genius and of the world".[137]

In the Scotland of 1792, Societies of the Friends of the People had sprung up and attracted both professional men and artisans. The leading light of the Glasgow association was Thomas Muir "the only son of a prosperous merchant...born in the High Street of Glasgow on 24 August, 1765...As a boy he attended the local Grammar School, later entering the University of Glasgow at the early age of twelve...When seventeen...he decided to study for the bar, which then offered in Scotland the best opportunities for young men of ambition and nimble wit".[138]

Muir graduated M.A. at Glasgow in 1782 and completed his studies at Edinburgh in 1787. At Glasgow, Muir had come under the influence of the liberal-minded John Millar, professor of law and government.[139]

Earlier in 1792 Scots radical politics had been exported to England where an émigré Scottish shoemaker, Thomas Hardy, founded the London Corresponding Society, introduced in the first chapter of this book.[140]

1792 proved to be a year of economic hardship in Scotland where a bad harvest sent the price of bread soaring. Radicals of all classes were restless. In May, as a result of the second part of the *Rights of Man* being published, the government issued a proclamation banning seditious meetings and publications, including Paine's treatise.

Just days after Wilson's arrest, on June 4, 1792, the weavers' strong opposition to the traditional King's Birthday Parade in Paisley made it the last ever held. Hungry crowds burnt Henry Dundas in effigy, and Sheriff Pringle sent in the troops. This action was criticised by Colonel Norman MacLeod, MP for Inverness who found much order, much coolness and great desire for reform in general. The people were neither very rich nor very poor; certainly not in the least like a rabble.[141] Their main concern was parliamentary reform.[142]

'Genius'[143].

A Hotbed of Genius (1986) has further stimulated and given direction to a continuing interest in Scotland [My wife's mother was a Glaswegian midwife]. It began with the history of medicine and found new life from the knowledge that William Redfern studied medicine in Edinburgh in 1822, returned in 1828-9 with his son, and died there in 1833.

The Scottish Enlightenment 1730-1790, subtitle of the book, became the text for David Daiches' introductory essay. With Peter Jones and Jean Jones, the three formed an editorial team for the Institute for Advanced Studies in Edinburgh in 1986. And, for the first time, visual arts were called upon to complement text in promoting 'understanding and enjoyment' of heritage.[144]

'[I]ntellectual, artistic, and technical advances' were made, not only in Edinburgh, but also in Glasgow, Aberdeen and Lowland Scotland.

While only four - David Hume, Adam Smith, Joseph Black and James Hutton - have individual entries in the book, Daiches found many others to populate his essay – encyclopaedist William Smellie (1740-95),[145] Henry Home, James Watt, and Robert and James Adam, selected from his first page. Key words, his section headings, include *precursors, the Historical Age, Moderatism, Scottish or British? Sense and sensibility, Ossian, Taste, morality and sentiment, Science and industry, Clubs and societies, Music,* and *Conclusion.*

The authors of the individual biographies, *David Hume* (1711-76), *Adam Smith* (1723-90), *Joseph Black* (1728-99), and *James Hutton* (1726-97), were in succession, Peter Jones (DH), D. D. Raphael (AS),[146] R.G.W. Anderson (JB), and Jean Jones (JH). Archie Turnbull contributed the final article, 'Scotland and America', and Peter Jones, a 'Conclusion'.

Reading *A Hotbed of Genius* led to a search for associated publications of a celebratory nature. *William Cullen* (1710-1790) was added to the four above.

David Hume (1977) attracted 200 scholars from Europe, North America, Asia and Australasia. Seven of eight invited plenary session addresses, with some additions, were published in that collection.[147]

Adam Smith was the subject of a bicentenary exhibition and catalogue, *Morals, Motives & Markets* (1990).[148] *Adam Smith Reviewed,* symposium papers sharing similar aims, followed (1992).[149]

This latter text was typical of the whole collection, 'not concerned to establish a hagiography' but 'to recreate the context in which Smith was writing...and to assess the cogency and value of his ideas from the perspective of today' (Ibid. x).

Further, as Nidditch pointed out in his Preface to Hume's *Enquiries...*(1974), "Students of philosophy should be urged not to assume that current editions of philosophical classics are everywhere or equally reliable; and they should be led to appreciate the work of textual scholarship (concerned with the history and establishment of texts, and the provision of glosses and other annotations) that is necessary for the faithful preservation and the understanding of the classics".

To this end, and for David Hume, the L.A. Selby-Bigge's texts, further refined by P. H. Nidditch; *Enquiries...* (3rd edition) appeared in 1975, and, *A Treatise...* in 1978. For Adam Smith, Oxford Published 'The Glasgow Edition' of his works in the 1970s.

Joseph Black, introduced by Anderson, above, had found an earlier reference in the latter's study of *The Playfair Collection and the Teaching of Chemistry at the University of Edinburgh 1713-1858* (1978).[150] Anderson also contributed 'An Outline Biography' to *Joseph Black 1728-1799 A Commemorative Symposium,* title of papers published in 1982.[151]

James Hutton 1726-97 The Founder of Modern Geology was the work of Donald B. McIntyre and Alan McKirdy. Published in 1997 it was commissioned to mark the bicentennial of the death of Hutton.[152]

Professor McIntyre also published a 'most comprehensive bibliography and books and articles on Hutton or containing significant references to him'. Jean Jones described this work as of 'first importance to historians of science' (1986:136). A précis of this work opened *James Hutton - Present and Future,* a collection of ten papers, edited by G.Y. Craig and J.H. Hull and published in 1999.[153]

Typically, as a member of the *Hotbed of Genius,* Hutton's studies ranged widely; in his case over medicine, chemistry, industry, farming, agriculture, soil, and geology.[154]

So it would be found for *William Cullen* [1710-1790] *and the Eighteenth Century Medical World*; "A bicentenary exhibition and symposium...[held] in 1990', was published in 1993.[155]

David Hume's commemorative text has a reference to 'Burke's maxim: we must all obey the great law of change'.[156] 'Hume's Science of Politics' had in mind, according to Duncan Forbes, "special circumstances in eighteenth-century Scotland that brought the facts of change home to men's minds in specially compelling ways, and...the need for change and the fate of those who are unwilling or unable to adapt to change".

Forbes observed this as 'a recurring theme in Scott's Waverley novels and expressed in Adam Smith's detached observation'. Forbes also saw Burke's maxim as both 'a recommendation and a warning, it implies resistance and defence mechanisms and the consequent need for programme, propaganda and rhetoric'.

"Smith...had begun his career as an expert in the science of rhetoric, and the Wealth of Nations is propaganda as well as science: the science is *ipso facto* programme and propaganda. Likewise, studying Hume widely surely involves examining his philosophy in the light of the science of rhetoric and its history".[157]

Finally, reference to the work of Roger L. Emerson will bring this section to a conclusion. Emerson contributed to Doig et al. (1993) positioning Cullen among 'Medical men, politicians and the medical schools at Glasgow and Edinburgh 1685-1803'. In Stewart and Wright (1994) he confronted "The 'affair' at Edinburgh and the 'project' at Glasgow: the politics of Hume's attempts to become a professor".

Emerson's volume of *Essays on David Hume, Medical men and the Scottish Enlightenment: 'Industry, Knowledge and Humanity'* brings his studies to 2009. [158]

The papers are mostly, but not all, conference papers given over the last fifteen years and revised for this volume. Their settings and the themes of his book are described in three pages - positioning the Scottish Enlightenment in the world, Argyll's patronage, counting the enlightened, what students read, David Hume, numbering the medics, and 'What is to be Done About the Scottish Enlightenment?'

While outcomes from studying the 'hotbed' collection may be discerned in other chapters of this present book, one particular question may be asked now, and responded to at this point, to round of this discussion: Why did people go to Edinburgh (and Glasgow) medical schools to study chemistry?

By reference to the 'hotbed' collection a stream of awareness of the links begins with an idea to educate medical students at home instead of abroad.

Medical facilities included an infirmary and physic garden from which medicines could be extracted.

Extraction processes involved chemical equipment and procedures. The physic garden led to commercial manufacture of medicines on site.

The foundation professors of the medical school at Edinburgh were Dutch, who brought European chemical knowledge with them.

Cullen challenged and advanced beyond his predecessors taking Black as his student. They revised the Scottish Pharmacopoeia.

Black, motivated to find a cure for 'the stone', used chemistry to study an allied substance, quicklime. He discovered Carbon dioxide ('fixed air') along the way, and gave chemistry a quantitative direction, e.g. the use of the balance for weighing small samples. [The balance has a long history as I have found from current reading.]

Cullen and Black opened their courses to agricultural and industrial problems, which in turn increased student numbers, and attracted an international audience.[159]

Chemistry continued as part of the medical course, Black being followed by Thomas C. Hope. After Chemistry, Cullen moved first to Medical Theory (1766) and to Medical Practice (1773).

"The Scottish Martyrs".[160]

The first Convention of the Scottish Friends of the People opened in Edinburgh on 11 December 1792. Over 150 delegates representing 80 societies from 35 towns and villages attended. Their aim was to draw up a petition to send to the British Parliament in support of electoral reform.

Muir, the Glasgow barrister with a reputation as a man of principle, had helped organise many of the individual societies.[161]

"Spurred on by a country-wide political ferment the movement quickly spread to the provinces," according to John Earnshaw. "A General Convention of the "Scottish Societies of the Friends of the People" was called at Edinburgh on 11th December. The Convention, attended by some one hundred and sixty delegates, included Margarot and Gerrald who represented the London affiliated societies. During the three-day assembly, Muir, one of the most prominent delegates, insisted on reading an inflammatory address from the United Irishmen of Dublin.[162] This imprudent action, coupled with the French form of personal address and procedure, which the assembly adopted, alarmed the authorities who had insinuated their spies into the assembly. To Robert Dundas - lord advocate of Scotland and bitter enemy of reform - drastic action seemed necessary. By mischance written evidence that Muir had distributed seditious pamphlets fell into the hands of the public prosecutor. This was all that was needed. Muir was arrested on 2 January 1793, interrogated and released on bail".[163]

"On New Year's Day the government opened a terrific offensive against all reformers, democrats, levelers, revolutionists and, for that matter, against all opponents of Henry Dundas. Suspected printers, ministers, lawyers, weavers and workmen were rounded up; sentences of from three to fourteen years in the penal colonies were handed out for the possession of seditious writing; the letter of the law against treasonable practices was enforced with an addled efficiency that suggested an intelligence system that had gone mad".[164]

Cantwell referred to this madness. Among the unpublished sources for his biography of Wilson were "a collection of reports from British intelligence agents in Scotland to the Home Office in London, 1792-1793-1794, entitled *Correspondence-Home Office*".[165] The single volume reports for the years 1789-92 grew to three volumes a year after Dundas became Home Secretary in 1791.

No report on Wilson was included but his confidant in the affairs of the weavers, William Mitchell, turned out to be a government agent.[166] Had Mitchell acted as agent provocateur for Wilson's uncharacteristic act of blackmail? Whatever the prime cause, Wilson was in gaol when the New Year's Day attack was made on Scotland's democrats, and he may have been overlooked as a result.

Muir could have remained abroad but chose to return to face the court against the advice of his friends. In Scotland he felt the wrath of Lord Justice-Clerk Braxfield.[167] "Robert Burns was moved to write *Scots Wha Hae*, in protest. This song was immediately banned as seditious".[168] Muir and the other Scottish Martyrs have their memorial on Edinburgh's Calton Hill,[169] and are remembered in 'Botany Bay' to which they were sent as convicts.[170]

The Agitation of the 1790s.

Thomas Hardy, introduced by Thompson in the first paragraph of his book, returned to open his fifth chapter.[171] In the interim, Thompson had shown that 'the Dissenting and libertarian traditions' reached "far back into English history".[172] "[T]he agitation of the 1790s, although it lasted only five yeas (1792-6) was extraordinarily intensive and far-reaching. It altered the sub-political attitudes of the people, affected class alignments, and initiated traditions which stretch forward into the present century. It was not an agitation about France, although French events both inspired and bedevilled it. It was an English agitation, of impressive dimensions, for an English democracy".[173]

A quieter, but none the less critical, statement of contemporary political interest is to be found in Thomas Bewick's *Memoir*,[174] to which I had come in the first place through my interest in birds. Bewick's *History of British Birds* was first published in 1797. In Newcastle, following a severe illness, Bewick, "all mind and memory", worked on his production of Aesop's Fables, and the enrichment of his memoirs with a critical commentary on the war years. Bewick introduces his friends, "a set of staunch advocates for the liberties of Mankind", who met at the Blue Bell, the Sign of the Unicorn and the News Room, Newcastle, throughout the Napoleonic Wars.

Bewick is scathing in his criticism of "Mr Pit" for having first advocated parliamentary reform in 1781 and in office 'changed sides'. George III offered the Prime Ministership to him in December 1783 but Pitt continued to support this reform in 1784 and won much support throughout the country while Fox attacked such reforms as plans "to destroy not the form, but the essence of the House of Commons". Briggs held it to be "misleading to ignore the mood of 1784, although less misleading than to overlook, as nineteenth-century historians did, the absence of modern party ties and the crucial influence of patronage in assuring the election result".[175]

"For all Pitt's successes, the real victor in the election of March 1784 was neither the 'people' nor the young prime minister, but George III who had chosen Pitt as the agent of his plans to break what he regarded as a concerted attempt to undermine the Constitution". "[A]lthough [Pitt] went on to give to the office of prime minister a significance that it had never hitherto possessed, he never tried to assert his claims as prime minister against the King. Nor did he go on pressing for long in the new Parliament for the parliamentary reforms which he had advocated so eloquently in 1782 and 1783 but which he knew the King did not like".[176]

The turning point on this crucial issue came in April 1785 when proposals Pitt made to give seventy-two additional members of Parliament to London and the counties by arranging a voluntary and compensated surrender of the franchise in thirty-six decayed boroughs, were defeated in the House of Commons by 248 votes to 174. Pitt made considerable personal efforts to carry this reform, asserted Briggs. This defeat prevented Parliament from gradually and peacefully reforming itself,[177] leaving the way open to more radical movements.

'Constitutionalism', as argued by George III, above, 'was the flood-gate which the French...broke down. But the year was 1792, not 1789, and the waters which flowed through were those of Tom Paine'.[178] An earlier treatment of this theme may be found in the second chapter of this book, with Paine being prosecuted by government and an era of repression under way.

Thompson described 1792 as 'the *annus mirabilis* of Tom Paine. In twelve months his name became a household word. There were few places in the British Isles where his book had not penetrated. It served as a touchstone, dividing the gentlemen reformers and patrician Whigs, from a minority of radical manufacturers and professional men who wrought an alliance with the labourers and artisans, welcomed Paine's social and economic proposals, and looked in the direction of a republic.

Pitt's long-delayed decision to prosecute Paine signalled the opening of the era of repression. Outlawing Paine (and the banning of the *Rights of Man*) was preceded and accompanied by a sustained effort by authority to meet the reformers in the field'.[179]

Thompson pointed to the distribution of *Rights of Man* and the promotion of anti-Jocobin societies as proceeding nation wide. In England "the revolutionary impulse had scarcely begun to gather force before it was exposed to a counter-revolutionary assault backed by the resources of established authority".[180]

In weathering the storm, the London Corresponding Society emerged with significant changes in emphasis and tone. Paine's name and republicanism gave way to purifying the Constitution. Scotland, Sheffield and Norwich - not London - set the pace. The great majority of the reformers in the societies of 1793 were artisans, wage-earners, small masters and small tradesmen. Economic grievances and social remedies joined French forms of organisation and of address as new themes.[181]

Of Certain Radicals.

Joseph Gerrald, Maurice Margarot and John Thelwall were among members of the professions taking a leading part under the banner theme of "restoring the 'purity' of the Constitution".[182] Gerrald and Thelwall 'were closer than any others to having the metal of national leaders and theorists'. Gerrald 'advocated most forcefully the dangerous proposal of Paine - the calling of a National Convention of British reformers. It was this threat, of a general combination of reformers, and - an even more serious, and growing, threat - of an alliance between English and Scottish reformers and the United Irishmen, that determined the Government to act'.[183]

As for John Thelwall, five letters to him from the poet, Samuel Taylor Coleridge,[184] belong to this decade and may serve as his introduction.[185] Each letter is in reply to and is inspired by Thelwall. There is a friendship and understanding between the two, of seriousness tempered by good humour.

For instance, on November 19 [1796] Coleridge wrote from Oxford Street, Bristol, to Thelwall, saying "...Your portrait of yourself interested me. As to my face, unless when animated by immediate eloquence, expresses great sloth, and great, indeed, almost idiotic good-nature. 'Tis a mere carcass of a face, fat, flabby, and expressive chiefly of inexpression. Yet I am told that my eyes, eyebrows, and forehead are physiognomically good; but of this the deponent knoweth not".[186]

I.A. Richards described Coleridge differently. "In person he was a tall, dark, handsome young man, with long, black, flowing hair; eyes not merely dark, but black, and keenly penetrating; a fine forehead, a deep-toned, harmonious voice; a manner never to be forgotten, full of life, vivacity, and kindness; dignified in person and, added to all these, exhibiting the elements of his future greatness".[187]

Thelwall and Coleridge agreed that "[i]t is the principal felicity of life and the chief glory of manhood to speak out fully on all subjects"; that "[h]e who thinks and feels will be virtuous; and he who is absorbed in self will be vicious, whatever may be his speculative opinions". References are made by them to poetry, their own and others, and to matters of life, death and the hereafter.

It seems that this text has been diverted from Thelwall, to Coleridge. Be patient, for the latter also had a place in the great controversy over the French Revolution. As evidence of a general criticism of English social structure, Coleridge and Southey planned to form an ideal community in America.[188] It would consist of twelve couples. This was in June 1794, after Coleridge had walked to Oxford to meet Southey.[189] Following marriage and the birth of his first son, in September 1797, Coleridge moved to a cottage at Nether Stowey, while the Wordworths, William and sister Dorothy, moved to Alfoxden just three miles away.[190]

"Soon came a visit from 'Citizen Thelwall,' a leading anti-Government democratic agitator. Coleridge had been disagreeing with him for some time in more and more friendly letters. His visit created local alarm. Wordsworth's coming had been bad enough, with his mysterious solitary walks toward the sea. (A French invasion, we must remember, was expected.) But now! Soon there was an agent observing and reporting on their doings, conversation, and visitors. This agent seems to have been a capable and sensible man, and in a conversation struck up on the road found Coleridge no friend to Jacobinism".[191]

On moving to Stowey, Coleridge had written: "I have accordingly snapped my squeaking baby-trumpet of sedition, and have hung up its fragments in the chamber of Penetences". The influence of Nether Stowey worked on Thelwall, too (p.306).[192] "Walking with Thelwall in the Quantocks in the summer of 1797, the poets came to a beautiful secluded dell. 'Citizen John,' said Coleridge, 'this is a fine place to talk treason in'. 'Nay, Citizen Samuel', replied Thelwall, 'it is rather a place to make a man forget that there is any necessity for treason'."

Be that as it may, Coleridge's and Wordsworth's earlier support of the French Revolution was well known. In 1795, Coleridge delivered an address at Bristol,[193] which in spite of its reasonableness and criticism of the same Revolution was considered to have 'Treason in it'. Because it was written "at one sitting between the hours of twelve at night and the Breakfast Time of the day, on which it was delivered...no literary Vanity prompted me to the printing of it - the reasons which compelled me to publish it forbad me to correct it..."

Coleridge left it to the reader to decide on those reasons but the previous paragraph provides a clue. This letter was written from 25 College Street, Bristol. Coleridge reported, "the opposition of the Aristocrats is so furious and determined, that I begin to fear, that the Good I do is not proportionate to the Evil I occasion- Mobs and Mayors, Blockheads and Brickbats, Placards and Press gangs have leagued in horrible Conspiracy against me- The Democrats are as sturdy in the support of me - but their number is comparatively small. Two or three uncouth and untrained Automata have threatened my Life- and in the last Lecture the Genus infirnum were scarcely restrained from attacking the house in which the "damn'd Jacobin was jawing away".[194]

Thelwall in a tour of East Anglia delivered "twenty-two lectures in Norwich; but at Yarmouth he and his audience were brutally assaulted by ninety sailors, armed with cutlasses and bludgeons, who had been sent for this purpose from a naval frigate lying in harbour".[195]

Liberty and the law.[196]

Ian Gilmour had no qualms about labelling Hanoverian England's "criminal law...the most violent feature of English life".[197] He looked at "legitimacy in dispute" from "The Glorious Revolution" to "Jacobitism and the 'Forty-five'".[198] In the second part, Gilmour turned to "powers and grievances" pausing to seriously consider - the army and the riot act, crime and the criminal law, the press gang, the game laws and cruelty to animals, election skulduggery, food riots, industrial disputes, and duelling.

The third and final section is headed "Avoidance of Revolution" to which reference was made in an earlier chapter. [199]

One of the resources of established authority brought to bear upon the London Corresponding Society was the law, Thompson argued. English law provided for summary convictions by local magistrates but "the Law Officers of the Crown were reluctant to advise major prosecutions".

"The law of sedition was indefinite", and "Fox's Libel Act (1792) [made] the jury the judge of the matter as well as of the fact". "It was, perhaps, Fox's greatest service to the common people, passed at the eleventh hour before the tide turned towards repression. Thus, in England, the Government was faced with a series of obstacles: an indefinite law, the jury system (which humiliated authority...twice...), a small but brilliant Foxite opposition...[including] Thómas Erskine (who led the defence in several trials), [and] a public opinion saturated with constitutional rhetoric and willing to spring to the defence of any invasion of individual liberties".[200]

"But Scottish law was different. Here the judges were docile or partisan, the juries could be picked with impunity. Here also the Scottish 'Friends of the people' had held a National Convention in December 1792. The Scottish trials of 1793-4 were aimed not only at the very vigorous Scottish Jacobin societies, but also at the societies in England".

Thompson continued. "The first blow was struck in August 1793, when Thomas Muir, the most gifted Scottish leader, was sentenced to fourteen years transportation after a scandalous mock trial. Braxfield, the Lord Justice-Clerk, was more virulent in his conduct than the prosecution.

Donald B. McIntyre included Lord Braxfield (Robert Macqueen) among 'Some Notable Edinburgh Characters: chiefly Lawyers and Disputants'. Master Horner in the following reference was the father of Francis and Leonard Horner.[201]

"Come awa', Maaster Horner, come awa', and help us to hang ane o' thae damned scoondrels," he whispered to a juror who passed behind the bench. In his charge to the jury he treated Muir's ability and his propaganda among "ignorant country people, and among the lower classes, making them leave off their work", as an aggravation:

"Mr Muir might have known that no attention could be paid to such a rabble. What right had they to representation? A Government...should be just like a corporation; and in this country, it is made up of the landed interest, which alone has a right to be represented",[202] an idea that has already been noted, above.

"One thing", he informed the jury, "Required 'no proof': the British constitution is the best that ever was since the creation of the world, and it is not possible to make it better". His learned fellow judges concurred in all of this. One of them - Lord Swinton - opining that the crime of sedition included "every sort of crime, murder, robbery, rapine, fire-raising...If punishment adequate to the crime...were to be sought for, it could not be found in our law, now that torture is happily abolished".[203]

Thompson had it, that "In September a second blow followed: the Rev. T. F. Palmer, an English Unitarian minister and Fellow of Queen's College, Cambridge, then ministering in Dundee, was tried at Perth. His "crime' was that of encouraging the reading of Paine, and membership of the Dundee Friends of Liberty - described as a society of 'low weavers and mechanics'. A bench of crocodiles wept copiously as they sentenced him to their 'mildest punishment' of seven years transportation to Botany Bay".[204]

As explained by Thompson, above, a sharper breed of lawyers produced less subservient jurors who thwarted attempts to bring down the leadership of the London Corresponding Society. Even Pitt was called to show his earlier involvement with the basic principles of Parliamentary reform for which the Society's leaders were now before the Courts. Nevertheless the Society's open existence was coming to a close. Having provided encouragement by example to the people of the ships, the London Corresponding Society faded away, with the memories of the fleet mutinies of 1797.

Enclosures.

Alice Clark described *Husbandmen* as 'the most numerous class in the village community. Possessed of a small-holding at a fixed customary rent and with rights of grazing on the common, they could maintain a position of independence'.[205]

Without the common, enclosures forcefully separated families from land and living and from the moral economy of primary production. Rootless, they were pushed into towns towards the proliferating factories. Here again the law was no friend to the poor.

Enclosures of commons seem to be far removed from working class concerns such as silk production and ship building yet they had in common the stripping away of non-monetary customary forms of payment to workers. Hobsbawm pointed to contrary outcomes. "In terms of economic productivity this social transportation was an immense success; in terms of human suffering, a tragedy, deepened by the agricultural depression after 1815 which reduced the rural poor to demoralized destitution. After 1800 even so enthusiastic a champion of enclosure and agricultural progress as Arthur Young was shaken by its social effects".[206]

Christopher Hill and Enclosures.

"Popular revolt was for many centuries an essential feature of the English tradition, and the middle decades of the seventeenth century saw the greatest upheaval that has yet occurred in Britain".[207] As Christopher Hill declared, "the long-term consequences of the Revolution were all to the advantage of the gentry and merchants, not of the lower fifty per cent of the population on whom" he focussed.[208]

According to Hill there were two revolutions in mid seventeenth-century England. "The one which succeeded established the sacred rights of property (abolition of feudal tenures, no arbitrary taxation), gave political power to the propertied (sovereignty of Parliament and common law, abolition of prerogative courts), and removed all impediments to the triumph of the ideology of the men of property - the protestant ethic. There was, however, another revolution, which never happened, though from time to time it threatened. This might have established communal property, a far wider democracy in political and legal institutions, might have disestablished the state church and rejected the protestant ethic".

Hill noted, that "Before 1641, and after 1660, there was a strict censorship. In the intervening years of freedom, a printing press was a relatively cheap and portable piece of equipment". Radical ideas were published. Class hostility exposed.[209]

A 'bitter and distrustful' attitude of English common people towards the gentry and nobility had been noted in 1614. These sentiments were reciprocated, according to Hill. "This class antagonism was exacerbated by the financial hardships of the years from 1620 to 1650" reported "as economically among the most terrible in English history".[210] At the same time "[t]he essence of feudal society was the bond of loyalty and dependence between lord and man", between master and servant, which was loosening by the sixteenth century.

No longer outlaws, masterless men, "alone or with a consort"[211] were increasing in numbers and were the subject of Hill's third chapter, in which he categorised them. First were "rogues, vagabonds and beggars, roaming the countryside in search of employment, too often mere unemployable rejects of a society in economic transformation, whose population was expanding rapidly.[212] Other vagabonds found London "what the greenwood had been for the medieval outlaw - an anonymous refuge. There was more casual labour in London than anywhere else, there was more charity, and there were better prospects for earning a dishonest living". This "was a large population, mostly living very near if not below the poverty line little influenced by religious or political ideology".[213]

Protestant sectaries formed the third category of masterless men. These people had opted out of the state church, so closely modelled on the hierarchical structure of society, so tightly controlled by parson and squire. Sects were strongest in the towns, where they created hospitable communities for men, often immigrants, who aspired to keep themselves above the level of casual labour and pauperism: small craftsmen, apprentices, serious-minded laborious men" who "organised social services, poor relief etc. for their members: they provided social insurance in this world as well as in the next".[214]

Commons and Commoners.

Hill's fourth category was the "rural equivalent of the London poor", the "cottagers and squatters on commons, wastes and in forests".[215] These are the people who will introduce enclosures as the next great disturbance to be discussed in this chapter.

Like Hill's first two categories, "these were victims of the rapid expansion of England's population in the sixteenth century; sometimes the victims, sometimes the beneficiaries of the rise of new or the growth of old industries. Unlike the relatively stable and docile populations of open arable areas, these men...often had no lords to whom they owed dependence or from whom they could hope for protection. They might exist for long enough to establish a precarious customary claim to continuance", and labourers were not prevented from erecting a cottage close to mineral works, coal mines, quarries, etc. These people "were liable to suffer from large-scale schemes for agricultural betterment...Meanwhile they existed, in the interstices of society, but undoubtedly growing in numbers by migration".[216]

Hill confronts a range of contemporary opinion in coming to terms with commoners, forests and commons.[217] Ideas as early as the 1530s for carving new holdings from the waste to settle the poor were at odds with royal policies of disafforestation, enclosure and draining of the fens. The Good Shepherd might have provided a table for the poor in the presence of their enemies but this beneficence or providence was not to last.

In a later chapter concerning *Levellers and True Levellers,* Hill argued that "Winstanley's conclusion...was absolutely right", "that communal cultivation of the commons was the crucial question, the starting point from which common people all over England could build up an equal community".

"Winstanley", Hill continued, "had arrived at the one possible democratic solution which was not merely backward looking, as all other radical proposals during the revolutionary decades - an agrarian law, partial inheritance, stable copyholds - tended to be. The economic arguments against those who merely defended commoners' traditional rights in the waste were overwhelming. England's growing population could be fed only by more intensive cultivation, by bringing marginal land under the plough. Enclosure by men with capital, brutally disregarding the rights of commoners, did at least do the job; in the long run, its advocates rightly claimed, it created more employment. But in the short run it disrupted a way of life, causing intense misery; and the employment which it did ultimately create was not of a sort to attract free commoners".[218]

"The radical agrarian programme was defeated...After 1649 the Rump of the Long Parliament did nothing to encourage agrarian reform, despite continued protests, as when Colonel John Pyne, radical M.P. for Poole, denounced "the taking away the right of the poor in their commons". On the contrary, acts were passed for fen drainage and to protect deer against poachers. The Barebones Parliament appears to have taken no notice of a scheme for nationalizing forests, fens and waste lands throughout England, and letting them with first offer to the poor. J.P.s restricted the right to gather fuel from the waste. The bill introduced into Parliament in 1656, commonly referred to as the last legislative attempt to prevent enclosure, actually proposed to regulate commons and commonable land so as to prevent depopulation whilst improving the waste".[219]

Christopher Hill revisited these studies of seventeenth century England in 1976. His first mention of "enclosures", is to "gentlemen leaders of the House of Commons and their clerical allies" turning "a blind eye to anti-enclosure riots", among other matters in 1640-42.[220]

"I have argued elsewhere", Hill said, "that the main long-term significance of the English Revolution was neither constitutional nor political nor religious but economic. In trade and agriculture it cleared the way for the capitalist development which made it possible for England to become the country of the first Industrial Revolution".

Hill argued that the "defeat of the radicals in the Revolution ensured the triumph of capitalist agriculture, at the cost of a disruption of traditional ways of life; the home market expanded because of enclosure and the subjugation of men and women to what they regarded as the slavery of wage labour".[221]

The agricultural boom, which followed, solved the problem of feeding an increasing population. "England became a corn-exporting country, and agriculture became the country's greatest capitalist industry. The total standard of living rose, but the profits of this boom went to the rich. The poor were dispossessed or forced into wage labour. This contributed to the decline of the size of the Parliamentary electorate, and enhanced the control over it of the well-to-do. Gregory King's table of 1696 suggests that paupers and wage-labourers may have amounted to half the population. They were wholly dependent on their superiors, incapable of political independence. In the eighteenth century they would be called the mob".[222]

A "Commercial Revolution" with English merchants buying colonial goods cheap and selling them dear is marked by a doubling of tonnage in the port of London between 1640 and 1680.[223] "The profits of this monopoly of imperial trade were founded largely on slavery; this cannot too often be emphasized, in view especially of the coy silence of many orthodox economic historians on the subject".[224]

African slaves in the New World had become, like the poor in Europe, the new 'milch cows of the rich'.

J.L. and Barbara Hammond: enclosures, 'a gigantic disturbance'.

In Britain, village labourers, a lower social order, would continue to lose their rights to the commons with enclosures, which literally drove, and then fenced them out. Enclosures were "assumed by the enlightened opinion of the day to be beneficent and progressive, [but were] none the less a gigantic disturbance".[225]

Between the years 1700 and 1844, 2 706 Acts of Parliament affected four and a quarter million acres of "Common Field and some Waste". Over the same period, 1 385 Acts of Parliament affected one and three quarter millions of Waste only.

Together these total 4,000 Acts and 6,000,000 acres.[226] Enclosures then marked "a national revolution, making sweeping and profound changes in the form and the character of agricultural society throughout England".[227]

These authors argued, that "if agriculture suddenly became a great industry, multiplying England's resources, as some say, twenty fold, an equitable readjustment would have increased the prosperity of all classes engaged in that industry".[228] In fact, the wages of village labourers were capped, and topped up by charity, on the one hand, and on the other, poorer and demoralised, they were fed into new industrial towns based on steam power. Their social futures were as black as the coal they used. [229]

Hammond, et al. compared an enclosed with an unenclosed village.[230] In the former "the normal labourer did not depend on his wages alone. His livelihood was made up from various sources". What these sources were, are described in their loss to the labourer, which follows.

"In an enclosed village at the end of the eighteenth century the position of the agricultural labourer was very different. All his auxiliary resources had been taken from him, and he was now a wage earner and nothing more. Enclosure had robbed him of the strip that he tilled, of the cow that he kept on the village pasture, of the fuel that he picked up in the woods, and of the turf that he tore from the common. And while a social revolution had swept away his possessions, an industrial revolution had swept away his family earnings. To families living on the scale of the village poor, each of these losses was a crippling blow, and the total effect of the changes was to destroy their economic independence".

J. M. Neeson leaves no turf unturned, as it were, in a challenging study of *Commoners: Common Right, Enclosure and Social Change in England, 1700-1820.* For example, lack of imagination led to historians failing to understand the value of peasant access to commons and waste. Gleaning, mentioned above, is given in detail as one example of common right exercised in a wider context.[231]

Clark wrote of husbandmen's children gathering 'scraps of wool from the brambles on the common'.[232]

Enclosures provide an obvious field for study, a balanced report proving useful to the position argued. As a discrete chapter (9), 'Resisting enclosure' followed the 'decline and disappearance' of the commons, in the sense caused by parliamentary enclosure. This ended Part II of this study.

'Making freeman of the slave' [*Made freeman of the slave,* John Clare,[233] quoted in context (p.297)] is a sole concluding chapter in Part III. There the argument flowers for commoners defined as peasants.

Little if anything is taken from the Hammonds' 'gigantic disturbances' by a 'revisionist wave' of literature. Jerome Blum placed the first 'stirrings' in the interwar and war years, followed by a 'barrage' 'after...World War II'.

Blum advanced a useful observation with much wider application, in noting how 'The debate about parliamentary enclosures can serve as a textbook example of the ebb and flow of historians' evaluations of the significance of an historical phenomenon'. [234]

Changes in the Landscape of a Once Forested Land.

There are other sources than the written word, important as they are, for information on early farm practice. W.G. Hoskins found evidence in the landscape for this pre-enclosure world. The ancient pattern was in places fixed under grass. Hoskins read the "complexity of...medieval and earlier landscape in the intricate pattern of ridge-and-furrow where the old-time arable had been converted to pasture and the plough ceased to disturb the soil".[235]

Hoskins described its beginnings. "Until well on in time the greater part of the English landscape was unplanned, above all in the Highland Zone of the west and north of the country. Here the fields, the winding lanes, the hedge banks and the wriggling walls, were the work of millions of now-unknown peasants and their families, working with the only tools they possessed – the axe, the mattock and the spade. Hence the smallness of fields created in this way, and their irregular shape as they met obstacles and moved around them rather than waste time moving a huge tree or a massive boulder. It was a landscape made piecemeal, almost yard by yard".[236]

Jacquetta Hawkes's book, *A Land*, told the story simply and well, and of her thoughts on reading her book, for the first time for a quarter of a century. She said it had come "directly out of my being: emotion had aroused my imagination and imagination had kindled both memories of childhood...and my study...of the world's past".[237]

That earlier landform had to be read with many aids, geological and geomorphological, with fossil pollen analysis among them. Comparisons with existing glacial and other landscapes across the earth were instructive. Later, Charles Darwin's life and work was evidence of the process of one man's learning about, and of coming to terms with, this vast information source.[238] Like other eighteenth and nineteenth century people, he experienced and in turn contributed to 'the shock of the new', and suffered the disturbance of religious and other dogmas.[239]

Diminishing forests also tell a story of man's impact on the land. Derek Ratcliffe[240] in a classic book on the Peregrine Falcon told how early and later Stone Age people colonised Britain as the ice retreated. Their cumulative effect on the forests was minor. People of the bronze and later iron ages with better tools cleared more forest but it was their use of timber as metal-smelting fuel that had the more profound effect.

"Deforestation had become significant in Roman times and it continued to accelerate through later centuries, reaching a peak in the Middle Ages and finally leaving a country largely denuded of its woodlands by 1800".[241] Wooden ships, war and expanding navies made a large contribution to this decline. "Man thus incidentally provided good Peregrine habitat in plenty," according to Ratcliffe, "a vast expanse of open or only partly wooded country which the bird especially favours in its hunting" with "an abundance of prey species in most districts".[242] Nature herself provided some protection of nesting sites in wild mountains and precipitous cliffs.

The taming of the first Peregrine went unrecorded but falconry has been followed for thousands of years. Art and literature recorded what Frederick II described as 'the noblest of all arts'[243] taking us back to early Egyptians and Chinese. Marco Polo described the use of Falcons and other hawks in China in the hunting of the great Khan.

Ratcliffe gave as the greatest impulse to falconry the returning Crusaders of the thirteenth century, following which it persisted for some four hundred years in Europe.[244] But, habits change. In England, Falcon and Hawk shared with Commoner the effects of extensive land enclosures of the late 1700s.[245] Each was ruthlessly excluded from game reserves. Douglas Hay researched poaching and the game laws at a specific site, Cannock Chase.[246] Hay concluded. "The acts of revenge [of poachers or commoners who had suffered for their landlord's game] challenge an historiography that is increasingly complacent about the social harmonies of that society".[247]

John Clare (1793-1864).[248]

There is symmetry in this chapter - early and late - in the stories of Alexander Wilson and John Clare. Each shared an intimate early life experience with a primal space, geographically distinct and circumscribed by walking distance.[249] Each was working class and suffered for it, found consolation in the natural world, closely observing and recording its sounds, forms, and colours; and at the same time responding imaginatively while yet holding firmly to basic human rights.

Wilson, and Clare, in turn, also suffered separation from an earlier love by the barrier of social status.[250] Each would suffer critical 'put downs'. Wilson was to be overshadowed by Audubon,[251] and Clare by Wordsworth and Coleridge. But each now has an assured place in his respective sphere - ornithology and poetry. Which, of course, was no consolation to either, when living!

William George Hoskins, who added landscape to my first experience of Clare through his bird poems, selected his verse to head a chapter in his "Parliamentary Enclosure".[252]

"Inclosure, thou'rt a curse upon the land,

And tasteless was the wretch who thy existence plann'd".

To Clare, Hoskins gave the credit for describing in prose and poetry what the change to the heath lands meant in *detail.* Clare's view was 'truer' than Crabbe's, being "the peasant's view from the inside, born in it and part of it". "Clare was the great exception, an articulate peasant", sharp of eye and ear and with the ability to record his observations.

Sir Harry Godwin, botanist, paid tribute to Clare's power of visual observation, when writing of the now extinct "meres" or freshwater lakes of Fenland. An idea on certain preconditions for the existence of one of the meres was "elegantly supported by a letter written by the country poet, John Clare, in 1825 in which he mentions that Whittlesey 'is also a place very common for the cranberry that trails to the brink of the mere'". The cranberry's habitat was confirmed as "a plant of acidic Sphagnum bogs" the precise requirement for the "conjecture" to which Godwin alludes.[253]

Hugh Haughton held that Clare produced "the one genuine attempt in the period to reproduce the song of the nightingale, as it were, verbatim".[254]

Eric Robinson wrote of the natural affinity the environment movement has, with both Clare's nature poetry and his sense of loss through enclosure. Robinson pointed to other aspects of Clare's literary work and shared in the task of selecting "from over two thousand poems and several hundreds of passages of prose and letters...an anthology" of Clare's *Political Verse and Prose* under the title, *A Champion for the Poor.*[255] His great satirical work, "The Parish", of over 2000 lines is to be found there.

Christopher Hill, who devoted the penultimate chapter in *Liberty Against the Law* to John Clare, had this to say of him.

"So Clare lamenting the final triumph of enclosure over the poor, and Clare fighting for freedom to write as he wished, offered a fitting conclusion to the story I have tried to tell of the defeat of freedom by law, property and accepted middle-class standards. As a contributory factor to his madness,[256] Clare cherishing a hopeless passion for Mary Joyce, a girl who was socially too superior for him to be able to marry her, also makes a relevant point. Clare's was not a sentimental romantic nostalgia. It was a practical, personal sense of shared loss. The things he loved, and which inspired him to write, were doomed; but he retained solidarity with the victims of transportation and imprisonment, and with the Swing rioters[257] executed for opposition to the "vast numbers of newly-made laws that took away rights from the common people". Although he often expressed himself cautiously, Clare retained strong social and political feelings".[258]

'The Dark Side of the Landscape'.

Clare had his moments of opportunity when patrons opened the door to publication of some of his poetry, to visits to London, and to books. But he was still of the rural poor, with all of its poverty and separateness. This chapter concludes with a reference to "The rural poor in English painting 1730-1840", by John Barrell.[259] He argued that the "vision of rural life" presented "can be understood only by understanding the constraints - often apparently aesthetic but in fact moral and social - that determined how the poor could, or rather how they could *not* be represented".

Barrell looked at the "minute social distinctions and nuances of status", [which Asa Briggs had described in a different context] and which he said "needed a novelist like Jane Austen to trace the delicate pattern".[260] But Barrell held that the "poor" were "coming to be thought of as a class, as the distant generalised objects of fear and benevolence" in eighteenth-century literature.[261] A dividing line made "brilliantly if misleadingly clear" by the need to keep "the labouring poor alive by supplementing their wages by public or private charity".

The poor themselves were aware of their eroded rights, conscious of needing charity even when employed, and resentful of the demeaning "postures" they had to assume to receive it. This, Barrell argued, was "class-consciousness".[262]

In this perceptive study the author focussed on the agricultural worker and the art of rural life. He concluded that the social conflict in the countryside "is largely ignored by the poetry of rural life...and it never breaks the surface of rural life, except...in a number of paintings by George Morland".[263]

Barrell continued. "For the most part the art of rural life offers us the image of a stable, unified, almost egalitarian society; so that my concern in this book is to suggest that it is possible to look beneath the surface of the painting, and to discover there evidence of the very conflict it seems to deny".

The paintings discussed were produced for the rich, and the above constraints "governed how the labouring, the vagrant, and the mendicant poor could be portrayed so as to be an acceptable part of the *décor* of the drawing rooms of the polite, when in their own persons they would have been unlikely to gain admission even to the kitchens".

Barrell suggests "that we should ask ourselves whether we do not still, in the ways we admire Gainsbrough, Stubbs, and Constable, identify with the interests of their customers and against the poor they portray".[264]

The reader is reminded that Gainsborough claimed to take as little account as possible of figures in the landscape, while in the work of Constable, with which the tradition closes, the figures are so small as to almost escape notice. Again "tattered clothes, heavy boots and agricultural implements" distinguish this tradition.[265]

"The demand for both poetry and painting to offer a more English image of rural life was understood to be the same thing as the demand for a more actualised image of that life".[266]

Barrell describes "Clare's poem...speak[ing] to us of a developing class-consciousness in the rural poor - the perception of the difference between what they might be, and what others force them to be".[267] "The "rough rude ploughman" is, then, "the necessary tool of wealth and pride" (lines 14-15), and Clare was rapped over the knuckles for saying so by his evangelical patron Lord Radstock, who accused him of "radical and ungrateful sentiments"[268] – lacking, that is, that air of submissiveness that was also missing from Morland's alehouse labourers.

Time would tell how many of the labouring poor, both rural and urban, "lacking that air of submissiveness" would find themselves in a convict transport on the way to "Botany Bay". David Kent, in his introduction, described Joseph Mason's 'real offence, for which he could not be openly charged, was that he was a radical, a critic of the *status quo* which condemned rural labourers in southern England to live in desperate poverty and kept them politically powerless to alter their circumstances'- in 1830.[269]

"The insignificance of mere sympathy as a political or economic force has rarely been better illustrated than in 1830, when the bulk of the counties' rulers agreed that the labourers' demands were just, indeed modest, and ought to be conceded, though the government in London, full of ideology and the fear of revolution, took a different view",[270] as it had done before, and would do again.

Chapter 8

WOMEN ABOARD, SHIPS AT SEA AND 'THE SHIP-OF-LIFE'

Ships at Sea.

"The British Royal Navy in the Age of Sail - ruler of the waves and protector of the world's largest empire - has always been accounted a strictly male preserve, Britain's strongest bastion of male exclusivity. The belief was ancient and ubiquitous that women had no place at sea. They not only were weak, hysterical,[1] and feckless and distracted the men from their duties, but they also brought bad luck to the ships they traveled (sic) in; they called forth supernatural winds that sank the vessels and drowned the men".

Suzanne J. Stark had long contemplated the subject of women in the Royal Navy when she published that opening paragraph in 1998.[2] Accounts may be found in her book of "women in disguise in naval crews", and "The Story of Mary Lacy, Alias William Chandler", but there is more to this book than intriguing stories. It serves to introduce the social conditions of women in the late eighteenth century.

Before taking up that theme, a moment considering a special case should not go amiss. Should women have travelled on those allied naval vessels, which took part in voyages of discovery in the eighteenth and early nineteenth centuries? Authorities thought not! Certain women - and some men - held the contrary view.

The first Western woman to see and sail across the Pacific was Jeanne Baré (Bonnefoy) in male disguise, a member of the French explorer Bougainville's expedition of 1766-69.[3]

Rose de Freycinet was disguised to go aboard the French ship, *Uranie.* Her presence had the full co-operation of the expedition's leader and captain of the ship, Louis de Freycinet, her husband. Although this caused a storm it was nothing compared to the joys and travails of their shared expedition, which lasted from 1817-1820 and included shipwreck.[4]

In England, Anne Chappelle and Matthew Flinders, married on Friday, 17 April 1801, and by Monday were on board the *Investigator* at the Nore. However, their undisguised intention to sail together received short shrift from the Admiralty. Anne Flinders was left behind.[5]

Elizabeth Waterhouse married George Bass on the 8 October 1800, but with no thought of sailing off together. Thoughts only came later with the anguish of separation. By then of course Bass had turned from discovery to commerce, and eventually disappeared somewhere, perhaps in the Pacific Ocean.[6]

In 1792 Mary Ann Parker was given two weeks to make up her mind to sail with her husband, John, captain of HMS *Gorgon* on a voyage around the world. She decided to go, leaving two children behind. Mary's account of her journey when published was financially timely as her husband died in 1775 leaving a large family.[7]

Whether women went aboard, or stayed behind, life would not be easy for them. Or would it? Hear what NAM Rodger has written.

"Unfortunately there has been virtually no research undertaken into what one might call the female half of the naval community as a whole: not the minority of women who went to sea, but the wives and mothers who stayed at home, bringing up small children, earning their living as best they might while their men were at sea, enduring years of absence and uncertainty. They represent an enormous void of ignorance, and our knowledge of the social history of the Navy will never be complete until someone fills it".[8]

In the minutes of William Redfern's court martial there are references to two women, Mrs Holland and Mrs Evans on board H.M.S. *Standard* at sea with the North Sea Fleet in 1797.[9] Mrs Holland was alleged to have spoken out in the Galley. Mrs Evans was the wife of John Evans, seaman, who went to the Committee looking for her to see if she had been sworn. He was asked, "Did they swear her?" Evans replied, "Yes". On being asked, "What oath did your wife take?" Evans replied, "The same that we took but I don't know exactly what it was. It was to stand true to the Cause until we had obtained the King's Pardon".[10]

Possibly, another reference was to a "prisoner's wife [who] was doing something at the stove" and "speaking against the business we were going about".[11] As neither *Holland* nor *Evans* was among the names of those listed in either one of the two courts martial of people arrested on *Standard,* this suggests a third woman aboard.[12]

These specific references to women at sea aboard a Royal Navy battleship may be compared with those of historians Stark (1998), Lewis (1960), Kemp (1970), Lavery (1995), and more lately, Rodger himself (2006).

Perhaps the person who gave Redfern a midwifery text on the eve of his joining the Navy was aware of the presence of women on board such ships.

What did the three male authors have to say about women in the Fleet? Lewis referred to "the whole illogical system of indiscriminate pressing, with its corollary of not allowing the men shore-leave when in port".[13] Kemp, looking back to the 1750s, discussed wives and prostitutes as "the anodynes, which made naval life bearable for the men in wartime".[14] Lavery gave the usual reasons for women being on seagoing Navy ships.[15]

Rodger mentioned their presence on Royal Navy ships for the periods 1660-88 (page134), 1689-1714 (212-3), 1763-92 (407), 1803-15 (505-6), and 1793-1815 (526-7).[16]

Our historians agreed that while women and very young children were few in number on ships at sea, young boys were common. Those women who were carried to sea were more likely to be wives of officers, petty officers, or soldiers. The latter would be marines, or soldiers in transit to distant stations.[17]

The wives of the first group had definite roles aboard ship. Looking after the sick and wounded was one of them. There is an account of women being stationed in the cockpit to assist the surgeon during a battle. Another refers to the refusal of service medals to two women who had served on a battleship.

Women could be granted supernumerary status for victualling and receive two thirds of the full allowance. Apparently these attached women helped the men with odds and ends, sewing, etc. for which they received payment from the seamen on their rare pay days.

Stark confirmed, that "there were women living and working in naval ships from the late seventeenth century to the middle of the nineteenth, although their presence on board was officially ignored and even hidden".[18] Some women in male disguise might be among them.

There was another class of ship for which "women were actually mustered, victualled, and paid" and to which Stark drew attention. These were hospital ships, where nurses and laundresses, either or both, were employed and paid able seamen's wages.

Specific references are made to women mustered in hospital ships for the years 1696, 1703, 1705, 1731, 1743, 1747, and 1749 and earlier still between the years 1756-63 throughout the Seven Years War. A nurse's task was to feed her patient and keep patient and bed linen clean. They had a difficult time. Their presence was resented by some officers, strongly supported by one particular surgeon, and no doubt appreciated, too, by many an unnamed seaman at the end of his tether.[19]

The small number of women at sea, at any time, may be compared with the hundreds present when the ships docked.[20] In the main, these were prostitutes, unknown and unnamed. Among them, one young woman was found to be heavily pregnant but gave birth ashore the next day. According to Stark, this account was a unique first hand report of an individual prostitute on board. [21]

Some gave birth on the ship[22] between the guns on the gun deck, giving life to the expression "son-of-a-gun". No 'daughters-of-a-gun'? The gun deck was the site of a variety of engagements, in battle with the enemy, and by night the slinging of hammocks; in port this deck was frequented by women in their hundreds. Wives, mistresses and prostitutes engaged in talking, singing, dancing and sharing the hammocks.

Stark described the process of giving shore leave as initiating "The Prostitutes Retreat to Shore".[23] For acceptance by authority, shore leave awaited a return to a volunteer Navy. This in turn followed the end of the war with France in 1815, with a reduced demand for seamen to man the ships, and the end of impressment and quotas.

While the conditions of war prevailed, so did "the prime reason why a woman joined the navy or marines" which "was to escape the restricted economic and social status assigned to women". Stark went on to say, that it "was, however, only the most daring and unconventional woman who was willing to take the extraordinary step of changing her gender role in order to gain the social and financial advantages of a man".[24]

Stark continued this theme, contrasting the life of a seaman for males with that for females. Men found it restricting. Women found social freedom there, denied to women outside where most profitable jobs and many recreational and social activities were forbidden.

"On shipboard a woman seaman was able to join the men as an equal in both work and play. She was no longer treated with condescension by her male peers".

Alice Clark, in her classic (economic sociology) text based on specific primary records of named individuals, *Working Life of Women in the Seventeenth Century* (1919), revealed earlier root causes for such pronounced trends.[25]

Lewis, not for any philosophical reason but purely on numbers at sea, placed women last among the categories of the crew.[26] In action, the behaviour of women was highly commendable.[27] Women brought powder to the guns which required scrambling up and down ladders from deck to deck. It was none the less dangerous for being a task women shared with boys. There was the constant risk of explosion and fire. Women gave sustenance to the wounded, in the blood and anguish of the cockpit, and helped the surgeon there.

There was "a number of genuine applications from women" for the "1847 Naval General Service Medal [open] to all survivors who could prove their presence at any of the specified actions in the Revolutionary and Napoleonic Wars". These, Queen Victoria ruled against,[28] even though recommended by her very own Royal Navy. What was the precedence this noble lady did not wish to establish? [29]

One woman, who went to sea as the pregnant wife of an A.B., gave birth to a son on HMS *Tremendous* a few days before the Glorious First of June battle in 1794. Being male, it was her "son-of-a-gun" who got the medal.[30]

Stark's book has its surprises, and moments of high drama and tragedy. It takes the reader back to Spithead, this time as the site of the accidental sinking of two famous ships. The earlier one is marked on the *Admiralty Chart 394* and is the Elizabethan wreck site of the ship *Mary Rose*. The second ship, the *Royal George*, was lost at Spithead on 29 August 1782 to be commemorated in a poem by William Cowper.

"Down went the *Royal George*"[31] and Admiral Kempenfelt too, with his crew of eight hundred men. "As she lay at anchor, 'slightly careened', undergoing some repairs, the ship's frames being completely decayed, the bottom suddenly dropped out of her, the result of building vessels with unseasoned timber during the Seven Years War and afterwards.[32]

Stark, discovered that "four hundred prostitutes [and] four hundred Bibles - the first allotment of Bibles donated for the uplift of seamen by the Naval and Military Bible Society" - were also lost.[33]

Women were shown to have had a long association with seamen, sailors and ships, changing little from Pepys's time to the close of the Napoleonic Wars. The continuing links were war and the failure to provide shore leave for seamen.[34]

Some men solved their personal problems by "running", a decision made easier by the crowding environment of men-of-war ships. Those who stayed, as working parts of a man-o-war - not inappropriately named - presented their commanding officers with a difficult choice - allow women on board, in port, or face a mutiny.

The Navy *Regulations* made it clear "That no Women be ever permitted to be on Board, but such as are really the Wives of the Men they come to; and the Ship not be too much pestered even with them. But this Indulgence is only tolerated while the Ship is in Port, and not under Sailing Orders".

What was the context of such an order? The words quoted formed the fifth of the "Rules for preserving Cleanliness" on ships, rules that were "to be punctually complied with".[35]

In her study of the wives of seamen, Stark came to an understanding that their roles changed with circumstance, wives becoming prostitutes, and prostitutes the result of husbands absent at sea, together with the need to provide for their children, and their poverty.[36]

This gives credence to Stark's picture of such prostitutes at that time as "undersized, often sickly teenagers" reflecting the youthfulness of the seamen. Less credibly, those portrayed by George Cruikshank and Thomas Rowlandson were "large, muscular, buxom woman in their thirties or forties, with coarse features and leering expressions".[37]

Writing of the prostitutes of Portsmouth and Plymouth who would have engaged the seamen of the Channel Fleet, Stark considered that though they "made up a considerable part of the population of those towns, they formed no cohesive group and had no political power and next to no legal rights. For that matter, few women, regardless of their social station, controlled their own lives, but respectable women wėre protected by their status within society".

"Prostitutes", on the other hand, according to Stark, "were particularly powerless; not only were they female and part of the great majority of the illiterate, unskilled underclass, but they lived outside the bounds of acceptable cultural standards. Prostitutes were open to ridicule and degradation and to both physical and emotional abuse that would not have been countenanced if directed to respectable women".[38]

Women on the Ships at Spithead and the Nore.

On 15 April 1797 at Spithead, the petitions were to be sent to London.[39] On that day women were to be removed from all the ships. They were there in hundreds as shore leave had been denied to the seamen.

The Navy's refusal to allow men to go ashore gave rise to the fourth Spithead grievance.[40] There, the seamen, "guardians of the land", made "a natural request, and congenial to the heart of man" to be granted an "opportunity to taste the sweets of liberty on shore".

These seamen, in seeking shore leave, asked "That [their] lordships will be so kind as to look into this affair, which is in no wise unreasonable; and that we may be looked upon as a number of men standing in defence of our country; and that we may in somewise have when in any harbour, and when we have completed the duty of our ship, after our return from sea".

So much did they desire this leave that the seamen were prepared to make the request more attractive to their Navy Lords by suggesting limits and inviting punishment for transgression. Namely, "that no man may encroach upon his liberty, there shall be a boundary limited, and those trespassing any further, without a written order from the commanding officer, shall be punished according to the rules of the navy".

Since the request went unanswered at Spithead, it became Article 2, at the Nore,[41] "That every man, upon a ship's coming into harbour shall have liberty (a certain number at a time, so as not to injure the ship's duty) to go and see their friends and families; a convenient time to be allowed to each man".

Born from dissention, the unconditional surrender of ships and mutineers at the Nore elbowed grievances aside. Shore leave was not considered. The practice of bringing women to the ships, in port, would continue.

The Navy was much more concerned with apportioning blame and punishment after the Nore mutiny - figuratively speaking, separating 'sheep' from 'goats' and sorting 'lambs' for branding or slaughter - whipping and hanging mutineers. An animal analogy is not too far stretched as live animals were kept on board Navy ships at that time. Officers liked fresh meat and pigsties occupied a site where a sick bay for seamen should have been. St Vincent took appropriate action, as noted in the fourth chapter, above.

"Sophia, a Person of Quality".

"Sophia, a Person of Quality", would not have been surprised by the conspicuous bravery of women in a war at sea. In her book, *Woman not Inferior to Man,* published in 1739, "Sophia" argued that a woman could be as brave as a man.[42]

According to Dale Spender there is a consensus that this book was written by Lady Mary Wortley Montagu, although Lady Mary did not claim it.[43] Dale Spender considered this to be understandable, "given its challenging contents", which provided "a sustained, systematic and satirical thesis, a comprehensive overview of patriarchy".[44]

"Sophia" asked, in arguing for women's equal qualification for military office, "Are there not strong and weak of both sexes?" She pointed to a "very vulgar error" that "helped confirm the *Men* in the prejudiced notion of *Women's* natural weakness. "When they mean to stigmatise a *Man* with want of courage they call him *effeminate,* and when they would praise a *Woman* for her courage they call her *manly*".

"The real truth is", Sophia claimed, "That humanity and integrity, the characteristics of our sex, make us abhor unjust slaughter, and prefer honourable peace to unjust war". She turned men's notions on their heads. *Effeminate* would now signify the highest praise of man's "good nature and justice". A *Woman* who espoused "the injustice and cruelty of the *Men's* nature, should be called a *Man*".[45]

Broadening this discussion, Christine Battersby discerned "stereotypically 'feminine' characteristics (intuition, emotion, imagination, etc.)' among "the qualities praised by the advocates of genius". According to Battersby, by 1800, "there was general agreement that not reason alone made man more than an animal, but "genius". However "a new rhetoric of exclusion developed in the eighteenth century"...that praised 'feminine' qualities in male creators...but claimed females could not - or should not - create".[46] Children. Yes. Ideas. No.

Suzanne J. Stark - 'Female Tars' Revisited.

Female tars in Stark's study bear witness to 'Sophia's' claim that some females are equal to males in their physical capacity and ability to survive on active service in the Navy. "In the Napoleonic Wars a black woman known as William Brown served in the navy for a dozen years, perhaps more, qualifying as able seaman and captain of the foretop.[47] Brown was one of four women seamen discussed in some detail and selected from twenty verified accounts of "women in disguise in naval crews".

Stark's questions, stated briefly, asked how did they get by, why did they volunteer, and what happened when their gender became known.[48] The absence of proof of identity and medical inspections on joining,[49] and the loose dress of seamen, overcame initial problems.

Urination and menstruation presented ongoing difficulties. The use of the "heads" (toilets), and tubes, in some cases, overcame the first. "[B]ad diet and strenuous physical activity" could have inhibited menstruation,[50] and the "psychological distance", or space, seamen maintained between one another, led them to ignore "any strange behaviour or evidence of sickness in their mates".

Discovery followed when an ordered flogging required stripping to the waist. Sexual harassment sometimes ensued.[51] Otherwise, leaving the Navy incurred no fines and was administratively straightforward. To Stark's reasons, already given above, for the "most daring and unconventional woman" joining the Navy, may now be added this singular advantage that a woman could leave the Navy whenever she wanted by revealing her true identity.[52]

Woman not Inferior to Man.

It is useful to read what Spender made of the book, *Woman not Inferior to man,* in her *Women of Ideas* republished in 1982,[53] but dating back to 1739. By that time the narrowing of work opportunities for women had already come into play, as revealed by Alice Clark (above).

Spender placed "Sophia" in the context of "Mary Wollstonecraft and her Foremothers" who included Alphra Behn, Mary Astell, "Sophia", Catherine Macaulay and Olympe de Gouges.[54] These women appeared out of the past, as Spender engaged with the theme - not hers - of Wollstonecraft as "first, and alone" in her protest.

Spender, in her evaluation of *Women not Inferior to Man* pointed to similarities in argument and style between "Sophia" and Mary Astell. Sophia's "Introduction" according to Spender, "is concerned with how it is we come to know what we know, the origin of our beliefs, and the way they influence our behaviour, the role that men play in formulating and imposing their beliefs on those who would possibly otherwise not share them, and the conviction that all the pieces fit together to ensure that males emerge as superior in a structure they have created".[55]

Furthermore, the analysis "Sophia" made, "ranges from the construction of knowledge, to women as sex-objects and reproductive machines, from women's intellectual competence to their exclusion from public office". "Sophia" "repeatedly urged women to examine the advantages men gain when women accept the male version of the nature of the universe. She repeatedly exhorts women to put forward and to validate a women's version which is in the interest of women, and not to be intimidated by men's claims of reason and logic, claims which it suits men to make".[56]

Sophia, in discussing the attitude of men to women takes as her starting point men "suffering sense to be led away captive by prejudice, and sacrificing justice, truth, and honour, to inconsiderate custom". Men are "hurried away by appearances" and "seemings".

"As they suppose without reason, so they discourse without grounds; and therefore would have as strongly maintain'd the negative of what they assert, if custom, and the impression of the senses had determin'd them to it after the same manner".

The *Antipodes* illustrates her point. Only custom (ignorance) and "the seemings of reason" had opposed its existence. Where there was once heresy, is now belief. "Nothing but the height of madness, or the depth of ignorance can now countenance a doubt of it".

Arguing from appearances the "celestial orbs move around the earth" yet "if we maturely consider" the earth revolves around the sun. A similar problem arises when a moving coach passes houses along the way. Once it is accepted that it is the coach that is moving all is clear.

Next comes the problem a clock poses for the "wild savages in the Indies. Unaware of the mechanism they attribute movement of the hands to spirits. This is followed, appropriately, with a reference to the "animal creation" as automata. Sophia said Des Cartes invented this idea to "amuse and impose upon fools".

Men of Religion are no more guided by reason than in any other profession. Custom rules. It was the faith of their forefathers. They condemn all beside it as erroneous.

Just so, man can seldom be induced to do justice to any other nation, even where truth is on its side.

Many, both men and women have been led to believe that the inequality of stations created by man is in men themselves.

Sophia saw "interest" and "custom" at the fountainhead of "this diversity of vulgar errors".

She now wishes to have a judgement made as to the equality of men and women and desired her witness to be "*undisguised truth*". Both women and men were excluded as prosecutors as being too involved in the outcome. She proposed *rectified reason* as the more *impartial judge.* If, "*reason* should declare us inferior to *Men* we will cheerfully acquiesce to the sentence". On the contrary, *Men* will exercise all their authority in "restoring [women] to the state of equality *nature* first placed [them] in".

Before the case opened, there was a need, argued Sophia, "to clear our ideas from all that is huddled and confused, by separating the fictitious from the real, the obscure from the evident, the false from the true, supposition from matter of fact, seemings from entities, practice from principle, belief from knowledge, doubt from certainty, *interest* and *prejudice* from *justice* and sound *judgment*".

Sophia continued, "To this end therefore we must examin[sic.], in order, what are the *general notions* which the *Men* entertain of *our sex*; on what grounds they build their opinions; and what are the effects to us and to themselves of the treatment we receive from them, in consequence of their present opinion".

The first chapter ends with Sophia promising, in "this little treatise...[to] examin, whether there be any *essential difference between the sexes* which can authorize the *superiority* the *Men* claim over the Women; and what are the causes of, and who are accountable for, the seeming difference which makes the sum of their plea".

"Women were long relegated to the shadows of history",[57] and many more 'Sophias' would need to shine light upon such darkness.[58]

Or as Clark had it, 'Hitherto the historian has paid little attention to the circumstances of women's lives, for women have been regarded as a static factor in social developments...[while] the most superficial consideration will show how profoundly women can be changed by their environment'.[59]

Why the Poor Should Be Content.

Archdeacon William Paley's transparent case of pressure to conform will be introduced below to confirm in one particular case the truth of Sophia's belief. It will demonstrate, too, an aggravation of the condition of that large fraction of the population, "the labouring part of the British public", that was female.

From the working poor came the prostitutes, the convicts, men and women who helped found the Australian nation, and of whom more will be heard in this book. Convicted men were already part of William Redfern's social milieu, in a prison hulk. Not only male convicts but women too, would become his patients or workers on his farm, in the fledgling colony of New South Wales.

Briggs set the structural scene for Paley's intrusion. "By Divine decree rather than by human contrivance, the poor, the greater part of society, were placed under 'the superintendence and patronage of the Rich'. In turn, the rich were charged by 'natural Providence, as much as by revealed appointment, with the care of the Poor'". Briggs gave as source for his quotes *The Works of Joseph Butler.*[60] In all cases "the principal duty of the poor was to be content with their lot".

In case the poor had any doubt about how they should behave, William Paley sent them a message. This was his celebrated *Reasons for Contentment* (1781).[61] Here are its concluding paragraphs.

"When compared with the life of the rich, it is better in these important respects. It supplies employment. It promotes activity. It keeps the body in better health, the mind more engaged, and, of course, more quiet. It is more sensible of ease, more susceptible of pleasure. It is attended with greater alacrity of spirits, a more constant cheerfulness and serenity of temper. It affords easier and more certain methods of sending children into the world in situations suited to their habits and expectations. It is free from many heavy anxieties which rich men feel; it is fraught with many sources of delight which they want".

Perhaps Paley had a point. Mary Wollstonecraft similarly dismissed rich women as beyond the pale and directed her *Vindication* to women of the middling class, with all their "follies".[62]

"If to these reasons for contentment," Paley continued, "the reflecting husbandman or artificer adds another very material one, that changes of condition, which are attended with a breaking up and sacrifice of our ancient course and habit of living, never can be productive of happiness, he will perceive, I trust, that to covert the stations or fortunes of the rich, or to however to covert them, as to wish to seize them by force, or through the medium of public uproar and confusion, is not only wickedness, but folly; as mistaken in the end, as in the means; that it is not only to venture out to sea in a storm, but to venture out for nothing".

How true! Particularly when applied to landowners enclosing commons. No more acute condemnation is required of their destruction of an "ancient course and habit of living" of poor men, women and children. Described as 'gigantic disturbances', above, such enclosures had the full support of the elites of Paley's Church of England in the House of Lords. One law for the rich, and another for the poor!

It is remarkable that copies of William Paley's letter, and the reply to it by "a poor labourer",[63] are readily available on microfilm in public libraries throughout the world, the State Library, Sydney, among them.[64]

As explained in the notes this was because Somerton Foxwell collected ephemeral materials such as pamphlets and broadsides, as well as books, acknowledging that "If any partiality has been shown, it has been in the desire to put in evidence the scanty and obscure literature which gives a clue to the opinions of the almost inarticulate masses of the people".[65]

Archdeacon Paley's intention was clear, of its time, and reflected the stance of the governing class. His second paragraph belongs with those other examples of repressive politics and policies directed against "stirring" sections of the working community, which have found a place in this book. Both the "wickedness" and "folly" of those not contented was there for all to see, said Archdeacon Paley. And, on the contrary!

This is the same Paley who saw the hand of God in nature's design. He was not the only one who saw rich and poor as part of that design and celebrated the difference. In *Reasons for Contentment* it was his Christian task to keep the design intact.

Edmund Burke, in reflecting "on the Revolution in France" and nearing the end of a discourse on that subject, had similar warnings to leave with his readers.[66]

"Good order", according to Burke, "is the foundation of all good things. To be enabled to acquire, the people, without being servile, must be tractable and obedient. The magistrate must have his reverence, the laws their authority. The body of the people must not find the principles of natural subordination by art rooted out of their minds. They must respect that property of which they cannot partake. They must labour to obtain what by labour can be obtained; and when they find, as they commonly do, the success disproportioned to the endeavour, they must be taught their consolation in the final proportions of eternal justice. Of this consolation, whoever deprives them, deadens their industry, and strikes at the root of all acquisition as of all conservation".

Conor Cruise O'Brien, as editor, noted Mary Wollstonecraft's comments on this passage. "This is contemptible hard-hearted sophistry, in the specious form of humility, and submission to the will of Heaven".[67] Yet, in some of Burke's earlier stances, Wollstonecraft had found much to admire, and for good reason.

A Vindication of the Rights of Woman.[68]

To Mary Wollstonecraft[69] there was no doubt that women had rights to life as persons. She looked for something beyond the biological and contemporary social definitions of eighteenth century womanhood discussed by Stark.

"After considering the historic page, and viewing the living world with anxious solicitude, the most melancholy emotions of sorrowful indignation have depressed my spirits, and I have sighed when obliged to confess that either Nature has made a great difference between man and man, or that the civilization which has hitherto taken place in the world has been very partial".[70]

With these words, Wollstonecraft opened the *Author's Introduction* to her book, *A Vindication of the Rights of Woman* published in London in 1792. It contains a dedication to M. Talleyrand-Perigord, *Late Bishop of Autun,* France. There, she asked him to "weigh what I have advanced respecting the rights of woman and national education".[71]

After studying the literature on education, Wollstonecraft reached "a profound conviction that the neglected education of my fellow creatures is the grand source of the misery I deplore, and that women in particular, are rendered weak and wretched by a variety of concurring causes originating from one hasty conclusion. The conduct and manners of women, in fact, evidently prove that their minds are not in a healthy state...One cause of this barren blooming I attribute to a false system of education, gathered from the books written on this subject by men who, considering females rather as women than human creatures, have been more anxious to make them alluring mistresses than affectionate wives and rational mothers".[72]

Women are treated "as a kind of subordinate beings, and not as a part of the human species, when improvable reason is allowed to be the dignified distinction which raises men above the brute creation, and puts a natural sceptre in a feeble hand". [73]

Wollstonecraft, too, discussed the relative physical strengths of men and women though her approach is somewhat different from "Sophia". She acknowledged "that the female in point of strength is, in general, inferior to the male". "But not content with this natural pre-eminence, men endeavour to sink us still lower, merely to render us alluring objects for a moment..."

Women, "intoxicated by the adoration...[of men] do not seek to obtain a durable interest in their hearts, or to become the friends of the fellow-creatures who find amusement in their society".[74]

Wollstonecraft takes up the complaint against masculine women, and asks where are they to be found? Are the complaints against women's ardour in hunting, shooting and gaming? She is in favour of the description "masculine women" if it implies "imitation of manly virtues, or, more properly speaking, the attainment of those talents and virtues, the exercise of which ennobles the human character, and which raises females in the scale of animal being, when they are comprehensively termed mankind", in these qualities some may "wish with me, that they may every day grow more and more masculine".[75]

Wollstonecraft does not follow "Sophia" in turning upside down the meanings of "effeminate" and "manly", accepting common usage.

She noted, "instruction which has hitherto been addressed to women, has rather been applicable to *ladies*". "The education of the rich [*ladies*] tends to render them vain and helpless". Wollstonecraft dismisses them and pays "particular attention to those in the middle class, because they appear to be in the most natural state".[76] These are the women to whom her remarks were addressed.

"My own sex, I hope, will excuse me, if I treat them like rational creatures, instead of flattering their *fascinating* graces, and viewing them as if they were in a state of perpetual childhood, unable to stand alone. I earnestly wish to point out in what true dignity and human happiness consists".[77]

"I wish to persuade women to endeavour to acquire strength, both of mind and body". "Dismissing, then, those pretty feminine phrases, which the men condescendingly use to soften our slavish dependence, and despising that weak elegancy of mind, exquisite sensibility, and sweet docility of manners, supposed to be the sexual characteristics of the weaker vessel, I wish to show that elegance is inferior to virtue, that the first object of laudable ambition is to obtain a character as a human being, regardless of the distinction of sex, and that secondary views should be brought to this simple touchstone".[78]

On Rearing Children.

To end her book, Mary Wollstonecraft presented "Some instances of the folly which the ignorance of women generates; with concluding reflections on the moral improvement that a revolution in female manners might naturally be expected to produce".[79]

For various reasons, Men have endeavoured to perpetuate Women's "weakness of mind and body", she argued. She followed by asking whether it was a natural state for women to be too weak physically "to suckle their children" and of such "weakness of mind to spoil their tempers"? [80]

One such folly related to "the rearing of children" that "has justly been insisted on as the peculiar destination of women". "The ignorance that incapacitates [women] must be contrary to the order of things. And I contend that their minds can take in much more, and ought to do so, or they will never become sensible mothers".[81]

Wollstonecraft put reason to contend with such follies. "But, fulfilling the duties of a mother, a woman with a sound constitution may still keep her person scrupulously neat, and assist to maintain her family, if necessary, or by reading and conversation with both sexes, indiscriminately, improve her mind. For Nature has so wisely ordered things, that did women suckle their children, they would preserve their own health, and there would be such an interval between the birth of each child, that we should seldom see a houseful of babes".[82]

Again, "we shall not see women affectionate till more equality be established in society, till ranks are confounded and women freed, neither shall we see that dignified domestic happiness, the simple grandeur of which cannot be relished by ignorant or vitiated minds; nor will the important task of education[83] ever be properly begun till the person of a woman is no longer preferred to her mind. For it would be as wise to expect corn from tares, or figs from thistles, as that a foolish ignorant woman should be a good mother".[84]

"Let woman share the rights, and she will emulate the virtues of man; for she must grow more perfect when emancipated, or justify the authority that chains such a weak being to her duty. If the latter, it will be expedient to open a fresh trade with Russia for whips..."[85]

Jane Austen, Mary Wollstonecraft, and Margaret Kirkham.

It is to Margaret Kirkham that this account now turns.[86] "The resemblance between Wollstonecraft and Austen as feminine moralists is so striking that it seems extraordinary that it has not always been recognised, but that is to leave out of account the Great Wollstonecraft Scandal of 1798".

Kirkham, herself, took into "account...the extent to which Wollstonecraft in *Vindication*, and the whole line of English feminism from Astell to Austen, relies upon rationalist eighteenth-century argument about ethics, and uses it to promote the idea that women are accountable beings of the same kind as men".

But in the context of Wollstonecraft's own sexuality there was a double standard. What was acceptable for men was not for women. Thomas Trotter, however, took the line of male accountability in his medical *View...*of 1807.

"It is too often the case", Trotter argued, "that the sordid parent winks at the son's indiscretions with the sex, rather than consent that he should marry the woman he loves, without a rich dower. And while by this growing custom, a certain number of defenceless females are doomed to all the horrors of prostitution, in order to gratify the passions of the young, and the avarice of the old, it is one grand step to the degeneracy of the species".[87]

Kirkham's "Great Wollstonecraft Scandal of 1798", when "the full fury of the anti-feminist backlash was let loose", followed the publication, in January 1798 by William Godwin, of the *Memoirs of the Author of a Vindication of the Rights of Woman.* In that year Mary Wollstonecraft conceived Godwin's child out of wedlock, married him, and died of puerperal fever eleven days after the birth of a daughter, Mary (Shelley).[88]

Godwin, against advice, published details of Wollstonecraft's "relationships with Imlay, her suicide attempts, her having conceived his child before marriage", and alleged rejection of Christianity, giving rise to the epithet, "atheist whore". Kirkham believes it was Joseph Johnson, her publisher, who wrote in her defence.[89] But it was too late. The whips were out. They did not come from Russia as Mary Wollstonecraft had envisaged, but from England, and they struck at any woman, who simply "emulate[d] the virtues of man".[90]

Richard Holmes's perceptive account of Wollstonecraft's experience of living in Paris, will appear later in this chapter.[91] Here it was important to note his more recent contribution to the Wollstonecraft/Godwin theme.[92]

Child Birth, Roy Porter and 'A Touch of Danger'.

There were many tasks Mary Wollstonecraft's better-educated women might attempt, given freedom. "Women might certainly study the art of healing and be physicians as well as nurses. And midwifery, decency seems to allot to them though I am afraid the word midwife, in our dictionaries, will soon give place to *accoucheur,* and one proof of the former delicacy of the sex can be effaced from the language".[93]

Roy Porter includes these three, "decency", midwives and accoucheurs, in a chapter headed "A touch of danger: The man-midwife as sexual predator". He grounded his study in the practice of medicine, "least prestigious of the learned professions", a failure in the fight against disease and death, and constantly liable to the lash and lampoon.[94] "[P]ublic suspicion of the medical profession ran deep".[95]

Over time, this changed into a suspicion of the practitioner as a corrupter of morals and a threat to female modesty. Christianity's distrust of the flesh sloughed sex off to the medical fraternity where were to be found the treatment of sexual defects and disease, the vindication of sexual pleasure as healthy, and the mechanics of reproduction.[96]

"The Discourse of Medicine and Science" had long "defined the feminine ideal in such a way as to fit it within the narrow sphere assigned to women by the social order. The happy, healthy woman was by definition the mother..."[97]

Then, in the last quarter of the 18th century a concern for "privacy and decency" was discerned in medical ethics and public opinion. "Propriety was context-dependent and subject to the mode". Bosoms but not ankles might be revealed.[98] The physician was expected to keep his distance. The patient's face and a history of the illness satisfied the medical examination. Later on, physical methods such as palpation and auscultation and the stethoscope were considered to be invasions of the space of patients.[99]

The royal touch, however, might cure scrofula. The implication of the fact that kings could cure by touch was that no one else might, according to Porter. When this practice ceased, touch healing spread to laymen. Mesmer, the "hypnotist", eventually gave up touching, but mesmerism was opposed for its tendency to sexual licence. "A greater premium came to be placed on physical privacy" and in "the new cult of sensibility" with its "heightened perceptions of the delicate nuances of body sensation and nervous response. In such an atmosphere, the body easily became wholly identified with sexuality".[100]

Porter's article was left at a focus of public debate on the propriety of the man-midwife's intimate involvement in the birthing process, even if sight unseen beneath a modesty protecting sheet. In that debate, Mary Wollstonecraft's 'decency' seemed to allot the task to women, as of yore. To liven that debate, Porter added a conspiratorial twist involving women of class, eminent male practitioners and the concealment of illegitimate babies.[101]

William Smellie.

" 'Touching' became a fresh cause celebre in the eighteenth century when the man-midwife became socially conspicuous, both numerically and, more so, as a perplexing figure in the public mind and an anomaly in the medical profession".[102] One of these man-midwives was the Scottish country surgeon William Smellie, a particular target for an opposition both male and female.[103]

William Redfern also worked as a male midwife. He was given an edited edition of Smellie's midwifery text in 1797, just prior to his joining the Navy. This book was inscribed by hand - "The gift of Mr John McMillin to W. Redfern Januarii 30th 1797".[104]

While Smellie's original work was in large folio, the Redfern edition of 1783 was in octavo, which required the plates to be redrawn by Andrew Bell (1726-1809). As this edition was directed to the Edinburgh students, it is probable that Professor Alexander Hamilton was the editor, as he was of the 1788 edition. Each had an additional fortieth plate, illustrating Thomas Young's improved instruments.[105]

The midwifery course at Edinburgh University "was taught by Thomas Young from 1756 to 1780, when he was joined by Alexander Hamilton; in 1800, Hamilton's son James took over the professorship".[106] William Redfern attended his lectures, but towards the end of his life.[107]

As mentioned earlier, Redfern's book is now in the History of Medicine Library, Royal Australasian College of Physicians, Sydney, Australia. It is the more valuable to this study since Redfern is recognised as Australia's first obstetrician,[108] and because it is one of only three known books from Redfern's Sydney library to have survived.[109]

"Smellie had his detractors, shrill and malicious ones like Mrs Nihell the midwife and Dr John Burton, a jealous and much inferior obstetric author and forceps-designer who was later caricatured by Sterne as Dr Slop in *Tristram Shandy*".[110] Mrs Nihell apparently took exception to Smellie's large hand, describing it as *a delicate fist of a great horse-godmother*.[111] Johnstone provided context for such opinions in a chapter 'The Crusader and his Antagonists'.

Ludmilla Jordanova saw in the divided image of male/female midwife a broader social and cultural context.[112] Furthermore, in her concluding chapter, 'Cultures of Kinship', she detailed the life of Ann Ford who would marry Philip Thickness. Jordanova's purpose was 'to indicate how what might appear to be abstract concerns could be grounded in the lives of real people, and also to convey something of the affect with which they were invested. It was not just that man-midwifery was controversial, that feelings about it ran high, but that these were precisely focused on the physical and moral intrusion that a man touching a particular woman constituted, and on the contagious quality of this intrusion, which could spread, like an infectious disease, to a whole nation'.[113]

Observation and critical thinking, associated with developments in the science and art of medicine, were spreading to midwifery, and calling into question the education of midwives. As were "prominent midwives like Mrs Cellier and Mrs Nihell. There was no proper organization of the training of midwives or control over their practice. The Bishops remained the licensing authorities in England".[114]

What of men as midwives? Their role became fashionable in Europe, and later in Britain, after Louis XIV employed a man-midwife.

A "much more specific influence resulted from the disclosure of the secret of the midwifery forceps. An instrument of that sort clearly called for more knowledge and skill in its use than could be expected of a [woman] midwife".[115] Of course, if women were allowed to study anatomy and medicine as part of their general education, as Wollstonecraft wished, they would be heading in that direction after taking an advanced midwifery course.[116]

Smellie's admonishment to the male accoucheur reads - "that he will assist the poor as well as the rich, behaving always with charity and compassion. He ought to act and speak with the utmost delicacy of decorum, and never violate the trust reposed in him, so as to harbour the least immoral or indecent design; but demean himself in all respects suitable to the dignity, of his profession".

As this is from the book given to William Redfern it is assumed that he was influenced by it.

Smellie, in case notes published in his midwifery texts told how "within four years of settling in practice" in Lanarch, the town of his birth, "he was being called into consultation by midwives in the neighbouring towns".[117] It was such experiences that challenged Smellie to ask questions and to search for answers as to why the particular need had arisen for his advice and assistance.

In using his own powers of observation and in thinking for himself, Smellie was reflecting a trend in medical practice, documented in the work of the Naval surgeons, in previous chapters of this book. At the same time he was working with women who were traditional midwives and learning from them. Surely his outline of the qualities preferred in a midwife, and some gentle advice to both men and women, involved in her work, reflect that experience. But Mary Wollstonecraft would not have been amused by Smellie's intrusion, and condescension.

"A Midwife, though she can hardly be supposed mistress of all these qualifications, ought to be a decent sensible woman, of a middle age, able to bear fatigue..".[118]

Marguerite du Coudray.

Some years after reading Redfern's copy of Smellie's midwifery text and Johnstone's biography at the History of Medicine Library I attended a book sale. There I happened upon a book by Nina Rattner Gelbart.

This book seemed to contradict the commonly held opinion, mentioned above, that the King's midwife was a male. Here was a woman, du Coudray.[119]

I bought the book to find an answer. Each midwife, male and female, served the King of France but in different ways.

There were further surprises. Du Coudray, like Smellie, used 'machines' and their own prepared texts in teaching midwifery, sharing a common focus on the interests of the unborn and mothers to be.

Gelbart estimated that Du Coudray and her disciples had trained ten thousand women during the midwife's lifetime.[120] This provides something of the measure of her outstanding achievement. Smellie, no drudge either, was able to claim at one point of his teaching that he had "given upwards of two hundred and eighty courses of Midwifery, for the instruction of more than nine hundred pupils, exclusive of female students; and in that series of courses one thousand one hundred and fifty poor women have been delivered in presence of those who attended me; and supported during their lying-in by the stated collections of my pupils; over and above these different cases to which we are often called by midwives, for relief of the indigent".[121]

Biographical details are fragmentary for both Du Coudray and Smellie. The Scotland into which William Smellie was delivered at birth, in 1697, "was in a state of the direst poverty. A series of hungry years in which the corn never ripened had brought death through sheer starvation to many thousands of its population of about a million, and had reduced even more to abject beggary".[122]

"Intellectually Scotland was at a very low ebb. Undernourishment had, as always, bred spiritual apathy, and of literary or cultural activity there was no vestige".[123] Yet Smellie was able to attend in his native town, Lanarch, a grammar school described later as "the most celebrated school in the west of Scotland", where he was able to acquire elementary mathematics, "a good working knowledge of Latin, and probably some knowledge of French since he did not hesitate to go to France...and to attend lectures there". [124]

In 1720, by then 23 years old, Smellie worked as a country doctor in the town of his birth probably after serving an apprenticeship. In 1733 he became a member of the Faculty of Physicians and Surgeons of Glasgow.[125] After 18 years at Lanark, Smellie moved to London but his curiosity for innovation was not satisfied and it was then he went to Paris.

Smellie could well have been in Paris in the year of graduation of Angelique Marguerite le Boursier (Du Coudray) in 1740.[126] Le Boursier had completed a three-year apprenticeship in midwifery with Anne Bairsin, and passed her qualifying examinations at the College of Surgery.[127] She then began to practise as a certificated midwife, one among some two hundred registered midwives in Paris at that time.[128]

After sixteen years of work and study in the capital, "destiny led Le Boursier to the provinces" in 1756.[129]As a gesture to those who had invited her, the midwife offered to teach the women of the countryside.[130] Selected on their character and financed by local donations these often poor barefooted peasants provided a daunting teaching challenge.

Birthing Machines Used by Smellie and du Coudray.

For Smellie, in Paris, what was new in teaching midwifery was the 'machines', to which Le Boursier was similarly attracted. What were these "machines" and how were they used?

In his discussion of the accoucheur, Smellie wrote of his 'machines'.

"In order to acquire a more perfect idea of the art, he ought to perform with his own hands upon proper machines, contrived to convey a just notion of the difficulties to be met with in every kind of labour; by which means he will learn how to use the forceps and crotchets with more dexterity, be accustomed to the turning of children, and consequently be more capable of acquitting himself in troublesome cases, that may happen to him when he comes to practise among women..."[131]

There is a record of the sale of one of Smellie's "exquisite artificial machines, in imitation of the living subjects".[132] These involved "uncommon labour and application".[133] Johnstone devoted a chapter to "Smellie's 'machines' and antenatal teaching" where he brought together notes by former students, and descriptions from friend and foe alike.[134]

From a student: "They are composed of real Bones, mounted and covered with artificial Ligaments, Muscles and Cuticle, to give them the true Motion, Shape and Beauty of natural Bodies, and the Contents of the Abdomen are imitated with great Exactness. Besides his large Machines (which are three in number) he has finished six artificial Children with the same minute Proportion in all their Parts; so that with the apparatus he can perform and demonstrate all the different kinds of Delivery with more Deliberation, Perspicuity and Fulness than can be expected on real Subjects".[135]

From a contemporary pamphlet: "The Uterus Externum and Internum [sic] are made to contract and dilate according to the Difficulty intended for the Delivery. The Children for these Machines are likewise excellently contrived, they having all the Motions of the Joints. Their Craniums are so formed as to give way to any Force exerted, and are so Elastick that the Pressure is no sooner taken off than they return to their natural Equalities".[136]

A former postgraduate student, Dr Peter Camper, noted that Smellie made use of cadavers in his lectures. He also used plain paper to demonstrate "the stretching or enlargement of the uterus in the various months of gestation", "and in the same way the thickness of the uterus, the difference of the cervix and the change in the os tincae are noted and made clear by colours". [137]

Smellie was not involved in reproducing numbers of his machines as was Du Coudray, who left "machines" behind as she moved on. His movements were restricted to a few changes of address in London, and in any case the "machines" went with him.

Gelbart said that in using the word "machine" Du Coudray was speaking "the language of enlightenment and reform, one well understood by the men she seeks to impress", although foreign to her students, "mes femmes".[138] Of Du Coudray's machine we have one extant example[139] and her own clear description.[140]

"I took the tack of making my lessons palpable by having them maneuver [sic] in front of me on a machine I constructed for this purpose, and which represented the pelvis of a woman, the womb, its opening, its ligaments, the conduit called the vagina, the bladder and *rectum intestine*. I added a model of a child of natural size, whose joints I made flexible enough to be able to put it in different positions; a placenta with its membranes and the demonstration of waters that they contain; the umbilical cord composed of its two arteries and of the vein..."

"[I]f I could not make these women very skilled, I would at least make them feel the necessity of asking for help soon enough to save the mother and children".

Du Coudray, on the move, needed to keep making machines, hundreds of them. One was left with a surgeon of her choice at each of the places where she taught, so that her work could be continued. It is reasonable to suggest that the need for new machines paved the way for innovation. Certainly Du Coudray went out of her way to inspect rival "machines" which, with her own "hands on" experience, could also have prompted changes to the current model. Numerous references are made to the "machines" in Gelbart's biography, and may be found in the index differentiated between "Obstetrical mannequins (du Coudray's)", and "Anatomical models" for those developed by other people.

Du Coudray's Book.

"Le Boursier du Coudray's textbook, the *Abrégé de l'art des accouchements,* has just been printed in the capital (1759)".[141] The author, Gelbart, draws the reader in to share the "momentous occasion". "It is published", she wrote, "on the rue St. Jacques by the widow Delaguette, official printer/bookdealer of the Royal Academy of Surgery, with royal approbation and privilege, and sells for 50 sous, or two and one-half livres. This is a momentous occasion; plans for the book have been in the works for years. Some ambivalence about the audience for the volume is evident in its full title" which is figured on the opposite page of Gelbart's book.

This full title reads in translation - "Abridgment of the Art of Delivery, in which we give the necessary precepts to put it successfully into practice. We have joined to it several interesting Observations concerning singular cases. A work very useful to young Midwives, and generally to all Students of this Art who wish to become skilled in it". Gelbart observed that the "work is supposedly for women, but it is also for men; it is an abridged, practical manual".

But Gelbart is mindful of the fact that few of Du Coudray's country students can read. "Why", Gelbart asks, "has the book suddenly appeared now, a year and a half after permission was first granted to print it?"

Gelbart gave reasons for "the midwife's decision to go public, to bother publishing, and to become an author". Du Coudray's success in Auvergne, her official support, "the favourable reception of her machine in Paris, the popularity of her innovative lessons and demonstrations", and "her broadening fame" all spur her on. As does her fight for a pension. Since France's entry into war with England in 1756 Du Coudray "reframed birthing as a matter of state".

In 1757, Du Coudray put her lesson notes together as a book and set off for Paris. Machine and book were Du Coudray's contribution to the war effort, saving babies for the French navy. This lent a prop to the crown and achieved the desired results. Approval to publish by Morand, her former anatomy professor, was followed by funding (later increased), a set of notes and observations to her text by her other teacher, Verdier, and the censor's approval of the longer version of her book.

"At the end of this year she will be charged by the king to launch a nationwide teaching tour". Du Coudray featured the *Abrégé* in her "mission statement" for that royal project.

For Gelbart the *Abrégé* was "pivotal in the fashioning of the midwife's special part in the obstetrical mobilization of the country...a passport...not just locally but nationally in the modernization and medicalization of France". Her dedication to the intendent of Auvergne, Ballainvilliers, gives to him the honour of conserving His Majesty's subjects, no less glorious than victory in battle.

Gelbart wrote of the midwife as being "up there in loyalty and importance with military generals, sustaining and defending her country. They kill foes, while she repairs, restores, preserves life. They do warfare, she does welfare".[142]

The midwife aims to please many publics at once from doctors, surgeons and apothecaries, seeking harmony with them, and with the Church, by keeping baptism in mind throughout and after the birthing process. Most of all, with her book, she strives to bridge groups.

Du Coudray "is female, but not antagonistic to men; Parisian, but adaptable to the provinces. She is superior, but never scornful of her students, conveying to them her conviction that they can learn to do what needs to be done to save numerous babies from the jaws of death. She is schooled, but not so urbane that she cannot appreciate the robust earthiness of peasants. She can use the common terms for body organs as fluently as the learned ones, and does. She can use units of measure from town or country, describing cervical dilation by the size of a coin here, the size of a fish's open mouth there. The midwife's book, as she says on the first page, is not an obstetrical treatise...The Abrégé is an abridgment, a different, new genre, a practical how-to manual, possibly the first of its kind in France. In fact, this text will generate a fad: short, clear, accessible childbirth booklets, often in question-and-answer catechism form, proliferate during the rest of the century".

Journalists recognise its usefulness and review it in the daily papers. Other journal reviews proliferate. Gelbart devotes a page to them. Concluding overall that the Abrégé had certainly attracted attention, and that at "a time when women writers are mostly ignored and denied the courtesy of a reply".[143]

The adulation of the present would lessen over time but "The Abrégé is to become a key player in Du Coudray's odyssey", with five new, carefully timed editions to come over the years. The little volume serves its readers and its author well. She aims at other publics, as well as her peasant audience.

Gelbart concludes this important chapter in her book with the words, "Of course, not everyone likes what they hear".

In the section that follows, attention will focus more on the contents of Smellie's books because of the Redfern link. Their students were certainly different as was the form and format of Smellie's original edition. Du Coudray solicited donations so that copies of her book could be given to her students on graduation. Poverty was a problem to be overcome. The timing and length of her courses took into consideration the demands placed by the home upon the young women who attended. Peak times of demand for the labour of women on farms had to be respected. Du Coudray preferred to teach younger women, even if barefooted peasants, than older midwives, fixed in their ways. Smellie would have found his students to be generally "better-off", and even included those from the country.

Smellie's Treatise.

As a matter of interest it was Smellie's friend Tobias Smollett, the novelist, who wrote the prefaces.[144] "I at first intended to have published this Treatise in different lectures," Smellie wrote, "as they were delivered in one course of Midwifery; but I found that method would not answer as well, in a work of this kind, as in teaching: because, in the course of my lectures, almost every observation has a reference to the working of those machines which I have contrived to resemble and represent real women and children; and on which all the kinds of different labours are demonstrated, and even performed, by every individual student.

"I have, therefore, divided the whole into an Introduction and Four Books, distinguished by Chapters, Sections, and Numbers; and have industriously avoided all theory, except for much as may serve to whet the genius of young practitioners, and be as hints to introduce more valuable discoveries in the art".

Smellie was referring to his original Treatise, which was published successively over the years 1751-2 to 1769 as a series. The last did not appear until the year after his death. A set of anatomical tables, or illustrations, with explanations, was an integral part of this project. The whole treatise was brought together in one volume in Redfern's copy, with the separate sections within it, called "books".

In the Redfern copy the first of three chapters in Book I is concerned with "The Structure & Form of the pelvis so far as it is necessary to be known in the Practice of Midwifery". In the second chapter Smellie writes "Of the External and Internal parts of generation proper to Women". This first book concludes with a discussion of "Pregnancy from preconception".

The first chapter of Book II confronts "diseases incident to pregnant Women, being either such as immediately proceed from Pregnancy, or such as may happen at any other Time; and if not carefully prevented or removed, may be of dangerous Consequence both to Mother and Child. Chapter II is about diseases incident to pregnant women, while "miscarriages" form the subject of the concluding chapter.

Book III opens with the examination or "touching" of the pregnant woman. The following chapter, "Of the different positions of natural labours", is in four sections. Eighteen sections are required for a discussion of "laborious labours". The last two chapters deal with "preternatural labours", and twins.

Book IV treats "Of the management of Women from the Time of their Delivery to the End of the Month with the several diseases to which they are Subject during that Period". Chapter II, "Of the management of new-born Children with the diseases to which they are subject", follows. Chapter III moves on to consider "the requisite Qualifications of Accoucheurs, Midwives, Nurses who attend lying-in Women, and wet and dry Nurses for children".

"Anatomical Tables, and Explanations and an abridgment of the practice of midwifery intended to illustrate the treatise and cases conclude the volume.

"The first table Represents, in a front view, the Bones of a well formed Pelvis". There are "33 drawings of child in utero", "4 tables of instruments" and an additional table by "the late Dr Thomas Young" of improved instruments.[145]

For Redfern's book, Andrew Bell, an engraver, had redrawn the plates in conformity with its smaller size. The original plates, published separately, were "as large as the human subjects".[146],[147] These tables, i.e. plates, were "engraved by Mr Grignion" from twenty-five drawings by Jan van Rymsdyk and eleven by Dr Peter Camper,[148] who appeared in the discussion of Smellie's "machines".

Smellie disabused anyone who might have thought "that this treatise is cooked up in a hurry", by informing his reader "that above six years ago I began to commit my lectures to paper for publication: and from that period have from time to time altered, amended, and digested what I have written, according to the new lights I received from study and experience. Neither did I pretend to teach Midwifery till after I had practised it successfully for a long time in the country: and the observations I now publish are the fruits not only of that opportunity, but more immediately of my practice in London during ten years".[149]

"These considerations, together with that of my own private practice, which hath been pretty extensive, will, I hope, screen me from the imputation of arrogance with regard to the task I have undertaken; and I flatter myself that the performance will not be unserviceable to mankind".[150]

Women, Men, and Medicine.

This training of midwives was almost a unique case of medical education for women. Across the field, according to Antonia Frazer, in "The Modest Midwife", men were favoured over women in medicine even in the previous century, because their education had given them Latin, a key to medical literature.[151]

Mary Astell campaigned against this inequality, which Mary Wollstonecraft saw as a reason for men taking over a traditional field of women's work, midwifery. She too argued for equal education for women and men in the eighteenth century.[152]

"One develops a great sympathy for the polemics of feminist writings when they challenge the insidious disappearance of women from history". In this quote, Johanna Geyer-Kordesch reminds one of Davis and Farge, above.

What was missing from homeland and colony was the contribution typical of women healers from the Middle Ages to the 17th century outside the university medical tradition. As medical knowledge increased in the 17th and 18th centuries the debarring of women from centres of medical learning helped create 'the women's sphere' - in the home.[153]

Ironically it was amongst the Nonconformist and separatist sects of a century filled with religious controversy that some ground was reclaimed. What eventually turned the tide for women's rights were ideas on natural law and democracy that also fed into the great revolutions, America (1776) and France (1789) and belated European revolutions of 1848.[154]

The mythologising of sexuality has to do with its power; the politicising of gender roles has to do with social purposes, not least of them the dignity and autonomy of individuals".

Furthermore, "The economic input and the public impact of women in philanthropy in the nineteenth century was also pivotal for social hygiene and public health, yet historians never seem to discuss the skills women learned in home management. As opposed to their organizational skills outside the home".

For reasons made clear, in this same context, by Outram, below, it would take time, and the determination of interested women. Geyer-Kordesch's account validates the efforts by women on the continent to achieve a medical education, after which it moves on to Britain and America.

Anne Witz noted "a relative neglect of the history and nature of women's participation in the professions" in sociology, and turned to an analysis of "male and female professional projects in the emerging medical division of labour". Her study examined "the relationship between gender and professionalism in medicine, midwifery, nursing and radiography".[155]

Little had changed by 1858 when the Medical (Registration) Act "set up a male monopoly and...effectively excluded women from access to the ranks of the medical profession".

"Women were excluded from medical education and examination in all of the institutions which made up the nineteen portals of entry onto the medical register". But, as Witz pointed out the "male monopoly over legitimate medical practice was quickly challenged by aspiring women doctors".[156]

"It is at the point when women challenged gendered exclusionary practices that the precise mechanisms through which men were able to institutionalise male power within professional projects are thrown into sharp relief, and it becomes possible to identify the institutional arenas within which male power and privilege were most effectively organised and defended". The effort, frustration and eventual success of Elizabeth Garrett, "the pioneer of the medical movement in England", to achieve a medical education and registration exemplifies the process of exclusion.[157]

Ann E. Clark (1844-1924), "the first woman in the Society of Friends to qualify in medicine in Great Britain", blocked in England, took advantage of a decision by Edinburgh to admit a small group of women to the medical school. That university changed its mind, part way through the course, and "Ann Clark transferred to the University of Berne, Switzerland, where she received her M.D. in 1877. After taking "her M.R.C.P. in Dublin and undertaking special studies in Paris, Vienna, and Boston, she went to Birmingham where she spent the rest of her professional life".[158]

Witz turned to a review of women's medical contribution in the pre-modern era, which included the work of Ehrenreich and English, placed by Witz among 'a small body of feminist analyses' of 'the twin processes of professionalization and masculinisation that marked the transition from pre-modern to modern medical practice'.[159] Her conclusion was that "the bulk of women's healing activities had been circumvented within the domestic arena" and did not survive as "the dominant location of medical services" shifted "from the private domestic to the public market arena".[160]

Female midwifery was a special case where "vast numbers of women earned their living" in pre-modern times[161] and many continued to do so. In the late nineteenth century in Britain "it was estimated that in small towns midwives attended only between five and ten per cent of confinements; in large provincial towns and in villages this could be anywhere between thirty and ninety per cent of confinements".[162]

Mary Lindemann has some useful comments in a brief reference to midwives.[163] "More Europeans came in contact with midwives than with any other medical practitioner...The era of midwifery reform and the rise of the man-midwife occurred in the eighteenth century. For the preceding centuries, midwives were (almost) unchallenged in the birth chamber".[164]

"Before embarking on a discussion of midwifery in early modern Europe, one should recognise that childbirth is not a pathological process: that is, pregnancy is not an illness. Feminist historians first argued that, by defining childbirth as a medical event, it more easily became the province of male physicians and surgeons. The majority of births (one historian estimates over 90 per cent) were uneventful whether attended by a physician, a midwife or a stork. Still, some births (perhaps as many as 3 per cent) were difficult and an ability to turn the child in utero could spell the difference between a live birth or tragedy for mother or child or both. Likewise the forceps, despite the dangers of introducing infection, tearing delicate membranes, or injuring the child, could result in the live birth of otherwise undeliverable children. Thus, the answer to the old question of whether man-midwives or midwives were the better birth attendants, is not simple. Some midwives were indeed dirty, ignorant, and dangerous; some man-midwives saved lives with their forceps; and some births were doomed to disaster no matter who attended".[165]

Nevertheless, as has already been noted in the references to Smellie in Britain and Du Coudray in France, male medical practice was encroaching on a traditional female role. The voluntary decisions of the midwives in Lanark to call on Smellie, and Du Coudray's deference to the surgeons, were at the heart of the processes of exclusion, inclusion, demarcation, etc., which would increasingly threaten midwives and make them subservient at work to male obstetricians.[166]

French Women of the Revolution.

Can one forget terror, and the guillotine hanging over the heads of men and women of the revolution in France? "14,080 death sentences [alone, were] passed between March 1793 and August 1794".[167]

Du Coudray was spared the guillotine but suffered nonetheless from having been the King's midwife. She died in her seventy-ninth year, hounded by the tax men on a night when she was alone. Du Coudray, the "once-trusted agent of the dethroned, beheaded, and vilified king" had been rejected by the Revolution. The Coutanceaus, her niece and nephew, though commended for their service to the French Republic, were thus denied Du Coudray's material legacy. Instead, they were well served by one "of an intangible kind", "her knowledge and technique, her sense of purpose, her wholehearted belief in the bien de l'humanite".[168]

Blood Sisters is a confronting collection of first-hand accounts of the terror written by women of all political persuasions. Marilyn Yalom was driven "to know how French women, as distinct from their male counterparts, had remembered the Revolution".[169]

Marie-Antoinette, Queen of France, Olympe de Gouges, and Mme Roland was each guillotined within a span of three weeks for stepping out of the "natural sphere" of their sex, according to the newspaper, *Le Moniteur*, which admonished women to remain silent at popular assemblies.[170]

Olympe de Gouges had directed her brief *Declaration of the Rights of Woman and Female Citizen* to Marie Antoinette. De Gouges's pamphlet was published in 1791.[171]

Mary Wollstonecraft dedicated her *Vindication of the Rights of Women* to Talleyrand, whom she had met in London.[172] A French edition of *the Rights of Women* had already appeared in Paris, and "had attracted the attention of the Girondists" who "were particularly interested in social and educational reform".[173]

Wollstonecraft decided in November 1792 to go to Paris. This "thirty-three years old, unmarried, and that rarest of things in eighteenth-century

England, a woman freelance reviewer and writer, living entirely by her pen", set off " 'alone - neck or nothing is the word'".[174]

In Paris, she made contact with the Girondists through Madame Roland. One result was that "Condorcet...commissioned her to draw up a paper on female education..."[175] This flirtation with the 'revolution' ended with Robespierre's attack on the Girondists, which "dampened [her] enthusiasm and considerably modified her opinion about the ease with which human civilizations could undergo important changes".[176]

Marilyn Yalom and Dorinda Outram, in turn, - each at home in *French* as in *English* - devoted a chapter to Madame Roland. Her "life...has always attracted attention. Partly this has been due to the enormous volume of self-documentation which she produced. She is probably the most extensively intimately documented woman of the French eighteenth century".[177]

Outram approached Mme Roland through "her attitudes to her own physicality and to that of men and other women", material of prime importance to understanding "on many levels". This was "an area neglected in the historiography at large, and in studies of Mme Roland in particular", and which Outram claimed to have been excised from early editions and generally neglected since.[178]

Mme Roland, then, was the source of a significant contribution to Outram's study, *The Body and the French Revolution.* "One of the major themes...has been the construction of human bodies, predominantly male, as arenas of public authority".[179]

Outram, in the penultimate chapter of her book, charted "in the case of a woman...the interaction of physical self-consciousness, reactions to the physicality of others, and the delineation of the public realm".[180] "These interactions emerge far more clearly and directly in the case of Mme Roland than in the case of many of the male actors...so far considered".[181]

In her later text, *The Enlightenment,* Outram "argues fairly consistently for a view of the Enlightenment as paralysed by its own social, political, and intellectual constructions in its attempts to change the world".[182] Some of the ideas underpinning this view are already there in this work published in the bicentennial year of the French Revolution.

"[A]lthough the French Revolution may have been the point in time at which the middle class[183] began to be constituted," Outram wrote, "it is as well to remember how profoundly conservative an event that Revolution actually was. While changing the form of government, challenging the political culture of the old regime and destroying many of its actual representatives, it thrust the bourgeoisie into power in a way which did not entail the inclusion in the political nation, except very briefly, of elements in society - the workers, peasants and women - which had been excluded under the old regime. As we have seen, while using a universalistic political discourse, it excluded workers and peasants from formal political participation on the basis of criteria (poverty, illiteracy) which made a mockery of a 'natural right' of all 'citizens' to *act* politically. Even more interestingly, the middle-class revolution in France developed an ideology whereby women were excluded by virtue of characteristics ascribed to them which defined them as different from men and *hence* defined their political unacceptability".[184]

"Nowhere was this process of exclusion and differentiation more marked than in the case of the most important word of the Revolutionary political vocabulary: 'virtue'. We have already seen how strong was the presupposition that political revolution could only take place if the niche formerly occupied by women's vice was taken over by male virtue".[185] There was an immense gulf between public male virtue personified by Brutus and private female virtue as shown by Lucretius.[186]

"The existence of this continuum between virtue as chastity or female fidelity within marriage, and virtue as the upholding of the republic at whatever private cost, carries a whole series of messages: that female chastity is the prerequisite for political innovation undertaken in the name of the general will and against monarchy; that women threaten the revolution, because any deviation from chastity/virtue involves the collapse of republic/virtue; and because through their unrestrained sexuality women can personalize politics and factionalise it with competition for their 'favours' (a significantly two-edged word). Virtue, far from being the linchpin of a monolithic 'discourse of the Revolution', in fact bisected the apparently universalistic discourse of the general will into distinct political destinies, one male and the other female'.[187]

Outram was "led back to the essential paradox that the French Revolutionary middle class probably actually produced an intensification of the pre-existing patriarchal political culture which they alleged they were attempting to replace".[188]

This story is continued by Linda Colley who pointed out that not only in France, but, throughout Western Europe, Great Britain and North America, "the debate over women's proper place in society had become increasingly intense as the eighteenth century progressed". In all of these areas, women were formerly excluded from exercising political rights, and in England and Wales the restrictions on them were harsher in some respects than elsewhere".[189]

Flora's English daughters, London University College, and Women Medical Students.

The process of social change is highly complex. Progress may be unpredictable and nonlinear but is not beyond the capacity of women and men to achieve it - finally!

"Botany became part of the gender economy for women in England, and they could make it work for them. During 1790-1830 women were particularly visible as writers of botany books".[190]

Ann B. Shteir spoke of "women who wrote about botany in genres such as verse, juvenile natural history books, novels, and introductory books for family-based education (p.3)".

"The stories of Maria Jacson, Agnes Ibbetson, and Elizabeth Kent all intersect with science culture and literary culture, extending from the Enlightenment decades across the Linnaean years and into romanticism.[191] These three women stand at the heart of this study of Flora's English daughters: working within changing parameters of beliefs about women, gender, and science, each struggled to make her contribution, and each also made botany a resource for herself. Each can be said to have had a career as a botanical writer".[192]

"From 1760 to 1830, the gendered shape of botanical culture gave women access to botany, but after 1830 the same gendering was inverted to deny them access. Women elbowed in but were elbowed out".[193] London University and its first professor of botany, John Lindley, were instrumental in this change.[194]

Shteir's reading of the effect of the new university on women in botany is in keeping with the ideas that gave it birth. After situating John Lindley as the first professor of botany at London University, Shteir quoted from his inaugural lecture delivered on Thursday, April 30, 1829.[195]

Lindley "aligned himself with Continental theories and roundly rang an ani-Linnaean theme. He argued that the 'science' of botany should concern plant structure rather than identification - should be botany according to the newer Continental mode rather than on stale and static Linnaean lines. Linnaeus was a figure of historical importance, 'a person exactly adapted to the state of science of the time in which he lived,' but 'a more advanced state of science' called for another system.

"Lindley acknowledged that the Linnaean system had the merit of simplicity, but he considered it to be superficial knowledge: 'The principles of Linnaean classification produced the mischief of rendering Botany a mere science of names, than which nothing more useless can be well conceived'.

"Instead, Lindley called for using a system based on plant structure: 'Let the vegetable world be studied in all its forms and bearings, and it will be found that certain plants agree with each other in their anatomical condition, in the venation of their leaves, in the structure of their flowers, the position of their stamens, in the degree of development of their organs of reproduction, in the internal structure of those organs, in their mode of germination, and finally in their chemical and medicinal properties".[196]

To Shteir, these arguments were less than a botanist's decision about the shortcomings of a particular technical taxonomy and more about the pro-Continental reformist attitudes of the new London University. To her it read like a profession of faith from within a broader sociopolitical credo.[197]

"London University founded in 1826, represented all that was new and radical and commercial in imperial London. This meant being opposed to the Tory-Anglican alliance and committed instead to reform and to training professionals for a new world of knowledge, including applied science.

"Science was one of the professional tools for the enlightened and secular reformers of the 'godless college', as the non denominational London University was called. The Benthamites of the new university 'repudiated the aristocratic ideal of polite knowledge as an embellishment to a gentleman's education and sought to create a serious body of knowledge useful to the reformers in government and the professions...[they aimed to] turn...middle-class students into a professional elite, a new middle management".

Lindley's botany belongs to that larger agenda, and Lindley himself, described by a biographer as 'a first class fighting man', represents the emergence of a new generation. These new orientations led particularly to repudiating botany as polite knowledge and to embodying it rhetorically as 'feminine'".[198]

Jim Endersby's *Imperial Nature: Joseph Hooker and the Practices of Victorian Science* appeared in 2008 (some years after the first drafts of this chapter). Lindley's hostility to the Linnaeans, associated with his belief that botany was in decline, is in evidence in *Imperial Nature.*

Lindley might have been a little more understanding of *Flora's English daughters* and of their career as botanical writers, for he, himself, "partly depended on selling books...for his income", as did the Hookers.[199]

Lindley's *Ladies' Botany,* in the form of letters "addressed to a lady on the botanical education of her children" at once mimicked a popular style but turned potential readers to the Natural System of Botany. His claim that the method of Linnaeus had universally given way among Botanists was disingenuous, to say the least, according to Endersby, who recorded its continuing use through the 1830s to the 1850s, and even later.[200]

London University while rejecting the Oxbridge pattern had not embraced women. Elizabeth Garrett's attempt to enter the medical school failed as late as 1862. A separatist move, the London School of Medicine for

Women was established in 1874. Four years later the University of London became the first British university to admit women to its degrees.[201]

As Witz pointed out, "male power in the institutional sphere of civil society is not routinely exercised as force or physical and verbal intimidation, but simply by changing the rules". This time it worked for women.

However, fighting for equal rights to a medical education was not without its personal dangers though bringing greater credit upon those who supported it, whether women or men, than its opponents in the two following cases.

"In November 1870 the 'indignities' (Lutzker, 1974) and 'petty annoyances' (Thorne, 1915) to which the women were increasingly subject came to a head in the riot at Surgeon's Hall, where the women were to sit an examination. A dense crowd had gathered outside the hall and the gates were slammed in their faces by a number of young men 'who stood within, smoking and passing about bottles of whisky, while they abused us in the foulest possible language (Jex-Blake 1886:92). One of the medical students already in Surgeon's Hall came to their aid and opened the gate for them. During the examination a sheep was pushed in by the rioters. When the examination was over, the women left protected against the rioters by a bodyguard (armed with osteological specimens, recalled Isabel Thorne) of some of their fellow students (Jex-Blake 1886: 93, Thorne, 1915: 14)".[202]

Imagine now a November morning of the previous year across the Atlantic Ocean. Would matters be different there?

To the delight of Dean Ann Preston of the Woman's medical College of Pennsylvania, she had permission to bring her women students to attend the Saturday teaching clinics of the Pennsylvania Hospital. A clipping from that city's *Evening Bulletin* described what happened.

"The students of the male colleges, knowing that the ladies would be present, turned out several hundred strong, with the design of expressing their disapproval of the action of the managers of the hospital particularly, and of the admission of women to the medical profession generally".

"Ranging themselves in line, these gallant gentlemen assailed the young ladies, as they passed out, with insolent and offensive language, and then followed them into the street, where the whole gang, with the fluency of long practice, joined in insulting them".

"During the last hour missiles of paper, tinfoil, tobacco-quids, etc., were thrown upon the ladies, while some of these men defiled the dresses of the ladies near them with tobacco juice".

Regina Markell Morantz-Sanchez claimed the event's historical importance in 1869, was to show that public sympathy was with the women. The behaviour of those men received a poor press. The women kept their hard won permission to attend the clinics.[203]

Interestingly, three women who appear above opened another book on women's march to equality of opportunity as women scientists, who, of their own free will chose to live alone, or in a relationship with another person, male or female.

Dorinda Outram, joint editor, opened *Uneasy Careers* with 'Before Objectivity', women in 'Early Nineteenth-Century' France. Ann B. Shteir followed with 'Botany in the Breakfast Room', and Regina M. Morantz-Sanchez, The Many Faces of Intimacy'.[204]

Chapter 9

EARLY CONVICT FLEETS & CONSEQUENCES

The Health of Convicts. I.

Alan Frost[1] has Arthur Phillip, born on 11 October 1738, entering the Greenwich Hospital School, "a charity for the sons of seamen" on 22 June 1751, having been at sea from the age of nine years.[2] On 1 December 1753, he was apprenticed on a vessel working seasonally between Arctic whaling[3] and European coastal trading.[4]

"By the summer of 1755, Phillip's youthful experience had begun to offer that sense of the world's expanse and variousness, of the diversity of men and their societies, that distinguishes the true voyager. It was to be this sense, more than any other single attribute, that would one day bring him safely through a scarcely-travelled sea".[5]

At seventeen, he joined the *Buckingham*, a 68-gun battleship, as a "captain's servant", in a squadron commanded by Admiral John Byng.[6] By 1759, Phillip was a midshipman. He experienced the Royal Navy during the Seven Years War 1755-60, and in Europe.[7] *An Anatomy of the Georgian Navy* in this war may be found in N.A.M. Rodger's classic *The Wooden World*.[8]

Phillip's need for a wider experience was to be partially satisfied in the West Indies. There from 1760 to 1763, he gained experience of the Royal Navy's dual roles, protecting trade routes and making war, under extreme conditions of tropical heat, limited rations of food and water, and disease - malaria and yellow fever.

As fourth lieutenant of a man-of-war he had "a substantial hand in the management of a large ship", and experienced "a real authority over men". Frost, in a useful discussion of Royal Navy discipline at the time, concluded that Phillip was learning "to keep the precarious balance between exemplary justice and understanding mercy, and thereby obtain a communal effort".

Greg Dening was also drawn to this theme, in his study of William Bligh, embedded in the eighteenth century Royal Navy. He examined discipline in the light of the experiences of the fifteen British naval vessels that had entered the Pacific between 1767 and 1795.[9]

Dening's conclusion, which follows, came from this and other readings. "The violence of discipline was not inevitable. Any captain could have known how to be a 'gentleman', how to manage the symbolic environment of his wooden world...Any captain could have discovered some social contract with his people, could have known how far his own person intruded on his role. Any captain could have known what Admiral Collingwood knew: that he would be the cause of his own mutiny. Any captain could have known how much he was the cause of the pain of those he flogged, how much he was the hangman of those who mutinied".[10]

Philip was also becoming aware of the human implications of the slave base of the American colonies. "This evil commerce and the lot of slaves made an abiding impression on Phillip. Twenty-five years later, when about the business of founding a colony, and conscious of Lord Mansfield's historic judgement abolishing the holding of slaves in England, his comment was, "there can be no Slavery in a Free Land - & consequently no Slaves".[11]

[Some there are who may detect a contradiction here. If you put too fine a point on it convicts in New South Wales were not slaves. But did you have to be legally constituted a 'slave' to be one? Did a convict in colonial America become a slave by being sold? Could a convict in New South Wales - to whom Phillip would restore civil rights – and not sold, be considered a slave?

There are moments when early chapters of this book may bring, to some minds, words such as 'Slave', 'slavery' and being 'enslaved' as applicable to persons not legally defined as 'slaves' but so affected.]

With peace came a short-lived marriage from 1763 to 1769, and life in the country. Ill health, stints in France, recruiting in England, which included his leadership of a press gang,[12] ended with Phillip on the half-pay register until 1775, about the time of Redfern's birth.

At this point Frost contemplated possible "engineering and military studies" undertaken by Phillip, and this knowledge and his language skills being put to use spying on the "French navy's dockyards and arsenal at Toulon".[13]

Phillip, and the Portuguese Navy.

Phillip achieved a captain's appointment in the Portuguese Navy due largely to Augustus Hervey, one of the Lord Commissioners, according to Frost. Hervey did not tell why the British authorities were willing that he should serve Portugal: "that he was an intelligent man, whose knowledge of languages permitted him to move freely about the European world and its extensions; that his naval and military expertise enables him to assess accurately the utility of harbours and the effectiveness of fortifications as he did so; that he was an officer who could be relied upon to report his observations discreetly; that, in effect, he was one from whom in time might come most useful information concerning 2500 kilometres of South American coastline, concerning the Spanish fortifications and forces about the River Plate estuary, concerning the geography, products, and economies of the Spanish and Portuguese colonies in America".[14]

Be that as it may, in 1778, Phillip left the Portuguese "extremely satisfied with [his] conduct" and his service.[15]

His experiences in Brazil had strengthened his earlier opinion, first formed in the West Indies, against slavery in a free land.[16] His future work in founding a colony stood to gain from his critical observation of sites and his experience of the fundamental issues involved in maintaining a human settlement.[17] But, whatever he did "he likely would do it against persistent ill-health".[18]

Frost details the next period of Phillip's life as contrary to that of "many a capable junior officer whom fate decreed should remain undistinguished and unpromoted".[19] Even without a patron, by then, he had had a succession of postings advancing "steadily in rank, from first lieutenant to master and commander to post captain in charge of a small battleship", a fourth rate '64'.[20] (Redfern's personal contribution to the Nore mutiny was on another '64', HMS *Standard*.)

Evan Nepean, John Blankett and Philip Gidley King became acquaintances in this period.[21] The first and the last of them have already entered this book and will return.

"After 1782, [Phillip] was one whom fate impelled to a unique endeavour, and the remembrance of nations. As now appears, his secret advice and service were the key to his passing from the one phase to the other".[22]

Transportation of Convicts.

Arthur Phillip was named leader of the first fleet of convict transports to sail to Botany Bay, and governor to be, of a proposed colony to be founded there.[23] Thomas Townshend, Viscount Sydney of the Home Office, made the announcement in August 1786.

As Frost noted, at the time of his writing, "precise reasons for the colonization of New South Wales have become a matter of very considerable controversy". Arguments for colonization developed around three themes, "the dumping of convicts", ideas related to "trade", and "strategic' planning".[24]

Frost also claimed that the mounting of the First Fleet, had "yet to be adequately described and analysed". Decisions regarding its adequacy needed to reflect some "800 relevant documents" rather than the 100 then used. Frost gave notice of his own work in progress and his agreement with Wilfred Oldham's thesis, refuting the view that the expedition was poorly mounted.[25]

Roger Knight noted that had Oldham's PhD (1933) thesis been published, "fewer inaccurate books on the First Fleet would have appeared".[26]

Who Were the Convicts? (Robson's answers)

For many years a debate has also ensued around the convicts themselves. George Rudé provided an overview of the debate to 1978, beginning with the impressions of the early governors and their mixed reactions to convicts in general and to some in particular.[27] For example Governor Macquarie's belief that "tried good conduct should lead a man back to that rank in society which he had forfeited" benefited both "William Redfern, the naval mutineer and James Meehan, an Irish rebel of 1798".[28]

As earlier, Governor King had done for Redfern, to be revealed in the chapter that follows, here.

Rudé contrasted Macquarie's approach to that of Commissioner Bigge, and the Reverend Samuel Marsden. (Of Bigge, more later in Vol. II) Marsden "believed that man was born in sin and that convicted felons, being more sinful than others, were utterly beyond redemption whatever their previous station in life".[29]

Like the Hammonds in England, some Australian historians began to see the convicts as more sinned against than sinning, as noted above.[30] In this context, Rudé referred to a paper by George Arnold Wood (1922) and two studies by T.J. Kiernan (Irish convicts, 1954).

A.G.L. Shaw (1953) was the first historian to challenge the rosy view, opening "a new critical, and more discriminating, assessment of the nature of the convicts". Shaw argued that, "most convicts, far from being the innocent victims of an unjust system, were urban thieves, pickpockets, and shoplifters, the product of urban overcrowding and unemployment...[and] far from being first offenders". [31]

Manning Clark came to broadly similar conclusions based on sampling of shiploads of convicts, arriving from 1813 to 1840. Clark saw these convicts as commonly thieves and young, of both sexes.

Shaw's ideas were widely disseminated through his entry in the ten volume *Australian Encyclopaedia* published in 1958.That article did two services to the memory of William Redfern, first by giving him credit for the positive impact of his report on convict ships, and second by including him among a list of about 1000 convicts who were essentially "political offenders".[32]

The list included: "The Scottish 'martyrs' of 1794; the naval mutineers of 1797 (including the surgeon William Redfern); the Irish rebels of 1798, 1803 and 1848; the agricultural rioters of 1830; the Tolpuddle 'martyrs' of 1834; the Canadian rebels of 1839, and the Chartists of 1842 - all these comprise a formidable-looking list".[33]

L.L. Robson (1965) followed some relatively minor amendments made by Shaw and Clark in their longer studies of the 1960s but "his study is far more detailed and specific than those that came before him and his conclusions are based on a far wider range of questions".[34]

Rudé lists these questions as: "where did the convicts come from? what crimes had they committed, including the one that led to transportation? how many were men and how many were women? how many were English and how many Scots or Irish? to which colonies were they sent? what happened to them when they got there? what further offences were committed in the colony? how old were they? what was their occupations, their marital status, the length of their sentence, their religion and place of birth? and why did they commit the crime that brought them to Australia?"[35]

Robson's answers covered the following categories: Numbers and destination; Place of trial; Age, and marital status; Social class, and occupation; Religion; Literacy; Nature and causes of crime for which sent out; Previous convictions; Offences in the colony; and English and Irish. Rudé was critical of Robson's categories and presentation on the grounds that change over time remains hidden, and occupations based on the United Kingdom census of 1951 have little in common with pre- or early industrial society.[36]

Who were the convicts? (Linebaugh's Answers)

Rudé would have found his criticisms met in Linebaugh's study, *The London Hanged,* discussed earlier in this book. To ask "who were the convicts?" could lead to the same sources that Linebaugh had found.

Edward Thompson had provided a stimulus to Linebaugh's quest by suggesting that it would be tempting to follow "the eighteenth-century inarticulate" "into the archives of crime". By doing that, Linebaugh discovered most had a biography and was able to conclude that the "London hanged" were "makers" as well as "takers". As "makers" they were defined as members of a working, and not a criminal class. [37]

Linebaugh's work is relevant to the line of research, presented in *Convict Workers,* edited by Stephen Nicholas (1988).[38] Michael Flynn, in his study of *The Second Fleet,* took issue with Stephen Nicholas. He also placed his critique in the context of "Convicts and Historians",[39] as had Rudé (above) travelling the same ground and with matching conclusions, in the main.

The Nicholas study found, "a surprisingly small proportion of the convicts were totally unskilled labourers", and "most of the convicts possessed work skills and had been employed before their transportation".[40] Nicholas admitted to being "a captive of our economic questions, quantitative data and statistical techniques in the same way that the old historiography is shaped by the framework and data employed by these older historians".

"The arguments presented...are controversial", Nicholas conceded. "Many will be criticised. Some, it is hoped, will be sustained by more detailed empirical investigation. But the book will have served its purpose if it unshackles Australia's 'founding fathers and mothers' - the transported convicts - from a history which ignores their human capital, and implicitly discounts their contribution to our economic and social development".

"Finally", according to Linebaugh, "the struggles of the hanged, like those of their class, inspired their rulers to initiatives of their own...we consider the history of the condemned as part of an eighteenth-century working class". With that argument, *The London Hanged* takes up the problem with which *Albion's Fatal Tree* closed, namely, what was the relationship between crime and the working class?" [41]

Hay, in his preface, to the latter text told how, "All the contributors to this book have been associated at one time in the Centre for the Study of Social History at the University of Warwick. We were all concerned with the social history of eighteenth-century England. And we were all centrally concerned with the law, both as ideology and as actuality and with that century's definition of crime".

Thompson and Linebaugh were contributors to that book and their work has impacted on the one you are reading, as you would be aware. In Thompson's *Whigs and Hunters* (1975) the study of law is at the centre again. There he maintained that whether "the actuality of the law's operation in class-divided societies has, again and again, fallen short of its own rhetoric of equity, yet *the notion of the rule of law is itself an unqualified good*" [my italics].[42]

Linebaugh's study has not entered into the Australian debate - criminal nor working class - as to the source of its convicts. It should have, as his work sourced material common to each study and came down conclusively on the side of convicts as a subset of workers.

The debate has advantaged individual convict records as research has focussed on them for evidence to support one side or the other of the argument. More usually though, research had the immediate intention of providing as complete a picture as possible of the convicts assembled on one ship or in one particular fleet, and the consequences to the individual, or to the whole, of his or her presence there.

One wonders whether evidence for crime and criminality among convicts misleads. It can mislead, but not everyone, and not all of the time.

In Linebaugh's work on the imposition of the wage it was apparent that workers in the shipbuilding trade had been underpaid for generations, in money terms. The negotiated taking of "chips" had only partly compensated for the difference. As the gap increased, between what was owed and what was given, so did the "taking". Authority reacted, vexatiously for the workers, by making the taking of "chips" - payment in kind - a criminal act.

While St Vincent came down heavily on striking workers at the shipyards he also widened his attack to include the dockyard clerks. "If all the clerks in the dockyards were dismissed, with annuities" he said, "payable on one condition only", "that they reside fifty miles from any dockyard", "the public would benefit exceedingly".[43]

Furthermore, "If the great families lived like tapeworms in the body politic the royal dockyards nursed a voracious species of shipworm, boring creatures whose tunnels to the Treasury had often been started by a great-grandfather. Samuel Pepys knew them when he was secretary to the Admiralty. They "stole" naval property. Knowing from the inside what the Navy needed, they cornered that article on the outside and bought it from themselves at huge profits. They drew pay from jobs they never went near...They took rebates from contractors and accepted inferior materials", and so on.[44]

J.H. Plumb, writing of the mutinies at Spithead and the Nore, noted: "the financial resources of the armed forces were the object of deliberate and calculated plunder" in 1797, with Britain at war and the seamen asking for a legitimate pay rise after 140 years.[45]

Do such notions suggest an unconvicted criminal class, this time in high society? Or, were such miscreants a subset of this class, as the convicted were of the working class?

Unearned *perquisites* had long been considered undesirable, but not criminal.[46] Nor was capital punishment or transportation considered appropriate punishment for such crimes against society. Why was this? [T]he

Honourable P.M. Woodward, a onetime Justice of the Supreme Court of New South Wales, provided an explanation:

"The number and nature of the crimes listed as felonies in the British criminal code were the direct consequence of the constitution and function of the eighteenth century Parliament. At that time the House of Commons was in no sense representative of the community as a whole. The members all belonged to the propertied class, voted into Parliament by a constituency restricted by limited property qualifications or representing rotten boroughs without any constituents at all. The members of the House of Lords were hereditary peers or senior members of the Anglican establishment. It is not surprising that a very large percentage of the legislation endorsed by these two houses should have had the protection of property as its sole objective".[47]

[For a present day comparison see "white-collar crime".[48]]

The Poverty Line.

H.A.L. Fisher, in 1946, opened the third book of his *History of Europe* with a brief statement headed "Strands of History". In it he demonstrated how "free trade" on the one hand, and the defence of labour against "capitalist exploitation", on the other, had produced a society where "material enjoyments were alike vastly more numerous and better distributed than ever before".

"Yet the problem of poverty was not solved", Fisher continued. Nor has it been, even today.[49] "Every workman had [has] a pistol pointed at his heart. A change of fashion, the bankruptcy of an employer, the failure of a distant harvest, the crash of a bank, the fraud or improvidence of a group of speculators, might throw him out of employment and reduce his family to want".

"The 'condition of the people question', though always of the first importance, was never steadily and continuously kept in the forefront of political attention. Other causes or diversions, more melodramatic and attractive, such as the rivalry of nations, the thirst for empire, the appetite for markets, were apt to ensnare the attention of statesmen or inflame the passion of mobs".[50]

Bound for 'Botany Bay'.

The next task is to review the experiences of convicts in the process of transportation to New South Wales. The sea, never far away, returns to our story. Convicts on the high seas, and in port, replace the seamen in our focus. But it will be well to keep their story in mind.

Charles Bateson's study of *The Convict Ship* takes the reader to "the dramatic story of a single phase of the convict transportation system - that of the actual conveyance of the prisoners to Australia from England and Ireland between the years 1787 and 1868. ... It is a history which has many dark and sombre hues - a story of hardship and human suffering, of disease and callous brutality, of mutiny and shipwreck, of cowardice and courage".[51]

For the ships of the First Fleet, on their journey to New South Wales,[52] Bateson's summary account reads as follows - "The *Sirius* and her convoy anchored in Botany Bay on January 20, 1788, barely 48 hours after the *Supply*. ... It was a magnificent feat of navigation and seamanship".[53]

Bateson considered the fleet's health record as even more remarkable.[54]

Surgeon Bowes noted some factors contributing to this good health record. One was government provision for the convicts - better than normally provided for marines going overseas on service - surgeons and officers paying strict attention to convicts, "keeping themselves and their berths well aired and perfectly clean", and "remarkably fine weather".[55]

Bowes contended that not all convicts had been "in the perfectly healthy state" on boarding that government had intended. *Alexander,* with "malignant disorders" from the beginning, continued to be a problem ship. Phillip had also "stamped the magistrates 'with infamy' " for sending women aboard the *Lady Penrhyn,* naked and filthy.[56] Clothing stores intended for later use in the colony had to be taken to clothe them.

Frost and His 'Botany Bay Mirages'.

Alan Frost, in arguing in *Botany Bay Mirages* against "an indescribable hopelessness and confusion" in getting the First Fleet under way, raised both general and specific issues.[57] First, it was wrong "to measure the thoughts and actions of people in the past by a measuring rod of [modern] knowledge and experience".[58] Secondly, organising that Fleet was a complex task. Frost pointed to effective shortcuts adopted at the time to achieve desired ends. Both "points of authority in the bureaucracy" and "lines of communication" needed to be understood.[59]

"The Home Office was responsible for convicts, so that it told the Treasury and Admiralty what was needed. The Treasury authorised the expenditure of funds. The Admiralty passed on requests for ships, goods and food to the Navy Board, which then ordered them". This apparent rigidity was loosened by direct and informal communication at a ministerial level between Lord Sydney, William Pitt and Admiral Lord Howe and through the permanent Heads of the departments. These were Evan Nepean (Home Office), George Rose and Thomas Steele (Treasury), Philip Stephens (Admiralty) and Sir Charles Middleton (Navy Board).

Eventually "Nepean, Middleton and Phillip adopted the procedure, which had served Cook so well, of Phillip's calling at the offices to say what was needed, seeing the necessary requests were issued and then seeing that they were fulfilled".[60]

Frost made the issue of good food a central consideration in the question of whether the *First Fleet* was well prepared. It is timely, then, to revisit some earlier discussion in this book relative to food and health at sea. The first point to note is the date. *First Fleet* preparations were under way in 1786. That was still ten years before Royal Navy ships could be assured of a supply of lemon juice.

Take note again, that in 1797, it was Royal Navy seamen, not convicts, who, while in port, were being denied fresh meat and vegetables, each a potential source of vitamin C. Yet, there was Phillip, supported by Surgeon William Balmain (*Alexander*), years before, asking for fresh meat for both marines, and convicts. Phillip extended his initial request to cover the whole time "they remain[ed] at Spithead, and that a small quantity of wine be allowed for the sick". Within a month these items were forthcoming.[61]

In looking at Phillip's food requirements after sailing, Frost acknowledged that the contractor had not conceptualised the voyage adequately. The model contract did not provide for either antiscorbutics or "necessaries" for the sick. Phillip argued that "the garrison and convicts are sent to the extremity of the globe as they would be sent to America - a six-weeks' passage".[62]

Of course, Phillip was correct. Watt, in hindsight, set the health requirements of such great ocean journeys.[63] He made some interesting comparisons.

Watt and the Polynesian Seafarers: A Positive Comparison.

"The experiences of the Polynesians illustrate the medical challenge of ocean exploration, for survival at sea depends upon the character of pre-embarkation health, adequate supplies of clean water, food of adequate quantity and quality, protection from the environment, a high standard of hygiene and discipline, the intelligent anticipation of health hazards, accident prevention and skilled care of the sick and injured. This presumes the need for a surgeon".

"Judged by these criteria, on almost every score, Polynesians had the advantage over Europeans", Watt declared. "They were an active people, largely free of pre-existing disease and their high fibre, predominantly vegetarian, diet with abundant fresh fruit ensured that body stores of vitamins were at maximum capacity, whereas those of European sailors, frequently victims of the press gang, had often been depleted by a previous voyage or the rigours and food shortages of European winters superimposed upon the sequelae of acute and chronic illness".

"The Polynesians kept river water fresh in large gourds or bamboo and seaweed containers which, towed astern, were cooled by the sea during the night. Europeans were condemned to drink stinking water, smelling of casks, or tasting of tar or sulfuretted hydrogen and the problem was never satisfactorily resolved until the advent of steam ships, which were able to provide clean water by condensation. Before that, diarrhoea and dysentery due to contaminated or infected water was common. Dysentery, or 'flux' as it was called was also caused by spoiled provisions contaminated by vermin and hastened the onset of scurvy by raising the pH of the intestinal contents and destroying vitamin C". [64]

Phillip's Experience with Scurvy.

What had been Phillip's experience of scurvy on the high seas? Frost, early in his biography of Phillip, discussed sickness in Admiral John Byng's squadron in terms closely related in sources and conclusions to those to be found in earlier chapters of this book. Frost concluded that Lind's preference for lemon and orange juice and fresh vegetables, together with Lind's "regimen" for maintaining a healthy ship environment, "were not widely followed in the ships of Byng's squadron". As a result, Phillip, who was there, would have encountered crews "weakened by illness", including scurvy.[65]

The next reference to scurvy, "rife among his crew" (not included in Frost's index) occurred in Phillip's own ship, *Europe*, a "64", en route to India via South America, in 1783. At Rio de Janeiro, Frost made no mention of either oranges or the curing of scurvy, but Phillip was aware of the availability of citrus fruits there, and would later make use of such knowledge as he did at the Cape, some years previously.

Then, Phillip was returning in company with eleven other ships from Madras. "By the time they [reached the Cape of Good Hope on 9 December, 1783] about 1800 of the crew were afflicted with scurvy, and there had been many deaths". Recovery of the sick followed, thanks to the forethought of members of the Dutch East India Company who had laid out a garden "to succour 'worn-out and scorbutic sailors' ".[66]

A further reference to scurvy (again missing from his index) may be found in Frost's chapter, *The First Fleet*, where Phillip is reflecting upon the thought that "Sickness must be the Consequence in so long a Voyage", of some six months. Frost quoted Phillip's conclusion. "Scurvy must make a great ravage amongst people naturally Indolent, & not cleanly".[67]

No doubt Phillip's awareness, and his plans and action aimed at averting such a disaster, led to Frost's conclusion, "it is in its health record that the voyage is most remarkable".[68] "Phillip and his captains and surgeons lost only forty-eight persons from embarkation - thirty-six male and four female convicts and five children of convicts, and one marine, one marine's wife, and one marine's child". Possibly, as few as a third of these, died of scurvy. By contrast, Anson, in 1740-44, lost 626 of 961 men to scurvy.[69] That was the tragedy that had stirred Lind to action and no doubt was exercising Phillip's mind in planning to prevent a recurrence.

He would have known that scurvy proliferated at that time close by in the Channel Fleet. The reasons, which involved Captain Cook, were argued earlier in this book and revolved around an undeserved support for essence of malt as antiscorbutic, an idea, which was 'taken on board' literally, by the Royal Navy. The *First Fleet* received a ton of the stuff. It was not an unmixed curse, however.[70]

Phillip held his ground. He fought to the end and won the right to purchase provisions *en route*.[71] These would include effective antiscorbutics, fresh vegetables and fruit. Phillip made use of earlier knowledge of lemons and oranges being available in Rio, noted above. Citrus fruits were common to both Portuguese and Spanish cultures, an Islamic inheritance, and taken to other places apart from the Americas.

Phoebe Lloyd, in a different contextual link to this book, has a reference to the Spaniards at that time as "the most expert agriculturalists in Europe", having "absorbed all the [Muslim] Moors could teach them", and as people who had "carried their expertise across the Atlantic". Lloyd described the convent gardens of Mexico, "planted with figs, grapes and pomegranates, their walks shaded by lemon and orange trees".[72]

Just so, "a long, shady avenue, lined on both sides with orange and lemon trees" impressed Rose de Freycinet in the East Indies, on a tour of the town of Umata, in the Caroline Islands, again, a reminder of [Moor] Spanish influence.[73]

Nevertheless, it has been suggested that the great Spanish navigator, Alexandro Malaspina, "had preferred the opinion of a commissioned officer and experienced navigator [Cook] to that of one whom he must have considered as a humble naval surgeon [Lind]".

"Clearly, to a man like Malaspina, the remedies of the North, recommended by Cook, had a prestige and a value which those of the South had not, although it was in Southern Europe that lemons and oranges grew and their effect against scurvy had been known for a long time". Fortunately the doctors who went with Malaspina had this traditional knowledge and had also read both Lind and Blane.[74]

If you are still reluctant to bestow an accolade on Phillip for his assiduity in forestalling scurvy, compare the responses of Flinders and Baudin to this same challenge, more than ten years later, on their journeys to, and around, Terra Australis.[75] And, if you wish, follow through the nineteenth century experience with scurvy in the convict ships with Bateson, and in Arctic exploration with Carpenter, Watt, and others.

At Port Jackson, where "Captain Baudin arrived in *Le Geographe* on the 20th [June, 1802]...a boat was sent from the *Investigator* to assist in towing the ship up to the cove. It was grievous to see the miserable condition, to which both officers and crew were reduced by scurvy; there being not more out of one hundred and seventy, according to the commander's account, than twelve men capable of doing their duty. The sick were received into the colonial hospital; and both French ships furnished with everything in the power of the colony to supply".[76]

In Flinders' case there is a mixed account of scurvy and its prevention. References to the 'Sick and Hurt Board', 'concrete acid of lemon, or other antiscorbutics' and 'Dr Blane'[77] appear in a letter to Banks about preparations for the *Investigator* journey.[78] Following an early report of good health on *Investigator*, Flinders gives the reader some concern that he too is confused in his understanding, as was Cook. Lemon and orange juice was not to be left out of Lind's teaching. How else can one interpret the following entry of Friday 16 October 1801?

"Within the tropics, lime juice and sugar were made to *suffice* as antiscorbutics; on reaching a higher latitude, sour krout and *vinegar* were substituted; the essence of malt was *reserved* for the passage to New Holland, and for future occasions".[79] All of this suggests a *reversed* order of antiscorbutic effectiveness and confusion with the proven and useless aids in curing scurvy. [My italics.]

James D. Mack noted, "the first sign of scurvy mentioned in the log" was a reference by Flinders in March 1803 to his "being lame at this time in both feet, with scorbutic ulcers".[80] In his *Journal*, a few pages later, Flinders reported "a lameness in both feet from incorrigible scorbutic ulcers" and "the debilitated state of my health, as well as many others in the ship".

On 26 March...Flinders requested Surgeon Bell to examine the crew and advise him on their fitness to continue without interruption. Bell found twenty-two men showing symptoms of scurvy, 'such as spongy gums and livid sores on the legs'.[81]

Mack included a more extensive report made by Bell,[82] pointing out that it was more than nineteen months since they had left England, receiving port refreshments at only Madeira and the Cape of Good Hope. Because of the situation at Port Jackson they were unable to obtain any animal food and but few vegetables. For the last eight months, "fruit and vegetables, the best antiscorbutics, formed no part of what was procured". Since they also had an outbreak of "violent diarrhoea...with symptoms of fever", this would also have imposed an added strain on any remaining bodily reserve of vitamin C.[83]

John Cawte noted that Flinders encounter with the Malay trepang gatherers was at a time when "he and probably most of his crew were affected by scurvy", from which "Indonesian colonisers of the Pacific never suffered" as they relied on the tamarind as an anti-scorbutic", carrying the pods with them.[84] Tamarind seeds dropped at Indonesian campsites along the coast of Arnhem Land have since grown into trees. Today, Aborigines make use of their fruits as a medicine, and tamarind continues to be a feature of Malaysian and Indonesian cookery.[85]

'No History Without Health': Bryan Gandevia:.

Dr Bryan Gandevia, distinguished physician and medical historian, conceived a challenging and inclusive title, "No History Without Health", in his contribution to a study of the topic, *Science Under Scrutiny*.[86] There he argued the "historiographic role of the history of medicine", the latter being defined as embracing "not only problems of disease and its management but also the concept of 'positive health' ". "Given a holistic definition, the history of medicine permeates all aspects of history".

Holding to the belief that "one may see history simply as the story of man's endeavour to adapt himself to his environment", Gandevia placed certain conditions on its acceptance such as "the indices of adaptation". These "must ultimately be primarily medical, again using that term in a broad sense to include indices of health as well as of disease, in populations or societies as well as individuals".

To illustrate this idea, Gandevia cited studies made of "the heights of the convict children transported to Australia *circa* 1820-1840. Boys aged between 13 and 18 years were approximately 6-9 cm shorter than other recorded series of children in Britain of about that period, and even shorter than grossly underprivileged children in various institutions. The short stature reflects their social and physical environment, perhaps particularly its nutritional component".[87]

A rapid increase in height in the first generation of Australian born children reflected the influence of a changed environment. A figure, in the form of a parallelogram had *ENVIRONMENT* and *HEALTH* facing one another at the vertical apices, and *Social* and *Physical* at the horizontal. This demonstrated an interacting or 'feedback' conception of the role of the history of medicine. Arrowed connecting lines to the four factors indicate two-way flows of influence.

An extended discussion of environmental factors and their quantitative or qualitative indices was strengthened by original studies of epidemics in Sydney's early convict period.[88]

Settlement at Sydney: Studies of Mortality, 1788-1792.

"The mortality over the first five years or so of settlement at Sydney offers a fascinating field for study. There was initially a small epidemic of dysentery and scurvy. This epidemic occasioned little concern and it soon settled down. Mortality for the next two years was negligible despite the fact that towards the end of that period the settlement was on the verge of starvation.

"The figure [Home, 1983] then shows a dramatic increase in mortality with a rapid decline over two or three months to levels which are again very low. This epidemic involved only second fleet arrivals, and the shape of the epidemic curve (a dramatic upsweep with a subsequent steady decline) strongly suggests that the epidemic commenced prior to the arrival of the fleet; in fact, other evidence indicates that this is so. The deaths in this case were probably due to multiple diseases but primarily to the introduction of these diseases amongst an overcrowded, malnourished and ill-treated population transported in the most unhygienic circumstances.

"Despite another period of inadequate rations, the mortality rate then returns to the same level as before. Following the arrival of the third fleet, there is a remarkable epidemic extending over a period of nearly a year. Detailed analysis has indicated that almost all those who died were drawn from those who arrived on the third fleet. There are no medical descriptions of the illness or illnesses from which the people suffered, although there are some lay observations concerning the manner of death. Again the mortality is independent of the ration level, so that lack of food or malnutrition was not the sole cause of death although both may have contributed to deaths from other causes".

"The mortality experience of convicts arriving on the early fleets is summarised in a *Figure* [Home, Fig. 3]. *This shows the survival rates, and the outstanding feature is the extraordinary high survival rate for the first fleet, a survival rate unlikely to have been reached had these convicts remained in Britain* [My italics]. The horrible mortality of the second fleet is clearly indicated and it will be noted that this group never really adapted to its environment, in that after arrival the survival rate continues to fall at a greater rate than that for the first fleet. The third fleet mortality is obviously high but it is not possible to follow those involved for very long after their arrival in the colony".[89]

"Death and disease greatly influenced the development of the first Australian settlements but no detailed study of mortality over the critical years

1788-1792 has previously been made" i.e. until Gandevia and Cobley published in 1974.

Gandevia and Cobley (1974).

That study will now provide a focus for convict health in Sydney in the first years of white settlement. There, as Gandevia said, "Contemporary records are reviewed in an attempt to establish the causes of mortality and to explain the epidemiological data, including the low mortality in inter-epidemic periods".[90]

He addressed Procedures; Pattern of Mortality,1788-1792; Mortality in Relation to Fleet of Arrival; Mortality by Ship of Arrival; Infuence of Sex, Age and Place of Origin; Record of Individual Deaths; Contemporary Observations on Mortality; The First Epidemic, January-June; The Second Epidemic, July-August 1790; The Third Epidemic, August 1791-July 1792[91]; Inter-Epidemic Deaths and Conclusion[92].

Watt, 'The Colony's Health'.

Gandevia and Cobley (1974) was described 'a classic paper' by Sir James Watt, invited to contribute to the Australian Academy of the Humanities' bicentennial conference, "Terra Australis to Australia". Watt's paper "The Colony's Health" was published in a report of the conference (1989),[93] and in a separate Journal (1989).[94]

Three of Watt's five categories will be accessed here: "pre-embarkation considerations", "conditions on the voyage" and "the quality of medical practice". [Watt's "philanthropic network" will be discussed in a later stage of this study.] Gandevia and Cobley have already covered Watt's remaining category, "Life in the colony".

Watt: 'Pre-embarkation Considerations'.

Watt first noted differences between the health of convicts and that "of officers, marines, soldiers and their families...and seamen and free settlers". In this book, Royal Navy ships at sea revealed a similar disparity between seamen and officers. Diet, living conditions, habits, and state of mind [including educational background], each contributed to observed differences.

Pre-embarkation considerations took into account "the social and economic status and the previous medical history of the colonists", as well as the convicts. Watt used naval statistics, from Blane and Lewis, which have earlier featured in this book. To these he added a reference to "sickness accounting for 88% of all deaths" in the army, to show the general effect of time spent in the services on officers, seamen and marines. Major Grose, and naval surgeons Considen and Balmain were named in this category.[95]

The convict background was "related to the social and economic situations which often drove them to crime and most particularly to their period of incarceration in prisons and prison hulks". Dr Lettsom, a distinguished Quaker physician, provided Watt's single and indelible illustration of the plight of one family of London's poor.

Prisons, aided by "avaricious jailors", compounded the health problems of the gaoled poor by ignoring "orders regarding [rations], hygiene, disinfection, clothing and heating. This resulted in rheumatism and chest complaints, including tuberculosis, and encouraged the spread of scabies, smallpox, typhus fever and other infectious diseases. These the convicts often brought on board the transports". In this context he referred to "Gerrald, one of the 'Scottish martyrs', [as having] contracted tuberculosis and died within two years of his arrival in the colony".

Watt generally agreed with Frost (1994:ch.1) that conditions in the hulks had improved by the time of the First Fleet, but included a complaint by Dr John Lind of "the Gaol Distemper" in the *Firm* prison hulk in February 1786. Epidemics of "gaol" or typhus fever continued to occur in both land prison and hulks. It was imported into the *Alexander* from the hulks at Woolwich.[96]

Also, Sir Jeremy Fitzpatrick,[97] first met in chapter seven, and who will soon come to our attention again, below, continued his campaign against 'gaol fever' until he was retired on half pay, in 1802.[98]

Phillip "recognised that the success of the colony would depend largely upon the health of the colonists". He therefore asked for convicts to be selected for their vigour and skills and being free of venereal disease. Phillip wanted over-crowding to be avoided and convicts to arrive on board washed and cleanly clothed. Watt confirmed that there was no such selection as old, feeble and ill convicts appeared on board.

Watt: 'Conditions on the Voyage'.

Watt looked particularly at the effect of the voyage on the subsequent health of convicts and their usefulness to the colony and to this end was particularly mindful of "the nature, terms and execution of the contract, the priorities of masters and agents and the medical arrangements".[99]

He contrasted the character and achievement of William Richards junior, contractor for the First Fleet and for the *Lady Juliana*, which had good health records, with instructions to masters by Calvert, Camden and King, contractors for the disastrous Second and Third Fleets. Strong humanitarian principles stood out on the one hand, and profit motives, slave trade experience, and no incentives to maintain the convicts in health, on the other.

The profit motive found expression in "withholding rations", and "curtailing space and accommodation as masters stuffed their ships with goods for sale in New South Wales. This affected ventilation and hygiene, dictated ports of call, the number of days in harbour and the availability of fresh food". "Under such conditions, epidemics spread rapidly and often carried long-term implications for the colony's health".

In spite of care, "Typhus fever, mumps, malaria, dysentery and scurvy were experienced by the First Fleet".

Watt detailed the story of typhus, on the *Alexander,* which deceived both White and Balmain but not the Physician, whom White found on board, and whom Watt thought could have been Robert Robertson, "a most experienced clinician and an authority on typhus fever, who was at Portsmouth at the time".[100]

He cited Charles Fletcher's warning, "no disease was more misleading, for it assumed different guises and was subject to frequent relapses". This observational error, in the case of the *Alexander,* led to typhus spreading to the marines, sixteen of whom were admitted to hospital before sailing and several died. As well, Altree, a young naval surgeon caught the disease, and suffered a slow recovery.

The mumps epidemic was serious. "Blane...observed how rapidly such epidemics could spread throughout a squadron" [as noted earlier (ch.20)]. The effects of the mumps virus were detailed. Described as one possible cause of childless marriages in the colony, it was also held responsible for the death of Captain Shea of the Marines (1790) and the insanity and death of Lieutenant William Maxwell (1791).

Watt: 'The Quality of Medical Practice'.

Watt's assessment was that the "quality of medical practice was governed by the resources available and the professional competence of the colony's surgeons who were predominantly naval".

It was Watt's considered opinion that "Naval medical practice, under the influence of percipient naval writers such as James Lind, William Northcote, Charles Fletcher and Sir Gilbert Blane was often more advanced than that of contemporary orthodoxy[101] represented by the College of Physicians and the Royal Society".[102]

While Watt presented the medical men of the First Fleet, and those who arrived about the same time in other ships, as members of a team, individual differences in skill and character were not overlooked. John Pearn held, that "differences rather than similarities, characterized our medical forbears in this country".[103]

Such differences contributed to some confusion in the supply of medical materials to the First Fleet. Medical arrangements for the convicts rested with the Home Office, whose Under Secretary, Evan Nepean, took advice from Sir Joseph Banks, President of the Royal Society. The Admiralty was responsible for warships.

However, an early (August 1786) request was made to the Sick and Hurt Board to inspect instruments, medicines, etc. being ordered for sick convicts. Nothing came of that, but following a new request, the Treasury asked the Admiralty to supply medicines for the convicts. Sir Charles Middleton took this matter up and immediately ordered medical supplies on "the scale laid down for a second rate battleship with 750 men" [A *74*, a two-decked ship like *Standard* but larger and much preferred by commanders].

One month later the Surgeon General, John White, submitted his own list. This had the effect of cancelling Middleton's generous order, which was replaced by White's more restricted list. The marines' medical needs, overlooked at first, but remedied later, would thereby cause some storage problems.

Nonetheless, Watt accepted that "Surgeon General John White proved to be an efficient and energetic administrator, a competent and humane clinician and a perceptive observer who made a careful study of natural history".[104] White built a hospital to replace the tents and made available facilities on the warships. Surgeon Worgan,[105] on the *Sirius*, successfully attended Lieutenant Collins, who had been dying from an obstinate dysentery. In 1790, "[t]he *Justinian* storeship brought out Samuel Wyatt's prefabricated hospital...which was speedily erected to take the huge influx of invalids from the Second Fleet".

"Subsequently, hospitals were built at Parramatta and Norfolk Island, and White, with his small medical team, coped admirably with the epidemics of 1788, 1790 and 1791-2".

The medical team, so described by Watt, "consisted of Dennis Considen, his first assistant, William Balmain, his second, Thomas Arndell, the third, and John Turnpenny Altree, not yet fully recovered from the typhus fever he had contracted in the *Lady Penrhyn*. Altree served on Norfolk Island until his return in 1791, with Thomas Jamison, first surgeon's mate of the *Sirius,* who joined the team as an assistant surgeon. That left George Worgan in the *Sirius* with his second mate John Lowes, and James Callan, surgeon of the *Supply*".

"The team was augmented by three convict surgeons. John Irving, the first Australian emancipist, who had demonstrated his ability on *the Prince of Wales* transport, served at both Sydney and Norfolk Island and was reckoned by Clark "the best surgeon amongst them". Daniel Kelly, who arrived in 1790 or 1791, was emancipated on 4 June 1793 and was praised for his medical work at Toongabbie despite his ill-treatment at the hands of John Macarthur. John Francis Molloy, however, who arrived in the *Pitt* in 1792, was found woefully lacking in professional skill when entrusted with the medical care of the Hawkesbury settlement".

"The New South Wales Corps provided a valuable addition to medical manpower, for its surgeons, John Harris and Edward Laing, quickly displayed their personal integrity and professional abilities. Harris carried out an exceedingly hazardous high amputation of the thigh, with complete success, in a soldier with a gunshot wound and Laing treated 100 dysentery cases with only two deaths from factors outside his control".[106]

Pearn: 'Gentlemen of the Faculty'.

Gentlemen of the faculty: a synopsis of the First Fleet surgeons; Comparisons and contrasts of the personalities who were the founders of medicine in Australia is an essential reference (Pearn 1988).

Clearly and succinctly presented in tabular form, Pearn provided a wealth of information. "Table 1: First Fleet ships..." linked surgeons to ships. "Table 2: Summaries of the careers and activities of the surgeons of the First Fleet" were collected under nine headings: *Career, Time in Colony, Explorations, Scientific contributions, Patronymic legacy, Magisterial offices, Land holdings in N.S.W., Notes* and *References.* There is a brief but useful accompanying text.

As Pearn observed, "No contemporary descriptions of the personalities of the First Fleet surgeons have yet been found, and their biographies lack this crucial contemporary evidence of them as "real and living" persons (such descriptions are available, for example, in the case of Henry Cowper who was the first official surgeon appointed at the Moreton Bay settlement in 1825).[107]

Watt: 'The quality of medical practice' (resumed).

Returning now to James Watt. "The absence of clinical records creates difficulties in assessing the scope and efficacy of medical care but a number of indicators permit some conclusions to be drawn. For instance, White's list of medicines for the First Fleet bore little resemblance to the standard naval list, but followed closely that recommended by William Northcote and we can presume he therefore followed Northcote's guidelines for the treatment of dysentery. In fact Edward Laing, who described the dysentery epidemic of 1792 in great detail, confirms this".

"White's second list from Sydney, dated 12 July 1788, shows what had been used and re-ordered and what new medicines he required in the light of experience. It included a variety of mild and strong purgatives, soothing enemas and opium used in the treatment of dysentery, tonics for convalescents and heart patients, medicines for the treatment of urinary disorders such as that from which Phillip suffered, expectorants for chest complaints, mercury ointment for the treatment of syphilis and concentrated lemon juice for the treatment of scurvy. This he had omitted previously despite its unequivocal recommendation by both Blane and Northcote as the only effective antiscorbutic".[108]

"In fact, if White had a weakness, it lay in his management of nutritional disorders and it is significant that, in the First Fleet, only White, in the *Charlotte*, and Irving, the convict surgeon of the *Prince of Wales*, had cases of overt scurvy. Considen, in the *Scarborough*, had the best record and seems to have been the best clinician, both in Sydney and Norfolk Island, and was also a skilful dentist. He carried out clinical trials of the medicinal plants found by White on his expeditions..".

"The most imponderable member of the medical team was William Balmain, another naval surgeon. He had difficulty in coping with the mumps and typhus epidemic in the *Alexander* transport and White had found it necessary to keep the ship under surveillance throughout the voyage. This seems to have changed White's initially favourable impression of Balmain and his subsequent experience of Balmain at Sydney Hospital seems to have caused him to oppose his later appointment as Surgeon General. He may have been justified, [Watt said], because deaths from dysentery at Norfolk Island reached a peak from 1794 to 1795 during Balmain's period there and fell rapidly when Jamison succeeded him. Nevertheless, Balmain became a respected and successful Surgeon General, though lacking White's humanity. For instance, he refused to attend Skirving, one of the "Scottish martyrs" who died of dysentery. Balmain may have been a better surgeon than physician because, when Phillip was pierced through the right shoulder by an Aboriginal spear, Balmain enlarged the wound, removed the contaminated barbs and had the satisfaction of seeing the wound heal by first intention, although it appears to have been quite superficial".

"Thomas Arndell, however, a kind hearted doctor who had charge of the hospital at Parramatta for three years, was a reluctant surgeon, except in the art of blood-letting. He learnt the hard way when he hesitated to amputate the arm of the botanist, David Burton, who died as the result of gangrene following a severe gunshot wound. The next such injury was treated by immediate amputation with a happier outcome".

"As epidemics were brought under control, trauma and other alcohol-related conditions increased in the colony following Grose's policy of establishing a currency in rum. Surgeons participated in social initiatives and exercised an influential role as magistrates, while hospitals became centres of refuge and skilled attention for convicts and Aboriginals alike".[109]

To the above, Watt added the concept of a *philanthropic network.* Those involved had significant influence in London affecting the appointment not only of surgeons but governors too. In turn, such appointments had their effect on the colony's health. One idea supported was that transportation offered convicts an opportunity to reform and become responsible citizens under the influence of a different environment.[110]

Watt gave his opinion of the epidemic that decimated the local Aboriginal population following the white settlement. "[T]here is no unequivocal evidence of the epidemic being caused by smallpox and...the surgeons acted entirely in a caring, compassionate and professional manner towards the Aborigines".

Finally came the two most unexpected conclusions to his study, "necessity rather than criminal propensity created the bushranger and...rum, by supplying the missing dietary calories, provided the energy which finally broke the vicious cycles of malnutrition and its sequellae to enable the colony to survive at the price of a generation of addicts".

William Noah's diary of the 'Hillsborough', 1798 to 1799.

(Note: Sir Jeremiah Fitzpatrick)

The *Hillsborough* Transport, not part of any of the first three convict fleets, was notorious for the deaths of 95 convicts on the way to the Colony.[111] Most of those who survived were sent to hospital on arrival. Governor Hunter described the survivors as "the most miserable and wretched convicts I have ever beheld".[112] Six of these convicts died, too.

No wonder, for as the convict diarist, described the experience, "Monday ye 29 Inst...We had now got to the End of a Long & Painfull tedious Voyage where Every Distress was to be meet with Heat Cold Hunger Thirst want of Remant Air &ca witch Created in us poor Convicts filth Verming & all kind of Diseases wich caus'd a Hundred poor Souls to be Buried in the Bowels of the Deph"[113]

The diarist, "William Noah, the author *of A Voyage to Sydney in New South Wales in 1798 & 1799,* was a native of Shropshire. In April 1797 he was sentenced to death at the Old Bailey for stealing two thousand pounds weight of lead, value £23 from his neighbour, Cuthbert Hilton, a plumber of No. 18 Princess Street, Westminster. Evidence given at the trial shows that Noah was a dealer in lead and old iron. In his own list of convicts sent from Newgate 18th October, 1798 he gave his occupation as silversmith. He was forty three years old at the time of his trial".[114]

The Noah's published diary there is little in the way of punctuation. The use of capitals is typically eighteenth century. Spelling hardly ever gets in the way of legibility.

"*Dear Sister*. I must acquaint you that I was Convicted as being an Assesary after the fact of Robbing Mr Cuthbert Hilton on 20 of April 1797 & on Wednesday Evening the 17th of October 1798 an Order Came to Newgate for me and 22 more Convicts to get ready to set off on the Next Morning when we where [were] calld up at 5 & Irond two together & at 8 proceeded in 4 Coaches attend'd by the City Constables to Black fryers Bridge where we alightd & was put on board a Sand Lighter & Dropt down the Thames..."

Here is a list of some of Noah's references to objects and matters as they appear to his sight or register on his mind. Convicted, dates, emotions (remorse, disagreeable), irons, place names, weather, food and drink, control (constables), solidarity (among convicts), convicts-coming aboard, soldier guards, vermin (from Hulks), hope (to live by), visitors (convict wives and relations), visitors (items smuggled in), smuggled items (Captain's & officers' opinion), loss of liberty to have visitors, last farewell, convict management (choose 6 convict sweepers and overseer to be on deck), visitor (Noah's wife), 'going on deck', mess of 6 men (items for use), sickness (recovery sick and hospital on gun deck), mess for the voyage (soap, pepper etc.), Sir Jerome Fitzpatrick[115] (grievances heard), anchor (Bower), convict (clothing issue), barbers (hair cut), weighd Anchor, Plumb Pudding, River money (paid to ship's company), pilot (Downs), convicts assist with anchor (served with butter), hospital (on Gun Deck), 12 seamen escape in boat, centinal, Mates, bread issue, convicts refused short weight, other food allowance listed...

The visits of Sir Jeremiah Fitzpatrick, Inspector-General of Health, are highly significant to the Redfern story (see the following chapter). Noah mentioned the first on October 26 while they were in the Thames. He inspected again in November on 20, 22, 28 and 30, and in December on 19 and 20.

On the first visit he "very Attentively heard several grievances". One was against the overseer, Wheeler, who had struck another with a centinel sword. Fitzpatrick promised "to all redress". They were also allowed "at Night a Burner down each Hatchway & a Centry plac'd over each".

On Sir Jeremiah's next visit, *Hillsborough* was at the Mother Bank, Portsmouth opposite Rye. He looked over the sick and ordered nine to Langston. Next day the convicts were "on deck while they smoked the ship".

Bateson made clear what was amiss.

"The *Hillsborough* was a large and roomy ship, and, according to the Transport Commissioners, had been fitted out on an improved plan, the bars of the prison being built far apart to admit the air more freely. She embarked

152 prisoners at Gravesend, and when she arrived at the Motherbank on November 17, 1798, her master William Hingston, reported to the Transport Board's agent at Portsmouth, Captain Charles Patton, that one convict had died and several other were sick".[116]

The dead convict would have been "Robert Penn alias Fish a Gentle young Man who was Capital Convicted at the Old Bailey for robbing his Master and took it so much to Hart as to Occasion his Death". Noah had recorded his death on Thursday, November 15, 1798. On Tuesday October 30 he had included a reference to "Convicts that were Ill sent into an Hospital provided for that purpose on the Gun Deck".

Hingston's report of the death of a convict probably resulted in the next visit, on November 20, of Sir Jeremiah Fitzpatrick[117], "who had inspected the ship in the Thames, ordered the sick to be transferred to a hospital ship, and urged most strongly that the ship's complement of convicts should not be made up from the prisoners in the Langstone Harbour hulks, aboard which the gaol fever, or typhoid, had raged in a malignant form for some time. His advice was disregarded, as were his further protests after the Langstone convicts had been embarked. He insisted, however, that five prisoners, all in an advanced stage of the disease, should be disembarked, and all five died within a few days".[118]

Two days later 61 convicts arrived from the Lion Hulk, Portsmouth. Sir Jerome returned that day. Frost and snow was perhaps the cause of an issue of cloath. A heavy fall of snow prompted an issue of fresh beef and broth that continued on to December 20.

90 convicts arrived new clothed from Langton hulks two days later. The same day women were admitted on board to the seamen. On the 28 Oct., Sir Jerome came again and ordered several convicts to the Sick Hulk or Hospital Ship. While the entry next day was "Nothing remarkable", on the following day Sir Jerome visited and ordered 18 of the sick to go back. The same number arrived that day from the Hulks.

On Wed.19 Sir Jerome ordered 10 out of the ship. Next day he brought 6 from the Lyon and one from Lefortune which made our compliment 300 men prisoners. Sir Jerome Fitzpatrick and Captain Ramson our ship Husband whose loss we much experienced bid us a Final Leave and wish us all success in our Long and tedious Voyage.

Particulars of the *Hillsborough* have not been found. She was shown as being of 764 tons, with William Hingston as Master and John Justice Wm Kunst[119] as surgeon.[120]

"James Duncan's contract of 1798 for the *Hillsborough*," was on a similar basis to that of "William Richards, jun., in 1792 for the transportation of convicts from Ireland'. There were some variations in the payments to

Duncan. £17 was increased by £1 for each convict embarked. £5 for each prisoner landed in satisfactory health was reduced to £4 10s 6d.[121] "In addition...the contractors were paid freight on such government stores as were shipped, the rate for the *Hillsborough* being £8 per ton.[122]

Bateson believed that this method of remunerating the contractors was certainly preferable to the flat per capita payment for each convict embarked. It provided the contractors with a financial incentive to treat the convicts humanely. The embarkation payment may have been too high and the disembarkation payment too low, but at least dead convicts no longer were more profitable than the living".[123] Obviously, it did little good, for the convicts on *Hillsborough.*

With government approval Duncan's contract allowed him to engage 30 men, over and above the 48 men forming the ship's company, to serve as guards. Each of the guards received £5 each per calendar month from the date of embarkation of convicts to their disembarkation in the Colony.[124]

Counting the crew on page nine of Noah's published account gives a total of 73, with six entered at the Cape of Good Hope. As this figure is close to the total of 78 for crew and guard, in Duncan's contract, it can be assumed that the guard on *Hillsborough* would have been close to the 30 allowed. This guard was not commanded by a military officer because it had been provided by the contractor. The master was responsible for its direction, conduct and discipline.[125]

Since the guard was under Hingston's direct control, it made him personally responsible for a mutiny, and equally for the fact that when on deck the convicts were so well secured that they could not move.

Hillsborough was among a group of ships that did not have on board a naval surgeon or a naval agent at that time. Lack of such supervision partly, but not completely, explained the deaths and the sickly and emaciated convicts who arrived in the Colony.[126]

"The heavy death-roll on the *Hillsborough* - 95 out of 300 men embarked - was due to an outbreak of typhus which no amount of supervision could have checked, although the British authorities might have prevented it, Bateson argued, by heeding Fitzpatrick's advice, 'not to embark prisoners from Langstone Harbour, where the gaol fever had been raging with much virulence'.[127]

Still, the fact that, excluding the *Hillsborough,* the mortality rate of the remaining five transports of the unsupervised group was one to every nine men embarked is sufficient proof that the absence of supervision was an important, perhaps the primary, factor in the high death-roll".[128]

Hillsborough arrived on the same day as *Albion*, 29 June 1799. "Governor Hunter directly refers to the 'fever' on these vessels by the well-established name of 'gaol fever'.

Sir Jerome Fitzpatrick (following Noah's spelling) would reappear in a book by Frank Clune.[129] In Clune's book, the actors' stories would be embellished with material gathered from their countries of origin and destination. Clune spun a good tale and was a popular author. Intrigued by William Redfern, contributions to his story appeared in the first chapter. (Separately, Clune told the story of the Scottish Martyrs.)

Two-year old Sarah Wills, sailed on *Hillsborough* with Sarah, her mother, in a deck cabin. They came, free. Thomas Wills, father and husband, was in a prison below.

1797 had special significance for Wills and Redfern as the year of their convictions, Wills for highway robbery and Redfern for mutiny.

Redfern was not on *Hillsborough.* Why was he in Clune's book?

It was the Wills' story that put him there. Sarah (Sally) Wills, the *Hillsborough* two-year old, who came free, at fourteen would marry the former convict, William Redfern.

Chapter 10

TRANSPORTATION - A NEW BENCHMARK

The Health of Convicts. II.

Governor Lachlan Macquarie reported that surgeon William Redfern was sent to Sydney Cove "at his own particular request to Sir Jeremiah Fitzpatrick, then Inspector of the Transport Service".[1]

Credibility for this claim is increased by Noah's revelation of the accessibility of Fitzpatrick to convicts, in the previous chapter. Redfern left the hulk in June 1801 and Fitzpatrick was retired on half pay in the following year. It was a timely move.

Oliver MacDonagh, Fitzpatrick's biographer, reported "The bulk of his work was in preventive public medicine".[2] "He probably graduated (in medicine) on the Continent (most likely in Paris) in the later 1760s".

"It may well be doubted," MacDonagh argued, "whether any officer in the central government service of either kingdom in the late eighteenth century was better equipped than Fitzpatrick in the field of public health".

Fitzpatrick "even hinted broadly that, trained in observation and enumeration as they were, doctors constituted the best pool of general administrative talent".[3]

C. J. Cummins confirmed it for the Colony of N.S.W. where "early colonial doctors...because of status and education...proffered leadership and occupied important positions in the social and political structure of the Colony" (Preface, above). Later, exemplified in William Redfern's life on Norfolk Island and on the mainland.

To return - Redfern had now been incarcerated, some time after his court martial in 1797, in a Portsmouth hulk. Taking his chance in the Colony was a more and more attractive option. All that was required was to expedite his sentence, transportation the result of his being thrown upon the King's clemency.

But there was more to it than that. The death threat was still hanging around his neck. He knew nothing to the contrary. That is what he told Commissioner Bigge years afterwards.

Whether Redfern's request to Fitzpatrick involved other convicts, is not known, but fourteen mutineers, in addition to Redfern, were on board the *Minorca.* They had come from different Navy ships.

In the Colonial Secretary's *Indents of Convict Ships 1801-1804,* the names of these convicts are listed together, the date and name of the ship on which they faced court martial, and their sentence.[4]

Noah's diary has two references to one of these convicts, Thomas McCann, a Nore mutineer. On November 17 the Captain called him "on Deck when he stated Every Grievance and was promised redress". On December 16 Noah recorded McCann being sent off the ship as "the Seamen reported him to the Captain as a Dangerous Man & without he was removed they would not go out in her". Their main concern was, that as McCann was "allways forward in wanting redress to the Grievances" of the prisoners, he might lead the convicts to take the ship. Perhaps it might have been better for all on board if he had stayed.

It would be difficult to describe the sense of relief welling up in William Redfern with the knowledge that the noose was off his neck and he was on board a brand new purpose built convict transport heading for Botany Bay.

Continuing efforts being made to avoid past errors in the transport of convicts appeared to peak about that time. Some of their plans, of course, went astray, as *Hillsborough* proved.

Serendipitous too that it was Sir Jeremiah Fitzpatrick himself who had set the medical scene hour by hour and day by day that would keep that and its cousin ships exceptionally healthy all the way to the Colony.

Was Sir Jeremiah instrumental, too, in having Redfern keep the record of the convict sick along the way?[5] He was both compassionate and passionately driven to relieve the suffering of the powerless - children, prostitutes and convicts. Lending an ear and responding, as detailed by Noah in the preceding chapter.

MacDonagh had made the point that Fitzpatrick got to know the incarcerated from his inspections. This is confirmed by Fitzpatrick's practice, regular inspection and close observation of school,[6] hospital, hulk, and transport.[7]

Was Redfern's record keeping, Sir Jeremiah's last 'cocking of the snook' at the insensitive powerful - the powerfully insenstive? To be sure he had made a wonderfully new and promising opening for one powerless 'political convict', William Redfern. One thing was missing, peace.[8]

It remains now to consider the meaning of the words "the record of the sick", since the focus in this book has now changed to "convicts in transports" from "seamen in Royal Navy ships of war".

Theory and Practice of Health in the 18th Century.

A theory of disease needed to be constructed and defended in the eighteenth century. In this context it was not sufficient to know that the juice of lemons and oranges cured scurvy. New discoveries in science from Newton, and from gases to electricity, were drawn upon in the construction of medical theory. Much time and energy was wasted on sterile endeavors in system building.[9]

"It is a humbling moral to the story", wrote Kenneth Carpenter, "that, after all the attempts to apply new scientific concepts and hypotheses, the final solution came from the rejection of theory and a return to the practical experience of previous centuries".[10]

Miasma was one concept of the origin of disease that remained active. Its persistence may be discerned in the following planning and instruction to maintain a healthy environment on board ship in port and at sea. Preventing disease from being generated within the ship itself and from the bodies of sick people was a primary intention.[11] Another, of course was to prevent sick people from coming aboard. Whatever, "prevention *was* better than cure". Really?

"Only in a few diseases was a cure possible at that date", confessed the "Most distinguished and influential of all naval physicians", Sir Gilbert Blane.[12]

For scurvy, "Blane was one who had the necessary humility and could say: 'Lemons and oranges...are the real specifics...[as] first ascertained and set in a clear light by Dr. Lind. Upon what principle their superior efficacy depends...I am at a loss to determine'".[13]

Blane, who has featured in earlier chapters, returns in an enhanced position of power. His will to effect change remained strong. Now, he moved to improve health on convict transports. To this task he brought a lifetime of experience in improving the health of seamen in the Navy.

"After later disasters", Watt wrote, "the advice of Sir Gilbert Blane was sought and he recommended far-reaching improvements in convict transportation. He was closely associated with the philanthropists, their naval sympathisers and like-minded colleagues in the Medical Society of London. He was also friendly with Sir Evan Nepean, Under-Secretary at the Home Office when the First Fleet sailed and later Secretary of the Admiralty. In turn, Nepean was associated with Wilberforce, Admiral Lord Gambier, Thornton and Pitt, the Prime Minister, in the Society for the Propagation of the Gospel. The influence of the philanthropists and their allies upon the health in the settlement was therefore significant".[14]

This provides evidence of what Dorothy Porter described as "a high-period of public health" which "began around the end of the eighteenth century".[15]

Lord Pelham & Sir Jeremiah Fitzpatrick.

Lord Pelham's letter, which follows, has Sir Jeremiah Fitzpatrick taking pride of place in a fresh move to protect the health of convicts on three new purpose built transports. Pelham[16] considered the detailed instructions set out below, a "striking triumph and vindication" of Fitzpatrick's efforts. It "represented the apotheosis of Sir Jeremiah's career as a regulator of health on transports. Never before had he had such liberty in preparing them for the voyage, or in laying down the mode of their sanitary government on the high seas".[17]

This occurred in 1801 when "the transport commissioners made it clear to a new under-secretary at the Home Office that, so far as they were concerned,"

"the Inspection of Troops, under order for Embarkation, respecting their Health, is particularly committed to Sir Jerome Fitzpatrick".[18]

Lord Pelham's letter revealed what the authorities had in mind for three equally seaworthy convict transports, one of which brought convict William Redfern to Port Jackson.[19] As Home Secretary, Pelham targeted the masters and surgeons of the convict transports, *Canada, Minorca,* and *Nile 1* in his letter from Portsmouth, dated 10 June 1801.

It was considered "right and necessary to impose certain rules and to point out certain regulations for the health, good order, and regularity of those ships". The Home Secretary entertained "a just opinion of the judgement and capability of Sir J. Fitzpatrick, Inspector-General of Health, who has signified to us that the above-named transports are completely fitted by the Hon'ble Transport Commiss'rs, and supplied with every necessary requisite for the purposes of health and comfort for all persons embarked therein and intended to be conveyed to his Majestie's settlement of New South Wales".[20]

Transport Commissioners' Supplies.

Among the supplies were those "comprehending diet of various kinds, and suited to such changes as the constitution may undergo by the voyage and climate, as also with a proper selection of medicines; with the means of cleanliness of their persons, comprehending soap, combs, razors, and also those for fumigation, ventilation, scrubbing, cleansing, the perfect purification of and convenient supply of water, together with every necessary for the hospital, including changes of bedding, sheeting, hospital cloathing, proper diet and drinks for the diseased and convalescent, and, in short, that no one matter is defective for the prevention or the remedies of disease".

The Obligations of Surgeons and a Log-book or Diary.

Lord Pelham noted: "Therefore, as considered necessary by the said Sir J. Fitzpatrick, we demand of you, and each of you, a strict adherence to the following obligations, and that you minute their observance in your log-book or diary, and report the same, with other matters as have been in a former direction enjoined on you by the Hon'ble Transport Board, to the Chief Governor of New South Wales, and reserve certified copies of the same for our inspection on your return..." and hence followed a list of instructions.

A Brief Summary of Pelham's Instructions.

Among instructions for the *Minorca* and her two sister ships this is the most detailed set. Marginal headings accompanied the printed version in *Historical Records of NSW* and provide a useful table of contents:- *Health of convicts, Health of convicts on voyage out, Cleaning and fumigating, A diary to be kept, Cleanliness the parent of health, The between decks to be swept and scraped, Berths to be washed, and bedding aired, The wind-sails, Treatment of the sick, Hospital furniture and requisites, Fresh air, Fumigation* and *Antiscorbutics.*

The Transport Commissioners to Acting-Governor King.

Two days before Lord Pelham's letter, on 8th June, the Transport Commissioners wrote from the Transport Office to Acting-Governor King, in New South Wales. King's reply was dated 2nd February, 1802, reflecting the measure of time and distance by wind in the sails of ships.[21]

"Sir,

We herewith, enclose to you, Copies of the Instructions which we have given to the Master and Surgeon of each of the three Convict Ships, Minorca, Canada and Nile 1 ...

We are, etc.,

Rupert George, Ambrose Serle and Wm Ay. Otway".[22]

Enclosures to Masters[23] and to Surgeons.

There were two enclosures, separate instructions to the masters and to the surgeons of the transports.

The first, a letter addressing Transport Commissioners to Masters of the Convict Ships, Minorca, Canada, and Nile 1. Transport office, 8th June, 1801, from Rupert George, John Schanck, Wm. Ay. Otway".

The second, a letter to the Surgeons,[24] from the Commissioners, of the same date, to "inform you that you are to keep a Diary during the Voyage to New South Wales..." with explicit details of what was to be recorded.

While masters and surgeons were to be held accountable, and their obligations were widely spread across the range of provision, these two officers might gain as well as lose from their efforts.

The reasons for and the nature of the medical diary Redfern was to keep are now clear.

The Convict Ships and Contracts.

Instructing master and surgeon was one thing, but how did the ships themselves contribute to the health of those who sailed in them?

"From the outset the contracts were drawn up with meticulous care", and "as practical experience revealed defects and deficiencies, the authorities endeavoured to render the contracts more stringent and comprehensive". The "contract with Brown, Welbank & Petyt, agents for the owners of the transports *Coromandel* and *Perseus*, is typical of the form which the charter-parties had assumed within little more than a decade of the First Fleet's departure, and it is significant of the determination to take every precaution and to provide for every contingency, at least on paper, that little alteration subsequently had to be made in the form of the charter-parties".[25]

The selection and appointment of surgeons for the ships was another matter and one to which Bateson devoted a chapter of his book. As his material is relevant to Redfern's own work on this subject, and is, itself, quoted by Bateson, it will be held over for a later chapter when the Redfern Report on Convict Transports is to be discussed.

The transfer of the medical administration of the Navy from the Sick and Hurt Board to the Transport Board, was discussed in an earlier chapter where it was shown to have had a positive influence on the health of seamen.[26] The Transport Board's involvement with transportation helps to explain Blane's positive impact on convict health, and for all of those who came free on these same ships.[27]

It is appropriate to revisit briefly the experiences of the early convict fleets described in the preceding chapter and to throw a little light on the discussion of "private versus public". Bateson, in his second chapter, *The Contractors*, discussed "[t]he "fitting out, assembling, provisioning and despatch of the First Fleet" as involving "many government departments and private contractors, but predominantly...the Royal Navy".[28] The government had turned from private contract, the basis for shipping convicts to the Americas, "to the principle of direct naval responsibility".[29]

After the foundation of the Colony the government returned to private contract, as in the American period. On "the ground of economy" it stayed with it, "even when its inherent defects became only too obvious".[30]

"Nearly all the evils associated with the actual conveyance of the convicts had their origin in the contract system. It was responsible for incalculable human misery, suffering and loss of life. The authorities were aware of the dangers, but although they genuinely strove to avoid them, the precautions taken to ensure the humane treatment of the prisoners on the voyage were at first inadequate".[31]

Michael Flynn, according to Brian H. Fletcher, saw the Second Fleet "as an avoidable 'human tragedy on a great scale'" [and] "as a compound of government cost-cutting, official carelessness and private greed".[32] It was, too, a continuing episode in the "interconnection between the Government and private enterprise",[33] of which the three ships, presently under discussion were also a part. It will be interesting to see how well these ships travelled to Port Jackson, for their success or otherwise will be a measure of the effectiveness of the latest measures of the Government to overcome past errors.

William Redfern Aboard the Convict Transport 'Minorca'.

Minorca, Nile 1, and *Canada* left Spithead on 21 June 1801, joining a convoy of 300 ships. Sailing via Rio de Janeiro the three convict transports, still together, reached Port Jackson 176 days later on 14 December 1801.

Bateson, whose research on *The Convict Ships 1787-1868* is daunting,[34] saw this latest venture as providing a new bench mark, and that with the exception of "a few minor amendments, the 1830's are identical with that of 1801".[35] This meant that Redfern would gain, at first hand, experience of the new procedures and standards. In time, it will become clear what use Redfern would make of this new knowledge.

Certainly in his inspections of arriving convict transports he would have had in mind Fitzpatrick's original instructions, alive and well practised in his benchmark journey to the Colony. Not for him to accept the incompetent.[36]

The Healthiest and Best Conditioned Convicts to Arrive.

John Leith as master of *Minorca,* and Geo. Longstaff as surgeon[37] would each receive his rewards, for on 2 February, 1802, Acting-Governor King wrote to Under Secretary King advising "of the arrival of the *Canada, Minorca* and *Nile 1* with the persons and provisions stated in the enclosed account. The passengers were all in good health, and the convicts the healthiest and best conditioned that ever arrived here, being all fit for immediate labour".[38]

These last four words also appeared in a separate letter to the Transport Commissioners, of the same date. King prefaced them with this statement, "It is necessary that I should remark the great attention shown by the Masters of those Ships, to those under their Care, who were all landed in high health..." That "The above Ships were Cleared before the time limited for their coming on Demurrage[39] was expired", was added to King's report, indicating that the ship itself had been kept clean on the way out.[40]

A fitting finale to Sir Jeremiah Fitzpatrick's life work.

Convict Ships as General Carriers.

There are a number of additional references to the three ships in the *Records*[41] that are deserving of mention, for convict transports were not restricted to the carriage of convicts to the Colony. Other passengers included the military and free settlers, which, of course reinforced the need to keep convict ships healthy.

From this source has been gleaned arrival dates and ship particulars such as the cargo carried and the condition of the convicts; ship departure dates and particulars - despatches carried, indent papers of convicts, instructions to masters and surgeons. Spirits, beef and pork were among the provisions carried.

The Victualling Board wrote to Governor Hunter on 13 May 1801 detailing the amounts of beef and pork supplied for the subsistence for nine months of the Convicts that were coming on the three ships. Ship Masters' names as well as those of five Board members are to be seen in this letter.[42]

On May 23 the Transport Commissioners advised that 208 Male and 100 Female Convicts were about to leave the River for Portsmouth on the three ships. The *Minorca* was to bring a Copy of the Charter Party, an Invoice of Medicines put on board for the use of the Convicts during the Voyage, and an Invoice and Bill of Lading of "110 Sets of Cloathing for Male Convicts". There was a postscript adding a list of Medical Necessities for the use of the Convicts on the voyage and another table, which extends our knowledge of the three ships to include their tonnage, M 407, C 403 and N 322. (Copies of these papers had not been found.[43])

The transport *Nile 1* brought an important letter relating to the continuing use of the Public Seal, from the Duke of Portland to Acting-Governor King.[44] There was a letter advising of a passage for Major Johnston and Captain Prentice on the *Minorca.*[45] An enclosure with a batch of official letters was a list which "specified the names, ages, dates and places of sentence of two hundred and eighty-five convicts, thirty-eight of whom were sentenced to transportation for life, six for fourteen years, and two hundred and forty-one for seven years. In addition, there were fifteen mutineers, five sentenced to transportation for life, and ten for seven years. One of these, of course, was William Redfern, who, although he assisted the surgeon, remained a convict.

A letter from Under Secretary King to Acting-Governor King advised of the settlers going out and signified that they should receive the usual rations of provisions and the indulgences that had been granted to persons in a like situation. These settlers were strongly recommended, having various handicraft and agricultural skills that would increase the manufactures and produce of the Colony.[46]

One enclosure is a table giving a "General Account of Persons and provisions landed from the *Canada, Minorca* and *Nile 1* Transports, Jany. 2d 1802". It is signed, John Palmer, Commissary.[47] King acknowledged the Provisions from the Victualling Board per *Canada* on February 2nd 1802.[48] In another letter he pointed out that the indents of the convicts on *Canada* and *Nile 1* were not sent.[49] Only *Minorca*'s was received.

A list of shipping returns provides additional information on the three ships.[50] Each entered Port Jackson on 14 December, 1801, when bonds were given. Each carried 10 guns. *Minorca* had a crew of 30, *Nile 1* had 24 and *Canada,* 32. All three ships were built in Newcastle, the first two were completed in 1799 and *Canada* in 1801. They were owned by F. and T. Hurry, and registered in London to carry general cargo from that city. In an appendix to the table most interesting lists were provided of the general cargo carried by the three ships.[51]

Separate tables detail the amount of spirits imported into the colony by these ships and an account for payment by the Commissary to Mr Jno. Leith, of the *Minorca,* for £240 for 800 gallons of spirits and £29 19 7 for 1070 lb. of sugar. This series of references ends with an Outwards Shipping Return showing the *Canada, Nile 1* and *Minorca* left Port Jackson on 6 February 1802, carrying Ballast, and bound for China.[52] By then, all the prison structures would have been removed.

Ian Nicholson reported the three ships as reaching Dover from China on 11 February 1803 having travelled in company, throughout the journey home,[53] as they had done on their trip to Port Jackson. Remembering their design origin it was useful to record no lessening in sailing efficiency in the search for a better health environment. In practice, and in each case, human management was an additional critical factor

Norfolk Island - The First White Settlement.

Redfern's journey did not end at Port Jackson. He and the other mutineers were bundled off to Norfolk Island[54]. While he is on his way there, some thought might be given to its natural history. After all, he was going to be on that island for some time.

On the 17 January 1801, the year that Redfern left England and sailed to Port Jackson, that "settlement was menaced with destruction by the shock of an earthquake, which was felt severely through the whole colony, but providentially, produced no injury. A slight concussion had been felt in the month of June 1788; but never, until this moment, had the alarm been repeated. The affrighted inhabitants rushed out of their houses, in momentary expectation of destruction; nor did they dare to return until the shock had passed by, and the apprehensions which it had produced had entirely subsided".[55]

This earth tremor serves to remind us of the Pacific rim of volcanoes with which Australia and western Pacific islands have been associated during both active and quiescent episodes.[56] Long before, Norfolk, and the smaller Phillip Islands had arisen from a mid-ocean ridge, associated with sea floor spreading, and vulcanism.[57]

This was part of an ongoing process, which led to the recent 'fiery birth of a Pacific isle witnessed by Australian scientists and attracting media attention.[58]

On the other side of the world fishermen had a close encounter of a similar kind.[59]

"In the early morning of 14 November 1963 the seamen of the fishing-boat *Isleifur II* from the Westman Islands had been paying out their line on the bank south-west of Geirfuglasker. When this was completed at 6.30, they went down into the forecastle for a hot cup of coffee. Shortly after someone sniffed a sulphurous smell in the air. ...".[60]

Norfolk Island measures eight kilometres by five, is about 3450 hectares in area, and lies 1360 kilometres east from Port Jackson.[61]

In time, a diverse landscape developed with reasonably fertile soils and a climate conducive to plant growth. The process of change was assisted by the "progenitors of all living things" on the island.[62] In the initial pre-human colonization plant material floated ashore rafting in seeds, insects and spiders. All three of which could have been airborne as were migrant and vagrant birds that carried on their feet, the spores of algae, mosses and ferns.[63]

No humanoids saw Norfolk rise from the Pacific Ocean some three million years ago, but there is evidence of recent pre-European discovery and settlement by Eastern Polynesians, Pacific Islanders.[64] They and others added items to the biological mix of species on the Island.[65]

Ruddy Turnstones from the Arctic and Double-banded Plovers from New Zealand were among waders sighted on Norfolk on two visits to the island by the author and his wife. [66] The White-faced Heron (1910) and the Australian Kestrel (1969) appear to have been self-introduced, their first sightings have been recorded.[67] Crimson Rosellas came as cage birds from the Australian mainland.

When Captain James Cook rediscovered the island on his second Pacific journey, on Monday 10th October 1773, he named it Norfolk.[68] Cook with others from *Resolution* landed on the island and gave individual accounts of what they found and collected there. It was a genuine *Terra nullius,* an "empty unowned land", which the mainland certainly was not, though, long claimed to be.

Large trees that covered the Island acquired the common name, *Norfolk Pines*.[69] Called "Spruce Pines" by Cook, who envisaged a future for them as ship's timber, he had his carpenter prepare a topg[allant] mast or "yard", at once. This pine would prove indifferent for masts. Even so, the ship's carpenter preferred timbers he knew.

The name, "James Lind", appeared in the early days of preparation of Cook's second voyage providing food for thought. Daniel Solander,[70] of Cook's first journey, wrote to Lind in December 1771, as a friend, asking whether he would accompany Banks and Cook on their second Pacific voyage as astronomer. Banks warmly supported the proposal although he had not met Lind.[71]

Cook, you will remember, had rejected Lind's rob of lemon, as had Blane, for good reasons. Lind's 'rob' was inert (heat destroyed its vitamin C). But, Banks, on the *Endeavour* with Cook, did have a supply of lemon juice prepared differently from Lind's boiled preparation. Dr Hulme had recommended it in a letter to Banks,[72] who used it to good effect to cure his own scurvy. Mr Monkhouse prescribed the same juice for Dr Solander with equal success.[73]

Imagine Lind and Cook on the one ship. It was not to be. Solander's "Lind" in any case, was not the scurvy cure man. There was a difference of twenty years in their ages.[74] And, as it happened, Banks fell out with the Admiralty over his participation in the second Cook voyage[75] and took

Solander and the younger Lind to Iceland. Believe it or not, to study volcanoes, objects of special interest at the time.[76]

William Wales (c.1734-1798) was Lind's replacement in Cook's party. Bernard Smith developed an argument to support the likely influence of Wales on the imagination of the young Coleridge.[77] Wales, an experienced astronomer and scientist, kept a journal in astronomical time and had earlier observed the transit of Venus at Hudson's Bay.[78]

In spite of the difference of opinion over Lind's concoction ('rob'), Cook shared common ground with him on the subject of vegetables, particularly "greens'.[79] As on the *Endeavour* voyage, every opportunity was taken to collect them, whether wild or cultivated. Cook, Wales, and the two Forsters, father and son, all looked for them. The growing points, or crowns of Cabbage Tree Palms were included. Wales found wood sorrel, sow-thistle and samphire. Forster, Jnr pulled up succulent plants growing on the beach to boil in their soups and recorded dining on palm 'cabbages', fish, and birds, that included indigenous pigeons.[80]

La Perouse who arrived at Botany Bay six days after Arthur Phillip, had also visited the Island but had not made a landing owing to the rough seas and powerful surf. Frank Clarke reminded us that La Perouse described Norfolk as "only a place fit for angels and eagles to reside".[81] Clarke also gave the flax growing on the island as a reason for the French interest, and of Phillip losing no time in establishing a settlement there.[82]

Publishers were not slow to provide accounts of the new colonies at Port Jackson and on Norfolk Island. In 1789, John Stockdale published *The Voyage of Governor Phillip to Botany Bay*, a compilation. According to James Auchmuty,[83] historian and editor, it was reprinted three times in the year after its first publication, translated into French and German, pirated in Dublin and reprinted by another publisher. At about the same time that Stockdale was preparing his second edition (1790) he was issuing another in weekly parts for the less affluent reader. The third edition and its reprint and the pirated Dublin editions all appeared in 1790. This was the escape literature of the time.[84]

Norfolk Island, 'Phillip to King'.

Phillip's Instructions to King, and the first accounts of the settlement on Norfolk Island may be found in *The Voyage of Gov. Phillip...*[85]

"With these instructions you will receive my Commission, appointing you to superintend and command the settlement to be formed in Norfolk Island, and to obey all such orders as you shall from time to time receive from me, his Majesty's Governor in Chief, and Captain general of the territory of New

South Wales and its dependencies, or from the Lieutenant-Governor in my absence," Phillip commanded...

"Given under my hand, at Head Quarters in Port Jackson, New South Wales, this 12th Day of February, 1788".

(Signed) Arthur Phillip.

William Redfern arrived on Norfolk Island just short of fourteen years after the first white settlers. The pattern of early settlement was visible and there were enough long-term settlers to find time and place for some likely stories. Commandant King[86] and Lieutenant Ralph Clark[87], each in his journal, has left detailed and intriguing contemporary accounts of this early European colony.

At daybreak on 6 March 1788 King went ashore from the *Supply.* Except for the women, the convicts, originally selected on the surgeon's advice, came ashore. They were in two boats, with tents, a quantity of each kind of provisions and the most useful tools. After landing with great ease the people were instantly set to work clearing away ground for the tents. The Colours were hoisted, and before sunset every thing and person belonging to the settlement were onshore and the tents pitched.

King was Superintendent and Commandant over a petty officer, a surgeon's mate, two marines, two men who understood the cultivation of flax, and nine male and six female convicts. Among them was a carpenter and a sawyer. [88] Their next daunting task was clearing a space for a garden among the huge pines that covered the island.

To reduce manageable trees to sawn timber, a sawpit was required. Peter Linebaugh described the pit sawyer's work in the eighteenth century Navy yards around London, as both 'arduous' and 'impressive'.[89]

The whip saw used for rough or planking work possessed a blade 7 or 8 ft. in length that was supported in a wooden frame. Two men operated it. The top man sharpened the teeth, marked the timber with a chalked line along its length, and held the tiller. The pitman held the box end of the saw and worked from the bottom of the sawyer's pit - a cavity dug in the ground about 12 ft. long, 6 ft deep and 2 ft. wide. He also positioned the log on its rollers.

The sawyers determined the rate of work...depending on the grain...and the shape of the piece to be sawn...using piece-rates to their own advantage.[90]

On Norfolk, by Monday 17 March 1788, three men had started digging the first sawpit. The work continued on Tuesday and was completed the next day. Near the sawpit, a Norfolk Island Pine had been felled. One hundred and fifteen feet long and two feet three inches in diameter, at breast height, it was sawn into planks and scantling for a Store House. Commenced on 21 March, the building was completed by sunset on 1 April 1788.

Descriptions of the timber cut, its quantity and uses are there. It might have been intended for a barn in Arthur's Vale or a barracks. Timber for export to Port Jackson and palings for fences were also cut. Shingles were split for roofing.

With the help of these pits, sawyers produced a variety of sawn timber. King described it variously as boards, joists, planks, plates, scantlings, sleepers, uprights, weather boarding, 3/4 boards for lining, and other stuff. Lengths were also cut for poles, for splitting into shingles and for palings. Three-inch planks and spars were sawn expressly for export to Port Jackson.

King gave the total production of sawn timber over four work periods in 1788. These were 898 feet - 13 to 19 April; 866 feet - 20 to 27 April; 1479 feet - 17 May to 2 June, and 877 feet - 1 to 17 June. While sawyers and carpenters were the key workers, others had a role. Women convicts dragged away branches for burning.

There are references to the people, sawyers, carpenters and blacksmiths. A catamaran and a coble were built, and a boat shed and new carpenter's house. Cellars were dug under houses and chimneys erected. Tents went up and the Governor's portable house was assembled.

Houses were built for Commandant King, the surgeons, and the commanding officer of troops, Lieutenant Cresswell as well as for a guard, the sergeant of marines, Stephen Donovan, midshipman of the *Supply*, and officers. A sentinal box and a storehouse were not overlooked, nor, over time, were houses for the storekeeper, settlers, surgeons and mates in cleared spaces among the pines that provided the timber.

Together with later additions and replacements, King's plans formed the built environment that Redfern and the other mutineers would experience when they came ashore. Copies of early first settlement illustrations may be found in the study published by Philip Cox and Wesley Stacey.[91]

Lieutenant Clark at Charlotte Field.

Major Ross placed Clark in charge of 'the little Town', which included the positioning and constructing of roads and buildings.[92] By 4 December 1790, Clark had started the road and clearing for the first houses, and had two house frames ready to assemble. He hoped to have four houses ready for thatching the next week.

On 13 December Clark reported the frame of his fifth house was up. He described it as 20 feet long by 12 feet broad, larger than each of the other four, 14 feet by 10. Next day, Clark set a gang of twelve men to work in an 'Ende[a]vour to make Bricks', and on the next, 15 December, had a saw pit made at Charlotte Field. He intended to send a 'pair of Sawyers ther[e]' the next day.

Clark ordered a leg iron for one convict carpenter, absent without leave, and 50 lashes each for two others who neglected their work. Another carpenter was ordered to receive 100 lashes for shirking and abuse. Yet, on 17 December, having discovered that "Sixteen of the men who have worked very hard all day...have nothing to eat", Clark responded by ordering them "two pounds of potatoes a pi[e]ce". The frame of the tenth house went up on 28 December and two days later Clark was telling the carpenters how he wanted a bridge built. In January 1791, he was giving orders for "a gaol, a pair of stocks and a neck coller for the Ladies".[93]

Providence, and the Birds of Norfolk Island.

Clark, in his last *Journal* entry for January 1791, reported the punishment of convict Jas. Robinson, "Coxwin of the Coble, for killing Pidgeons". He received 50 Lashes. This seems strange considering that 172,184 Mt Pitt birds were killed at that time. A special dispensation for the "pidgeons" came from the surgeon, who alone could order them to be killed, as "pidgeons" were "the only fresh thing that will make a little weak soup for the Sick". [94]

Clark made clear, his own and the settlement's indebtedness to the Mt Pitt birds. "[I]f it had not been for the great aboundance of Birds which resorted to Mount Pitt about Sun Set the greatest part of use would have been in our graves before the Arrival" of the store ships. "[F]rom the latter end of April until the Middle of July no Smaller a number...than five thousand was Kild a night". "[T]hey never came in from Sea...until about Sun Set when the[y] generally hovered about the mount for an hour before the[y] came down which was as thick as a Shour of hail". This reminded Clark of the biblical "Shour of quails".[95] The Mt Pitt Birds, too, were hailed as Providence Birds.

Other birds appear to have fed the settlement. Clark referred to one resembling in form the Mt Pitt Bird, but with white feet, and the habit of remaining in its nest burrow during the day. He called it a "flying Sheep" or "mutton bird". These "were also in great abundance for Six weeks when their Young tooke flight and the[y] all left use".[96]

A House for D'Arcy Wentworth.

Lt. Ralph Clark's *Journal* entry for Tuesday, 1 February 1791, stated that he had "been at Charlotte Field Since day break and am Just Returned -- Orderd a Fraim of Mr. Wentworths house to be begun..". On Tuesday 22 February, 1791, Clark recorded having "got the Fraim of Mr. Wentworths house up...hope that it will be Soon finished for him to get into it as it is very disagreeable for him to be obliged to walk out ther[e] every day to See the Sick...got all the working women out from her[e] to Charlotte to assist the women there to carry flax for thatching the Houses..".[97]

By Thursday 3 March, 1791, the Carpenters were employed "putting the Logs round Mr. Wentworths house..". "[G]ot Mr Wentworths House So Fare finished that he may goe into it to morrow if Majr. Ross thinks proper..".[*Journal* for Thursday 7 April, 1791.] Clark's final reference to D'Arcy Wentworth occurred on Monday 6 June, 1791 - "walkd out to Queensborough after dinner and ordered Sarah Lyons to Receive 50 Lashes for abusing Mr. Wentworth...She only received 16 as Mr. Wentworth begd that She Might be forgiven the other thirty four which She was.."..

According to Clark, Charlotte Field was renamed Queensborough on 30 April 1791.

The First Cellar on Norfolk Island.

Cellars on Norfolk Island came by chance, as explained by King in his diary entry of Wednesday, 23 April 1788. This subject is of more than passing interest as both of Redfern's houses on the Island had cellars, as had the house he would build on the mainland, at *Campbellfield,* years later.

King tells how, "On digging about 2 feet under my house, I find the bottom is sand & a loose sand stone I therfore (sic) dug a cellar under a small part of it but the deeper I went I found the bottom dryer & judged it to be a very proper place to put the provisions in, as it will be both safe & dry & will add much to the security of the provisions in being under my immediate care and inspection & will prevent the building another Store house, for a considerable time I therefore broke two men off from clearing away...& began digging a cellar under the house the whole length & breadth of it viz. 24 feet by 12, & 5 feet deep".

As the cellar seemed such a good idea, King had one dug under the surgeon's house to store his supplies, too.

This introduction to the First Settlement of Norfolk Island ends here. In general, life on the Island was a microcosm of that on the mainland.[98] Over time the population would rise and fall away until the Island was abandoned.

Wright shows a population peak of 1,115 in October 1791, a decline to 889 by October 1791 and a second peak of 1,102 in August 1804.[99] From March 1805 to June 1807 it remained in the 820s. With accelerating evacuation of the Island the numbers were down to 255 by November 1810. By then Redfern would be on the mainland and the time would be approaching when a clearing party, would raze the buildings to deny the French.[100]

William Redfern Arrives.

The *Harrington*, a Calcutta built Snow of 180 tons under Wm. Campbell, Master, sailed for Norfolk Island from Port Jackson on 30 December 1801. Carrying Redfern, twenty-two convicted mutineers from *Minorca* and *Canada*, and despatches it reached the Island on 8 January 1802.[101]

[*Harrington* left for Port Jackson on 16 January 1802, arrived on 24th and left again on 20 February under ballast, hunting for seals.]

Redfern's name first appeared in the *Norfolk Island Victualling Book* on 9 January 1802.[102] Since all the mutineers were sent to Norfolk it cannot be argued that Redfern was specially selected on account of his medical expertise. However, this would almost certainly be the reason for him being detailed to assist the surgeon, James Mileham,[103] who had been sent to Norfolk to relieve Thomas Jamison. The latter's presence on the Island resulted from the wreck of *Sirius*, on which he had been surgeon's mate.

Jamison left in October 1799 for the mainland, where Phillip had appointed him an assistant colonial surgeon. From this position he rose to become principal surgeon. Jamison held degrees of BA 1768 and MA 1772 from the University of Dublin. Ford recognised him as the Colony's first medical journalist on the strength of an article on smallpox in the Sydney *Gazette* on 14 October 1804.[104]

On Norfolk Island, time and tide, were of the essence. Convicts were sentenced to 'do time', seven years to 'life'. Even so, time would free many of them.[105] Tide held sway over their coming and going. King's party was lucky coming ashore. *Sirius* grounded and was wrecked but no lives were lost. Others were not so lucky. The tide was against them.

"The frequency of storms from the south, combined with the long fetch (to Antarctica and beyond) produces very large swells in Sydney Bay", that prevent ships from unloading.[106] A second point for this risky operation was at Cascades, north of the Island. At times, it gained some relief from the swell.

As noted earlier, La Perouse did not land, while Cook came ashore at a protected cove to the north-west but was confronted by steep cliffs. In bad weather, ships stood off, or, like *Supply* and *Sirius,* were blown out of sight of the Island.

Captain William Scott, of HMS *Porpoise* left Sydney on 27 May 1802 and arrived Norfolk Island on 6 June.[107] Bad weather forced the ship to stand off for twenty-two days. One attempt to land failed. Scott refused permission for the occupants to return on board and the whaleboat was forced to make a risky landing on Phillip Island.

Surgeon Tom Roberts of the New South Wales Corps, impatient after being cooped up on *Porpoise* for three weeks, made another attempt to land on 19 June.[108] It was against the odds and also against every signal to desist, including the firing of a musket. With the whaleboat smashed to pieces in the surf, all those aboard were drowned, including the surgeon.

Major Foveaux, in his military capacity, at once appointed Redfern to take Surgeon Robert's place.[109] On being informed, Acting Governor King on the mainland ruled that the establishment would not allow it, as it was a Corps position. Nevertheless, a note that Foveaux wrote some years later showed that Redfern continued to work for the Military on Norfolk Island without pay.[110]

Foveaux, in his civil capacity, as Commandant, placed Redfern in charge of the hospital.[111] Surgeon Mileham had left the Island for Sydney in March of that year. Wright showed that the number of male Government servants (convicts) employed at the hospital had grown from 3 (1797) to 5 (1800).[112]

By February 1805, Surgeon James Davis was in charge, with D'Arcy Wentworth as Asst. surgeon and Wm Redfern his assistant. Mary Bolton was a convict nurse.[113] George Guy, who had served his time, worked in a dispensary, and there were other assistants to the surgeons. John Barry was overseer.[114]

The placement of the hospital and the associated surgeon's dwelling house may be seen in "A Map of Settlement of Sydney, Norfolk Island, 1793".[115] Only four patients were listed as "Sick in Hospital" on 6 November, 1800 and again on February 1805, with a total population ranging from 900 down to 800 over that period.[116]

Mary Bolton could have filled the role of midwife, since in 1805 there were one hundred children under two years of age on the stores. In the same year there were two hundred children of all descriptions off the stores. Most of the children were born on Norfolk. Fifty died there. They were among one hundred and ninety-three deaths, over twenty-six years.[117]

King provided Collins with an 'Account of births and deaths from November 12, 1791, to September 31, 1796', during which time there were 137 deaths: I (Civil), 4 (Military), 94 (Convicts) and 38 (Children) died. Children were between 1 month and 2 years of age, and 23 of them died from teething problems.

Causes given for all other deaths were: Dysentery 45, Cholera morbus 1, obstipation 1, Fevers 7, consumptions 8, Debility 22, Lues venerea 5, Dropsy 3, Putrid sore throat 1, Convulsions and epilepsy 4, Surfeit 2, scalded 1, abscess and canker 2, Eruptions, scald head and mortifications 3 Iliac passion 1, Shot 1, casualties 2, executed 1, suicide 2, Ophthalmia 2. [118]

Redfern would have assisted at births as he was not amiss to midwifery. His reputation in that area would be confirmed on the mainland, later. There is no evidence of Redfern studying midwifery in his period of initial medical training. Not surprisingly as Commissioner Bigge was not very interested in such details. On the other hand, Redfern's successful practice in the colony, and the ownership of a basic text, are suggestive. Studies in midwifery at Edinburgh University, later in life, give point to this line of thought.

In London, towards the end of the eighteenth century lectures were available in a range of medical courses within and without hospitals and unrestrained by university curricula. Not uncommonly, an Edinburgh graduate conducted such courses. Smellie's midwifery venture discussed earlier is an outstanding example.

William Redfern had an interesting story to tell of an anatomy lecturer. Depending on the fee paid the course was either practical and hands on, or what you might expect from 'talk and chalk'. [The account has greater relevance to Book 2.]

Colonial Surgeons at that time, had started their Royal Navy careers as surgeons mates. [In the Army, called assistant medical officers.] Some few had a university background apart from Edinburgh as you may have noticed, above.

"The strength of an Edinburgh [University] education," Roy Porter explained, "lay in imparting the elements of anatomy, surgery, chemistry, medical theory and practice. After three years, an Edinburgh man trained in medicine and surgery was ready to go out into the world to practice the new trade of "general practitioner" or family doctor. Those falling sick in 1810 in Newcastle, Newfoundland or New South Wales would most probably have been seen by Edinburgh doctors".[119]

Acting as assistant to the surgeon, on the convict transport to Sydney, was a lucky break, a change of fortune, indeed, for William! In addition to practice he would have had access to his own and the surgeon's books. The surgeon, himself, stood to gain from William's insights medical and convict. Especially his ability to mingle freely and to communicate with the convicts

Following his conviction and transportation, Redfern had to confront his exile, a kind of death. Separation from parents, sisters, brothers, nieces, nephews, and friends, felt complete. He would be "tyrannized by distance". Letters were virtually at the will of the wind in traveling from one hemisphere to the other in wooden sailing ships.

No doubt a little 'put out' on learning that Port Jackson was not the end of his journey, and having to go aboard a small 'boat', as it were, he may have wondered if it would ever reach such a tiny speck on the map, Norfolk Island.

As each day passed on the *Harrington* from the mainland the distance from the bustle of London Town was magnified. With home now but a distant thought, his loss of freedom and civil rights pressed upon him.

As bad as things were, the air was fresh and the Island environment more bracing than the Hulk's mud flats.

Still, the place was a gaol, clearly circumscribed. A vast moat of wild seas hemmed it in. There was no escape.

While he did not know it, that first settlement on Norfolk was closer to the mainland in many more ways than the second one. Nor did he know what he might make of it all. How might ebullience and resilience work out?

Acting-Governor King, on the mainland introduced a certificate of conditional freedom for good conduct. On 21 November 1802 Commandant Foveaux, on Norfolk Island, gave one such certificate to William Redfern, in his first year on the Island.

Acting-Governor King approved. No wonder. King had inspected the medical diary, which Redfern had kept on the *Minorca.* Convict or no, he was well educated, and knowledgable in the medicine of his time, and would have produced a very creditable account. Add to Redfern's medical knowledge and skills the "Medicines, Instruments [and] Books", that he had with him, and put yourself in the Governor's place. Would you, too, agree?[120]

In due course King went further. He advised Foveaux that he might bestow on William Redfern one of the blank free pardons he was sending. The only condition was that he continued to perform his medical duties to Foveaux's satisfaction. Accordingly, Redfern was emancipated on 19 June 1803, for being "so useful in doing the duty of Surgeon".

The first Australian emancipist was another convict surgeon, John Irving, who had also served on Norfolk Island. He was considered by Clark to be "the best surgeon amongst them".[121]

David Richards found the first settlement on Norfolk Island (1788-1814), over time, to have been "served by 16 medical men - 5 or possibly 6 of whom, were or had been, medical transportees". Richards considered that "most were not formerly qualified". "They came involuntarily, either as colonial medical officers assigned to a tour of duty or as convicts".[122]

Redfern, by now, would have been taking satisfaction from his earlier decision to exchange imprisonment for transportation. His resilience had helped overcome past adversity, the possible outcome of that other Redfern characteristic, his ebullience. Bubbling up like a cork pushed into water.

On Norfolk, Redfern consciously set to work to "better [his] condition".[123] A decision not unusual for surgeons and others on the Island, described by Parsons as "the hot house...with its continual gossip, constant innuendo, and incessant struggle for profit, patronage and position".[124]

While being a surgeon had drawn him in to the mutiny at the Nore, and to rejection, on Norfolk Island it would bring him further acceptance in charge of the hospital. Perhaps Foveaux was also taken by Redfern's resilience, his lightening step, and more purposeful stride, as he set out for the forty-eight acre farm he had purchased on 9 July 1802.[125]

Redfern *had* to walk. Only Foveaux had a vehicle.

King and Foveaux - Governor and Commandant.

Was there a precedent for King's positive attitude to William Redfern? Do you remember King supporting striking seamen, against the purser, and Phillip himself? That was ten years before the Great Mutinies of 1797 when such complaints and much more serious ones from seamen in Royal Navy ships on active duty were accumulating unread in the Admiralty offices. It was a time when the advice of Admirals was ignored. Practical advice that if acted upon might have forestalled the mutinies.

King put removing causes above punishing strikers at the time of the First Fleet. Howe spoke man to man to the mutineers at Spithead achieving reconciliation by removing causes. Government, in refusing Howe's offer to conciliate at the Nore, moved to punish the mutineers, victims of their own poor management decisions.

What can be said about Foveaux, equally positive about Redfern?

What did T.G. Parsons have to say? "Despite a scholarly entry in the *Australian Dictionary of Biography* by Professor Brian Fletcher", "Foveaux is still portrayed [1988] as brutal and sadistic, a man who gloried in the use of the lash and the abuse of convict women".

"This portrait is based almost completely on two pieces of evidence, *The Recollections*...of Robert 'Buckey' Jones,[126] and the *Memoirs*...of General Joseph Holt. Neither of these works is convincing,"[127] Parsons wrote.

The character of Foveaux was central to any satisfactory assessment of Redfern's character. There was no escaping him or his problematic position.

Take the extreme position of 'monster'. What kind of a person might a "monster" seek as a friend, and what kind of a person might seek to befriend one?

Parsons, again, saw the ready acceptance of negative perceptions of Foveaux, as allied with those of the NSW Corps as "scum of the earth". Yet, Parsons' research showed the Corps to be "more nearly a cross-section of British society than scholars have been prepared to admit".[128]

Similarly extreme positions were taken about Royal Navy seamen at the time of the Napoleonic Wars. Their description as "scum of the earth" was obviously wrong and proven to be. [For which see the second chapter of this book.]

Such negativity was reinforced by "the many brilliant graphic artists at work in Britain at this time".[129] Linda Colley believed that they were not "able to forge a convincing and uncondescending image of the plebeian patriot". Nor of the prostitutes in chapter eight.

Again, while the Corps military officers were dominated by a code of honour,[130] most were obliged to engage in economic activities to sustain their careers.[131] Parsons developed this theme in a separate publication in the same year.[132]

Working against Parsons was a widespread perception that Norfolk Island settlements were bad "news", anyway. As Valda Rigg said, "the first convict settlement has been subsumed into the reputation of the second".[133] The first settlement was perceived as no different from the second, "a hell on earth", "place of ultra-penal punishment".

One stereotype fed on the other, making bad, worse, and any correction or revision the more difficult. This is not dissimilar to the task of separating the great fleet mutinies of 1797 - beneficial to the Royal Navy in the longer term - from the stereotypical non Navy short term and selfish mayhem of the single ship mutiny.[134]

Rigg, while not accepting the First Settlement as "idyllic", spoke more in terms of "their contribution to agriculture...that at times provisioned both Norfolk Island and Port Jackson, their emotions and aspirations, and their family life as well as their material circumstances".

Nevertheless while far removed "from the horrific and brutalised experience of the second settlement", founded upon Commissioner Bigge's recommendations, the first settlement was also, but to a lesser extent, a place of secondary punishment, as pointed out by Castles.[135] A younger legal historian, Bruce Kercher also confirmed a great difference between the first and second settlements on Norfolk Island.[136]

Let Wright as author of one volume, and Nobbs, as editor of the other, be credited with ending any doubt about the First Settlement being closer in kind to that on the mainland.

"Major Foveaux appears to have received much unfair abuse over the years", Wright announced, pointing to General Joseph Holt as the source of the initial criticism.[137]

Wright's Foveaux was not the monster of stereotypical caricature so many people loved to hate. "The records", Wright said, "seem to show Major Foveaux as a very able administrator who was willing to take, and then live by, very difficult decisions when the occasion arose. On Norfolk Island he pressed ahead with needed public works, building schools, barns, roads and public buildings, although Governor King may not have appreciated his clearing of 100 acres of pine-clad ground at Anson Bay in January 1802".

In Wright's opinion, Foveaux's lengthy "position paper" of 26 March 1805 gave "the last authoritative word on the destiny of the First Settlement, and provides the 'raison d'etre' for its termination".

"Foveaux's views were accepted over those of King, and when Bligh arrived at Port Jackson, he had very explicit instructions from Wm Windham to evacuate the whole of Norfolk Island community, together with the full details of compensation to be awarded".[138]

Wright, having this record in mind, considered it "paradoxical that during the last hundred years Joseph Foveaux has received so much abuse over his administration of Norfolk Island...For the last half of the twentieth century, historians and popular writers have universally condemned him".

In the end, Wright proved that the "Bucky" Jones and Joseph Holt material were forgeries and fictions. He made them available on the worldwide web with an opening statement of Foveaux's achievement, more extensive than the earlier quote from his book.[139]

Anne-Maree Whitaker, biographer of Foveaux.

Anne-Maree Whitaker expressed profound gratitude to Reg Wright, on the second page of her biography of Foveaux, for exposing the source documents for what they were, "forgeries that tell us nothing about the real Joseph Foveaux".[140]

Whitaker's portrait of Foveaux provides a positive resolution to problems presenting from earlier demonic sketches. Foveaux and Redfern can now face each other as human beings individually different as birth and living might have determined.

In this context Foveaux's Whiggish leanings come to attention. Did they incline towards sympathy for one who had suffered "Tory" punishment, ill deserved as it had been? Mirroring the parallel acceptance of "mutineers" by Acting-Governor King.

It was King, too, who introduced a staged approach to emancipation through a conditional certificate that recognized and encouraged progress in that direction.

Foveaux, nevertheless, was wary of a contingent of United Irish prisoners who landed on Norfolk Island. Initially, he made a mental note that "a strict hand and watchful eye shall be kept" over them. This fell away over the next six weeks allowing the Irish prisoners to plan a revolt. Though the uprising was nipped in the bud, with named leaders arrested after a prayer meeting, the outcome could have been bloody. The civil and military officers were assembled and decided on capital punishment for Peter McClean and John Wollaghan (Houlahan).[141]

Other natives of Ireland faired differently. Whitaker noted that the appointments of "William Redfern a native of Belfast" with his assistant "Bryan O'Connor, a United Irishman from Cork", effectively promoted the two erstwhile rebels to the civil establishment, and thus to the social circle centred on Government House. This also included Commissary Broughton and his de facto wife Elizabeth Heathorn, and Ensign Lawson and his de facto wife Sarah Leadbetter.[142]

"Two words, *power* and *patronage,* in the title of Whitaker's *Foveaux* have different associations throughout her book. As well as receiving patronage, Foveaux extended it to others. If ever Redfern had a patron, it was Foveaux, whether on, or off, Norfolk Island. Patronage is a two-way process, which may or may not bring credit to either bestower or recipient. It seems that both Foveaux and Redfern came out of the exchange with credit.

Patronage cultivated a wide field, particularly in the eighteenth and well into the nineteenth centuries. "In the last two decades of the eighteenth century and the first twenty years of the nineteenth", according to Asa Briggs, "the gradual reduction of patronage" was one of "five factors making for change" in governing. Patronage from a peak of influence "was ceasing to be the only cement which held the English political system together".[143] Briggs had described the joint secretary of the Treasury in 1822, as "(thereby patronage secretary)".[144]

Hazel King opened her paper, "Pulling Strings at the Colonial Office" by quoting the historian J.H.Plumb to the effect that "in eighteenth-century England, patronage went naked and quite unashamed - it scarcely bothered to wear a fig-leaf". In the nineteenth-century, "patronage was essential for a man who wanted to get a colonial appointment or other favours; but from the cases of [Governors] Brisbane and Goulburn, it can be seen that patronage would not necessarily save him from recall. Patronage could help a man to promotion; but for promotion more than patronage was usually needed - experience, proven ability, good timing and good luck".[145]

Each of these came to Redfern's assistance on the Island, contributing to his success, and thereby reinforcing ties to his patron, Foveaux. In the light of the above discussion, Redfern's emancipation appears to have been both deserved and honourable.

There is now the question of Foveaux's asthma to be considered. Mentioned in passing by Fletcher,[146] and without a source in my *Journal* article; again in Wright's "Shipping Movement" and in Nobbs,[147] it was fully aired in Whitaker.[148]

Wright's "Shipping Movements" revealed that the Brig *Dart,* with D. McLennan, as Master, left Otaheite on 5 September 1803 and arrived at Norfolk Island on 21 Sept. The *Dart* left next day for Sydney, arriving on 30

Sept., carrying "seal skins, salt, pork and passengers". "Col. Foveaux badly effected by asthma, Alex Dollis & family and Wm Redfern" were the passengers. Whitaker added "Mrs Sherwin, two-year-old Ann, and their servants including William Blake and George Lewis".

Obviously Redfern had previously discussed Foveaux's asthma and the curative effect of a sea voyage. But ship arrivals were unpredictable. The last ship to call, the *Harrington,* had left on 21 June of that year. Now the timely arrival of the *Dart* presented an opportunity.

Foveaux wrote to King, advising him that his asthma was getting worse, had confined him to his house and asked to be relieved of his command of the Island.[149] At the same time, he asked Redfern for a medical report which was handed to Foveaux next day,[150] 22 September 1803, at Norfolk Island. Bear in mind that Redfern had already received his pardon.

The party returned to Norfolk Island in the ship *Union,* Master J. Pendleton. It left Sydney on 19 January and arrived at Norfolk Island on 9 February, 1804, returning to Sydney with 55,055 lbs of salt pork.[151]

Whitaker provides an interesting account of Redfern's activities at Port Jackson.

Redfern's Land and Enterprise.

R. J. Ryan has a brief history of the granting and recording of land grants in the introduction to his useful book on that subject. The story of Redfern's land may be found there, starting from its original grant, 14 February, 1792, and including his purchase, and sale on 8 September, 1804 for £160 Stg. to William Thompson.[152]

Selling his land may have had something to do with Lord Hobart's decision to evacuate Norfolk Island in favor of a settlement in Van Diemen's Land. The intention of this decision was to forestall the French and for the same reason the First Settlement buildings would be razed. It may also have been influenced directly by Foveaux, who supported the evacuation.

While Redfern's interest in land on the Island was minuscule compared to the land he accumulated on the mainland, it is useful to understand the colonial background. "The power to grant land[153] was one of the many responsibilities entrusted to Arthur Phillip as the first Governor of New South Wales.

After his departure from the colony, this power devolved to his successors. There is considerable evidence of irregularity and abuse of the system following Phillip's departure. The condition for granting land was set down quite clearly in George III's instructions to Phillip. Emancipated convicts, "from their good conduct and a disposition to industry" were to be given land according to the following schedule:

"To every male shall be granted 30 acres of land, and in case he shall be married, 20 acres more; and for every child who may be with them at the settlement at the time of making the said grant, a further quantity of 10 acres, free from all taxes, quit rents, or other acknowledgements whatsoever, for the space of ten years; Provided that the person to whom the said land shall have been granted shall reside within the same and proceed to the cultivation and improvement thereof".[154]

Land grants were later extended to "non-commission officers and private marines" under certain conditions and eventually, and controversially, to officers serving in New South Wales.[155]

In the discussion that follows, one of the primary objectives is to position on the Island the two houses that Redfern owned. Wright makes a critical contribution to this end by having Settlers' Blocks superimposed on a 1971 map of Norfolk Island. The resulting map is printed as end papers in Wright (1986).[156]

Deputy-Surveyor Charles Grimes surveyed the Island between 1792 and 1794 from the *Sirius* according to Bernard Dowd.[157] Grimes' 1794 "Plan of Settlers Lots" "identifies 95 blocks fronting the various creeks on either side of the road from Sydney to Phillipburgh and Queensborough". Wright argued for the creek system as "the major topographical feature for the early surveyors".[158]

Of the 95 blocks, landholders were restricted to 88. But more than this number were being farmed as some landholders leased parts of their blocks to people whose primary employment in the community was not farming.[159]

Wright shows the Lot number, size and occupier of the settlers' blocks in 1796 in a Table (7). From this material it may be seen that Wentworth's block (88), an original grant to John Hayes, was west of present day St Barnabas Church, which brings it to the western edge of the Island and its high cliffs.[160] It cannot be assumed that there was a house on that block and that Redfern subsequently owned it.

According to Ryan (1981) the land Redfern bought and later sold had been purchased by D'Arcy Wentworth from Joseph McCaulden. In material sourced to Deputy Surveyor Grimes Report of Ground granted to settlers in 1793, McCaulden's original grant was Lot 66.

From Wright's endpaper map it can be seen that the Sydney-Queensborough Road formed the southern boundary of this lot, part of which now lies under the eastern end of the airport landing strip. The long axis of Lot 66 pointed towards *The Stables,* at Longridge.

For further details of the ownership and fracturing of McCaulden's original grant of 23 March 1796 it is necessary to return to Ryan. McCaulden was to pay a rental of one shilling per year after five years commencing 14 February, 1792. The land was "sold by the grantee to Mr Darcy Wentworth and by him to Thomas Coller, who sold 18 acres to James Dyas and Charles Cooper". The remainder went "for £47 to Mr Fane Edge, who also purchased the other 18 acres". Edge "sold 12 acres to Richard Morgan and the other 48 were knocked down to William Redfern on 9th July, 1802". He "sold the same for £160 Stg. to William Thompson on the 8th September 1804. The grant document was "torn up this 6th October, 1821. (Signed) F. Goulburn". [161]

Thomas Collier(?) came out on *Neptune*; James Dyus and Charles Cooper, on *Salamander* - but, at different times; and Richard Morgan on *Alexander*. Of four William Thompsons, all came as convicts, and two were on the Island at the time of the sale from Redfern. Fane Edge was a member of the 102nd Regiment.

As Joseph McCaulden was a marine, a member of the 102nd Regiment, it will be necessary to turn again to the conditions of the grants. Officers and marines were not eligible at first but this was changed later to include "the several non-commissioned officers and private marines" who may wish to remain when the detachment is relieved, "as also such other persons as may be disposed to become settlers".[162]

Wright included McCaulden among 22 marine/seamen settlers for Norfolk Island discharged at Sydney 10 & 12 December 1791 They sailed January 1792. Wright estimated 63 ex-sailors and Marines and 53 ex-convicts, settled at Norfolk Island in 1791-2 (*Victualling Books.*) In May 1792, 111 settlers occupied 4,130 acres.[163]

There is a reference in a Redfern *Letter 2,* below, to his 'pretending' to Piper that Wentworth owned one of the houses credited to Redfern. Assuming that Piper would fall for this, one could accept that Wentworth had originally owned it.

Ralph Clark, you remember, had built a house for Wentworth at Charlotte Fields, changed to Queensborough, later in the same year, 1791.

Tentatively it may be suggested that if Redfern were to convince Piper that one of the two Redfern houses still belonged to Wenworth it might well have been on either Lot 66 or 88. I lean towards 66, which was closer to the main settlement. The houses for which Redfern was credited when he was sent off the Island in 1808 are described in *John Piper's Norfolk Island Returns*[164] a a house 1: 24 feet by 12 feet, and a house 2: 33 feet by 12 feet. Attached, were

"A Salting House, 20 feet by 14 feet, battened with boarded and shingled roof and flagged floor" and "A small boarded shed and shingle privy".

This return shows that Redfern had no horses, asses, oxen, calves, sheep - either full or half grown, lambs or goats, but did have 62 hogs. In the next column, under the heading "Acres of Corn", has been entered - 4730 lbs, with the word "alive" above it. Under total amount, next column, appears L88/13/9 (the math is correct). Apparently Redfern had no "acres of corn".

It would appear then, that Redfern was concentrating on hogs, and either had an enclosure on one of his blocks, or leased some land, and bought corn to feed them. Since Redfern had continued to sell grain and swine meat to the Commissariat Stores after selling his land, he must have been in the business of buying and selling the local product of free, emancipated and convict small farmers.

His mentors in selling to the Government Stores were Surgeons Thomas Jamison[165] and D'Arcy Wentworth[166], each of whom had served on the Island and had been so engaged. The point of the exercise was to accumulate Commissariat Stores certificates that would become payable in sterling funds. Local paper money, or promissory notes, was heavily discounted in the Colony against sterling.

However there was another dimension to this matter as explained by Butlin. "[T]he two ways by which most salaries were collected in New South Wales were to pay them to local importers for goods and to discount them with local merchants or others. By 1806 at the latest the second practice was well-established...D'Arcy Wentworth acted as intermediary on a large scale. For a number of years William Redfern at Norfolk Island bought the bills of officials, remitted them to Wentworth in Sydney, whence they were remitted to William Balmain in London for collection".[167]

The lesson was clear to Redfern. In many ways, Norfolk Island was his "schoolroom". There he learned survival skills that would serve him well on the mainland when he returned.

Smallpox Vaccination.

Several references have been made to smallpox in this book. Blane and Trotter in the Navy had actively supported vaccination with cowpox, as against inoculation with live smallpox. Trotter had arranged for an early recognition of Edward Jenner's work by having a gold medal struck and presented to him. The brief two years or so that it took to have Jennerian vaccination adopted by the Royal Navy was a vast improvement on the forty-year lag for the issue of lemon juice against scurvy.

In the convict settlement at Port Jackson, Surgeon Thomas Jamison was appointed acting surgeon-general in June 1802 during Balmain's absence.

Jamison shares with Surgeons Harris and Savage the first successful vaccination of children against smallpox in the colony on the mainland. There has been some controversy about the source of the cowpox vaccine. This may be resolved by a careful reading of Governor King's letters to Lord Hobart in May of 1803.[168]

On 9 May, 1803, King asked Lord Hobart to send vaccine material to the Colony. Ten days later King advised Hobart of the receipt of vaccine matter from the Jennerian Society and of the unsuccessful vaccination of a number of children. King again asked for fresh vaccine to be sent. However, two days later, on the 21 May, he received a letter from Jamison advising that the vaccine had taken. Twelve days after vaccination, Jackson's child showed a positive response. Mr Savage took vaccine matter from the pustule and subsequently 400 children were vaccinated with cowpox against the smallpox.

King wrote again to Hobart on 14 August 1804 confirming the early success with vaccine brought from the *Coromandel* and advising that two lots of vaccine had been sent to Norfolk Island. Evidently the first attempts did not succeed for Foveaux wrote to Governor King on 20 December 1804 as follows - "Agreeable to your instructions I directed the Surgeon to make experiments of the Vaccine Matter, for inoculating the Children for the small pox, it having failed in the first instance, he has made trial of that sent by the Integrity, which I hope will succeed". Success was reported from Norfolk Island in February 1805. The third attempt took advantage of children with cowpox arriving from the mainland, probably in the previous month.

Redfern was probably involved. At that time, Redfern, and D'Arcy Wentworth (having returned to Norfolk Is. in May) were shown as assistant surgeons, with James Davis[169] as surgeon in charge. [Redfern's advice to Macquarie that he had received two heifers "as a reward for his exertions in carrying on the Inoculation of the Cow-pox" could have applied to his later work on the mainland.]

On Norfolk Island, Redfern took sick parades and was not afraid to exempt sick convicts from work, when such a decision was warranted, according to Holt, an Irish political prisoner on the Island.[170] The implication was that Redfern needed courage to make such decisions. This, in itself, also acted to denigrate Foveaux. 'Bucky' Jones also played this game. Now D'Arcy Wentworth shared with William Redfern a more humane attitude to convicts.

While the general run of surgeons did not like to have to attend floggings there was something to be said for their presence. Hernia sufferers, commonly former sailors, were exempted. Flagellation could be stopped on medical grounds and even medical assistance provided. The final hurt for those whipped was to have salt rubbed, or at least, thrown over their wounds.

Contrary to painful experience, and the expression - "rubbing salt into the wound" - salt did help in wound cleaning at least.

The reference to Joseph Holt brings to mind an earlier chapter. Holt was a political prisoner having been connected with the Irish rebellion of 1798. Redfern knew of him on Norfolk Island and later at Port Jackson, where he bought Holt's flock of sheep.

Maurice Margarot, one of the Scottish Martyrs, was eager to meet Joseph Holt when he arrived at Sydney Cove on 11 January 1800. Holt reached Norfolk Island on 10 May 1804 with D'Arcy Wentworth on the ship *Betsy.* Margarot arrived in August 1805 in the small brig *Venus* and stayed only until 16 October when he left on HMS *Buffalo* for Van Diemen's Land.

Did Redfern get to meet Margarot in that short time? It would be interesting if he did, and more interesting still, to know what they might have discussed. Particularly in view of Michael Roe's opinion that "Margarot's feeling for social justice was true and in him the intellectual 'left' came to Australia".[171] The second part of that sentence would need to be understood in the context of late eighteenth century radicalism as essentially concerned with parliamentary reform and its consequences.[172]

The Redfern Letters from Norfolk Island (Letter 1: 'Redfern to Wentworth').

Two surviving letters from Redfern to Wentworth, after the latter left the Island, attest to a growing friendship and mutual financial dealings. Holt's belief that the two had links with the north of Ireland - more likely to be true than false - probably strengthened their friendship. These letters are from a later period of Redfern's stay on the Island. They came to my attention in the beginning phase of this study in the late 1960s through catalogues in the Mitchell Library, Sydney, New South Wales. The first, dated 16th September 1807 is from the "Wentworth Papers".[173] And referred to how he was "shocked at the unworthy treatment"[174] he had received and that "ample redress for the indignity you have suffered" would be attained.[175]

It appears that D'Arcy Wentworth had written to Redfern giving an account of the way Governor Bligh had treated him. Redfern's condemnation of the perpetrator is somewhat extreme - "As lamentable a species of depravity as can possibly be attendant on the most degenerate state of Human nature". Such words would not want to fall into the hands of the wrong person. Perhaps Redfern, out of concern for his friend D'Arcy had simply allowed his pen to run away with him. (Or was there another reason? Was he worrying about his own future, or his boat, then under construction?)

After that first outburst, Redfern calmed down, consoling D'Arcy with the thought that his friends had stuck by him and that His Majesty's Ministers would provide "ample redress for the indignity [he] had suffered". Redfern then turned to more mundane affairs by enclosing a number of bills and a statement of affairs between them indicating that he "holds my note for £101.15. 0 and any other Notes of Mine in your possession to be delivered to me, or their amount deducted from the sum of our general acct to which I put my Signature as acceptance of, on the day you embarked here for Port Jackson: for should you go to Europe, or any Accident happen to either of us, the note or notes might be liable to be twice demanded seeing that they still stand against me, notwithstanding that they are included in the general amount already alluded to and consequently form a part of it".

In this context, *consolidate* probably involved bringing all Island farming and other activities under government control as part of the staged evacuation of Norfolk Island. Compensation, in money or kind, was made later for any dispossession, as in Redfern's case. The reference to "our general account" points to a partnership between Redfern and Wentworth.

The references to accounts add to other indications, from his Norfolk Island experiences, of a primary and ongoing interest in his financial affairs. Further evidence of book keeping will appear later, together with a pride in his ability to live within his means. Matters of solvency are very much to the fore in his concern for the status of individual accounts.

Redfern shows in this letter an awareness of the working of a cashless society through paper currency, or bills. He is particularly aware of the problems of a joint account being open to accidental losses from either side. Such foresight runs contrary to an ebullient nature but is certainly at one with the extraordinary threats facing Wentworth on the mainland with his conflict with Governor Bligh, with Redfern about to be uprooted from Norfolk Island.

Redfern has turned to a number of requests, which are mostly self-explanatory. For personal use, there is "tea and sugar", "some paper", "Account Books" and "Hops", to make beer. "Iron Hoops" were for wooden casks into which would go his pickled pork.

Note that "iron large enough to make axles and other necessary parts" is "for one of our Timber Carriages". This is further confirmation of a joint business venture, and one large enough to require more than one carriage, or cart. Their business was most likely related to grain and pork if the following is to be interpreted correctly.

Redfern's market report to Wentworth advised him that the export market for 'hogs', that is, as pickled pork will come to a close. Not only would they stand to lose on their joint venture, but Redfern, while still able to eat pork, would find it increasingly difficult to have poultry on his table for a change.

It was well that Redfern asked D'Arcy Wentworth for his advice. It would be needed sooner than he might have thought.

Who was "My Lady" of William Redfern's Letter?

A most tantalising question arises from the concluding paragraph of this letter. 'My Lady', whom Redfern mentioned, knew D'Arcy Wentworth and Maria Ainsley well enough to send them greetings and gifts.

Redfern had sailed back to Norfolk Island from Port Jackson on 9 February 1804 after accompanying a sick Foveaux to the mainland. Wentworth was back on the Island for a second time in May of the same year. Wentworth left the Island in the ship *Argo* on 30 March 1806, and was back on the mainland by 7 April.[176]

For part of that period, at least, the two couples were together, and still were on 15 September 1807 when the letter was written, and probably continued on into the next year.

As part of the search for the identity of Redfern's "Lady", the services of the Mitchell Library were called upon. Marjorie Hancock, Deputy Mitchell Librarian, at the time, had catalogues and indexes in the Library searched "for information concerning William Redfern's first wife, but [had] only found the following references, which confirm the facts you already know".

Marjorie Hancock's reply was dated 19 October 1964 and contained the following references to their searches.

"T. D. Mutch's Biographical Index contains the following entry, listing William Redfern and his wife among the settlers embarked on board the Estramina for the Derwent. (Redfern, William - Bigge Appendix Box 12/ p.152). List of settlers embarked on board the Estramina schooner for the Derwent, 15 May 1808. William Redfern - individuals not holding land, 1 wife 1 servant".[177]

In addition, Mrs Hancock quoted from *The Australian Encyclopaedia* (1958 volume 7, pp.395-7). "[Redfern] appears to have married twice although nothing is known of his first wife except that she accompanied him on his return to Sydney from Norfolk Island in 1808". The source of that information was Edward Ford's 1953 paper. In 1967, Ford had nothing more to add in his *Redfern* entry in the *Australian Dictionary of Biography* (1788-1850, vol 2).

Reg Wright noted in his book, *The Forgotten Generation of Norfolk Island and Van Diemen's Land* (1986 p. 39), that on the voyage southwards he [Redfern] was credited with an unknown wife and servant". [Table 14, the 4th Embarkation list (p.111)]. No names were entered for wife and servant.

In the same list there are two other instances of missing names - one a wife, the other a child. In Table 10, Wright provides "Various listings of five embarkations Norfolk Island to Derwent - 1807/1808". For the *Estramina*, on which Redfern left Norfolk Island on the 15 May 1808 the figures are for women - 13/13/12 [3 records]. Table 14 lists 10 women named and 2 unnamed, a total of 12. However the totals indicate a real person, although unnamed, occupied each blank space on the indent.

Wright discovered other discrepancies and made an attempt "to synthesize the passenger lists using victualling and other records. It seems reasonable", Wright argued, "to assume that between 567 and 578 persons were transformed to the Derwent in 1807-08. The difference of 11 persons between Archives and Mitchell Library records could be explained by the presence of 11 convicts on the *Porpoise* not noted on the latter records. Although their names do not appear on the passenger list, the two "Irish Exiles: William Maum and Michael Dwyer, were reputedly sent o the Derwent on *Porpoise*". To these names, Wright added seven others suggested by the Victualling lists.[178]

O'Donohoe (1986) looked at the links between men and women in Norfolk Island's First Settlement. Immediately preceding the main text are two pages of names headed "Unattached Families". Introductory notes on the first page stated that there were nine females with children and six males unattached. On the second page is a list of "Males known to have partners but whose identities were not found". William Redfern's name does not appear on either page.

This is encouraging. In the body of the text, which is arranged alphabetically, William Redfern's name appeared bracketed with *Sarah McHenry*. For each, the date of arrival is 1801 and the date of departure 15. 5.1808. No ship's name, nor any other information is provided on the entry lines but underneath is the following -

"The *Estramina*'s list had William Redfern with a wife. He boarded on 6.5.1808 and so did Sarah McHenry, the only persons to do so".[179]

Whatever the results, of any further searches, it can be concluded that Redfern was attracted to the opposite sex. It may also appear from another of his letters to D'Arcy Wentworth that he did not consider all women on the Island to be "damned whores". But the women were different, even if, as Redfern pointed out, certain men were the prime cause of some of them being as they were. Before turning to that letter, what can be said about the relations between the sexes on Norfolk Island?

In the first place there was not a normal distribution of women and men. In the foundation party it was about 1:3 (1788). By 1804 it was still around that proportion with 186 women out of an adult population of 773. Of those women, 146 were free and 40 were convicts.

In the foundation party, Ann Innet, 'the matron of the group' became the mistress of Commandant Philip Gidley King and gave birth to the first child born on the Island. Two other women married convicts. By 1804 there were 311 children, 68 of whom lived with their mothers. Marriage or strong bonds would reduce the number of unattached women still further.

On the other hand, if "the military on Norfolk Island found itself largely excluded from access to women" then the ratio of women to convict men would increase. "As a result the 1790s was marked by increasing tension and frustration on the military side and jealousy and suspicion on the part of the free and convict settlers who complained incessantly about soldiers attempting to 'seduce' their wives. This unrest was a major cause of civil-military conflict in 1793-94".[180]

Wright estimated that somewhere between 2,850 and 3,000 individuals lived on Norfolk Island...during the 26 years of the First Settlement. "There were at least 1,700 males, 460 women, and 690 children. Over 320 men from the N.S.W. Corps served on the Island". [181]

Are we to accept those 460 women as "damned whores"? I think not, even if they were described as such. Just as circumstances, male demand coupled with extreme poverty, could move women into whoredom, opportunities of a different kind allowed another response. Did such opportunities arise?

Major Ross's General Order of 8 January 1791 aimed at forming "family units" essentially to "take wives and children off the store". One result was to show that convict men and convict women were prepared to live together and to form lifelong associations. This was regardless of church sanctions,[182] and questioned the relevance of such descriptions as "whores" (Ralph Clark et al.) and "concubines" (Samuel Marsden).

E.P.Thompson discovered that "reading the history of women as one of unrelieved victim-hood...can make for good polemics. But it is scarcely flattering to women". He realized this when "An elderly self-educated villager, with a keen weather-beaten face, became tense, and at length burst out: "We women knew our rights, you know. We knew what was our due". They instructed Thompson that working women had made their own cultural spaces, had means of enforcing their norms, and saw to it that they received their "dues". Their dues might not have been today's "rights", but they were not history's passive subjects".

If not whores, can it be assumed that the women of the First Settlement on Norfolk Island, like their sisters in twentieth century North Lincolnshire, were not completely passive subjects? How could they be, with supply and demand working to their advantage.

Reading *The Forgotten Generation of Norfolk Island and Van Diemens Land* is to see evidence of men, and of women, behaving badly towards one another. At the same time the disinclination of so many of the Islanders to leave, suggests that many other men and women, had settled into a steady relationship, and did not want it to be disturbed by what might prove to be an unsettling move.

'Redfern to Wentworth' (Norfolk Island Letter 2).

This is an intriguing letter, which also has something to say about the relations between the sexes on Norfolk Island. More importantly, in a biography of Redfern, it provides insight into his understanding of part of that reality. Unfortunately almost nothing is known about Redfern's own relationships with Norfolk Island women.

The name of the person, to whom this letter is written, is not given in the letter. Nor is the date. On the strength of internal and external evidence certain conclusions have been reached. Some time in May 1808, around the 19th, is suggested here as a likely date for the letter. D'Arcy Wentworth was the person to whom the letter was directed. This has been assumed previously but formerly argued here.

A missionary, James Elder, asked Captain Piper to recommend a young woman from the Island as a suitable wife. The person suggested by Piper, was considered by Redfern to be unsuitable for the reasons he gave, and did not reflect too well upon Piper.[183] "Elder applied to the great Personage for a character, and he received for answer as Elder himself said, that those Girls were unknown to every thing vicious - from his friends Mr & Mrs Mitchell".[184]

Redfern was led into an unguarded and therefore unwise discussion with the missionary, Elder, who was aware of the reputation Piper had for philandering when on the mainland. Suddenly aware of his position, he had Elder sworn to secrecy, and then confirmed Elder's worst fears about Piper's advice. Elder replied that a Person had informed him of the reports in circulation, which he found to be very general, and therefore would drop the affair.[185]

Piper's punishment of Redfern was dismissal and banishment. He was to go on board "the first Vessel for the Derwent". Whatever the reason, whether it was as Redfern told it, or not, Commandant Piper was angry.

Piper had first to reverse an earlier decision that Redfern should remain on the Island and the older Surgeon move to Van Diemen's Land.[186] Secondly, by giving the Derwent as Redfern's destination he was cutting him off from wider opportunities that might be available to him on the mainland. Thirdly, by describing Redfern as "a danger to society", in his 1808 *Return,* he was making more difficult Redfern's chances of being restored to society, sometime in the future.

Piper tightened the screw still further. He removed Redfern's "servant" and "family" from the Store. This meant that the longer he took to leave the Island, the more it would cost him for their upkeep. "Being on the Store" was a legitimate cost to Government for his services as surgeon. Next, Piper forced Redfern to sever his connection with a boat-building project that was nearing completion. Redfern had a share in a vessel and he would rather sell out than be an obstacle its launch.[187]

Redfern's reaction stands to his credit, disposing of his share in the boat with the interest of his co-builders in mind. Again, although under pressure from Piper and smarting from Elder's betrayal of his good intentions, Redfern made some thoughtful moves to regain lost ground.

It is timely to consider where, if at all, D'Arcy Wentworth fits into these events. The original letter being with the Darcy Wentworth papers, is not in itself sufficient proof that it was written to D'Arcy. However, consider the following argument for that idea.

Redfern's previous letter to his friend and business partner, D'Arcy Wentworth, asked specifically for his advice on whether he should "come to Port Jackson - and what pursuits would be the most eligible". This was the object that Piper had frustrated by his decision to send Redfern to the Derwent.

Wentworth, alone, would have understood at once the depth of Redfern's disappointment. More to the point, he would have been willing and able to do something to help Redfern after he had left Norfolk Island. After all they were friends as well as business partners.

No one else comes to mind as a person to whom Redfern would have written such a letter. Who, more than Wentworth, would have been 'astonished' by Piper's action? Consider the way Redfern brought Island people and events into play in his letter. He was obviously writing to someone to whom those people and events were known, Wentworth, for example, who had lived on the Island on two separate occasions.

What of Piper's philandering at Port Jackson and again on Norfolk Island?[188] Even there, Redfern was sure of his ground and felt confident that he could talk about Piper in the way he had - if it were Wentworth to whom he was writing.

Again, the joint business venture points to Wentworth as the person for whom Redfern was "holding a house in trust". This business connection would help convince Piper that Redfern was making an honest claim. He was not of course. Redfern excused his lie on account of Piper's vindictiveness. "Two wrongs were making a right".[189]

Redfern had been busy intending to get off the Island as quickly as possible. Captain A. Bristow,[190] who had arrived at Norfolk in April, was prepared to offer a berth to Redfern, to accept his letter, and to deliver it into D'Arcy Wentworth's hands. This placed Bristow in a position to confirm or deny Redfern's account of the Elder story as he was 'acquainted with the whole of it'.

Redfern's attempt to go direct to Port Jackson failed. Piper ordered him to leave on *Estramina.* Thus, Redfern embarked on 17 May 1808 on *Estramina,* which left Norfolk Island on 19 May, reaching Hobart in Van Diemen's Land on 5 June. However, he arrived, uncontested, at Port Jackson on 21 June 1808, on the same ship. He did well to place his trust in Captain Bristow, who must have delivered his letter, almost certainly to D'Arcy Wentworth. Who else could have delivered him safely to Port Jackson? The Captain? Wright has him listed as Oxley, but E.W.Dunlop (ADB2) has Oxley at Norfolk Island in 1806, on his way to England in 1807, and returning in November 1808, too late for *Estramina*'s May/June trip with Redfern.

The names of Redfern's wife and servant remain as an *Estramina* secret. However, it is possible that this servant was James Sheers, junior. Reg Wright thought that he "may well have become Australia's first native-born surgeon but died November 1814 at the age of 21 years as "First Medical Apprentice to Dr Redfern".[191] James was brother to Mary Ann Shears, who at fourteen years of age became the mistress of Commander Captain John Piper. Four children were born to this couple before their formal marriage in 1916, and ten more afterwards.[192]

'Endeavour 3' - a note.

Phillip's restrictions on boat building on Norfolk Island were made clear to King and subsequently to commandants who followed him.[193] Graeme Andrews suggested that Piper probably reflected the sense of isolation of the Islanders when he allowed a boat to be built.[194]

Bligh was not impressed when alerted, probably by his son-in-law Captain Putland, in command of the *Porpoise* (2) who visited Norfolk Island in June/July, and again in October 1807.[195]

As noted in the previous chapter, Piper forced Redfern to give up his share in the boat, being built with Robert 'Buckey' Jones, beachmaster John Drummond, and boat builder Thomas Ransome. The schooner, *Endeavour*

3, of 50 tons was successfully launched and departed the Island under Captain M. Davis, with a crew of four, on 19 November 1808, arriving Sydney on 29 December.

Redfern would have had mixed feelings when it turned up. Having been associated with the building of a sea-going ship brought deep satisfaction. He knew he had helped to save the project from Commandant Piper's threats by selling his third share. That was a bit hard on Redfern. Perhaps he would have been pleased by the positive tone of the *Gazette* report.[196]

Continued in Volume II

Jones AR (2019) Better than cure: Volume II: Wellbeing in the Colony
ISBN: 978-0-6484471-9-1

About The Author

Arthur Raymond Jones was born in Cessnock, NSW. He first became interested in William Redfern as Principal of Minto Public School which was opposite the historic precinct of William Redfern's farm and home.

Since that time his insatiable desire for historical investigation and evaluation of evidence has seen him present and publish on Redfern's expertise, interests and endeavours, including Redfern's studies at Edinburgh University and his valuable contributions to the early colony of New South Wales. Better Than Cure, published in two volumes, is the culmination of more than 55 years' work.

Throughout his career, Arthur, who has enjoyed a long-term and passionate interest in libraries, participated in the establishment of local and school libraries, and built opportunities for community development through his contributions to local government and urban planning. He was an Alderman on Campbelltown Council from 1971 to 1977 and a member of the Macarthur Development Board from 1981 to 1987. He is also a Life Member of the Campbelltown and Airds Historical Society. In keeping with his love of libraries and early memories of books, which to him were uncommon but highly valued, he and the Jones family have donated his personal library of research material that underpins Better Than Cure, to the Campbelltown City Library, NSW.

Combined Bibliography

for:
Volume I (*Wellbeing in the Wooden World*)
&
Volume II (*Wellbeing in the Colony*)

ADB1

Australian Dictionary of Biography, General editor, Douglas Pike, 1788-1850, volume I, A-H. Section editors, A.G.L. Shaw 1788-1825 & C.M.H. Clark 1826-1850, Melbourne University Press, 1966.

ADB2

Australian Dictionary of Biography, General editor, Douglas Pike, 1788-1850, volume 2, I-Z. Section editors, A.G.L. Shaw 1788-1825 & C.M.H. Clark 1826-1850, Melbourne University Press, 1967.

Australian Dictionary of Biography, Volume 3: A-C: 1851-1890: section eds. N.B.Nairn, A.G.Serle, & R.B.Ward, Melbourne University Press, Carlton, Victoria, 1969.

Australian Dictionary of Biography, Volume 4: D-J: 1851-1890: section eds. N.B.Nairn, A.G.Serle, & R.B.Ward, Melbourne University Press, Carlton, Victoria, 1972.

AE

The Australian Encyclopaedia, Vols 1-10. Alec H. Chisholm, Editor-in-chief, et al. Angus & Robertson Ltd, Sydney, 1958.

ASHM

Australian Society of the History of Medicine.

B&P

Companion Encyclopedia of the History of Medicine, vols 1 & 2, Routledge, London, 1997(1993).

BT

Bigge, John Thomas. *Appendix* [indexed], *B.T. Boxes 1-36 / CY Reel,* microfilm.

{Appendix [*Evidence*] to the Bigge Reports, P.R.O., London, [available in Australia as] B[onwick] T[ranscripts], hard copy, Boxes 1-36 / or as microfilm, CY reels. See Redfern to Bigge, below.}

CAHSI

Campbelltown and Airds Historical Society Incorporated.

DNB

The Dictionary of National Biography, ed. Sidney Lee Vol LII Shearman to Smirke London, 1897.

Gill

Gill, Conrad. *The Naval Mutinies of 1797...,* University of Manchester Publications, Manchester, 1913.

HRA

Historical Records of Australia

HRNSW

Historical Records of New South Wales

IGI

International Genealogical Index.

LAH

Library of Australian History.

L&C:

Lloyd, Christopher & Jack L.S. Coulter. *Medicine and the Navy 1200-1900, Vol III* - 1714-1815, E. & S Livingstone Ltd., Edinburgh and London, 1961.

M&D

Manwaring, G.E. & Bonamy Dobrée. *The Floating Republic: An Account of the Mutinies at Spithead and the Nore in 1797*, Penguin Books, London, 1937 (1935).

MJA

Medical Journal of Australia

ML

Mitchell Library, Sydney, New South Wales.

ODNB

The Oxford Dictionary of National Biography, online *ODNB*, ed. Brian Harrison, Oxford University Press, 2004.

OPMHA

Occasional Papers in Medical History Australia, series 1-9, Australian Society of the History of *Medicine*, Biennial Conferences. [Series ended at 6th Biennial Conference of ASHM, 1999 (Health&History, 1999, 1:222-226).]

PRO

Public Records Office

RAHS

Royal Australian Historical Society

RACP

Royal Australasian College of Physicians

Ritchie

Ritchie, ed. 1, 1971

Ritchie, John, ed. *The Evidence to the Bigge Reports, New South Wales under Governor Macquarie, Volume 1, The Oral Evidence,* Heinemann, Melbourne, 1971.

Ritchie, ed. 2, 1971

Ritchie, John, ed. *The Evidence to the Bigge Reports, New South Wales under Governor Macquarie, Volume 2, The Written Evidence,* Heinemann, Melbourne, 1971.

SOED 1 & 2

The Shorter Oxford English Dictionary on Historical Principles, revised & edited C.T.Onions, Third Edition, *volumes I,* A-Markworthy, & II, Marl-Z and Addenda, Oxford, At the Clarendon Press, 1974.

Unpublished papers

Ann Coats & Philip MacDougall. eds. *The 1797 Mutinies – Papers of the Spithead and Nore Bicentenary Conferences, 1997,* mentioned in Rodger, 2006. [Subsequently published.]

Jones, Arthur. *Bibliography of a life and the times of William Redfern.*

Jones, Arthur. *Chronology of a life and the times of William Redfern.*

Jones, Arthur. *Courtmartial of William Redfern, 1775-1833*: Synopsis and study.

Jones, Arthur. *Index to four papers about William Redfern, 1775-1833.* 52pp.

Jones, Arthur. *Index to author's daybooks (1 to 20): reading and research about William Redfern, 1775-1833.* 62pp.

A

Abir-Am, Pnina G. and Dorinda Outram. eds. *Uneasy Careers and Intimate Lives: Women in Science 1789-1979*, Rutgers University Press, New Brunswick and London, 1987.

Abbott, Ian. "Origin and spread of the cat, *Felis catus*, on mainland Australia, with a discussion of the magnitude of its early impact on native fauna", in *Wildlife Research* 29, 2002.

Ackerknecht, Erwin H. *A Short History of Medicine*. The Johns Hopkins University Press, Baltimore, 1992.

Adam, Alexander and Allen Fisk. *Adam's Latin Grammar* (simplified)...Facsimile of the 3rd ed., New York, 1827. Nabu Public Domain Reprints, printed by Lightning Source UK Ltd 17 Jan 2011.

Adorno, Theodor W. and Max Horkheimer, trans. by John Cumming. *Dialectic of Enlightenment*, Verso, London, 1979.

"Agriculture" [entry by W.T.T.] in *The Encyclopaedia Britannica*, 1875.

Allaby, Michael. ed. *The Oxford Dictionary of Natural History*, Oxford University Press, Oxford, 1985.

Al-Hassani, Salim TS et al. eds. *1001 Inventions* [not to be taken literally]: *Muslim Heritage in Our World*, 2nd ed., Foundation for Science, Technology and Civilisation, Manchester, 2007.

Almanack. 1806, facsimile edition, The Trustees of the Public Library of NSW, Sydney, 1966.

Anson, George. *A Voyage round the World in the years MDCCXL, I, II, III, IV*, compiled under the direction of Lord Anson by Richard Walter, chaplain, intro. John Masefield, Heron Books, London, c.1912.

Antill, John Macquarie & Rose Antill-de Warren. *The Emancipist: An Historical Drama In Three Acts*, Angus & Robertson, Sydney, 1936.

Aplin, Graeme. ed., *Sydney Before Macquarie: A Difficult Infant*, NSW University Press, Kensington, 1988.

Armstrong, David. *Political anatomy of the body: Medical knowledge in Britain in the twentieth century*, Cambridge University Press, London, 1983.

Armstrong, David. *An Outline of Sociology as Applied to Medicine*, 3rd ed., Wright, London, 1990.

Armstrong, Edward A. *The Folklore of Birds: An Enquiry into the Origin & Distribution of some Magico-Religious Traditions*, Houghton Mifflin Company, Boston, *The Riverside Press, Cambridge*, 1959.

Atkins, Susanne et al. eds. " 'Outpost Medicine', Australasian Studies on the History of Medicine", Third National Conference of ASHM, Hobart, February 1993, *OPMHA*, University of Tasmania and ASHM, 1994.

Atkinson, Alan. *Camden: Farm and Village Life in Early New South Wales,* Oxford University Press, Melbourne, 1988.

Atkinson, Alan. *The Europeans in Australia: A History: Volume I,* Oxford University Press, Melbourne, 1998.

Atkinson, James. *An Account of the State of Agriculture & Grazing in New South Wales...*1826, facsimile edition with Introduction by Brian H. Fletcher, Sydney University Press, 1975.

Auchmuty, James J. "D'Arcy Wentworth (1762?-1827)" in *ADB2.*

Auchmuty, James J. 'The editor's introduction", ix-xiii, in *The Voyage of Governor Phillip to Botany Bay...,* 1970.

Audubon's Birds of America, George Dock jr, text. Harry N. Abrams. New York, 1979.

Austin, A.G. *Australian Education 1788-1900, Church, State and Public Education in Colonial Australia,* Sir Isaac Pitman & Sons, Ltd, Melbourne, 1961.

Austin, A.G. *Select Documents in Australian Education 1788-1900,* Sir Isaac Pitman & Sons, Ltd, Melbourne, 1963.

B

Backhouse [James] *&* [George Washington] *Walker in Illawarra & Shoalhaven 1826,* Edgar Beale & Winifred Mitchell (Introduction) & Michael Organ (Dedication). eds., Illawarra Historical Society, 1991.

Baehre, Rainer. "The Medical Profession in Upper Canada Reconsidered: Politics, Medical Reform, and Law in a Colonial Society". A paper presented to the annual meeting of the Canadian Society for the History of Medicine, 5 June 1993. *Canadian Bulletin of Medical History,* 12: 1995: 101-24. Online at

http://www.cbmh.ca/archive/00000313/01/cbmhbchm_v12n1baehre.pdf

Baer, Marc. *Theatre and Disorder in Late Georgian London,* Clarendon Press, Oxford, 1992.

Banks, Joseph. *The Endeavour Journal of Joseph Banks 1768-1771* [in 2 volumes], J.C.Beaglehole, ed., The Trustees of the Public Library of New South Wales in association with Angus & Robertson, Sydney, 1962.

Barker, Francis, et al. *1789: Reading Writing Revolution, Proceedings of the Essex conference on the Sociology of Literature July 1981,* University of Essex, 1982.

Barnard Eldershaw. M[Pseudonym used by Marjorie Barnard & Flora Eldershaw]. *The Life and Times of Captain John Piper,* ill. Adrian Feint, Ure Smith, Sydney, in assn. with The National Trust of Australia, N.S.W., 1973 (1939).

Barr, John. *Britain Portrayed: A Regency Album*, The British Library [Board], London, 1989.

Barrell, John. *The dark side of the landscape: The rural poor in English painting 1730-1840*, Cambridge University Press, Cambridge, 1987.

Barrett, Jim. *Cox's River: Discovery, History and Development*, Graphic Workshop, Armadale, 1993.

Bashford, Alison & Claire Hooker. eds. *Contagion: Epidemics, history and Culture from smallpox to anthrax*, Pluto Press, Annandale, NSW, 2001.

Bassett, Marnie. *The Governor's Lady: Mrs Philip Gidley King, An Australian Historical Narrative*, Melbourne University Press, Carlton, Victoria, 1992.

Bateson, Charles. *The Convict Ships 1787-1868*, Brown, Son & Ferguson, Ltd., Glasgow, 1985 (1959).

Battersby, Christine. *Gender and Genius: Towards a Feminist Aesthetics*, Indiana University Press, Bloomington and Indianapolis, 1989.

Baudin, Nicolas. *The Journal of Post Captain Nicolas Baudin Commander-in-Chief of the Corvettes, Geographe and Naturaliste...* Translated from the French by Christine Cornell, With a foreword by Jean-Paul Faivre, Libraries Board of South Australia, Adelaide, 1974.

Baxter C.J. ed. *Musters and lists NSW and Norfolk Island Sydney: Australian Biographical and Genealogical Record* in association with the Society of Australian Genealogists, 1988.

Beaglehole, J.C. "On the Character of Captain James Cook" in *The Geographical Journal*, Vol CXXII, Part 4, December 1956. On line, at NZETC

http://www.google.com.au/search?hl=en&source=hp&q=NZETC&btnG=Google+Search&aq=f&aqi=g3&aql=&oq=&gs_rfai=

Beaglehole, J.C. "The Young Banks", introduction to *The Endeavour Journal of Joseph Banks 1768-1771*, 1962.

Beasley, A.W. *Fellowship of Three* [Hunter, Cook & Banks], Kangaroo Press, 1993.

Bellot, H. Hale. *University College London 1826-1926*, University of London Press, London, 1929.

Bennett, J.M. "Bigge, John Thomas (1780-1843)", in *ADBI*, Melbourne University Press, London. 1966.

Bennett, J.M. & Alex C. Castles. *A Source Book of Australian Legal History*. The Law Book Company Ltd., Sydney, 1979:247-254.

Benson, Doug & Jocelyn Howell. *Taken for Granted: The bushland of Sydney and its suburbs*, Kangaroo Press in assn with Royal Botanic Gardens, Sydney, Kenthurst, 1990.

Berezin, Mabel. "Emotions and the Economy" in Neil J. Smelser & Richard Swedberg. eds. *The Handbook of Economic Sociology*, second edition, Princeton University Press, Princeton and the Russell Sage Foundation, New York, 2005.

Bernier, Olivier. *The World in 1800*, A Robert L. Bernstein Book, John Wiley & Sons Inc., New York, 2000.

Berriot-Salvadore, Evelyne. "The Discourse of Medicine and Science", in Davis & Farge, 1994.

Betts, Jonathan. *Harrison, John.* National Maritime Museum, Greenwich, 3rd ed. 1997.

Bewick, Thomas. *A Memoir of Thomas Bewick Written by Himself*, ed. and intro. Iain Bain, Oxford University Press, London, 1975.

Bewick, Thomas, Iain Bain, ed., and introduction. *A Memoir of Thomas Bewick, written by himself*, Oxford University Press, London, 1975.

Bigge, John Thomas. *Report of the Commissioner of Inquiry into the State of the Colony of New South Wales, 1822*, Libraries Board of South Australia, Adelaide, 1966.

Bigge, John Thomas. "Report of the Commissioner of Inquiry into the State of the Colony of New South Wales, 1822", in *British Parliamentary Papers, Colonies, Australia, I.*, Shannon Irish University Press, 1968.

Bigge, John Thomas. *Report of the Commissioner of Inquiry, On the State of Agriculture and Trade in New South Wales,* 1823, Ordered by the House of Commons to be printed, 13 March 1823.

Bigge, John Thomas. *Appendix*, indexed, [Evidence] to the Bigge Reports, P.R.O., London, [available in Australia as] B[onwick] T[ranscripts], hard copy, Boxes 1-36, or as microfilm, CY reels.

Black, Jeremy & Roy Porter. eds. *The Penguin Dictionary of Eighteenth-Century History*, Penguin Books, Harmondsworth, 1996.

Joseph Black 1728-1799: A Commemorative Symposium, A.D.C.Simpson, ed. The Royal Scottish Museum, Edinburgh, 1982.

Blake, William. *Milton*, ed. and commentary by Kay P. Easson and Roger R. Easson, Thames and Hudson, London. 1979.

Blanco, Richard L. *Wellington's Surgeon General: Sir James McGrigor*, Duke University Press, Durham, N.C., 1974.

Blanco, Richard L. "The Soldier's Friend-Sir Jeremiah Fitzpatrick, Inspector of Health for Land Forces", in *Medical History*, xx, 1976:402-421.

Blane, Gilbert. *Observations on the Diseases Incident to Seamen*, Second edition, with corrections and additions, London, Cooper, 1789.

Blewett, Graham. *Ferries and Farms: A History of Lugarno*, Copyright © 2000; http://www.nsw.nationaltrust.org.au/lugcontents.htm.

Boime, Albert. *Art in an Age of Revolution 1750-1800.* The University of Chicago Press, Chicago and London, 1987.

Bonwick, James (1817-1906). Guy Featherstone in *ADB3,* 1851-1890.

Bonyhady, Tim. *The Colonial Earth,* Melbourne University Press, Carlton South, 2001.

Booty, John E. "The Anglican Tradition", in Numbers & Amundsen, 1986.

Bostock, John. *The Dawn of Australian Psychiatry: An account of measures taken for the care of mental invalids from the time of the First Fleet, 1788, to the year 1850, including a survey of the overseas background and case notes of Dr F. Campbell, Glebe, NSW,* Australasian Medical Publishing Company, Sydney, 1968.

Boulding, Kenneth. *Economics as a Science,* McGraw-Hill, 1970, cited by Frank J. B. Stillwell, 1974.

Bower, Peter. *Turner's Papers: A Study of the Manufacture, Selection and Use of his Drawing Papers 1787-1820,* Tate Gallery, London, 1990.

Bracegirdle, Brian. "The Microscopical Tradition", in Bynum & Porter, *I,* 1997.

Braithwaite, Helen. *Romanticism, Publishing and Dissent: Joseph Johnson and the Cause of Liberty,* Palgrave Macmillan, Basingstoke, U.K., 2003.

Brand, Stewart. *The Clock of the Long Now: Time and Responsibility,* Weidenfeld & Nicolson, London, 1999.

Brandt, Allan M. "Sexually Transmitted Diseases" in Bynum & Porter, 1997.

Braverman, Harry. *Labor and Monopoly Capital: The Degradation of Work in the Twentieth Century,* Monthly Review Press, New York, 1974.

Bridges, Peter. *Foundations of Identity: Building Early Sydney 1788-1822,* Hale & Iremonger, Sydney, 2001 (1995).

Briggs, Asa. *The Age of Improvement 1783-1867,* Longman, London, 1978.

Briggs, Asa, introduction. *The Grand Panorama of London from the Thames in 1844,* a wood engraving published originally for Pictorial Times. [This edition] Sidgwick & Jackson, London, 1977(1972).

Broad, Jacqueline and Karen Green. eds. *Virtue, Liberty, and Toleration: Political Ideas of European Women, 1400-1800,* Springer, Dordrecht, The Netherlands, 2007.

Broad, Jacqueline and Karen Green. *A History of Women's Political Thought in Europe, 1400-1700,* Cambridge University Press, 2009.

Broadbent, James and Joy Hughes. eds. *The Age of Macquarie,* M.U.P., Carlton, 1992.

Broadbent, James & Joy Hughes. Elizabeth Farm, Parramatta: A History and a Guide, Historic Houses Trust, 1984.

Broadbent, James, Suzanne Richard & Margaret Steven. *India, China, Australia: Trade and Society 1788-1850,* Historic Houses Trust of New South Wales, Sydney, 2003.

Brome, Vincent. *The Other Pepys,* Weidenfeld & Nicolson, London, 1992.

Bronowski, Jacob. *The Ascent of Man,* British Broadcasting Corporation, 1973.

Brook, J & J.L. Kohen. *The Parramatta Native Institution and the Black Town: A History,* New South Wales University Press, Kensington, 1991.

Brown. A.J., H.M. Sherrard and J.H. Shaw. An Introduction to Town and Country Planning, Angus & Robertson, Sydney, 1959 (1951).

Browning, Elizabeth Barrett. *Sonnets from the Portuguese,* introduction by Dorothy Hewlett, decorated by Reynolds Stone, Dante type, bound in silk, The Folio Society, London, 1962.

Brownlee, Walter. *The Navy that Beat Napoleon,* Cambridge University Press, Cambridge, London, 1980.

Brunton, Paul, ed. and intro. *Awake Bold Bligh! William Bligh's letters describing the mutiny on HMS Bounty,* Allen & Unwin, State Library of New South Wales, Sydney, 1989.

Bryson, Anna. "The Rhetoric of Status: Gesture, Demeanour and the Image of the Gentleman in Sixteenth-and-Seventeenth-Century England" in Gent & Llewellyn, ed.1990.

Buchan, William. *Domestic Medicine,* 8th edition, London, 1784 (1st edn.1769).

Buchan, William. *Domestic Medicine or the Family Physician...*The second American edition, 1774, privately printed for the members of The Classics of Medicine Library, Gryphon Editions, New York, 1993.

Bunyan, John. *The Pilgrim's Progress,* Hugh Ross Williamson, intro. Fount, *HarperCollins* Publishers, London, 1979 (I, 1678; II, 1684).

Burke, Edmund. *A Philosophical Enquiry into the Origin Of Our Ideas of the Sublime and Beautiful,* 2nd ed. 1759.
http://www.english.upenn.edu/~mgamer/Etexts/burkesublime.html

Burke, Edmund. *Reflections on the Revolution in France and on the Proceedings in Certain Societies in London Relative to that Event, 1790,* ed. & intro. Conor Cruise O'Brien, Penguin Books, London, 1986 (1790).

Burke, Peter. *The Art of Conversation,* Cornell University Press, Ithaca, New York, 1993.

Burke, Peter. *Celebrated Naval and Military Trials,* W.H. Allen & Coy, London, 1876.

Burnby, Juanita. 'An Examined and Free Apothecary' in Nutton & Porter, 1995.

Burnham, John C. "A History of Medical Practitioners and Historians as Writers of Medical History" in Individuals & Institutions in the History of Medicine, *OPMHA9*, ASHM, 1999.

Burnham, John C. "A Brief History of Medical Practitioners and Professional Historians as Writers of Medical History" in *Health and History: Bulletin of the Australian Society of the History of Medicine, v1: 4*: 1999.

Burnswoods, Jan & Jim Fletcher. *Sydney and the Bush: A pictorial History of Education in New South Wales*, NSW Department of Education, Sydney, 1980.

Butlin, S.J. *Foundations of the Australian Monetary System 1788-1851*, Sydney University Press, Sydney, 1968 (1953).

Bynum, W.F. "Nosology" in Bynum & Porter, 1997.

Bynum, W.F., Anne Hardy, Stephen Jacyna, Christopher Lawrence & E.M. Tansey. *The Western Medical Tradition 1800-2000*, Cambridge University Press, Cambridge, 2006.

Bynum, W.F. & Roy Porter. eds. *Companion Encyclopedia of the History of Medicine, vols.1 & 2*, Rutledge, London and New York, 1997 (1993).

Bynum, W.F. & Roy Porter. eds. *Medicine and the Five Senses*, Cambridge University Press, Cambridge, 1993.

Bynum, W.F. & Roy Porter. eds. *William Hunter and the Eighteenth-Century Medical World*, Cambridge, 1985.

Byrne, David. "The Royal Navy in Jane Austen's Lifetime 1775-1817", in *Sensibilities*, The Jane Austen Society of Australia, 10, 1995.

Byrne, H. memorial to Frederick Goulburn, 30 August 1822. NSW Col Sec In Letters mem. 1822, A+B no 37 p.1 CS Mem 5.

Byrne, Paula J. *Criminal Law and Colonial Subject: New South Wales, 1810-1830*, Cambridge University Press, Melbourne, 1993.

C

Cage, R.A. "The origins of poor relief in New South Wales, an account of the Benevolent Society, 1809-62" in *Australian Economic History Review*, 1980.

Calton Hill Burial Grounds. "New Calton Burial Ground" in *Calton Hill Conservation Plan,* Architectural Gazetteer, Appendix 7.00 (page 50), prepared for Edinburgh City Council, August 1999 [Accessible online].

Campbell, John. "Early Developments in Australian Obstetrics" in John Pearn ed., 1988.

Cantwell, Robert. *Alexander Wilson: Naturalist and Pioneer*, [includes a portrait, 8 colour plates of birds by Wilson, 16 b.w. ills. by the artist and decorations by Robert Ball], J. B. Lippincott Company, Philadelphia and New York, 1961.

Carlquist, Sherwin. *Island Life: A Natural History of the Islands of the World*, illustrated by the author, et al., American Museum of Natural History, The Natural History Press, New York, 1965.

Carpenter, Kenneth E. "Exploring New Vistas in History and Economics": *The Goldsmiths'-Kress Library of Economic Literature*, Published [Woodbridge, Conn.]: Research Publications [198-] No. 26. 33/3, State Library of NSW, Sydney.

Carpenter, Kenneth J. *The History of Scurvy and Vitamin C*, Cambridge University Press, New York, reprinted with corrections, 1987.

Carpenter, Kenneth J. "Nutritional Diseases" in Bynum & Porter. eds. 1997.

Carter, Harold B. *The Sheep and Wool Correspondence of Sir Joseph Banks 1781-1820*, The Library Council of New South Wales in Association with the British Museum (Natural History), London, 1979.

Carter, Paul. *The Road to Botany Bay: An Essay in Spatial History*, Faber & Faber, London, 1988.

Castles, Alex. *An Australian Legal History*. The Law Book Company, Sydney, 1982.

Cawte, John. *Healers of Arnhem Land*, UNSW Press, Sydney, 1996.

Cawte, John. *The Last of the Lunatics*, Melbourne University Press, Carlton South, 1998.

Cecil, David. *A Portrait of Charles Lamb*, Constable, London, 1983.

Chisholm, Alec H., ed. in chief, *The Australian Encyclopaedia, 10 vols*, Angus & Robertson, 1958.

Clark, C.M.H., *A History of Australia I: From the earliest times to the Age of Macquarie*, Melbourne University Press, Carlton, 1979.

Clark, Ralph. *The Journal and Letters of Lt. Ralph Clark 1787-1792*, Paul G. Fidlon & R.J. Ryan. eds. Australian Documents Library in association with LAH, Sydney, 1981.

Clark, Robert A. & J. Russell Elkinton. *The Quaker Heritage in Medicine*. The Boxwood Press, Pacific Grove, CA, 1986 (1978).

Clarke, Frank. 'The Reasons for the Settlement of Norfolk Island' in Nobbs, 1988.

Clifford, Harold Trevor. *Thomas Parmeter, Poetaster and Rhymist*, National Library of Australia Cataloguing-in-publication Entry, De Quiros Press, St Lucia, 1997.

Clayson, Christopher. 'William Cullen in eighteenth century medicine' in *William Cullen and the Eighteenth Century Medical World*, 1993.

Clune, Frank [& P.R. Stephensen]. *Bound for Botany Bay: Narrative of a Voyage in 1798 Aboard the Death Ship Hillsborough*, Angus & Robertson, Sydney, 1964.

Clune, Frank. *Rascals, Ruffians and Rebels of Early Australia*, Angus & Robertson, North Ryde, 1987.

Clune, Frank. *The Scottish Martyrs*, Angus & Robertson, Sydney, 1969.

Coats, Ann & Philip MacDougall. eds. *The 1797 Mutinies - Papers of the Spithead and Nore Bicentenary Conferences, 1997* [unpublished] in Rodger, 2006.

Cobbett, William. *Cobbett's England: A selection from the writings of William Cobbett*, ed. & intro. John Derry, engravings by James Gillray, The Folio Society, London, 1968.

Cobbett, William. *A French grammar; or, plain instructions for the learning of French. In a series of letters...*, Charles Clement, London, 1824.

Cobley, John. *The Crimes of the Lady Juliana Convicts - 1790.* 1989.

Cohen, Michele. *Fashioning Masculinity: national identity and language in the eighteenth century*, Routledge, London, 1996.

[Coleridge, Samuel Taylor]. *The Portable Coleridge*, ed with an introduction by I.A.Richards, Penguin Books, Harmondsworth, 1978.

Colley, Linda. *Britons: Forging the Nation 1707-1837*, Vintage, London, 1996; New Pimlico ed. 2003.

Colonial Secretary *Indents of Convict Ships 1801-1804*, 4/4004 COD 138.

Collins, David. *An Account of the English Colony in New South Wales, etc.*, vols I and II, London, 1798, reproduced by the Libraries Board of South Australia, Australiana Facsimile Editions No. 76, 1971.

Collins, Gillian. *Walter Bromley - An Enigmatic Reformer*, The British & Foreign School Society; online at http://www.bfss.org.uk.

Collins, Randall. "Emotional Energy as the Common Denominator of Rational Action" in *Rationality and Society*, Vol 5, No 2, 203-230 (1993) discussed in Berezin, 2005: 109, 124). Available on the internet.

Colonial Secretary, *Index to the Colonial Secretary's Papers, 1788-1825*, on line.

Colquhoun, Patrick. *Treatise on the Commerce and Police of the River Thames, 1796*, Rav/FM4/2 no. 18053, Goldsmiths Kress Library of Economic Literature,

Combe, William. *A History of Madeira*, Ackermann, London, 1821.

Comte, August. *Positive Philosophy, II*, in Coser, 1977.

Connelly, Frances, et al. *My Country is the Whole World: An Anthology of Women's Work*, Cambridge Women's Peace Collective, Pandora Press, London, 1984.

Conrad, Lawrence I. "Arab-Islamic Medicine" in Bynum & Porter, 1997.

Cook, James. *Journal during his First Voyage Round the World made in H.M. Bark, Endeavour 1768-71*, etc. Australian Facsimile Editions No 188, Libraries Board of South Australia, Adelaide, 1968.

Cook, James, 1728-1779. *"Captain Cook's journal during his first voyage round the world, made in H.M.Bark "Endeavour", 1768-71. A literal transcription of the original mss. with notes and introduction edited by Captain W.J.L. Wharton. London, Elliot Stock, 1893".* Australiana Facsimile Editions No. 188, Reproduced by the Libraries Board of South Australia from a copy held in the State Library of South Australia, Adelaide, Libraries Board of South Australia, 1968.

Cook, Tim, ed. and intro. *The Wordsworth Book of Restoration and Eighteenth-Century Verse*, Wordsworth Poetry Library, Wordsworth Editions Ltd, Ware, 1997.

Cooke, Terry S. Wills. *The Currency Lad: A Biography of Horatio Spencer Howe Wills. 1811-1861 and the Story of his immediate family 1797 to 1918, using contemporary letters, documents, daguerreotypes, paintings and photographs, 1997.* Online, 'Wills, Horatio Biography currency_lad.pdf (page 1 of 311)'.

Cooter, Roger. "War and Modern Medicine", Table I, in Bynum & Porter, 1997.

Corbin, Alain. *The Lure of the Sea: The Discovery of the Seaside in the Western World 1750 -1840*, translated by Jocelyn Phelps, Penguin Books, London, 1995.

Corbin, Alain. *The Foul & the Fragrant: Odour and the Social Imagination*, Papermac, Macmillan Publishers Ltd, London, 1996.

Cordingly, David. *Nicholas Pocock 1740-1821*, Conway Maritime Press in association with The National Maritime Museum, London, 1986.

Coser, Lewis A. *Masters of Sociological Thought: Ideas in Historical and Social Context*, 2 ed. Harcourt Brace Jovanovich, New York, 1977.

Court Martial. "Minutes of the proceedings of a court martial..." *PRO/ADM 1/534.* [Copy held by the History of Medicine Library, RACP, Sydney.]

Courtney, Nicholas. *Gale Force 10: The Life and Legacy of Admiral Beaufort 1774-1857*, Review, Headline Book Publishing, 2003.

Covacevich, Jeanette. et al. eds. *History, Heritage and Health, Proceedings of the Fourth Biennial Conference of the ASHM*, [containing] Papers presented at Norfolk Island, 2-9 July, 1995, *ASHM*, Brisbane, 1996.

Cowlishaw, L. "The First Fifty Years of Medicine in Australia", in *The Australian and New Zealand Journal of Surgery*, 1936.

Cowper, William. "Loss of the Royal George" [poem] in Tim Cook, ed. and intro. 1997.

Cox, Michael L. "Fingersmiths, Female Factories and the Famous", in Covacevich, et al. eds. 1996.

Cox, Philip & Wesley Stacey. *Building Norfolk Island*, Thomas Nelson, Australia, Ltd., Melbourne, 1971.

Craig, David. *Scottish Literature and the Scottish People 1680-1830*, Chatto & Windus. London, 1961.

Crawford, Catherine. "Medicine and the Law" in Bynum & Porter, 1997.

Crawford, Patricia. "Sexual Knowledge in England, 1500-1750", in Porter & Teich, 1994.

Crawford, Richard, ed. *Young & Free: Letters of Robert and Thomas Crawford 1821-1830*, Self-published, Macquarie, ACT, 1995.

Creese, Richard, W.F. Bynum and J. Bearn. eds. *The Health of Prisoners: Historical Essays*, Amsterdam-Atlanta, GA, 1995.

Crittenden, Victor. *The Voyage of the First Fleet 1787-1788*, Mulini Press, Canberra, 1981.

Croft, David. "Agriculture" in Marriott, 1998.

Crystal, David. *The Stories of English* [Title given in two typefaces: bold and regular], Allen Lane, an imprint of Penguin Books, London, 2004:5.

Cuffley, Peter, *Cottage Gardens in Australia*, The Five Mile Press, Hawthorn, Victoria, 1986.

Cullen, William. *The First Lines of the practice of Physic V1, volume I*, with notes by John Rotheram, M.D., Samuel Campbell, New York, 1793, facsimile edition printed by Kessinger Publishing Rare Reprints, 2007(?), [www.kessinger.net].

Cullen (1710-1790), William. in David Daiches, Peter Jones and Jean Jones. eds. *A Hotbed of Genius: The Scottish Enlightenment 1730-1790*, Edinburgh University Press, Edinburgh, 1986.

Cullen, William and the Eighteenth Century Medical World, A bicentenary exhibition and symposium arranged by the Royal College of Physicians of Edinburgh in 1990. A. Doig, J.P.S. Ferguson, I.A.Milne and R. Passmore. eds., Edinburgh University Press, 1993.

Cummins, C.J. "The Administration of Lunacy and Idiocy in N.S.W. 1788-1855", *Australian Studies in Health Service Administration, No.2,* School of Hospital Administration, The University of New South Wales, Kensington, 1968.

Cumpston, J.H.L. [intro. and ed. M.J.Lewis]. *Health and Disease in Australia, A History*, A.G.P.S., Canberra, 1989.

Cunningham, A.E. ed. *Patrick O'Brian: A Bibliography and Critical Appreciation*, British Library Publishing Division, 1994.

Cunningham, Peter and David S. Macmillan, ed. *Two Years in New South Wales*, Royal Australian Historical Society and Angus & Robertson, Sydney, 1966 (1827).

Cunnington, Cecil Willett and Phillis Cunnington. *The History of Underclothes*, Dover Publications, Inc., New York, 1992.

D

Daiches, David, Peter Jones, and Jean Jones. eds, for the Institute for Advanced Studies, *A Hotbed of Genius: The Scottish Enlightenment 1730-1790 (1986)*, Edinburgh University Press, Edinburgh, 1986.

Daiches, David. 'The Scottish Enlightenment' in David Daiches et al. 1986.

Damousi, Joy. Depraved and Disorderly: Female Convicts, Sexuality and Gender in Colonial Australia, Cambridge University Press, Cambridge, 1997.

Damousi, Joy. "The emotions of history" in Stuart Macintyre, ed. 2004.

Darwin, Charles. *The Expression of the Emotions in Man and Animals*, John Murray, London, 1872; Facsimile edition, Gryphon, New York, 1994.

Davidson, Basil. *The Story of Africa* [book of the television series AFRICA, a Mitchell Beazley Television-RM Arts Channel Four Television co-production in association with the Nigerian Television Authority], Rigby, 1984.

Davis, Natalie Zemon & Arlette Farge. eds. [Georges Duby & Michelle Perrot, eds for the whole] *A History of Women in the West, III. Renaissance and Enlightenment Paradoxes.* The Belknap Press, Harvard University Press, Cambridge, Massachusetts, 1994.

Defoe, Daniel. *The History of the Remarkable Life of John Sheppard (Large Print)*, The Echo Library, Cirencester, 2005.

Defoe, Daniel. with woodcuts by Peter Pendrey. *A Journal of the Plague Year: Being observations...* The Folio Society, London, 1960.

Defoe, Daniel. (P.N. Furbank et al. eds.) *A Tour through the Whole Island of Great Britain.* The Folio Society, London, 2006.

De Freycinet, Rose. *A Woman of Courage, The Journal of Rose de Freycinet on her Voyage around the World 1817-1820,* Translated and edited by Marc Serge Riviere, National Library of Australia, Canberra, 1996.

De Gouges, Olympe. *The Rights of Women* [Paris, 1791], trans. by Val Stevenson, Pythia Press, London, 1989.

De Moore, Greg. *Tom Wills: His Spectacular Rise and Tragic Fall,* Allen & Unwin, Crows Nest, NSW, 2008.

Dening, Greg. *Mr Bligh's Bad Language: Passion, Power and Theatre on the Bounty*, Cambridge University Press, Cambridge, 1993.

Desowitz, Robert. *Tropical Diseases from 50,000 BC to 2500 AD*, Flamingo, London, 1998.

De Volney, Constantin. *The Ruins: or, A Survey of the Revolutions of Empires*, translated from the French, fifth edition, to which is added The Law of Nature by the same author, J. Johnson, London, 1807.

De Volney, C. *The Ruins or Meditations on the Revolutions of Empires and The Law of Nature,* trans. Levrault, Paris *1802,* [now] in The Echo Library edition, Teddington, Middlesex, 2007.

De Vries, Susanna. Strength of Spirit: Pioneering Women of Achievement from First Fleet to Federation, Millennium Books, Alexandria, 1995.

De Vries-Evans, Susanna. *Pioneer Women, Pioneer Land. Yesterday's tall poppies*, Angus and Robertson, Sydney, 1987.

De Waal, Frans. "Joint Ventures Require Joint Payoffs: Fairness among Primates", in *Social Research*, vol73, no2, Summer 2006; Online accessed,

http://www.emory.edu/LIVING_LINKS/pdf_attachments/dewaal_socialresearch2006.pdf

Diamond, Jared. *Guns, Germs, and Steel: The Fates of Human Societies*, W.W. Norton, New York, 1997.

Diene, Doudou. ed. *From Chains to Bonds: The Slave Trade revisited,* UNESCO Publishing and Berghahn Books, Paris and New York, 2001.

Digby, Anne. *Making a medical living: Doctors and patients in the English market for medicine, 1720-1911,* Cambridge University Press, Cambridge, 1994.

Doig, Andrew. 'Dr Black, a Remarkable Physician' in *Joseph Black 1728-1799: A Commemorative Symposium,* 1982.

Doig, A., J.P.S. Ferguson, I.A. Milne and R. Passmore. eds. *William Cullen and the Eighteenth Century Medical World,* A bicentenary exhibition and symposium arranged by the Royal College of Physicians of Edinburgh in 1990, Edinburgh University Press, Edinburgh, 1993.

Donald, Beverley. *Hargrave Park? Never Heard of it: The story of a forgotten suburb,* Casula Powerhouse, Liverpool, 2007.

Dow, Gwyneth M. *Samuel Terry: The Botany Bay Rothschild,* Sydney University Press, Sydney, 1974.

Dow, Gwyneth M. "Terry, Samuel. (1776?-1838)" in *ADB2.*

Dudley, S. F. 1953, in "James Lind: Laudatory address", Proceedings Nutrition Society, 12:202-9, in Carpenter, 1987.

Dugan, James. *The Great Mutiny,* Andre Deutsch, London, 1966.

Dunlop, Norman J. "William Redfern, the First Australian Medical Graduate, and His Times", in *Journal and Proceedings,* RAHS, vol. XIV, part II, 1928.

Dyster, Barrie. *Servant & Master: Building and Running the Grand Houses of Sydney 1788-1850,* Historic Houses Trust, University of NSW Press, Sydney, 1989.

E

Earle, Augustus (1793-1838), in *ADBI.*

Earle, Augustus. *The Wandering Artist: Augustus Earle's Travels Around the World 1820-29,* A National Library of Australia Travelling Exhibition, Patricia R, McDonald, Curator, David Ellis, Exhibitions Manager, Andrew Rankine, Designer, 1994.

Earnshaw, John. "Thomas Muir, Scottish Martyr", [*Studies in Australian and Pacific History -No. 1,* General Editor - Walter W. Stone], The Stone Copying Company, Cremorne, N.S.W., 1959.

Eldershaw, M. Barnard. *Phillip of Australia.* The Discovery Press, Penrith, 1972 (1938).

Elias, Norbert. Van Krieken, Robert, Routledge, Abingdon, Oxon, 1998: Digital Printing 2007.

Elias, Norbert. "Studies on the Genesis of the Naval Profession", in *British Journal of Sociology,* 1950.

Elias, Norbert. Edited and with an introduction by René Moelker and Stephen Mennell, *The Genesis of the Naval Profession,* University College Dublin Press, 2007.

Elkinton, J. Russell. "Quakers in Medicine", in Robert A. Clark & J. Russell Elkinton, *The Quaker Heritage in Medicine,* The Boxwood Press, Pacific Grove, CA, [1978]1986.

Ellis, E.S. Foreword by T.K.Penniman. *Ancient Anodynes: Primitive Anaesthesia and Allied Conditions,* Wm. Heinemann, Medical Books Ltd, London, 1946.

Ellis, M.H. "The Foundation of Campbelltown, Some Casual Notes" in *Journal and Proceedings, Campbelltown and Airds Historical Society,* vol 1, no 1, 1948.

Ellis, M.H. *Francis Greenway.* The Discovery Press, 1972.

Ellis, M.H. *John Macarthur.* The Discovery Press, Penrith, 1972 (1955).

Ellis, M.H. *Lachlan Macquarie: His Life, Adventures and Times,* Angus & Robertson, Sydney, 1970.

Ellis, MH. *Letter to A.R. Jones.*

The Encyclopaedia Britannica: A Dictionary of Arts, Sciences, and General Literature, Ninth Edition, Volume I, Adam & Charles Black, Edinburgh,[1875]:291-416.

Emerson, Roger L. *Essays on David Hume, Medical Men and the Scottish Enlightenment, 'Industry, Knowledge and Humanity',* Ashgate Publishing Ltd, Farnham, Surrey, 2009.

Endersby, Jim. *A Guinea Pig's History of Biology,* Harvard University Press, Cambridge, Massachusetts, 2007.

Endersby, Jim. *Imperial Nature: Joseph Hooker and the Practices of Victorian Science,* University of Chicago Press, Chigaco, 2008.

Estensen, Miriam. *The Life of George Bass: Surgeon and sailor of the Enlightenment,* Allen & Unwin, Crows Nest, N.S.W., 2005.

Estensen, Miriam. *The Life of Matthew Flinders,* Allen & Unwin, Crows Nest, N.S.W., 2002.

Evans, Eric J. *The Forging of the Modern State: Early industrial Britain 1783-1870,* Longman, London, 1986 (1983).

Evans, George Ewart, ill by C.F. Tunnicliffe. *The Horse in the Furrow,* Faber & Faber, London, 1986 [1960].

Evans, Susanna. Historic Sydney as seen by its Early Artists, Doubleday Australia, Lane Cove, 1983.

Evatt, Herbert Vere. *Rum Rebellion, A Study of the Overthrow of Governor Bligh by John Macarthur and the New South Wales Corps...,* Angus & Robertson, Sydney, 1938.

F

Fara, Patricia. *The Story of Carl Linnaeus and Joseph Banks: Sex, Botany & Empire,* Icon Books, Cambridge, 2004.

Farley, Maree M. "Thomas Parmeter, Convict Doctor (c.1790-1836)", in *History, Heritage and Health: Proceedings of the Fourth Biennial Conference of the Australian Society of the History of Medicine,* 1996.

Faulkner, H.W. Locational Stress on Sydney's Metropolitan Fringe, A thesis submitted for the degree of Doctor of Philosophy, The Australian National University, Canberra, December, 1978.

Fenner, Frank. *Nature, Nurture and Chance: The Lives of Frank and Charles Fenner,* ANU E Press. The Australian National University, Canberra, 2006.

Fetter, Frank Whitson. *The Economist in Parliament 1780-1868,* Duke University Press, Durham, North Carolina, 1980.

Ferngren, Gary B. "The Evangelical-Fundamentalist Tradition", in Numbers & Amundsen, 1986.

Fidlon, Paul G. & R. J. Ryan. eds. *The Journal and Letters of Lt. Ralph Clark 1787-1792,* Australian Documents Library, in association with LAH, Sydney. 1981.

Fidlon, P.G. & R.J. Ryan. eds. *The Journal of Philip Gidley King: Lieutenant, R.N. 1787-1790,* Australian Documents Library, Sydney, 1980.

Fischer, Lewis R, Harald Hamre, Poul Holm, Jaap R. Bruijn eds. *The North Sea. Twelve Essays on Social History of Maritime Labour, Stavanger,* Norway, 1992.

Fisher, H.A.L. *A History of Europe* (complete edition in one volume), Edward Arnold & Co., London, 1946.

Fisher, John. "Origins and Early Development of the Veterinary Profession", (2002), in *Milestones in Australian Veterinary History,* on The Australian Veterinary History Society website, October, 2005.

Fisher, John. "Veterinary Surgeons in early New South Wales: a preliminary survey", in *The Australian Veterinary History Society Newsletter,* no. 8, Nov. 1993.

Fisher, Richard B. *Edward Jenner 1749-1823,* Andre Deutsch, London, 1991.

Fisher, Susanna. *The Makers of the Blueback Charts: A History of Imray, Laurie, Norie & Wilson Ltd,* Regatta Press Ltd, Ithaca, New York, 2001.

Fletcher, Brian H. "Foreword" in Flynn, 2001.

Fletcher, Brian H. *Landed Enterprise and Penal Society: A History of Farming and Grazing in New South Wales Before 1821,* Sydney University Press, Sydney, 1976.

Flinders, Matthew. Dr Stephen Murray-Smith, intro., T.M.Perry, discourse, Annette Macarthur-Onslow, ill. *A Biographical Tribute to the memory of Trim, Isle de France, 1809,* John Ferguson, Halstead Press, Sydney, 1985.

Flinders, Matthew. *A Voyage to Terra Australis...in the years 1801, 1802, and 1803...in His Majesty's Ship The Investigator ...etc. etc. Vol. I, G. & W. Nicol, London, 1814.* [Facsimile reprint, Libraries Board of South Australia, 1966.]

Flinders to Banks, [letter] 8 February 1801, ML, Sydney, mentioned in James D. Mack, Matthew Flinders, The Discovery Press, Penrith, 1976.

Flood, Josephine. *Archaeology of the Dreamtime,* Collins, Sydney, 1983.

Flood, Josephine. *The Moth Hunters, Aboriginal Prehistory of the Australian Alps,* Australian Institute of Aboriginal Studies, Canberra, 1980.

Flower, Cedric. *Duck and Cabbage Tree: A Pictorial History of Clothes in Australia 1788-1914,* Angus and Robertson, Sydney, 1968.

Flynn, Michael. *The Second Fleet: Britain's Grim Convict Armada of 1790.* LAH, Sydney, 2001.

Flynn, Michael. *Settlers and Seditionists: The People of the convict ship Surprise 1794*, Angela Lind, Sydney, 1994.

Fogarty, Ronald. *Catholic Education in Australia 1806-1950 vol I, Catholic Schools and the Denominational System*, Melbourne University Press, Melbourne, 1959.

Duncan Forbes. "Hume's Science of Politics" in G. P. Morice, ed. *David Hume: Bicentenary Papers*, [from a conference, to commemorate the bi-centenary of the death of David Hume, sponsored by the University of Edinburgh, in conjunction with its Institute for Advanced Studies in the Humanities] The University Press, Edinburgh, 1977.

Ford, Edward. "The Life and Work of William Redfern", *Bulletin of the Post-Graduate Committee in Medicine*, University of Sydney, Australasian Medical Publishing Co. Ltd., Glebe, Sydney, 1953.

Ford, Edward. *Thomas Jamison and the Beginning of Medical Journalism in Australia*, Australasian Medical Publishing Company, Glebe, 1954.

Ford, Edward. "Medical Practice in Early Sydney..." in MJA, II, 9 July 1955.

Ford, Edward. "The Charles Mackay Lecture", *Medical Practice in Early Sydney: With special reference to the work and influence of John White, William Redfern and William Bland*, Australasian Medical Publishing Company Ltd, Sydney, 1955.

Ford, Edward. *Bibliography of Australian Medicine, 1790-1900*, Sydney University Press, 1976.

Ford, Edward. "Retirement of Professor Sir Edward Ford" [author, a colleague] in *The Gazette*, University of Sydney, vol 2, no 4:214-5, 1967.

Foreman, Amanda. *Georgina: Duchess of Devonshire*, HarperCollins, London, 1999.

Foreman, Laura & Ellen Blue Phillips. *Napoleon's Lost Fleet: Bonaparte, Nelson, and the Battle of the Nile*, Discovery Communications Inc., London, 1999.

Forster, Frank M.C. "Dr William Smellie and His Contribution to Obstetrics", in *The Australian and New Zealand Journal of Obstetrics and Gynaecology*, Vol. 3, No. 3 - September 1963.

Forster, Frank M.C. *Progress in Obstetrics and Gynaecology in Australia*, John Sands Pty Ltd, Sydney, 1967.

Forster, Frank M.C. "Midwifery and Gynaecological Care in the Early Years of Settlement", in *Progress in Obstetrics and Gynaecology in Australia*, John Sands Pty Ltd, Sydney, 1967.

Fosdick, Harry Emerson. *A Guide to Understanding the Bible: The Development of Ideas within the Old and New Testaments*, Student Christian Movement Press, London, 1938.

Foster, A.G. "The Sandhills, an Historic Cemetery", *Journal of the Royal Australian Historical Society*, 1919.

Foster, William C. *Sir Thomas Livingston Mitchell and his world, 1792-1855*, Institution of Surveyors, NSW, Sydney, 1985.

Foucault, Michael. "The Politics of Health in the Eighteenth Century", in *The Foucault Reader*, Paul Rabinow, ed. Pantheon Books, New York, 1984.

Foveaux, J. Letter book. *A1444*:42. ML, Sydney.

Foveaux, J. "Certificate" in W. Redfern, "Memorial to Governor Macquarie: 1810. The Memorial gave reasons for the grant as non-payment on Norfolk Island for his work with the military and loss of property on leaving the Island. 4/1827 CS mdms no. 271

Fraser, Antonia. Charles II: His Life and Times, Weidenfeld & Nicolson, London, 1993a.

Fraser, Antonia. *The Weaker Vessel: Woman's lot in seventeenth-century England*, Mandarin, London, 1993.

Fridriksson, Sturla. *Surtsey, Evolution of life on a Volcanic Island*, A Halstead Press Book, John Wiley & Sons, New York, 1975.

Frost, Alan. *Arthur Phillip 1738-1814: His Voyaging*, Oxford University Press, Melbourne, 1987.

Frost, Alan. *Botany Bay Mirages: Illusions of Australia's Convict Beginnings*, Melbourne Univ Press, Carlton, 1994.

G

Gandevia, Bryan. "Health and Disease at Botany Bay", in D. J. Anderson, ed. *The Botany Bay Project*, [title and publishers], [Sydney], 1973.

Gandevia, Bryan. "No History Without Health", in Home, 1983.

Gandevia, Bryan. *The Sir Edward Ford Bequest*, History of Medicine Library, RACP, 1987.

Gandevia, Bryan. "Socio-Medical Factors in the Evolution of the First Settlement at Sydney Cove 1788-1803"[Based on a paper read before the Society 29 January 1974], in *Journal & Proceedings*, RAHS, Vol.61 Pt 1, March, 1975.

Gandevia, Bryan, Alison Holster & Sheila Simpson. *An Annotated Bibliography of the History of Medicine and Health in Australia*, RACP, Sydney, 1984.

Gandevia, Bryan & John Cobley. "Mortality at Sydney Cove, 1788-1792", in *Australian and New Zealand Journal of Medicine*, 1974.

Gandevia, Bryan. with the research assistance of Sheila Simpson, *Tears often Shed: Child Health and Welfare in Australia from 1788*, Pergamon Press, Rushcutters Bay, 1978.

Garneray, Louis. Translated from the French with foreword and notes by Richard Rose. *The Floating Prison: The remarkable account of nine years' captivity on the British Prison Hulks during the Napoleonic Wars: 1806 to 1814,* Conway Maritime Press, London, 2003.

Garran, J.C. & L. White. *Merinos, myths and Macarthurs: Australian graziers and their sheep, 1788-1900,* A.N.U. Press, 1985.

Gascoigne, John. *Joseph Banks and the English Enlightenment: Useful Knowledge and Polite Culture,* Cambridge University Press, Cambridge, 1994.

Gatrell, V.A.C. *The Hanging Tree: Execution and the English People 1770-1868,* Oxford University Press, Oxford, 1996.

Gelbart, Nina Rattner. "Female Journalists" in Davis & Farge, eds. 1994.

Gelbart, Nina Rattner. *The King's Midwife: A History and Mystery of Madame du Coudray,* University of California Press, Berkeley and Los Angeles, California, 1998.

Genealogical Research Directory, see Johnson, Keith A. & Malcolm R. Sainty.

Gent, Lucy & Nigel Llewellyn. eds. *Renaissance Bodies: The Human Figure in English Culture c. 1530-1660,* Reaktion Books, London, 1990.

George, Dorothy. *England in Transition: Life and Work in the Eighteenth Century,* Penguin Books, London, 1953 [1931].

Gerth, H.H. & C.Wright Mills. *From Max Weber: Essays in Sociology,* trans., ed. and intro. by Gerth & Mills, Routledge & Kegan Paul, London, 1977.

Gesner, Peter. "The Pandora project: reviewing genesis and rationale" in The Bulletin of the Australian Institute for Maritime Archaeology, 12, 1, 1988.

Gesner, Peter. "Situation report: HMS Pandora", in *Bulletin Australian Institute for Maritime Archaeology,* 14, 2, 1990.

Gill, Conrad. The Naval Mutinies of 1797..., University of Manchester Publications, Manchester, 1913.

Gilmour, Ian. Riot, Risings and Revolution: Governance and Violence in Eighteenth Century England, Pimlico, London, 1993.

Gittins, Ross. "Yes, you can legislate for morality", in *The Sydney Morning Herald,* "Monday Comment", August 26, 2002.

Goddard, Jonathan Charles. 'The navy surgeon's chest: surgical instruments of the Royal Navy during the Napoleonic War' in *Journal of the Royal Society of Medicine,* Volume 97, April 2004:191-197;

http://www.ncbi.nlm.nih.gov/pmc/articles/PMC1079363/pdf/0970191.pdf, accessed on line 25 July 2012.

Godwin, Sir Harry. *Fenland: its ancient past and uncertain future*, Cambridge University Press, Cambridge, 1978.

Goldsmid, John Marsden. *The Deadly Legacy: Australian History and Transmissible Disease*, NSW University Press in association with the Australian Institute of Biology, Kensington, NSW, 1988.

Goldsmiths'-Kress library of economic literature: microfilm, State Library of NSW, Sydney, see Carpenter, Kenneth E.

Goodin, V.W.E. "Reddall, Thomas (1780-1838)" in *A.D.B.2*: 1788-1850.

Gordon, Douglas. *Medical Journal of Australia, 2*, 1963 in J.G.Steele, Appendix I, 1975.

Gould, Rupert T. *John Harrison and his Timekeepers*, National Maritime Museum, London, 1978. (Reprinted from *The Mariner's Mirror*, Vol. XXI, No.2, April 1935.)

Grant, Jacqueline. Sarah Grant, ed. *Providence, The Life and Times of John Grant 1792-1866*, self-published, Orange, 1994.

Green, H. M. *A History of Australian Literature, Volume 1*, Angus & Robertson, 1961.

Griffiths, David Clyde. selected and edited. *Documents on the Establishment of Education in New South Wales 1789-1880.* Australian Council for Educational Research, Melbourne, 1957.

Griffiths, Geoff and Terry Cass. *Campbellfield, A Heritage Study*, for the Ministerial Development Corporation, N.S.W. Government, 1996.

Grogan, R.S. "Diseases and Casualties of the Kokoda Buna Campaigns" in *OPMHA 7*, 1996

Guelke, Leonard. *Historical Understanding in Geography: An idealist approach,* Cambridge University Press, Cambridge, 1982.

Guerini, Vincenzo. A *History of Dentistry: from the Most Ancient Times until the End of the Eighteenth Century,* Philadelphia and New York, Lea and Febiger, 1909.

Guest, James. "Frederic Wood Jones..." in "The Impact of the Past upon the Present", *OPMHA 5*, Perth, 1991:186.

Gunson, Niel. *Messengers of Grace: Evangelical Missionaries in the South Seas*, Melbourne/New York, Oxford University Press, 1978.

Gunson, Niel. 'British Missionaries and Their Contribution to Science in the Pacific Islands' in MacLeod and Rehbock, eds.1994.

Gunson, Niel. "Cover, James Fleet & Henry, William", in *ADBI.*

Gunson, N. "Crook, William Pascoe", in *ADBI.*

Gunson, N. "Elder, James (1772-1836)"

Gunson, N. "Williams, John (1796-1839)", in *ADB2.*

H

Hagger, Jennifer Therese. *Australian Colonial Medicine,* Rigby, Adelaide, 1979.

Halliday, R.W. and A.O. Watson. ed. *A History of Dentistry in New South Wales 1788-1945,* Australian Dental Association (NSW Branch), Sydney, 1977.

Hamblyn, Richard. *The Invention of Clouds: How an Amateur Meteorologist Forged the Language of the Skies,* Picador, 2001.

Hamilton, James. *Faraday: The Life,* HarperCollins, London, 2003.

Hammond, J.L. & Barbara Hammond. John Rule, ed. *The Skilled Labourer,* Longman, London and New York, 1979.

Hammond, J.L. & Barbara Hammond. *The Village Labourer Vols I & II,* Guild Books. The British Publishers Guild, Longmans, Green, London, 1948 (1911).

Hancock, W.K. *Professing History,* Sydney University Press, Sydney, 1976.

Hannaway, Caroline. "Environment and Miasmata", in Bynum & Porter, *I,* 1976.

Hardy, John & Alan Frost. *Studies from Terra Australis to Australia,* Australian Academy of the Humanities, Canberra, 1989.

Harrison, John. Jonathan Betts. National Maritime Museum, Greenwich, 3rd ed. 1997.

Harte, Negley and John North. *The World of University College London: 1828-1990,* University College, London, 1978 (1991).

Harte, Negley. *The University of London 1836-1986, an illustrated history,* The Athlone Press, London, 1986.

Hartley, L.P. *The Go-Between,* Readers Union, Hamish Hamilton, London, 1954.

Hartley, L.P. *The Go-Between,* Penguin Books in association with Hamish Hamilton, Harmondsworth, 1958.

Haughton, Hugh. "Progress and Rhyme" in Hugh Haughton, Adam Phillips & Geoffrey Summerfield. eds. *John Clare in Context,* Cambridge University Press, Cambridge, 1994,

Hawkes, Jacquetta. *A Land,* David & Charles, London, 1978 (1951).

Hawkins, Ralph. *Convict Timbergetters of Pennant Hills,* Hornsby Shire Historical Society, 1994:133.

Hay, Douglas et al. *Albion's Fatal Tree: Crime and Society in Eighteenth-Century England,* Pantheon Books, New York, 1975.

Hay, Douglas. "Poaching and the Game Laws on Cannock Chase", in Hay et al. 1975.

Henderson, Ronald F. *Australian Government Commission of Inquiry into Poverty, First Main Report*, Australian Government Publishing Service, Canberra, April 1975.

Henderson, Graeme. *Maritime Archaeology in Australia*, University of Western Australia Press, Nedlands, 1986.

Henderson, Graeme & Myra Stanbury. *The Sirius, Past and Present*, Collins, Sydney, 1988.

Herbert, Chris. *The Geology and Resource Potential of the Wianamatta Group*, Bulletin No.25, Department of Mineral Resources and Development, Geological Survey of New South Wales, Sydney, 1979 (manuscript dated 1976).

Herda, Phyllis. et al. eds, *Vision and Reality in Pacific Religion: Essays in Honour of Niel Gunson*, Macmillan Brown Centre for Pacific Studies and Pandanus, Books, A.N.U., Canberra, 2005.

Herman, Arthur. *The Scottish Enlightenment: The Scots' Invention of the Modern World*, Fourth Estate, London, 2003.

Herman John. *Painted Panorama 1800-1870*, Paintings from the Mitchell and Dixson Collections of the State Library of New South Wales, exhibited at The Blaxland Gallery, in commemoration of Grace Brothers' Centenary, 1885-1985, catalogue published 1985.

Hermes, Neil. *Birds of Norfolk Island*, Wonderland Publications, Norfolk Island, 1985.

Hibbert, Christopher. *Nelson, A Personal History*, Viking (Penguin), London, 1994.

Hill, Christopher. *Change and Continuity in Seventeenth-Century England*, London, Weidenfeld and Nicolson, 1974.

Hill, Christopher. *Some Intellectual Consequences of the English Revolution* [A Curti Lecture]. The University of Wisconsin Press, Madison, 1980.

Hill, Christopher. *Liberty Against the Law: Some Seventeenth-century Controversies*, Allen Lane, The Penguin Press, London, 1996.

Hill, Christopher. *The World Turned Upside Down: Radical Ideas During the English Revolution,* Penguin Books, London, 1991(1972).

Hill, Stephen. *The Tragedy of Technology: Human Liberation Versus Domination in the Late Twentieth Century*, Pluto Press, London, 1988.

Historic Buildings, Parramatta. Helen Baker, compiler. Presenting six interesting examples of Colonial Architecture at Parramatta, Vol I, Cumberland County Council, 1961.

Historic Buildings, Central Area of Sydney, Vol II, Cumberland County Council, 1962.

Historic Buildings, Windsor and Richmond. Helen Baker, writer, Rachel Roxburgh, research. State Planning Authority of NSW, 1967.

Hoare, Merval. *The Discovery of Norfolk Island,* Australian Government Publishing Service, Canberra, 1974.

Hoare, Merval, "The Island's Earliest Visitors", in Nobbs, ed., 1988.

Hobbes, Thomas. *Leviathan,* Dent: London and Melbourne, 1983[1651].

Hobsbawm, Eric J. *The Age of Revolution 1789-1848,* A Mentor Book, New York, 1962.

Hobsbawm, Eric J, *Nations and Nationalism since 1780,* Cambridge, 1990.

Hobsbawm, Eric & George Rudé, *Captain Swing,* Phoenix Press, London, 2001[1969].

Holden, Robert. *Orphans of History: The Forgotten Children of the First Fleet.* The Text Publishing Company, Melbourne, 1999.

Holder, R.F. *Bank of New South Wales: A History, vol 1*:1817-1893, Angus & Robertson, Sydney, 1970.

Holland, Francis Ross. Jr. *America's Lighthouses: An Illustrated History,* Dover Publications Inc, New York, 1988 (1972).

Holmes, Richard. *The Age of Wonder: How the Romantic Generation discovered the Beauty and Terror of Science,* Harper Press, London, 2008.

Holmes, Richard. *Coleridge, Early Visions,* Flamingo, HarperCollins, 1999.

Holmes, Richard. *Footsteps: Adventures of a Romantic Biographer,* Penguin Books, Harmondsworth, 1985.

Holmes, Richard. *Sidetracks: Explorations of a Romantic Biographer,* Harper Collins Publishers, London, 2000.

Holmes, Richard, ed. *Mary Wollstonecraft, A Short Residence in Sweden, Norway and Denmark,* and William Godwin, *Memoirs of the Author of 'The Rights of Woman',* Penguin Books, 1987.

Holmes, Richard. *Shelley The Pursuit,* New York Review Books, New York, 1994 [1974].

Holmes, Richard. *Wellington, The Iron Duke,* HarperCollins, Hammersmith, 2003.

Home, R.W. *Science Under Scrutiny,* D. Reidel Publishing Company, Lancaster, 1983.

Hoorn, Jeanette. *Australian Pastoral, the Making of a White Landscape,* Fremantle Arts Centre Press, Fremantle, 2007.

Hooper, Judith. *Of Moths and Men: An Evolutionary Tale.The untold story of science and the Peppered Moth,* W.W. Norton & Company, New York, 2002.

Hopkins, Eric. *Industrialisation and Society: A Social History, 1830-1951,*Routledge, London, 2000.

Hoskins, William George. *English Landscapes,* British Broadcasting Corporation, London, 1976.

Hoskins, William George. *The Making of the English Landscape,* Penguin Books, Harmondsworth, 1978 (1955).

Hoskins, William George. Introduction by Keith Thomas. *The Making of the English Landscape.* The Folio Society, London, 2005.

Howse, Derek. *Greenwich time, and the discovery of the longitude,* Oxford University Press, Oxford, 1980. [Gift of Frank McNeale.]

Hughes, Robert. *The Fatal Shore: A History of the Transportation of Convicts to Australia, 1787-1968,* Collins Harvill, London, 1987.

Hugill, Stan. *Sea Shanties,* with drawings by the author [photographs courtesy The National Maritime Museum, London; and words and music], Barrie & Jenkins, London, 1977.

Huisman, Frank & John Harley Warner. eds. *Locating Medical History: The Stories and Their Meanings,* The Johns Hopkins University Press, Baltimore and London, 2004.

Hume, David. *Enquiries Concerning Human Understanding and Concerning the Principles of Morals,* [Reprinted from the Posthumous edition of 1777 and edited with Introduction, Comparative Table of Contents, and Analytical Index by L.A.Selby-Bigge] Third Edition with text revised and notes by P.H.Nidditch, [Open University Set Book], Clarendon Press, Oxford, 1988 (1975).

Hume, David. *A Treatise of Human Nature,* Edited, with an Analytical Index, by L.A.Selby-Bigge, Second Edition with text revised and variant readings by P.H.Nidditch, Clarendon Press, Oxford, 1978 (1888).

Hume, David. *A Treatise of Human Nature,* [sourced to the three volumes published in London, 1739-1740] Dover Publications, New York, 2003.

Hume, David. An introductory note by John B. Stewart. *An Enquiry Concerning the Principles of Morals,* [Reprinted from the edition of 1777] Open Court Publishing, Chicago, 1966.

Hume, David. *Bicentenary Papers,* G. P. Morice, ed. [from a conference, to commemorate the bi-centenary of the death of David Hume, sponsored by the University of Edinburgh, in conjunction with its Institute for Advanced Studies in the Humanities] The University Press, Edinburgh, 1977.

Hunter, Clark. ed. *The Life and Letters of Alexander Wilson,* American Philosophical Society, Independence Square, Philadelphia, 1983.

Hunter, Ernest. "Back to Redfern: Autonomy and the 'Middle E' in relation to Aboriginal health", *An AIATSIS Research Discussion Paper,* Number 18, July 2006, Australian Institute of Aboriginal and Torres Strait Islander Studies, Canberra, 2006.

Hutton, James. G.Y. Craig and J.H. Hull. eds. *James Hutton - Present and Future*, The Geological Society, London, 1999.

Hutton, James, Donald B. McIntyre and Alan McKirdy. *James Hutton: The Founder of Modern Geology* (1726-97), The Stationery Office, Ltd., 1997 (the bicentennial of Hutton's death).

I

Ihde, Erin. *A Manifesto for New South Wales: Edward Smith Hall and the Sydney Monitor 1826-1840*, Australian Scholarly, Melbourne, 2004.

Irvine, Nance, ed. *Dear Cousin: The Reibey Letters, Twenty-two letters of Mary Reibey, her children and their descendants, 1792-1901*, Janet Press, Sydney, 1995.

Irvine, Nance. ed. and with commentary. *Mary Reibey, Molly Incognita, 1777 to 1855, and Her World*, LAH, North Sydney, 1982.

Irvine, Nance. ed. and with commentary. *The Sirius Letters: The Complete Letters of Newton Fowell, Midshipman & Lieutenant aboard The* Sirius, *Flagship of the First Fleet on its Voyage to New South Wales*, The Fairfax Library, Sydney, 1988.

Isaacs, Jennifer. comp. & ed. *Australian Dreaming, 40,000 Years of Aboriginal History*, Lansdowne Press, Sydney, 1987.

Isaacs, Jennifer. *Bush Food: Aboriginal food and herbal medicine*, 1987.

J

Jack, Sybil M. "Why the status of the midwife declined and male accouchers came to dominate childbirth from the seventeenth century in Europe: some suggestions", in Individuals & Institutions in the History of Medicine, Proceedings of the 6th Biennial Conference of ASHM, *OPMHA 9*, Sydney, 1999. [Papers ordered by author surname.]

Jackson, Christine E. *Bird Etchings, The Illustrators and Their Books 1655-1855*, Cornell University Press, Ithaca and London, 1989.

Jackson, E. Sandford. "Henry Cowper, Surgeon, and His Times", in *Transactions of the Third Medical Congress* (British Medical Association), 1929. and J.G.Steele, *Brisbane Town in Convict Days 1824-1842*, University of Queensland Press, Queensland, 1975. This last has a copy of Gordon's *M.J.A.* article as "Appendix 1".

Jacyna, Stephen. "Medicine in transformation, 1800-1849" in Bynum et al., 2006.

James, C.R.L. *The Black Jacobins: Toussaint L'Ouverture and the San Domingo Revolution.* A Vintage Book, 1963.

James, William. *The Naval History of Great Britain: From the declaration of war by France in 1793 to the Accession of George IV, Vol II,* A new edition to 1827 in six volumes, London, 1886.

Jamison, Thomas. "General observations on the smallpox", *Sydney Gazette,* 14 October 1804.

Jenkyn, Thomas, W. ed. *A Book of English Prose,* Thomas Nelson and Sons, London, 1909.

Jenner, Edward. *An Inquiry into the Causes and Effects of the Variolae Vaccinae, a Disease Discovered in some of the Western Counties of England particularly Gloucestershire and known by the name of the Cow Pox,* Printed for the Author, London, 1798.

Jenner, Edward. *The Note-book of Edward Jenner,* in the possession of the Royal College of Physicians of London, with *an Introduction on Jenner's work as a Naturalist* by F.Dawtrey Drewitt, Oxford University Press, London, 1931.

Jennings, Charles. *Greenwich: The Place Where Days Begin and End,* Little, Brown and Company, London, 1999.

Jinks, Catherine. *The gentleman's garden,* Allen&Unwin, Crows Nest, NSW, 2002.

Johnson, Keith A. & Malcolm R. Sainty. eds. *Genealogical Research Directory,* North Sydney, 1991.

Johnston, George. *A Charge of Mutiny: The Court Martial of Lieutenant Colonel George Johnston for deposing Governor William Bligh in the Rebellion of 26 January 1808,* introduced by John Ritchie, National Library of Australia, Canberra, 1988.

Johnstone, R.W. *William Smellie: The Master of British Midwifery,* E. & S. Livingstone Ltd., Edinburgh, 1952.

Jones, A. "Mutinies, Small and Great", in Pearn, J., Carter, P. & Phillips, G.E., eds. *Programme and Abstracts* (1995:95), [for] Mutiny and Medicine: An International Conference on the History of Medicine 1995, ASHM, 1995.

Jones, Arthur R. "William Redfern (1775?-1833), Mutineer to Colonial Surgeon in New South Wales", [in two parts] *Journal of Medical Biography,* 1999; Part I, 7: 35-41 and Part II, 7: 78-85, The Royal Society of Medicine Press Ltd, London.

Jones, Arthur R. "Surgeon William Redfern in London and Edinburgh (1828-1883?) *Journal of the Royal Australian Historical Society,* 2017; Vol. 103 Part 2, pp 201-211.

Jones, Colin. "Charity Before c.1850" in Bynum & Porter, 1997.

Jones, David J. *A Source of Inspiration & Delight: The Buildings of the State Library of New South Wales since 1826*, Library Council of N.S.W., Sydney, 1988.

Jones, Owen. ed. and contributor, "The Principal in Retrospect and Today", in *The School Principal: A Symposium*, F.W. Cheshire, Melbourne, 1962.

Jones, Peter. 'The aesthetics of Adam Smith' in P. Jones and Andrew S. Skinner, *Adam Smith Reviewed*, 1992.

Jordanova, Ludmilla J. "Guarding the Body Politic: Volney's Catechism of 1793", in Barker et al. 1789.

Jordanova, Ludmilla. *Nature Displayed: Gender, Science and Medicine 1760-1820*, Addison Wesley Longman, London and New York, 1999 edition; digitally printed on demand in 2012.

K

Kass, Amalie M. "The Obstetrical Casebook of Walter Channing1811-1822", *Bulletin of the History of Medicine*, 1993.

Kass, Terry. *Sails to Satellites: The Surveyors General of NSW (1786-2007)*, NSW Department of Lands, Bathurst, 2008.

Karskens, Grace. *The Rocks: Life in Early Sydney*, Melbourne University Press, Carlton, Victoria, 1997.

Kartzoff, M. *Nature and a City: The Native Vegetation of the Sydney Area*, Edwards & Shaw, Sydney, 1969.

Kastner, Joseph. Text by J.K., commentaries by Miriam T. Gross. *The Bird Illustrated, 1550-1900*; From the Collections of the New York Public Library, Introduction by Roger Tory Peterson, Harry N. Abrams, Inc. New York, 1988.

Kastner, Joseph. *A World of Naturalists*, John Murray, London, 1978.

Keane, John. *Tom Paine: A Political Life*, Bloomsbury, London, 1995.

Kemp, Peter. *The British sailor: A social history of the lower deck*, J. M. Dent & Sons Ltd, London, 1970.

Kenny, M.J.B. "Hall, Edward Smith (1786-1860)" in *ADBI*.

Kent, David & Norma Townsend. *The Convicts of the Eleanor: Protest in Rural England New Lives in Australia*. The Merlin Press, Pluto Press Australia, 2002.

Kent, David & Norma Townsend. eds. *Joseph Mason: Assigned Convict 1831-1837*, Melbourne University Press, Carlton South, 1996.

Kercher, Bruce. *An Unruly Child: A History of Law in Australia*, 1995.

Kercher, Bruce. Perish or Prosper: The Law and Convict Transportation in the British Empire, 1700-1850, *Law and History Review* 21.3 (2003: 154 pars. 4 Jan 2006.

http://www.historycooperative.org/journals/1he/21/3/forum_kercher.html.

Kenyon, J.P. *Stuart England*, in the series, "Pelican History of England", Harmondsworth, 1982 (1978).

Keynes, Geoffrey. ed. *Blake, Complete Writings with variant readings*, Oxford University Press, Oxford, 1971.

Keynes, Randal. *Annie's Box: Charles Darwin, his daughter and Human Evolution*, Fourth Estate, London, 2001.

King, Charles James. "The First Fifty Years of Agriculture in New South Wales" in the *Review of Marketing and Agricultural Economics*, 1948.

King, Hazel. *Colonial Expatriates: Edward and John Macarthur Junior*, Kangaroo Press, Kenthurst, NSW, 1989.

King, Hazel. "Pulling Strings at the Colonial Office", in Journal and Proceedings, RAHS vol 61, pt. 3 September 1975.

King, Philip Gidley. *The Journal of Philip Gidley King: Lieutenant, R.N. 1787-1790*, Paul G. Fidlon & R.J.Ryan, eds, Australian Documents Library, Sydney, 1980

Kirkham, Margaret. *Jane Austen, Feminism and Fiction*. The Athlone Press, London, 1997.

Knight, Frank. The Clipper Ship, Collins, St James's Place, London, 1973. [Donated Frank McNeale].

Knight, Roger. "The First Fleet: Its States and Preparation, 1786-1787" in Hardy & Frost, 1989.

Kociumbas, Jan. *The Oxford History of Australia*, Volume 2 1770-1860 Possessions, Oxford Univ Press, Melbourne, 1992.

Kociumbas, Jan. *Australian Childhood: A History*, Allen & Unwin, St Leonards, 1997:

Kowaleski-Wallace, Elizabeth. *Consuming Subjects: Women, Shopping, and Business in the Eighteenth Century*, Columbia University Press, New York, 1997.

Kramnick, Isaac. "English Middle-Class Radicalism in the Eighteenth Century" in Literature of Liberty, Vol. 3, No. 2: Summer, 1980, [The Online Library of Liberty].

L

Lacour-Gayet, Robert, James Grieve. translation. *A Concise History of Australia,* Penguin Books,

Harmondsworth, 1976.

Lau, D.C. trans. and introduction. *Confucius: The Analects Lun Yu.* The Folio Society, London, 2008.

Laugesen, Amanda. *Convict Words: Language in Early Colonial Australia,* Oxford University Press, South Melbourne, 2002.

Laut, Peter. *Agricultural Geography: Vol.2 - Mid-latitude Commercial,* Thomas Nelson, Melbourne, 1970 (1969):

Lawrence, Christopher. *Medicine in the Making of Modern Britain, 1700-1920,* Routledge, London and New York, 1994.

Lawrence, C.J. "William Buchan: medicine laid open" in *Medical History,* 1975.

Lawrence, Ghislaine. "Surgery (Traditional)" ["Operative Surgery to 1800"], in Bynum & Porter, 1997.

Lawrence, Susan C. "Entrepreneurs and Private Enterprise: The Development of Medical Lecturing in London, 1775-1820", *Bulletin of the History of Medicine,* LXII, 1988.

Lawrence, Susan. "Anatomy and Address: Creating Medical Gentlemen in Eighteenth-Century London", in Nutton & Porter, eds., 1995.

Lavery, Brian. *Nelson's Navy: the ships, men and organisation 1793-1815,* Conway Maritime Press Ltd, London, 1995(1989).

Lavery, Brian. *Nelson's Navy: The Ships, Men and Organisation 1793-1815,* Naval Institute Press, Maryland [USA], 1995 (1994).

Leavitt, Judith Walzer. *Brought to Bed: Childbearing in America 1750 to 1950,* Oxford University Press, New York, 1986.

LeFanu, W.R. *A Bio-bibliography of Edward Jenner 1749-1823,* Harvey & Blythe, Ltd, London, 1951.

Leopold, Aldo. *A Sand Country Almanac and Sketches Here and There,* Oxford University Press, Oxford [New York], 1987[1949].

Leapman, Michael. *The Ingenious Mr Fairchild: The Forgotten Father of the Flower Garden,* Headline Book Publishing, London, 2000.

Leavitt, Judith Walzer. *Brought to Bed: Childbearing in America 1750 to 1950,* Oxford University Press, New York, 1986.

Levere, Trevor H. *Transforming Matter: A History of Chemistry from Alchemy to the Buckyball.* The Johns Hopkins University Press, Baltimore and London, 2001.

Lewis, Michael. *A Social History of the Navy 1793-1815,* Ruskin House, George Allen & Unwin Ltd, London, 1960.

Lewis, Milton J. intro. and ed. Cumpston, J.H.L. *Health and Disease in Australia, A History*, A.G.P.S., Canberra, 1989.

Lewis, Milton J. "Introduction", in Individuals & Institutions in the History of Medicine..., *OPMHA8*, ASHM, 1999.

Lewis, Milton. *Thorns on the Rose: The History of Sexually Transmitted Diseases in Australia in International Perspective*, Australian Government Publishing Service, Canberra, 1998.

Lind, James. *An Essay on the Most Effective Means of Preserving the Health of Seamen in the Royal Navy and a Dissertation on Fevers and Infections together with Observations on the Jail Distemper and the proper means of preventing and stopping its infection*, printed for J. Murray, London, 1779.

Lindemann, Mary. *Medicine and Society in Early Modern Europe*, Cambridge University Press, Cambridge, 1999.

Linebaugh, Peter. *The London Hanged: Crime and Civil Society in the Eighteenth Century*, Penguin Books, Harmondsworth, 1993.

Linebaugh, Peter & Marcus Rediker. *The Many-Headed Hydra: Sailors, Slaves, Commoners, and the Hidden History of the Revolutionary Atlantic*, Beacon Press, Boston, 2000.

Linebaugh, Peter. "The Ordinary of Newgate and His Account" in J.S.Cockburn, ed., *Crime in England 1550-1800*, Princeton University Press, Princeton, New Jersey, 1977.

Linebaugh, Peter. "The Tyburn Riot Against the Surgeons" in Hay et al., 1975.

Liston, Carol. *Campbelltown: The Bicentennial History*, Allen & Unwin, North Sydney, 1988.

Liston, Carol. "Colonial Society" in James Broadbent & Joy Hughes, *The Age of Macquarie*, Melbourne University Press, in association with Historic Houses Trust of New South Wales, 1992.

Liston, Carol. *Sarah Wentworth, Mistress of Vaucluse*, Historic Houses Trust, Glebe, 1988.

Lloyd, Christopher C. *The British Seaman: 1200-1860: A social survey*, Collins, London, 1968.

Lloyd, Christopher. ed. *The health of seamen: selections from the work of Dr James Lind, Sir Gilbert Blane and Dr Thomas Trotter*, the Navy Records Society, London, 1965.

Lloyd, Christopher. ed. "Introduction", to *Sir Gilbert Blane*, etc., 1965.

Lloyd, Christopher. *Lord Cochrane, Seaman, Radical, Liberator*, Henry Holt and Company, New York, 1998 [1947].

Lloyd, Christopher C. "Victualling of the Fleet (18th and 19th centuries)", in Watt, et al. 1981.

Lloyd, Christopher & Jack L.S.Coulter. *Medicine and the Navy 1200-1900, Vol III - 1714-1815,* E. & S. Livingstone Ltd., Edinburgh and London, 1961.

Lloyd, Phoebe. "Philadelphia Story" in *Art in America,* Nov 1988.

Lobban, Robert Dalziel. *Edinburgh and the Medical Revolution,* Cambridge University Press, New York, 1980.

Longford, Elizabeth. *Wellington: Pillar of State,* Granada Publishing Ltd., Panther Books, St Albans, Herts, 1975.

Loudon, Irvine. *Medical Care and the general practitioner: 1750-1850,* Clarendon Press, Oxford, 1986.

Loudon, Irvine. "Medical practitioners 1750-1850 and the period of medical reform in Britain", in Andrew Wear, ed. 1992.

Lovejoy, Paul E. "The African Diaspora: Revisionist Interpretations of Ethnicity, Culture and Religion under Slavery 1", *Studies in the World History of Slavery, Abolition and Emancipation, II,* 1, 1997.

Low, Donald A. *The Regency Underworld,* Sutton Publishing, Stroud, Gloucestershire, 1999.

Lowenthal, David. *The Past is a Foreign Country,* Cambridge University Press, Cambridge, 1985.

Luxford, Yvonne. "Birth of a Nation: Convict Midwives", in Jeanette Covacevich, et al. eds. *OPMHA 7,* 1996: 73-6.

M

Macalpine, Ida & Richard Hunter. *George III and the Mad-business,* Pimlico, London, (1969) 1995.

Macarthur Onslow, Sibella. ed. *Some Early Records of the Macarthurs of Camden,* Rigby, Sydney, 1973 (1914).

McCarthy, Louella. Compiler for the Organising Committee of the 6th Biennial Conference of the Australian Society of the History of Medicine Inc., Dr Judith Godden, Chair. "Individuals & Institutions in the History of Medicine, Proceedings of the 6th Biennial Conference of the Australian Society of the History of Medicine", *Occasional Papers in Medical History Australia No 9,* Sydney 7-10 July 1999.

McCubbin, Charles. *Australian Butterflies,* Nelson, Melbourne, 1971.

McDaniel, W.B. 2d. "The place of the amateur in the writing of medical history" in *The Bulletin of the History of Medicine,* American Association of the History of Medicine and the Johns Hopkins Institute of the History of Medicine, volume 7, 1939.

MacDonagh, Oliver. *The Inspector General: Sir Jeremiah Fitzpatrick and Social Reform, 1783-1802,* Croom Helm Ltd, London, 1981.

MacDonagh, Oliver. 'Envoi: humanity, economy, policy: on common sense and expertise in the life of Sir Jeremiah Fitzpatrick', in Roy MacLeod, ed. *Government and Expertise: Specialists, Administrators and Professionals.* Cambridge University Press, Cambridge, UK, 1988 (2003). Google books.

McDonald, Angus. "Early American Soil Conservationists" in *USDA Miscellaneous Publication No. 449,* Washington, D.C.: Soil Conservation Service, U.S. Department of Agriculture, 1941, reprinted 1986. [Website in endnote 40, Ch. 13].

MacDonald, Helen. "Legal Bodies: Dissecting Murderers at the Royal College of Surgeons, London, 1800-1832" in *Traffic: An Interdisciplinary Postgraduate Journal,* No. 2. 2003.

MacDonald, Michael. "Religion, Social Change, and Psychological Healing in England, 1600-1800", in Sheils, *The Church and Healing,* 1982.

McGrigor, Sir James. *The Autobiography and Services of Sir James McGrigor Bart. Late Director-General of the Army Medical Department,* London, 1861. [Not sighted. References in Blanco (1974) are to this edition and cited as, *McGrigor (page).*]

McGrigor, Sir James, Mary McGrigor. ed. *The Scalpel and the Sword: The Autobiography of the Father of Army Medicine,* Scottish Cultural Press, Dalkeith, 2000.

McGrigor Sir James. Richard L. Blanco. *Wellington's Surgeon General: Sir James McGrigor,* Duke University Press, Durham, N.C., 1974.

McIntosh, A.M. "The Life and Times of William Bland", *Bulletin of the Post Graduate Committee in Medicine,* University of Sydney, Sept 1954.

Macintosh, Neil K. *Richard Johnson, Chaplain to the Colony of New South Wales. His Life and Times 1755-1827,* Library of Australian History, Sydney, 1978.

Macintosh, Stuart. "Introduction" to Ernest Scott, *The life of Matthew Flinders,* Angus & Robertson, HarperCollins Publishers, 2001.

McIntyre, Donald B. and Alan McKirdy. *James Hutton: The Founder of Modern Geology.* The Stationery Office, Edinburgh, 1997.

Macintyre, Stuart. ed. *The Historian's Conscience: Australian historians on the ethics of history,* Melbourne University Press, Carlton, 2004.

Mackaness, George. "Some Letters of Rev. Richard Johnson, B.A., First Chaplain of New South Wales", collected and edited with notes, commentary and introduction by Mackaness, 1978.

McLaughlin, John Kennedy. McLaughlin cited Windeyer, "'A Birthright and an inheritance': the Establishment of the Rule of Law in Australia", 1 *Tasmania Univ. Law Rev* 635, 1961.

McLachlan, Noel D. "Eagar, Edward (1787-1866)", *ADBI.*

McLachlan, Noel D. "Edward Eagar, a Colonial Spokesman", *Historical Studies*, Volume 10, No. 40. May 1963.

McLachlan, Noel D. *Waiting for the Revolution: A History of Australian Nationalism*, Penguin Books Australia, Ringwood, Victoria, 1989.

McLaughlin, John Kennedy. *The Magistracy in New South Wales, 1788-1850*, [Thesis submitted pursuant to the requirements for the Degree of Master of Laws], University of Sydney, August 1973; accessed online15-17 September 2007.

See http://www.forbessociety.org.au/documents/magistracy.pdf.

McLeod, Judyth. Keith A McLeod. photography. *Heritage Gardening, With an Illustrated Directory of Heirloom Flowers, Fruit and Vegetables*, Simon & Schuster, East Roseville. 1994.

MacLeod, Roy and Philip F. Rehbock. eds. *Evolutionary Theory and Natural History in the Pacific: Darwin's Laboratory*, University of Hawai'i Press, 1994.

McLoughlin, Lynne. "Landed peasantry or landed gentry: A geography of land grants", in Aplin ed. 1988.

McNeil, David R. "Medical Care Aboard Australia-Bound Convict Ships 1786-1840", in *The Bulletin of the History of Medicine*, 1952.

Macquarie, Elizabeth. "Elizabeth to Sarah Redfern", 9 February 1824, Redfern Papers, *MSS 2381/1*, ff 1-4.

Macquarie, Lachlan. *Journals of his Tours in New South Wales and Van Diemen's Land 1810-1822*, The Trustees of the Public Library of New South Wales, Sydney, 1956. (Now, online.)

Macquarie, Lachlan. *A Letter to the Right Honourable Viscount Sidmouth in Refutation of Statements made by The Hon. Henry Grey Bennet, M.P. etc*, Richard Rees, London, 1821.

Magee, Reginald. "Weapons and Wounds circa 1790", in History, Heritage & Health: Proceedings of the Fourth Biennial Conference of ASHM, 1996.

Magnusson, Magnus. *The Clacken and the Slate: The Story of the Edinburgh Academy 1824-1974*, Collins, London, 1974.

[Malaspina, Alexandro]. De Zulueta, Julian & Lola Higueras. "Health and Navigation in the South Seas: The Spanish Experience" in Watt et al. 1981.

Mann, D.D. *The Present Picture of New South Wales*, John Booth, London, 1811, with an introduction by Brian Fletcher, John Ferguson, Sydney, 1979.

Mann, Julia de L. *The Cloth Industry in the West of England From 1640 to 1880*, Alan Sutton, Gloucester, 1987[1971].

Manwaring, G.E. & Bonamy Dobrée. *The Floating Republic: An Account of the Mutinies at Spithead and the Nore in 1797*, Penguin Books, London, 1937 (1935).

Marcus, G.J. *Heart of Oak: A Survey of British sea power in the Georgian era,* Oxford University Press, London, 1975.

Marriott, Joan. ed. *Cowra on the Lachlan,* Cowra Shire Council in conjunction with Cowra and District Historical Society, 1998.

Marty, Martin E. & Kenneth L. Vaux. eds. *Health/Medicine and the Faith Traditions: An Inquiry into Religion and Medicine,* Fortress Press, Philadelphia, 1982.

Martyr, Philippa. *Paradise of Quacks: An Alternative History of Medicine in Australia,* Macleay Press, Sydney, 2002.

Matthews, Peter Hans and Andreas Ortmann. 'An Austrian (Mis)Reads Adam Smith: A Critique of Rothbard [Murray Newton] as Intellectual Historian', *Review of Political Economy,* vol. 14, issue 3, 2002 (2000).

Mazrui, Ali A. *The Africans: A Triple Heritage* [book of the television series The Africans, jointly produced by the British Broadcasting Corporation and Weta (Public Broadcasting Service)], B.B.C. Publications, 1986.

Melbourne, A.C.V. *William Charles Wentworth,* The Discovery Press, by arrangement with Queensland University Press, Penrith, 1972 (1934).

Melville, Herman. "Billy Budd: Sailor [an inside story] What befell him in the year of the Great Mutiny etc.," in *Three Stories,* The Folio Society, London, 1967.

Melville, Herman. sel. and ed. by Harold Beaver. *Billy Budd, Sailor and Other Stories,* Penguin Books, London, 1985.

Micale, Mark S. *Hysterical Men: The Hidden History of Male Nervous Illness,* Harvard University Press, 2008.

Miller, Jonathan & Borin Van Loon. *The Strange Case of Charles Darwin & Evolution,* Writers and Readers, London, 1982.

Minorca [Convict transport]. *John Leith, log. India Office Records,* IOR L/Mar/B/335A, filmed Oct 1983; a microfilm copy, AJCP, M1624, at the, Sydney, NSW

"Minutes of the proceedings of a court martial..." *PRO/ADM 1/534.* Copy held by the History of Medicine Library, R.A.C.P., Sydney.

Montagu, Lady Mary Wortley. *The Lover: A Ballad,* in Tim Cook, ed. and intro. 1997.

Montagu, Lady Mary Wortley. *The Turkish Embassy Letters,* Introduction by Anita Desai; Text edited and annotated by Malcolm Jack, Virago Press, London, 1994.

[Montagu, Lady Mary Wortley, attributed]. *Sophia, a Person of Quality. Woman Not Inferior to Man: or A short and modest Vindication of the natural Right of the Fair-Sex to a perfect Equality of Power, Dignity, and Esteem, with the Men,* Printed for John Hawkins, London, MDCCXXXIX

(1739), a facsimile reprint of the 1743 edition for the International Women's Year, Bentham Press, London, 1975.

Moorehead, Alan. *The Fatal Impact: The Invasion of the South Pacific 1767-1840,* [original publisher Harper & Row, New York, 1966] this edition created and produced by Mead & Beckett Publishing, Sydney, 1987.

Moorehead, Alan, ill. intro., *Darwin and the Beagle,* Hamish Hamilton, London, 1970.

Morantz-Sanchez, Regina Markell. *Sympathy and Science: Women Physicians in American Medicine,* Oxford University Press, New York, 1987.

Moss, David J. *Thomas Attwood: The Biography of a Radical,* McGill-Queen's University Press, Montreal & Kingston, London, Buffalo, 1990.

Munro, Craig. *Inky Stephensen: Wild Man of Letters,* University of Queensland Press, St Lucia, 1992.

Murray, Venetia. *High Society in the Regency Period 1788-1830,* Penguin Books, London, 1999.

Mutiny on the Bounty 1789-1989. An International Exhibition, to mark the 200th Anniversary, 1989, and a book of the exhibition with the same name, Published by Manorial Research PLC in association with the National Maritime Museum, London, 1989.

Mutiny on the Bounty: the story of Captain William Bligh seaman, navigator, surveyor and of the Bounty mutineers, an exhibition at the State Library, Sydney, and a book of the exhibition with the same name, Published by the State Library of New South Wales, 1991.

Myles, Helen & Isabel Tarrago. *Some Good Long Talks,* Women's Health Policy Unit, Queensland Health, 1992; Network of Women in Further Education, online.

N

Nash, Roderick Frazier. *The Rights of Nature: A History of Environmental Ethics,* Primavera Press. The Wilderness Society, Leichhardt, N.S.W. 1990.

Neal, David John. *The Rule of Law in a Penal Colony: Law and Power in Early New South Wales,* Cambridge University Press, Cambridge, 1991.

Neale, Jonathan. *The Cutlass and the Lash, Mutiny and Discipline in Nelson's Navy,* Pluto Press, London, 1985.

Neale, W. J. *History of the Mutiny at Spithead and the Nore,* 1842.

Nicholas, Stephen, ed. *Convict Workers: Reinterpreting Australia's past,* Cambridge University Press, Cambridge, 1989.

Nicholson, Ian. *Log of Logs,* Roebuck Society, Nambour, Queensland, 1993.

Nicolson, Malcolm. "The art of diagnosis: Medicine and the five senses" in Bynum & Porter, 1997.

Noah, William. *Voyage to Sydney in the Ship Hillsborough 1798-1799, and A Description of the Colony*, LAH, Sydney, 1978.

Nobbs, Raymond, ed. *Norfolk Island and its First Settlement 1788-1814*, LAH, North Sydney, 1988.

"Norfolk Island victualling book", 1802: 147, in Baxter CJ, ed. *Musters and lists NSW and Norfolk Island Sydney*, Australian Biographical and Genealogical Record in association with the Society of Australian Genealogists, 1988.

Norrie, Philip. *Vineyards of Sydney*, Horwitz Grahame, Sydney, 1990.

Numbers, Ronald L. & Darrel W. Amundsen, *Caring and Curing: Health and Medicine in the Western Religious Traditions,* Macmillan Publishing Company, New York, 1986.

Nussbaum, Felicity A. ed. *The Global Eighteenth Century.* The Johns Hopkins Press, Baltimore and London, 2003.

Nutton, Vivian & Roy Porter. eds. *The History of Medical Education in Britain*, Rodopi, Amsterdam & Atlanta, G.A. (Clio Medica 30/The Welcome Institute Series in the History of Medicine), 1995.

O

O'Brian, Patrick. *The Nutmeg of Consolation*, Harper Collins, London, 1997.

O'Brien, Denis Patrick. *The Classical Economists Revisited*, Princeton University Press, Princeton and Oxford, 2004 (1975).

O'Donnell, Ruan. *'Desperate and Diabolical': Defenders and United Irishmen in Early NSW,* accessed, 11 November 2007.

http://members.pcug.org.au/ppmay/defenders.htm,

Oeland, Glenn. "William Bartram: A Naturalist's Vision of Frontier America" in *National Geographic*, March 2001.

O'Farrell, Patrick. *The Irish in Australia,* N.S.W. University Press, Sydney, 1993[1986].

Oldfield, Audrey. *The Great Republic of the Southern Seas: Republicans in Nineteenth-Century Australia*, Hale & Iremonger, Alexandria, NSW. 1999.

Osborne, Graeme and William Frederick Mandle. *New History: Studying Australia Today*, George Allen & Unwin, North Sydney, 1982.

O'Shaughnessy, Peter. *A Rum Story: The Adventures of Joseph Holt Thirteen Years in New South Wales (1800-12)*, Kangaroo Press, Kenthurst, 1988.

Outram, Dorinda. *The Body and the French Revolution: Sex, Class and Political Culture*, Yale University Press. New Haven and London, 1989.

Outram, Dorinda. *The Enlightenment*, [in the series] "New Approaches to European History", Cambridge University Press, Cambridge, 1995.

Outram, Dorinda. *Panorama of the Enlightenment.* The J. Paul Getty Museum, Los Angeles, Thames and Hudson Ltd, London, 2006.

P

Pakenham, Thomas. *The Year of Liberty: The History of the Great Irish Rebellion of 1798*, Phoenix, London, [1969] 1992.

Paine, Thomas. *Common Sense and The Crisis*, Anchor Books, New York, 1973.

Paine, Tom. *Rights of Man* [with an Introduction by Derek Matravers], Wordsworth Classics of World Literature, [Everyman edn, 1915], 1996.

Paley, William. *Reasons for contentment: addressed to the labouring part of the British public*, Printed for R. Faulder, London, 1793: Goldsmiths'-Kress library of economic literature: no.15768, microfilm, RAV/FM4/2, State Library of NSW. Sydney.

[Paley, William.] Poor labourer, author. *A letter to William Paley, M.A., Archdeacon of Carlisle, in answer to his Reason [sic] for contentment, addressed to the labouring part of the British public / from a poor labourer.* Printed by J. Ridgway, London, 1793: Goldsmiths'-Kress library of economic literature: no. 15764, microfilm, RAV/FM4/2, State Library of NSW, Sydney.

Palmer, Richard. "The Church, Leprosy and Plague", in Shiels, ed. *The Church and Healing*, 1982.

Parker, Irene. *Dissenting Academies in England, Their Rise and Progress and their Place among the Educational Systems of the Country*, Cambridge: at the University Press, 1914; facsimile copy, Pranava Books, 272330, India.

Parsons, George. "The commercialism of honour: Early Australian capitalism 1788-1809", in Aplin, ed., 1988.

Parsons, T. George. "The New South Wales Corps on Norfolk Island 1792-1810" in Nobbs, 1988: 84-6.

Parsons, Vivienne. "Thomas Jamison (1745-1811)", in A.D.B. vol 2:1788-1850.

Pascoe, Charles Eyre. *The Joyous Neighbourhood of Covent Garden: A Literary Souvenir of the Tavistock Hotel, done in celebration of its hundredth anniversary*; John Jellicoe, ill. Chiswick Press, London, 1887.

Pearn, John Hemsley. "Gentlemen of the faculty: a synopsis of the First Fleet surgeons: Comparisons and contrasts of the personalities who were the founders of medicine in Australia", in *The Medical Journal of Australia, Vol 149*, December 5/18, 1988.

Pearn, John Hemsley. *In the Capacity of a Surgeon: A Biography of Walter Scott, Surgeon and Australian colonist, and first civilian of Queensland...*, University of Queensland, Brisbane, 1988.

Pearn, John Hemsley. ed. *Pioneer Medicine in Australia*, Amphion Press, Brisbane, 1988.

Pelling, Margaret. "The meaning of contagion", in *Contagion: Epidemics, history and Culture from smallpox to anthrax*, Alison Bashford & Claire Hooker. eds. Pluto Press, Annandale, NSW, 2001.

Pelling, Margaret. "Contagion/germ theory/specificity" in Bynum & Porter. eds. 1997.

Perlin, John. *A Forest Journey: The Role of Wood in the Development of Civilization*, W.W. Norton & Company, New York 1989.

Perry, T. M. *Australia's First Frontier: The Spread of Settlement in New South Wales 1788-1829*, Melbourne University Press in assn with The Australian National University, 1965 (1963).

Pescott, R.N. *Emancipist and Autocrat: The Life of Doctor William Redfern and his relationship with Governor Macquarie in the society of New South Wales* [A study towards an M.A. Thesis, A.N.U.], a roneoed copy, 10 May 1970.

Phillip, Arthur. *The Voyage of Governor Phillip to Botany Bay...*1789, Australiana Facsimile Editions, Hutchinson of Australia, Melbourne, 1982 (1968).

Phillip, Arthur. *The Voyage of Governor Phillip to Botany Bay...*[1789], with an Introduction and Annotations by James J. Auchmuty, RAHS and Angus and Roberstson, Sydney, 1970.

Phillips, Gael & John Pearn. "A convict and colonial pharmacopoeia..." in J. Covacevich, et al. OPMHA 7.

Phillips, Gael E. & John H. Pearn, "'Oral History' - Memorials to Three Pioneer Australian Dentists" in Susanne Atkins, et al. eds. 1994.

Pickstone, John, "Medicine, Society, and the State', in Roy Porter. ed. *The Cambridge Illustrated History of Medicine*, Cambridge, New York, 1996.

Piper, J. *Norfolk Island returns 1808*, a "List of settlers etc. embarked on board the Estramina Schooner for the Derwent 15 May 1808". *CY Reel 1303 BT 12*:152a,b. ML, Sydney.

Plowright, John. *Regency England: The age of Lord Liverpool*, Lancaster Pamphlets, Rutledge, London and New York, 1996.

Plumb, J.H. *England in the Eighteenth Century*, Penguin Books, (1963) 1981.

Pockley, R.V. *Ancestor Treasurer Hunt: The Edward Wills Family and descendants in Australia, 1797-1976*, Wentworth Books, Sydney, 1976.

Pockley, R.V. *Ancestor Treasure Hunt: The Antill Family, England 833-America 1680, Australia 1809,* Wentworth Books, 1978

Pollard, N.S. "William Cowper (1778-1858)" in *ADBI.*

Pool, Bernard. "Navy Contracts in the Last Years of the Navy Board, 1780-1832", in *The Mariner's Mirror*, vol.50, 3, 1964:161-176.

Porter, Dorothy. "Public Health" in Bynum & Porter, *2*, 1997.

Porter, Dorothy & Roy Porter. *Patient's Progress: Doctors and Doctoring in Eighteenth-century England,* 1989.

Porter, Ian Alexander. "Thomas Trotter, M.D., Naval Physician" in *Medical History, 7*, 1963.

Porter, Roy. "A touch of danger: The man-midwife as sexual predator," in Rousseau & Porter. eds, 1987.

Porter, Roy. "Introduction", to Thomas trotter, *An Essay Medical Philosophical, and Chemical on Drunkenness and its Effects on the Human Body*, Longman, Hurst, Rees and Orme, London, 1804, reprinted by Routledge, London, 1988.

Porter, Roy. *The Enlightenment,* MacMillan Press Ltd, London, 1990.

Porter, Roy. *Disease, medicine and society in England, 1550-1860*, 2nd ed. [Prepared for the Economic History Society], Cambridge University Press, Cambridge, 1995.

Porter, Roy. *London, A Social History*, Penguin Books, Harmondsworth, 1996.

Porter, Roy. *The Greatest Benefit to Mankind: A Medical History of Humanity from Antiquity to the Present*, HarperCollins, London, 1997.

Porter, Roy. "Medicine and Faith" (ch. iv), in *The Greatest Benefit to Mankind: A Medical History of Humanity from Antiquity to the Present,* HarperCollins, London, 1997.

Porter, Roy. "Religion and Medicine" in Bynum & Porter, 1997.

Porter, Roy. *Enlightenment: Britain and the Creation of the Modern World,* Penguin Books, 2001.

Porter, Roy. "Secularization" in Ch 9, and "Rationalizing Religion" Ch.5, in Porter, 2000.

Porter. Roy. *Bodies Politic: Disease, Death and Doctors in Britain, 1650-1900*, Reaktion Books, London, 2001.

Porter, Roy. *Flesh in the Age of Reason: How the Enlightenment Transformed the Way We See Our Bodies and Souls*, Penguin Books, London, [published posthumously] 2004.

Porter, Roy. *The Making of Geology: Earth science in Britain 1660-1815,* Cambridge University Press, Cambridge, 2008 (1980, 1977).

Porter, Roy. ed. *The Cambridge Illustrated History of Medicine,* Cambridge University Press, Cambridge, 1996.

Porter, Roy & Dorothy Porter. *In Sickness and in Health: The British Experience, 1650-1850,* Fourth Estate, London, 1988.

Porter, Roy & G.S. Rousseau. eds. *Sexual underworlds of the Enlightenment,* Manchester University Press, Manchester, 1987.

Porter, Roy & Mikulas Teich. *Sexual Knowledge, Sexual Science, The History of Attitudes to Sexuality,* Cambridge University Press, Cambridge, 1994.

Porter, Roy & Lesley Hall. *The Facts of Life: The Creation of Sexual Knowledge in Britain, 1650-1950,* Yale University Press, New Haven and London, 1995.

Portraits. William and Sarah Redfern. See *ML Portrait Index Catalogue.*

Post Office, Sydney, NSW. *The History of the G.P.O., The City's Centrepiece,* Australia Post, Hale & Iremonger, Pty Limited, Sydney, 1988.

Priestley, Joseph. Peter Miller, ed. *Political Writings.* Cambridge University Press New York, 1993.

Priestley, Joseph. *An Essay on the First Principles of Government, and on the nature of Political, Civil and Religious Liberty,* including Remarks on Dr Brown's *Code of Education,* and on Dr Balguy's *Sermon on Church Authority,* the Second Edition, corrected and enlarged, printed for J. Johnson, No. 72, in St Paul's Church-Yard, 1771, reprinted in Priestley, Joseph. Peter Miller. ed. 1993.

Proudfoot, Helen, Anne Bickford, Brian Egloff and Robyn Stocks. *Australia's First Government House,* Allen & Unwin in conjunction with the Department of Planning, North Sydney, 1991.

Proust, A.J. ed. *A Social and Cultural History of Medicine in New South Wales in the 19th Century: Southern Tablelands and Monaro,* self-published, Forrest, A.C.T. 1999.

Pugh, R.B. assisted by Elizabeth Crittall. eds. *The Victoria History of the Counties of England,* Vol 7, *Wiltshire.*

Q

Quakers, Religious Society of Friends. *This we can say: Australian Quaker Life, Faith and Thought,* Australian Yearly Meeting of the Religious Society of Friends (Quakers) Inc, Armadale North, Victoria, 2003

R

Rack, Henry D. "Doctors, Demons and Early Methodist Healing", in W.J.Sheils, ed., 1982.

Ratcliffe, Derek. *The Peregrine Falcon,* ill. by Donald Watson et al., T & AD Poyser, Calton, 1980.

Rathbone R. *A Very present Help, Caring for Australians Since 1813. The History of the Benevolent Society of N.S.W.* Sydney: State Library of New South Wales Press, 1994.

Redfern [William] to [Governor] Brisbane, 1 Nov. 1824. AA NSW Fiche 3107, 4/1839A.

Redfern [William] Letter to Bigge 5 February 1821, BT Box 26 / CY1446, pp 6186-6222. [An unconnected page is inserted between 6219 and 6220.]

Redfern, William. *Letter to D'Arcy Wentworth 16 Sept 1807,* Wentworth Papers, ML A751: 201-203, Sydney.

Redfern, William. *Letter to [D'Arcy Wentworth] [19 May 1808],* Darcy Wentworth Papers, ML A4073: 15ff., Sydney. [See ch. 10, above, for this date based on internal evidence]

Redfern, William. [His] *Will,* [attached] to a "Grant of land at Sydney", *AR17/2, ML.* Feb. 1 1834, attested copies.

Redfearn, Fred. AR 17/4, ML, Sydney: 3 letters.

Redfern, William. Minutes of the proceedings of a court martial...PRO/ADM 1/534. Copy held by the History of Medicine Library, RACP, Sydney.

Rediker, Marcus. *Between the Devil and the Deep Blue Sea, a study of Merchant Seamen, Pirates, and the Anglo-American Maritime World, from 1700 to 1750,* Cambridge University Press, New York, 1993 [1987].

Rediker, Marcus. *The Slave Ship: A Human History,* Viking, the Penguin Group, New York, 2007.

Regulations and Instructions relating to His Majesty's Service at Sea. The Thirteenth Edition, London, 1790.

Rice, Tony. Introduction by Dr David Bellamy, *Voyages of Discovery, Three Centuries of Natural History Exploration,* The Natural History Museum, Scriptum Editions, London, 2000.

Rich, P. et al. "Prehistory of the Norfolk Island Biota", in R. Schodde, et al. A Review of Norfolk Island Birds: Past and Present, Australian National Parks and Wildlife Service, Canberra, 1983.

Richards, David. "Medical Men at Norfolk Island: The First Settlement, 1788-1814" in OPMHA7, "History, Heritage and Health", Proceedings of the Fourth Biennial Conference of ASHM, Papers Presented at Norfolk Island, 2-9 July, 1995, ASHM, Brisbane, Australia,1996: 409-11.

Richards, David. "Medical Men in Tasmania 1803-1870", in *OPMHA 6,* 1993.

Richards, David. "Medical Transportees to Australian Colonies: 1788-1868", in OPMHA7.

Richardson, Joanna. *The Brownings: A Biography Compiled from Contemporary Sources,* The Folio Society, London, 1986.

Rienits, Rex & Thea. *Early Artists of Australia,* Angus & Robertson, Sydney, 1963.

Rigby, Brian. "Volney's Rationalist Apocalypse: Les Ruines..." in Barker et al.1982.

Rigg, Valda. "Convict Life: A 'Tolerable Degree of Comfort'?" in Nobbs, 1988:97ff.

Rimmer, W.G. *Portrait of a Hospital, the Royal Hobart,* Hobart, 1981.

Ring, Malvin E. *Dentistry: An Illustrated History,* Harry N, Abrams, Inc., New York, 1985.

Risse, Guenter B. "Medicine in the age of Enlightenment", in Wear, ed. 1992.

Guenter B. Risse. "Cullen as clinician: organisation and strategies of an eighteenth century medical practice", in A. Doig et al eds. *William Cullen and the Eighteenth Century Medical World,* Edinburgh University Press, Edinburgh, 1993.

Ritchie, John. *Punishment and Profit: The Reports of Commissioner John Bigge on the Colonies of New South Wales and Van Diemen's Land, 1822-1823; their origins, nature and significance,* Heinemann, Melbourne, 1970.

Ritchie, John. ed. *The Evidence to the Bigge Reports, New South Wales under Governor Macquarie, Volume 1, The Oral Evidence,* Heinemann, Melbourne, 1971.

Ritchie, John. ed. *The Evidence to the Bigge Reports, New South Wales under Governor Macquarie, Volume 2, The Written Evidence,* Heinemann, Melbourne, 1971.

Ritchie, John. *Australia as once we were,* Heinemann, Melbourne, 1975.

Ritchie, John. Introduction and ed. *A Charge of Mutiny: The Court Martial of Lieutenant Colonel George Johnston for deposing Governor William Bligh in the Rebellion of 26 January 1808,* National Library of Australia, Canberra, 1988.

Ritchie, John. *Lachlan Macquarie: A Biography,* Melbourne University Press, Carlton, 1988.

Ritchie, John. *The Wentworths: Father and Son.* The Miegunyah Press, Carlton South, 1997.

Robinson, Eric, "Introduction" in Dawson, P.M.S., Eric Robinson & David Powell. *John Clare: A Champion for the Poor, Political Verse and Prose*, Mid Northumberland Arts Group, Carcanet Press, 2000.

Roddis, Louis H. *A short history of nautical medicine*, Harper & Brothers, New York, 1941.

Rodger, Ella Hill Burton. *Aberdeen Doctors at Home and Abroad: The Narrative of a Medical School*, William Blackwood and Sons, Edinburgh and London, 1893.

Rodger, Nicholas A.M. *The Admiralty*, T.Dalton, Lavenham, 1979.

Rodger, Nicholas A.M. *The Wooden World: An Anatomy of the Georgian Navy*, W.W.Norton and Company, New York, 1996 (1986).

Rodger, N.A.M. "Shipboard Life in the Georgian Navy, 1750-1800; the Decline of the Old Order?" in Fischer, Lewis R, et al. eds. 1992.

Rodger, N.A.M. "The Naval World of Jack Aubrey" reprinted [from Cunningham, 1994] in Patrick O'Brian, *The Nutmeg of Consolation,* 1997 (1991).

Rodger, N.A.M. *The Command of the Ocean, A Naval History of Britain, 1649-1815*, W.W. Norton & Company, New York, 2006.

Rosen, Sue. *Losing Ground: An Environmental History of the Hawkesbury-Nepen Catchment*, Hale & Iremonger, Sydney, 1995

Rosenberg, Charles E. *Explaining Epidemics and Other Studies in the History of Medicine,* Cambridge University Press, New York, 1995.

Rosenberg, C.E. "Medical Text and Social Context: Explaining William Buchan's *Domestic Medicine" in Bulletin of the History of Medicine,* 1983.

Rosenman, Helen. trans. and retold account. *Two Voyages to the South Seas: by Captain Jules S.-C Dumont D'Urville 1826-1829 and 1837-1840,* Melbourne Univ. Press, 1992.

Rosner, Lisa. *Medical Education in the Age of Improvement: Edinburgh Students and Apprentices 1760-1826*, Edinburgh University Press, 1991.

Rousseau, G. S. & Roy Porter. eds. *Sexual underworlds of the Enlightenment*, Manchester University Press, Manchester, 1987. See also under Porter, Roy, [G.S.Rousseau &] eds. 1987.

Le Roy, Paul Edwin. "The Emancipists, Edward Eagar and the struggle for civil liberties" in *JRAHS*, Vol.48, Pt.4. Aug.1962.

Rudé, George. *The Crowd in History: A study of Popular Disturbances in France and England, 1730-1848*, Serif, London, 1995(1964).

Rudé, George. *Protest and Punishment: The Story of the Social and Political Protesters transported to Australia 1788-1868*, Oxford University Press, Melbourne, 1978.

Rudé, George. *Revolutionary Europe 1783-1815*, Fontana Press, London, 1985 [1964].

Russell, Kenneth Fitzpatrick. *British Anatomy, 1525-1800: A bibliography of Works, Published in Britain, America and the Continent*, 2nd ed., St Paul's Bibliographies, 1987.

Ryan, David G. "The Original Forests", in the journal, *Australian Forest Growers*, 1993/1994.

Ryan, R.J. ed. *Land Grants 1788-1809*, Australian Documents Library, Sydney, 1981.

S

Sainty, Malcolm R. & Keith A. Johnson. eds. *Census of New South Wales*, November 1828, LAH, 1980.

Sainty, Malcolm R. & Michael C Flynn. *Index to the Australian Dictionary of Biography, volumes 1 & 2 (A to Z - 1788-1850)*, Library of Australian History, Sydney, 1991.

Schaffer, Irene. *Land Musters, Stock Returns and Lists, Van Diemen's Land 1803-1822*, St David's Park Publishing, Hobart, 1991.

Scott, Ernest. *The life of Matthew Flinders, with an introduction by Prof. Stuart Macintyre*, Angus & Robertson, An imprint of HarperCollins Publishers, Sydney, 2001.

Serullaz, Arlette et al. *French Painting: The Revolutionary Decades 1760-1830*, catalogue, ill. in colour (39), black and white (55) and with notes by J[acques] V[ilain] at the Art Gallery of New South Wales exhibition, 1980.

Shaw, A.G.L. "Convicts and Transportation", in Chisholm, 1958.

Sheedy, Kieran. *The Transportation of Michael Dwyer and the Wicklow Rebels.* The Woodfield Press, Dublin, 1997, in Donald, 2007.

Sheils, W. J. ed. *The Church and Healing: Papers read at the twentieth summer meeting and the twenty-first winter meeting of the Ecclesiastical History Society*, The Ecclesiastical History Society, Oxford, 1982.

[Ships] ML. "General Card Index: Ships".

Shteir, Ann B. *Cultivating Women, Cultivating Science: Flora's Daughters and Botany in England 1760 to 1860*, The Johns Hopkins University Press, Baltimore, 1996.

Shuster, R.R. & Shuster, S. "Buggery in the British Merchant Navy in the Mid 19th Century" in History, Heritage & Health; Proceedings of the Fourth Biennial Conference of ASHM. The Australian Society of the History of Medicine, Brisbane, 1996.

Sidney, Algernon. Thomas G. West. ed. "*Discourses Concerning Government*, Liberty Fund, Indianapolis, 1996.

Sigerist, Henry E. Elizabeth Fee and Theodore M. Brown, eds. *Making Medical History: The Life and Times of Henry E. Sigerist.* The John Hopkins University Press, Baltimore & London, 1997.

Sigerist, Henry E. *A History of Medicine, vol 1: Primitive and Archaic Medicine,* Oxford University Press, New York, 1951.

Sigerist, Henry E. *A History of Medicine, vol II: Early Greek, Hindu, and Persian Medicine,* Oxford University Press, New York, 1961.

Simpson, Margaret. *Old Sydney Buildings: A Social History,* Kangaroo Press, Kenthurst, 1995.

Smellie, William. *William Smellie's Treatise on the Theory and Practice of Midwifery with a set of Anatomical Tables,* published in Edinburgh, Nov. 1783.

Smellie, William. *A Sett of Anatomical Tables with Explanations, and an Abridgement, of the Practice of Midwifery...* [facsimile reproduction from a 1st ed. folio copy of 1754, donated to the Postgraduate School of Obstetrics and Gynaecology], University of Auckland, Auckland, 1971.

Smith, Adam. The Theory of Moral Sentiments, Glasgow Edition, D.D.Raphael and A.L.Macfie. eds. Oxford University Press, 1979 (1976). This edition authorized by OUP for reprinting by Liberty Fund Inc., Indianapolis, in 1982.

Smith, Adam. *The Theory of Moral Sentiments,* "Great Books in Philosophy", Prometheus Books, New York, 2000 (1759). [In this study, displaced by the Glasgow Edition.]

Smith, Adam. *An Inquiry into the Nature and Causes of The Wealth of Nations* (1776), Glasgow Edition, General editors R.H.Campbell and A.S.Skinner, textual ed. W.B.Todd, Oxford University Press, 1979 (1976). This edition authorized by OUP for reprinting by Liberty Fund Inc., Indianapolis, in 1982.

Smith, Adam. *An Inquiry into the Nature and Causes of The Wealth of Nations* (1776), The University of Chicago and Encyclopaedia Britannica, Inc., Chicago, 1971 (1776). [In this study, displaced by the Glasgow Edition.]

Smith, Adam. A Primer. Eamonn Butler, with a commentary by Craig Smith, The Institute of Economic Affairs, Great Britain, 2007. Published in Australia by The Centre for Independent Studies, St Leonards, Sydney, June 2008.

Smith, Adam. David Daiches Raphael, *The Impartial Spectator: Adam Smith's Moral Philosophy,* Clarendon Press, Oxford, 2007.

Smith, Adam, Reviewed. Peter Jones and Andrew S. Skinner, eds, Edinburgh University Press, 1992.

Smith, Adam 1723-90, Morals, Motives & Markets, The Adam Smith Bicentenary Committee exhibition organized by Jean Jones and designed by

Sandy Hamilton. Catalogue text by J. Jones, and design by S. Hamilton, Royal Museum of Scotland, 17 July-2 Sept 1990.

Smith, Adam. The Essential Adam Smith, with Introductory Readings. Heilbroner, Robert L. & Laurence J. Malone, Oxford University Press, Oxford, 1986.

Smith, Bernard. *European Vision and the South Pacific 1768-1850...,* Oxford University Press, 1969.

Smollett, Tobias. *The Adventures of Roderick Random,* ed. intro. notes by Paul-Gabriel Bouce, Oxford University Press, World's Classics, Oxford, 1988.

Sobell, Dava & William J.H. Andrews. *The Illustrated Longitude,* Fourth estate, London, 1998.

Solander, Daniel. *Collected Correspondence 1753-1782,* ed. and translated by Edward Duyker and Per Tingbrand, The Miegunyah Press, Melbourne University Press, 1995.

Spender, Dale. *Women of Ideas: And what men have done to them,* From Aphra Behn to Adrienne Rich, Routledge & Kegan Paul, London, 1982.

Spigelman, J.J. Chief Justice of NSW. *Foundations of the Freedom of the Press in Australia - The Inaugural Australian Press Council Address,* Sydney, 20 November 2002, Website of the Supreme Court of NSW.

Stark, Suzanne J. *Female Tars: Women Aboard Ship in the Age of Sail,* Pimlico, London, 1998.

Steel, Tom. *Scotland's Story,* Fontana/Collins, London in association with Channel Four Television Company Ltd and Scottish Television PLC, 1985.

Steele, J.G. *Brisbane Town in Convict Days 1824-1842,* University of Queensland Press, Queensland, 1975.

Stewart, C.P. & Guthrie, D. ed. *Lind's Treatise on Scurvy,* Edinburgh, The University Press, 1953.

Stilwell, Frank J.B. *Australian Urban and Regional Development,* Australia and New Zealand Book Company, Sydney, 1974.

Stower, Caleb. *The Printers Grammar: Or introduction to the Art of Printing: Containing a Concise History of the Art, with the Improvements in the Practice of Printing, for the last Fifty Years.* B. Crosby and Co., London, 1808, republished by Gregg Press Ltd in association with The Archive Press Ltd, London, by permission of the St Bride Foundation from the original in its possession, 1965.

Summers, Anne. *Damned Whores and God's Police: The Colonization of Women in Australia,* Penguin Books Australia, Ringwood, Victoria, 1980, [and revised ed. 1994].

Sutton, Harvey. *Lectures on Preventive Medicine,* Consolidated Press, Sydney, 1944.

T

Tanner, Howard. *Towards an Australian Garden*, Photography by Richard Stringer, Valadon Publishing, Woollahra, 1983.

Tawney, R.H. *Religion and the Rise of Capitalism: A Historical Study*, Penguin Books, Harmondsworth, 1977 (1922).

Tench, Watkin. *Sydney's First Four Years...* Published in association with the Royal Australian Historical Society, Angus & Robertson, 1961.

Thackray, Arnold. ed., *Constructing Knowledge in the History of Science, Osiris*, A Research Journal devoted to the History of Science and its Cultural Influences, second series, volume 10, 1995.

Thompson, E.P. "The Crime of Anonymity", in Douglas Hay et al. *Albion's Fatal Tree: Crime and Society in Eighteenth-Century England*, Pantheon Books, New York,1975.

Thompson, E.P. *Customs in Common*, Penguin Books, London, 1993.

Thompson, E.P. *The making of the English working class*, Vintage Books, New York, 1966.

Thompson, E.P. *Whigs and Hunters, The Origin of the Black Act*, Pantheon Books, New York, 1975.

Thompson, E.P. *Witness Against the Beast: William Blake and the Moral Law*, Cambridge University Press, Cambridge, 1993.

Thorne, Alan & Robert Raymond. *Man on the Rim: The Peopling of the Pacific*, Angus & Robertson, North Ryde, N.S.W., 1989.

Thorne, R.G. *The House of Commons 1790-1820*, (series, *The History of Parliament*), published by the History of Parliament Trust, Secker & Warburg, London, 1986.

Tomaselli, Sylvana. "Virtue", in Black & Porter, 1996.

Townsend, S.L. "Obstetrics through the Ages", in *Medical Journal of Australia*, 1952.

Trevelyan, George Macaulay. *England Under the Stuarts*, The Folio Society, London, 1996 (1904: rev. 1946, 1925).

Trohler, Ulrich. PhD thesis. *Quantification in British Medicine and Surgery 1750-1830*, 2006 (1978), accessed 24 July 2012, www.jameslindlibrary.org.

Trotter, Thomas. *An Essay Medical, Philosophical, and Chemical on Drunkenness and its Effects on the Human Body*, Longman, Hurst, Rees and Orme, London, 1804, reprinted by Routledge, London, 1988.

Trotter, Thomas. "Medicina Nautica: State of Health of the Fleet" [Extracts from], in Lloyd, 1965.

Trotter, Thomas. *A View of the Nervous Temperament; being a practical enquiry into the increasing prevalence, prevention, and treatment of those diseases commonly called nervous, bilious, stomach and liver complaints;*

indigestion; low spirits; gout, etc., A reprint of the 1807 edition, Longman, Hurst, Rees, and Orme, London, 1807. This is a volume in the Arno Press collection, Classics in Pyschiatry. Arno Press, A New York Times Company, New York, 1976.

Turner, A.J.

Turner, John. *Joseph Lycett: Governor Macquarie's convict artist*, Hunter History Publications, Newcastle, 1997.

Turner, J.S., Courtney N. Smithers & Ruurd D. Hoogland. eds. *The Conservation of Norfolk Island*, The Australian Conservation Foundation, Inc. Special Publication No.1, c.1968.

U

Uglow, Jenny. *The Lunar Men; The Friends who made the Future 1730-1810*, Faber and Faber, London, 2002.

Underwood, John. *Madeira [photographs]*, Sunflower Books, London, 1983.

Underwood, John & Pat. *Landscapes of Madeira: a Countryside Guide* (Landscape Countryside Guides), Third edition, revised and enlarged, Sunflower Books, London, 1988.

V

Van Zuylen, Gabrielle & Claire de Virieu photographer, *Alhambra: A Moorish Paradise*, Thames & Hudson, London, 1999.

Varman, Robert V.J. "Material Life Including the Evidence from Archaeology" in Nobbs, ed. 1988.

Vattel, Emmerich De. *The Law of Nations* [The 6th American edition of 1844 was entitled "The Law of Nations or Principles of the Law of Nature, Applied to the Conduct and Affairs of Nations and Sovereigns"], Washington D.C.; Carnegie Institution, 1916.

Versluysen, Margaret Connor. "Midwives, medical men and 'poor woman labouring of child': lying-in hospitals in eighteenth-century London", in Helen Roberts, ed. *Women, health and reproduction*, Routledge & Kegan Paul, London, 1981.

Virgil [Publius Vergilius Maro], *The Georgics*, translated into English verse by K.R.Mackenzie; soft-ground etchings by Nigel Lambourne, The Folio Society, London, 1969 (29 B.C.E).

W

Wallis, P.J. & R.V. with assistance...*Eighteenth Century Medics, Project for Historical Biobibliography*, Newcastle Upon Tyne, 1988.

Ward, John Manning. "Foundation of the University of Sydney", in *JRAHS*, vol xxxvii, 1951.

Ward, John Manning. *James Macarthur: Colonial Conservative, 1798-1867*, Sydney University Press, Sydney, 1981.

Warner, John Harley. "The History of Science and the Sciences of Medicine", in *Osiris*, vol. 10, 1995.

Warner, Oliver. *Fighting Sail: Three hundred years of warfare at sea*, Cassell, London, 1979.

Watmore, Pamela & Aileen Robertson. "Pioneers", *Family Roots*, Cowra, revised ed. 1986.

Watson, J[ames] Frederick [William]. *The History of the Sydney Hospital from 1811 to 1911*, W.A. Gullick, Government Printer, Sydney, 1911.

Watson, James Frederick William, 1878-1945. *ADB 12*, 1990, online edition: 12.04.08.

Watson, James Frederick William, 1878-1945. National Library of Australia, "Finding Aids, Manuscripts, online", accessed 12.04.08.

Watt, James. "The Burns of Sea Battles", *Problems of Medicine at Sea*, National Maritime Museum, Greenwich, London, Maritime Monographs and Reports, No 12, 1974.

Watt, James. "Medical Aspects and Consequences of Captain Cook's Voyages", *Conference on Captain James Cook and His times*, Simon Fraser University, Burnaby, B.C., Canada, 1978.

Watt, James. "Some Consequences of Nutritional Disorders in Eighteenth-century British Circumnavigations", in Watt et al. *Starving Sailors*, 1981.

James Watt, "Health and Settlement 1788-95: Surgeons and the Environment" in the *Australian and New Zealand Journal of Surgery*, 1989.

Watt, James. "Health and Settlement 1788-95: Surgeons and the Environment", in *Aust. N.Z. Surg.*, 1989a.

Watt, James. "The Colony's Health," in Hardy & Frost, 1989b.

Watt, James. "Voyaging to New Zealand: The Medical Challenge", in the *Australian and New Zealand Journal of Surgery*, 1991.

Watt, J., E. J. Freeman, and W.F. Bynum. eds. *Starving Sailors: The influence of nutrition upon naval and maritime history*, National Maritime Museum, 1981.

Watts, Ruth. "Joseph Priestley, (1733-1804)", in *Prospects: the quarterly review of comparative education*, vol. XXIV, no.1/2, 1994:343-53, UNESCO, International Bureau of Education, Paris, 1999.

Wear, Andrew. "The History of Personal Hygiene" in Bynum & Porter *2.*

Wear, Andrew. ed. *Medicine in Society: Historical essays,* Cambridge University Press, Cambridge,1992.

Weatherburn, A.K. *George William Evans: Explorer,* Angus & Robertson, Sydney, 1966.

Weber, Eric & Leen De Vreese, "The Causes and Cures of Scurvy: How Modern was James Lind's Methodology?" in *Logic and Logical Philosophy,* vol 14, 2005:55-67,

Weidenhofer, Margaret. The Convict Years: Transportation and the penal system 1788-1868, Lansdowne Press Pty. Ltd., Melbourne, 1973.

Wentworth, William Charles. *Australasia,* University of Sydney Library, Sydney, 1997, online at http://setis.library.usyd.edu.au/ozlit.

Wentworth, William Charles. *Statistical, Historical and Political Description of the Colony of New South Wales...* G. and W. Whittaker, London, 1819; facsimile edition, 1978.

Wesley, John. *Primitive Physic: An Easy and Natural Method Curing Most Diseases,* Wipf and Stock Publishers, Eugene, Oregon, 2003 (1791).

Western, Charles Callis. *Substance of the Speech...in the House of Commons, May 1814 on the Subject of the Corn Laws,* London, 1814, Digitized by Microsoft from a copy in the University of Toronto.

Whitaker, Anne-Maree. ed. & intro. *Distracted Settlement: New South Wales after Bligh, from the Journal of Lieutenant James Finucane 1808-1810,* The Miegunyah Press, Carlton South, 1998.

Whitaker, Anne-Maree. *Joseph Foveaux: Power and Patronage in Early New South Wales,* UNSW Press, Sydney, 2000.

Whitaker, Anne-Maree. *Unfinished Revolution: United Irishmen in New South Wales 1800-1810,* Crossing Press, Sydney, 1994.

White, John. *Journal of a Voyage to New South Wales,* biographical intro. Rex Rienits, ed. Alec H. Chisholm, Angus & Robertson, in assn with the RAHS, Sydney, 1962.

Wiener, Martin J. "The Health of Prisoners and the two Faces of Benthamism" in Richard Creese, W.F.Bynum & J. Bearn, eds. *The Health of Prisoners, Historical Essays,* Amsterdam & Atlanta, GA (Clio Medica 34/The Welcome Institute Series in the History of Medicine), 1995.

Wilkinson, Lise. "Epidemiology", Ibid. Bynum & Porter, 2, 1997.

Will and land grants. *ML Ar17/2.* "Grant of land at Sydney", 1 February 1834, and attested copies.

Willett, C. and Phillis Cunnington. *The History of Underclothes,* Dover Publications, Inc., New York, 1992 (1951).

Williams, Glyndwr & Alan Frost. eds. *Terra Australis to Australia,* Oxford University Press in association with the Australian Academy of the Humanities, Melbourne, 1988.

Williams, Gwynn A. *Goya and the Impossible Revolution,* Allen Lane, 1976.

Wilson, Adrian. "William Hunter and the Varieties of Man-Midwifery," in Bynum & Porter. eds, 1985.

Wilson, Leonard G. "Fevers", in Bynum & Porter, vol 1, 1997.

Windschuttle, Keith. *The Killing of History: How a discipline is being murdered by literary critics and social theorists,* Macleay Press, Paddington, NSW, 1996.

Winspear, Rosalind. "A College benefactor: Frank Forster - obstetrician, gynaecologist, medical historian and bibliophile", *Comment,* in *The Australian and New Zealand Journal of Obstetrics and Gynaecology,* 2004.

Winton, Ronald. *Why the Pomegranate? A History of the RACP,* R.A.C.P., Sydney, 1988.

Withers, Charles W.J. "On Georgics and Geology: James Hutton's 'Elements of Agriculture' and Agricultural Science in Eighteenth-Century Scotland" in *The Agricultural History Review,* The British Agricultural History Society, Volume 42, Part I, 1994.

Withers, Charles W.J. "William Cullen's Agricultural Lectures and Writings and the Development of Agricultural Science in Eighteenth-Century Scotland" in the *The Agricultural History Review,* The British Agricultural History Society, Volume 37, Part II, 1989.

Witz, Anne. *Professions and Patriarchy,* Routledge, London, 1992.

Wollstonecraft, Mary. *A Short Residence in Sweden, Norway and Denmark,* [published jointly with William Godwins's Memoirs...,] ed. Richard Holmes], Penguin Books, London, 1987.

Wollstonecraft, Mary. *A Vindication of the Rights of Women,* ed. and intro., Miriam Brody, Penguin Books, Harmondsworth, 1992 (1792).

Woodward, P.M. "The Law in 18th Century England" (Foreword) by John Cobley. *The Crimes of the Lady Juliana Convicts - 1790,* LAH, Sydney, 1989.

Woolley, Benjamin. *The Herbalist: Nicholas Culpepper and the fight for medical freedom,* Harper Perennial, Hammersmith, 2004.

Wordsworth, William. "Preface to Lyrical Ballads" in *Famous Prefaces,* The Harvard Classics, 1909-14, Bartleby.com, Great Books Online.

Worgan, George B. *Journal of a First Fleet Surgeon,* The Library Council of New South Wales, in association with the LAH, Sydney, 1978.

Wright, Judith. *Collected Poems 1942-1970,* Angus & Robertson, Sydney, 1975.

Wright, Reg. "Shipping Movements, 1788-1814", in Nobbs, 1988.

Wright, Reg. *The Forgotten Generation of Norfolk Island and Van Diemen's Land*, LAH, Sydney, 1986.

Wujastyk, Dominik. "Indian Medicine", in Bynum & Porter, 1, 1997.

X

No Entries

Y

Yalom, Marilyn. *Blood Sisters: The French Revolution in Women's Memory*, Pandora, London, 1995.

Yarwood, A.T. *Samuel Marsden: The Great Survivor*, Melbourne University Press, Carlton, 1977.

Young, Maxine. "The British administration of New South Wales 1786-1812" in J.J.Eddy & J.R.Nethercote.

eds., *From Colony to Coloniser*, Hale & Iremonger, 1987.

Z

Zinsser, H. *Rats, Lice and History*. Boston: Atlantic Monthly Press, 1935.

Notes

Preface & Introduction Notes

1 Blane, 1789:222.

2 Rodger, 2006. See ch. 29, "Infinite Honour", and ch. 32, "A Thinking Set of People".

3 Crystal, David. *The Stories of English.* Allen Lane, an imprint of Penguin Books, London, 2004:5.

4 Frost, 1994:112, 252 n6. Frost's source was: Hancock, 1976:61.

5 Hartley, 1954:"Prologue", 1.

6 Lowenthal, 1985:xvi.

7 Parsons, in Aplin, 1988:104, 117n12.

8 Lowenthal, 1985:xix.

9 Atkinson, 1998:xviii.

10 Ibid.

11 Cummins, 1968:1-2.

12 Berezin, in Smelser and Swedberg, eds. 2005:109-27. A newspaper article by Ross Gittins, Economics Editor of the *Sydney Morning Herald,* brought this book to my attention.

13 Smith, [1759]2000:3. See also Berezin, above, 2005:113, for the notion that "the two works are more intricately connected than scholars had previously understood".

14 Gatrell, (1994)1996:v-x. See Darwin, ([1872]1994); and Collins (1993), mentioned in Berezin, 2005:109, 124, and published on the internet.
[Professor Katherine Samaras dramatized a present day 'better than cure' theme, and more, 'health as a resource' at TEDxSydney: https://www.youtube.com/watch?v=FoV3YCQSSzk. Last accessed 22 November 2014.]

15 Dr Brian Turner suggested that this 'Introduction' should be separated from an earlier first chapter and provided a convincing argument. I thank him for it.

16 In the late 1960s Minto would become a critical site for a district centre (later rejected) as part of the three cities plan of development for the Campbelltown, Camden and Appin areas.

17 S. Elliott Napier. 'William Redfern: The Story of His Life', in *The Sydney Morning Herald,* 22 & 31 July [22 (original form)], and 9 October (addenda), 1926. Digital copies required rewriting against the original page. Napier, an experienced journalist, takes precedence over Dunlop in publishing the earlier study. Not surprisingly Napier stressed the friendship between Macquarie, Antill and Redfern.

18 Dunlop, 1928:57-105. Page references to "Dunlop, 1928" are to this edition. See also Dunlop's "A Postscriptum", *Journal and Proceedings,* 1928:299.

19 Ford, 1953:1-36.

20 Clune, Frank [and P.R.Stephensen], 1964. See also *ADB on line* for Clune, Francis Patrick (Frank) (1893-1971).

21 Pescott, 1970:1-124.

22 Grant, 1994. Jacqueline's husband is a descendant of John Grant.

23 Jones, 1999:7:35-4, and 1999:7; 78-83.

24 Rudé, 1978:238.

25 Ibid. See 1-10, for a discussion of the problem of definition, 8-10 for the citation and a reference table.

26 Ford, 1953:1.

27 Ford, 1955:41-54.

28 Dr Bryan Gandevia, personal communication.

29 Frank Fenner, *Nature, Nurture and Chance*, published by ANU E Press, 2006:34.

30 Anonymous (a colleague). "Retirement of Professor Sir Edward Ford", in *The Gazette*, University of Sydney, vol 2, no 4:214-5, 1967. This story was repeated in Ford's "Obituary", the *Sydney Morning Herald*, Tuesday, 2 September 1986. The same notion of shared responsibility for health has been propagated within civil society. The William Redfern Oration commemorates the man, and an idea - preventive medicine.

31 Grogan, R.S., in *OPMHA,* 1996:140-1.

32 See also Ben Haneman, "Sir Edward Ford (1902-1986)" in *Health & History*, Bulletin of the Australian Society of the History of Medicine, 1999, *1*: 208-211.

33 Fenner, 2006:chapter 3, pp. 35-6.

34 Clune, 1964, opp. p.128. Sheila Sim also photographed the grave in January 1998.

35 Roger Pescott to Arthur Jones, 19 October 1969.

36 *PRO/ADM 1/534*, "Minutes of the proceedings of a court martial..." [Copy held by the History of Medicine Library, R.A.C.P., Sydney]. "The Redfern letter" is discussed in chapter 6, following.

37 In hindsight, but with all due deference to the late Roy Porter, *The Making of Geology*, 2008 (1980):80. Such an interaction (dialectic) was earlier in evidence in Jones (1999) between the views of the author and the Commissioner (Bigge).

38 Dunlop, Norman John, 1867-1928, "Obituary", *The Medical Journal of Australia*, 23 February 1929:258-61.

39 Ford, Sir Edward (Ted) (1902-1986) *ADB* online. See also Fenner (2006:35-6).

40 Bryan Gandevia, review of Ford's (1976) *Bibliography...* in *The medical Journal of Australia,* 9 July 1977. Gandevia had already published an annotated bibliography and would move on to a *Bibliography of Australian & Health Services to 1950* published by A.G.P.S. Canberra, 1988.

41 Gandevia, 1987. See also "Sir Edward Ford: a biographical note", in *Ford and Australian Medical History,* History of Medicine Library, R.A.C.P., 1978.

42 Winton, 1988:"The Library", 75-86.

43 Clune, 1964:5.

44 Tim Peach, manager, the State Library Bookshop, Sydney, alerted me to the fact that Clune had a ghost writer. Munro, 1992:305, listed Clune books ghosted by Stephensen.

45 Carol Liston has Sarah as 'colonial-born' in "Colonial Society" (ch.2, p.30), Broadbent and Hughes, 1992.

46 Munro, 1992:172. Stephensen was a "Quixotic figure", a former Queensland Rhodes scholar, "admired by D.H.Lawrence, parodied by Aldous Huxley, trailed by MI5, and vilified as a traitor in his own country"; he had been a "scholar, writer, publisher, company director and Communist Party activist", Ibid. 3-11. See *ABD on line* for Stephensen, Percy Reginald (1901-1965).

47 Ibid. 172.

48 Grant. 1994.

49 Ibid. 35.

50 Watmore, Pamela & Aileen Robertson. *Pioneers, Family Roots,* Cowra.

51 'Ronald Mervyn McGreal (1906-92) became the first Secretary of the Library Board of New South Wales in 1945. He played a significant part in the Camp Library Service during World War II, and was Deputy Principal Librarian of the Public Library of New South Wales, 1959-71' (David Jones in *The Australian Library Journal* August 1995:147n8).

52 *Campbellfield,* the Redfern house at Minto, is the subject of an appendix in Volume II of: *Better than Cure The life and times of the ebullient and resilient William Redfern 1775-1833.* Brief references are made to associated historical, architectural and conservation studies.

53 Antill, and Antill-deWarren, 1936. The authors, Major General Antill and his daughter [claimed to be adopted, for which see Pockley, 1978:76] were descendants of Major Antill, who married a sister of Sarah Wills, wife of Redfern. A print of a coat of arms bearing the name "William Redfern" appears in a bound volume of *The Emancipist* held by the Mitchell Library, Sydney (A822/A). See an endnote about this coat of arms where it is considered in the text, below.

54 An unsuccessful search was made at the time for a primary reference to *Minto* as a place name in New South Wales, such as is available for Airds (Macquarie, *Journals of His Tours...*1956:17). Revisiting this matter in 2011,

I had no more success with the Geographical Names Board of NSW (Carol Jarvis, 2 September 2011). Here is a sequence of events within which *Minto* must have been applied to an area of land, recorded, and placed on a map. The County of Cumberland was proclaimed by Governor Philip at the colony's foundation. In course of time, districts were recognised and named within the County of Cumberland. Wells, 1970 (1848:262, 9) has Minto and Airds as 'One of the original districts'. Why are there no straightforward answers for *Minto* as there are for Airds? That is my problem. Who gave it that name, when, and where was it recorded? From 1825 the colony was to be divided into parishes, hundreds and counties (Terry Kass, 2008:12). Wells, 1970 (1848:262)

55 As Minto burst from its village constraints in later years a number of new schools were built. One, close to the Redfern cottage, commemorates Sarah Redfern. The name, "Campbellfield", was given to a neighbouring school to the south.

56 Rachel Roxburgh, National Trust of Australia (N.S.W.), Women's Committee: House Inspection No 51, Sunday, 9 August, 1964:Minto and Campbelltown. In the National Trust Notes (No 51) it was incorrectly claimed that Commissioner Bigge had appointed the new Principal Surgeon. Chapter 15, below, has the correction.

57 For *saggart* the best I could obtain at the time was 'priestly', which fits with the intention of the original gift, and from talking with Teaching Nuns. No Church document was found. Since then computers and Wikipedia have strengthened the derivation with the following: "Saggart (Irish*: Teach Sagard,* meaning 'priest's house') is an outer suburban village in South Dublin County, Ireland, south west of Dublin city". This Wikipedia site (Saggart) was accessed 12 Jan. 2011. [Saggar (SOED, 1974) refers to a particular way of using clay in firing ceramic wares, a process used by a potter-in-residence at Campbelltown Art Gallery some time back.]

58 Pescott's study (1970) would provide some leads in due course.

59 Antill and Antill-de Warren, 1936.

60 Ellis, 1948:2-12. Reprinted 1991.

61 Ibid. See p.17 for the house, and pp.15-18 for the context.

62 Dr John Turner, historian, writer and commentator on Hunter Valley history, had conducted a number of study tours of Norfolk Island. See his book, *Joseph Lycett,* 1997, for references to Redfern's report on convict transports. Dr Turner died, 1998, aged 64.

63 Some trepidation, about my entry into this new field, was reduced by my reading of W.B. McDaniel, 2d, "The Place of the Amateur in the writing of Medical History", *The Bulletin of the History of Medicine*, 1939:7:687-695. It is of interest that his article was published in the year of this *Bulletin*'s foundation. The preceding article was by the noted medical historian, Henry Ernest Sigerist.

64 Winton, 1988:82. The library acquired this name in 1982, but the decision to form an historical library goes back to May 1954, with Professor Ford appointed Curator of the Library at the same time (Ibid. 40).

65 Bryan Gandevia, Alison Holster and Sheila Simpson, 1984:vi. [Time passes, as have Bryan, Alison and Sheila (AJ 2011).] Brenda Heagney knew them well. Bryan Gandevia, 1925-2006 (*H&H,* vol 8, no 2, 2006); Alison Holster, 1934-2008 (*RACP News,* Oct/Nov 2008, p.30).

66 "Annual Report", R.A.C.P., 1986, quoted in Winton, 1988:83.

67 Brenda Heagney tells the story of her professional career, as 'one of the longest serving medical librarians' in NSW, in *HLA News,* June 2009.

68 See Edward Ford, "Cowlishaw, Leslie (1877-1943)" in *ADB online.* See also a reference to Cowlishaw's library at the Royal Australasian College of Surgeons mentioned inter alia by James Guest in *OPMHA 5,* Perth, 1991:188.

69 See Alison Holster's entry, *Brian Price Billington,* in the RANZCP College Roll.

70 Gandevia in Home, 1983:81-98. The Australian context of the debate between Medical History and History of Medicine may be seen in the series *Occasional Papers on Medical History Australia,* which had its beginning in the Australian Medical Association, Victorian Branch and the Medical History Unit, University of Melbourne, and has continued with papers presented at Biennial Conferences of the Australian Society of the History of Medicine. For critical comment see also Diana Dyason (1984), Neville Hicks (1982) and Brian Dickey (1984). The two last are included as references to the first of these three authors.

71 Further to the preceding note, see Lewis, 1999 (v-vi). Note particularly Gandevia's early involvement in Melbourne medical history activities and again, after moving to Sydney in 1962 (vi, n3, passim); in an international context see Burnham, (Lewis, 1999, 43-47), and Warner, *Osiris,* vol. 10, 1995:164-193. Professor Warner gave the plenary address at the 1995 conference of A.S.H.M., where I had the pleasure of meeting him.

72 A. Jones, in Pearn, J., Carter, P. and Phillips, G.E., 1995:95.

73 Ian Jones, my son, designed the poster bearing in mind the material I had selected, and in the end mounted it on a board 31 x 100 cm.

74 Bryan gave me his copy of Gordon C. Sauer's *John Gould The Bird Man, A Chronology and Bibliography,* inscribed, "For Arthur Jones - In appreciation of his research and his generous help", 19 December 1994.

75 Ackerknecht, 1992 (1982 revised edn.):153.

76 See in particular, for *Fitzpatrick,* Blanco (1976), and MacDonagh (1981), and, for *McGrigor,* autobiography (1861, 2000), and biography (Blanco, 1974).

77 Carter, 1979.

78 Gill, 1913.

79 Brunton, 1989:1.
80 Ibid. n7.
81 Dening, 1993:146.
82 Lavery, 1995:245-51, "Fleets" in Nelson's Navy, first published in Great Britain, in 1989, by Conway Maritime Press.
83 Ibid. 350.
84 Windschuttle, 1996:70.
85 Manwaring and Dobrée, 1937.
86 Rodger, 2006.
87 Ibid. 448, 448n33.
88 Ibid. 448n35.
89 Trotter, 1976(1807): 154-5.
90 This Redfern study falls naturally into two parts (published as separate volumes).

Chapter 1 Notes

1 Harold B. Carter (1979:viii)
2 Dunlop, 1928:62. See also *Historical Records of Australia, Series I,* vol.vi: 745; Bigge (1822) 1968:84.
3 Dunlop, 1928:299.
4 Ibid. Dr Archie A. Scot Skirving, F.R.C.S., Edinburgh, did the research, which was passed on by his brother, Dr Robert Scot Skirving of Sydney. The Edinburgh Registrar-General's office records were searched. There, a notice in the records of Calton Burying Ground stated that "William Redfern, aged fifty-eight years, formerly a surgeon living at 18 Lothian Street, Edinburgh was buried in the New Ground in a grave purchased for his executors by Mr David Walker. The cause of death is not shown. The entry is dated 23 July, 1833". The grave could not be found at that time.
5 Dunlop, 1928:87.
6 Ford, 1953:12.
7 Ibid. 31.
8 Chisholm, ed. 1958, 7:395-7.
9 *ARJ 17/4,* Mitchell Library, Sydney: Fred Redfearn - 3 letters; 16 April 1955 is in reply to Fred's letter of 21 March 1955. This gives particulars of the Muster Log of HMS *Standard,* 1797. Fred and I corresponded from 1964 to 1967.
10 Clune, 1964:142.
11 Ibid. 128, a photograph of Redfern's grave is inserted after that page.
12 Rillie, James. From a letter to Fred Redfearn, who sent me a copy on 10 April 1967.
13 Ibid. For an update on the Burial Ground, see City of Edinburgh Council website, 1999:54-7.
14 Clune, 1964:142.

15 Dunlop, 1928:299.
16 Clune, 1964:108.
17 Ibid. 142.
18 Pescott, 1970:2-4; 3n2.
19 Sarah left Sydney on 10 March 1833 on *Norfolk* (Dunlop: 100; Clune: 142).
20 William Lachlan Macquarie Redfern married a Miss Walker of Glasgow.
21 For Dr Iggo's confirmatory letter see Jones, 1999,7:83,n86. The wording is almost an exact copy of that in Dunlop: 299, above.
22 Redfern's date of birth will be 1774 or 1775. The question mark will go.
23 Clune, 1964:108.
24 Pescott, 1970:3. See also Redfern's *Will.*
25 Tom Murray, personal communication. There is a reference to Tom in Johnson & Sainty, eds. 1991.
26 Pockley, 1978:65-75. For Antill's exchange of his diary for 20 of John Lewin's drawings see *Macquarie's Journals of his Tours...*1956:254, "Notes on the illustrations". See Bernard Smith for his evaluation of the "considerable historical importance" of Lewin's paintings, in which may be traced "the rude yet distinct beginnings of an Australian school of landscape painting" (Smith, 1960:174).
27 *Bigge Transcripts*, Vol 128:60940/180.
28 Bigge, *Report*, 1822, 1968:88.
29 I referred to these matters in 2010 when presenting a paper, *William Redfern and Lachlan Macquarie, the best of friends,* at Campbelltown's celebration of the *Macquarie Bicentennial.* Inter alia, I quoted a friend of Macquarie, Sir James McGrigor, on the negative qualities of young army officers [at issue, here], when not in the field (McGrigor, 2000:135, last paragraph).
30 *Ar17/2* M.L. "Grant of land at Sydney", with *Will* attached; Feb. 1 1834, attested copies.
31 M. H. Ellis, letter to the author. See also M. H. Ellis, 1970 [1947], where Ellis described Redfern as "tawney" (230), while W.C. Wentworth was "thatched in curious auburn hues" (231). Michael Persse gave Wentworth auburn hair in *A.D.B. 2*:1788-1850. Tawney, as colour, could range from brown to yellow.
32 Holt and D'Arcy Wentworth travelled to Norfolk Island on the ship *Betsy* in 1804.
33 Clune, 1987[1968]: 180; O'Shaughnessy, 1988:91,187.
34 O'Farrell, 1993[1986].
35 Whitaker, 2000:70.
36 Whitaker, 1994. Holt (67-8) is again the source for Redfern being Irish. In Whitaker (1994:189), Redfern's name appears in the context of the

assimilation of the Irish. In a general reference to Redfern (Ibid. 197-8) the source is *ADB II.*

37 Pearn, 1988:31,192.

38 Correspondence commenced in 1994 between the author and Dr Betty Iggo, about "Redfern at Edinburgh University" from which these facts were obtained. See chs 17 and 21, below.

39 For Howe, father (George) and son (Robert), see *ADB 1*, 1788-1850:557-9.

40 Porter "[M]edicine was, in fact, far more than a placebo, or just a bedside manner" (See above, Ch.04:'Medical Education Ashore').

41 Redfern's description of Bigge reveals a sharp eye - "The quiver of your lip, the curl of your nose, the expression of your eye". Howe was no better than Bigge at drawing out Redfern's medical skills. Neither mentioned how Redfern used his five senses, or palpation, perhaps. For this, in a wider context, see Malcolm Nicolson's 'preliminary sketch', "The art of diagnosis: Medicine and the five senses" in Bynum and Porter, 1997:801-25; and also Bynum and Porter, eds. 1993.

42 Dunlop, 1928:85.

43 Ford, 1953:20.

44 Pescott, 1970:46-7.

45 Ritchie, 1971, vol.1:120.

46 Jacyna, Stephen. "Medicine in transformation, 1800-1849", in Bynum et al., 2006:19.

47 Dunlop, 1928:104.

48 Ibid. 98-9. See Porter, below, "[M]edicine was, in fact, far more than a placebo, or just a bedside manner", at that time.

49 See chapter 6 in Volume II: *Better than Cure The life and times of the ebullient and resilient William Redfern 1775-1833*, "Redfern to Bigge", 5 February 1821.

50 Clune, 1964:176.

51 See chapter 10 in Volume II: *Better than Cure The life and times of the ebullient and resilient William Redfern 1775-1833*, for details.

52 Norrie, Philip. *Vineyards of Sydney*, Horwitz Grahame, Sydney, 1990.

53 J.C. Beaglehole, "On the Character of Captain James Cook" in *The Geographical Journal*, Vol CXXII, Part 4, December 1956:417-29. A copy was loaned by my neighbour, Frank MacNeale, RN, RAN. Notes checked against New Zealand Electronic Text Centre: http://www.google.com.au/search?hl=en&source=hp&q=NZETC&btnG=Google+Search&aq=f&aqi=g3&aql=&oq=&gs_rfai= [NZETC]. Accessed 12.05.2010.

54 Sir James Watt. "Some Consequences of Nutritional Disorders in Eighteenth-Century British Circumnavigations" in J. Watt, et al. *Starving Sailors*, 1981:65-9.

55 Hobsbawm, 1962; Boime, 1987.
56 Briggs, 1978 (1959).
57 Thompson, 1966:"Preface", 9-14.
58 Braithwaite, 2003:xii-xiv.
59 Estensen, 2005:passim; more precisely, chapter 5, and other references to his books.
60 Ibid. 15 - Gilbert Blane commented favourably on "Bass's reputation as a surgeon".
61 *BT,* Box 6, 2487-2509, Reel CY 1551.
62 Ford, 1953:12.
63 Dunlop, 1928:62.
64 See the *Preface,* above.
65 Gill, 1913:44.
66Ibid.
67 Gilmour, 1993:423. The author "served as Secretary of Defence under Edward Heath in 1974 and was appointed Lord Privy Seal and Deputy Foreign Secretary in Mrs Thatcher's first cabinet" (Ibid. half title page).
68 Manwaring and Dobrée, 1937 [1935]. Republished 1987, The Cresset Library, Century Hutchinson Ltd.; paginated as for the original Geoffrey Bles edition1935.
69 Smollett, 1988:85-88. See also Rodger's criticism, 1996:14, "As [Smollett] had served one voyage as a surgeon's mate he was not wholly unacquainted with the Navy, but he remains a poor, or rather an over-rich, substitute for documentary evidence".
70 Dugan, 1966.
71 See Clune, 1964:107-15, for this and the following paragraph.
72 Joseph Gurney (1744-1815) and William Brodie Gurney (1777-1855) were active at the time. See also Ritchie, ed. 1988, following his "Introduction", where a "Mr Bartrum...attended on behalf of Governor Bligh, by Permission of the Court" to make a short hand record of the court-martial of Lieut,-col. Geo. Johnston.
73 Thomas Redfern of Trowbridge, William of this book, and Robert. Evidence for Robert is his death certificate, a copy of which was sent to me by Jane Beck (received 28 October 1994). Robert's son William, was born in Philadelphia (Ibid. 1994).
74 Loudon in Wear, ed. 1992:224-5. See also Loudon, 1986.
75 Wallis, 1988. [Copy accessed at Society of Australian Genealogists, Sydney.]
76 Ritchie, 1971, 1:132-36, "Evidence of William Redfern, 26 June 1820" [amended].
77 Ibid. 136-9, "William Redfern's Notes on the [draft] Minutes of his Evidence", 8 February 1821.

78 Jane Beck, personal communication. Redfern's letter to Bigge apparently had the required effect in this instance. The corrected minute shows "Company of Surgeons". Redfern was appointed surgeon's first mate on H.M.S. *Standard.*

79 John Redfern [not related] gave me a copy of the reply he received from the Royal College of Surgeons of England, confirming date and outcome of the examination. Additionally, a copy of page 150 of the Examination Book was included. The top of the page contains names from a previous examination, it is assumed. These have been ruled off from the list containing Redfern's name, which appears under the heading - "At a Court of Examiners holden at the Theatre the 19th day of January 1797".

80 Ritchie, 1971, 1:138.

81 Ritchie, 1970:159.

82 Ritchie, Volume I, 1971:xiii-xiv.

83 Ibid. Volume I:1971:136-9, "William Redfern's Notes...", 8 February 1821.

84 Christopher Clayson, 'William Cullen in eighteenth century medicine' in *William Cullen and the Eighteenth Century Medical World*, 1993:93.

85 Bigge, 1966.

86 ML A1190, Governors' Despatches, Vol.1, 1813-1816, p.55.

87 In a later chapter may be found a reference to Royal Navy medical practice at sea surpassing that on land in the late eighteenth century.

88 Loudon, 1992:222-3.

89 Digby, 1994.

90 W.F. Bynum, "Roy Porter, obituary", in the *Guardian*, Tuesday 5 March 2002. Roy Porter was found dead beside his bicycle on 3 March 2002. He was on his way to his garden plot.

91 Ibid.

92 Lawrence, Christopher, 1994:19. See also Susan Lawrence, 1988:171-92, and in Nutton and Porter, eds, 1995.

93 Pickstone, in Porter, ed., 1996:304-341. See also Nutton and Porter, eds, 1995.

94 McGrigor, *The Autobiography*...2000:89;81.

95 Jacyna, 2006:29.

96 See Smollett, 1988:85-88 above.

97 Liston, 1992:21. Liston did not give a reference.

98 Pescott, 1970:42.

99 See Irvine Loudon, "Why are (male) surgeons still addressed as Mr?" *British Medical Journal*, on line, 23 December 2000.

100 Cohen, 1996:1. Described by its author as being "about the construction of the gentleman", it has challenging ideas about the influence of woman's presence on men in France, and in England, about language, and the silencing of women.

101 Ford, 1953:12.
102 Juanita Burnby, 'An Examined and Free Apothecary' in Nutton and Porter, 1995:18,23.
103 Loudon, 1992:225.
104 Ibid. 223-4.
105 Jenkyn, ed.1909:117-22, for Coleridge; Ibid. 140-5, for Lamb. See also Holmes, 1999:23-38; and Cecil, 1983:22-31.
106 Smith, 1960. Smith provided a reference, p.39n3, to an original idea he had conceived, that Wales might have influenced Coleridge's *Rime of the Ancient Mariner*. It was "Wales's scientific enthusiasm for the study of the atmosphere [that] became a source of inspiration", p.50.
107 Rosner, 1991:passim.
108 Lobban, 1980:42.
109 Rosner, 1991:73.
110 Pescott, 1970:4.
111 Melbourne, 1972 [1934]: 36. Wentworth entered Peterhouse College in 1823, where after a month he announced the completion of a poem on the theme of Australasia. For more detail see Ritchie, 1997:201-2. A copy of the poem may be seen on line.
112 Wentworth, 1819:facsimile edition, 1979. Revised edition 1824.
113 Ritchie, 1988:139. Redfern is included among Macquarie's "intimate circle".
114 Ritchie, 1970:122.
115 Ibid. 122n72.
116 Ritchie, 1988:136.
117 Ibid.
118 It was Ritchie who suggested Pescott's title, "Emancipist [Redfern] and Autocrat [Macquarie]", and who supervised, encouraged and took a "meticulous interest" in his study. This was acknowledged by Pescott, 1970:ii.
119 Ford, 1953:25.
120 Irvine, 1995:60.
121 Thompson, 1993:xii.
122 Ibid.
123 Ibid. 9.
124 Dunlop, 1928:63.
125 The Scottish pronunciation of *Smellie* is closer to *Smily*. Brenda Heagney, personal communication.
126 Loudon, "Childbirth" in Bynum and Porter, 1997:1052.
127 See Charles Darwin, who described Sir Charles Bell as "so illustrious for his discoveries in physiology, published in 1806 the first edition, and in 1844 the third edition of his 'Anatomy and Philosophy of Expression', 1994 (1872):2. Lobban (1980:46) had Charles Bell attending the wounded immediately after the Battle of Waterloo. After operating night and day for a

week his arms were "powerless with the exertion of using a knife", a process in which he was renowned for his speed.

128 Russell, 1987:xxxvi. I had access to a set, not Redfern's, in the collection of the History of Medicine Library, RACP, Sydney.

129 Elizabeth Windschuttle. *Taste and Science: The Women of the Macleay Family 1790-1850*, Historic Houses Trust of New South Wales, Glebe, 1988.

130 Russell, 1987:xli.

131 Bryan Gandevia, personal communication. I sighted and photocopied Ford's card.

132 I have not identified this W. Bell.

133 See Bligh, in A.D.B. I:1788-1850, 1966.

134 Cowlishaw, vol 6, 1936/7:10. Other references to Redfern appear between pp. 9-13.

135 Pescott, 1970:42 gave "Macquarie to Bigge", 6 November 1819, *HRAI*, vol x:221-2. This will prove to be a highly significant reference later in this book, in the context of Macquarie, Redfern and Bigge.

136 Ibid. 223-4.

137 Cable, K.J. "Fulton, Henry (1761-1840)", *ADBI*, 1966.

138 Ellis, 1970:483-4.

139 ML, A4073, *D'Arcy Wentworth Papers*, "Redfern to [Wentworth]". While undated, and although Wentworth was not named, Redfern's response is appropriate to the occasion.

140 Wright, 1988:220-1. A third visit from *Porpoise* (2) was made in December, without Putland. See also Wright, 1986:103, who suggested that had Bligh not been so keen to relocate the Islanders to the Derwent he may not have been deposed. *Porpoise* (2) would have been in the harbour with naval officers and Marines on hand.

141 Ritchie, 1988:31.

142 Nobbs, 1988:146.

143 Imagine my surprise on being told by Alison Holster, former librarian of the History of Medicine Library, that the book in question was on display in an exhibition of works forming part of David Scott Mitchell's original bequest, in the library that bears his name. An email from Paul Brunton, senior Curator, Mitchell Library, Sydney, provided background to the book's rediscovery.

144 Evatt, 1938.

145 As argued in the introductory chapter, Macquarie had blundered.

146 Beaglehole, J.C. "The Young Banks", 1962:1.

147 Carter, Paul. 1988:17.

148 Ritchie, 1997:199-200.

149 Ritchie, 1988:193n3; see also endnote 270n3, "Anon. to L. Macquarie, c.1815-18", Brisbane Collection, A XLIII, Box 29, ff.1-20, Mitchell Library, Glasgow.

150 Liston, 1992:22n6; see also Ritchie, 1988:193n3, above.
151 Grant, 1994.
152 McIntosh, 1954, No. 6. See also, Ford, 1955, above.
153 See Ford, 1955, above.
154 Proust, 1999:38, gave A.M. McIntosh as his source, as did John Cobley, in his entry, William Bland (1789-1868). *ADB I.*
155 Ritchie, 1971, 1:120. An extract from William Bland's answers to Bigge's questions on colonial medical matters appeared in the same volume, 143-5.
156 Jones, A.R., unpublished, *Cumulative Index to four short works about William Redfern, surgeon, 1774?-1833.* Grant's book was omitted as it had its own index. I am indebted to my eldest son, Howard, who introduced me to Macintosh computers and has never failed to solve my computing problems. When set in normal style, 12 point Helvetica font, the *Cumulative Index* spread over thirty-five A4 pages. Key words gave page references to Dunlop, Ford, Clune and Pescott, in columns, in that order, as single line entries. The usefulness of this index may be imagined.
157 A print of a coat of arms bearing the name "William Redfern" appeared in a bound volume of *The Emancipist* held by the Mitchell Library, Sydney (A822/A). That the coat of arms belonged to our William Redfern is the more likely in view of this Antill/Redfern connection. No reference to it was found in the family history section of the State Library of NSW. Three spellings were considered - Redfearn, Redfern and Redferne. Elvin's *Dictionary of Heraldry* would lead one to believe that the animals of the cat family pictured, were *leopards*, one of which held up a *fern* frond. The upper part of the shield is formed by the bases of two inverted right-angled triangles that form the shape of a letter "W', with outer sides, parallel. Within the triangles, two leopards face each other while holding up a central anchor, an "emblem of hope". The caduceus sign of the modern physician has a tree, as the rod, with entwined serpents, against a light background, triangular in shape with a rounded base, its apex pointing to and touching the base of the anchor. The symbolic references to Redfern and to his profession are clear. ('Coat of arms', or 'bookplate', or both? See Mark J. Ferson, in *Health & History.* 1999. 1:347-357.)
158 Tomaselli, in Black and Porter, eds, 1996, gave J.G.A.Pocock's *Virtue, Commerce and History...*1991, as an additional reference.
159 Wollstonecraft, 1992 (1792).
160 Outram, 1989.

Chapter 2 Notes

1 Manwaring, G. E. and Bonamy Dobrée, 1937:34-5. Spithead is an anchorage between Portsmouth Harbour and the Isle of Wight for which, see *Admiralty Chart*, SC394, 1995 edition. William Heather's chart of 1797 may be seen online at

http://www.geog.port.ac.uk/webmap/hantscat/html/maptype.htm; accessed 16 June 2008. For William Heather, see Fisher, 2001.

2 For dress of seamen, see Dugan, 1966:93n, and Lloyd, 1968:236.

3 Private enterprise boats, floating shops, carrying provisions, vegetables, etc., to ships for private sale. See *S.O.E.D.* for evolution from dirt-boats, 1685-1769.

4 Gill, 1913:6. [Hereinafter abbreviated to Gill.] "[Lord] Bridport had been made Commander-in-Chief in May 1795. His predecessor, "Lord Howe had been compelled to retire...from a severe attack of gout".

5 Gill, 1913:11. Bridport ascertained that the first petitions were sent to the Admiralty late in 1796. They were disregarded. Later, 11 petitions, sent to Howe are preserved. They were sent to Bridport just before the mutiny (Ibid. 11n1).

6 Word usage is blurred in the literature - "seaman" [Royal Navy] and "sailor" [other].

7 Manwaring and Dobrée, 32n. The source given was C.S.P. Dom., 1652-3:43.

8 Gilmour, 1993:418n73; 492 also gave Gill and Manwaring and Dobrée as core references. N.A.M. Rodger (2006:chapter 29) puts the question beyond doubt. Rodger's studies to the mid 1700s, published first in 1986 (1996:346) moved on to 1797, published in Lewis R. Fischer, et al., eds, *The North Sea. Twelve Essays on Social History of Maritime Labour,* Stavanger, Norway, 1992:29-36. [In 2012 I acquired a copy of Fischer (1992).] Rodger acknowledged this 1992 publication in "The Naval World of Jack Aubrey" in A.E. Cunningham, ed. 1994, reprinted in Patrick O'Brian's *The Nutmeg of Consolation,* 1997:317-338. I thank Ian and Christa Binns for a collection of Patrick O'Brian's Georgian Navy books.

9 Dugan, 1966:54ff, "The Humble Petition" (Ch3).

10 'On Institutions' in Norbert Elias, *The Genesis of the Naval Profession* (2007) edited and with an introduction by René Moelker and Stephen Mennell, now to hand (2011). Since then I have read Robert van Krieken's account of Norbert Elias [2007(1998)]

11 Thompson, in Hay et al., 1975:255. "The anonymous threatening letter is a characteristic form of social protest in any society which has crossed a certain threshold of literacy, in which forms of collective organized defence are weak, and in which individuals who can be identified as the organisers of protest are liable to immediate victimization". These petitions were not threatening, however.

12 Neale, Jonathan, 1985, passim. For Neale, see Rodger, 2006(2004):836.

13 Ibid. 152-5. Dugan provided details of Howe's earlier career, including his meetings with Benjamin Franklin in London, his subsequent resignation over the pursuit of a punitive war against the American Colonists, and his status as

'the sailors' friend' after the *Janus* affair. See also Warner, 1979:122-142. Dr Thomas Trotter held Admiral Howe in high regard.
14 *Queen Charlotte*, had been Howe's flagship at the *Battle of the 1st June 1794* (Manwaring and Dobrée, 140).
15 Lavery, 1995 (1989): 145-6".Marines are often associated with the suppression of mutiny, and this role was vastly expanded during the Napoleonic Wars", but they "were not always effective in suppressing mutiny. At Spithead and the Nore, they often took a full part alongside the seamen". "Some marines were commended for their loyalty, but others were hanged or flogged for supporting the mutiny [at the Nore]". Probably the marines had received a pay rise before the seamen to encourage their loyalty to the Captain.
16 In her chapter 'Textiles' [seventeenth century], Clark wrote of 'pauperisation of large numbers of women' from inadequate wages. Here, a century later, her words could equally apply to the wives of seamen, viz. 'Instead of the independence and self-reliance which might have been secured through adequate wages [of her husband in the Royal Navy] mothers were not only humiliated and degraded, but their physical efficiency and that of their children was lowered' (Clark, 1968 (1919): 147).
17 Lloyd, 1968:235. "[H]ard work at sea so soon ruined even adequate clothing, that the purser was authorised to sell slops [i.e. replacement clothing items], taking a shilling in the pound discount for his pains".
18 Manwaring and Dobrée, 32n17. Source given as *Admiralty Documents* in the Public Record Office (Ad. 1/5125), *Petitions to the Admiralty 1793-1797.*
19 Gill, 359, "Appendix A.1". "From the *Defence* to the Admiralty": "The petition was drawn up on the *Queen Charlotte* and sent to the other ships to be copied. This copy may serve, therefore, as an example of the earlier petitions, written before the Mutiny had been organized. The original manuscript was sent to the Admiralty with Sir Peter Parker's dispatch A 354, A.S.I. 1022 [*Admiralty Secretary In-Letters*]".
20 See Thompson, 1993:33, in the context of "Patricians and Plebs", "a man put, perforce, into the stance of soliciting favours will not reveal his true mind".
21 Manwaring and Dobrée, 76n; Neale, 1842:47. Neale's source was given as "the Commons Journals, 52, p.503". To M&B, 'significant', no doubt because on 23 April a committee of the Privy Council had been set up to investigate the sailor's wage claim, and that these figures show conclusively the tardiness of the Royal Navy in the matter of paying sailors. See in particular the first amount due being to "ships paid off".
22 Gilmour, 1993:16. Reluctance to pay seamen had a history. "Adam's fine screen outside the Admiralty was built to keep out sailors agitating for their pay. Presumably it was cheaper than paying them".

23 Gill, 7, 14. In 14n2, Gill wrote, "Bridport called at Portsmouth on 3 March; and one bundle of petitions may have been sent to Howe then".

24 Gill, 6. From 7-10 March.

25 Gill, 14. See also Gill, 6 and 6n2. Bridport's squadron, known as the Grand Fleet, consisted of 16 ships of the line and some frigates and smaller vessels. The battleships are listed by name in the footnote. Gill, 6, Rear-Admirals Gardner, Colpoys and Pole served under Bridport.

26 Gill, 6.

27 Lavery, 1995:300-5,"Blockade" - disliked by both officers and men, unfairly described as 'Channel gropers' (p.305); see also Marcus, 1975:171ff.

28 Manwaring and Dobrée, 32-3ff.

29 Manwaring and Dobrée, 33n18.

30 Rodger, 1979:69. Spencer appointed 19 December 1794:82, "only thirty-six, Spencer's birth and wealth had already placed him in the inner circle of the Whig aristocracy. He was in some ways another Sandwich - like him a scholar, with the finest private library in Europe". See Foreman, 1999, for family and society background. Georgina was Spencer's sister.

31 Manwaring and Dobrée, 33

32 Gill, 97-8. Increases that resulted from meeting the Mutineers' demands are set out there.

33 Manwaring and Dobrée, 33n19. Manwaring and Dobrée comment (p.270), "This letter [from Spencer to Bridport] has not before been noticed".

34 Manwaring and Dobrée, 20-23. See Captain Pakenham's 1796 letter to Spencer discussed below.

35 Manwaring and Dobrée, 34. Howe, because of his gout, would not return to his former post.

36 See above reference.

37 Dugan, 1966:147, took Fox's statement in Parliament - "All I know is what I have seen in the papers" - to indicate that he did not receive the Petitions. For Fox, see Foreman (1999), above.

38 Manwaring and Dobrée, 36.

39 Manwaring and Dobrée, 37n reads: "Men's wives - perhaps a courtesy title - were allowed to stay on board when the ship was in port". See also Gill, 19n. Sending the women ashore, suggested to Gill,"the seamen were prepared for violent measures". See also Ch.7, below.

40 Manwaring and Dobrée, 37.

41 Dugan (1966:82) has Admiral Parker expressing "resentment that Lord Bridport had not informed him about the seamen's petitions". This statement, quite apart from being unsourced, cannot be used to imply, as Dugan did, that Bridport was aware of what was going on.

42 Manwaring and Dobrée, 38; see also Gilmour, 1993, "combinations" in the context of eighteenth century "Industrial Disputes", ch.12; "The acts were repressive but seldom invoked. Most combinations were already illegal...and

trade unionism proceeded irrespective of the new legislation", "Before and after the Combination Acts, the authorities often preferred conciliation to violence".

43 Manwaring and Dobrée, 38-9.

44 Manwaring and Dobrée, 39

45 Manwaring and Dobrée, 38

46 Manwaring and Dobrée, 40ff.

47 Thompson, E.P. *Customs in Common,* 1993:185ff. "We have been warned in recent years, by George Rudé and others, against the loose employment of the term "mob". I wish in this chapter to extend the warning to the term "riot", especially where the food riot in eighteenth-century England is concerned" (Ibid). The word "mutiny" will receive critical attention in chapter 5, below.

48 Dugan, 1966:93, described this meeting as "the first expression of universal male suffrage that Britain had ever seen".

49 Manwaring and Dobrée, 42.

50 Manwaring and Dobrée, 50-1, Appendix II (259-60).

51 The grievances will be discussed in chapters 2 and 3, below. The wages claim will lead into a discussion of the 1790s in Britain. Other grievances will be considered in the context of Naval health and medicine serving at the same time to provide background for understanding William Redfern's work as a surgeon's mate.

52 Manwaring and Dobrée, 'From the *Annual Register*, 1797, State Papers, 380'.

53 Lloyd, 1965:See 238n; "Trotter hardly refers to the Mutinies of 1797 in his *Medicina Nautica,* but in his pamphlet, *A Practical Plan for Manning the Royal Navy* (Newcastle, 1819), he made this claim".

54 Rodger, 2006:446. At Spithead, bounties were not listed among grievances (Ibid. 447). Spithead and Nore omitted impressment and flogging as grievances.

55 Ibid. 443. See also Elias, 2007, passim. Only recently coming to my attention (2011), Elias provided an historical study of the Navy as a profession, or institution, from Elizabethan times, with due regard to commerce and with useful comparison and contrast with continental navies, or lack of them, including Dutch, French, Spanish and German. Not simply descriptive, Elias combined this knowledge with a Continental (later English) background - birth, languages, culture, politics and history - to pinpoint important linkages especially power and change.

56 Lewis, 1960:135-40.

57 Ibid. 135-139

58 Elias provides understanding, in 'The Growing Costs of the Naval Establishment: Elizabeth and Cromwell Compared' (115-120) with 'Appendix...Royal Navy Personnel 1789-1816' (128).

59 Lewis, 1960:116-127, "The Quota". Lewis looking at the increasing demand for seamen against the supply, agreed that a quota system was needed, but described this first attempt at National Service a failure.
60 Lavery, 1989:117-128. Part V, "Naval Recruitment" includes I, "The Problem", 2 "The Press Gang, and Other Methods". See, Brownlee, 1980:20-1, for a summary.
61 Gilmour, 1993:Ch.8. "The Press Gang" was only "slightly less violent than the criminal law", Ibid. 184-192. See also Marcus, 1975:107, the Thames in 1793 and 1803. On the latter occasion "close on a thousand seamen were taken in a single night".
62 Rodger, 1996:150. See "Manning", Ch. v in part A: "The problem" and C: "Impressment".
63 Gill, 283.
64 Hibbert, 1994:32-3, tells of Nelson impressing seamen from returning merchant ships.
65 Ibid.
66 Rediker, 1993 [1987]. Ibid. Ch.1:"The seaman as man of the world (10-76)":32. See also, Gilmour (1993:416), who reported pay for Merchant Navy seamen as four times that offered by the Royal Navy, pre 1797.
67 Lavery, 1995:118, for this paragraph.
68 Adam Smith, Glasgow Edition of *Wealth of Nations,* Liberty Fund, 1981:464-5.
69 Rediker, 1993 [1987]: 4-5.
70 Ibid. 6-7.
71 Ibid. 5.
72 Rediker, 1993:110, 205, for the origin of the word "strike".
73 Linebaugh, Peter, 'The Tyburn Riot Against the Surgeons' in Hay et al., 1975:79. The other four kinds of solidarities were "the family, the personal friends, fellow workers, [and] the Irish".
74 Linebaugh, 1993:123-4, in "The Picaresque Proletariat During the Robinocracy [Robert Walpole,P.M.1720-50]".
75 Rediker, 297-8.
76 Lavery, 1995:269-73, "The Merchant Marine". For his reference to wages, 272, Lavery gave as his source, "Parliamentary Report no 5071, 1800, on the Coal Trade".
77 See various references to Jesse Lemisch in Rediker,1993. Looking at the positions taken by Linebaugh & Rediker, above, it is not surprising that they jointly published *The Many-headed Hydra,* 2000, a study of the lives of *Sailors, Slaves, Commoners* of the Atlantic over two centuries. More recently, in 2007, Marcus Rediker published *The Slave Ship...*2007. Both books reached me in 2009 with this present book nearing completion.
78 Rodger, 1996:11. Again see Rodger, 2006.
79 Dugan, 1996:473-4, "Appendix I".

80 Neale, 1985:passim.

81 Gill, 260-79. "Clearly, 'the spirit of tyranny and oppression' was thoroughly subdued", and removed "in consequence of the mutinies..." (Ibid. 279).

82 The idea of customs being 'invented' brings to mind and gains credence from *The Invention of Tradition,* 1992 (1983). Terence Ranger makes reference in passing, to 'invented traditions of the new ruling classes [being] to some extent balanced by the invented traditions of industrial workers' (Ibid. 1992:211).

83 Thompson, 1993:1, and 2-15, "Introduction: Custom and Culture".

84 Ibid. 3, 'oral tradition', 4-5:'classic struggles'.

85 Ibid. 6, not self-defining, 7:'located within'.

86 Ibid. Ref. 7-9; 9-10, for the addition.

87 Rediker, 1993:234-5.

88 Foreman and Phillips, 1999:108. See also Neale, 1985:68-118; chs 5 & 6 for the mutiny on HMS *Culloden* in 1794.

89 Gilmour, 993:417* (footnote).

90 Thompson, 1993:191.

91 Manwaring and Dobrée, 45.

92 Manwaring and Dobrée, 20-1.

93 See Neale, 1985, for the effect of the deliberate rolling of canon balls along decks, in the dark. For rolling balls in a less intimidatory situation see seamen at play with Flinders' cat, *Trim* (Flinders, 1985:18-9).

94 Rodger, 2006 [2004]: 490.

95 Each had decided not to keep their ships at sea continuously, as the copper on their bottoms allowed, and military strategy demanded. This was a calculated risk. The French did escape from Brest at times.

96 Gill, 8ff.; Manwaring and Dobrée, 23ff, Ch 2".The Ferment Works"; Dugan, 1966:53ff., Ch 3, "The humble petition".

97 Rodger, 1996 [1986]: 188-204, "Straggling and Desertion"; 354-59, "Appendix", IV-VI.

98 For a biography of Thomas Trotter, see Ian Alexander Porter, *Medical History,* 7:155-64, 1963; see also Roy Porter, "Introduction", in Trotter, 1804, reprinted by Routledge, London, 1988.

99 Rodger, 1996:194-5

100 Lewis, 1960:133-5; Admiral P. Patton's figures also quoted in Lavery, 1994:143-4.

101 Corbin, *The Lure of the Sea,* 1995:Chapter 1, "The Roots of Fear and Repulsion", which includes the sea itself.

102 Rodger, 1996:207, is talking about "natural" discipline' from the "fear of drowning".

103 Lavery, 1989:193.

104 Ibid. 194-9. "Watches", etc. in Part IX: "Shipboard Life", I: "The Organisation of the Crew".

105 Lloyd, 1968:232-3. John B. Hattendorf's informative introduction to the 1998 edition of Lloyd's *Lord Cochrane*, is essential reading, in view of the importance of Lloyd's continuing contribution to this present study.
106 Gill omitted *Impetueux* (74) but included *Nymphe* (36). Manwaring and Dobrée, showed two delegates for *Impetueux*.
107 Dugan, 1965. Appendix 3. From the number of guns it is possible to determine which are line-of-battle ships.
108 Lewis, 1960:25-6, described "rating" "as an overworked, omnibus word, used in all sorts of different connections. Everything and everybody was 'rated'.
109 Lavery, 1989:35-57 in Part II: "Types of Ship" provides more than enough information on this subject. The Rating System is discussed on page 40.
110 Embroiled, in the inclusive sense, either for or against, officer or seaman.
111 Brunton, 1989:1
112 Manwaring and Dobrée, 257-8 Appendix I, list of delegates: 43-46 delegates discussed
113 Lavery, 1989:137n23(Adm1, 5125), and 137n24 (Manwaring and Dobrée, 262-3), each in "The Status of the Petty Officer". Lavery's edition of Manwaring and Dobrée, is different from that used in Note 39 as the source of the List of Delegates.
114 Brownlee, 1980:23-5; see "Jobs" for this paragraph. Brownlee, a Master Mariner, has produced an excellent concise presentation of "the ships, the men, and the main strategies of the British Navy that defeated the French in the Napoleonic wars" (p2) [48pp].
115 Lavery, 1989:137. Lavery said four were Midshipmen but five are clearly shown on the list.
116 Manwaring and Dobrée, gave as their sources in 41n (271), Information from the Muster Books and their own Appendix I (256-7) where a table of information about the Delegates may be found.
117 Rodger, 2006:448.
118 Ibid. 449.
119 Rodger, 2006:448, 448n36, 724n36, which reads, "See the Bibliography under Brown, Coats, Doorne, MacDougall and Neale". Coats, Doorne and MacDougall each contributed to Ann Coats and Philip MacDougall, eds., *The 1797 Mutinies - Papers of the Spithead and Nore Bicentenary Conferences, 1997* [N.A.M.R. added, 'forthcoming: I am grateful to authors and editors of this collection for the opportunity to read and cite it in advance of publication']. [[Further, from a reply to an email I sent to Ann Coats on 23 September 2006, the collection remained unpublished. From a later Google search I found a 2011 publication date and placed an order. A copy arrived on 1.12.2011 too late to influence this biography. A.J.]]

120 Ibid. Gill described "bad food and low wages" as "objective causes" of "disaffection" while the "vague but heartening ideals of the [French] Revolution' provided a "subjective" cause (viii-ix).
121 Keane, 1995:307, 592n113-4. Keane gave as his reference, W.S.Lewis, ed., *Horace Walpole's Correspondence, vol 11* (New Haven, Conn., 1973), 239.
122 Keane, 1995:307-8 for this and the following paragraph.
123 Gill, viii-ix, Preface. Gill's statement continues, "and that nearly all of the seamen in the Channel and North Sea fleets were in some degree affected by them". See also Gill, Book VI, "The Political Aspects of the Mutinies", Chs XXII-III, pp.299-323.
124 Briggs, 1978 [1959]: 13.
125 Lewis, 1960:124.
126 Ibid. 124-5.
127 See Manwaring and Dobrée, 43 and Dugan, 1966:94. Neither appears to have done a thorough search of individual backgrounds. However, each confirms the presence of Irishmen amongst the delegates. Rodger (2004[2006]:449) accepts "four out of thirty-three were Irish".
128 Gilmour, 1993. Ch. 18, 391-431; Ireland and the mutinies, 414-423.
129 Gilmour, 423. See Hobsbawm and Rude, 2001[1969], for an interesting parallel: Ch.12, 239-50. There, the role of "blacksmiths, carpenters and artisans - men who were in a somewhat superior condition of life", i.e. different, from farm labourers in the agricultural "Swing" Riots that climaxed in 1830.
130 Ibid. 417, for this, and the three following paragraphs.
131 Thompson, 1966:167, has 11 500 Irish sailors and 4 000 Irish Marines in the Navy.
132 Gill, 36-9. The seamen interpreted Gardner's aim as an attempt to sow division and mistrust in the fleet. His angry outburst on being outwitted by the Delegates did not help. Gill assessed Gardner's "well-meant effort" as "one of the most disastrous incidents of the year". Furthermore "the feeling of suspicion" aroused, combined with events of the following two weeks, ended in "the second outbreak of mutiny at Spithead and St Helens" (39).
133 Manwaring and Dobrée, 43, where ship by ship the Delegates are briefly described and their qualities assessed.
134 Dugan, 94.
135 See Gill, 317n1. Dugan, 63-4, Joyce, "the leading spirit" served a sentence for sedition, lost his tobacco shop in Belfast.as a result.
136 For this quote see Gilmour, 1993:418, 492n72. His note contains references to Manwaring and Dobrée, Gill, and several other sources. On the Delegates maintaining the internal discipline of the Mutineers, see Manwaring and Dobrée, 44-6, 46ff, 58.
137 Gill, 30

138 Heilbroner, and Malone, 1986:3. There, by way of 'locat[ing] Smith in his times', these commentators claimed, that "Adam Smith [1723-1790], like all his contemporaries, believed firmly in the need for a well-defined social hierarchy and a firm adherence to the principle of property". Later, on the same page, comes their understanding that "all of the philosophes [of the Enlightenment], including Smith, share one limit to their social imaginations...an inability to imagine that the lower orders might some day exercise sovereignty over society. Democracy, with all its implicit threats to property and hierarchy, was not yet on the political agenda and would not be put there until the French Revolution".

139 Thompson, 1966:13.

140 Ibid. 1966:18. "London Corresponding Society" hereinafter referred to as "LCS".

141 Thompson, 1993:125-6.

142 Ibid. xvii. See Volney, 1807. [This copy held by the State Library of NSW.] For further discussion of Volney see Rigby (22-37), and L. J. Jordanova (12-21), in Barker et al. 1982. Volney was described by Thompson as "the French revolutionary and atheist thinker" (128); "It was a book more positive and challenging, and perhaps as influential, in English radical history as Paine's *Age of Reason*, which it preceded by several years" (199-203ff.). [See *Bibliography* for a new edition, 2007.A.J.]

143 Volney, 1807:106-113.

144 Thompson, E.P.1993:199n7. Perhaps few had read the book but many would have seen catching handouts and paste ups from both Paine and Volney as this note suggests. It reads, "The confrontation between the 'distinguished class' and the 'people' was circulating as a fly-sheet perhaps as early as December 1792'. [PRO reference and acknowledgment followed]. See the reference to non-readers having the texts of prints read to them, outside print shops, in Baer, 1992:256. This, too, is the point made in the case against Muir, in Flynn (1994:xix), of reading Volney to people.

145 Volney, *The Ruins...* The Echo Library edition, Teddington, Middlesex, 2007:196.

146 Thompson, 1966:345-429, for a detailed discussion of Methodism.

147 Ibid. 1966:345-6. See also the previous note for detailed supporting argument.

148 Gerth and Mills. *From Max Weber:* 1977:18; 320ff. Note particularly Weber (321, 321n35 & 459), where he makes a point of repeating, "it is not the ethical doctrine of a religion, but the form of ethical conduct upon which premiums are placed that matters".

149 Rodger, 2006 (2004): 452.

150 Dening, 1993:passim.

151 Ibid. 1993:378. Dening gives as reference, Norbert Elias, "Studies on the Genesis of the Naval Profession", in *British Journal of Sociology*, 1950, 1:291-

301. Since writing that end note I have read the 1950 Elias *Journal* study twice, in the above context, and as published in Norbert Elias, edited and with an introduction by René Moelker and Stephen Mennell, *The Genesis of the Naval Profession*, University College Dublin Press, 2007. This reveals the editors' acceptance of Elias' intention, given in a footnote to the first page of the 1950 article, that there would be three papers in all. The second and third were never published. It remained to find them. That story may be read in the *Introduction* (2007, 1-24). In 'Tensions and Conflicts' Elias wrote, "One should not think that strife was incompatible with amity or rivalry with collaboration' (2007:72) and follows with questions. The first, 'But how should one proceed?'"

152 Dening, 1993:379. Attributed to Peter Stallybrass and Allon White, 1986:80.

153 Dening, 1993:379. Dening gave six references for this quote.

154 Ibid. 379.

155 Ibid. 156.

156 "The tarred pigtail had not yet appeared". See "dress of seamen" (Dugan, 1966:93n).

157 For this quote see Gilmour, 1993:418, 492n72. His note contains references to Manwaring and Dobrée, Gill, and several other sources. On the Delegates maintaining the internal discipline of the Mutineers, see Manwaring and Dobrée, 44-6; 46ff; 58.

158 Briggs, 1978 [1959].

159 Hobsbawm, 1990:91, cited in Colley, 1996:387.

160 Thompson 1966:147ff. For more about Binns see Dugan (1966:[in England] 68-9, 362n, 378-80 [tried for sedition], 385-6, 393, 412, 451-2, [in America] 468-9, 469n.

161 Gilmour, 1993:443, n32, 495. The introductory sentences, of the paragraph from which that quote was taken, read as follows: "Pitt was well aware of the armed forces' crucial role not only in repelling invasion but also in preserving the political system from internal revolt. Yet the government's handling of the army and navy was much more negligent than its treatment of the lower classes. By turning a blind eye to all the warning signals of impending trouble in the fleet, it precipitated mutinies which laid Britain open to invasion and which were politically - as well as militarily - the most perilous moment of the revolutionary decade"(Ibid).

162 Colley, 1996:297ff. "Manpower", and the three "Appendix" entries.

163 Hobsbawm, 1962:104, [Weidenfeld and Nicolson, 1995 reprint:79]. For a different context see Marc Baer's study of the 1809 London theatre riots (1992:245). Baer wrote of people in "both celebratory and protest crowds" as carrying "strong controls against participating in the breakdown of social order". He went on, "It has been argued in this book that the essence of these controls...lay in a particular perception of the past and an essential theatricality

of life. By appealing to the past to frame the debate for the present, such beliefs disallowed a radically different future".

164 Gill, 27-8. Petty officers' support of the men discussed briefly, but more fully at 28n1, shows both support and restraint. On the other hand at 20n1 petty officers were reported as handing to the first-lieutenant of the *Defence* a copy of a petition, and a letter dated 15 April. Lavery, 1989:137:"The position of the petty officer was often quite difficult, especially when the officers tried to use them as spies against the men. This apparently happened aboard the *Prosperine* in 1797, when the crew complained of four petty officers 'continually going fore and aft the deck to listen to what is said, which is repeated by them to the commander".

165 Manwaring and Dobrée, 254-5. See also opening section of a following Chapter, "Woman aboard".

166 See Rediker, 1993:297-8, for a discussion of the idea that the sea is, or is not, a "wet nurse to democracy". Rediker argued that it was, "because maritime commerce mobilized thousands of men who spent much of their lives...battling 'authority and privilege'".

167 Herman, 1967:148. For an interpretation of the story see also *Billy Budd, Sailor and Other Stories*, sel. and ed. Harold Beaver, London, 1985:49. "In the very perception, however, that a modern tragedy has no need of tragic heroes; that agony and destruction are inherent in a man-of-war, madness in the floating hulk of our black civilization - the bitter seed of the tale lies buried".

168 Gill, 20. See also Gill, 3-15.

169 Manwaring and Dobrée, 60. Lady Spencer considered "That a mutiny of this extent should have been brewing for 3 months, and not one word of it to have transpired, is most wonderful".

170 Evidence for such contact between ships may be inferred from Gilbert Blane's observation of how rapidly "epidemics could spread throughout a squadron". See also Sir James Watt, 'The Colony's Health' in Hardy and Frost, 1989:140.

171 Manwaring and Dobrée, 58

172 Gill, 288.

173 Gill, 18 and 18n4, Admiralty Secretary Minutes 136, 15 April.

174 Gill, 18

175 Gill, 42-4

176 Gill, 19-20.

177 Gill, 21n.In this note, Gill drew attention to the mistaken view, widely held, that the mutiny broke out on the 15 April. Gill also inclined to the view that Bridport never gave a general order to prepare for sailing as he did not mention it in his letters. Gill concluded his note by saying that 'it seems quite probable that the mutiny began when Gardner tried to take his squadron to St Helens', as instructed (Gill, 18). Manwaring and Dobrée, 41.

178 Manwaring and Dobrée, 254-5".That sailors on attesting now take the Oath of Allegiance is largely due to the impression made on the authorities by the awed seriousness with which the sailors in the mutinies regarded the swearing of an oath". An observation first made by the magistrates Graham and William sent down to Sheerness to spy on the mutinies (Ibid).
179 Gill, 26
180 Ibid.
181 Gill, 30
182 Gill, 30n1 provides brief biographies of Spencer, Arden, Young and Marsden who formed the Admiralty Deputation. See "Appendix".
183 Gill, 31
184 Gill, 32
185 Gill, 34
186 Ibid.
187 Gill, 35
188 Ibid.
189 Gill, 36-37
190 Gill, 38
191 Ibid.
192 Ibid.
193 Gill, 39
194 Gill, 47-8
195 Gill, 41; Manwaring and Dobrée, 73.
196 Gill, 40-1:Manwaring and Dobrée, 74.
197 Gill, 42.
198 Gill, 48.
199 Gill, 47.
200Gill, 103-4. Gill argued that 'the policy of the Plymouth mutineers was always directed from the Grand Fleet' at Portsmouth. M & D: 78-9, for details of the Plymouth mutiny.
201 Gill, 51-2,52n1; Manwaring and Dobrée, 87.
202 Manwaring and Dobrée, 79-80.
203 Gill, 48.
204 Ibid.
205 Gill, 48-9, and 52; Manwaring and Dobrée, 81-2.
206 Gill, 48.
207 Gill, 56.
208 Gill, 57.
209 Gill, 58-9.
210 Gill, 68-71; 96-7; Manwaring and Dobrée, 97.
211 Gill, 94-96.
212 Gill, 67-8, 96.
213 Gill, 96-7.

214 Manwaring and Dobrée, 89-91. See 89n, "These numbers are uncertain; the returns differ. The man Bover, killed was not a Delegate, as is always stated".

215 Gill, 58-66. This forms a chapter, "The Mutiny on the London". Footnotes to this chapter carry on a debate about eyewitness and other accounts. 64n2 provides in tabular form seven different versions of the events relating to persons "killed and wounded".

216 See Elias (2007), 'The Development of the Midshipman' (chapter 3) as a significant role, but not straightforward, in 'The Genesis of the Naval Profession'.

217 Manwaring and Dobrée, 91 n 111. In this note the authors said: "Accounts are confused. The one here is taken, as well as from the sources already quoted, from Hannay, Tunstall and Neale; and especially from Colpoys' letter to Nepean of 8/v/97. See Ralfe, *Naval Biography, III*, 172-4. [This is typical of the careful nature of their research.]

218 Gill, 48, and see also his 'Note 3. On the Estimates' (97-8), cited below.

219 Manwaring and Dobrée, 100-1

220 Neale: 66-89 in Manwaring and Dobrée, 101. See below, the note to Bridport's thirty copies of an Act, which retells Gill's account of the passing of the "seamen's bill".

221 Gill, 65-6.

222 Manwaring and Dobrée, 101-2, for information, in the next two sentences.

223 Manwaring and Dobrée, 102.

224 Gill, 70.

225 Manwaring and Dobrée, 102ff.

226 Ibid.

227 Ibid.

228 Manwaring and Dobrée, 103.

229 Manwaring and Dobrée, 103-5.

230 But safer for an Admiral, Bridport, than a surgeon's mate, Redfern, to utter them at his court martial, in a few months time, for mutiny at the Nore.

231 Gill, 72-3, 72ns 1-2, and 73ns 1-2. Gill wrote that with the mutiny "thus peacefully going forward, the "seamen's bill" was passing quickly through the necessary stages in Parliament. It will be remembered that the vote, which was so urgently needed, was delayed, partly through the slowness of parliamentary procedure and partly through sheer misfortune, until 8 May. On that day Pitt moved in a committee of supply that £372,000 should be granted to defray the cost of the proposed increase of wages and victualling for the remainder of the year" (72n1, gives the source as Parl. Hist., vol xxxiii. 477-483). Brought before the House of Commons, a bill based on the committee's resolution passed without opposition (73n1, gives the source, Ibid. 483-489). After a short debate, the Upper House passed the bill unanimously (73n2, Ibid. 489-

493). It was then an Act of Parliament and thirty copies were taken to Bridport on the 10th (73n3).
232 Gill, 97-8, "Effect on the Estimates".
233 Gill, 73.
234 Manwaring and Dobrée, 105-10; 117.
235 Gill, 74.
236 Manwaring and Dobrée, 110-122, "Gala Days", the concluding chapter of Part I, "The Breeze at Spithead". Part II, "The Floating Republic", which has the Nore story.
237 Manwaring and Dobrée, 112. Examples are given of Howe's difficulty with words.
238 Gill, 74-5.
239 Manwaring and Dobrée, 113.
240 Ibid.
241 Manwaring and Dobrée, 114.
242 Gill, 75; Manwaring and Dobrée, 114-7.
243 Manwaring and Dobrée, 114-8.
244 Manwaring and Dobrée, 115-6.
245 Admiral Young to Sir Hugh Seymour, 26/v/98, Barrow, 339, in Manwaring and Dobrée, n139, 273.
246 Gill, 77; Manwaring and Dobrée, 116.
247 Manwaring and Dobrée, 116-7.
248 Manwaring and Dobrée, 117.
249 Gill, 78.
250 Ibid.
251 Ibid. 79n3.
252 Manwaring and Dobrée, 118.
253 Manwaring and Dobrée119, n144, given as a quote from Neale, 124. "That place for the whole incident, which the critical reader can accept or not as he pleases".
254 Manwaring and Dobrée, 119-22.
255 Gill, 80, 131; Manwaring and Dobrée, 120.
256 Gill, 79-81.
257 London Chronicle 15 May, Gill, 81, and Manwaring and Dobrée, 121.
258 Manwaring and Dobrée, 122, "An act of total oblivion".
259 Colley, 1996:229; 430n40; "Sailors and marines join Royal Parade"; "In December 1797, George III would process in state through the London streets past a crowd of well over 200,000 people to give thanks at St Paul's cathedral for British naval victories over the Dutch, French and Spanish fleets. Royal Thanksgivings for military victories had occurred in Britain before (though not since Queen Anne's reign), but the press rightly detected that more was involved here than just a return to old, indigenous traditions. The Naval Thanksgiving, the Morning Chronicle judged, was a 'Frenchified farce',

not least because it broke with normal British practice and copied Revolutionary French precedent (and advertised the Royal Navy's return to loyal obedience after the recent mutinies at Spithead and Nore) by including in its ranks 250 ordinary sailors and marines. The king himself had been responsible for this innovation and for the initial decision to hold a thanks giving".

Chapter 3 Notes

1 State Papers, 380, *Annual Register,* in Manwaring and Dobrée, 1937:260-1, Appendix II. The Delegates' names appear in Appendix I (Ibid. 257-8).
2 Lloyd, 1968:247. To appreciate Lloyd's judgement here, see numerous references to him throughout this book, and to "Professor Hattendorf's examination of [his] distinguished career as a naval historian" in *Lord Cochrane* (Lloyd, 1998:x, xiii-v.). How close the seamen were to Edmund Burke's "Men have no right to what is not reasonable" (1986:154).
3 Manwaring and Dobrée, 46-8.
4 Manwaring and Dobrée, 58. For this the authors gave Ad.1/5125, adding the following note - "Not dated; but it seems plausible to place it here". The next quote in this chapter supports this conclusion.
5 Manwaring and Dobrée, 65.
6 Kemp, 1970:174, considered the Spithead mutiny to have given rise "to some remarkable literary efforts on the part of the seamen", exemplified by this petition.
7 Ibid. 173.
8 Briggs, 1978(1959): 12. Briggs used the term "social pyramid", "which few contemporaries believed could or should be converted into a cube". In his first chapter, "Economy and Society in the 1780s" in England (1978:ch. 1), Briggs provided a view of its working through contemporary eyes.
9 Manwaring and Dobrée. See opening sentences in the first chapter of their book.
10 Briggs, 1978(1959): 137.
11 Ibid.
12 Briggs, 1978:140n1.
13 Briggs, 1978:139.
14 Briggs, 1978:140.
15 For Edward Thompson's contribution, (1966), to this discussion, see below.
16 James, C.R.L.,1963:200, cited Fortescue, *History of the British Army*, vol. IV, pt.1:546; "The cost in San Domingo alone had been £300,000 in 1794, £800,000 in 1795, £2,600,000 in 1796 and in January alone in 1797 it was more than £700,000". That year the British Government decided to withdraw from San Domingo.
17 Briggs, 1978:129.

18 Discussed more fully in chapter 11, Volume II, *Better than Cure The life and times of the ebullient and resilient William Redfern 1775-1833.*
19 Ibid.
20 Ibid. 168.
21 Ibid.
22 Ibid.
23 Briggs, 1978:170.
24 Thompson, 1966:104 for this specific reference, and 102ff for the Chapter, "Planting the Liberty Tree".
25 Braithwaite, 2003:passim. A very useful text in this context, it places the publisher Johnson at the centre of dissenting religious publishing and questions the meaning and use of the word, "radical" at that time. The main aim was parliamentary reform.
26 See "*Church and King* Riots" (135-148), chapter nine in George Rudé, *The Crowd in History,* 1995(1964); Rudé discussed common elements in conservative riots in Europe by way of introduction to this study which is especially relevant to this present context.
27 See Thompson, 1966:105-6, for references in this paragraph.
28 Braithwaite, 2003:113, refers to the attack on Priestley's house and laboratory in the context of the Birmingham riots. See also a brief but acute reference in Bronowski, 1973:144, where the Unitarian, Joseph Priestley, is held to have described his laboratory as "one of the most carefully assembled...in the world".
29 Thompson, 1966:116
30 Ibid.
31 Ibid. 1966:108n1; 86-103; 108-113.See also for a discussion of Tom Paine, *Rights of Man, I & II.*
32 Ibid. 1966:106-7, references in this paragraph. This theme is adjourned to chapter 4.
33 Manwaring and Dobrée, 16
34 Gilmour, 1993:423
35 Gilmour, 1993:vii, "Preface".
36 Gill, 32. The Delegates demanded that 'the supplies of fresh beef must not be curtailed by the substitution of flour for part of the fair share of meat". [There is some confusion in the footnotes on this page with three numbered in the text - 1, 2, and 1, again. Note 1 at the foot of the page is correct. Note 2 refers not to '2' in the text but to the second use of '1'.]
37 Gill, 300, quotes from a letter, in his discussion of "The political aspect of the mutinies". His problem was to find a "theoretical principle", as prime cause for the mutinies, in the absence of an "outward event", arousing "unusual discontent". Gill found his "principle" in the revolutionary ideas that had produced in the seamen "their desire for greater liberty and better treatment" (Ibid. 314).

38 Gill, 288.
39 Lewis, 1960:442,"Appendix III". Lewis, and Hodge (1855), used different methods to achieve comparable results.
40 Ford, 1976:262 - item 2070, drew attention to the equal relevance, to Government emigrant ships, of Redfern's 1814 *Report* on convict transports. It should be remembered, too, that convict transports also carried, in addition to convicts, crew, from officers to seamen, guards, free settlers, supplies, trade goods and mail.
41 Rodger, 2006:580; 582-3. See also, for example, ch.19, "The Great Wheels of Commerce and War: Administration 1715-63".
42 *Regulations and Instructions relating to His Majesty's Service at Sea*, [1790]. Copy read at the History of Medicine Library, RACP, Sydney. NSW.
43 Lloyd, Christopher C. "Victualling of the Fleet (18th and 19th centuries)", in Watt et al., eds, 1981:9.
44 Dening, 1993:22-3,69,84,107.
45 Fidlon & Ryan, eds, 1980:7. John White, Surgeon-General to the First Fleet where this incident occurred, dismissed it as having arisen "more from intoxication". In a note to this comment, Alec H. Chisholm, the editor of White's *Journal* (1962:51n) drew attention to Lieut. King's more informed comment.
46 Crittenden, 1981:15. See also Reg Wright (1986:19).
47 Lloyd, 1981:11.
48 Beaglehole, 1962, Vol 1:393. Banks' comment was, "Our *bread* indeed is but indifferent, occasioned by the quantity of Vermin that are in it, I have often seen hundreds nay thousands shaken out of a single bisket (sic)". Banks had them identified. Beaglehole added a footnote, explaining that one pest was a flatbodied pseudoscorpion that fed on the eggs, etc. of the other pests.
49 Ibid. 10-11.
50 Ibid. 10.
51 Ibid. 14. See also Sue Shephard, ch.12, "Canning" 2000:221ff, and Whitaker, 1998:12-3, for the description of a "sirloin of beef which was roasted in London. It was bought at Hoffmans in Bishopsgate Street, who preserves meat so effectually by packing it in a tin case hermetically sealed, and then covered with tallow and enclosed in a wooden box, that it will keep upwards of a year perfectly sound". Seamen had a long wait for tinned beef.
52 Brand, 1999:16. See Hill, 1988:2, for the continuing problem of "the most sophisticated of productive technological systems...subject to design faults and minor human error, the human consequences of which can be of megalithic proportions".
53 Anson, c.1911(1748): 151, had lost by then, 626 of 961 people from scurvy during and after sailing around Cape Horn.
54 Sir Gilbert Blane writing much later than Lind saw 'Ambiguity of Language' as a 'Source of Medical Error'. See 'Elements of medical logic: illustrated by

practical proofs and examples' (1822:243ff.), a Google Book accessed 18 May 2010.

55 Lind, James, *A Treatise of the Scurvy* [First edition reprint] in Stewart, C. P. & Douglas Guthrie eds. A Bi-centenary Volume, Lind's *Treatise*, The University Press, Edinburgh, 1953.

56 Carpenter, 1987:vii.

57 McCord, C.P., "Scurvy as an occupational disease", The Sappington Memorial Lecture, *Journal of Occupational Medicine, I*: 1959:316, cited in Carpenter, Kenneth J. 1987:253. See also a figure of one million for the shorter period 1600 to 1800 in Roddis. 1941:145.

58 Beaglehole, ed., 1962:vol II: 301; vol I: 250-1.

59 Quoted from Lind's *A Treatise of the* Scurvy, by C.P.Stewart, in the latter's introduction to the reprint of Lind's *Treatise* in Stewart and Guthrie, 1953:365.

60 Carpenter, 1987:200. See ascorbic acid's "role in the final stages of the production of collagen, the principle protein in connective tissue".

61 "Elixir of Vitriol [flavoured sulphuric acid] having been recommended by the College of Physicians as an efficacious Medicine in Scorbutick Cases, and the same being made a Part of the Invoice of the Surgeon's Sea Chest; the Captain is to order the Surgeon to observe such printed Instructions as will be given to them by the Commissioners of the Sick and Hurt for their Guidance in the Practice and Care of it *(Regulations and Instructions...)*". This was the standard treatment for scurvy in the Royal Navy for 100 years following the advice of the College of Physicians in the mid-1600s. See also Carpenter, K.J., "Nutritional Diseases" in Bynum and Porter, eds. 1997:1:468.

62 See U. Trohler, 'The history of clinical effectiveness' in *Proceedings of the Royal College of Physicians of Edinburgh*, Supplement, Volume 31, 2001:42-45, and his PhD thesis University of London, 1978, 'Quantification in British Medicine and Surgery 1750-1830 with special Reference to its Introduction into Therapeutics', accessed on line 23 July 2012, www.jameslindlibrary.org/pdf/theses/troehler-1978.pdf.

63 Carpenter, 1997.

64 Lawrence, Christopher, in "The Impact of the Past upon the Present", *OPMHA* Perth, July 1991:227-232.

65 Carpenter, 1987:57.

66 Dudley, S. F., 1953a, "James Lind: Laudatory address", in Carpenter, 1987:73. Dudley is quoted as saying, "This contempt of public opinion, social status, and honours is not so uncommon among real scientists. It is a kind of pride...which is to be deplored in so far as it holds up the development of social science and social health".

67 *S.O.E.D.* 1974. *Rob* described as "The juice of a fruit, reduced by boiling to the consistency of a syrup"; *SOED* 2007 has for *rob*, 'origin Medieval Latin

from Arabic *rub*'; I found *rubb* in Ibn Battuta, *Rihla* (Gibb, 1999). For its effectiveness etc., see Carpenter, 1987:233, and 226; 69, 74, 94, and 83.

68 Blane, 1789 [2nd edn.]:499-502ff.,"Observations on the Scurvy".

69 Brunton described Cook's error as 'a classic illustration that in medicine correlation is not necessarily causation', in his article 'The scourge of scurvy' (*State Library of New South Wales Magazine*, July 2008:16-17; See also, p.75, above.).

70 See Lloyd, 1965, for references to scurvy by Lind, Blane and Trotter.

71 Beaglehole, 1962:243-4 and: 251.

72 See Dr Nathaniel Hulme's letter to Banks, in Beaglehole, 1962:vol II:301.

73 Ibid. 393. This page also contains a reference to the American naturalist John Bartrum, who will be mentioned in a later chapter.

74 Ibid. 65.

75 Watt, J. et al. 1981:201, para.17. But, see Carpenter (1987:87) -"In 1778, Hulme, who had earlier urged the use of lemon juice in the Navy, now recommended "salt of tarter" (potassium carbonate) mixed with weak spirit of vitriol as an effervescing drink and therefore a good source of fixed air (Hulme, 1778). Watt has characterized this change as showing that he "lacked the moral fibre to sustain a correct but unpopular theory (Watt, 1979:85)".

76 Frost, 1994:114-25 starts from the idea 'that good food is an important aspect of health care'. The paragraph that follows on vitamin C is from Frost (1994, 120).

77 There is no entry for *Frederick Thomson* in Ford (1976), nor in Gandevia, Holster and Simpson, (1984).

78 Lloyd and Coulter, 1961:319-327, provide a detailed discussion of the involvement of Blane and Trotter in the issue of lemons and lemon juice to the Fleet, source of the attached *Table*. [Lloyd and Coulter, vol III, hereinafter referred to as Lloyd and Coulter, 1961]. Lloyd's collected extracts from Lind, Blane and Trotter have the story in their own words (Lloyd, ed. 1965).

79 Lloyd, 1965:298fn.

80For these two extracts, see Trotter, in Lloyd, 1965:298-9.

81 Hibbert, 1994:33.

82 Watt, Sir James. "Some Consequences of Nutritional Disorders in Eighteenth-century British Circumnavigations" in Watt et al. 1981:51.

83 Manwaring and Dobrée.260

84 Anson, c.1911 1748:100-3;109-11; the island on which Anson landed was Juan Fernandes, where Alexander Selkirk had been marooned.

85 Lloyd, at this point, continued with a discussion of scurvy in the Royal Navy. This will be taken up at a later stage.

86 Trotter, Thomas. "Medicina Nautica: State of Health of the Fleet", in Lloyd, 1965:223.

87 Flinders, 1966:42, Tues. 3 Nov. 1801.

88 Coleridge, in Jenkyn, 1909:117ff.
89 See Lloyd, 1981:12-13, for this, and the preceding quotation.
90 Lloyd and Coulter, 1961:158. The reference given for this item is Blane, Sir G. (1815), "Statements of the Comparative Health of the Navy", in *Medical-chirurgical Transactions,* 6, 490-573.
91 Watt, J. et al., eds. 1981:69.
92 Risse, Guenter B., "Medicine in the age of Enlightenment", in Andrew Wear, ed. 1992:149.
93 Ibid. 171-2. See a French parallel in Gelbart: 1998, in a later chapter of this book.
94 Ibid. 172
95 Ibid. 171
96 Burnham, in *Health and History* 4, 1999:250-273, and in *OPMHA no* 9:1999. See also Warner, in *Osiris,* 2nd Series, vol. 10, 1995. Warner and Burnham each delivered plenary addresses at International Conferences of the Australian Society of the History of Medicine, Warner, at Norfolk Island in 1995, and Burnham, in Sydney, 1999. See also Lindemann, 1999. Her primary goal was "to 'mainstream' the history of medicine" (Introduction, 1).
97 Ibid. Burnham, vol. 4:273. See also W.B.McDaniel, 2d. 1939:7:627-662.
98 Lloyd, ed. 1965.
99 To these three (ref. Lloyd and Coulter, Ch.3, 38-48), I would now add Robert Robertson, first alerted by Watt (Bk 1, Ch.9, below) and now by Ulrich Trohler 2006 (1978), whose thesis was downloaded in July 2012 from www.jameslindlibrary.org.
100 The 1779 edition contained "a new Chapter on the Means of Obtaining fresh Water at Sea...in which the Author vindicates his Claim to the important Discovery of freshening Sea-water by Distillation", making use of materials available on ships. See 1779:148-151, for details. For Lind's support for a rival claim see Stewart and Guthrie, 1953:172. Baudin, Solander, and Flinders each refer to stills for obtaining freshened water. Copies of their journals were read while staying with Drs Ian and Lyn Abbott, Perth, Western Australia.
101 Lloyd and Coulter, 386-7,"Printed Sources". The 1779 edition of *Lind's Essay on the Moat Effective Means of Preserving the Health of Seamen, etc.* is not included, but is the text I studied at the R.A.C.P. History of Medicine Library, Sydney.
102 Ibid. 381-2.
103 The State Library of N.S.W. reported its acquisition of Trotter's three volume *Medicina Nautica* [with Lind and Blane books] in *SL* magazine, July 2008, accessed on line, 22 Oct. 2012.
104 Lloyd, 1965. This book was borrowed from the Biomedical Library of the U.N.S.W., Sydney. I have since bought my own copy.

105 Lind, *Essay...,* 1779:1-11, "Of Imprest Men", where Lind used the Nore guardship as his example of what was happening, how fatal were the effects, and how simple and effective the preventive methods.
106 Lloyd and Coulter, 3, Correspondence of the Sick and Hurt Board (*S and H*) was the chief original source of information in their first chapter. 'The Sick and Hurt Board' forms chapter 1 of Section I*, The Medical Department.* This contains six chapters - The Surgeon; The Physician; The Apothecary and Dispenser; The Cockpit, Sick Berth and Hospital Ship; Hygiene: Ships Ventilation and Clothing; and Victualling.
107 Ibid. 4. Such criticism was part of a wider picture of the times. The Navy as the largest purchasing department came in for a fair share of the 'virulent abuse of the other side' in Parliament. However, '[i]n 1783, William Pitt introduced a bill for the Reform of Abuses in Public Offices, mentioning that the Chief Clerk of the Navy Office with a salary of about £250, received £2500 per annum in gifts. This bill was rejected by the House of Lords but two years later (25 Geo.III,C.19) Commissioners were appointed 'to enquire into the Fees, Gratuities Perquisites and Emoluments...received...in Publick (sic) Offices...and to examine into any abuses'. '[A]n Order in Council of 8 June 1796 finally reorganized the Navy Board on the lines recommended by the Commission'. For the discussion from which this material is derived, see, Bernard Pool, in *The Mariner's Mirror*, Vol.50, No.3, August 1964.
108 Lloyd and Coulter. 5. As early as 1781 Dr Robert Robertson, later senior physician in the navy, was complaining of "the indigent and penurious establishment of the medical department of the Navy". The need to improve the status of naval surgeons was also taken up by Trotter, in Lloyd, 1965:244ff.
109 Lloyd and Coulter, 5. See also p.6. The S. and H. Board was not constituted to handle its business transactions, resulting in arrears of 'two and a half million pounds in 1792, and another one and a half since that date'.
110 Goddard, J.C., 'The navy surgeon's chest: surgical instruments of the Royal Navy during the Napoleonic War' in *Journal of the Royal Society of Medicine,* Volume 97, April 2004:191-197, accessed on line, 25 July 2012. http://www.ncbi.nlm.nih.gov/pmc/articles/PMC1079363/pdf/0970191.pdf.
111 Ibid. 8, source for the last two paragraphs. Dr Andrew Baird, 'at the instigation of Lord St Vincent' 'was the officer chiefly responsible for hospital inspection from 1800 until 1806, when he was joined by Dr Weir as Inspector of Naval and Prison Hospitals'.
112 Blane, 1789:Part II of the 1789 edition under the heading, "Of the Causes of Sickness in Fleets and the means of Prevention".
113 As noted above Pringle's words had undesirable consequences.
114 Read Blane again, replacing seamen/sailors with people, having in mind, children, women, and men. For which see, Puska, "Global Chronic Disease Prevention - From Science to Effective Programmes and Policies", *Redfern Oration,* Melbourne, 2007.

115 This of course serves as a reminder of Edward Ford, telling the general, that army health in the New Guinea campaign was the concern of everybody, not just the surgeons (see the opening chapter, above).
116 Lloyd, in Watt, 1981:201. See also *Appendix I, Summary of the Discussions*, para. 17.
117 Trotter, "Medicina Nautica", in Lloyd, ed., 1965:267, for the next two paragraphs.
118 Ibid. 1965:228:which included officer assistance to the wounded after the Battle of 1 June 1794.
119 Trotter, 1976 [1807]: 153-4. Here, one might refer to Roy Porter's *Introduction* to Trotter's other work, *Essay on Drunkenness*, 1988 (1804): 28ff., for "the debate over the gains and losses of man's emergence from 'rudeness to refinement' - Trotter himself picks up that famous phrase'".

Chapter 4 Notes

1 Gill, 52; Dugan, 131. See above.
2 Detailed in the previous chapter.
3 Dugan, 389-97, "The Mutineer Surgeon", has a reference to Redfern's care of the sick, 392. Note 1:Redfern was a surgeon's mate, not a "surgeon's assistant". Note 2:For Redfern's court martial see below.
4 See below.
5 Dugan, 131-2.
6 Manwaring and Dobrée, 72.
7 Rediker, 1993(1987): 86, 235,239; 244-5 the quote, from Edward Barlow. His *Journal* is listed third on the list of abbreviations (references) p. xv (Ibid.)
8 Gill, 268ff.
9 Certainly with regard to physical punishment, "No Commander shall inflict any Punishment upon a Seaman, beyond Twelve Lashes upon his bare Back with a Cat of Nine Tails, according to the ancient Practice of the Sea". (See below, *Regulations and Instructions*, 1790:46).
10 Ibid.
11 Manwaring and Dobrée, 17-21.
12 Lavery, 210-11.
13 Ibid. 173. See also Ibid. 275n66. Manwaring and Dobrée give as their source, Earl of Camperdown, *Life of Admiral Duncan*, 1898, chapter v (unless otherwise stated).
14 Ibid. 20-1.
15 Regulations and Instructions... [1790]: 45
16 Black and Porter, eds. 1996. See the entries for "honour" and "virtue" contributed by Sylvana Tomaselli.
17 Gill, 274-7.
18 James, Vol II, 1886, who found difficulty even mentioning the mutinies.

19 See Manwaring and Dobrée, "Preface", which contains their estimate of difference between their own and Professor Gill's "piece of research", mentioned in chapter one, above.
20 Watt, 1989:137
21 Lewis, in Watt, 1989. See also Lewis, 1960:442.
22 Trotter in Lloyd, 1965:306.
23 Ibid. 309. Appointment received 9.4.1794 (dated 3.4'.94.). Trotter served on the hospital ship, *Charon,* until injured "climbing up the side of the *Irresistible*...to attend a wounded officer", in 1795. "[U]ntil his retirement from the service in 1802, he served mainly ashore, though still in his capacity of Physician of the Fleet. It was during these years that he compiled his *Medica Nautica* in three volumes and was constantly agitating for improvement in the hospital and medical services. Many of his proposals...for improved pay and status were adopted in 1805, too late for any benefit to himself" (Lloyd, 1965:214-5, in "Editor's Introduction" to Trotter extracts.). When in 1805 he applied for an increase in his pension, it was refused (Ibid.).
24 It was only that year that the British Government decided to retreat from San Domingo. See James, C.R.L. above.
25 Lloyd and Coulter, 1961:159.
26 Ibid. 1961:p.135, for the first reference to the name, and 67, for the second, and S.O.E.D. for the mythological references.
27 Ibid. 1961:67-9. See also Lavery, 1995:216; 224. Hospital ships were of two kinds, mobile and stationary. *Charon* was of the former kind, following the Fleet. Stationary ships were at Chatham (74 gun ship), at Falmouth (50 guns), and one at Plymouth. The last two received sick from the Channel Fleet. Hulks were used as hospitals in dockyards lacking shore facilities.
28 Linebaugh, 1993:411-12 and 412n19, reminds his readers that "the West Indian campaign...cost England in Army and Navy little fewer than one hundred thousand men, about one-half of them dead, the remainder permanently unfitted for service" (Fortesque, 1915:vol iv, part 1).
29 Lloyd and Coulter, 172
30 Lloyd and Coulter, 68. The need for and absence of varied diets for hospital patients will arise in a later chapter as a problem for William Redfern at Sydney, N.S.W.
31 Lloyd and Coulter, 187. See also 185-290, Section III, "The Naval Hospitals".
32 Jennings, 1999:25, who described the hospital as, "Too grand, too awkward, too cold, too intimidating, too unfriendly for the pensioners it housed, it turned out to be an architectural masterpiece which failed the purpose for which it was built".
33 Lloyd and Coulter, 196.
34 Ibid. 218.
35 Ibid. 240ff., "Thomas Trotter".

36 Regulations and Instructions...[1790].
37 Ibid. 55-6.
38 Ibid. 131, Article 1-2. See 131-4 for "The Surgeons", Articles I-XI.
39 See "Clearing for action" in Brownlee (1980:30) for a brief description of the ship's preparation.
40 See Ghislaine Lawrence, "Surgery (Traditional)", in Bynum and Porter, 1997:976-980, for a brief survey of "Operative Surgery to 1800", and a discussion of instruments and procedures. See also Ellis, E.S. *Ancient Anodynes: Primitive Anaesthesia and Allied Conditions*, 1946. I thank Alison Holster for suggesting this book and Richard Bailey and Liz Wall for arranging a loan and time for me to read it.
41 Lloyd and Coulter, 57-64, 'The Cockpit'.
42 See Lawrence, 1997:961-83; 976-980, for references to treatment of wounds from the Greeks to the early nineteenth century.
43 Brownlee, 1980:48.
44 No doubt the daily morning meetings between Wellington and James McGrigor, his chief medical officer, contributed to this improvement. Prevention had a high priority on this officer's practice and took many forms including anticipation of need based on the morning's briefing. See mentions of McGrigor's autobiography and biography below.
45 Roger Cooter, "War and Modern Medicine", *Table I*, in Bynum and Porter (1997:1542). Cooter raises some critical issues in this paper. He suggests, for example, that "The actual practice of medicine and surgery in the armed forces also needs to be viewed in terms of immediate political and economic forces", contrasting amputation (Napoleonic Wars) with conservation of limbs (First World War). See R.D. Lobban (1980:46), for a reference to Sir Charles Bell (1774-1842) who went to Waterloo immediately after the battle and "for a full week...operated night and day until his arms were 'powerless with the exertion of using the knife'".
46 For details of wounds received, see Hibbert, 1994.
47 A useful brief description of the wounds inflicted, and treatments offered, may be found in Reginald Magee's paper, "Weapons and Wounds *circa* 1790", 1996:255-7. This article (255) details the movement of Nelson's fatal musket ball after it hit him.
48 See Foreman and Phillips, 1999:134-5, for an eyewitness account and painting, both by the Reverend Cooper Willyams, chaplain of the *Swiftsure*.
49 Watt, 1974.
50 Watt, 1974:3.
51 Ibid.
52 Ibid. 4-5.
53 Ibid. 3-6.
54 Ibid. 5, for the two following paragraphs.
55 Ibid. 5, for details.

56 Ibid.
57 Ibid. 17. Attributed to Sir James Earle and written some 200 years ago. Watt, 15-17, makes reference to the preceding period.
58 Lloyd and Coulter, 64-5.
59 Ibid. 65.The source for this quote is given as Lind, *An Essay*...London, 1774.
60 Lloyd and Coulter, 65. Here the source is Lind, J., (1763) *Two Papers on Fevers and Infection*, London: Wilson: 208.
61 Ibid. 65, see also 165.
62 Kid, 'a sailor's mess tub' *SOED* 2007.
63 Ibid.
64 Ibid. 66.
65 Jones, 1999; 7:36.
66 Lloyd and Coulter, 10.
67 *Bigge Transcripts*, CY Reel 1551, medical interviews, Redfern to Bigge, Notes on the Minutes of his oral evidence, 8 February 1821.See Chapter 1, Volume II of *Better than Cure The life and times of the ebullient and resilient William Redfern 1775-1833*, for a detailed treatment of the conflict between Bigge and Redfern. Bigge brought his secretary into the argument according to Redfern, hence his inclusion here.
68 Lloyd and Coulter, Points 1-5 appear on pages 11,12,13,15 and 33 respectively. This information accords with that given by Redfern with respect to dates and designations. For item 4, Redfern quoted from the "Office for Sick & Wounded Seamen 28 Jany. 1805", from the same Order in Council of 23 January 1805, used by Lloyd and Coulter.
69 This matter was raised in the opening chapter to be resolved later.
70 Ibid. 23-9, for the problems of surgeons in the early part of the century, and 29-37, for reform of the medical branch.
71 Ibid. 29.
72 Ibid. 31, for the content of this paragraph. For Trotter, see Lloyd, 1965.
73 Ibid. 37.
74 Porter, 1963.
75 Porter, 1995:62-3.
76 Watt, 1989. See the discussion of medical provision for the First Fleet (1788) to NSW in a later chapter.
77 Lloyd, in Watt et al., 1981:12.
78 Ibid. 1981:13. See also Lloyd and Coulter (183) with almost the same figures for 1779 and 1813.
79 S.O.E.D. 1975. 'Loblolly' given as 'thick gruel or spoon-meat, as used by seamen, etc., burgoo'; a "Loblolly boy" was a surgeon's attendant on shipboard"; also "*dialogue*, errand boy". This last, is precisely the meaning that applies to a significant moment in William Redfern's court-martial in the next chapter.

80 Wilson, "Fevers", in Bynum and Porter, vol 1, 1997:382-411.
81 Lloyd and Coulter, 1961:329. Their quote is from Zinsser, 1935:153.
82 This follows Lloyd and Coulter, broadened by a number of key references to Bynum and Porter, *Companion Encyclopedia...*1997, and Ackerknecht, *A Short History of Medicine*, 1992. [Scurvy will not be revisited here.]
83 Lloyd and Coulter, 1961:330.
84 Ibid. 330-1; See Porter, 1990:66-7, for a reference to the stimulation of "Enlightenment values" on medicine, and again in Porter's *Enlightenment*, below (ch.17). See also Ackerknecht, 1992:137-44.
85 Bynum and Porter, 1997. Redfern, being a miasmatist, I have taken the opportunity to extend the discussion of *miasmata* at this point, in anticipation of later need. For William Cullen, on this topic, see *The First Lines of the practice of Physic*, chapter IV, facsimile edition.
86 Bracegirdle, Brian. "The Microscopical Tradition", in Bynum and Porter, 1997, I: 112-4.
87 Dr Robert Robertson (1742-1829): Fever specialist, eighteenth-century medical experimenter, naval health reformer and senior physician in the Royal Navy medical department. Author, Bruce Hamilton Short, Master of Philosophy Thesis, School of Public Health, Faculty of Medicine, University of Sydney, November 2013. Accessed online 25.11.14. See my own reference to Roberston (Ch. 08:264, and 264n101).
88 Lloyd and Coulter, 345.
89 From my own reading of James Lind, "A Treatise of the Scurvy", 1st ed., reprinted in C.P.Stewart & Douglas Guthrie, ed., The University Press, Edinburgh, 1953. See confirmation in Lloyd and Coulter, vol. 3:1961:332; "Just as all sorts of dietary diseases were called scurvy, so the innumerable attempts to classify fevers resulted in 'a strange jumble'".
90 Hannaway, Caroline. "Environment and Miasmata", in Bynum and Porter, 1997, *I*:292-308.
91 Plumb, 1963:12. "The first noticeable thing about these towns [1714-42] would have been the stench". See Corbin, (1982) 1996.
92 Porter, Dorothy. "Public Health", in Bynum and Porter 1997:2:1232-8.
93 Gandevia, 1975:1-25; and 1973:59-63.
94 Observations I made while living nearby.
95 Porter, 1997:2:1237-8
96 Ibid. 1237-8. Not surprisingly Porter goes on to consider the effects of "a demographic explosion" with social consequences far beyond individual powers to overcome.
97 See also in chapter 7, below, Sir Jeremy Fitzpatrick, whom William Redfern met, to his advantage.
98 Regulations and Instructions...1790:200.
99 Lloyd and Coulter, 1961:348-358.
100 Fisher, 1991, opens with an 1803 description of smallpox.

101 Jenner, 1798. See also Lefanu, 1951, and Jenner, 1931. [Alison Holster loaned the last two books to me.]
102 See "Obituary for Professor Frank Fenner (1914-2010)", The Health Report, *ABC Radio National*, 29 November 2010. "A tribute to world renowned Australian scientist Professor Frank Fenner, who died recently. Professor Fenner helped rid the world of smallpox and Australia of a rabbit plague".
103 Montagu, 1994:80-2, the letter. Anita Desai told how Lady Mary was struck by smallpox, "the dread disease that had killed her brother". Treated by Hans Sloane and Dr Garth, she recovered, "but with her beauty marred: her eyelashes were gone, and her skin pitted" (xv). Malcolm Jack, ed., noted that Sarah Chiswell died from smallpox in 1726 (168n7).
104 Fisher, 1991:14 - A brief description is given of six weeks of preparation for Edward Jenner, when a schoolboy, before being inoculated with smallpox.
105 Wujastyk, Dominik. "Indian Medicine", in Bynum and Porter, 1997:765 *Inoculation*, wherein Lady Mary Montague is mentioned; see also Dorothy Porter, "Public Health", Ibid. 1236, and Lise Wilkinson, "Epidemiology", Ibid. vol 2, 1267-8.
106 Fisher, 1991:101, 114.
107 LeFanu, 1951:153. The letter was dated 20 February 1801.
108 Ibid. 46.
109 Ibid. 47.
110 An error, in Lloyd and Coulter, 1961:164n2, *Medicina Nautica*, II,28, and 351-2, was corrected in my own paper, which follows below.
111 Jones, 1999, 7:40 n.28.
112 Lloyd and Coulter, 1961:352-4
113 Lloyd and Coulter, 1961:353, here, and for the following paragraphs.
114 Porter, Roy. "Introduction", in Thomas Trotter, 1988.
115 Ibid. xxi.
116 Bewick, 1975:161. "I cannot however omit acknowledging the civilities of...Dr Thomas Trotter Esq. well known over all England as Physician to the Fleet".
117 Ghislaine Lawrence, "Surgery (Traditional)" in Bynum and Porter, *2,* 1997:979.
118 Ibid.
119 Watt, in Hardy and Frost, 1989:146, ns.103ff.
120 Lloyd and Coulter, 356, gave as a source for their two extracts William Turnbull, *The Naval Surgeon*, 1806, which may be read now as a Google Book where the above references may be found (111-3). Accessed 3 November 2011. Turnbull has a section on diseases of the Channel Fleet starting on p.116.

121 Kemp, 1970:48; 144-5, "sucking the monkey" - men encouraged the women to drain the coconuts and to fill them with rum before bringing them aboard.
122 Lloyd and Coulter, 356
123 Ibid.
124 Trotter, *On Drunkennes*: 1804:8
125 Ibid. 1804:172-4
126 Porter, Roy. *Introduction,* "Appendix", 1804, 1988:xlii-xliii. It is this focus, and the book's rarity, that led to its reprint in the Tavistock *Classics in the History of Psychiatry.*
127 Trotter, 1807, 1976.
128 Trotter, 1804:23.
129 Ibid. 48.
130 Watt et al., eds. 1981:68-9.
131 Lloyd and Coulter, 1961:335.
132 In each of two consecutive paragraphs in which the blockade is mentioned, Trotter, 1976:154-5, directed the reader to two footnotes. The first is to an original source, his observations on the "species of nervous disease" that he is discussing, *Medicina Nautica, vol. 3.* This is the context of the quote, in chapter one, about statesmen reading the medical history of fleets and armies. In the second footnote, Trotter gave "the fate of the cow-pock inoculation" as "proof of the indifference of politicians to the improvement of the health and safety of the community".
133 Ibid. 1976:155. Trotter wrote, "The practice of blockade has crept much into our naval system of late; yet it was abhorred by Howe and Nelson, as inconsistent with the genius of our seamanship". This is a criticism of St Vincent, to whom Trotter, was Fleet physician as well as to Howe. According to Lavery (1995:301), it was St Vincent who re-established the close blockade, to which Trotter took exception, first in the Mediterranean fleet off Toulon in 1795 and then in the Channel Fleet in 1800. "Strategic as well as disciplinary reasons were given for adopting it". It kept "the crews busy and unable to communicate with the shore and with other ships" and thereby reduced the likelihood of another Fleet Mutiny (Ibid.)
134 Ibid. n.354, which reads "Information from Librarian of the Royal College of Physicians".
135 PRO/ADM 1/534. See the Court Martial judgment and more lenient attitude to William Redfern in view of the circumstances mentioned in the text.
136Macalpine and Hunter, (1969) 1995:291.
137 Ibid. 291ff.
138 Ibid. 329.
139 Macalpine and Hunter, 1995:172ff for 'Porphyria'.

140 Ibid. 1995:174-5. See also, Porter, 2001:119-120. Porter commented, "treatment for insanity have frequently seemed indistinguishable from torture engines", and - "Therapy. Torture and sexual bullying dissolve into each other, and make bad worse; madness taints all it touches".

141 Lloyd and Coulter, 1961:335.

142 Trotter, one time physician to that fleet, wrote of attending "fifty thousand cases of the veneral disease", but gave neither place nor time (*View of the Nervous Temperament*, 1976(1806):112-3).

143 Ibid. 1961:169 in W. Turnbull. *The Naval Surgeon*, London: Phillips, 1806

144 Ibid. 1961:357, in a brief discussion of venereal disease, 357-8.

145 Ibid. 1961:32.

146 Ibid. 1961:32, from Trotter's memorial to St Vincent as First Lord in 1801. See p.109 for a panacea, Dr Ward's pills and flux medicines for 'rheumatic, scorbutic and venereal disease'. See pp.295-6 for the pill's prescription - 'antimony, dragon's blood (i.e. balsam) and wine'. The Admiralty ordered this pill for Anson's voyage when 1051 men of a total crew of 1955 died, mostly from scurvy (Ibid.).

147 Ibid. 1961:32, and 357.

148 Ibid. 1961:358, where the source of their quote is given as *Medicina Nautica*, I, 1790-1803:113. See Lloyd, 1965:229(1795).

149 Lewis, Milton James, 1998:22. This masterful work treats of The History of Sexually Transmitted Diseases in Australia in International Perspective.

150 Lavery, 1995:203-7.

151 Ibid. 203-4.

152 Redfern used this word in his *Report* on the three convict transports when discussing the effect of different materials, from which clothing is made, in retaining body exudations. "Cotton or linen, if worn on the person till it become filthy, will retain fomites, and communicate Contagion as certainly as Woolen". This was the earlier concern of Thomas Trotter, M.D. [Redfern's *Report* is the subject of a later chapter.] The internet reveals a continuing use of the term fomites in the U.S.A. as an inanimate carrier of disease, e.g. foot and mouth disease on human footwear.

153 Jones, 1999, 7:35-6, where the following references are given - Lind, *An Essay on ...Preserving the Health of Seamen*...1779:4-5; Blane, *Observations*...1789:252. See also Trotter T. *Medicina Nautica*, in Lloyd C, 1965:243.

154 Bower, 1990:17-8. Rags were also the sources of the artist Turner's papers. "[N]o industry works in isolation and the invention of Arkwright's Cotton Gin, in 1793, led to the wide availability in England of cotton clothing and materials, which as rags, would eventually filter through to papermakers a few years later". "The rags were sorted by women, who possibly had one of the worst jobs ever invented". "The rags were often filthy and needed

considerable washing". Workers were subjected to smell, contagious disease and serious lung conditions from rag dust (Ibid.).
155 Lavery, 1995:207.
156 Ibid.
157 Marcus, 1975:9-10
158 Porter, 1988:xxi.
159 Flinders, 1966 [1814]: 25.
160 Ibid. 29.
161 Ibid. 36
162 Lavery, 1995:208-11, "Rewards and Pleasures".
163 Ibid. 210-11:*Sex*.
164 Shuster and Shuster, 1996.
165 Rodger, 1996(1986): 80-1; see also 159.
166 Ibid. 211.
167 Brunton, 1989:1.
168 Flinders, 1966 [1814]:36.
169 See Elias (2007) for 'midshipman'.
170 Gill, 1813:386-90. See also Richard S. Holdstock, 'Ballads of the Great Mutiny of 1797' (13.8.06) in Rod Stradling, *Musical Traditions Internet Magazine*, accessed 25.11. 2014;
http://www.mustrad.org.uk/articles/mutiny.htm
171 Hugill, 1977.
172 Lavery, 1995:209, who gave as his source, for Edward Mangin's comments, NRS [Society for Nautical Research] *Five Naval Journals*, p.70.
173 Ibid. 211. Ideas from Lavery's text.
174 Lavery, 1995:209.
175 In the second chapter of this book, 'yarning' was selected for its relevance to the theme 'making a mutiny in 1797'.That reference is to Dening, 1993:379-80.
176 Dening, 1993:73
177 Ibid. 71.
178 Ibid.
179 Ibid.
180 Ibid. 71. See also 76ff.
181 Ibid. 73.
182 Ibid. 77.
183 Ibid. 80, which is the source of the quote that followed.
184 Ibid. 79. For example "[t]he ducking stool dangled from the same yard arm from which a man might hang".
185 Ibid. 80.
186 Carpenter, 1987:15-7. A facsimile excerpt is included. See note about beriberi, 16.
187 Ibid. 241-2

Chapter 5 Notes

1 H.M.S. the *Standard*: National Maritime Museum, 19 Nov. 1997 and 16 Dec. 1997, replies to my letter of 11 Nov'.97:In the first, Imogen Gibbon, Historic Photographs & Ship Plans, enclosed "a proforma detailing the plans we have for *HMS Standard*, a 64 gun ship, launched in 1782". My letter was then passed on to Ms. Lindsey Macfarlane, Picture Library, who wrote, "I have searched our catalogues and records for a picture of HMS *Standard* with no result. I have also searched for pictures of all the Intrepid/Magnamine Class ships on the enclosed list also with no result". In an attachment to the second letter is a list of all the I/M, 1765 Williams design 64s, Class ships with additional information viz. that *Standard* between 1799 and 1801 was hulked/a convalescent ship and broken up in 1816. Lavery, 1995:48 has a history of *64s*.

2 For Texel, the largest and most western island of an archipelago in the Wadden Sea, visit https://ageofsail.wordpress.com/category/geography/page/2/. For Texel Roads, ship assembly area, from Den Helder, and its naval base north of Amsterdam, past Texel to the south west of the island of Terschelling, see http://www.texel.net/en/about-texel/villages/oudeschild/: accessed 25.11.14.

3 Dugan, 1966:178. [Hereinafter the date of publication will be omitted.] For the Nore, see the *Admiralty Chart, SC1185, Small Craft Series*, 1995. See also William Heather's "Chart of the East Coast of England including the Entrances to the Thames", J. Stephenson, engraver, 1811. My nautical neighbour Frank, brought me a reproduction copy of this chart from England. A drawing of the Nore light-ship may be seen on this chart. It fits Holland's description of the first version of ship and light (1988:55).

4 Holland, 1988:55.

5 Ibid. 177.

6 Dugan, 177.

7 Marcus, 1975:See "seamanship", "a neglected branch of naval history" in his Preface ix-x; "London River", 176ff, for the reference to Cook see 214-5.

8 See "Blueback Charts" in Fisher, Susanna, 2001:passim.

9 Ibid. 178. Nevertheless increased wages were not "given" but had to be contested, as evidenced in Lavery, 1995:272.

10 Marcus. 178.

11 Dugan, 178.

12 Ibid. 178-9.

13 Rodger, 1986:194ff.

14 Manwaring and Dobrée, 1937:126.

15 Manwaring and Dobrée, 127-8. For Surgeon John Snipe, see previous chapter. A typed copy of his letter shows *John* Snipe as the author. Edward Ford, 1953, had *John* Snipe giving Manwaring and Dobrée, 1937, as his

source. Lloyd and Coulter, 1961:162, gave *John* Snipe as surgeon of the *Sandwich* at Sheerness. Dugan, 179, had *William* Snipe.

16 Manwaring and Dobrée, 127-8. There the source is given as Ad.1/727. See Manwaring and Dobrée, for note 2, 274, and Bibliography, 279, *Admirals' Despatches,* Nore, Buckner, Ad. 1/727-8.

17 Manwaring and Dobrée, 200.

18 Lloyd &Coulter, 1961:163.

19 Dugan, 187-8.

20 Gill, 1913:120-1. [Hereinafter the year of publicaton for Gill will be omitted.]

21 Lloyd and Coulter.1961, 372, Appendix B is a Table of the "Number of Seamen and Marines voted annually, with the Number of Sick sent on Shore". The source is given as "Blane, *Comparative Health,* Appendix". By converting the sick as a percentage of the number voted, the results for 1796, 1797, and 1798 are 16.86, 17.12, and 13.09. The general trend is downwards. 1797 is against that trend. But note the improvement in the following year. Was this a positive effect of the mutiny?

22 Lind, James. *An Essay on the Most Effective Way of Preserving the Health of Seamen and a Dissertation on Fevers and Infection,* etc., London, 1779:4ff. I read an original copy of this third edition at the History of Medicine Library. This is also the edition used by Christopher Lloyd in his book of extracts (Lloyd, Navy Records Society 1965).

23 Ibid. 177ff.

24 Neale, 1985:159, reported "the Admiralty was still frightened of the *Defiance*" [mutinied 1795 (see Neale for details)] and dispersed the crew, one hundred being sent to the *Director*.

25 Dugan, 126-7.

26 Ibid. 172-3.

27 The Pacific Ocean, too. See *Hillsborough* below.

28 Dugan, 177.

29 Gill, 101-3, includes a list of a dozen ships, 102, most of which were frigates or sloops, "a chance collection of ships belonging to different fleets". Gill's source was fn.1 *Cunningham,* 2-3. However, Dugan listed twenty, which included the ships from the North Sea Fleet.

30 Dugan, 200.

31 Ibid. 245-7.

32 References to N.A.M. Rodger (2006), below, are to the second of his three-volume history of the Royal Navy. For an earlier and similar statement, see N.A.M. Rodger, 'Mutiny or subversion? Spithead and the Nore', in Thomas Bartlett, et al. *1798, A Bicentenary Perspective,* 2003:549-564.

33 Rodger, 2006:448-9; see above, chapter 2.

34 Dugan, 224.

35 Marcus, 107.

36 Dugan, 178-80.
37 Ibid. 180.
38 See Gill, 104-5 for the effect of Gardner's dispute of 21 May.
39 Seamen were not required to swear an oath on entering the Royal Navy at that time. I leave it to you to decide upon a suitable swearing in ceremony for a seaman shanghaied into the Navy, or coerced by any other means.
40 Dugan, 180-1; Gill, 104.
41 Ibid. 181. Dugan did not provide a source for the original. His version is identical with the copy to be found in Gill, 117. There, its source is given as "Papers of the *Repulse*, no.7". Gill, 117, 117n1, told how Lord Keith was so impressed by "the great importance that the mutineers had attached to their oath of fidelity to the delegates" that he suggested seamen and marines "should be made to swear allegiance to King and Constitution". Manwaring and Dobrée, 254-5, discussed this matter in greater detail, adding as had Gill, that Magistrates Graham and Williams had a similar idea.
42 Gill, 107-8.
43 Gill, 79-81.
44 Dugan, 176. Spencer's note and the King's reply are each on this page but unsourced.
45 Gill, a brief summary, 141n1, and a longer discussion, 138-141. Manwaring and Dobrée, 144-6, articles, as copied here, with commentary. Dugan, 201-2, also listed the ships involved at that time.
46 Manwaring and Dobrée, 274, give *A[nnual] R[egister]* (Rivington's edition), 1797. (A.R.) (Not to be confused with Longmans), State Papers, 387, as their source. See also the Delegates, Manwaring and Dobrée, 201. By the 6 June when Lord Northesk, Captain of the Monmouth was invited to talk with them, they numbered sixty.
47 Dugan, 202.
48 Manwaring and Dobrée, 144-6.
49 Dugan, 251-2.
50 The two references to marines no doubt reflect the problems they faced and the support they had given to the mutineers. See the action on *Standard* in the North Sea, below.
51 Lavery, 1995:145-6.
52 Ibid. where Lavery gave as reference, J S Tucker, *Memoirs of the Earl of St Vincent*, 1844, vol 1, p.297. Lavery noted, "The marines were not always effective in suppressing mutiny. At Spithead and the Nore, they often took a full part alongside the seamen. Some marines were commended for their loyalty, but other were hanged or flogged for supporting the mutiny". See references to the marines in the *Minutes* of Redfern's court martial. Lavery also noted, 145, that marines "formed a major part of the First Fleet which founded the British colony of Australia, guarding the convicts who were sent there in 1787".

53 Minutes of the proceedings of a court martial...PRO/ADM 1/534. Copy held by the History of Medicine Library, R.A.C.P., Sydney.
54 Rodger, 2006:452-3, for this and the following paragraph.
55 Dugan, 487-9, Appendix 5, copy of the letter.
56 Manwaring and Dobrée, 250.
57 Ibid.
58 Dugan, 223, 237, 239.
59 Ibid. 240.
60 Linebaugh, 1993:409. Such medical metaphors, the stuff of Roy Porter's well illustrated book, *Bodies Politic...*2001, were "part of the verbal and visual language of the body politicized and of politics medicalized" in the art of caricature and cartoon.
61 Colley, 1996:304.
62 Ibid.
63 Gill, 144.
64 Gill, 146.
65 Gill, 148-9.
66 Ibid.
67 Gill, 149.
68 Gill, 150-1; See also Gill, 30n1 for biographical notes on these four Board members who also formed the Spithead deputation.
69 Gill, 151.
70 Gill, 152.
71 Gill, 169.
72 Gill, 177.
73 Gill, 162.
74 Gill, 152.
75 Gill, 155.
76 Gill, 241.
77 Gill, 211.
78 Gill, 177. See Cordingly, 1986:78-9, Plate VI, which shows a two-decker under sail, even though on this occasion it is a painting of an East Indiaman.
79 Dugan, 494-5, *Appendix 8,* in full.
80 Manwaring and Dobrée, 183ff, discussed the circumstances in a chapter headed *Melodrama.*
81 Gill, 211.
82 Gill, 188, 9n1. Wallace was from H.M.S. *Standard.*
83 Ibid.
84 Gill, 204.
85 Gill, 181.
86 Gill, 209n2, 241.
87 Gill, 206.
88 Manwaring and Dobrée, Ad. 1/727.

89 Manwaring and Dobrée, 1937:199-200.
90 Gill (219-221) referred specifically to water when discussing "Supplies running low". Cutting off supplies had given the government "a great advantage" and had probably led the delegates to consider an escape by sea (221). Dugan referred to delegate discussion of the Admiralty's stoppage of food and water (294-5ff).
91 Gill, 241.
92 Gill, 184.
93 Gill, 206-7.
94 Gill, 206.
95 Gill, 195-6; See also Marcus:182ff. Navigational aids were removed "several times in the sixteenth and seventeenth centuries".
96 Gill, 241.
97 Gill, 239.
98 Gill, 241.
99 Gill, 243.
100 Gill, 240.
101 Gill, 241.
102 Gill, 244; Clune, 1964:114.
103 Gill, 244.
104 Gill, Ibid; 188n1.
105 Muster Log, HMS *Standard,* ADM 1/5341 & IND 4778.
106 Gill, 241
107 Ibid.
108 Gill, 243.
109 Gill, 240-1.
110 Gill, 242.
111 Dugan, 395, 395n1.
112 Gill, Ibid.
113 Gill, 248, said *Standard,* Manwaring and Dobrée, 1937:237ff, *Sandwich,* and Dugan, 359 ff, said *Sandwich.*
114 Dugan, 415.
115 *Regulations and Instructions...*MDCCXC [1790]. In this transcription the long 's' is replaced with the modern 's'. Original spelling has been retained.
116 Attempts to put a name to Redfern's counsel have not been successful, nor has the search for relevant literature on Royal Navy courts martial in England, except for Ala Alryyes, dicussed in the following chapter ("War at a Distance: Court-Martial Narratives in the Eighteenth Century" in *Eighteenth-Century Studies,* 2008*).*
117 Jones, A. 'William Redfern'*, JMB*: 1999; 7:35-41. I gave as reference, n.28, "Trotter, T. *Medicina Nautica vol. II,* p.28, quoted in Lloyd C. & Coulter JLS, eds *Medicine and the Navy, vol. III,* 1714-1815, Edinburgh: E&S Livingston, 161:164n. It was not until 2008 that Mark S. Micale's

Hysterical Men appeared. While he included Trotter's writings he seems to have overlooked the above quote and the particular cause given for the hysteria described.

118 Rodger, 1986. Introduction, 11ff.

119 Ibid. 11.

120 Ibid. 346.

121 Briggs, 1978 [1959]: 8ff, which describes a comparative English social structure ashore, in the 1780s.

122 Rodger, 1986:29.

123 Ibid. 205, Chapter VI.

124 Ibid. 205.

125 Ibid. 206.

126 Ibid. 207.

127 Ibid. 210.

128 Ibid. 211n.

129 Ibid. 211.

130 Briggs, 1978 [1959]:13.

131 Rodger, 1986:212

132 Ibid. 1986:212. "Captain Augustus Hervey, as polished a sophisticate as any in the Service, punched his steward in the mouth in anger, while Captain Charles Middleton, an officer of real piety and a future First Lord of the Admiralty, kicked one of his warrant officers in the backside".

133 Ibid. 1986:216-7.

134 Ibid. 1986:217. This was Lord Howe, the conciliator, of previous chapters.

135 Ibid. 1986, 216n, and 399.

136 Kemp, 1970:145-9; For Middleton see 145-7, which include a number of his specific orders relating to clothing, cleanliness, vice and immorality, drunkenness, ventilation, leave related to good behaviour, reduction in flogging, wives only on board, and fighting among the crew. For Kempenfelt, at the time, flag captain to Admiral Hardy in the *Victory*, see 147-9, where his discipline implied constant employment that did not cut into meal times, repose, washing and mending [clothes]. He supported the idea of a uniform and recommended the introduction of canvas bags for the use of seamen. He also considered religion an essential part of discipline.

137 Ibid. 1986:218.

138 Ibid. 1986:220.

139 Ibid. 1986:222-3.

140 Ibid. 1986:229.

141 Ibid.

142 Ibid. 1986:229-30.

143 Ibid. 1986:233.

144 Ibid. 1986:230-1.

145 Ibid. 1986:232.

146 Ibid. 1986:233.

147 Ibid. 1986:237.

148 Ibid.

149 Dening, 1993:339-67, "Scene ii. *Reflection*: Representation and the contribution of Errol Flynn, Clark Gable, Marlon Brando and Mel Gibson to cultural literacy".

150 Lavery, 1995, "4 Mutiny and Desertion", agrees that such cases were rarer, 141, and seemed to be characteristic of small ships, 143.

151 *Mutiny on the Bounty 1789-1989,* 1989:116-23, and *Mutiny on the Bounty,* 1991:43-56. Books have shared articles. See also Dening, 1993:passim.

152 Peter Gesner, "The Pandora project: reviewing genesis and rationale" in *Bulletin Australian Institute for Maritime Archaeology*, 12(1): 27-36. Apart from its tragic overtones, "*Pandora* can be considered the best preserved site known to date for archaeological study of the material culture of day-to-day life in an 18th century British ship on a long sea voyage to the South Pacific", and described as a 'marine Pompei' [Bas Kist] 'with day-to-day activity snap-frozen due to a catastrophe'.152

153 Manwaring and Dobrée, 67; Lavery, 1995:143. Handed over to the Spaniards, *Hermione* was later recaptured. See Cordingly, 1986:78, 54, for a description and illustrations including *The cutting out of the Hermione* by marine artist Nicholas Pocock, 1740-1821. Captain Edward Hamilton of the frigate *Surprise* carried out "one of the most daring cutting out expeditions" with a hundred men in small boats, against a much larger force.

154 Rodger, 1986:238.

155 Brome, 1992:90 [All references to Pepys in this paragraph.]

156 Rude, 1964:254.

157 Fraser, 1993:433.

158 Rodger, 1986:238-9, to this, and the following sentence.

159 Rodger, 1986:243-4.

160 Rodger, 1986:346n, in his three-page conclusion, goes against the grain of this present book, stressing social cohesion over division, and arguing for a wooden world "built of the same materials as the wider world". However, Rodger accepted "that the Service which suffered the mutinies of 1797 must have been very different from that of forty years before", the period with which his book was concerned. This conclusion had four references to Ian R. Christie, *Stress and Stability in Late Eighteenth-Century Britain,* Oxford, 1984.

161 Rodger, 1986:346; *Conclusion.*

162 Rodger, N.A.M. "The Naval World of Jack Aubrey" in A.E. Cunningham, ed. *Patrick O'Brian: A Bibliography and Critical Appreciation*, British Library Publishing Division,1994.

163 Rodger, N.A.M. "Shipboard Life in the Georgian Navy, 1750-1800; the Decline of the Old Order?" in Fischer Lewis R, et al., eds, *The North Sea. Twelve Essays on Social History of Maritime Labour,* Stavanger, Norway, 1992:29-39.
164 Ibid. reproduced in full in Patrick O'Brian, *The Nutmeg of Consolation,* Harper Collins, London, 1997:317-338.
165 Ibid. 317-24.
166 Ibid. 324-6.
167 Ibid. 326-7.
168 Ibid. 328-334.
169 Lavery, 1989:142,141, in the context of "Mutiny and Desertion", pp.141-144.
170 Dugan, 152.
171 Gilmore, 1993:423, accepted that "the mutinies were not instigated by the United Irishmen or by the radical societies", 443, even though Valentine Joyce was "a United Irishman who had been imprisoned for sedition", 418. Sir Ian Gilmour a barrister, was Lord Privy Seal and Deputy Foreign Secretary in Mrs Thatcher's first cabinet.
172 For obvious reasons, repeated here, from Trotter, Thomas, *Medicina Nautica,* II, 28 in Lloyd and Coulter, 1961:164.
173 Dugan, 395n, where he argued that Professor A. Aspinall printed copies of 36 letters in George III's own handwriting, affirming the death sentence.
174 See chapter 15 (book 2).
175 Rediker, 1993:6. Rediker continued working in this field, published *The Slave Ship: A Human History,* in 2007, and with Peter Linebaugh, *The Many-Headed Hydra: Sailors, Slaves, Commoners, and the Hidden History of the Revolutionary Atlantic,* in 2000. These longer studies confirm and strengthen their earlier contributions.
176 Lewis, Michael. *British Ships and British Seamen,* The British Council, and Longmans Green, London, 1944[1940]: 20.
177 Lewis, 1960:58-59, 80-81 for references to "sea-shires" in this and the previous sentence. For detail, see his Ch. III: "The Lower Deck" and table, *Modes of Entry* 1812, 139.
178 Rediker, 116-152 "The Seaman as Wage Laborer".
179 Lewis, 1944[1940]: 23-4.
180 Rediker, 5. See the full paragraph in the first chapter of this book.
181 Ibid. 154; 155, following sentence.
182 Ibid. 163.
183 Ibid. 206.
184 Ibid.
185 Ibid. 154n.
186 Ibid. 201n56; Hay, in Hay et al.1975:253; see also Lloyd *English Seamen* 76, 89, 90.

187 Ibid. 201.

188 Manwaring and Dobrée, 18-20.

189 Watt, J. et al., 1981:13-14.

190 Rediker, 1993:228n44.

191 Ibid. 308-9.

192 See Rodger, above.

193 Rediker, 227-8.

194 Ibid. 228.

195 Ibid. 235.

196 Porter, 1994:139

197 Colquhoun, 1796; 136,153,155. See also State Library of NSW microfilm, RAV/Fn4/2 no 18053, with River Thames' statistics for the year 1797. [Herbert Somerton Foxwell's driven collecting, and the Goldsmith'-Kress microfilms.]

198 Porter, 1994:139ff.

199 Linebaugh, 1993:409. For Colquhoun, see also Low, 1999:12ff.

200 *Minutes*...PRO/ADM 1/534. Source: *History of Medicine Library*, Sydney. Royal Australian College of Physicians.

201 Ibid. 4 to 6.

202 Gilmour, 1993, included among such "possible causes", stressing the Government under Pitt turned "a blind eye to all the warning signals on impending trouble in the fleet, [and] precipitated mutinies which laid Britain open to invasion and which were politically - as well as militarily - the most perilous moment of the revolutionary decade, 443".

203 The actions of other mutineers being tried at the same time are mentioned but space does not allow equal treatment with Redfern, here, or in the next chapter.

204 Dening, 1993:55. Pasley was Matthew Flinders's patron; see Scott, 2001[1914]: 21-46, Ch.III. This includes the battle off Brest in 1794, 'the glorious First of June', under Admiral Howe, in which Flinders participated as an aide-de-camp to Pasley, who lost a leg there, in action. Flinder's journal on *Bellerophon* describes the action, Scott, 2001:37-45. Flinders named a Cape after Pasley, Ibid. 46.

205 Gower, Sir Erasmus (1742-1814) in *DNB.*

206 Markham, Captain John (1761-1827) in *DNB.*

207 Riou, Captain Edward (1758?-1801) in *DNB.*

208 Manwaring and Dobrée, 163.

209 Dugan in a rare footnote confirms this to be William Bligh of Cook's *Resolution*, *Bounty* and former Governor of NSW.

210 Manwaring and Dobrée, 225.

211 Burke, 1876:295-338.

212 Manwaring and Dobrée, 236.

213 Manwaring and Dobrée, 237.

214 Manwaring and Dobrée, 234-5 for both letters.
215 Manwaring and Dobrée, 194, 211, and 227.
216 Gill, 1913:88.
217 Gill, 1913:30n1 paragraph 5.
218 Rodger,1979:64.
219 Ibid. 65.
220 See Nepean, Evan (1752-1822) entry in the *Australian Dictionary of Biography* 1788-1850 vol 2, Douglas Pike gen. ed., Melbourne University Press, Carlton, 1967,2:281; see also Frost, 1994.

Chapter 6 Notes

1 This account of the minutes opened in the preceding chapter. How this copy of the *minutes* came to be in the *History of Medicine Library*, Royal Australian College of Physicians, Sydney is explained in the *Introduction* to this book. PRO/ADM 1/534.
2 Baer, 1992:11.
3 Dening, 1993:147. The full title was Mr Bligh's Bad Language: Passion, Power and Theatre on the Bounty.
4 See the previous chapter, 4:23ff, for background notes to these individuals.
5 Minutes...PRO/ADM 1/534. History of Medicine Library, Sydney.
6 Ibid.
7 See preceding chapter reference to 31 May 1797. Source is given as *Appendix 8 in Dugan, 1966.*
8 This copy of the Minutes had two introductory pages (i & ii) followed by a run from 1 to 145. Printed numbers were missing from 40 to the end and had to be checked against the text before page numbers were pencilled in. Redfern's defence submission is best slotted in between pages 96 to 115 which brings the total to 165. But, be advised that Redfern's defence is a separate 20-page document.
9 Captain Thomas Parr of His Majesty's Ship *Standard* appeared as Prosecutor. Witnesses were sworn, and questioned by Prosecutor, the court and prisoners as the need of the moment demanded. The Prosecutor's first question to each witness was "Do you know the prisoners?" The invariable answer was "Yes I know them all".
10 The first reference is identified here, as "A", and the last, "G". The pages of the minutes for Tuesday, 22nd August, 1797, from which that first précis came, are shown as M17-23.
11 Again, see Elias (2007) for understanding of the role of the midshipman.
12 Starting DAY 1:Tuesday, 22nd August, 1797. [My reference to the *Précis: A (first reference to William Redfern: M17-23 (Minute pages)*].
13 Parr's questions suggest that Fitzgerald was beginning to appear to him as a defence 'plant' among the prosecution witnesses claiming as he did that Redfern was always against the mutiny.

14 This is intriguing. Why would the captain raise this matter? Why have it included in the minutes? Was Parr's invitation connected with Redfern's desire to leave the Navy? Or, was it concerned in some way with the mutiny? No evidence throws light on either question. But, consider the following. Captain Parr, now Redfern's prosecutor, raised the matter with Redfern's mess-mate, in part because he, too, had been invited [my supposition] and would remember, and in part for the following reason. Parr had become aware of Redfern's hostility before the trial (see p.14). He thought that the reason for this hostility might become an issue, and took advantage of the presence of this witness to confirm that he had invited Redfern to dine with him, an action that could be interpreted as a friendly, and not a hostile gesture. On the contrary, note Redfern's statement (see p.11), through his counsel, of "Captain Parr strangely eager to convict [him] if possible".

15 *M23-38.* Continuing DAY 1:Tuesday, 22 August, 1797.

16 *M38-44.* Concluding DAY 1:Tuesday, 22 August, 1797.

17 This was the letter, mentioned in chapter one, that Clune did not find.

18 *M45-48.* Start of DAY 2:Wednesday, 23 August, 1797.

19 *M49-52.* Continuing DAY 2:Wednesday, 23 August, 1797.

20 *M64-68.* Continuing DAY 2:Wednesday, 23 August, 1797.

21 *M72-78.* Concluding DAY 2:Wednesday, 23 August, 1797.

22 Dugan, 1966:313. James Dugan has it that Thomas Cheeseman was a member of the committee but offered to testify against his mates. Captain Parr accepted his offer and he was promised a pardon. From the *Minutes* it seems that Cheeseman was a self-confessed committeeman. His name does not appear on either of the two *Standard* courts martial so Dugan's claim may well be correct.

23 Ibid. The first major source of information about Redfern is provided by these court martial *Minutes.* For that reason, together with the court's decisions and their longterm effects on Redfern, it was essential to make full use of the material they contained. This is the most detailed presentation of that material to date, although my unpublished work based on these minutes was written in 1995, and provided material for my first paper about William Redfern, 1999; 7:35-41, and for this chapter.

24 It would be interesting to know the precise moment when Redfern asked the loblolly boy to fetch his boots and shoes. Was it before, or after, Wallace shot himself? The implications are several. Some are dispelled by his request. *He didn't ask for his bag.* If he had asked for his bag, knowing that there were pistols in it, this might have implied that Redfern wanted to do something with them. No. He asked only for his boots and shoes. Whether or not the pistols were in his bag it can be assumed that Redfern was not suicidal. And this in turn might give substance to his claim that he saw his involvement as different in kind, and much less involved, than leading mutineers such as Wallace.

25 *Minutes* of Redfern references, pp. 17-23, Day 1, Tuesday 22 August 1797.

26 Ibid. 64-68, Day 2, Wednesday 23 August 1797.
27 Ibid. 23-38, Day 1, Tuesday 22 August 1797.
28 Ibid. 72-78, Day 2, Wednesday 23 August 1797
29 Ibid. 23-38, Day 1, Tuesday 22 August 1797.
30 Ibid. 45-48, Day 2, Wednesday 23 August 1797.
31 Ibid. 49-52, Day 2, Wednesday 23 August 1797.
32 Ibid. 72-78, Day 2, Wednesday 23 August 1797.
33 Ibid. 38-44, Day 1, Tuesday 22 August 1797.
34 Jones, 1999:7:35-41. "Redfern's cross-examination of witnesses was brisk and well sustained. However, as he had the benefit of counsel and accepted his advice, it is difficult to draw other conclusions from Redfern's performance in court or to determine his contributions to the 20-page defence submission, read by his counsel".
35 PRO/ADM 1/534. Redfern's "Submission" was of 20 pages while the total for the other five prisoners was little more than 5-6 pages.
36 *Minutes*: Mr Hamilton Fitzgerald, sworn (p.17), questioned about Redfern (18ff).
37 I am taking this as a reference to a pre-trial situation, mentioned above, where the Judge Advocate was required to interrogate those to be charged, prepare a statement of charges, and send it to the accused so that he could mount his defence. As pre-trial procedures, Redfern's remarks were not included in the minutes. It also supports my earlier contention that Captain Parr was aware of Redfern's negative reaction to being charged, as stated. This whole line of thought gains credence with the timing of the verbal attack on Parr, which coincided with criticism from within the panel of judges.
38 Redfern mentioned in his *Submission* a few items not included in the *Minutes.*
39 See Manwaring and Dobrée, 208-10. The escape of the mutineer ships from the Thames had been in the minds of the mutineers. There was talk of the *Standard* going to France. Apparently, Branscombe was using his charts to convince the committee of the navigational difficulties involved. To increase the difficulty, "Trinity House arranged to have the buoys and beacon lights of the outward passage removed". That work was completed by 9 June. Selected references to navigation in the Thames, follow. Nelson's "damned pilot...ran the Ship aground...below the Nore" on 12.4.1784, Hibbert, 1994:45. Marcus, 1975:176-92, discussed the "London River", including a history of Trinity House, responsible for buoys and beacons, maintaining the removal of these guides "effectually cut off the escape of the [Nore] rebel fleet" (185). Copies of William Heather's Thames entrance chart, 1811, and an *Admiralty Chart 1185*, 1995, were brought from England for me by Frank McNeale, RN, & RAN.
40 Ala Alryyes, "War at a Distance: Court-Martial Narratives in the Eighteenth Century" in *Eighteenth-Century Studies*, vol. 41, no 4, Summer 2008:525-

542; accessed 14 October 2009. Parker makes an appearance in the final paragraphs (Alryyes, 2008:) There is a reference to James Dugan (1965:417), which is identical with (1966:420-1).

41 For quotes in this and the preceding paragraph, see Alryyes, 2008:525-7. For following references, see 'Military Law and History', *Ibid.* 537-9.

42 Associated with a modern day hoax; refer to Google.

43 For Melville, Alryyes gave 'Billy Budd, Sailor,' in *Billy Budd, Sailor, and Selected Tales,* ed. Robert Milder (Oxford University Press, 1997), 343. [In the Penguin Books edition, Harold Beaver, ed.1985:389.]

44 Algernon Sidney. 'Speech on the Scaffold', in William Jennings Bryan, *The World's Famous Orations* (1906).
See *http://www.bartleby.com/268/3/14.html,* Bartleby.com, *Great Books Online.*

45 See Kenyon, 1982 (1978): 221, for Algernon Sidney, and the context of the Rye House Plot. See also Antonia Fraser, 1993a: 231-4. "There is no evidence that any of them [Essex, Russell, Sidney] were direct plotters. They were condemned for their general opposition; guilt by association" (Ibid. 231).

46 Further discussion may be found on *The Online Library of Liberty,* copyright 2004 Liberty Fund, Inc. Algernon Sidney, *Discourses Concerning Government (1698)* foreword by Thomas G. West; Updated: 9 August, 2004.

47 Smith, 1988 (1790):238-9.

48 This paragraph bears out the following sentence in Dening's reference in n.2. above - "The sailors showed that they knew that in the presentation of power the forecastle must be as dramaturgical as the quarterdeck".

49 "The verbal distinction damaged Mr Redfern's hopes to life", Dugan, 393, noted the court's question to the witness, Nicholson, "Did Redfern say 'by the consent' or 'by the order' of the ship's company".

50 *Redfern to Bigge,* Sydney, Feb 5 1821, *ML, BT* 26, pp. 6186-6222; CY1446. [Note, one page therein is not part of Redfern's letter.] A copy of Redfern's letter to Bigge also appears in Ritchie, 1971, vol 2:187-199.

51 *Redfern to Bigge,* Sydney, Feb 8 1821, Redfern, BT6, 2502-9,. See also 26 June 1820, 2487ff. See also Ritchie 1971:vol. 1:*The Oral Evidence,* 132-6, Q&A 1-40; Redfern's notes, 136-9.

52 The one exception was the marine, Captain M'Intosh, sent ashore by Captain Parr, himself, at the request of the men, while in the North Sea before coming down to the Nore.

53 Dugan, 313. This account continued over page.

54 It would be useful to check the records to see whether the alleged Redfern letter still exists. If there is a signature, it might be compared with that in his copy of the midwifery text, which is of the same year.

55 *HRAI vol x*: 224-31. Enclosure, No. 4, *Mr Commissioner Bigge to Governor Macquarie.* Commissioner Bigge is the subject of later chapters.

56 An echo of "the most awful crisis that these kingdoms ever saw", the words of Lord Arden, one of the Lords of the Admiralty (Rodger 2006 [2004]:448). See earlier chapters for his role in putting the mutinies down. He visited Spithead and the Nore as a member of an Admiralty committee, which met only with intermediaries. Admiral Howe, on the other hand, met face to face with the delegates.
57 Ibid.
58 Ibid.
59 Gilmour, 1993:vii.
60 Ibid. 443.
61 Gill, 22.
62 Ibid. 23n123n1. A.S.I. 107, J202, 16 April. This letter is Bridport's answer to the order of the 15th from the Admiralty, "to hold himself in constant readiness to put to sea at the shortest notice", Gill, 18.
63 Ibid. 23n2; A.S.I. 107, J205, 16 April.
64 Some twenty years after Bridport uttered them, these words are germane to Bigge's treatment of Redfern. See a later chapter.
65 Gilmour, 423, pointed out that neither concessions nor hangings would prevent further mutinies.
66 Hibbert, 1994:102.
67 Ibid. 102n29, 426. Hibbert gives as his reference Nicolas, [Sir Harris, ed., *Dispatches and Letters of Vice-Admiral Lord Viscount Nelson,* 7 vols., London, 1844-6] ii, 402. This idea echoes Admiralty attempts to have Admiral Duncan bring his North Sea squadron to attack the Nore mutineers. This was an enterprise, which received a luke-warm reception from Admiral Duncan, Manwaring and Dobrée, 163. Captain Bligh carried a fresh proposal - for the same action - to Yarmouth, but found Duncan's fleet at sea, Manwaring and Dobrée, 177-8.
68 Hibbert, 1994:102n29, 426, above.
69 See references in a previous chapter to the Spithead hanging of HMS *Montague* mutineers from the North Sea and the Nore. Sir Peter Parker was Port-Admiral at Plymouth when ships had been drawn into the Spithead mutiny. Now, Parker was ordering mutineers to be hung at Spithead. Bullying officers, unwanted by the seamen, and left behind as part of the settlement, were somewhat disgruntled. For an example of a "dam'd tarter", i.e. "bullying officer", in Nelson's Fleet in January 1797, see Hibbert, 1994:102-4.
70 Dugan, 258.
71 PRO/ADM 1/534:26.
72 Gill, 26.
73 Gill, 117, Papers of the *Repulse,* no 7.
74 Gill, 104; Dugan, 181.
75 Linebaugh, 1993:311, a reference to "the riots of the spring and early summer of 1768", Ibid. 310.

76 PRO/ADM 1/534:26. In this book see a reference to chapter 4.
77 Dugan, 1966:392. The correct title was "surgeons mate" when Redfern joined in 1797. For a more specific reference to the place of warrant officers, see Lavery, 1995:23, and 100-1. The first reference, under "The Naval Administration" shows the Navy Board responsible for appointing by warrant, but not examining surgeons. The second reference shows four levels of warrant officer. Surgeons, though warrant officers, shared with commissioned officers, entitlement to walk the quarterdeck, and live in the wardroom". Surgeon's mates might aspire to the quarterdeck but certainly occupied a lower level. "Literacy was one thing that all warrant officers had in common".
78 Clark, 1979 (1962): 98-9. Being "promoted" to "surgeon" by the mutineers did not count. Redfern remained a "surgeon's mate". Nonetheless, the point of both Clark's and Dugan's comments remains.
79 See chapter 9, for this matter.
80 Whitaker, 1994:67-8.
81 Frost, 1994:9-41.
82 PRO, Miscellaneous Convict Prison Registers 1802-1849, HO 9/8 Hulk Registers, Portland Hulk, moored at Portsmouth:
83 Avge Age, 16.4 ... 13(2),14,16,17,18(4),19:
Avge Age, 22.8 ... 20(4),21(2),22(4),23(3),25,26(3),29:
Avge Age, 32.4 ... 30(2),31(3),32(2),37,38:
Avge Age, 42... 41,42,44:50.
84 Louis Garneray. Translated from the French with foreword and notes by Richard Rose. The Floating Prison: The remarkable account of nine years' captivity on the British Prison Hulks during the Napoleonic Wars: 1806 to 1814, Conway Maritime Press, London, 2003.

Chapter 7 Notes

1 *1798, A Bicentenary Perspective*, Bartlett et al., eds. 2003:'A five-day academic conference commemorating the bicentenary of the 1798 rebellion was held between 19 and 23 May 1998...The event brought together international scholars, local historians and specialists in a diversity of areas, all of whom were trying to understand the cataclysmic events that brought eighteenth-century Ireland to such a violent close' (*Preface*). Unfortunately, not to hand when this chapter was written, and certainly not yet digested.
2 Pakenham, [1969] 1992:13.
3 Ibid. "Prologue", 17-19.
4 See Dugan, 1966:420-34, for Tone's last years.
5 Whitaker, 1994. "Between 1800 and 1806, six ships arrived from Ireland carrying just over 1000 convicts, of whom at least 400 were political prisoners. These Irish were different, both from their predecessors and from the general run of convicts. They were more educated and more articulate, as well as politically trained and (often) militarily experienced. They included a former

county sheriff, clergymen, schoolteachers, doctors, lawyers and a surveyor". (Ibid. v).

6 Pakenham, 1992:349-50,"Epilogue"; For an estimate of the total population of NSW in 1802, as 7,014, see Cumpston, intro and ed. M.J.Lewis, 1989:39.

7 Dugan, 1966:396-7.

8 Pakenham, 1992:350, which includes reference to Holt, Meehan, and to the memorial, which follow.

9 Blanco, *Wellington's Surgeon General: Sir James McGrigor,* 1974:38. (I have read, too, McGrigor's autobiography, edited by Mary McGrigor, republished in 2000.)

10 Ibid. 30.

11 Donald was son of Munro 1, who was succeeded by Secundus (II) and Tertius (III) as lecturers at Edinburgh University Medical School.

12 McGrigor (Autobiography), 2000:175.

13 Oliver MacDonagh, *The Inspector General,* 1981. Passim.

14 McGrigor, 80.

15 Ibid. 127; for this and the preceding paragraph.

16 Donald Munro, *An Account of the Diseases which were most frequent in the British military hospitals in Germany* (from January 1761 to the Return of the Troops to England in March 1763), to which is added 'An ESSAY on the Means of Preserving the Health of Soldiers, and conducting Military Hospitals', 1764. A Project Gutenberg EBook released February 21, 2010 [EBook #31338] and accessed 30 March 2011. See http://www.gutenberg.org and http://manybooks.net/.

17 For Bryan Gandevia Prize for Australian military-medical history, see http://www.awm.gov.au/research/grants/gandevia_prize.

18 Linebaugh, 1977:246-269. At 348n1, Linebaugh advised that "A more complete treatment of the subject may be found in his thesis, *'Tyburn: A Study of Crime and the Labouring Poor in London During the First Half of the Eighteenth Century'* (Warwick Univ. Ph.D. thesis, 1975)".

19 Linebaugh, 1993, xxiv-v, 'Introduction', for this and the two following paragraphs.

20 Ibid. 371-401, chapter 1, Volume II of *Better than Cure The life and times of the ebullient and resilient William Redfern 1775-1833.*

21 Ibid. 374.

22 Ibid. 378-382.

23 Wollstonecraft, 1987 [1796 MW and 1798 WG]. It was happy that the District Pilot Officer had been paid in honour, with a badge for his service, for his stipend left something to be desired. "Thus, my friend, you perceive the necessity of perquisites. This same narrow policy runs through every thing" (1987:67).

24 Linebaugh, 1993:378.

25 Ibid. 381.

26 Ibid. 374, "In eighteenth-century London, just as the necessary value of labour often appeared as 'crime', so the surplus value of the ruling class appeared as 'corruption', and nowhere perhaps was this more in evidence than in the dockyards". See Plumb, 1981:200ff; Dugan, 1966:435ff; Pool, 1964:161-176.

27 Linebaugh, 1993:400, saw Samuel Bentham as notable for work processes in the eighteenth-century shipyard, 382-90, as "the great innovator of dockyard development", 396-401, and as the first of three "capitalist interests" - technologists, economists and police, 429. For Frederick Taylor see the quote, 400, and Braverman, 1974:87, "Taylor [too] dealt with the fundamentals of the organization of the labor process and of control over it". Time and motion studies grew out of his original research.

28 Linebaugh, 1993:400-1.

29 Ibid. 401.

30 Ibid.

31 Jones, 1999; 7:81, "Private practice and the cost of medicines".

32 Low, 1999 [1982]:12-25, includes a portrait (1818).

33 Linebaugh, 1993:426-7.

34 Ibid. 427.

35 41 references to Patrick Colquhoun came up when his name was entered on Webcat, the online catalogue of the State Library, Sydney, NSW. These were all in microform, part of the Goldsmith'-Kress Collection, and ranged over the period 1783?-1806:35 (18th C), 6 (19th C). At the Library I concentrated on the 1800 edition of "A Treatise...[676pp. octavo]".

36 George, 1953 [1931]:147-155, 'Appendix'.

37 Gatrell, 1996.

38 Ibid. vi.

39 Ibid.

40 Ibid. 18.

41 Ibid.

42 Ibid. 18-9.

43 Ibid. 6-7.

44 Ibid. 7. Gatrell remarked, "How easily this extraordinary fact has been forgotten-that the noose was at its most active on the very eve of capital law repeals!"

45 Ibid. 7. In 7n11, Gatrell advised that "For these estimates and all English data in the following see App.2".

46 Ibid. 24 - but read the following paragraph, too.

47 Linebaugh, 1993:256. This opens an earlier chapter, titled "Silk Makes the Difference", a reference to a proverb, "We are all Adam's children, but silk makes the difference". As for "Chips and Ships" this chapter on 'silk' is rich in detail of production and human relations and spreads to encompass worldwide 'tumults' from Spitalfields to Bengal, 272.

48 Ibid.
49 Ibid. 285-7.
50 Ritchie, 1988:1.
51 See also Hugh Trevor-Roper, 'The Invention of Tradition: the Highland Tradition of Scotland' in Hobsbawm & Ranger ed. 1992 (1983), where the author argued that 'the whole concept of a distinct Highland culture and tradition is a retrospective invention' (Ibid. 15).
52 My original source for information about Alexander Wilson was Robert Cantwell's 1961 biography, which includes a portrait, 8 colour plates of birds, 16 b.w. ills. by the artist and decorations by Robert Ball, 1961. Kastner, 1978:329, described Cantwell's biography as "a work of high literary quality". Now, some years later, I have acquired a copy of Clark Hunter, 1983:8, who, while noting a few items missed by Cantwell, referred to them as "relatively trifling when set against the importance of his biography" which "brought to us a much fuller picture of the man and a great deal of new information". Finally, in 2013, Edward H. Burtt, JR and William E. Davis JR published *Alexander Wilson: The Scot who founded American Ornithology*. 'Wilson's entire scientific and ornithological career is contained within the pages of *American Ornithology*'. Wilson by publishing this work 'established American ornithology on the world stage' (Ibid. 285).
53 *The Shorter Oxford English Dictionary*, 1974:"Paisley, Name of a town in Scotland, used attrib. In P. shawl, a shawl in soft bright colours resembling a Cashmere shawl, orig. made at P.; P. pattern, the characteristic pattern of such a shawl; so P. cotton, velvet, etc., cotton, velvet, etc. having this pattern".
54 It was not surprising to find caged canaries in a coal mining area in those days as these birds were taken down the mines to test the air quality.
55 Wright, 1975:87-8.
56 For an English illustration see Jenny Uglow's biography of Thomas Bewick (2006), 'an early conservationist - up to a point' (370). Notwithstanding, Bewick's carefully observed end-block engravings of animals and birds, together with text, did much to develop an interest in nature from the earliest years, which had positive results for conservation in the longer term. Over a wider field, see Leopold, 1987[1949]: passim; particularly "The Land Ethic" (201-26). Nash (1990): passim, first published in the USA in 1989.
57 Hay et al., 1975:311; Appendix I, a. *Gleaning*.
58 Linebaugh, 1993:409, in "Sugar and Police: The London Working Class in the 1790s".
59 David Craig, 1961. Craig's aim was "to suggest the essentials of Scottish culture during the period, in relation to the literature and its public", 9. His 'social history' of literature did not aim "to cover the background", 11, but is useful in understanding Wilson's work. At a time when "'leaders of thought' had little sympathy with the popular stirrings", "popular poetry was at the root

of that awakening", 111. "Polite" culture opposed the vernacular of Burns and Wilson.

60 Hobsbawm, 1962:44ff; in the 1995 ed., 27ff.

61 Gilmour, 1993:3

62 Robert Macqueen (1722-1799). See references in McIntyre (1997).

63 Thompson, 1966:124

64 *The New Testament,* Matthew, 13:3.

65 Cantwell, 1961:16.

66 For Witherspoon in context, see Archie Turnbull, 'Scotland and America, 1730-90', in David Daiches et al. *A Hotbed of Genius,* 1986.

67 Ibid. 19. "Dr. Witherspoon's standing was high, not only in Paisley and Scotland, but throughout Britain. He was the leader of the democratic minority in the Church of Scotland, in a long-drawn-out dispute having to do with the rights of congregations to approve the ministers placed over them". See Craig, 1961:64, for an allied comment, on the philosopher Hume not realising that the "desire for a universal opportunity for religious debate was one of the best and most characteristic bents in the Scottish Reformation, and at the root of its revolt against the old Church thought". For an update on Witherspoon, see Herman, 2003:text and sources, 421-2. Herman wrote, "Most Americans are totally unaware of John Witherspoon's role in the making of their revolution and the Declaration of Independence. Even scholars rarely include him...Nevertheless, an academic subculture of Witherspoon studies continues to thrive". Authors and texts are listed.

68 Hobsbawm, 1962:47. "English education was a joke in poor taste, though its deficiencies were somewhat offset by the dour village schools and the austere, turbulent, democratic universities of Calvinist Scotland which sent a stream of brilliant, hard-working, career-seeking, and rationalist young men into the south country: James Watt, Thomas Telford, Loudon McAdam, James Mill".

69 For understanding, see Douglas Hay, "Poaching and the Game Laws on Cannock Chase" in Hay et al., 1975:189-253.

70 Hobsbawm, 1962:34. See Linebaugh 1993:410ff and Kowaleski-Wallace, 1997:37-51.

71 Cantwell, 43-5.

72 Ibid. 48. See also Craig, 1961:122, who has a reference to Wilson telling "in his journal how on his rounds peddling as a packman he carried prospectuses of his poems and canvassed for subscribers".

73 Cantwell, 49.

74 Ibid. 50-1 and 55-60.

75 Adam Smith, 1971:Opening ch. of Bk 1, 3:"Of the Division of Labour", has the manufacture of pins as an example of the way productivity is increased by the division of labour.

76 Comte, August, *Positive Philosophy, II*, p. 292, quoted in Coser, 1977:12. While Comte was concerned with the wider social function his description is equally true at this level.
77 Cantwell, 69
78 See Thompson, 1975:263-71, blackmailing. Thompson's conclusion, though not specific to Wilson's case, is relevant: "Letters of this kind offer a pathetic and ineffectual counterpoint to the real exchanges of influence and interest passing between the great" and the lowly. And again, "they may sometimes be seen as intrinsic to proto-democratic forms of organization, deeply characteristic of eighteenth-century social and economic relations".
79 Cantwell, 265-276. Wilson's poem, *The Shark: or Lang Mills Detected*, appears there with copies of Court Records of Wilson's Arrest, and other matters relevant to the case. The story is told in full in the text. Part of Wilson's punishment was that he had to burn his poem in public, but not before "printed copies...had been placed in every weaving shop in Paisley" (74). See also Craig (1961:87-91), who discussed Wilson and 'The Shark' in the context of "the number of poems concerned with the simple living-needs of crofters, labourers, weavers, the people generally".
80 Hunter, 1983:8.
81 Ibid. 36.
82 Ibid. 39. Hunter's discussion takes up pages 36-40. Appendix 1, 409-28, includes a copy of the poem *The Hollander* and court documents pertaining to the case.
83 Burtt and Davis accessed and reproduced 'the pencil sketches, pen and ink drawings, and draft paintings known to [them], for the plates in *American Ornithology'* (2013:63-279).
84 Cantwell, 1961:258
85 Oeland, 2001:123. See *also The Bulletin* and *The Ornithological Society* which bear Wilson's name to this day.
86 Marcus Rediker, *The Slave Ship*...2007; see also Linebaugh & Rediker, 2000.
87 Doudou Diene, "From the Slave Trade to the Challenge of Development: Reflections on the Conditions for World Peace", in *From Chains to Bonds: The Slave Trade Revisited*, UNESCO and Berghahn Books, 2001.
88 Davidson, Rigby, 1984:138.
89 Ibid. 1984:147; see 137-150,"The curse of Columbus".
90 Ibid. 147. See Robert Desowitz, *Tropical Diseases from 50,000 BC to 2500 AD* (99), where he pointed out that since black Africans "rarely died of yellow fever", "Their survival gave further proof of the economic advantage of their enslavement over that of the Amerindians and indentured whites".
91 Davidson 1984:142.
92 Ibid. 139.
93 Mazrui, 1986:159-60.

94 Ibid. 159.
95 Ibid.
96 Ibid. 77, for the question, and part answer; for more on racism see 26,102ff.
97 Ibid. 104.
98 Ibid. 109ff.
99 Nicephore Soglo, President of the Republic of Benin, 1991-96, in his Foreword to Diene, ed., 2001:xii.
100 Ibid. 125-138, Paul E. Lovejoy, "Conditions of Slaves in the Americas". See also Lovejoy, 1997.
101 De Gouges, 1989 [Paris, 1791.]: 19-20, a reference to 'men of colour on our islands' ruled by despots, and 'liberty'.
102 Hobsbawm. 1995, ed. 69.
103 James, 1963:passim. There, slavery is writ large. I thank my son, Ian, for bringing this book to my attention.
104 Ibid. 200, citing Fortescue, *History of the British Army, Vol. IV*, pt.1:496.
105 McIntyre, 1997:Preface. See also McIntyre in Craig & Hull, 1999:1, Abstract.
106 Bernier, Olivier, The World in 1800, A Robert L. Bernstein Book, John Wiley & Sons Inc., New York, 2000.
107 The authors in Nussbaum's collection 'confront the ways in which European knowledge is itself a situated knowledge, neither universal nor objective, and the ways that indigenous systems of belief are not inherently inadequate or naïve".
108 Paine, 1973. See also Keane, 1995. For the character of Paine and the author's absence of "sniping and sermonizing" see his Prologue, xvii.
109 Cantwell, 23-4
110 Porter, 1990:95pp. *Enlightenment: Britain and the Creation of the Modern World*, Penguin Books, 2001. *Flesh in the Age of Reason: How the Enlightenment Transformed the Way We See Our Bodies and Souls*, Penguin Books, London, [published posthumously] 2004. Finally, Porter's doctoral thesis in a more accessible form, reprinted by Cambridge University Press, Cambridge, 2008 (1980, 1977).
111 Porter, 1980:72ff.
112 Hobsbawm, 1962:38. "Yet in practice the leaders of the emancipation for which the enlightenment called were likely to be the middle ranks of society, the new, rational men of ability and merit rather than birth, and the social order which would emerge from their activities would be a 'bourgeois' and capitalist one".
113 Outram, 1995, offered "a succinct survey of Enlightenment historiography", according to Porter, 2001:488n12. See also Outram's later work, *Panorama of the Enlightenment*, Thames and Hudson Ltd, London, 2006.
114 Outram, 1995:12.

115 See Rudé, 1985 [1964], passim. See also Roy Porter, 2001:xix, for "enlightenment" in its British setting, although he admitted to "not giv[ing] much space to political debate, literature and the arts, to tides of taste, the commercialization of culture or the forging of nationalism". Porter gave his reasons, among them the availability of "splendid books [which] have appeared recently in all these areas".

116 Outram, 1995:98. See also Williams (1976) who provides a telling exposition of Outram's idea applied to Spain. While giving, that "'genius'...defies historical analysis", Williams held that "even 'genius' is located in time and place and works with [it]'. He went on, "Without [Goya's] commitment to Enlightenment in its peculiarly Spanish form, his work would lose half its power". Goya's major tension was between reason and unreason, e.g. The *Disasters of War,* Ibid. 1976:94-5, 162.

117 Outram, 1995:127, concluding paragraph.

118 See for example, Outram, *The Body and the French Revolution*, 1989.

119 See for the general case, Hammond and Hammond, 1948 (1911]: 34-6.

120 Wollstonecraft, 1992.

121 Outram, *On being Perseus: New Knowledge, Dislocation, and Enlightenment Exploration*, Preprint 60, Max Planck Institute for the History of Science, 1997 (18pp). Needless to say it formed a chapter in David Livingstone and Charles Withers, eds. *Geography and Enlightenment,* Chicago Press, Chicago, 1999. ('Geography' rounds out the collection of enlightenment subjects discussed below.

122 Daiches, in *A Hotbed of Genius*, 1986:14.

123 Roger L. Emerson. *Essays on David Hume, Medical Men and the Scottish Enlightenment*, 'Industry, Knowledge and Humanity', Ashgate, Farnham, 2009:(Ch. 2) 21-38.

124 Cobbett's England,1968:194-5.The original source for this article is given (1968:202) as - "To the Landowners on the Evils of Collecting Manufacturers into Great Masses", 17 November 1824, from his Political Works VI, 430-42.

125 Ibid. 197. This brings to mind the temperature below deck, from body heat, in crowded convict ships.

126 Ibid. 199.

127 For a parallel case in France, see Outram (1984:106; post 1815, Ch. V: *The Restoration and the crisis of patronage*). Georges Cuvier, the French scientist, a protestant, also supported the Lancastrian system. "To achieve the quickest results in the minimum time, it [the Société pour l'Instruction élémentaire] decided to use the Lancastrian or monitorial system of instruction. As the pupils taught each other at the minimum of expense and with surprisingly solid results, the idea spread well beyond Paris, and a networks of associations soon covered almost the whole of provincial France". The Lancastrian system will receive more detailed attention in Great Britain

and in colonial New South Wales in chapter 9, Volume II of *Better than Cure The life and times of the ebullient and resilient William Redfern 1775-1833.*

128 Gascoigne, 1994:passim. For these quotes see 'The limits of the English Enlightenment' (ch. 55).

129 Steel, 1985:215ff.

130 Ibid. 218

131 Keane, 1995:532. Wilson's lines quoted from Craig, 1961:77. I am indebted to Keane for this reference, which led me to Craig's work and a better appreciation of Alexander Wilson's poetry in the context of the times. Craig, 1961:324, has "buffet, wallop", for "lounder". The internet turned up the idea, "to punish", in "the sense of being treated like children by the Gods" in an *IJoST Forum* Article, Vol.1, no 1:B. Dunlop, Edinburgh, accessed through *Google,* 29 October 2002.

132 *Many a hundred.* For the original, see Craig, 1961:212.

133 Cantwell, 162, has the names "Bartram" and "Peale" but gives no specific reference. Hunter has a letter, "Wilson to Lawson, CVIII: Albany, 3 November 1808" which included "Peale", and "Benny". The latter, and a type-founder Ronaldson, are mentioned in references to naturally occurring antimony and lead, in Wilson letters, Hunter, 1983:247, 284, 287, and 290. References to Bartram in the notes will be retained on account of his importance to Wilson's development as a naturalist. For a study of Wilson against the background of a history of natural science of the New World see Kastner, 1978. For a recent brief account of the Quaker naturalist and botanist, Bartram, see Oeland, above, who credited Wilson with writing "a fitting epitaph...in a grateful letter...[in which he]...readily acknowledged Bartram's profound influence on his life and career. Time spent in the company of that kind old wanderer had sharpened Wilson's eye, and now, he wrote, 'I see new beauties in every bird, plant, or flower I contemplate'". See also Cantwell, 1961:279, in notes on subscribers to Wilson's *American Ornithology,* Appendix II, and Hunter, 1983.

134 Cantwell, 120-1.

135 Cantwell, 162.

136 Keane, 532.

137 These references to 'eyes' connect to Oeland, above.

138 Earnshaw, 1959:7-14.

139 Ibid. Thompson, 1966:124-5; 127. See also Clune, 1969, passim; Clune acknowledged Earnshaw's inspiration and encouragement. See also Earnshaw entries under individual names in *Australian Dictionary of Biography*, 1967, vols 1&2. Since writing this chapter I have found - Flynn, 1994, and Oldfield, 1999:19-40.

140 Thompson, 1966:124-5;127.

141 Steel, 1985:219. For comparison with a later reference to Redfern, see the use of the word "rabble", in the context of "colonial radicalism", which

subsumes the Scottish Martyrs. Years later, Professor John Manning Ward, 1981:36 and 34-7, argued that a meeting held in 1825 was not a "rabble", being composed of Redfern and other leading citizens. This meeting's purpose was to adopt an address to Governor Brisbane of New South Wales seeking his advocacy of Lord Bathurst, to introduce "trial by jury and a representative assembly of one hundred members".

142 See *Advertisement in* The Glasgow Advertiser *by Paisley Reformers*, Paisley, Saracen's Head Inn, 8 February 1793, in Hunter, 1983:429-32, Appendix 11.

143 This title inspired me to collect the books mentioned in this section for more detailed study. ARJ.

144 Daiches, David, Peter Jones, and Jean Jones, eds, Edinburgh University Press, Edinburgh, 1986. The visual arts were also to the fore in *Adam Smith* (1990) and *William Cullen* (1993:1-84); see below.

145 Obstetrician William Smellie (1697-1763), whose text William Redfern used, was a friend of Cullen (See Doig et al 1993:9; Portrait and note).

146 David Daiches Raphael, joint ed. *The Theory of Moral Sentiment*, and *Lectures on Jurisprudence* (Glasgow Edition); contributed to bicentenary collections of essays, and published *The Imperial Spectator: Adam Smith's Moral Philosophy* (2007).

147 G.P. Morice, ed., David Hume: Bicentenary Papers (1977). See also Hume and Hume's Connexions, M. A. Stewart and John P. Wright, eds. (1995). For an update see, Roger L. Emerson. Essays on David Hume, Medical Men and the Scottish Enlightenment, 'Industry, Knowledge and Humanity', Ashgate Publishing Ltd, Farnham, Surrey, 2009.

148 Adam Smith (1723-90), an exhibition organised by The Adam Smith Bicentenary Committee, 17 July-2 Sept 1990, Jean Jones, Sandy Hamilton, 1990.

149 *Smith, Adam, Reviewed.* Peter Jones and Andrew S. Skinner, eds., Edinburgh University Press, 1992.

150 R.G.W. Anderson, The Playfair Collection and the teaching of Chemistry at the University of Edinburgh 1713-1858, The Royal Scottish Museum, Edinburgh, 1978.

151 A.D.C. Simpson, *Joseph Black (1728-1799): A commemorative Symposium, 1978,* The Royal Scottish Museum, Edinburgh, 1982.

152 Donald B. McIntyre and Alan McKirdy, *James Hutton: The Founder of Modern Geology* (1726-97), The Stationery Office, Ltd., 1997 (the bicentennial of Hutton's death).

153 G. Y. Craig and J. H. Hull, eds. *James Hutton - Present and Future,* The Geological Society, London, 1999. The complete study - Donald McIntyre, *James Hutton's Edinburgh was* printed in *Earth Sciences History* Vol 16, no 2, 100-157 1997.

154 Culled from the above works.

155 A. Doig, J.P.S. Ferguson, I.A.Milne and R. Passmore, Eds. *William Cullen and the Eighteenth Century Medical World*: A bicentenary exhibition and symposium arranged by the Royal College of Physicians of Edinburgh in 1990, Edinburgh University Press, 1993.
156 Duncan Forbes, 'Hume's Science of Politics' in G.P. Morice, ed., David Hume: Bicentenary Papers (1977:42ff., 50).
157 See 1. Matthews and Ortmann (2000) for the rhetorical structure of *Wealth of Nations* downloaded from
http://world.std.com/~mhuben/reviews.html, 7 July 2012.
See 2. Ortmann and Baranowski, 2001,
http://home.cerge-ei.cz/ortmann/papers/09SchumpeterWrongYK.pdf, accessed on line, 7 July 2012.
158 Emerson, 2009. They surfaced while searching academia for Trevor Levere, one of two editors in the series 'Science, Technology and Culture, 1700-1945', to which Emerson's *Essays* belong.
159 Obviously R.G.W. Anderson was a primary source for Black, but contributed to the Cullen account, for which Doig et al. (*Cullen*: 1993) was an important source. Emerson contributed insights on the influence of Holland on early teachers of medicine in Scotland (Emerson, 2009:14-15), and on patronage (for which, see Emerson, 2009:27ff, and Doig et al. 1993:186ff). [Additionally, there are Hutton strands to chemical themes.]
160 Steel. 1985:218-224. "Scottish martyrs" named "Edinburgh martyrs".
161 Ibid. 219ff.
162 For useful background, see Elaine McFarland, "Scotland and the 1798 rebellion: The limits of 'common cause' " in Thomas Bartlett et al, eds, 2003.
163 Earnshaw, 1959:9
164 Cantwell, 73-4
165 Ibid. 307.
166 Ibid. 72-3
167 For Braxfield, character of, and references to, see Donald B. McIntyre, "James Hutton's Edinburgh: The Historical, Social and Political Background" (1997), above.
168 Steel, 221.
169 Clune, 1969, passim. Clune acknowledged Earnshaw's inspiration and encouragement. See Earnshaw entries under individual names in *Australian Dictionary of Biography*, 1967, vols 1&2. See also Michael Flynn, *Settlers and Seditionists: The People of the convict ship* Surprise *1794*, Angela Lind, Sydney, 1994:xx-xxi for portraits and monument.
170 Oldfield, 1999:19-40. John Earnshaw has Gerrald, with advanced tuberculosis, taken from his sick bed at Newgate gaol to the storeship *Sovereign*. At Port Jackson fellow martyrs and friends cared for him, as did "the liberal minded surgeon Bass". Gerald died on 16 March 1796 (Gerrald, Joseph 1760-1796 in *ADB1*). William Skirving died on 19 March 1796.

Again, Surgeon Bass of the *Reliance* was in daily attendance (Skirving, William in *ADB2*). Surgeon Balmain refused to attend him. Skirving had dysentery (Watt, in Hardy & Frost:149, 265n143).

171 Thompson, 1966:104

172 Braithwaite, 2003. See also, below, 'commons', 'commoners' and 'enclosures'.

173 Thompson, 1966:102.

174 Bewick, 1975, passim. For this reference see Ibid. 132-5. See references to Bewick in Thompson (1966:180-1, 219). [Thompson used a different edition of Bewick.]

175 Briggs, 1978:78-91

176 Ibid. 84

177 Ibid. 84-5. Pitt believed the urgent tasks of recovery and reconstruction were more important than 'prolonged discussion of general principles'.

178 Thompson 1966:104

179 Ibid. 111

180 Ibid. 113

181 Ibid. 122-3

182 Ibid. 122

183 Ibid. 123

184 Since writing the following notes on Coleridge and Thelwall, I have read Holmes, 1999 [1989]. "Pantisocracy", the subject of chapter 4 (Ibid. 59-88), runs on to the first few pages of the following chapter, where Coleridge's radical politics mix with his religious preaching (Ibid. 89-116). Coleridge, in London in 1794, had followed the treason trials at the Old Bailey of Hardy, Tooke, Thelwall and Holcroft (Ibid. 81).

185 Coleridge, Samuel Taylor. *The Portable Coleridge,* 1978:246, 250, 256.Letters dated June 22, 1796, November 19 [1796], December 17 and 31, 1796 and [October 16], 1797.

186 Holmes, 1999: opp. p.320, see the 1795 portrait of Coleridge, by Pieter van Dyke, subtitled "The young radical lecturer and poet in Bristol". (National Portrait Gallery, London.) This portrait also appears on the cover of Richards (1978).

187 Richards, ed. :1978:250-1.

188 Holmes, 1999:295 and 299, for the effect of Bartram's *Travels* on Coleridge and Asra (Sarah Hutchinson); see also Kastner (1978:110 ff.) for further comment on effect on Coleridge and Wordsworth.

189 Ibid. 3ff, and '236-7; 275, for the motives behind this idea', 'Pantisocracy', an idea which came to nothing.

190 Holmes, 1999:156-62, cited Edmund Blunden and E.L. Griggs, *Coleridge: Studies by Several Hands,* Constable, 1934:80-3, for references to Home Office [spy] reports on Coleridge and others. What the spy saw as mapping the countryside for French invaders, Holmes described as "a classic

description of Romantic poets at work, because it is recorded in absolute ignorance - or innocence - of the literary significance of what was being done". (1999:160). Coleridge, Wordsworth and Dorothy "began their work like plein-air painters, taking elaborate notes of the varied effects of light on the landscape, of plant and water, of wind and cloud and starlight. Night walks were as frequent as daylight ones...". (Ibid.)

191 Richards, 7.

192 Ibid. 7-8.

193 Ibid. 318-328 for a copy of the text of this Address Delivered at Bristol.

194 Ibid. 241-3.

195 Thompson, 1966:148.

196 William Redfern was briefly a magistrate in New South Wales. So this book looks to the law for an understanding of that role in a convict colony, with some concern for its victims. Among works studied, three are listed below. (1) Christopher Hill, 1996:ix-x, Preface. Hill said that he aimed 'to rescue the landless ex-peasantry from posterity's enormous silence'. This is from a sentence which opens with a reference to Edward Thompson's rescue of 'the poor stockinger' and others 'from the enormous condescension of posterity', in his *Making of the English Working Class.* (2) Douglas Hay, et al., 1975. Hay informed the reader that all the contributors were 'centrally concerned with the law'. Finally, (3) David Neal (1991:xii), where he acknowledged 'the seminal work on the rule of law in eighteenth-century England by Edward Thompson and Douglas Hay'.

197 Gilmour, 183.

198 Ibid. v, 'Table of Contents' for this list of headings for the three parts of his book.

199 Ibid. 414ff.

200 Thompson, 1966:123-4

201 McIntyre, in *Earth Sciences History*, 1997:100-157.

202 Thompson, 1966:124

203 Ibid. 124fn1, for source material.

204 Ibid. 124-5

205 Clark, 1968 (1919): 56.

206 Hobsbawm, 1962:69. While J.M.Neeson, 1996 (1993):, below, was critical of Hobsbawm and Rude (1969:

207 Hill, Christopher,1991[1972]:13

208 Ibid.

209 Ibid. 17

210 Ibid. 21.

211 Ibid. 50

212 Ibid. 40.

213 Ibid. 40-41

214 Ibid. 41-2. See also Thompson 1993: passim. [Born Feb. 3, 1924, Edward Thompson died August 28, 1993.]
215 Ibid. 39-56.
216 Ibid. 43 for this paragraph. For the attraction of the forests see pp.43-4. "Sylvan liberty is idealized in the ballads of Robin Hood, in Shakespeare's Forest of Arden and in the wise 'old men' who appear in Elizabethan and Jacobean pageants. This may relate to contemporary migration to forests in search of security and independence".
217 Ibid. 50-56, II - 'Forests and Commons' in chapter 3, 'Masterless Men', for the following summary.
218 Ibid. 130. This discussion (128-132) adds to an earlier treatment (50-56) under the same heading, 'Forests and Commons'.
219 Ibid. 5 5-6 for this paragraph and its references in Hill (1991)
220 Hill, Christopher, 1980:18.
221 Hill's reference here is to his *Change and Continuity...*1974, chap. 10. Hobsbawm commented on this contradiction, above.
222 Hill, 1980:34-6. See George (1953:147-155) for Gregory King's *Table,* an "estimate of the population and wealth of England and Wales at the end of the seventeenth century", with Colquhoun's estimates for the end of the eighteenth century for comparison.
223 Ibid. 36
224 Ibid.
225 Hammond and Hammond, 1948(1911) 34. For an account of the original contribution made by the Hammonds, their subsequent neglect and return to favour, see the general introduction and bibliographic note by John Rule in the 1979 edition of *The Skilled Labourer*, 1979. For another assessment see Hobsbawm and Rude (2001[1969]: 13ff.)
226 Hoskins, 1978 (1955):177-8, provides a different set of figures
227 Hammonds, 1948:34-5. See also Hoskins, 1978[1955]:177ff.for regional variation in the impact of enclosures upon the landscape.
228 Ibid. 1948:6, Preface to the Guild Edition.
229 Industrial melanism: In turn, dark forms of the light Peppered moth (*Biston betularia*) would stimulate studies of industrial melanism, which became embedded in the literature as classics of natural selection; Judith Hooper (2002) to the contrary.
230 Hammonds, 1948:102.
231 Neeson, 1996:312ff, 'gleaning', in 'Peasants and Common Right'.
232 Clark, 1968 (1919):64.
233 John Clare is featured in a following segment of this chapter.
234 Blum, Jerome. 'English Parliamentary Enclosure' in *The Journal of Modern History*, Vol. 53, No. 3 (Sep. 1981), pp.477-504, University of Chicago Press, 1981. Accessed 8 January 2012.
235 Hoskins, 1976:77; for 'ridge-and-furrow' see plate 53.

236 Ibid.
237 Hawkes, 1978 (1951):1. See also Jacquetta Hawkes, 'Prehistory' in *Prehistory and the Beginnings of Civilization Vol I* (History of Mankind: Cultural and Scientific Development), Published for The International Commission for A History of the Scientific and Cultural Development of Mankind, George Allen and Unwin Ltd, London, 1963.
238 Keynes, 2001:passim. See also Moorehead, 1970, and Miller and Van Loon, 1982.
239 Ibid. Keynes, 2001, and Miller and Van Loon, 1982.
240 Ratcliffe, 1980:32.
241 Ibid.
242 Ibid.
243 Ibid. 33. For Frederick II, see Elsa Guerdrum Allen, 1969 (1951): 390, 398, for references to Dr Casey Wood, being able to 'assemble the many parts [of Frederick's work] in several European languages, and render the whole into English'. First published in 1943 with Wood and F. Marjorie Fyle as translators. A copy of a later printing may be found on line as a Google book. Accessed 20 October 2011.
244 Ibid.
245 Ibid. 39, here refers only to traditional falconry. The link with Hawk and Commoner, was my addition.
246 Hay, in Hay et al. 1975:189-253
247 Ibid. 253. This is of interest in the context of class differences, if any, and possible effects, in the Royal Navy in the 18th Century (Rodger, 1996:344-6). Rodger held that 'in its fundamentals, in the ways in which people dealt with one another and thought of one another, the Royal Navy closely resembled British society ashore'. To Rodger, despite "great disparities of wealth, power and opportunity", society "displayed no great gulfs between classes", in mid-century. However he accepted that "the Service which suffered the mutinies of 1797 must have been very different from that of forty years before". Rodger's original study was not designed to find answers for the second half of the eighteenth century [as his later work did], but Hay's work is a pointer.
248 Craig, 1961:100. "The work and career of John Clare (often compared with Burns)", and Craig saw in it "a relevant contrast" to Scottish "vernacular poetry". Later, Craig wrote that Burns 'unlike Clare' was 'far from his me´tier' in attempting 'Augustan satires' (105).
249 As a teenager I got to know intimately a small area of bushland within walking distance of my own home. The effects of mine-drained water were visible. No 'crawchies' (crayfish) lived there. Wilson's bird drawings and Clare's bird poems first attracted.
250 Each came to my knowledge by chance discovery, but to a mind prepared by family and education to appreciate nature in general, and birds in particular. Thomas Bewick, who created wood engravings of birds and

animals, had a passing reference in chapter four. Thomas Trotter met him at Newcastle on Tyne. I read Iain Bain's biography and then his edited copy of *A Memoir of Thomas Bewick.* Recently I was reminded of their shared likes and dislikes, and intense feelings for their own intimately known piece of country. They also had in common a deep and intense opposition to enclosures.

251 Hunter (1983:7) credited Dr Allen with rescuing Wilson from the developing dominance of Audubon. A brief biography of Wilson completed Elsa G. Allen's paper, *The History of American Ornithology before Audubon,* Transactions of the American Philosophical Society, Russel and Russel, New York, 1961(1951): 552-569. (Copy to hand.) In claiming Wilson as 'Father of American Ornithology' Allen stressed his powers of 'scientific observation and literary expression' (569). Burtt & Davis (2013) 'realized that a book devoted to Wilson's role in the founding of American ornithology could illuminate the scientific and artistic gifts that he brought to the field (Ibid. 433)'. In turn these underline Wilson's position as 'Father of American Ornithology'.

252 Hoskins, 1978[1955]: Clare was quoted at the head of "Parliamentary Enclosure and the Landscape" (ch.6). Nine lines of Clare's verse tell of the loss of trees with enclosure (197). Three lines express the 'bareness of the countryside until the hedgerows grow (200). Finally Clare's diary records the presence of surveyors as an early warning of the coming of the railways (262). See also Hoskins, 1976:77-86.

253 Godwin, 1978:96

254 Haughton, Hugh, "Progress and Rhyme" in Hugh Haughton, Adam Phillips and Geoffrey Summerfield, eds. *John Clare in Context,* 1994:78. [A copy of this poem is in *John Clare's Birds* (1982)]. Christopher Hill had written his chapter about Clare before he saw the above text (Haughton, 1994). "Most of the articles in this useful book contain new information and fresh insights", Hill said. But as his "purpose was to place Clare in his historical context" Hill didn't feel the need to rewrite but did acknowledge and use some material in Haughton, et al. See "John Clare, 1793-1864" in Hill, 1996:311-24.

255 Robinson, Eric, "Introduction" in Dawson, P.M.S., Eric Robinson and David Powell, 2000:ix. In this context see also John Lucas, "Clare's Politics" in Haughton et al., eds.1994:148-177.

256 Porter, Roy, "'All madness for writing': John Clare and the asylum" in Haughton et al. 1994:259-278. Porter's "conviction [was] that we might usefully forget about Clare as suffering from a disease syndrome but read his despair essentially as a product of circumstances - above all, the circumstances of being permanently locked away - " (273). He concluded, "If Clare's story is one of madness and genius, it is no less one of madness and money", (274) i.e. extreme poverty.

257 Hobsbawm and Rude, 1969. See also David Kent and Norma Townsend (1996, and 2002), below.
258 Hill, 1996:323-4. In a footnote (324n46) Hill described John Lucas, "Clare's Politics", in John Clare in Context, p.168 and passim, as "an admirable corrective to the often-expressed view of Clare as non-political".
259 Barrell, 1987.
260 Briggs, Asa .1978[1959]:10. But see also his discussion of 'Rich and Poor' (57-65) and discussion of 'class' (65, and footnotes).
261 Barrell, 1987:3.
262 Ibid.
263 Ibid. 5
264 Ibid. 5. Barrell is not suggesting, he says, "that we should do anything else, merely that we should ask what it is that we do; to identify with the exhausted and underfed labourers is impossible for us, and would be insulting if it were not".
265 Ibid. 6
266 Ibid.
267 Ibid. 155-6.
268 Ibid. 155.
269 *Joseph Mason Assigned Convict, 1831-1837,* [J.M'.s memoir] ed. by David Kemp and Norma Townsend, 1996. See also Kent and Townsend, 2002.
270 Hobsbawn and Rude, 2001[1969]:17. See also, "Repression and Aftermath" (Pt 4) which includes a chapter on Australia.

Chapter 8 Notes

1 But, see references to hysterical seamen and Micale's *Hysterical Men* in chapter 5 (see earlier).
2 Stark, 1998.
3 Honore Forster. *Voyaging Through Strange Seas: Four Women Travellers in the Pacific.*
http://www.nla.gov.au/pub/nlanews/2000/jan00/story-1.pdf 4 June 2009.
4 [Rose de Freycinet] *A Woman of Courage: The Journal of Rose de Freycinet on her Voyage around the World 1817-1820.* Translated and edited by Marc Serge Riviere, illustrated, National Library of Australia, Canberra, 1996.
5 Miriam Estensen, *The Life of Matthew Flinders,* Allen & Unwin, Crows Nest, NSW, 2002:ch.14.
6 Miriam Estensen, *The Life of George Bass,* Allen & Unwin, Crows Nest, NSW, 2005.
7 Mary Ann Parker, A voyage round the world in the Gorgon man of war, Captain John Parker [1794-95] / performed and written by his widow, London, Printed by JohnNichols, 1795.

8 Rodger, 2006 (2004): 407.
9 PRO/ADM 1/534. See Jones, 1999:36; 36n22.
10 PRO/ADM 1/534:26.
11 Ibid. 59.
12 Ibid. Question - who was the prisoner? There is no *Evans* among those charged in the two *Standard* courts martial. Here they are - John Burrows, Joseph Hudson, William Redfern and Thomas Lunniss alias Linnes Bryan Finn and Joseph Glaves, the marines... William Holdsworth, Henry Freeman, John, alias Jonathan Davis, Bartholomew Connery, William Jones, Sampson Harris, and Thomas Stack, seamen. However, more seamen were arrested than were charged. See Dugan (1966:395-7).
13 Lewis, 1960:282.
14 Kemp, Peter. 1970:133. See 'anodyne' in a different context as book title in Ellis, 1946.
15 Lavery, 1995:112,113,131,140,141,147,203,210,210; nurses 133,216.
16 Rodger, 2006 [2004]. For the period 1660-88, see p.134; for 1689-1714 see p. 212-3; for 1763-92 see p. 407; 1803-15 pp.505-6; and 1793-1815 pp. 526-7).
17 Richard Parker, elected to lead the Nore mutiny was called to HMS *Montagu* to adjudicate a problem. Mrs Knight, the captain's wife on a day's visit to her husband at Yarmouth had been carried south to the Nore. She was soon released. (Dugan 1966:272.)
18 Stark, 1998:2.
19 Stark, 1998:68-71, makes a significant contribution to the earlier reference to hospital ships in this book, where the sources used, made no mention of women.
20 Stark, 1998:68-71; see also Byrne, 1995:40-61.
21 Ibid. 36-7.
22 Ibid. 61.
23 Ibid. 44-6.
24 Ibid. 92ff. "Why Women Joined the Navy or Marines", the source for the two following paragraphs. See Kowaleski-Wallace, 1997:129-143.
25 Clark, Alice. *Working Life of Women in the Seventeenth Century*, Reprints of Economic Classics, A.M. Kelley, New York, 1968 (1919).
26 Lewis, 1960:280-7,"The Ship Hierarchy, (g), The Women".
27 Kemp, 1970:170-1
28 Ibid.
29 Lavery, 1995:141. Two women, present at the Battles of the Nile and Trafalgar, were refused Naval General Service Medals because it would create a precedent, which would be followed by "innumerable applications" from many others.
30 Kemp, 1970:170-1.
31 Cowper, 1997:302-3.

32 Marcus, 1975:13. But, see Rodger 2006(2004): 375, for the coppering of the fleet and an inherent problem in the detail, reflecting both the "weaknesses as well as strengths and weaknesses of Middleton as a reformer".
33 Stark, 1998:38. The reference given is Ford K. Brown, *Fathers of the Victorians: The Age of Wilberforce,* Cambridge University Press, Cambridge, 1961:22.
34 Stark, 1998:5-20.
35 Regulations, 1790.
36 Stark, 1998:20-28. Alice Clark (1968:142) referred to 'poor Seamen and Soldier's wives' assisted by work in the silk industry by then (1714), a pauper trade.
37 Ibid. 36. Stark's material is relevant to a later discussion of female convicts in the context of Anne Summers, 1980, 1994.
38 Ibid. 28-46. This quotation, divided into two paragraphs, above, appears as one whole on pp. 28-9.
39 See above, chapter 2.
40 See 'Grievances', chs 3 and 4.
41 See 'Grievances', ch. 3.
42 "Sophia, a Person of Quality", attributed to Lady Mary Wortley Montagu, 1739. A facsimile edition was published in 1975 of the 1943 edition, which contains the reply of an anonymous Gentleman and a further riposte.
43 See Montagu's *The Lover: A Ballad* "published in 1747, [but] written much earlier", the lines point "And that my delight may be solidly fixed, /Let the friend and the lover be handsomely mixed".
44 Spender, 1982:53; 56-64. Spender wrote (pp.63-4): "'Sophia's' book could be published today and with the aid of a few minor editorial changes could pass as a contemporary feminist analysis of patriarchy. Inside feminist circles it could be perceived as radical - outside them as 'outrageous' and cause no doubt for the abuse and harassment typically heaped upon women who dare to assert such reasons in a male-dominated society. Her sanity would be called into question before her intellectual contribution was acknowledged".
45 Women and military office, a brief extract from *Sophia*...1975, *Women not Inferior to Man,* in Connelly et al., 1984:26-29
46 Battersby, 1989:2-3.
47 Stark, 1998:86. See Chapter 3, 82-122, for the discussion of "Women in Disguise in Naval Crews". Michael Lewis (1960) in his reference to William Brown described her "rating of Captain of the Main Top, [as] a post given to the most skilled and agile members of the crew".
48 Stark, 1998:82ff.
49 Stripping, washing and providing fresh clothing to new Navy recruits, recommended earlier by James Lind, above, was not yet universally applied, to the detriment of the health of seamen. The process was later applied to

some of the convicts destined for New South Wales, revealing one 'male' convict as a woman. See Irvine, 1982.

50 Frost, 1994:211-2; 264n2. A reference to "body fat...proportion (15-10 per cent) necessary to sustain menstruation and ovulation" – in this case to female prisoners in British gaols. The authors of the study, given by Frost, were R.E. Frisch and J.W. McArthur, 'Menstrual Cycles'. *Science*, 185 (1974), pp. 949-51.

51 Stark, 1998:88-91

52 Ibid. 92-7.

53 Spender, 1982:35-9ff.

54 Ibid. See *Index of Names,* 581ff. Follow entries for perceptive accounts of each of these women: Alphra Behn 1640-1689, Restoration dramatist; Mary Astell 1666-1731, feminist writer, equal educational opportunities for women; ['Sophia'] Lady Mary Wortley Montagu 1689-1762, aristocrat and writer [See also references to smallpox in this present work.]; Catherine Macaulay 1731-1791, History of England 8 vols.; Olympe de Gouges 1748-1793 [See reference in this chapter, below].

55 Ibid. 56.

56 I accept this reading, and have added argument developed by "Sophia", from the facsimile reprint, above.

57 Davis and Farge, 1994. Duby and Perrot, the general editors of the five-volume work, saw "this series as a provisional summary of the results achieved to date and as a guide to further research".

58 Updated briefly in later chapters eighteen, and nineteen.

59 Clark, 1968 (1919):1 (opening paragraphs).

60 Briggs, 1978:8-15. Joseph Butler was Bishop of Durham and influenced Adam Smith, among others.

61 Paley, 1793.

62 See Venetia Murray, 1999; see also Foreman, 1999.

63 William Paley, 'a reply by a Poor labourer 1793': Goldsmiths'-Kress library of economic literature: no. 15764, Microfilm, RAV/FM4/2, State Library of NSW, Sydney.

64 Carpenter, Kenneth E. [198-], No.26.33/3, State Library of NSW, Sydney. Herbert Somerton Foxwell (1848-1936) a professor at University College, London, was a compulsive collector of economic material, spending a large part of sixty years in his quest, and in some of those years averaging seven and a half miles a day on foot.

65 Ibid. Having run out of money Foxwell sold his first collection. It formed the nucleus of the Goldsmiths' Library at the University of London. With cash in hand he set out again. His second collection is now in the Kress Library of Business Administration, Harvard University. Microfilm copies have been sold around the world.

66 Burke, 1986 (1790):372.

67 Ibid. 398n200. O'Brien, the editor, gave as source, Wollstonecraft's *Vindication*.
68 Wollstonecraft, 1992:79
69 Ibid. Brody, ed. "Introduction": 8ff. Mary Wollstonecraft "became a member of a cosmopolitan London-based group which included Henry Fuseli, the Swiss painter, Joseph Priestly, the famous chemist and radical in politics and theology, William Godwin, the political philosopher, the poet William Blake and Thomas Paine, the international patriot". This group met in the rooms above the bookshop of a London bookseller, Joseph Johnson, "a man of liberal politics and a generous disposition". He encouraged Mary Wollstonecraft in her writing and published her work and was "the patron of many [other] aspiring and hungry young writers, one of whom was William Blake". For further insight into the work of members of the above group in the context of Johnson's liberalism and publishing, see Braithwaite, 2003, and Boime, 1987.
70 Wollstonecraft, 1992:79, *Author's Introduction.*
71 Ibid.
72 Ibid.
73 Ibid. 80.
74 Ibid.
75 Ibid. 80-1.
76 Ibid. 81.
77 Ibid.
78 Ibid. 82. See also Sylvana Tomaselli, who quoted Wollstonecraft - including this reference to "virtue" - in her entry, *Virtue*, in Black and Porter, 1996. See also later references to the social construction of "virtue", in this chapter, as having different meanings for men and women, e.g. Outram, 1995.
79 Wollstonecraft, 1992:307
80 Ibid. Ch. 13, "Some Instances...", 307–28.
81 Ibid. 321.
82 Ibid. 323.
83 See references to Mary Wollstonecraft in the context of the study and use of botany, etc. in Shteir, 1996.
84 Wollstonecraft, 1992:323-4.
85 Ibid. 327.
86 Kirkham, 1997:48, 171.
87 Trotter, 1976:33.
88 Kirkham, 1997:48.
89 Ibid. 48-9. For Joseph Johnson, see above, Braithwaite, 2003, in particular.
90 Wollstonecraft, 1992:327 - quoted above. See below, the reference to three women in the French Revolution, guillotined for not keeping silent.
91 Holmes, 2000:197-8, 199-266.

92 Holmes, 2000:198, convinced Penguin Classics to republish two books side by side, Wollstonecraft, and Godwin, 1987. He accepted the effect noted by Kirkham, above, of Godwin's *Memoir* but rejected criticism that the *Memoirs* had diminished and distorted Mary's real importance...to be taken seriously for her ideas" by directing attention to Godwin's first six chapters which "concentrate almost exclusively on Wollstonecraft's intellectual development". Again, Godwin regarded "the *Rights of Woman* as her major work"; Holmes, 2000:214, for each quote. In the short term, the effects were as Kirkham believed, and in the longer term, it is to be hoped, as Holmes argued.

93 Wollstonecraft, 1992:266

94 Porter, in Rousseau and Porter, ed. 1987:206-7. chapter 8:206-232.

95 Ibid. 207. See also Porter, 2001, chapter 5 in particular.

96 Porter, 1987:207-210. For an enlightening study of this subject, see Porter and Hall, 1995. Patricia Crawford contributes a useful paper, "Sexual Knowledge in England, 1500-1750", in Porter and Teich, 1994.

97 Berriot-Salvadore, in Davis and Farge, 1994:348-388.

98 See Willett and Cunnington, 1992:68-94; and 96-119; health-related.

99 Porter, 1987:212

100 Ibid. 213-5.

101 Porter, 1987:222ff.

102 Ibid. 215-224.

103 Ibid. 215ff; See 217 and 219-20.

104 William Smellie's Treatise...1783.

105 Johnstone, 1952:131. See 126ff for an evaluation of "Smellie's Greatness and Posthumous Fame", and contrasting views of the use of forceps, where Johnstone stressed Smellie's "wise rules and safeguards" that were not so well remembered. For more on the Smellie editions, see Russell, 1987.

106 Rosner, 1991:55.

107 See Dr Betty Iggo to AR Jones, results of research, 1994ff.

108 Forster, 1967:14, cited in Jones, 1999; 7:79.

109 It is interesting to muse upon these words and to consider the life of the text originally given to William Redfern and passed on by his wife Sarah to her sister, the wife of Governor Macquarie's aide-de-camp, Major Henry Colden Antill, from whose descendants it came to the History of Medicine Library.

110 Editorial comment in Smellie, 1 754(1971). Sue Prince allowed me to study her copy, published by the University of Auckland, New Zealand in 1971.

111 Townsend, 1952, 1:551-565.

112 See Jordanova, 1999 edition; digitally printed on demand in 2012. For male midwives see 'Part 1, Natural Polarities', in 'Chapter Two: Feminine Figures: Nature Display'd' (21-47).

113 See pp. 203-10, 210 for this quote. Smellie is mentioned on p211.
114 Johnstone, 1952:30ff.
115 Johnstone, 1952:30 for this and the preceding paragraph.
116 Jack, 1999. [Papers are arranged in alphabetical order of surname of author(s).]
117 Ibid. 12.
118 Smellie, 1783:326-7
119 Gelbart, 1998. See above references to Gelbart, and Coudray, in Sybil M. Jack, 1999.
120 Ibid. 277. "Epilogue", where Gelbart argued for du Coudray's positive impact on an increased life expectancy pinpointed from 1750.
121 Smellie, William, "Preface", in William Redfern's copy, Smellie, 1783.
122 Johnstone, 1952:2.
123 Johnstone, 1952:2.
124 Ibid. 7.
125 Johnstone, 1952:15.
126 Gelbart, 1998:19-21, for a discussion of the midwife's name. On her 'statement' dated 1 August 1760, she gave her name as Le Boursier du Coudray. Before this year, she was "Le Boursier", and after it, "du Coudray". "In more ways than one, then, this letter of 1760 marks a watershed", Gelbart said.
127 Gelbart, 1998:25.
128 See "midvives" in Lindemann, 1999.
129 Gelbart, 1998:60.
130 Ibid. 57-60. "Clermont, 9 May 1755". There, Le Bousier found "the indigent women of the countryside" "have become the real focus of her attention". Among these Auvergne women she "encountered for the first time the climate of terror and dread that hangs over childbirth in the countryside" (Ibid. 58-9). When the ruling of that year, "that midwives are not authorized to use obstetrical forceps", was added, Le Bousier decided to challenge the surgeons with her special teaching skills (Ibid. 60).
131 Smellie, 1783:325
132 Russell, 1987:34, item. No. 131. See also a brief reference to this sale in Johnstone, 1952:28.
133 Johnstone, 1952:20.
134 Ibid. 25-9.
135 Ibid. 25. See also p. 26, for additional description by Mrs Nihell, of the "scurrilous attack upon Smellie".
136 Ibid. 25.
137 Ibid. 26-7.
138 Gelbart, 1998:64
139Ibid. 62. Figure 5. "The only known extant example of Mme du Coudray's obstetrical "machine," made of wicker, fabric, leather, stuffing, and sponges.

She produced hundreds of these, but the others must have disintegrated with use. This one is preserved in the Musee Flaubert, Rouen".

140 Ibid. 6o-4, Paris, 13 May 1756.

141 Ibid. 72ff.

142 Ibid. 75.

143 This opinion is well-informed. See Gelbart's "Female Journalists" in Davis and Farge, eds. 1994:393, 420-35.

144 Johnstone, 1952:39.

145 Dr Thomas Young studied medicine at Edinburgh University. Later, as Professor, he taught Midwifery from 1756 to 1780, when he was joined by Alexander Hamilton (Rosner, 55).

146 Russell, 1987:179, Item no 753.

147 See note 85 for the book reference.

148 Russell, 1987:179, item no 753 for the reference to Grignion and Rymsdyk; and to p. 181, item no 766 for the no. of Rymsdyk drawings and the reference to the 'eleven drawings...by Peter Camper".

149 Smellie, in William Redfern's copy. See this and the following paragraph.

150 Johnstone, 1952:127, had accepted Smellie's "description of the mechanism of labour, [as] his greatest, most fundamental, and at the same time most far-reaching contribution to obstetrics". Forster, 1963:133, agreed, adding that certain details "were not generally accepted until the nineteen thirties when the radiologists proved [Smellie] right".

151 Frazer, 1993:509.

152 Porter, 2000:76n28, 508:"Between 1650 and 1800 female literacy in England increased from under 15 per cent to about 36 per cent", Margaret R. Hunt, *The Middling Sort*, 1996:85.

153 Geyer-Kordesch in Bynum and Porter *2*, 888-894. The remaining pages 895-914 take the struggle to the end of the 19th Century. Note the conclusion.

154 Ibid. 894.

155 Witz, 1992:79. The Introduction forms with Part I of this book a wide-ranging critical analysis of the grounds for, and the direction of, the author's study of "gender, closure and professional projects". Part II will provide a few brief references for our present purpose.

156 Ibid. 1992:73. American women's parallel experience may be read in Morantz-Sanchez, 1987.

157 Ibid. 1992:73ff.

158 Elkinton, J. Russell. "Quakers in Medicine", in Clark and Elkinton, [1978]1986 :49.

159 Witz, 75. See Ehrenreich and English, *Witches, Midwives and Nurses*, 1973, and their given source *Malleus Maleficarum, Hammer of Witches*; Christopher S. Mackay's 'complete translation' of *The Hammer* was published by Cambridge University Press in 2009 (to hand).

160 Ibid. 82. Witz presented the idea that "the arts of healing were practised throughout history by women" as the 'strong thesis' supported by Ehrenreich and English 1973, 1979, among others. Witz considered the 'strong thesis' to be open to criticism on the grounds that men as well as women were engaged in popular healing, that women form all classes practised medicine, and that women continued their work well into the eighteenth century (pp76-83). Roy Porter's article "The patient in England, c. 1660-c.1800", in Wear, 1992:91ff. provides evidence of these criticisms being taken into account but without denying the contribution of women. Porter considered that "There is...every reason to believe that the expansion of professional medicine in the eighteenth century stimulated rather than suppressed lay medication", but both by men and womep.108). Witz (81) considered an observation by A. Clark (1919), that "women were excluded from specialised sites of education" "was indeed important, and yet overlooked". Porter's article referred to the increasing number of 'everyday practitioners', better educated surgeon-apothecaries in the eighteenth century (100). Irvine Loudon considered the typical surgeon-apothecary of the second half of the eighteenth century was a grammar school, not a public school boy", in his article "Medical practitioners 1750-1850..." in Wear, above 1992:223-4. As educational requirements for medical practitioners rose, opportunities for women slipped further out of reach.

161 Witz, 1992:106. The source of the information is given as Clark, A. (1919) *Working Life of Women in the Seventeenth Century*, London: George Routledge, Reprinted 1981, London: Virago. [Subsequently I have obtained and read my own copy – Alice Clark. *Working Life of Women in the Seventeenth Century*, Reprints of Economic Classics, A.M. Kelley, New York, 1968 (1919).]

162 Witz, 1992:113-4. The C.J. Cullingworth reference is to "The Registration of Midwives", *Contemporary Review*, March 1878.

163 Lindemann, 1999:220-4.

164 Ibid. 220

165 Ibid. 220-1. Lindemann gave as a reference for this paragraph, Wilson, in Bynum and Porter, 1985:343-69.

166 Witz follows her analysis of the topic, *Medical Men and Midwives,* to the end of the nineteenth century.

167 Outram, 1989:109-10, presents the idea that without the guillotine "the great group executions of the Terror...would have been rendered more difficult, if not impossible..., as Samson's letter makes clear [on that and the previous page]".

168 Gelbart, 1998:274-5.

169 Yalom, 1995, has an "Annotated Bibliography of 87 French Women's Eyewitness Accounts of the Revolution", 267-97.

170 Ibid. 94.

171 De Gouges, 1989:Introduction:i-v.
172 Holmes, 1985:94. Holmes provides a useful account of the years Mary Wollstonecraft spent in Paris (71-132).
173 Ibid. 94-5
174 Ibid. 90. To Holmes, a Wollstonecraft letter, which included her decision to go to France, "was one of the most exciting documents [he had] ever read". "[O]n 9 April 1795, Mary Wollstonecraft finally left France. Instead of the tricolour cockade she now carried a small child wearing the bright red sash she had bought for her...Here was the only symbol of hope left to her". (Ibid. 130).
175 Ibid. 103.
176 Brody, Miriam, in her "Introduction" to Wollstonecraft*,* 1992:13.
177 Outram 1989:184-6. See these notes to chapter 8, *Words and Flesh,* for a concise biography and bibliography.
178 Ibid. 131.
179 Ibid. 124. See for comparison with another age, Anna Bryson in Gent and Llewellyn, 1990:136-153. According to Bryson, in this period "writings on gentlemanly manners show the emergence of the body as a central subject and organising principle in the ideal of 'courtesy' or, a significantly new term, 'civility'" (Ibid. 141).
180 Outram 1989:131.
181 Ibid. 131. Reasons for this conclusion are in the following pages of her book.
182 Outram, 1995:133, see under "Suggestions for further reading", "1 General surveys".
183 Outram, 1989:153-4, "relied throughout this book upon the definition of class produced by the French sociologist Pierre Bourdieu, in his book *Distinction,* where he uses the word 'class' not as a *group* label, but as a *location* label. Class for Bourdieu is located by the multiplicity of its practices, in their interrelationship rather than their specificity".
184 Ibid. 154
185 Ibid. 126.
186 Boime, 1990:391-89. For these two Roman republican figures, neo-classicism and male and female virtue, etc. see Boime's study in the context of the work of Jacques-Louis David. A poor illustration of David's *Ebauche* sketch for *Le Serment du Jeu de paume* (*The Oath of the Tennis Court*), the male "deputies act[ing] with the gestures of classical drama", may be found in Boime: 430, where individual actors are identified. Dorinda Outram's *The Body...,* has a much better reproduction of this sketch, reflecting one of the key images of her work, spread over the dust jacket. A more finished sketch was on display in 1980 at the Art Gallery of New South Wales exhibition of *French Painting: The Revolutionary Decades 1760-1830.* See the catalogue

compiled by Arlette Serullaz; also illustrated in colour in the *Exhibition Guide.*

187 Mary Wollstonecraft's later years fit this pattern. The uproar that followed Godwin's *Memoirs of the Author of 'The Rights of Woman'*, Holmes, 1987, show the close parallel that existed between the double standard in France, after the Revolution, and the contemporary English attitude to women and men.

188 Outram, 1989:155. For this discussion, see her final chapter, "The French Revolution, Modernity and the Body Politic" (153-164). See also the Montagu poem, in Cook 1997:283-4.

189 Colley, 2003. "Womanpower", 237-281.

190 Shteir, 1996:4. Earlier, Shteir, in '*Botany in the Breakfast Room*' (Abir-Am and Outram ed. 1987), accepted, and even extended women's contribution to Botany, through membership of families which included 'men at the heart of nineteenth-century botany' (p.34). Nevertheless Shteir contended that women's 'contributions were invisible in histories of botany until recently' (p.33) (Ibid. 1987).

191 Anticipating Richard Holmes, *The Age of Wonder*, 2008, and his references to 'Romantic Science' and 'wonder' in his 'Prologue', xv-xxi.

192 Shteir, 5.

193 Ibid. 169.

194 Ibid. 5. Shteir briefly put Lindley's aims in his own words, as distinguishing between 'polite botany', 'amusement for ladies', and 'botanical science', 'an occupation for the serious thoughts of man'.

195 Ibid. 260n15. Lindley, *Introductory Lecture...1829*, 1829:9-10.

196 Ibid. To this point the words within single inverted commas are Lindley's own.

197 Ibid. 156-7. Shteir's argument forms part of a chapter, 'Defeminizing the Science of Botany'.

198 Ibid. 156.

199 Jim Endersby. *Imperial Nature: Joseph Hooker and the Practices of Victorian Science*, University of Chicago Press, Chigaco, 2008:38ff for 'botany in decline' and 172ff for "The Linnaean 'Incubus' ".

200 Ibid. See 176, for *Ladies Botany*, and 175, for reference to Endersby's comments and continuing use of Linnaean system.

201 Witz, 1992:73-103.

202 Ibid. 90-1.

203 Morantz-Sanchez, 1987:8-9.

204 Pnina G. Abir-Am and Dorinda Outram, eds. *Uneasy Careers and Intimate Lives: Women in Science 1789-1979*, Rutgers University Press, New Brunswick, and London, 1987. (I found this book in 2011).

Chapter 9 Notes

1 Alan Frost, *Arthur Phillip 1738-1814:His Voyaging* (1987). Reading this chapter will confirm my indebtedness to Alan Frost, initially to his biography of Phillip, but to other publications acknowledged along the way. It can be said that he always had in mind the impact of health and medicine, as practised at the time, on people and events. Accordingly it was at the 1995 conference of the Australian Society of the History of Medicine on Norfolk Island that I met him.

2 Ibid. 2-9.

3 Ibid. 11-17.

4 Ibid. 18-23.

5 Ibid. 23.

6 Byng had the misfortune to face a court martial, which found him guilty and cost him his life.

7 Ibid. 33:24-33, for the events.

8 Rodger, 1996 (1986).

9 Dening, 113-156. The full text of this study of discipline is entitled "Scene ii. *Reflection*". [It follows "Scene i. *Narrative*".] This reference appears on the first page, 113, and the list of ships on p. 384.

10 Ibid. 156 for this quotation.

11 Frost, 1987:45, n.15, 278, "Phillip. Memorandum of c. September 1786, CO 201/2:92". See also Linebaugh (348-356) for former slaves in London, "a pan-African community", and its role in working-class action.

12 See Gilmour, 184-191, 'The Press Gang' for background.

13 Frost. 1987:49-55.

14 Ibid. 63-4. Generally restated on page 91.

15 Ibid. 91.

16 See for general background to Spanish and Portuguese colonies, "Another America" in Bernier, 2000:227-290.

17 Frost, 91.

18 Ibid.

19 Lavery, 1995:88ff. There is a useful discussion of promotion in part iv against which Phillip's experience in the Navy may be assessed. The section on "Commissioned Officers" is the more useful at this point.

20 Frost.1987:99.

21 Ibid. 100-1.

22 Ibid. 101. Further discussed, Ibid. 105-125, where Spanish affairs, and a voyage to India, further broaden his experience. See Ibid. 129-133 for among other things Phillip's employment by Nepean to spy once more on French naval preparation in the Toulon area.

23 Phillip, Arthur. *The Voyage of Governor Phillip to Botany Bay...*Original edition 1789, Facsimile Editions, 19781970.

24 Ibid. 291-2. The Decision to Colonize (291).

25 Ibid. 292-3. *The First Fleet* (292); See also Frost, 1994.
26 Knight, in Hardy & Frost, 1989:257n11.
27 Rudé, 1978: passim..:ch.1, 237-41.
28 Ibid. 237.
29 Ibid. 237-8.
30 Ibid. 238ff.
31 Ibid. 239
32 Shaw, 1958, vol.iii:25-38, includes bibliography. See pp. 25 and 31 for references to William Redfern.
33 Ibid. 31.
34 Rudé, 239. He noted that Robson's study was "limited to a sample of one in twenty of all convicts arriving in Sydney and Hobart".
35 Ibid. 239-40.
36 Linebaugh provides useful evidence of change. The "subject-matter of this book is presented in accordance with the advance of time" (xxv). 'Finance capitalism', 'mercantilism' and 'manufacture' provide a time sequence in which hangings are studied (xxv). He particularly stressed the need to take note of the specific nature of early industrial society.
37 Linebaugh, 1977:246-269; "The author of this *Account,* the Ordinary of Newgate, was the prison chaplain. Appointed by the Court of Aldermen of the City of London, he held office during good behaviour. He was always a clergyman of the established Church". Linebaugh (349n7) gave a House of Commons...*Report* (1837) for "a concise description of the office". However, "the Ordinary too was but a mere man, very much part of the crowd at Tyburn, and, as Hogarth showed, closer to the ragged ballad-monger than his stiff collar suggested" (Ibid. 269).
38 Nicholas, 1989.
39 Flynn, 2001.
40 Flynn, 2001:111 (last paragraph).
41 Hay et al., 1975. See also David Neal, 1991: xii; 202n6 for an acknowledgement of "the seminal work on the rule of law in eighteenth-century England by Edward Thompson and Douglas Hay".
42 Thompson, 1975:267, 266; see also preceding and following pages.
43 Dugan, 1966:245. See Rodger 2006:"Administration 1763-1792 (368-79)" and "[for] 1793-1815 (473-488)".
44 Dugan, 1966:445.
45 Referred to in Jones, 1999;7:35. Plumb, 1981[1950]:201-2.
46 See Pool, B., chapter 3, n100.
47 Woodward, "*The Law in 18th Century England*" (Foreword) in Cobley, 1989:14.
48 Gittins, Ross, Economics Editor. "Yes, you can legislate for morality" in *The Sydney Morning Herald*, 2002. There, Gittins wrote, "Have you noticed the way politicians change their tune when they switch from blue-collar to

executive crime? Apparently, if the crim[inal]'s wearing a suit at the time it makes all the difference". This was part of a debate about businessmen enriching themselves at the expense of shareholders to the tune of millions of dollars and whether Parliament should legislate to clearly make such behaviour criminal, impose more gaol sentences and fund more effective detection and enforcement agencies. Stronger moves are being made in this direction, since then, prompted by some extreme examples of white-collar crime, and not only in Australia.

49 What has changed? See Henderson, 1975:viii, "The elimination of poverty should be a vital national goal".

50 Fisher, 1946:791-3.

51 Bateson, 1985:Preface to first edition, 1959. Bateson has several references to Redfern; see under *Surgeons, Named*: 413. Bateson, 1969, reported that he had examined 600 microfilmed journals, P.R.O.Adm.104, of surgeons-superintendent from these ships.

52 Ibid. 94-119.

53 Ibid. 114.

54 Ibid. 115-6.

55 Ibid. 116.

56 Ibid. 99.

57 Frost, 1994:110-125.

58 Ibid. 112: a reference to Sir Keith Hancock's "rule of contextual congruity", in the preface, above. Subsequently I read the source book, Hancock's *Professing History* (1976).

59 Frost, 1994:111. See also Roger Knight, "The First Fleet: Its State and Preparation 1786-1787" in Hardy & Frost, 1989. Between pages 260-261 have been inserted, inter alia, Fig 29:'Administrative Structure Royal Navy 1660-1832' and Fig 30:'The Commissioning of the First Fleet 1786-87 (informal structure)'.

60 Ibid.

61 Ibid. 117-8

62 Ibid. 119

63 Watt, 1991, 61,147-150:148.

64 Ibid. 148. Watt provided the following references: Appleton, 1958:42; Buck, 1950:42; Lloyd and Coulter, 1961:3:90-1; Rutherford & Skinner, 1940:25; and Carre in Watt et al.1981:73-8. Watt's paper included early references to scurvy, to Maori sea rations, which provided "a healthy, nutritious and balanced diet", and to good hygiene on Maori ocean canoes.

65 Frost, 1987:27-29.

66 Ibid. 116, 120, and 121 provide references for the first, second and third sentences in this paragraph, and for the mention of gardens reference. Flinders benefited from garden produce at the Cape.

67 Ibid. 143; a discussion of scurvy. In the use of the word "indolent", Phillip is making the classic reversal of lethargy, an effect of scurvy, with a cause, discussed in an earlier chapter.

68 Ibid. 161.

69 Ibid. 162. See Frost, 1994:125.

70 Watt, 1978, "malt is a potential source of the B complex of vitamins which were also deficient in the seaman's diet, although its potency would obviously depend upon the conditions of storage and there are several references to its deterioration by the journalists". This paper is on file at History of Medicine Library, R.A.C.P, Sydney.]

71 Frost, 1994:122-4.

72 Phoebe Lloyd, 1988:158. This is an article about the early American artist Raphaelle Peale and his family. [Peale's father was a friend of Alexander Wilson, and a brother subscribed to his *American Ornithology*, Cantwell,1961. See also Gabrielle Van Zuylen and Claire de Virieu photographer, 1999.

73 De Freycinet, Rose. *A Woman of Courage,* 1996:79.

74 For these references to Malaspina, see Julian de Zulueta and Lola Higueras, Watt et al. 1981:85-99.

75 I had an opportunity to read facsimile editions of the two following works in a home library in Perth, Flinders, 1814, 1966, and Baudin, 1974.

76 Flinders, 230.

77 Flinders, Vol.2:201-3; Thurs.27January1803, Flinders named a projecting point, Point Blane (Gove P'r, Northern Territory) as a compliment to Dr (Now Sir Gilbert) Blane, of naval medical history fame.

78 *Flinders to Banks*, 1976 [1966]:60.

79 My italics. That lime juice was to *suffice* shows he is misreading Lind's text. Sour krout will be passed over, but *vinegar* was proved by Lind to be ineffective. Then to *reserve* essence of malt as something special is to repeat the error associated with Cook. Malt was of little or no use. There may well be something of Bligh's influence here, as Flinders was with Bligh on his second breadfruit expedition.

80 Flinders, *Journal*, vol.1, p.479, in Mack, 1972:145n12.

81 Mack, 1972:148n17, gives his reference as "P.R.O., Adm.55/76, 'Journal kept on board His Majesty's sloop Investigator...', p.8. Hereafter cited as Flinders, 'Journal', vol.II". For Flinders' medical condition see Prof. Stuart Macintosh, "Introduction" to Ernest Scott, 2001. Macintosh accepted Geoffrey Ingleton's diagnosis that Flinders died from 'gonorrhoea contracted at Tahiti while a midshipman with Bligh' (xii). See also Estensen, 2002:19.

82 Mack, 1972:148.

83 Watt, et al., 1981:201, paragraph 15. "The association of flux (diarrhoea) with scurvy was frequently reported in fleets and expeditions and appears to have been due to two causes". One resulted from "eating rancid fats". The

other was due to dysentery destroying ascorbic acid. Medicin General Carre described a vicious circle - "scurvy-prone sailors with low reserves of vitamin C readily acquired infections such as dysentery; this in turn required increased utilization of vitamin C by the body; however, dysentery also...destroyed vitamin C in the bowel and less of the vitamin was therefore absorbed; reserves were rapidly depleted and overt scurvy was manifested. After lemon juice was issued to the British Fleet, men were not only protected from scurvy, but also from other infections".

84 In the context of Polynesian ocean exploration see Watt, 1991.61.147-150. In a wider context see Blane, *Observations on the Diseases Incident to Seamen,* 2nd ed. 1789:23; Patients, who had recovered from scurvy 'by the use of limes' were given daily, a 'pint of wine, with an equal quality of water, made agreeable with sugar and tamarinds'.

85 See Cawte, 1996:75,7) and Isaacs, 1987:210, 229, 239); To Cawte's input add Watt's on Polynesian exploration in the Pacific, above.

86 Gandevia, in Home, 1983:81-98.

87 Ibid. 82.

88 Gandevia, in Home, 1983:81-98.

89 Ibid.

90 Gandevia and Cobley, 1974, 4, pp.111-125.

91 This idea of a psycho-social disease was developed by Bryan Gandevia, alone, in a subsequent paper. It will not be accessed here. See Bryan Gandevia, "Socio-Medical Factors in the Evolution of the First Settlement at Sydney Cove 1788-1803", Royal Australian Historical Society, *Journal and proceedings,* Vol.61, Pt.1., March 1975:1-25.

92 Collins, 1971:211. I had the satisfaction of checking the Collins' references in the facsimile edition, in context.

93 Watt, "The Colony's Health" in Hardy & Frost, *Studies from Terra Australis to Australia,* 1989. This book published the conference papers.

94 Watt, J, The Australian and New Zealand Journal of Surgery, 1989,59,923-931.

95 For army health and medicine, See *Wars...* in chapter 07, above.

96 See references in the account of *Hillsborough* later in this chapter.

97 Sir Jeremiah Fitzpatrick, as given by Oliver MacDonagh, in his biography, *The Inspector General: Sir Jeremiah Fitzpatrick and Social Reform, 1783-1802,* Croom, Helm, London, 1981.

98 Ibid.

99 Watt, 1989:139-141, for "Conditions on the voyage".

100 See White, 1962:47ff. for his account of meeting on the *Alexander* "a medical gentleman from Portsmouth" and confirmation that he and Balmain disagreed with the advice given. Watt's conclusions relative to Robert Robertson's expertise and being within reach at the time were born out by the DNB, 1885-1900, Vol 48 (Wikisource). Cook, G. (*Journal of Medical*

Biography, 2006:14:42-45) has Robertson an "18th-centuiry authority on 'fever'. Likewise the DNB had him publishing on 'fevers' in 1779, 1789 and 1790, and appointed to Greenwich Hospital in 1793.

101 Sir James McGrigor accepted this to be so, but spent his life bringing the Army into line. For Army surgeons, see McGrigor (2000:80-1; 133ff), and overall (Ibid. passim). See also his biographer, Blanco (1974,21ff.)

102 Watt, 1989:146-9, "The quality of medical practice".

103 Pearn, 1988:639-643. The references in this chapter, to studies by Gandevia, Pearn, and Watt, are obviously complementary.

104 See also White, 1790, 1962.

105 See Worgan, 1978.

106 This and the two preceding paragraphs were combined in Watt's original text.

107 Cowper was Redfern's second apprentice.

108 Watt's original paragraph has been split in two, here.

109 The most serious split is between author and end notes - 150 to this point, with 27 more to come - making reference to the originals, Watt, 1989a and b, the more imperative.

110 Watt's *philanthropic network* will be discussed in a later chapter.

111 Noah, 1978.

112 Governor Hunter's remarks are from a report to London on 27 July 1799, in an Introduction to the published Noah diary. This provides biographical references to Noah's life before and after coming to the Colony.

113 Noah, 1978:61.

114 Ibid. Introduction.

115 Sir Jeremiah Fitzpatrick.

116 Bateson, 1985 (1959):167-8.

117 Bateson has *Sir John Fitzpatrick,* throughout his book, as the 'Home Department's Inspector-General of Health'.

118 Ibid. 168.

119 Ibid. 179-82. Surgeon Kunst was having lunch on the convict transport *Hercules,* on 29 December 1801, in the vicinity of the Cape Verdes, when a mutiny occurred. 14 convicts died in "the bloodiest mutiny attempt...in a convict ship". This resulted in the convicts being kept confined for the rest of the journey. As a result 44 died and an equal number required medical treatment.

120 Ibid. 157-8.

121 Ibid. 20.

122 Ibid. 21. See "The Contractors", 10-22, for the history of variations in payments from ship to ship.

123 Ibid. 21.

124 Ibid. 26-7.

125 Noah, 1978:9-10. Bateson, 1985:26-7, for "Naval Agents and Guards".

126 Bateson, 45-7; for "Surgeons and Surgeons-Superintendent".
127 Bateson, 63.
128 Ibid. 46.
129 Clune, Frank [& P.R.Stephensen], 1964, 7ff).

Chapter 10 Notes

1 Macquarie, Lachlan, Gov. NSW. A Letter to the Right Honourable Viscount Sidmouth in Refutation of Statements made by The Hon. Henry Grey Bennet, M.P...London, 1821:38.
2 MacDonagh, Oliver. "Envoi: humanity, economy, policy: on common sense and expertise in the life of Sir Jeremiah Fitzpatrick", ch 13, in Roy MacLeod, *Government and Expertise: Specialists, Administrators and Professionals, 1860-1919*, Cambridge University Press, 2003:243, 244, 253, 251, sentence by sentence in that order; Google books on line, sighted 19.04.2010.
3 See also Oliver MacDonagh. *The Inspector General: Sir Jeremiah Fitzpatrick and Social Reform 1783-1802*, Croom Helm, London, 1981.
4 *Colonial Secretary Indents of Convict Ships 1801-1804* 4/4004 COD 138:p.51. Fifteen are bracketed as 'Mutineers'. Ford said fourteen (1953:11). Only Redfern was tried on Neptune. His sentence is shown as 'Life', i.e. 'transported for life'.
5 Macquarie, 1821:38.
6 See also Sir Jeremiah Fitzpatrick (with John Howard) in Donald H. Akenson *The Irish Education Experiment* (1970:35 and 68).
7 His regular practice from his earlier efforts in Ireland (MacDonagh, 1981).
8 The *Peace of Amiens*, 25 March 1802 to 18 May 1803.
9 Ackerknecht, 1992:128ff. Note also that, "In spite of the preoccupation with systems, the study of individual diseases and the isolation of new disease entities made continued progress in the eighteenth century" (Ibid. 131ff).
10 Carpenter, 1987:96
11 See chapter 3.
12 See Lloyd, ed., introduction to Sir Gilbert Blane, 1965:132-3.
13 Ibid. 96.A reference to Lloyd, C., ed. 1965:159-60.
14 Watt in *Aust.NZ.J.Surg.*1989.59:928.
15 Porter, 1997:1231; 1231-1261.
16 Thomas Pelham, 2nd Earl of Chichester (1756-1826), Home Secretary 1801 to 1803.
17 MacDonagh, 1981:277-8, a timely addition to the primary references which had earlier formed this chapter.
18 Ibid. 234.
19 *HRNSW* iv: 399-402
20 MacDonagh, 1981. For further details of Fitzpatrick's contributions to the maintenance of health on convict transports see, section II of 'Service and Servitude', 1796-1802 (Chapter 12:267-284).

21 *HRA*, iii: 97.

22 For the Transport Commissioners, here, and below, see selected sites from *Google* searches including Roger Morriss in *War in History* 2007;14; 310 (incl. A. Serle) at
http://wih.sagepub.com/cgi/content/abstract/14/3;310.
Ambrose Serle may also be approached through 'loyalist' or 'quotes' (refs to his book, "*Americans Against Liberty, Or An Essay on the Nature and Principles of True Freedom*". London: 1775. 1 reel(s). Serle (1742-1812) was a British civil servant and secretary to Lord Howe from 1776 to 1778. Commissioner in the British government Transport Office, and hymnist. This work is critical of America's continued use of slaves and its desire for independence from Britain. Title continues "Shewing [sic] that the designs and conduct of the Americans tend only to tyranny and slavery".
http://mulibraries.missouri.edu/specialcollections/index.htm-
Accessed 13 July 2009.
For Otway see http://www.otway.com/family/517.html - Accessed 13 July 2009. For John Schanck, see *Dictionary of Canadian Biography Online*; see also reference, "Grant, James (1772-1833)" in *ADB Online*. Both dictionaries accessed 13 July 2009. Schanck designed the *Lady Nelson* and his friend Grant commanded this ship.

23 Ibid. 97-8.

24 Ibid. 98.

25 Bateson, 1985:12ff.

26 Since writing this earlier chapter I have acquired Rodger's *Command of the Ocean*.

27 Ibid. 38-40.

28 Ibid. 10.

29 Ibid. 11.

30 Ibid.

31 Ibid. 12.

32 Fletcher, 2001.

33 Ibid. 2001:79, in the context of 'The Second Fleet in History', 77-88, and preceding pages, 1-76.

34 Ibid. 2001:79, where Flynn considered "Bateson's description of the investigation into the abuses on the fleet and the Trail trial is muddled and inaccurate".

35 Bateson, 1985:13n5, 314, compared *HRA I* iii 358-363 with later contracts.

36 Ellis, 1972[1955]: 528. Ellis, biographer of Macquarie and Greenway, talked of minds breaking down "of those who had made the early voyages in wet ships to Botany Bay and suffered its primal rigours". Redfern of course had not, but was still included.

37 Bateson. 338-9 for this paragraph.

38 *HRAI,* iii. 379.

39 Demurrage, in commercial usage (going back to 1641), refers to the "Detention of a vessel by the freighter beyond the time agreed on; the payment made in respect of this", *SOED.*
40 *HRAI,* iii. 381.
41 Ibid.
42 Ibid. 93.
43 Ibid. 94.
44 Ibid. 4.
45 Ibid. 107.
46 Ibid. 108-9.
47 Ibid. 380.
48 Ibid. 381.
49 Ibid. 403, see last paragraph.
50 Ibid. 452.
51 Ibid. 454.
52 Ibid. 639.
53 See Mitchell Library, Sydney, NSW, "General Card Index: Ships" for references to Minorca. See also in Ian Nicholson, *Log of Logs*, A Roebuck Book, for reference to a homeward journey log attributed to John Leith: India Office Records, IOR L/Mar/B/335A, filmed Oct 1983; a microfilm copy, AJCP, M1624, at the Mitchell Library, Sydney, NSW, was too faint for effective study.
54 This *first* European (British) Settlement on Norfolk Island was contemporary with the mainland settlement at Sydney Cove in 1788, and had a similar social mix. The first hand accounts of Arthur Philip, 1982 (1789), David Collins, 1971 (1798), Philip Gidley King*, Journal...1787-1790* (1980) and Ralph Clark, *Journal 1787-1792* (1981) should suffice to make this clear.
55 Mann, 1811, 1979.
56 Thorne and Raymond, 1989:38ff. for a specific geological reference.
57 Rich, in R. Schodde, et al., 1983:6-29.
58 CSIRO Australia (2000, May 25), 'Fiery Birth of New Pacific Island', accessed 22 February, 2011.
59 Fridriksson, Sturla. *Surtsey, Evolution of life on a Volcanic Island,* A Halstead Press Book, John Wiley & Sons, New York, 1975.
60 Ibid. Surtsey offered a pristine site for the study of the formation of island biota. See, http://www.vulkaner.no/n/surtsey/esurtseal.html.
For the Nomination of Surtsey for the UNESCO World Heritage List, see, Surtsey_nomination.pdf.
61 Hermes, 1985.
62 Turner, J.S., Courtney N. Smithers and Ruurd D. Hoogland, c.1968.
63 Carlquist, 1965:14-24ff.
64 Hoare, Merval, "The Island's Earliest Visitors", in Nobbs, ed., 1988:18ff.

65 The coming of man to the Pacific brought bananas on the one hand and weeds and insects on the other. See McCubbin, 1971:2ff. for the story of the American Monarch, Australia's Wanderer. Seeds of the Milkweed, the food plant of this butterfly were carried across the Pacific by boat, island by island. The butterfly, both wind blown and ship assisted, established itself on islands where the milkweed was then growing. Eventually it reached Australia.

66 Moorehead, 1970. Charles Darwin's *Beagle* journey and his accounts of plants and animals on islands of the Galapagos and Hawaii early attracted an interest in the study of these and other islands, mentioned by J.S.Turner et al above.

67 Hermes, 1985:10,32.

68 Hoare, 1974; reprinted, Greenways Press, Norfolk Island, 1985. It contains extracts from original texts relating to Cook's visit to Norfolk Island, is well researched and documented, with a select bibliography, and index. [Dr Turner and I met and talked with Merval Hoare on a visit to Norfolk Island in 1994.]

69 See Nobbs (1988) for illustrations of the Pines that featured on early prints.

70 For Daniel Carl Solander see *ADB2*:456-7.

71 Solander, 1995: Letter 99:289, 332. Ibid. 291n1 refers to James Lind MD, FRS, 1736-1812.

72 Banks, 1962. Hulmes's letter is in *Vol II*: 301. A note on his work on scurvy is in *Vol I*: 243n1-244.

73 Ibid. vol.1:393

74 Carpenter, 1987:80. James Lind, of scurvy cure fame, lived from 1716-94. His contemporary, 1736-1812, became Physician to the Household of George III, and as we have seen nearly accompanied Cook (Lloyd, 1965:2).

75 Banks, 1962:vol.1:71-81. This edition contains a silhouette drawing of the 'shadows' of Banks and Solander by James Lind.

76 Ibid. vol.2:81-94. Among the reasons given by Beaglehole for the visit to Iceland was, "The age was fond of volcanoes, and Iceland had a volcano, 83".

77 Smith, Bernard, 1969:39,39n. Smith, in his third chapter, Cook's Second Voyage, draws attention to his idea that Wales could have influenced Coleridge's Ancient Mariner. Coleridge attended Christ's Hospital school while Wales was master of the Mathematical School there from 1775-98. Coleridge, writing of his schooldays, told how "Two or three times a year the mathematical master beats up for recruits for the king's boys, as they are called; and all who like the navy are drafted into the Mathematical and Drawing Schools, where they continue till sixteen or seventeen years of age, and go as midshipmen and school masters in the Navy".

78 Hoare, 1985 [1974]:7-9.

79 Anson, c1912 (1748): 109 (grass), 109ff. (other plants). Anson, pre-Lind, with all the scurvy his crew suffered and died from, could not get his ships to

land soon enough to cure them with any plant food he could find, including grass.
80 See Nobbs, 1988:18-22, for "The Islands Earliest Visitors". Ibid. fig 65, has the pigeon, now extinct. See also John Hicks, "The Natural History of Norfolk Island", 159-172. Beryl Evans, and Owen, OA 1981 for services to conservation, provided a direct and useful introduction to the Island biota during a visit in 1994. For reference to Owen and photograph, see Jean Edgecombe, *Norfolk Island...*, Self published, Thornleigh, 1991:116.
81 Over time, a description wide of the mark, as Norfolk had no 'eagles' and no place for 'angels' in the 'hell' of the second settlement. ARJ (2014).
82 Clarke, in Nobbs, 1988:33n16. *HRNSW1*, part 2, 123, and 333 has the La Pérouse reference.
83 I had the pleasure of being present at meetings, chaired by Professor Auchmuty, of the Central Coast Branch of the Library Association. One of the planning tasks involved a Union Catalogue of books from local sources, business and other; a basic need in Newcastle with a young university.
84 For Auchmuty, James J., see the editor's introduction, ix-xiii, *The Voyage of Governor Phillip to Botany Bay...*, 1970.
85 Ibid. 38-9. "Instructions for Philip Gidley King, Esq., Superintendent and Commandant of the Settlement of Norfolk Island"; First accounts of that settlement, 47-52. See also, for the ongoing story, King, *The Journal of Philip Gidley King: Lieutenant, R.N. 1787-1790*, Fidlon, and Ryan, eds. Australian Documents Library, Sydney, 1980.
86 King, 1980.
87 Clark, 1981.
88 Wright, 1986:6ff.; Wright provided "a brief pen picture" of each of these first settlers.
89 Linebaugh, 1993:383.
90 Ibid. 383-4.
91 Cox and Stacey, 1971:7-21. Notes to the "Illustrations", Mitchell Library, Sydney, NSW, 92-3. See ill. 3n for details relating to a map of Sydney, Norfolk Island, 1793.
92 Clark, 1981:172ff.
93 Punishing women posed few problems for Clark, whose reference to convicts as "Ladies" is belied by other descriptions of them for which he is infamous. See Summers, 1980:11, but also 1994:2-3.
94 Clark, 1981:180; 31 January 1791.
95 Ibid. 292-3:Clark to Captain Campbell of the Marines, Port Jackson, 11 February 1791.
96 Ibid. 293. Clark underlined the difference between Mt Pitt birds and Mutton Birds by sending skins of each to his wife, Betsy, Clark: 161; Saturday 28 August 1790. See Robert V.J. Varman. "Material Life Including the Evidence from Archaeology" in Nobbs ed.1988:157; From a trench dug, and

subsequent "analysis of the bird bones...more than one species of bird [was] involved in the tragic slaughter". Among them were - Mt Pitt birds the Providence Petrel, *Pterodroma solandri,* two other species in that genus, and the Wedge-tailed Shearwater, *Puffinus pacificus.* Two other Shearwaters are known as Muttonbirds, the N.Z. Sooty, and the Tasmanian Short-tailed. Clark: 167-185, around 400 Tropic Birds were collected in one season; "for their feathers" see Ibid. 184.

97 Clark, 1981.

98 See Wright, 1986:passim. See also Nobbs, ed., 1988:passim.

99 *HRNSW 5,* 14 Aug. 1804:431 shows a total of 1,084, including 311 children. Wright, 1986:52, has 347 children in August for a total population of 1,102. In the following year at the Muster of 1 Feb 1805, there were 148 children on the stores and 212, off the stores, making a total of 360, *HRNSW 5,* 1 Feb 1805:549.

100 Wright, 1986. See ch. XIV, 'The Closure'.

101 Jones, 1999; 7:37, notes 40-41.

102 Ibid. "Norfolk Island victualling book"*, 1802*:147, in Baxter, 1988.

103 James Mileham, ship's surgeon, arrived on Ganges, 2 June 1798; "Thirteen convicts died on the passage, and many of the survivors were suffering from scurvy on arrival", Bateson, 1985:160. Mileham was an emigrant from France post revolution, and "though a very worthy man...very defective in medical knowledge", Richards, 1994:410.

104 Ford, 1954. This pamphlet contains a copy of Thomas Jamison's article, "General observations on the smallpox", *Sydney Gazette,* 14 October, 1804.

105 See Amanda Laugesen, 2002:For the word "free", its extensions and relativities, see "Introduction", xiiiff, and text, 89-100.

106 Henderson and Stanbury, 1988:95. [On the mainland, in later years, this same swell caused ships to take in coal from the Wollongong mines on the north side of sheltering capes.] See also, Graeme Henderson, Maritime Archaeology in Australia, University of Western Australia Press, Nedlands, 1986.

107 Wright, 1986:80-81.

108 Foveaux, J. *Letter book. A1444:*42. Mitchell Library, Sydney.

109 *HRA I,* 1917; x:275, 3 September 1804, 21 February 1820.*

110 Foveaux, J. "Certificate" in W. Redfern, "Memorial to Governor Macquarie: 1810. The Memorial gave reasons for the grant as non-payment on Norfolk Island for his work with the military and loss of property on leaving the Island. ML 4/1827 CS mdms no. 271.

111 Jones, 1999. *HR NSW,* 1897; v:306-9, 1 March 1805. D'Arcy Wentworth's pay shows this dual source.

112 Wright, 1986:55.

113 Ibid. 53,59:Mary Bolton was shown at the end of the list of "Occupations at Norfolk Island - Feb.1805", the only woman on the list. A note stated that

Mary Bolton had been hospital nurse on the Island for over eight years, Ibid. 142. In 1813 she appears as Samuel Day's wife, with two children, en route to Port Dalrymple, Ibid. 136.

114 Ibid. 53:55-61.

115 Cox and Stacey, 1971:ill.3n.

116 Wright, 1986:55, 59; Population, 52.

117 Ibid. 51.

118 Collins 1971 (1798):515-6.

119 Porter, 1997:291. Porter's year, 1810, may have been a little early bearing in mind the main source of supply was from surgeons on ships most of whom at that time started as surgeons mates. Redfern's connection with Edinburgh University Medical School came in the 1820s.

120 Redfern to Bigge, 5 February 1821:6196-222, *BT Box 26 appendix.*

121 Richards, David. "Medical Transportees to Australian Colonies:1788-1868", *Occasional Papers on Medical History Australia:7* (Series), see n. 83, above.

122 Ibid. "Medical Men at Norfolk Island...1996:409-11.

123 Redfern to Bigge, 5 February 1821, above.

124 Parsons in Nobbs ed., 95.

125 Ryan, 1981:76.

126 My Redfern study "*DayBook 3*" [unpublished] shows that I referred to the Robert Jones Recollections on 21.03.1994, made notes, but did not include Dr Gandevia's warning comment to be careful of Robert (Bucky) Jones Recollections (Rumsey Papers). Dr Gandevia had given me access to his filing cabinets, stored at the History of Medicine Library, while I was reading there.

127 Tasman G. Parsons, "The New South Wales Corps on Norfolk Island 1792-1810" in Nobbs, 1988:84-6. Parsons "demonstrated the falsity of [the] view" "that the N.S.W. Corps was composed of rapacious officers and a rank and file which was the refuse of society, the sweepings of the English prison system", Ibid. 95ns74,75. See below.

128 Parsons, in Nobbs, 1988:81.

129 Colley, Linda, 2003:406, endnote. Ch. 7:1. "The reasons for this were aesthetic as well as political", Colley wrote, giving John Barrell and Matthew Lalumia as sources. See Barrell, earlier in this book.

130 Ibid.

131 Ibid. 82

132 Parsons, in Aplin, ed. 1988:102-119.

133 Rigg, Valda, "Convict Life: A 'Tolerable Degree of Comfort'?" in Nobbs, 1988:97ff.

134 See earlier chapters of this book.

135 Castles, 1982:65. Castles showed that it was already a place of secondary punishment in the First Settlement. However, the reason convicts then felt it

to be "a very severe sentence" was "because it is a small spot and they have no chance of escaping", Hunter, and the *Report of the Select Committee on Transportation*,1812:21.
136 Kercher, 1995:35.
137 Wright, 1986:79 for this quote, 82, for that in the following paragraph.
138 Ibid. See chapter XI, "The Exodus"; see also 96, 99.
139 To be reached on the Whitaker website, 9 March 2004, on last check.
140 Whitaker, 2000:2, with references to Wright's work on this topic, which includes his M.A. Honours thesis, Macquarie University (NSW), 1997; Descent, vol 28, pt 3, 1998, and Tasmanian H.R.A. Papers and Proceedings, vol 46,no 3, 1999.
141 Whitaker, 2002:60-4. The abbreviated account follows Whitaker, who wrote, "These hasty executions were to haunt Foveaux for the rest of his career". ML sources were given for this comment in an endnote, 63n47.
142 Whitaker, 2000:70.Some points to be noted. The matter of Redfern's place of birth has been discussed above, in the opening chapter. Redfern had an appointment by warrant on *Standard*, as had the surgeon, a warrant officer. He had officer rank as a colonial surgeon. As I explained when discussing Redfern's trial he had a supporting Counsel who read the defence statement. How might one decide between Redfern and Counsel as the source of the reference to Algernon Sidney?
143 Briggs, 93:110-11.
144 Ibid. 186.
145 King, 1975.
146 *ADB1*, 1966:408.
147 Wright, in Nobbs, 1988:218.
148 Whitaker, 2000:75.
149 Whitaker, 2000:75n125, Foveaux to King, 21 September 1803, *Foveaux Letter Book, A1444*, ML. P.64. For "asthma" see also Ibid. n126.
150 Whitaker, 2000:75n129, Redfern memorandum, 22 September 1803, CO 201/30. PRO, p.60.
151 Whitaker, 2000:76, and Wright, in Nobbs, 1988:218, for the details.
152 Ryan, 1981:76.
153 Land grants in relation to Australia's indigenous people, the Aborigines, are discussed in a later chapter.
154 Ibid. xii-xiii.
155 Ibid. xiii-xiv.
156 Wright, 1986:See 'End Papers' for sources of information on Settlers' Blocks, and the composite map, Division of National Mapping, Canberra.
157 Charles Grimes (1772-1858), *ADB1*, 1966.
158 Ibid. 66-7.
159 Ibid. 67.

160 Ibid. 67-8. I was in this vicinity when visiting Norfolk Island as part of this study.
161 Ibid. 76.
162 Ibid. xiii.
163 Wright, 1986:64-5, for this paragraph.
164 Piper, J., C.Y. Reel 1303 BT 12:152a,b. Mitchell Library, Sydney.
165 Parsons, Vivienne, "Thomas Jamison (1745-1811)" in *ADB2,* 1967. "Jamison was deeply embroiled in trade. He was active in bringing wheat and pork from Norfolk Island settlers who, before the evacuation of the island, owed about £15000 to Jamison and other Sydney merchants".
166 Auchmuty, J.J. in "D'Arcy Wentworth (1762?-1827)", *ADB2* 1967:579-82. Wentworth had been on Norfolk Island from 1790 to 1796, returned on 8 May 1804 45 as assistant surgeon, with Redfern helping him. He was to leave again on 30 March 1806. [Collins, 1971(1798:474) reported Wentworth as appointed on 4 May 1796, by the governor as assistant-surgeon in the room of Mr Samuel Leeds, who came out with Governor Hunter and had returned to England 'to recover his health'.]
167 Butlin, S.J. 1968:56-7, fn32. This footnote leads to "Wentworth Papers" (Mitchell
Library).
168 *HRA vol iv* p.82:9 May 1803.
169 Richards, *David,* 1996:410. Richards described James Davi(e)s as having 'escaped detailed [biographical] scrutiny', but added that "under the alias of Christopher Sheakstone was tried at Kingstone-on-Thames on 23 Mar.,1791 and transported on the Pitt to arrive at Port Jackson in Feb.,1792". Collins recommended him to King "as well qualified for the position". The balance of the article generally matches the details in Wright (1986), and Nobbs, ed. 1988. James Davis boarded H.M.S. *Porpoise* at Norfolk Island on 26 December 1807 for the Derwent. His name appeared in the general muster in Van Diemens Land in 1818. See Wright, 1986, for the last two items.
170 *ADB1.* See "Holt, Joseph (1756-1826)" entry written by G.C.Bolton.
171 *ADB2.* See "Margarot, Maurice (1745-1815)" entry written by Michael Roe.
172 Braithwaite, 2003. See chapter 8 in Volume II of *Better than Cure The life and times of the ebullient and resilient William Redfern 1775-1833.* In a final reading of this chapter I took note of Johnston's thesis where he concluded for the period, post 1850s, "with few exceptions, Australian historians have not adequately contextualised colonial conservatism, liberalism and radicalism in its British setting. British colonies such as New South Wales and Victoria are all too often treated as closed, largely self-referencing, political systems".
http://www.library.unsw.edu.au/~thesis/adt-NUN/uploads/approved/adt-NUN20060908.134928/public/01front.pdf:

for Stuart Buchanan Johnson: *The Shaping of Colonial Liberalism: John Fairfax and the Sydney Morning Herald, 1841-1877*, A Thesis submitted for the Degree of Doctor of Philosophy at the University of New South Wales, 2006. Site visited 14 June 2008.

173 *Wentworth Papers, A751*:201-203, Mitchell Library, Sydney, N.S.W.

174 *Hannah and Sally* was an American trading and sealing Brig that came to Sydney via Rio in 1807. Later that year this ship apparently called in at Norfolk Island on its way to Canton.

175 Redfern was careful not to name names but his reference to 'Mr Lawson' and 'Brother officers' easily pointed to Bligh. Lawson had bought a commission in the NSW Corps and was stationed on Norfolk Island until 1806, so would have been well acquainted with D'Arcy Wentworth. As an officer he was acting on the latter's court martial in 1807, "on the eve of the rebellion against Governor Bligh in 1808". In 1813, Blaxland, Lawson, and Darcy's son, William, would cross the Blue Mountains.

176 On 7 June 1806, D'Arcy and Maria had a quantity of linen stolen from the garden of their house in Parramatta. Maria had put it out to bleach. See *The Sydney Gazette*, 31 August 1806, 3a.

177 This is a reference to the same *Return*, which provided information on Redfern's houses, etc. Under a subheading, "Individuals not holding land" Redfern's name appears. Beside his name under the column headed "Wife" is the figure "1". No children are shown and a second column headed "Servant".

178 Wright, 1986:105-6, but not Sarah McHenry

179 A Sarah McHenry and William Redfern connection has not been established to my satisfaction.

180 Parsons, in Nobbs, ed., 1988:88-90ff.

181 Wright, 1986:51.

182 Ibid. 63-5.

183 M. Barnard Eldershaw, 1973 (1939): passim; see also Marjorie Barnard's entry, "John Piper (17737-1851)", in the *ADB2* (1967). In these studies, two aspects of Piper as a 'lady's man' may be understood, the one sexual, the other platonic. His lively and open social behaviour attracted the friendship of men and women. His female correspondents included Elizabeth Macarthur, snr. and jnr., Mrs Marsden, and Governor King's wife. He collected seashells for Mrs Bligh while her husband was Governor. Piper formed a relationship with Mary Ann Shears, the fourteen-year old daughter of convicts. He would later marry her and have a large family. (See Wright, 1986:39-40). [On the mainland, Redfern, too, would marry a convict's daughter of the same age.]

184 Gunson, Niel. See his entry 'James Elder (1772-1836)' in *ADB1*:353. James Mitchell, also a former Tahitian Missionary, "had originally come to Australia with the First Fleet as quartermaster of the *Sirius*". On Norfolk Island, Mitchell was agent to Simeon Lord.

185 Ibid. Elder "served in the Tahitian mission from July 1801 until he returned to Sydney in March 1808. On 19 July 1808 he married Mary Smith...by whom he had ten children". Elder's "reserve and obstinacy were balanced by his intellectual gifts". According to the Redfern letter, above, Elder came from Otaheitie in the Whaler, *Seringapatam*, under Capt Clark. As this ship arrived at Norfolk Island on 24 April, 1808, a 'March' arrival in Sydney does not appear to be correct. As Clark had sailed for the South Seas, Elder could have found a berth on another ship to take him to Sydney in time for his July wedding, Wright in Nobbs: 221. This entry also has references to other missionaries and to early nonconformist church history in Australia, part of a later chapter.

186 *HRNSW 5*, King to Foveaux, 20 July 1804:405; "The duty of surgeon will be performed by a junior assistant from hence, and the eldest assistant now acting as surgeon at Norfolk Island will necessarily be removed to Port Dalrymple".

187 Wright, 1986:80. "Another substantial vessel built at Norfolk I. was the *Endeavour* schooner which was constructed by Robert Jones, John Drummond and Thomas Ransome. A Letter from Commandant Captain John Piper to Port Jackson dated 30 November 1808, advised that the vessel had just been launched".

188 Parsons, T.G. in Nobbs, 1988:81ff, has already been involved in this chapter in defending the character of Commandant Foveaux against the attacks made by Robert 'Bucky' Jones and Joseph Holt. James Mitchell joins them here in an attack on Foveaux's alleged attitude to women, Ibid. 88ff.

189 In Redfern's 'defence submission' at his court martial he showed a similar reaction when under stress, "deceiving or suffering", he said. "Some unguarded and doubtful expressions may have escaped me. It is remarkable that little if anything of this sort has been proved It should be considered I had no alternative but that of deceiving or suffering". After much thought, in each case, I believe the reason for his deceit was more a specific response to a particular event than a general character trait or weakness. Interestingly, Redfern, himself, was the source of the information on each occasion.

190 Captain Bristow, a whaler, visited NI in May 1804, November 1805 and April 1808.

191 Wright, 1986:40.

192 Ibid.

193 See Phillip's "Instruction to King": above.

194 Graeme Andrews, "The Impossible Port" in Nobbs, Ed.,:146-48. Andrews gives Cumpston as reference for "details of construction and subsequent career".

195 *The Sydney Gazette: and New South Wales Advertiser*, 7 June, 1807:vol v, no 215:3a; see for Oct. 1807, Wright, R. "Shipping Movements1788-1814", in. Nobbs: 221.

196 *Ibid.* 1 January 1809:vol vi no 26. Wright in Nobbs, 1988:221, gave Aaron Davis, as master. Aaron left the Island in Feb. 1805. A search of Wright, 1986 and Nobbs, 1988 associate Aaron with Mary Walker (Taunton) in Flynn, 2001:590-1. Assuming this material to apply, Aaron would not have been on Norfolk Island in 1809. Wright in Nobbs, 1988:148 gave M.Davis, as Captain of the *Endeavour*. I have not been able to find him.

www.ingramcontent.com/pod-product-compliance
Lightning Source LLC
Chambersburg PA
CBHW031934090426
42811CB00002B/180